Classroom Peanuts

HAHAHAHAHAHA
HAH HAHAHAHA
HAHA HAHAH

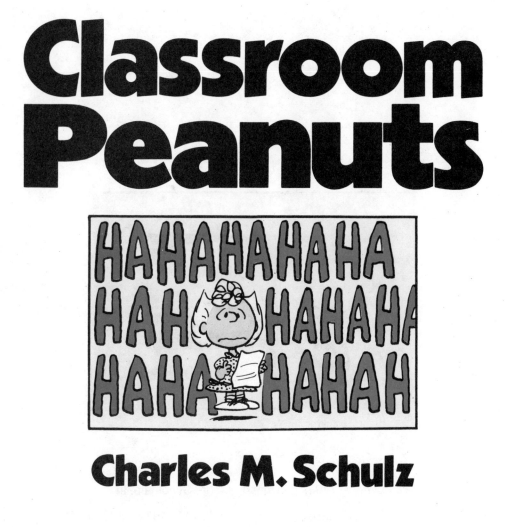

Charles M. Schulz

Holt, Rinehart and Winston / New York

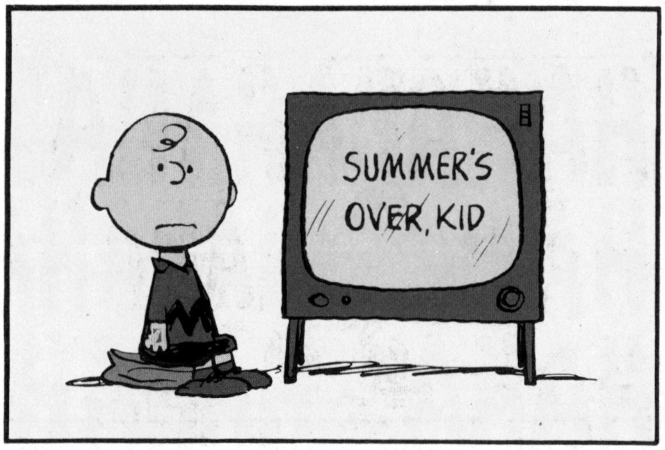
SUMMER'S OVER, KID

Published by Holt, Rinehart, and Winston, 383 Madison Avenue, New York, New York 10017.

Published simultaneously in Canada by Holt, Rinehart and Winston of Canada, Limited.

Library of Congress Catalog Card Number: 82-80108

ISBN: 0-03-061529-1

Printed in the United States of America

1 3 5 7 9 10 8 6 4 2

ISBN 0-03-061529-1

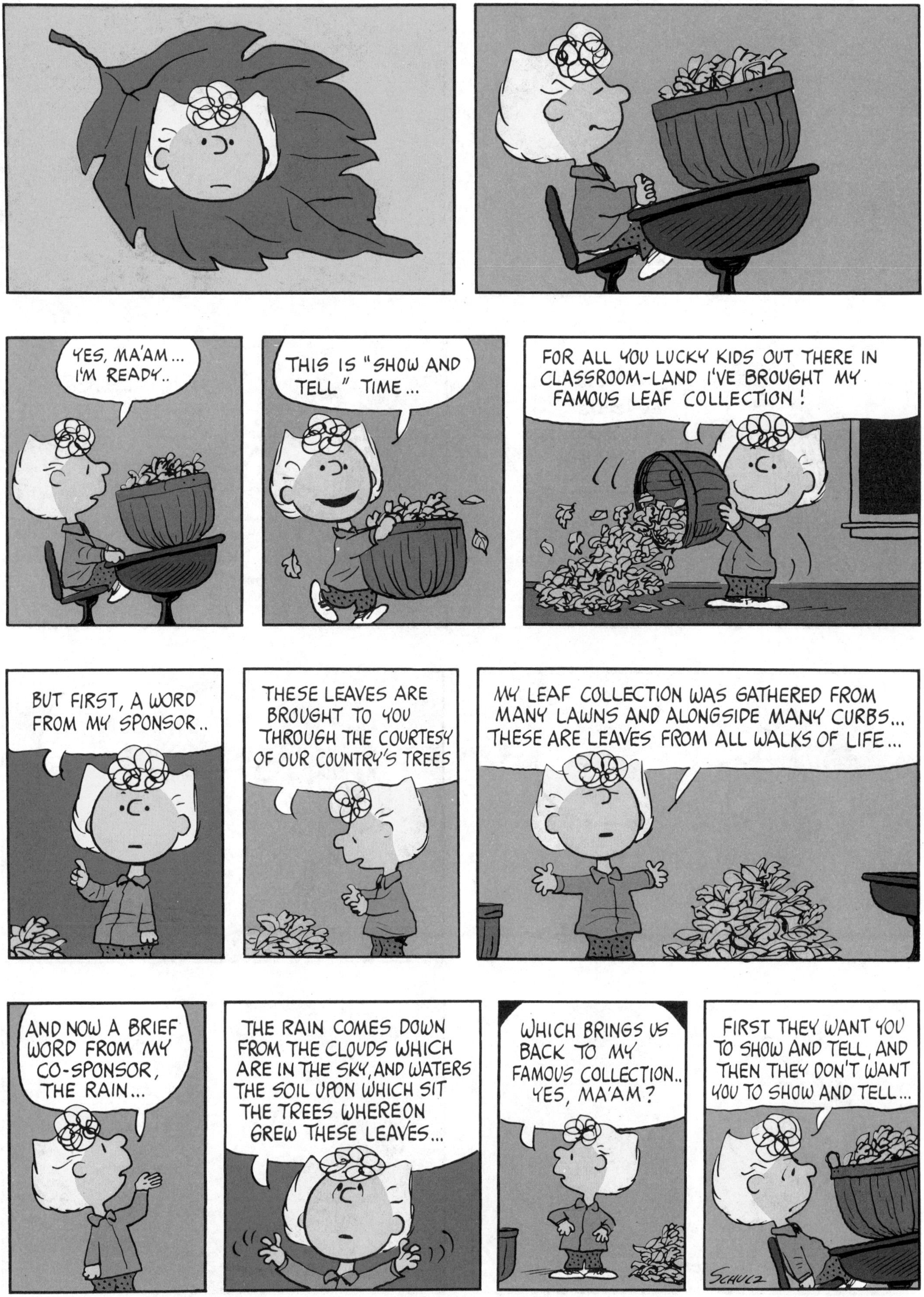
YES, MA'AM... I'M READY..
THIS IS "SHOW AND TELL" TIME...
FOR ALL YOU LUCKY KIDS OUT THERE IN CLASSROOM-LAND I'VE BROUGHT MY FAMOUS LEAF COLLECTION!
BUT FIRST, A WORD FROM MY SPONSOR..
THESE LEAVES ARE BROUGHT TO YOU THROUGH THE COURTESY OF OUR COUNTRY'S TREES
MY LEAF COLLECTION WAS GATHERED FROM MANY LAWNS AND ALONGSIDE MANY CURBS... THESE ARE LEAVES FROM ALL WALKS OF LIFE...
AND NOW A BRIEF WORD FROM MY CO-SPONSOR, THE RAIN...
THE RAIN COMES DOWN FROM THE CLOUDS WHICH ARE IN THE SKY, AND WATERS THE SOIL UPON WHICH SIT THE TREES WHEREON GREW THESE LEAVES...
WHICH BRINGS US BACK TO MY FAMOUS COLLECTION.. YES, MA'AM?
FIRST THEY WANT YOU TO SHOW AND TELL, AND THEN THEY DON'T WANT YOU TO SHOW AND TELL...
SCHULZ

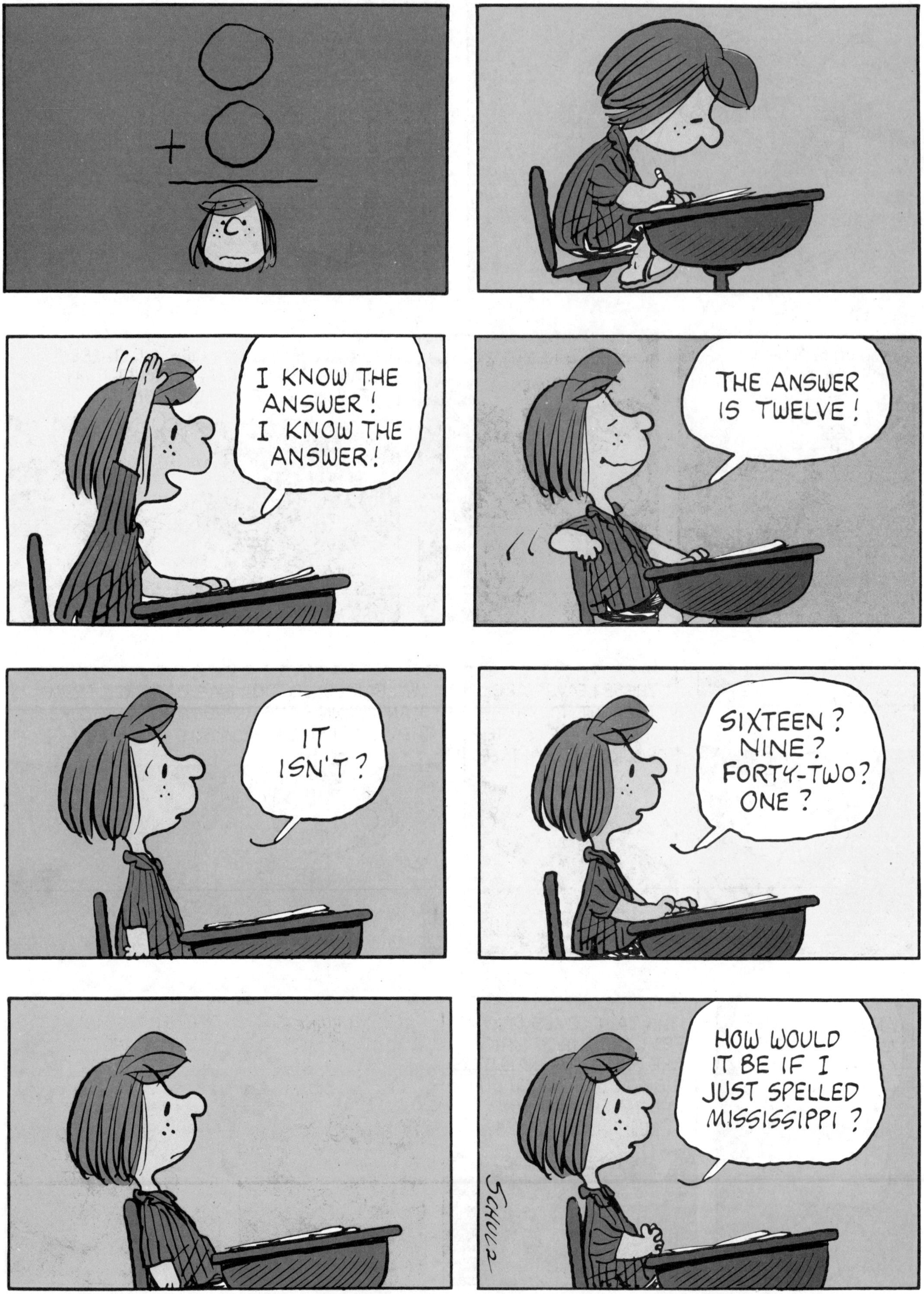
I KNOW THE ANSWER! I KNOW THE ANSWER!
THE ANSWER IS TWELVE!
IT ISN'T?
SIXTEEN? NINE? FORTY-TWO? ONE?
SCHULZ
HOW WOULD IT BE IF I JUST SPELLED MISSISSIPPI?

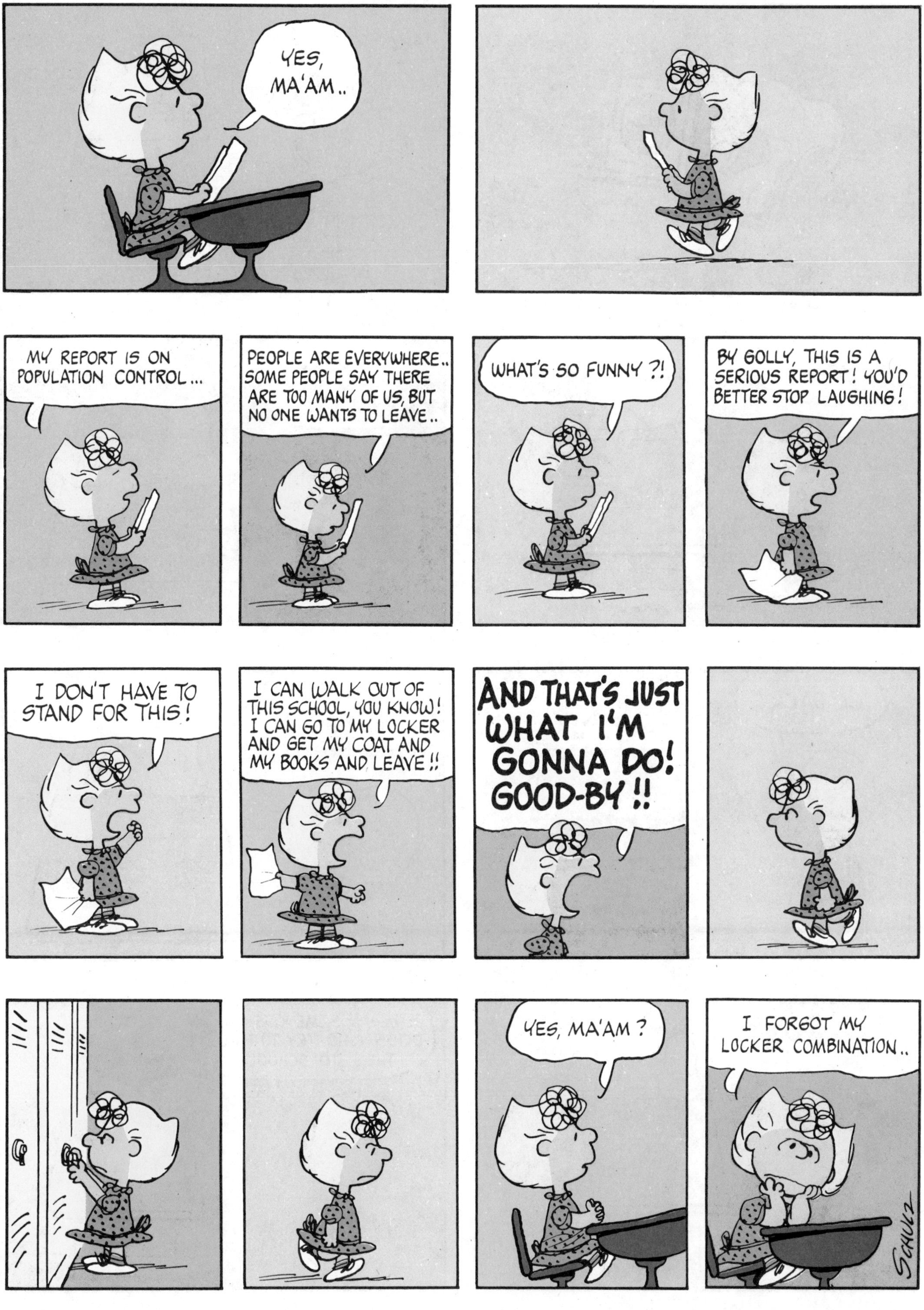
YES, MA'AM..
MY REPORT IS ON POPULATION CONTROL...
PEOPLE ARE EVERYWHERE.. SOME PEOPLE SAY THERE ARE TOO MANY OF US, BUT NO ONE WANTS TO LEAVE..
WHAT'S SO FUNNY ?!
BY GOLLY, THIS IS A SERIOUS REPORT! YOU'D BETTER STOP LAUGHING!
I DON'T HAVE TO STAND FOR THIS!
I CAN WALK OUT OF THIS SCHOOL, YOU KNOW! I CAN GO TO MY LOCKER AND GET MY COAT AND MY BOOKS AND LEAVE!!
AND THAT'S JUST WHAT I'M GONNA DO! GOOD-BY!!
YES, MA'AM?
I FORGOT MY LOCKER COMBINATION..
SCHULZ

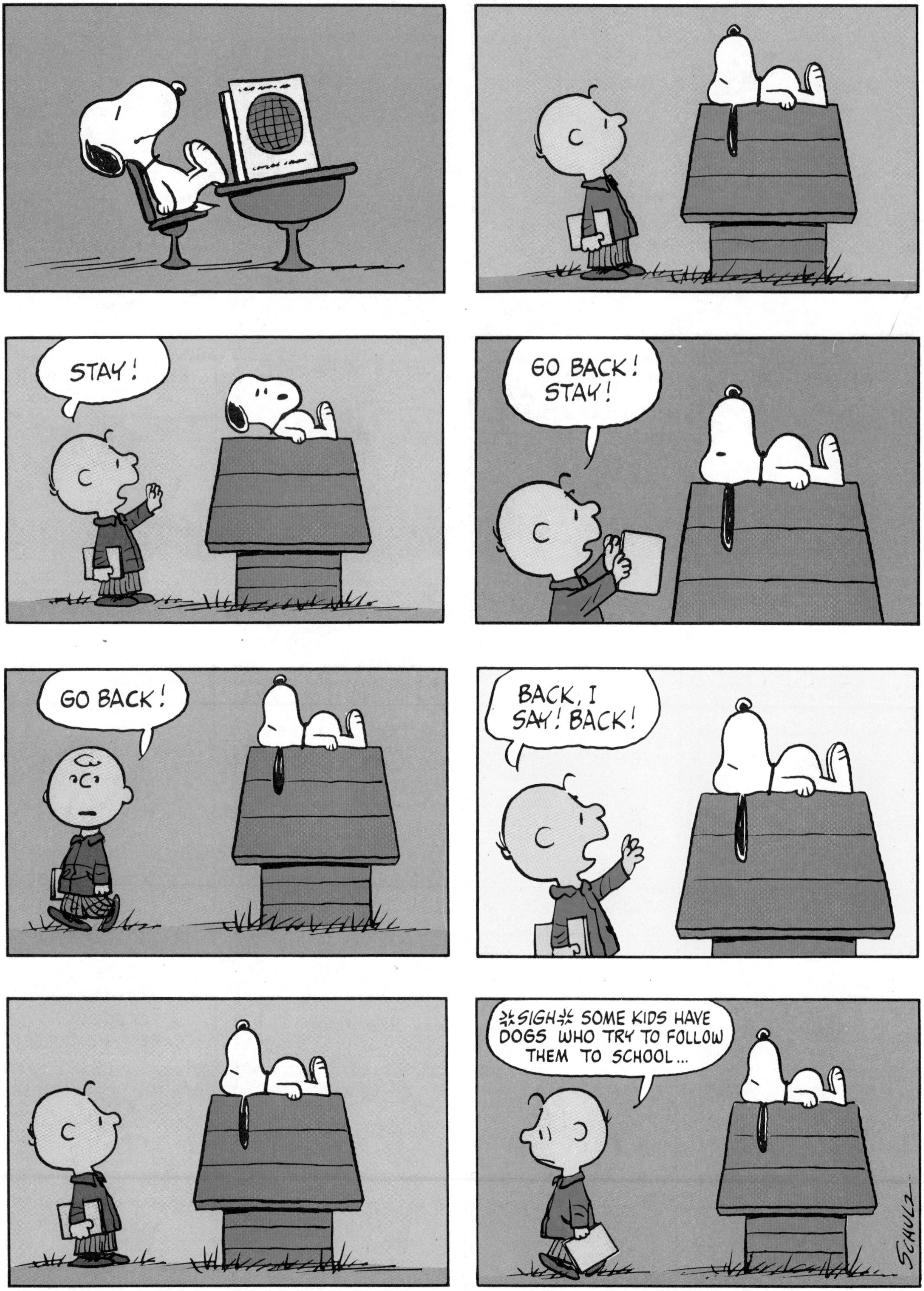
STAY!
GO BACK! STAY!
GO BACK!
BACK, I SAY! BACK!
SIGH SOME KIDS HAVE DOGS WHO TRY TO FOLLOW THEM TO SCHOOL...
SCHULZ

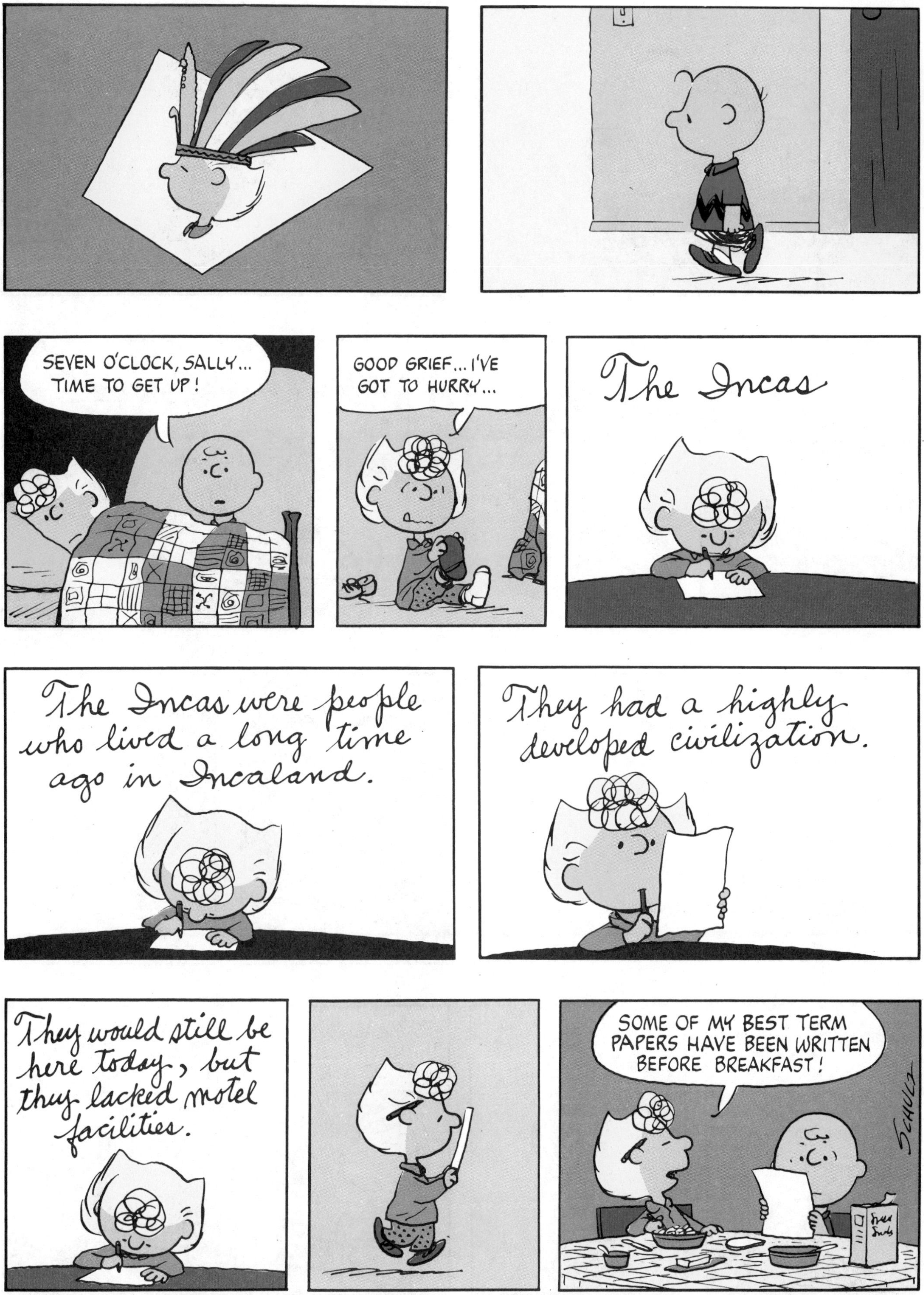
SEVEN O'CLOCK, SALLY... TIME TO GET UP!
GOOD GRIEF... I'VE GOT TO HURRY...
The Incas
The Incas were people who lived a long time ago in Incaland.
They had a highly developed civilization.
They would still be here today, but they lacked motel facilities.
SOME OF MY BEST TERM PAPERS HAVE BEEN WRITTEN BEFORE BREAKFAST!
SCHULZ

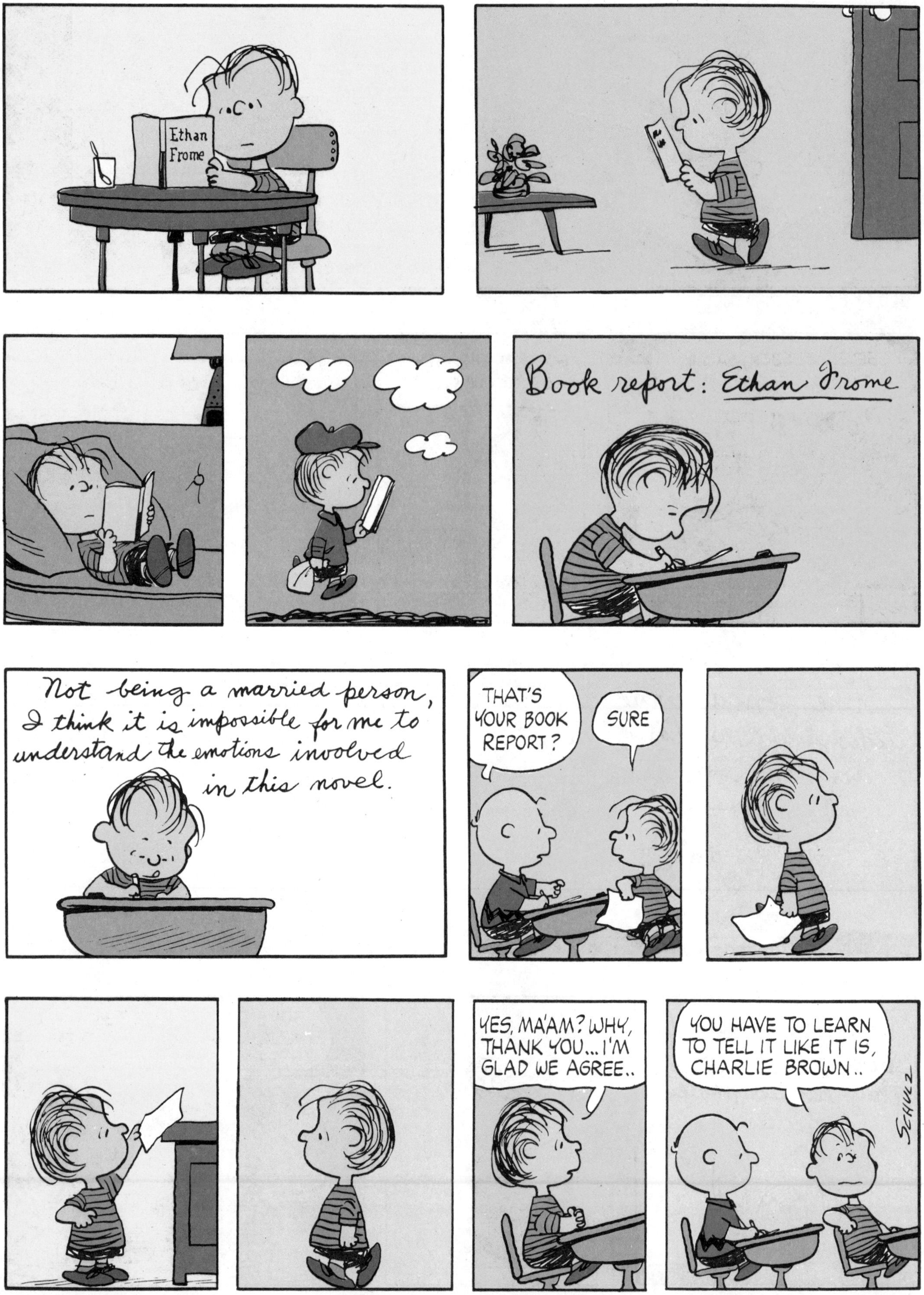
Ethan Frome
Book report: Ethan Frome
Not being a married person, I think it is impossible for me to understand the emotions involved in this novel.
THAT'S YOUR BOOK REPORT?
SURE
YES, MA'AM? WHY, THANK YOU... I'M GLAD WE AGREE..
YOU HAVE TO LEARN TO TELL IT LIKE IT IS, CHARLIE BROWN..
SCHULZ

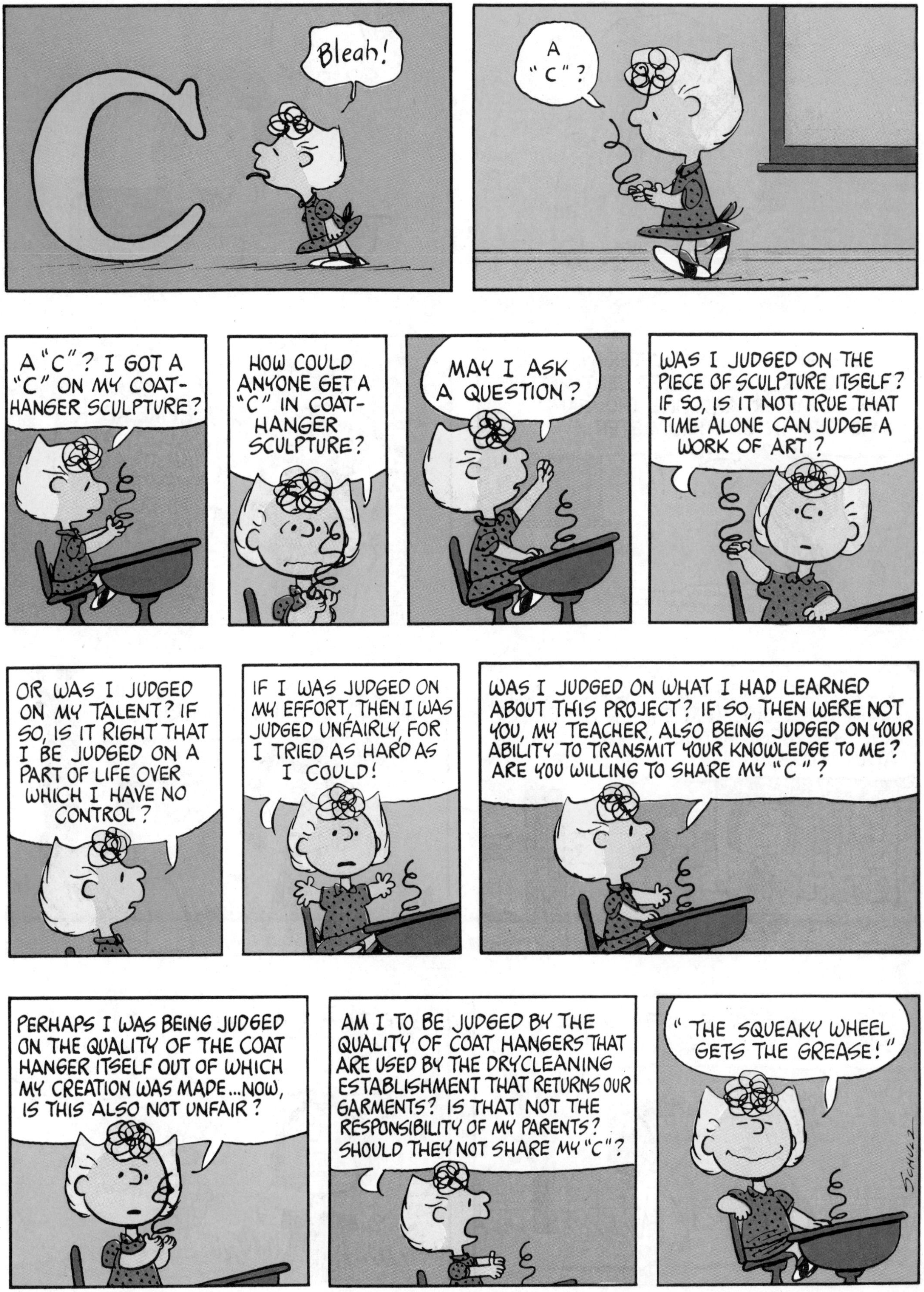

Bleah!
A "C"?
A "C"? I GOT A "C" ON MY COAT-HANGER SCULPTURE?
HOW COULD ANYONE GET A "C" IN COAT-HANGER SCULPTURE?
MAY I ASK A QUESTION?
WAS I JUDGED ON THE PIECE OF SCULPTURE ITSELF? IF SO, IS IT NOT TRUE THAT TIME ALONE CAN JUDGE A WORK OF ART?
OR WAS I JUDGED ON MY TALENT? IF SO, IS IT RIGHT THAT I BE JUDGED ON A PART OF LIFE OVER WHICH I HAVE NO CONTROL?
IF I WAS JUDGED ON MY EFFORT, THEN I WAS JUDGED UNFAIRLY, FOR I TRIED AS HARD AS I COULD!
WAS I JUDGED ON WHAT I HAD LEARNED ABOUT THIS PROJECT? IF SO, THEN WERE NOT YOU, MY TEACHER, ALSO BEING JUDGED ON YOUR ABILITY TO TRANSMIT YOUR KNOWLEDGE TO ME? ARE YOU WILLING TO SHARE MY "C"?
PERHAPS I WAS BEING JUDGED ON THE QUALITY OF THE COAT HANGER ITSELF OUT OF WHICH MY CREATION WAS MADE...NOW, IS THIS ALSO NOT UNFAIR?
AM I TO BE JUDGED BY THE QUALITY OF COAT HANGERS THAT ARE USED BY THE DRYCLEANING ESTABLISHMENT THAT RETURNS OUR GARMENTS? IS THAT NOT THE RESPONSIBILITY OF MY PARENTS? SHOULD THEY NOT SHARE MY "C"?
"THE SQUEAKY WHEEL GETS THE GREASE!"
SCHULZ

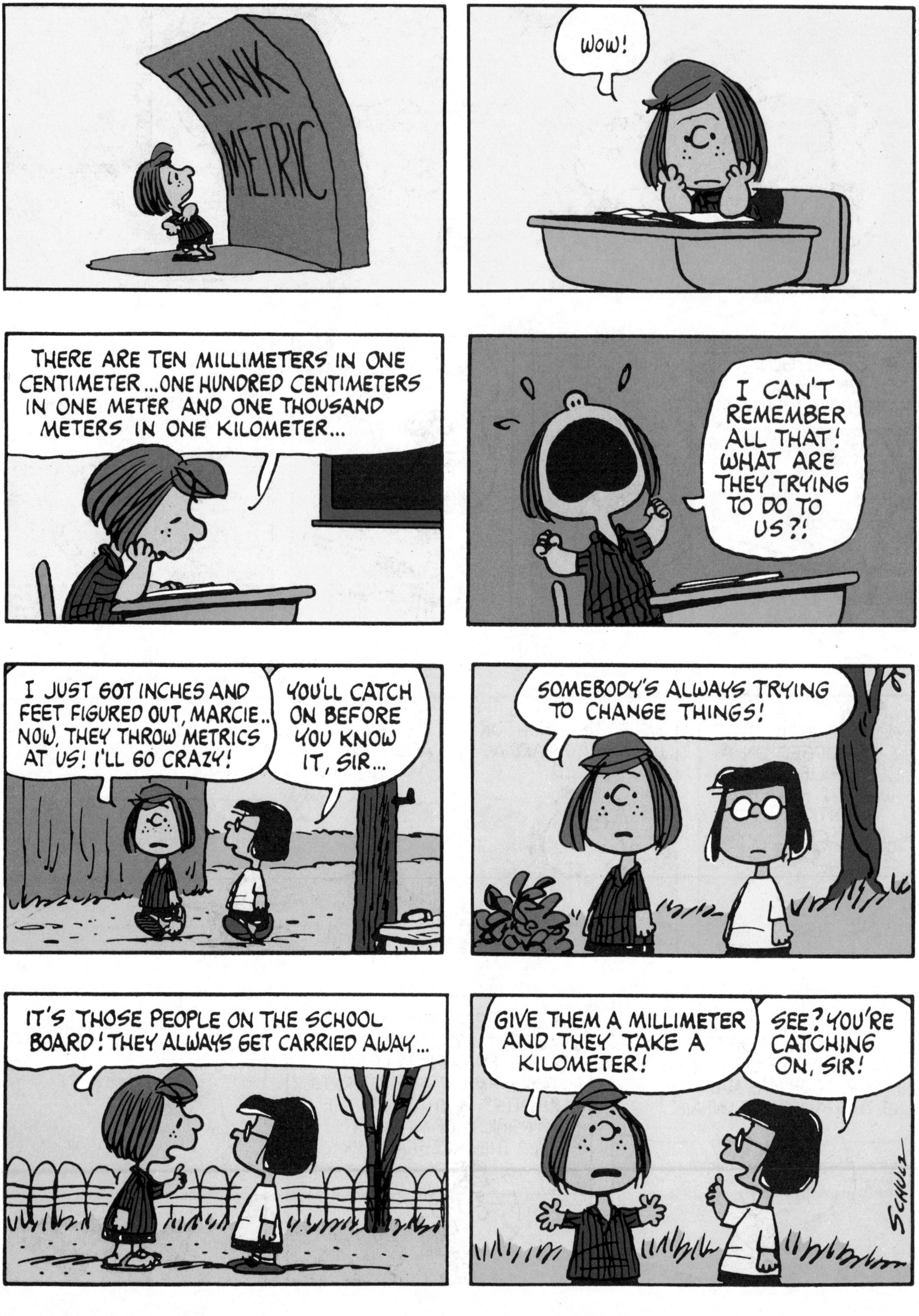
THINK METRIC
WOW!
THERE ARE TEN MILLIMETERS IN ONE CENTIMETER...ONE HUNDRED CENTIMETERS IN ONE METER AND ONE THOUSAND METERS IN ONE KILOMETER...
I CAN'T REMEMBER ALL THAT! WHAT ARE THEY TRYING TO DO TO US?!
I JUST GOT INCHES AND FEET FIGURED OUT, MARCIE.. NOW, THEY THROW METRICS AT US! I'LL GO CRAZY!
YOU'LL CATCH ON BEFORE YOU KNOW IT, SIR...
SOMEBODY'S ALWAYS TRYING TO CHANGE THINGS!
IT'S THOSE PEOPLE ON THE SCHOOL BOARD! THEY ALWAYS GET CARRIED AWAY...
GIVE THEM A MILLIMETER AND THEY TAKE A KILOMETER!
SEE? YOU'RE CATCHING ON, SIR!
SCHULZ

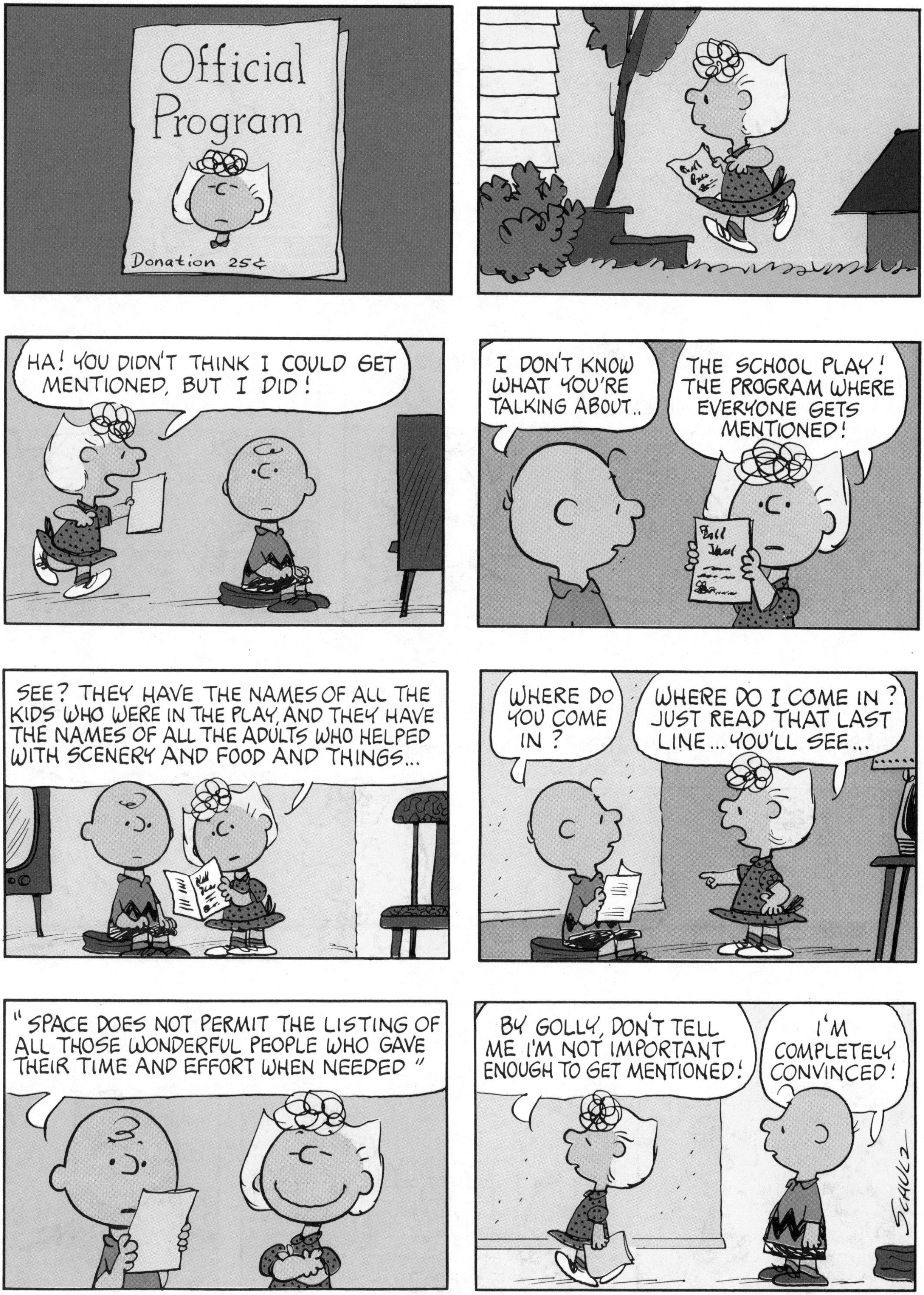
Official Program
Donation 25¢
HA! YOU DIDN'T THINK I COULD GET MENTIONED, BUT I DID!
I DON'T KNOW WHAT YOU'RE TALKING ABOUT..
THE SCHOOL PLAY! THE PROGRAM WHERE EVERYONE GETS MENTIONED!
SEE? THEY HAVE THE NAMES OF ALL THE KIDS WHO WERE IN THE PLAY, AND THEY HAVE THE NAMES OF ALL THE ADULTS WHO HELPED WITH SCENERY AND FOOD AND THINGS...
WHERE DO YOU COME IN?
WHERE DO I COME IN? JUST READ THAT LAST LINE... YOU'LL SEE...
" SPACE DOES NOT PERMIT THE LISTING OF ALL THOSE WONDERFUL PEOPLE WHO GAVE THEIR TIME AND EFFORT WHEN NEEDED "
BY GOLLY, DON'T TELL ME I'M NOT IMPORTANT ENOUGH TO GET MENTIONED!
I'M COMPLETELY CONVINCED!
SCHULZ

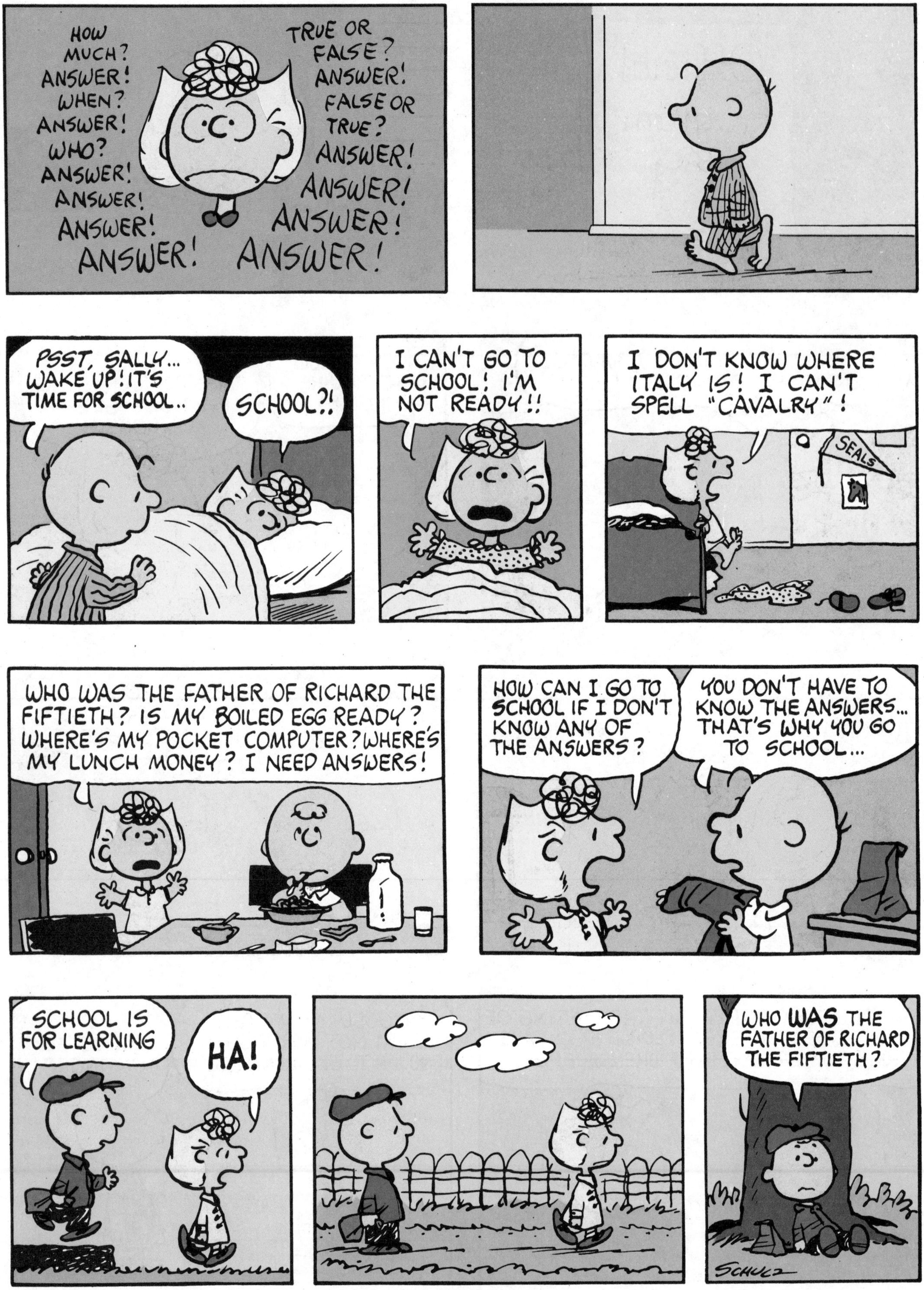
HOW MUCH? ANSWER! WHEN? ANSWER! WHO? ANSWER! ANSWER! ANSWER! ANSWER!
TRUE OR FALSE? ANSWER! FALSE OR TRUE? ANSWER! ANSWER! ANSWER! ANSWER!
PSST, SALLY... WAKE UP! IT'S TIME FOR SCHOOL..
SCHOOL?!
I CAN'T GO TO SCHOOL! I'M NOT READY!!
I DON'T KNOW WHERE ITALY IS! I CAN'T SPELL "CAVALRY"!
SEALS
WHO WAS THE FATHER OF RICHARD THE FIFTIETH? IS MY BOILED EGG READY? WHERE'S MY POCKET COMPUTER? WHERE'S MY LUNCH MONEY? I NEED ANSWERS!
HOW CAN I GO TO SCHOOL IF I DON'T KNOW ANY OF THE ANSWERS?
YOU DON'T HAVE TO KNOW THE ANSWERS... THAT'S WHY YOU GO TO SCHOOL...
SCHOOL IS FOR LEARNING
HA!
WHO **WAS** THE FATHER OF RICHARD THE FIFTIETH?
SCHULZ

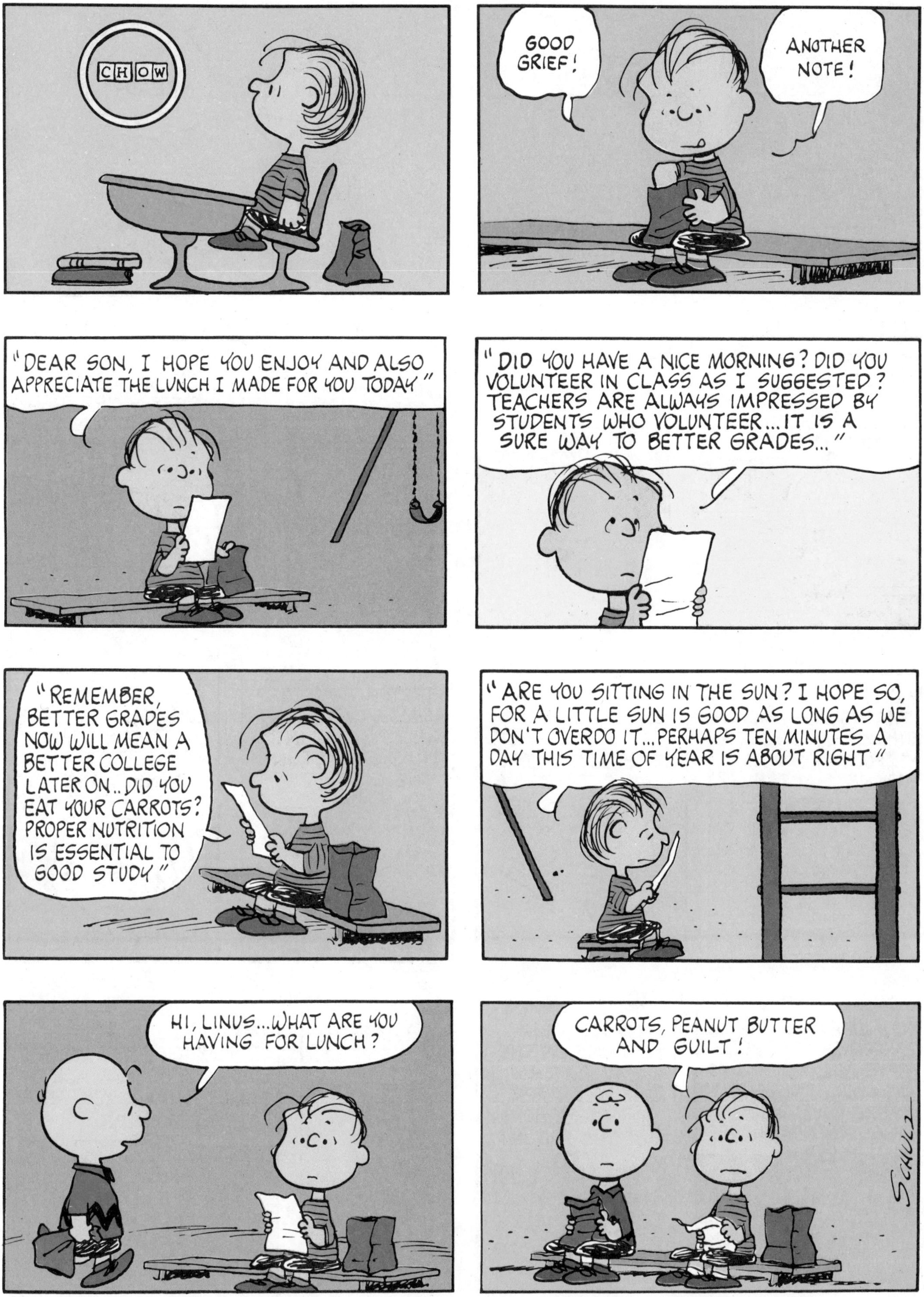
CHOW
GOOD GRIEF!
ANOTHER NOTE!
"DEAR SON, I HOPE YOU ENJOY AND ALSO APPRECIATE THE LUNCH I MADE FOR YOU TODAY"
"DID YOU HAVE A NICE MORNING? DID YOU VOLUNTEER IN CLASS AS I SUGGESTED? TEACHERS ARE ALWAYS IMPRESSED BY STUDENTS WHO VOLUNTEER...IT IS A SURE WAY TO BETTER GRADES..."
"REMEMBER, BETTER GRADES NOW WILL MEAN A BETTER COLLEGE LATER ON..DID YOU EAT YOUR CARROTS? PROPER NUTRITION IS ESSENTIAL TO GOOD STUDY"
"ARE YOU SITTING IN THE SUN? I HOPE SO, FOR A LITTLE SUN IS GOOD AS LONG AS WE DON'T OVERDO IT...PERHAPS TEN MINUTES A DAY THIS TIME OF YEAR IS ABOUT RIGHT"
HI, LINUS...WHAT ARE YOU HAVING FOR LUNCH?
CARROTS, PEANUT BUTTER AND GUILT!
SCHULZ

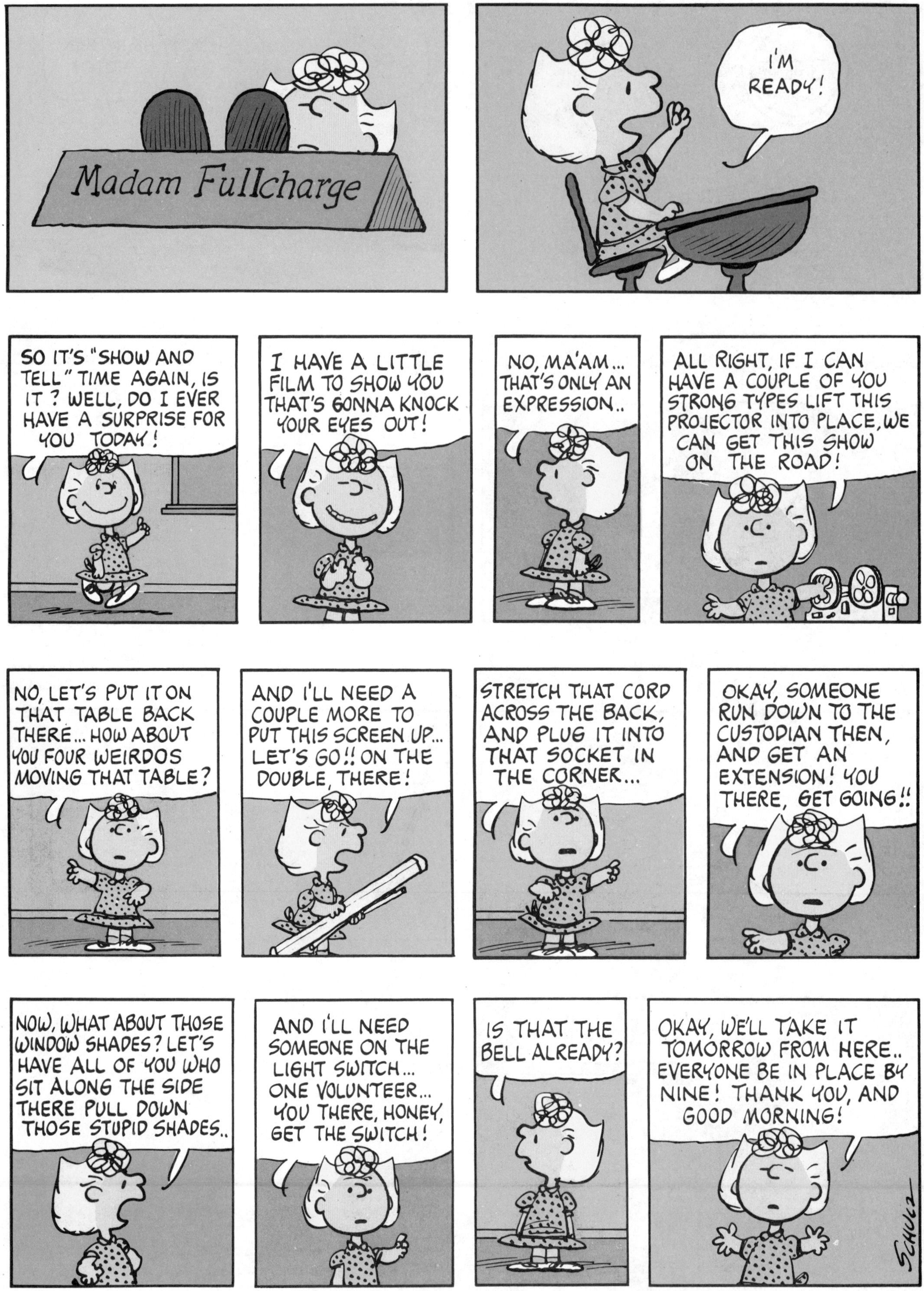
Madam Fullcharge
I'M READY!
SO IT'S "SHOW AND TELL" TIME AGAIN, IS IT ? WELL, DO I EVER HAVE A SURPRISE FOR YOU TODAY!
I HAVE A LITTLE FILM TO SHOW YOU THAT'S GONNA KNOCK YOUR EYES OUT!
NO, MA'AM... THAT'S ONLY AN EXPRESSION..
ALL RIGHT, IF I CAN HAVE A COUPLE OF YOU STRONG TYPES LIFT THIS PROJECTOR INTO PLACE, WE CAN GET THIS SHOW ON THE ROAD!
NO, LET'S PUT IT ON THAT TABLE BACK THERE... HOW ABOUT YOU FOUR WEIRDOS MOVING THAT TABLE?
AND I'LL NEED A COUPLE MORE TO PUT THIS SCREEN UP... LET'S GO!! ON THE DOUBLE, THERE!
STRETCH THAT CORD ACROSS THE BACK, AND PLUG IT INTO THAT SOCKET IN THE CORNER...
OKAY, SOMEONE RUN DOWN TO THE CUSTODIAN THEN, AND GET AN EXTENSION! YOU THERE, GET GOING!!
NOW, WHAT ABOUT THOSE WINDOW SHADES? LET'S HAVE ALL OF YOU WHO SIT ALONG THE SIDE THERE PULL DOWN THOSE STUPID SHADES..
AND I'LL NEED SOMEONE ON THE LIGHT SWITCH... ONE VOLUNTEER... YOU THERE, HONEY, GET THE SWITCH!
IS THAT THE BELL ALREADY?
OKAY, WE'LL TAKE IT TOMORROW FROM HERE.. EVERYONE BE IN PLACE BY NINE! THANK YOU, AND GOOD MORNING!
SCHULZ

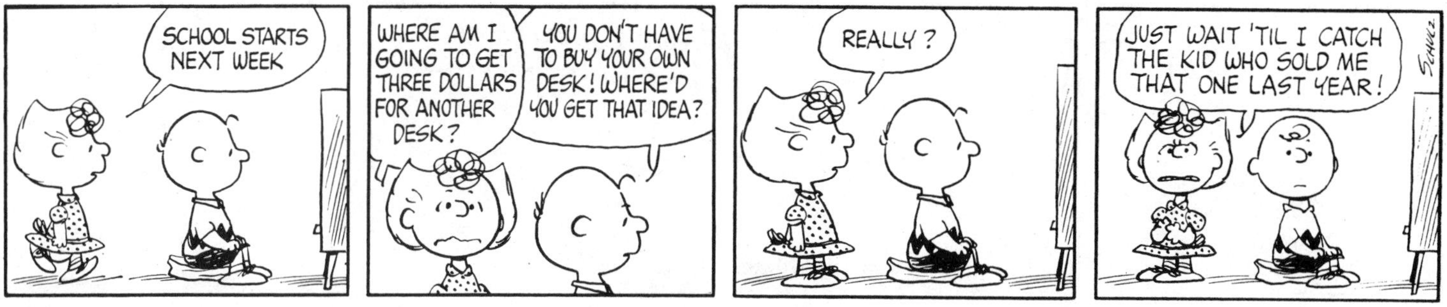
SCHOOL STARTS NEXT WEEK
WHERE AM I GOING TO GET THREE DOLLARS FOR ANOTHER DESK?
YOU DON'T HAVE TO BUY YOUR OWN DESK! WHERE'D YOU GET THAT IDEA?
REALLY?
JUST WAIT 'TIL I CATCH THE KID WHO SOLD ME THAT ONE LAST YEAR!

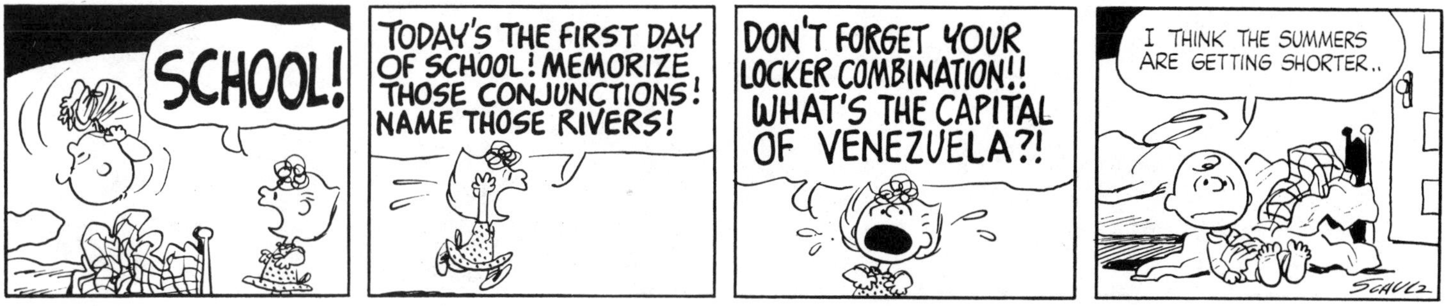
SCHOOL!
TODAY'S THE FIRST DAY OF SCHOOL! MEMORIZE THOSE CONJUNCTIONS! NAME THOSE RIVERS!
DON'T FORGET YOUR LOCKER COMBINATION!! WHAT'S THE CAPITAL OF VENEZUELA?!
I THINK THE SUMMERS ARE GETTING SHORTER..

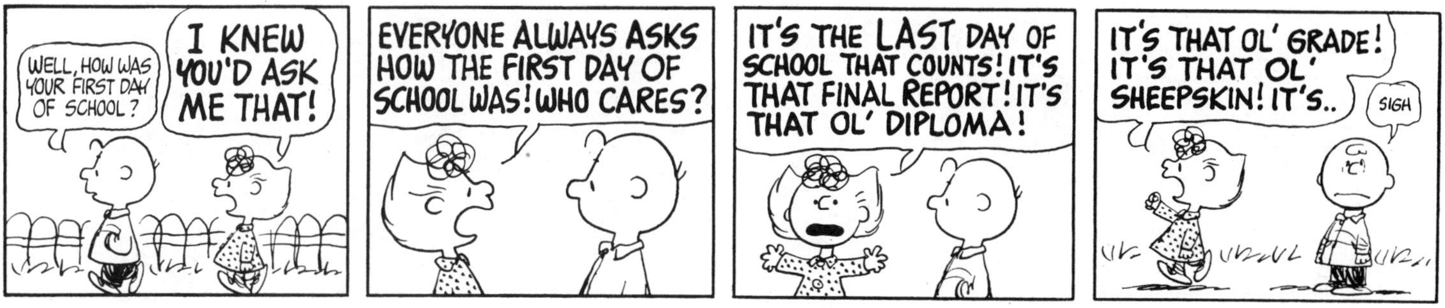
WELL, HOW WAS YOUR FIRST DAY OF SCHOOL?
I KNEW YOU'D ASK ME THAT!
EVERYONE ALWAYS ASKS HOW THE FIRST DAY OF SCHOOL WAS! WHO CARES?
IT'S THE LAST DAY OF SCHOOL THAT COUNTS! IT'S THAT FINAL REPORT! IT'S THAT OL' DIPLOMA!
IT'S THAT OL' GRADE! IT'S THAT OL' SHEEPSKIN! IT'S..
SIGH

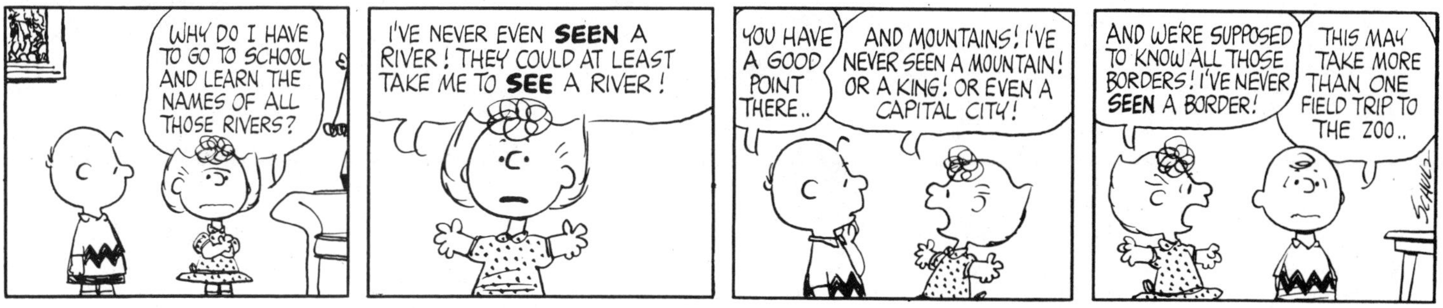
WHY DO I HAVE TO GO TO SCHOOL AND LEARN THE NAMES OF ALL THOSE RIVERS?
I'VE NEVER EVEN SEEN A RIVER! THEY COULD AT LEAST TAKE ME TO SEE A RIVER!
YOU HAVE A GOOD POINT THERE..
AND MOUNTAINS! I'VE NEVER SEEN A MOUNTAIN! OR A KING! OR EVEN A CAPITAL CITY!
AND WE'RE SUPPOSED TO KNOW ALL THOSE BORDERS! I'VE NEVER SEEN A BORDER!
THIS MAY TAKE MORE THAN ONE FIELD TRIP TO THE ZOO..

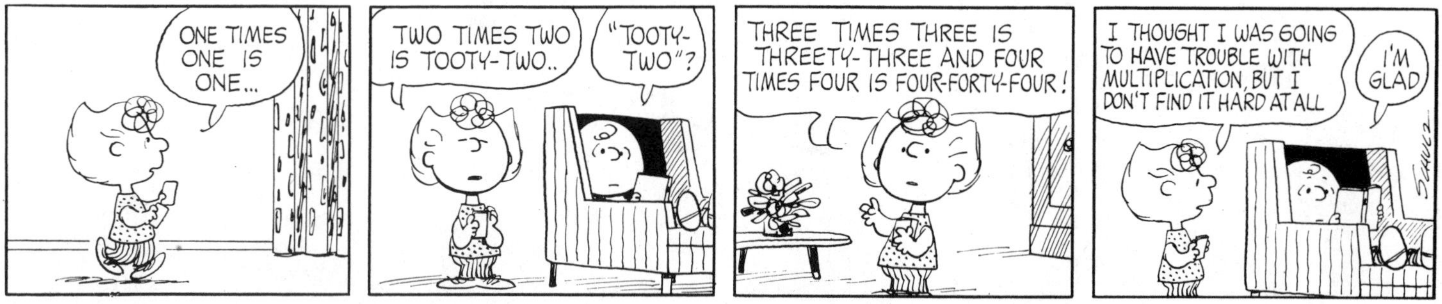
ONE TIMES ONE IS ONE...
TWO TIMES TWO IS TOOTY-TWO..
"TOOTY-TWO"?
THREE TIMES THREE IS THREETY-THREE AND FOUR TIMES FOUR IS FOUR-FORTY-FOUR!
I THOUGHT I WAS GOING TO HAVE TROUBLE WITH MULTIPLICATION, BUT I DON'T FIND IT HARD AT ALL
I'M GLAD

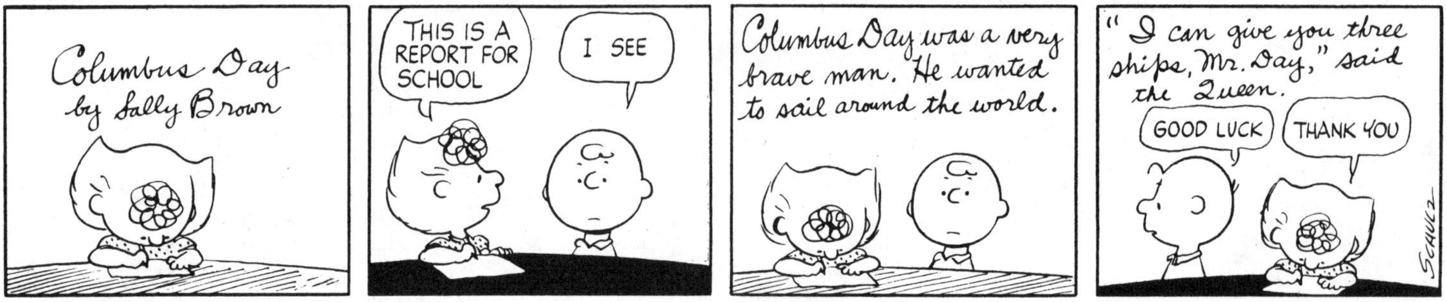
Columbus Day
by Sally Brown
THIS IS A REPORT FOR SCHOOL
I SEE
Columbus Day was a very brave man. He wanted to sail around the world.
"I can give you three ships, Mr. Day," said the Queen.
GOOD LUCK
THANK YOU
SCHULZ

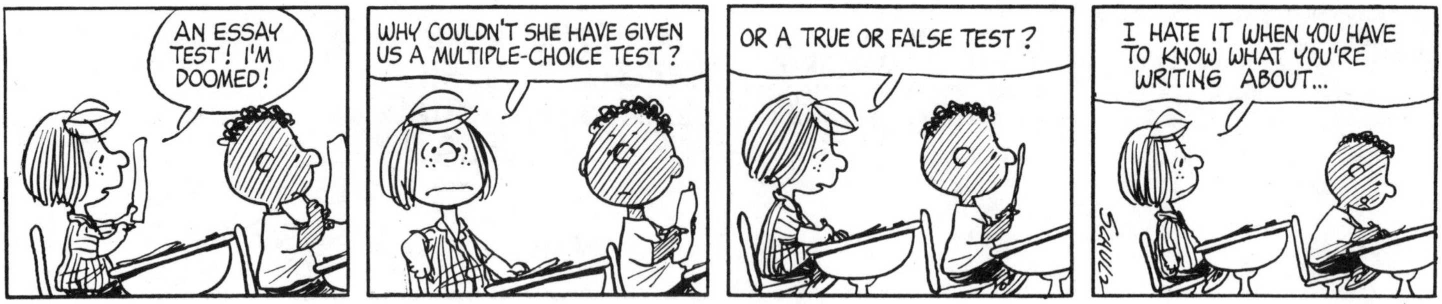
AN ESSAY TEST! I'M DOOMED!
WHY COULDN'T SHE HAVE GIVEN US A MULTIPLE-CHOICE TEST?
OR A TRUE OR FALSE TEST?
I HATE IT WHEN YOU HAVE TO KNOW WHAT YOU'RE WRITING ABOUT...
SCHULZ

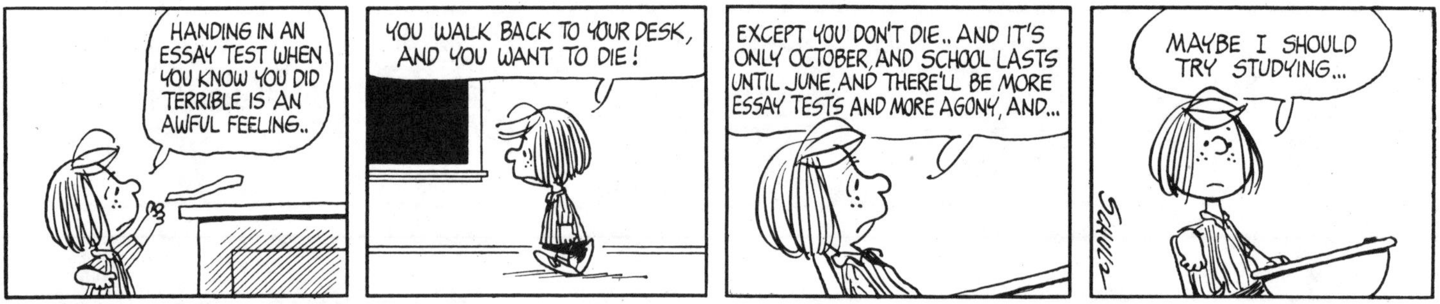
HANDING IN AN ESSAY TEST WHEN YOU KNOW YOU DID TERRIBLE IS AN AWFUL FEELING..
YOU WALK BACK TO YOUR DESK, AND YOU WANT TO DIE!
EXCEPT YOU DON'T DIE.. AND IT'S ONLY OCTOBER, AND SCHOOL LASTS UNTIL JUNE, AND THERE'LL BE MORE ESSAY TESTS AND MORE AGONY, AND...
MAYBE I SHOULD TRY STUDYING...
SCHULZ

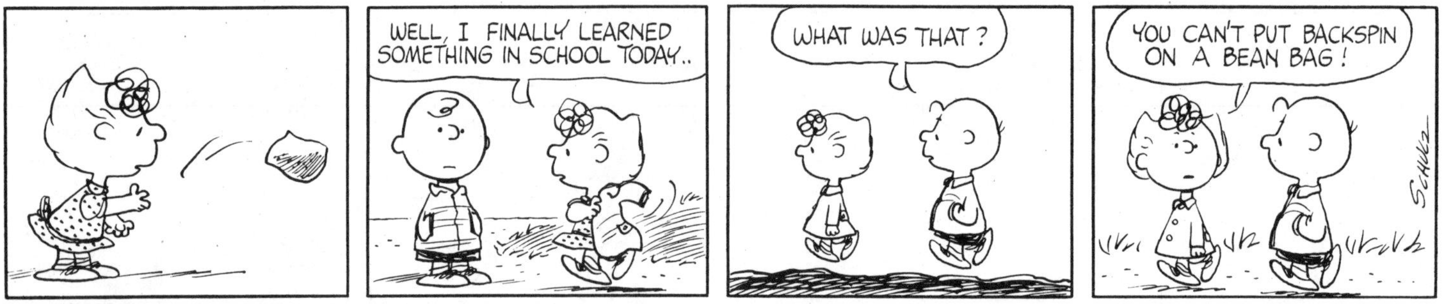
WELL, I FINALLY LEARNED SOMETHING IN SCHOOL TODAY..
WHAT WAS THAT?
YOU CAN'T PUT BACKSPIN ON A BEAN BAG!
SCHULZ

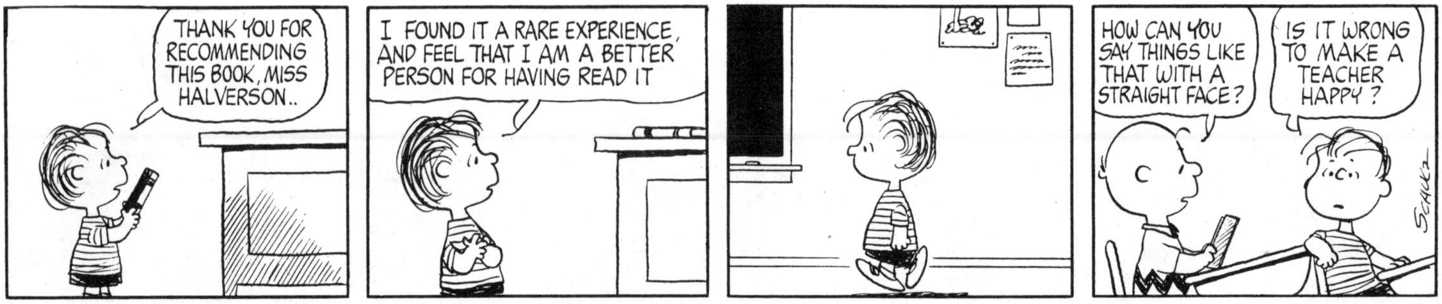
THANK YOU FOR RECOMMENDING THIS BOOK, MISS HALVERSON..
I FOUND IT A RARE EXPERIENCE, AND FEEL THAT I AM A BETTER PERSON FOR HAVING READ IT
HOW CAN YOU SAY THINGS LIKE THAT WITH A STRAIGHT FACE?
IS IT WRONG TO MAKE A TEACHER HAPPY?
SCHULZ

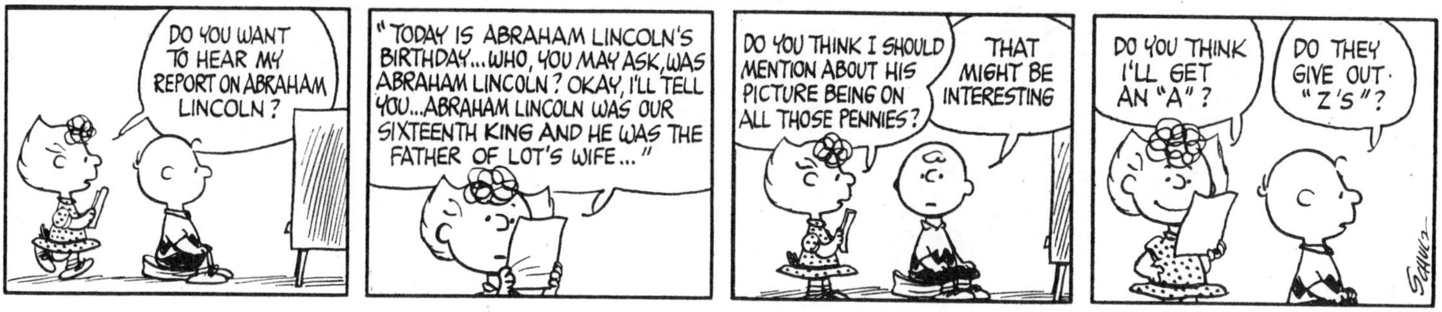
DO YOU WANT TO HEAR MY REPORT ON ABRAHAM LINCOLN?
"TODAY IS ABRAHAM LINCOLN'S BIRTHDAY...WHO, YOU MAY ASK, WAS ABRAHAM LINCOLN? OKAY, I'LL TELL YOU...ABRAHAM LINCOLN WAS OUR SIXTEENTH KING AND HE WAS THE FATHER OF LOT'S WIFE..."
DO YOU THINK I SHOULD MENTION ABOUT HIS PICTURE BEING ON ALL THOSE PENNIES?
THAT MIGHT BE INTERESTING
DO YOU THINK I'LL GET AN "A"?
DO THEY GIVE OUT "Z'S"?

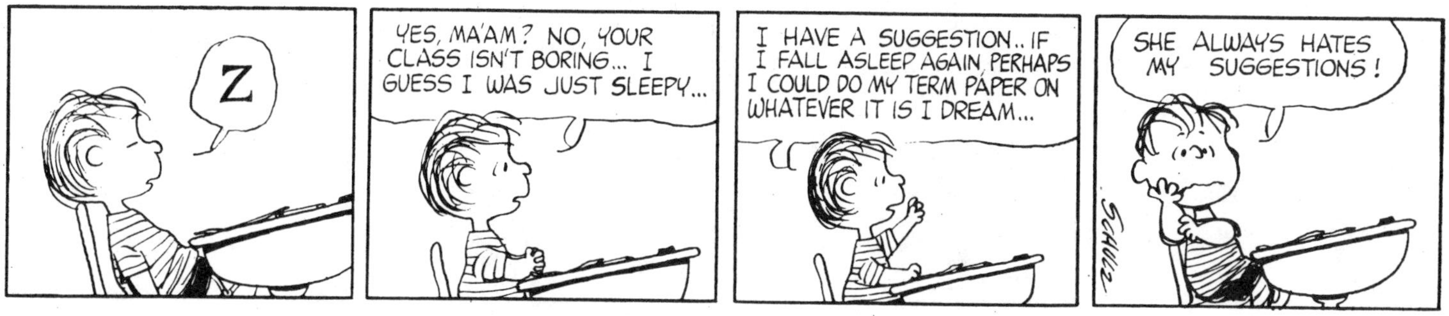
Z
YES, MA'AM? NO, YOUR CLASS ISN'T BORING... I GUESS I WAS JUST SLEEPY...
I HAVE A SUGGESTION.. IF I FALL ASLEEP AGAIN PERHAPS I COULD DO MY TERM PAPER ON WHATEVER IT IS I DREAM...
SHE ALWAYS HATES MY SUGGESTIONS!

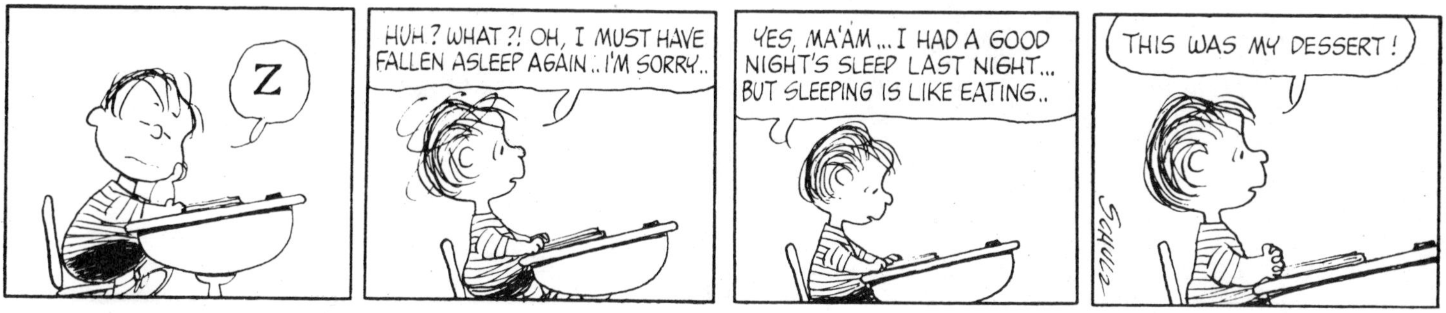
Z
HUH? WHAT?! OH, I MUST HAVE FALLEN ASLEEP AGAIN.. I'M SORRY..
YES, MA'AM... I HAD A GOOD NIGHT'S SLEEP LAST NIGHT... BUT SLEEPING IS LIKE EATING..
THIS WAS MY DESSERT!

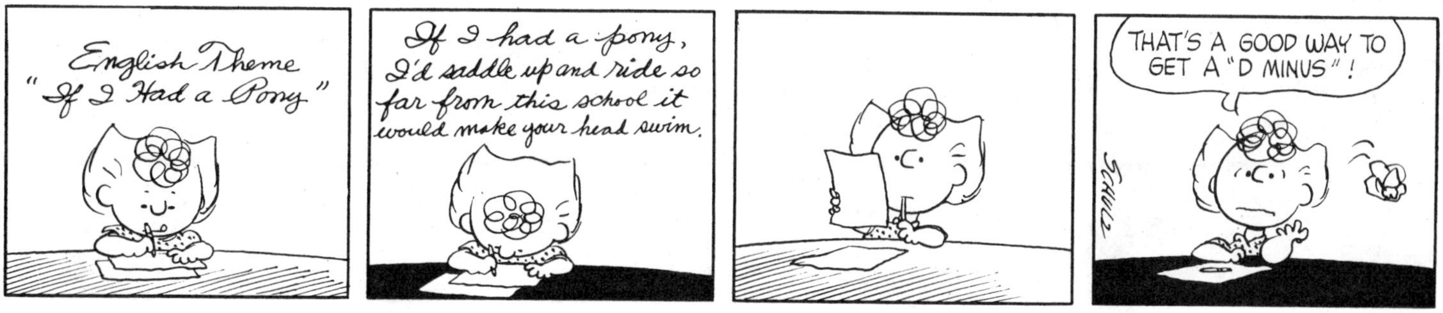
English Theme "If I Had a Pony"
If I had a pony, I'd saddle up and ride so far from this school it would make your head swim.
THAT'S A GOOD WAY TO GET A "D MINUS"!

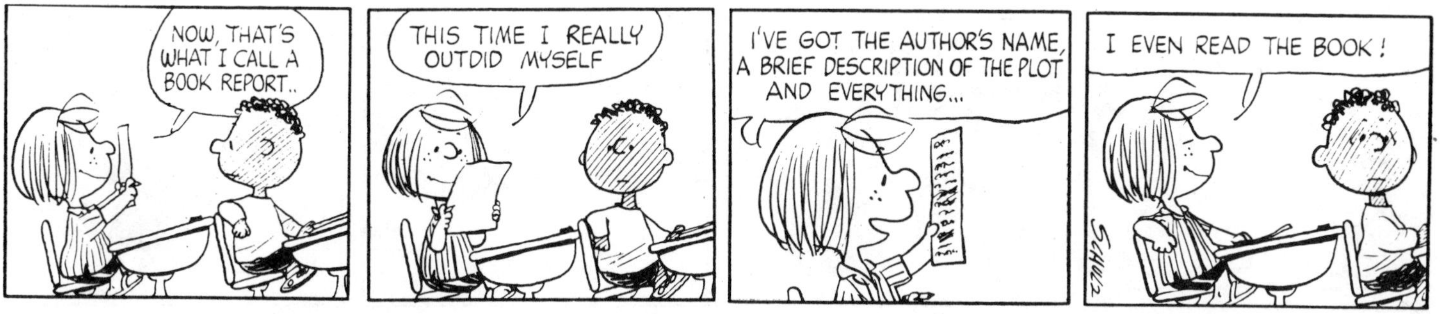
NOW, THAT'S WHAT I CALL A BOOK REPORT..
THIS TIME I REALLY OUTDID MYSELF
I'VE GOT THE AUTHOR'S NAME, A BRIEF DESCRIPTION OF THE PLOT AND EVERYTHING...
I EVEN READ THE BOOK!

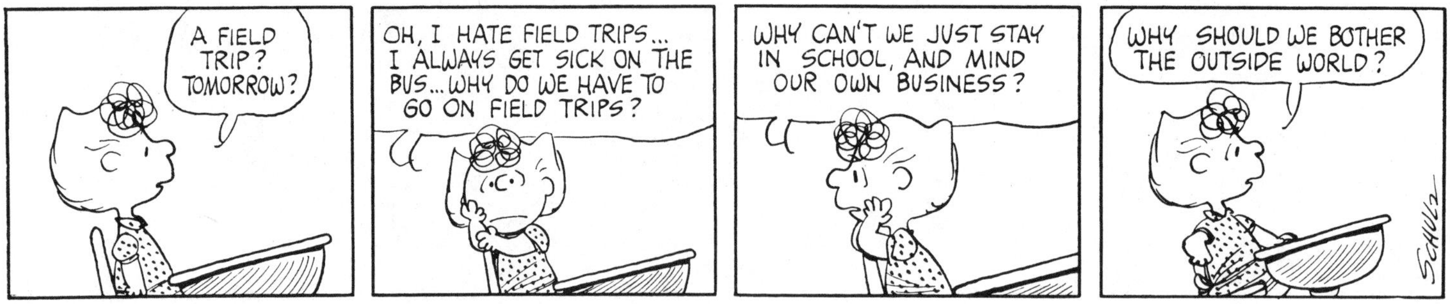
A FIELD TRIP? TOMORROW?
OH, I HATE FIELD TRIPS... I ALWAYS GET SICK ON THE BUS... WHY DO WE HAVE TO GO ON FIELD TRIPS?
WHY CAN'T WE JUST STAY IN SCHOOL, AND MIND OUR OWN BUSINESS?
WHY SHOULD WE BOTHER THE OUTSIDE WORLD?
SCHULZ

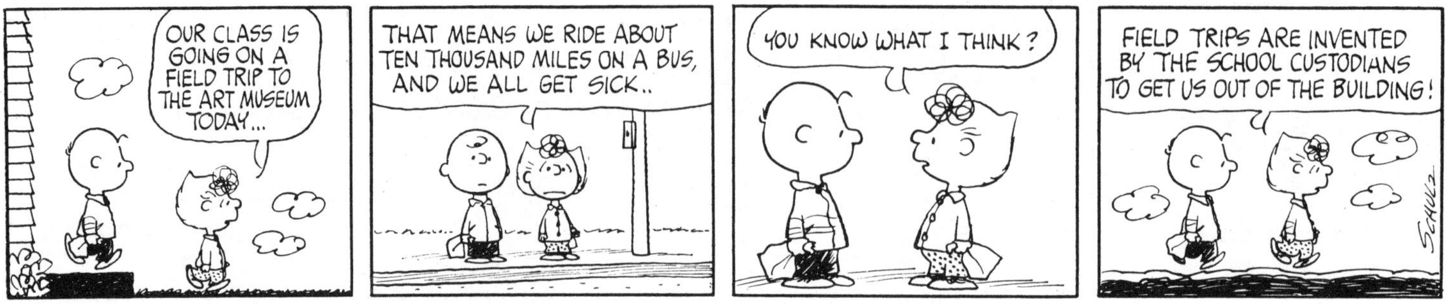
OUR CLASS IS GOING ON A FIELD TRIP TO THE ART MUSEUM TODAY...
THAT MEANS WE RIDE ABOUT TEN THOUSAND MILES ON A BUS, AND WE ALL GET SICK..
YOU KNOW WHAT I THINK?
FIELD TRIPS ARE INVENTED BY THE SCHOOL CUSTODIANS TO GET US OUT OF THE BUILDING!
SCHULZ

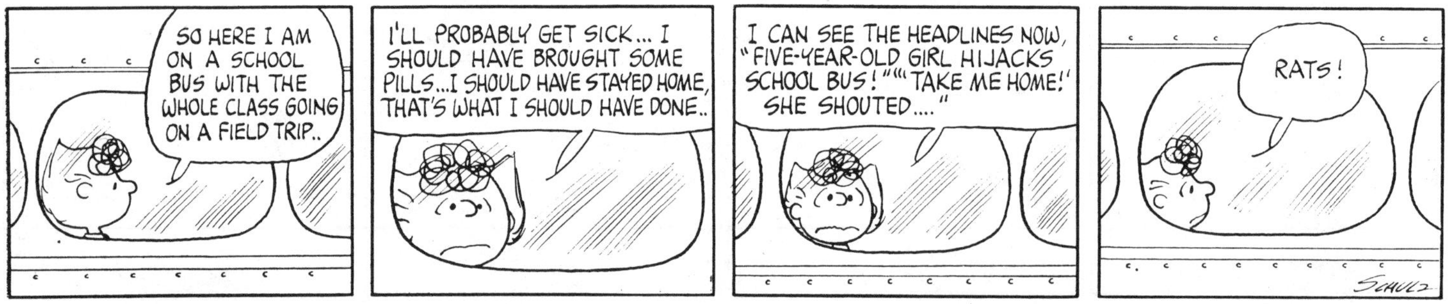
SO HERE I AM ON A SCHOOL BUS WITH THE WHOLE CLASS GOING ON A FIELD TRIP..
I'LL PROBABLY GET SICK... I SHOULD HAVE BROUGHT SOME PILLS... I SHOULD HAVE STAYED HOME, THAT'S WHAT I SHOULD HAVE DONE..
I CAN SEE THE HEADLINES NOW, "FIVE-YEAR-OLD GIRL HIJACKS SCHOOL BUS!" "'TAKE ME HOME!' SHE SHOUTED...."
RATS!
SCHULZ

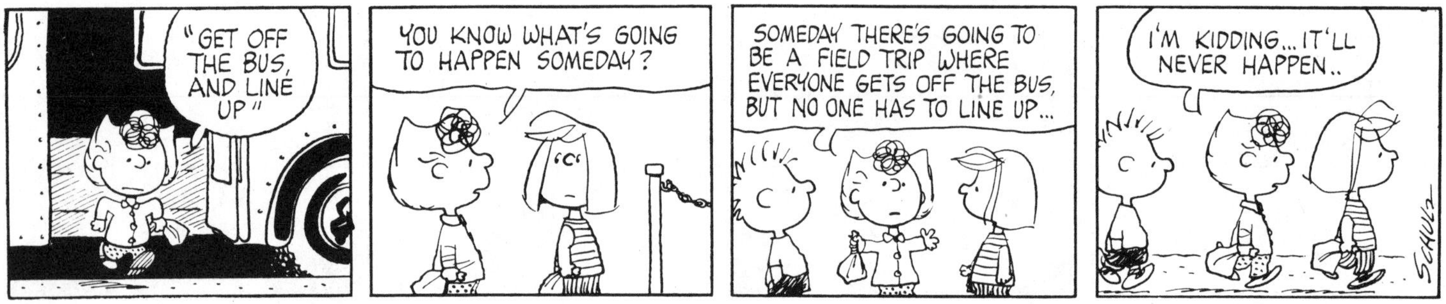
"GET OFF THE BUS, AND LINE UP"
YOU KNOW WHAT'S GOING TO HAPPEN SOMEDAY?
SOMEDAY THERE'S GOING TO BE A FIELD TRIP WHERE EVERYONE GETS OFF THE BUS, BUT NO ONE HAS TO LINE UP...
I'M KIDDING... IT'LL NEVER HAPPEN..
SCHULZ

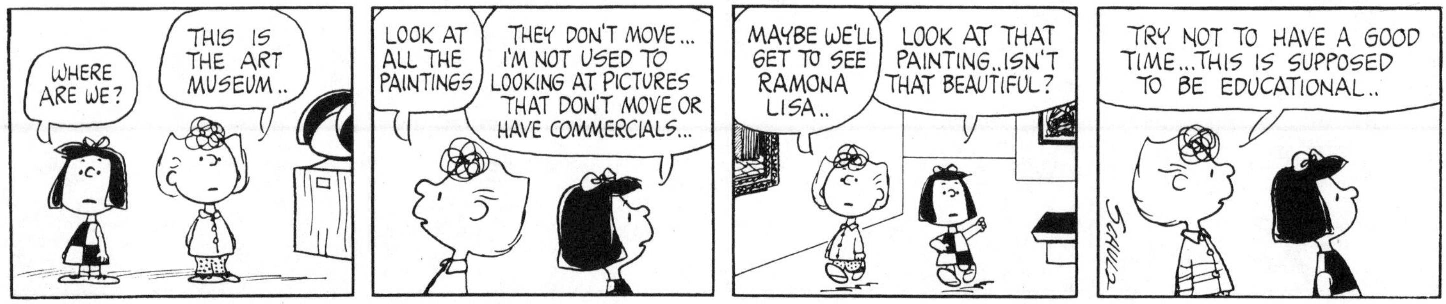
WHERE ARE WE?
THIS IS THE ART MUSEUM..
LOOK AT ALL THE PAINTINGS
THEY DON'T MOVE... I'M NOT USED TO LOOKING AT PICTURES THAT DON'T MOVE OR HAVE COMMERCIALS...
MAYBE WE'LL GET TO SEE RAMONA LISA..
LOOK AT THAT PAINTING.. ISN'T THAT BEAUTIFUL?
TRY NOT TO HAVE A GOOD TIME... THIS IS SUPPOSED TO BE EDUCATIONAL..
SCHULZ

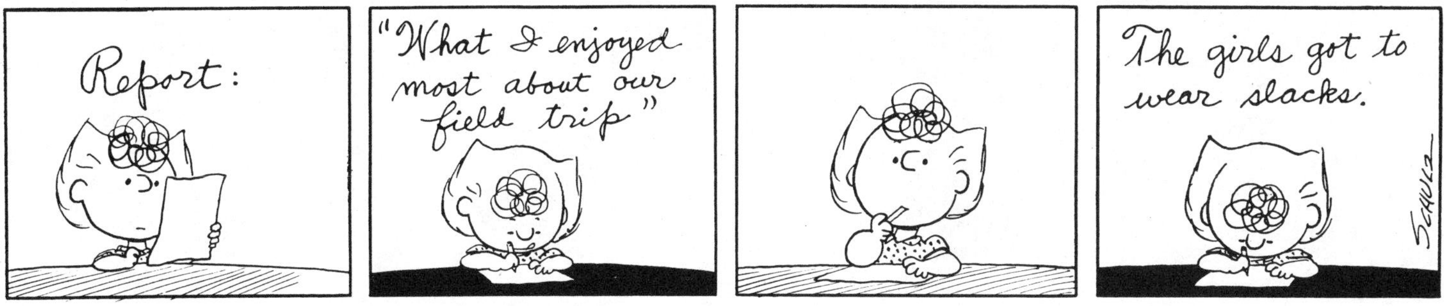

Report:
"What I enjoyed most about our field trip"
The girls got to wear slacks.
SCHULZ

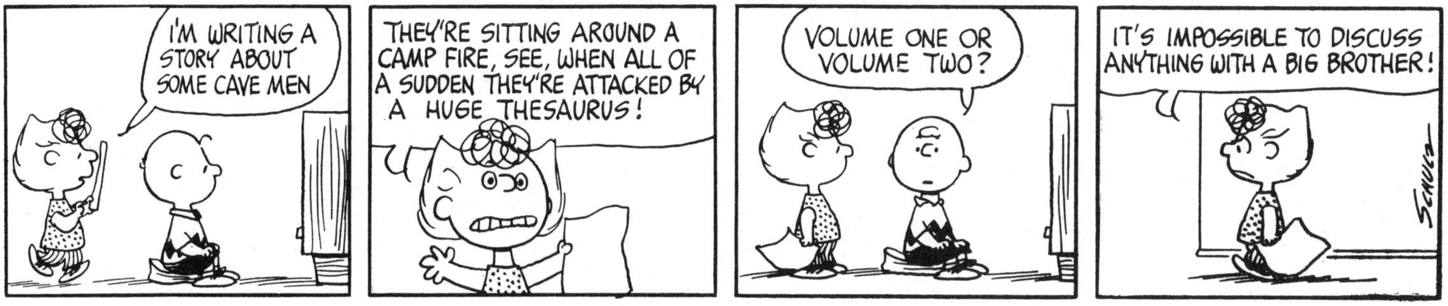

I'M WRITING A STORY ABOUT SOME CAVE MEN
THEY'RE SITTING AROUND A CAMP FIRE, SEE, WHEN ALL OF A SUDDEN THEY'RE ATTACKED BY A HUGE THESAURUS!
VOLUME ONE OR VOLUME TWO?
IT'S IMPOSSIBLE TO DISCUSS ANYTHING WITH A BIG BROTHER!
SCHULZ

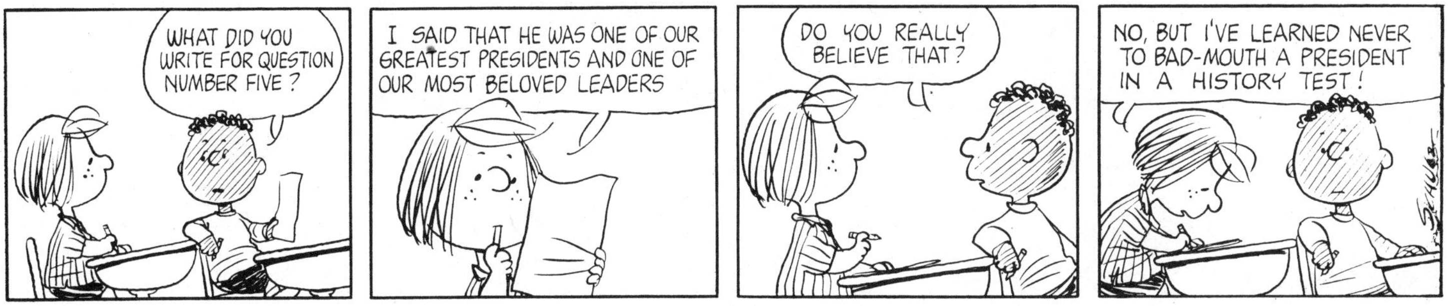

WHAT DID YOU WRITE FOR QUESTION NUMBER FIVE?
I SAID THAT HE WAS ONE OF OUR GREATEST PRESIDENTS AND ONE OF OUR MOST BELOVED LEADERS
DO YOU REALLY BELIEVE THAT?
NO, BUT I'VE LEARNED NEVER TO BAD-MOUTH A PRESIDENT IN A HISTORY TEST!

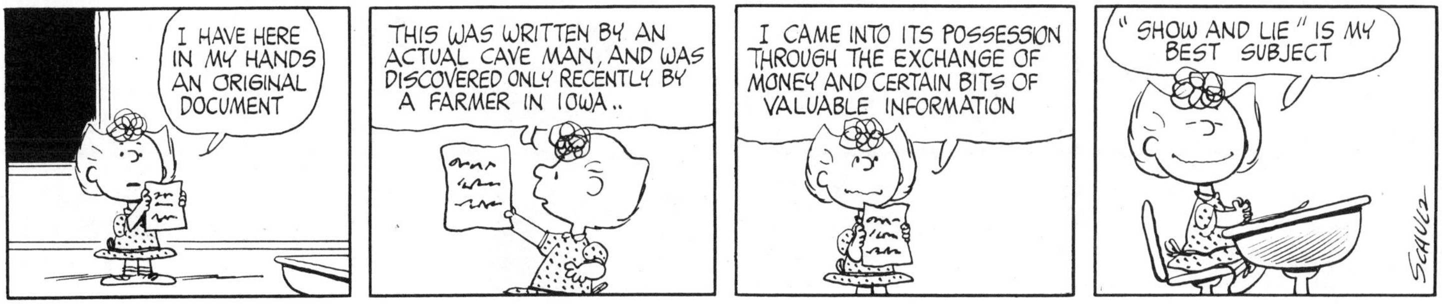

I HAVE HERE IN MY HANDS AN ORIGINAL DOCUMENT
THIS WAS WRITTEN BY AN ACTUAL CAVE MAN, AND WAS DISCOVERED ONLY RECENTLY BY A FARMER IN IOWA..
I CAME INTO ITS POSSESSION THROUGH THE EXCHANGE OF MONEY AND CERTAIN BITS OF VALUABLE INFORMATION
" SHOW AND LIE " IS MY BEST SUBJECT
SCHULZ

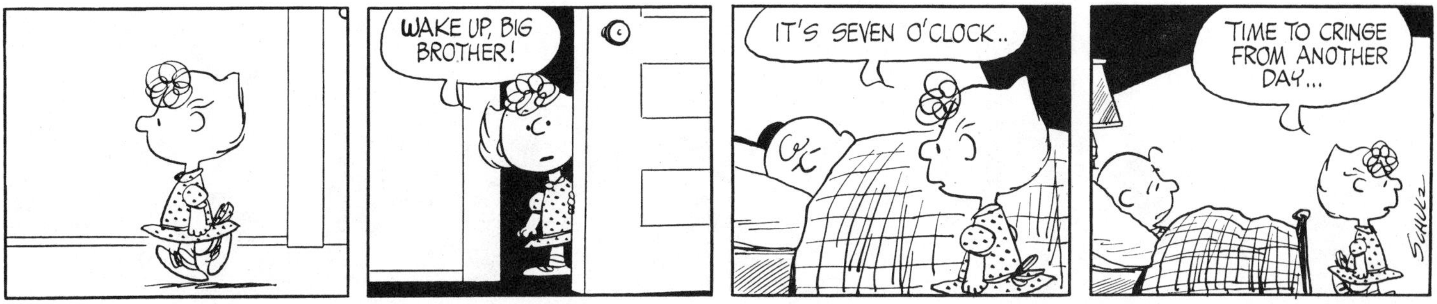

WAKE UP, BIG BROTHER!
IT'S SEVEN O'CLOCK..
TIME TO CRINGE FROM ANOTHER DAY...
SCHULZ

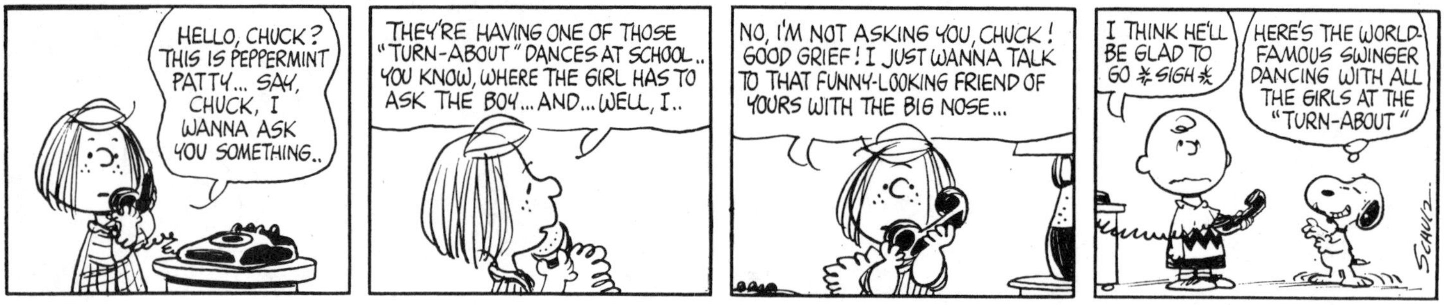
HELLO, CHUCK? THIS IS PEPPERMINT PATTY... SAY, CHUCK, I WANNA ASK YOU SOMETHING..
THEY'RE HAVING ONE OF THOSE "TURN-ABOUT" DANCES AT SCHOOL.. YOU KNOW, WHERE THE GIRL HAS TO ASK THE BOY... AND... WELL, I..
NO, I'M NOT ASKING YOU, CHUCK! GOOD GRIEF! I JUST WANNA TALK TO THAT FUNNY-LOOKING FRIEND OF YOURS WITH THE BIG NOSE...
I THINK HE'LL BE GLAD TO GO ✲SIGH✲
HERE'S THE WORLD-FAMOUS SWINGER DANCING WITH ALL THE GIRLS AT THE "TURN-ABOUT"
SCHULZ

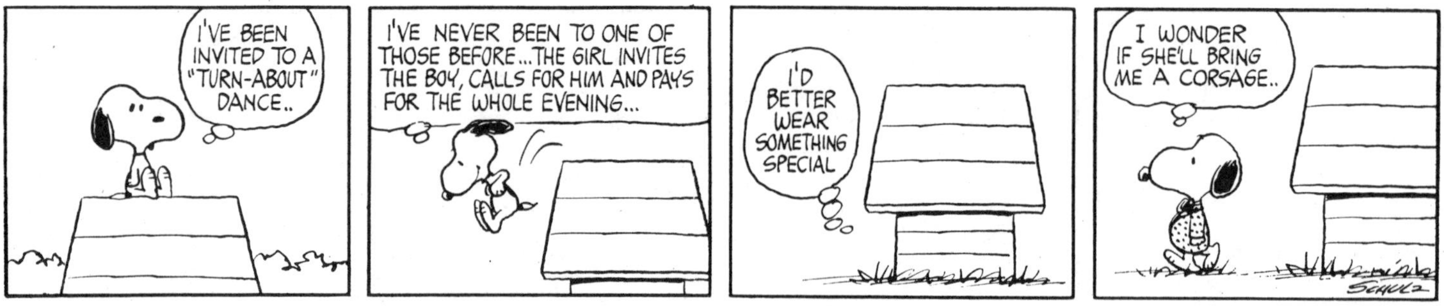
I'VE BEEN INVITED TO A "TURN-ABOUT" DANCE..
I'VE NEVER BEEN TO ONE OF THOSE BEFORE...THE GIRL INVITES THE BOY, CALLS FOR HIM AND PAYS FOR THE WHOLE EVENING...
I'D BETTER WEAR SOMETHING SPECIAL
I WONDER IF SHE'LL BRING ME A CORSAGE..
SCHULZ

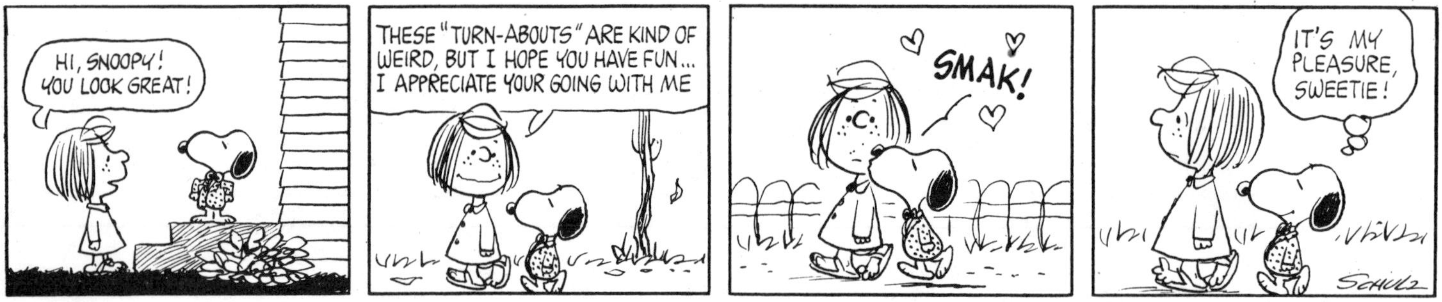
HI, SNOOPY! YOU LOOK GREAT!
THESE "TURN-ABOUTS" ARE KIND OF WEIRD, BUT I HOPE YOU HAVE FUN... I APPRECIATE YOUR GOING WITH ME
SMAK!
IT'S MY PLEASURE, SWEETIE!
SCHULZ

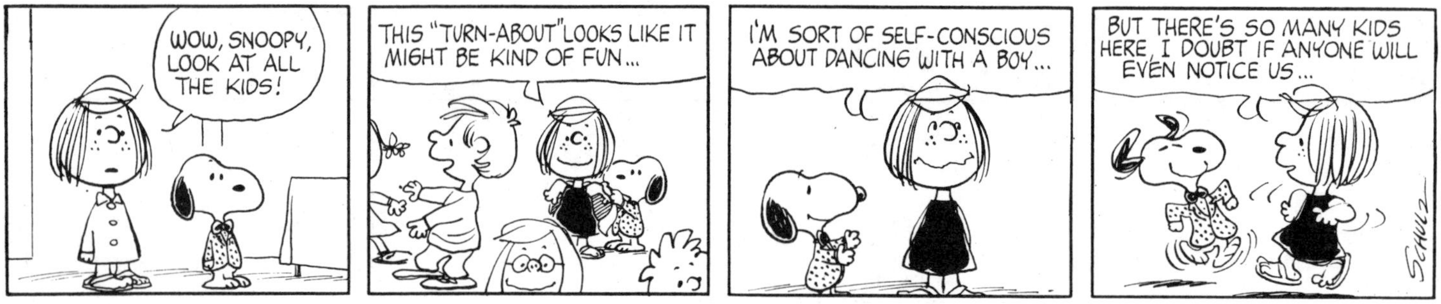
WOW, SNOOPY, LOOK AT ALL THE KIDS!
THIS "TURN-ABOUT" LOOKS LIKE IT MIGHT BE KIND OF FUN...
I'M SORT OF SELF-CONSCIOUS ABOUT DANCING WITH A BOY...
BUT THERE'S SO MANY KIDS HERE, I DOUBT IF ANYONE WILL EVEN NOTICE US...
SCHULZ

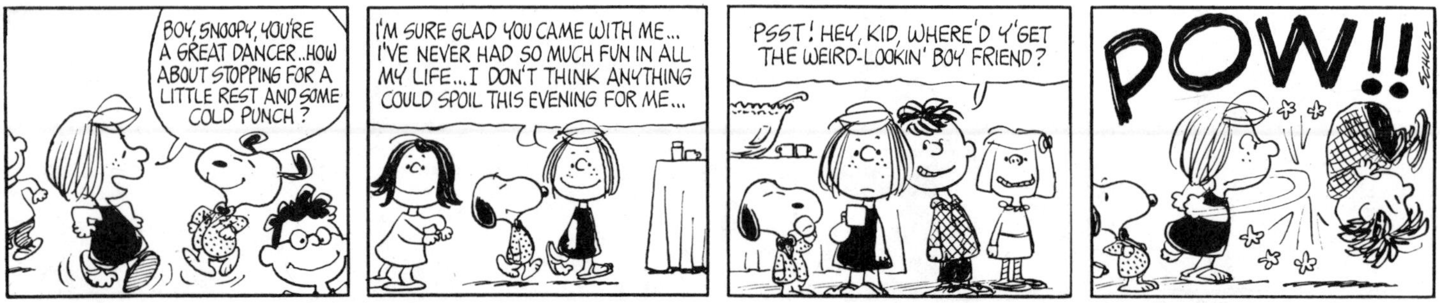
BOY, SNOOPY, YOU'RE A GREAT DANCER..HOW ABOUT STOPPING FOR A LITTLE REST AND SOME COLD PUNCH?
I'M SURE GLAD YOU CAME WITH ME... I'VE NEVER HAD SO MUCH FUN IN ALL MY LIFE... I DON'T THINK ANYTHING COULD SPOIL THIS EVENING FOR ME...
PSST! HEY, KID, WHERE'D Y'GET THE WEIRD-LOOKIN' BOY FRIEND?
POW!!
SCHULZ

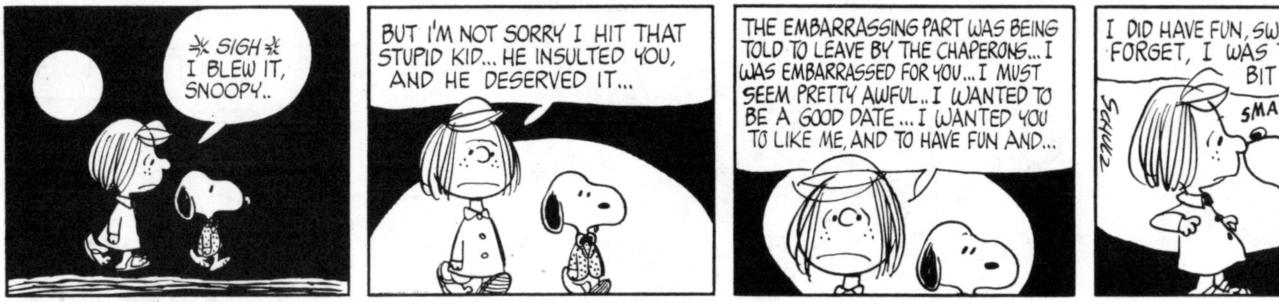

☼ SIGH ☼ I BLEW IT, SNOOPY..
BUT I'M NOT SORRY I HIT THAT STUPID KID... HE INSULTED YOU, AND HE DESERVED IT...
THE EMBARRASSING PART WAS BEING TOLD TO LEAVE BY THE CHAPERONS... I WAS EMBARRASSED FOR YOU... I MUST SEEM PRETTY AWFUL.. I WANTED TO BE A GOOD DATE... I WANTED YOU TO LIKE ME, AND TO HAVE FUN AND...
I DID HAVE FUN, SWEETIE... DON'T FORGET, I WAS THE ONE WHO BIT THE CHAPERON!
SMAK
SCHULZ

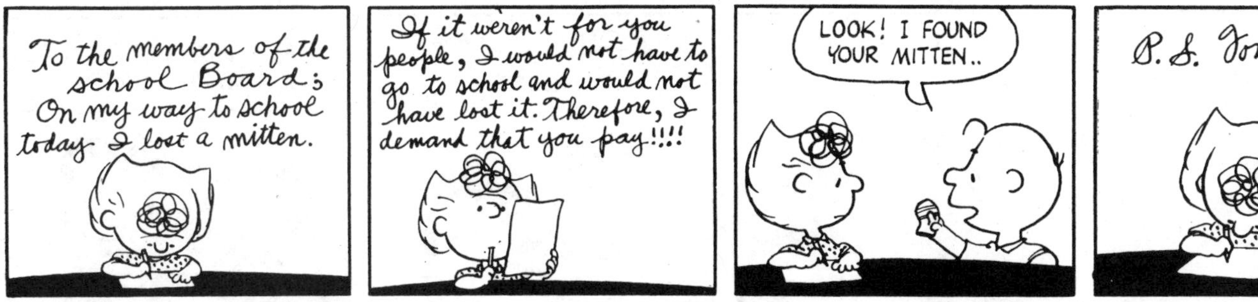

To the members of the school Board: On my way to school today I lost a mitten.
If it weren't for you people, I would not have to go to school and would not have lost it. Therefore, I demand that you pay!!!!
LOOK! I FOUND YOUR MITTEN..
P. S. Forget it.
SCHULZ

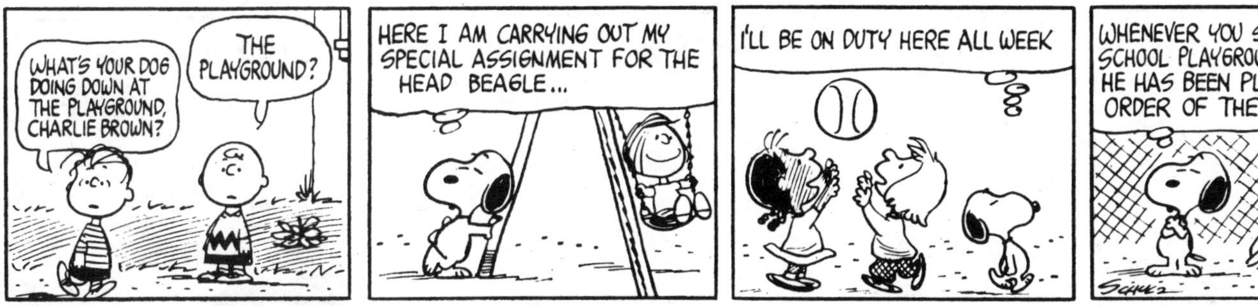

WHAT'S YOUR DOG DOING DOWN AT THE PLAYGROUND, CHARLIE BROWN?
THE PLAYGROUND?
HERE I AM CARRYING OUT MY SPECIAL ASSIGNMENT FOR THE HEAD BEAGLE...
I'LL BE ON DUTY HERE ALL WEEK
WHENEVER YOU SEE A DOG ON A SCHOOL PLAYGROUND, YOU KNOW THAT HE HAS BEEN PLACED THERE BY ORDER OF THE HEAD BEAGLE!
SCHULZ

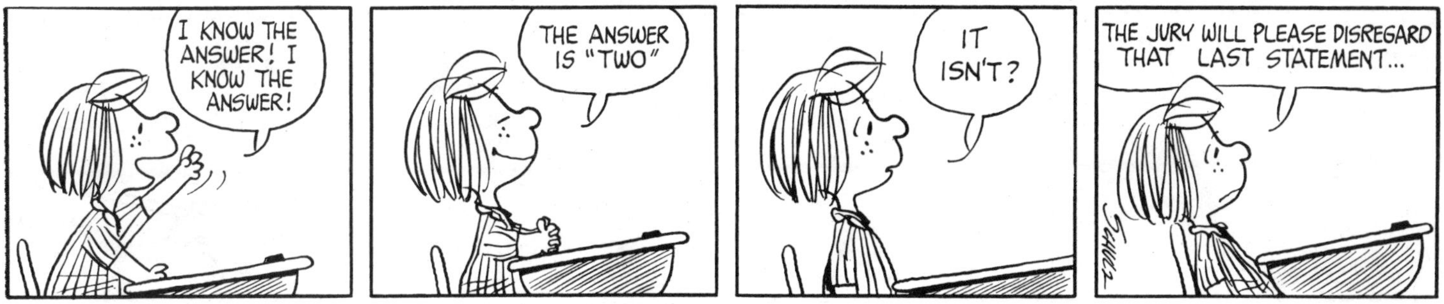

I KNOW THE ANSWER! I KNOW THE ANSWER!
THE ANSWER IS "TWO"
IT ISN'T?
THE JURY WILL PLEASE DISREGARD THAT LAST STATEMENT...
SCHULZ

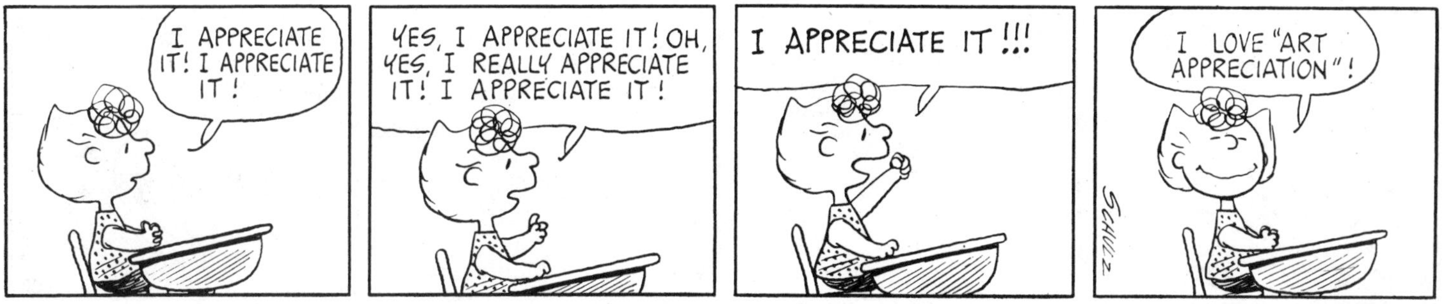

I APPRECIATE IT! I APPRECIATE IT!
YES, I APPRECIATE IT! OH, YES, I REALLY APPRECIATE IT! I APPRECIATE IT!
I APPRECIATE IT!!!
I LOVE "ART APPRECIATION"!
SCHULZ

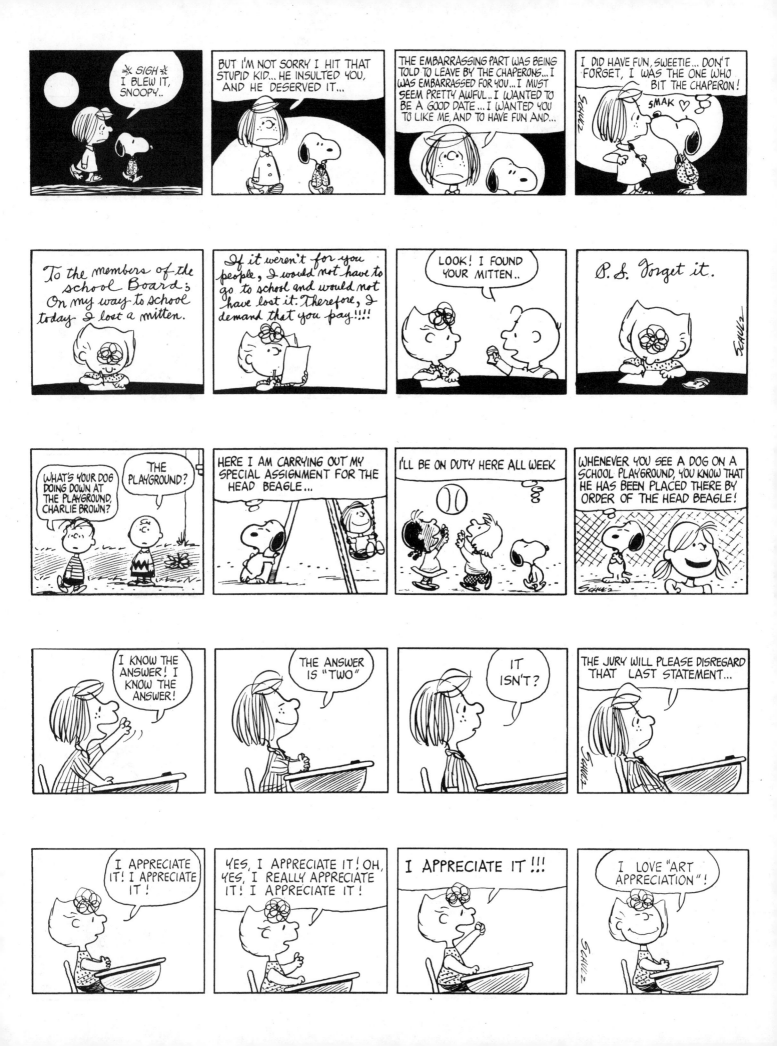

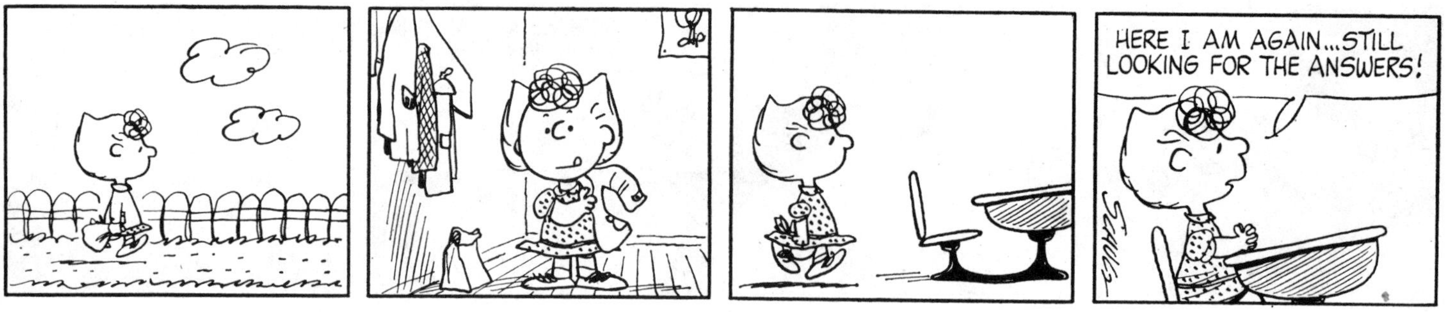
HERE I AM AGAIN...STILL LOOKING FOR THE ANSWERS!
SCHULZ

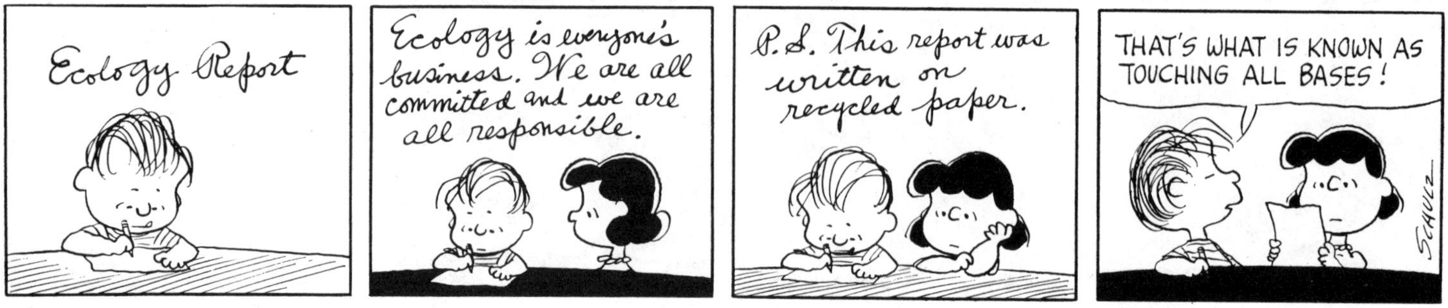
Ecology Report
Ecology is everyone's business. We are all committed and we are all responsible.
P.S. This report was written on recycled paper.
THAT'S WHAT IS KNOWN AS TOUCHING ALL BASES!
SCHULZ

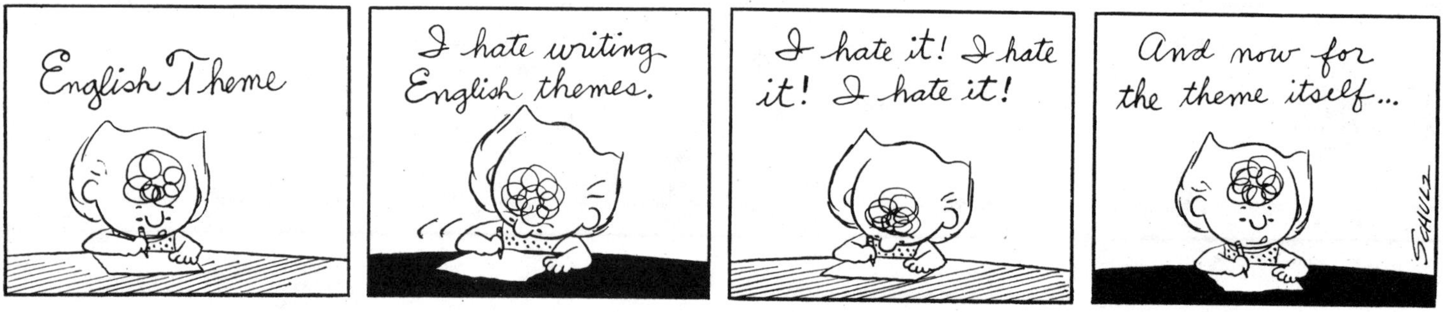
English Theme
I hate writing English themes.
I hate it! I hate it! I hate it!
And now for the theme itself...
SCHULZ

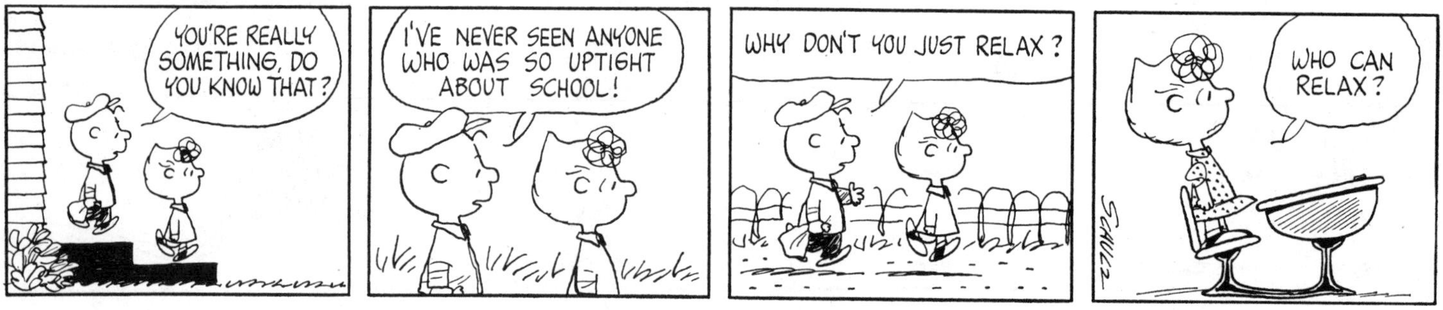
YOU'RE REALLY SOMETHING, DO YOU KNOW THAT?
I'VE NEVER SEEN ANYONE WHO WAS SO UPTIGHT ABOUT SCHOOL!
WHY DON'T YOU JUST RELAX?
WHO CAN RELAX?
SCHULZ

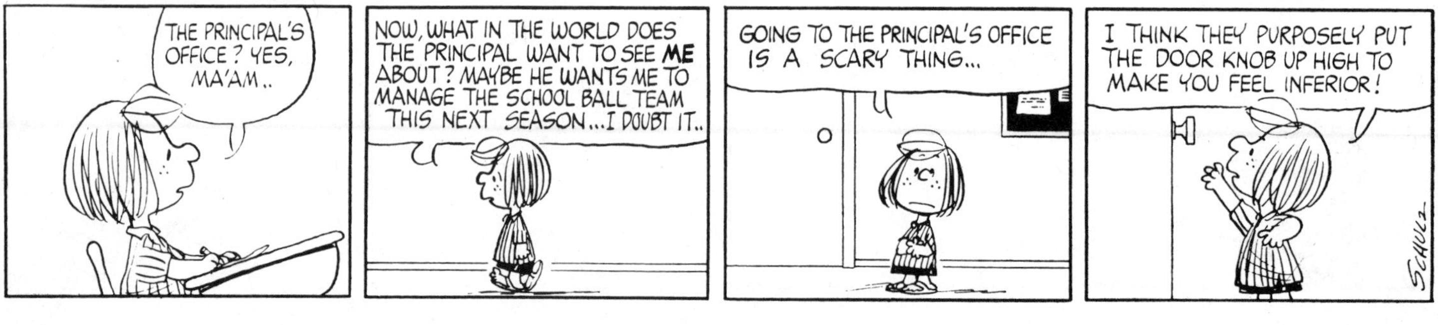
THE PRINCIPAL'S OFFICE? YES, MA'AM..
NOW, WHAT IN THE WORLD DOES THE PRINCIPAL WANT TO SEE **ME** ABOUT? MAYBE HE WANTS ME TO MANAGE THE SCHOOL BALL TEAM THIS NEXT SEASON...I DOUBT IT..
GOING TO THE PRINCIPAL'S OFFICE IS A SCARY THING...
I THINK THEY PURPOSELY PUT THE DOOR KNOB UP HIGH TO MAKE YOU FEEL INFERIOR!
SCHULZ

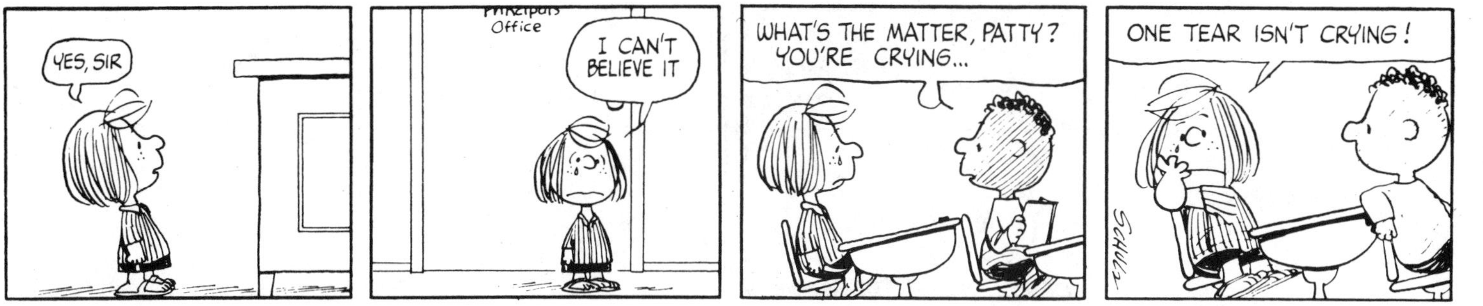
YES, SIR
Office
I CAN'T BELIEVE IT
WHAT'S THE MATTER, PATTY? YOU'RE CRYING...
ONE TEAR ISN'T CRYING!

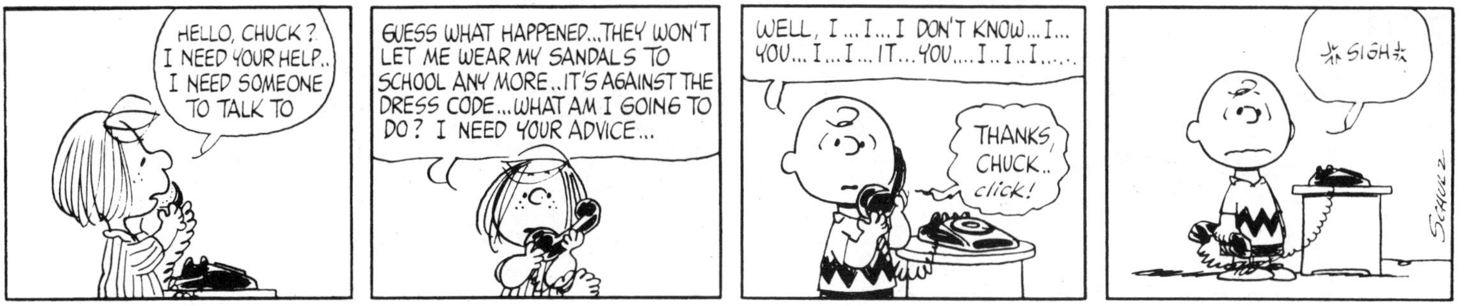
HELLO, CHUCK? I NEED YOUR HELP.. I NEED SOMEONE TO TALK TO
GUESS WHAT HAPPENED...THEY WON'T LET ME WEAR MY SANDALS TO SCHOOL ANY MORE..IT'S AGAINST THE DRESS CODE...WHAT AM I GOING TO DO? I NEED YOUR ADVICE...
WELL, I...I...I DON'T KNOW...I... YOU...I...I...IT...YOU....I..I..I.....
THANKS, CHUCK.. click!
SIGH

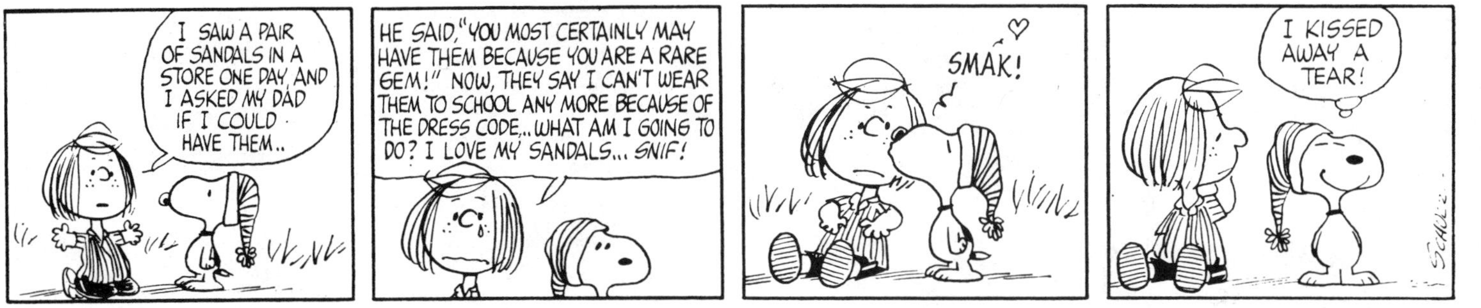
I SAW A PAIR OF SANDALS IN A STORE ONE DAY, AND I ASKED MY DAD IF I COULD HAVE THEM..
HE SAID, "YOU MOST CERTAINLY MAY HAVE THEM BECAUSE YOU ARE A RARE GEM!" NOW, THEY SAY I CAN'T WEAR THEM TO SCHOOL ANY MORE BECAUSE OF THE DRESS CODE.. WHAT AM I GOING TO DO? I LOVE MY SANDALS... SNIF!
SMAK!
I KISSED AWAY A TEAR!

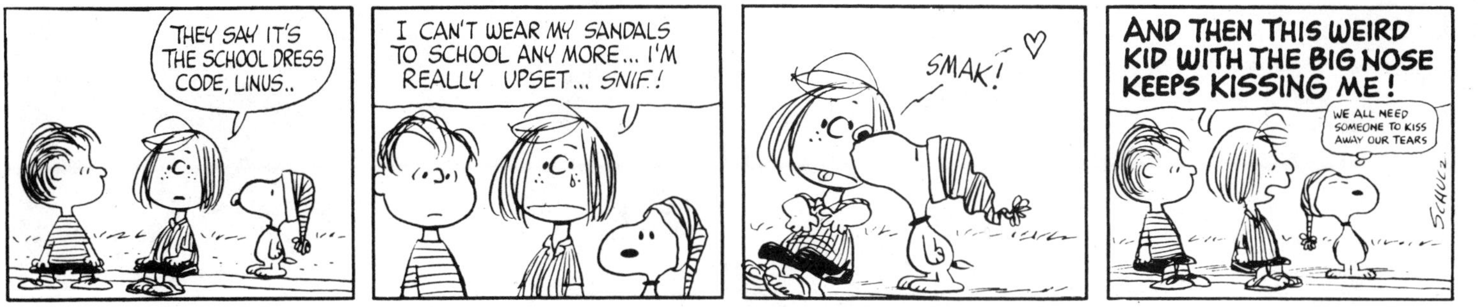
THEY SAY IT'S THE SCHOOL DRESS CODE, LINUS..
I CAN'T WEAR MY SANDALS TO SCHOOL ANY MORE... I'M REALLY UPSET... SNIF!
SMAK!
AND THEN THIS WEIRD KID WITH THE BIG NOSE KEEPS KISSING ME!
WE ALL NEED SOMEONE TO KISS AWAY OUR TEARS

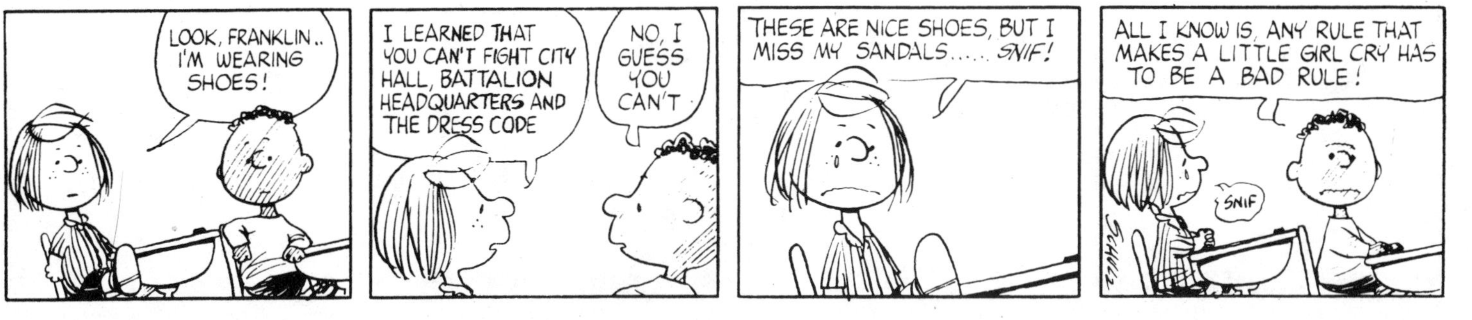
LOOK, FRANKLIN.. I'M WEARING SHOES!
I LEARNED THAT YOU CAN'T FIGHT CITY HALL, BATTALION HEADQUARTERS AND THE DRESS CODE
NO, I GUESS YOU CAN'T
THESE ARE NICE SHOES, BUT I MISS MY SANDALS..... SNIF!
ALL I KNOW IS, ANY RULE THAT MAKES A LITTLE GIRL CRY HAS TO BE A BAD RULE!
SNIF

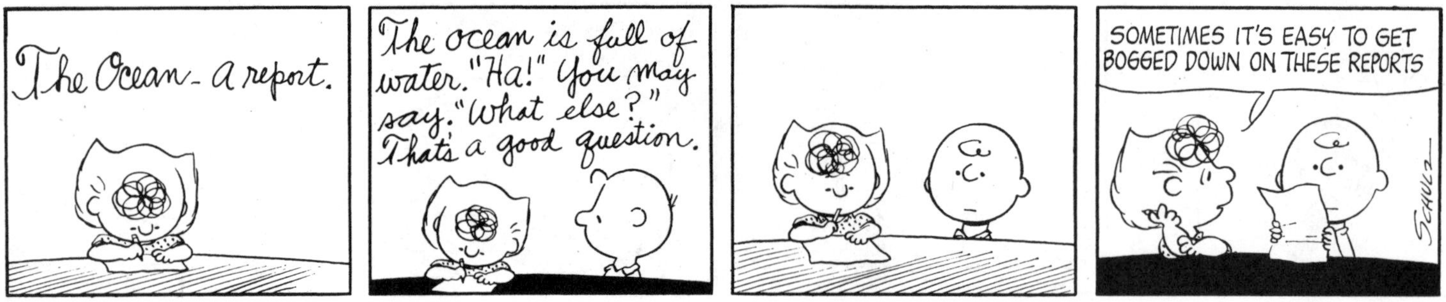
The Ocean - a report.
The ocean is full of water. "Ha!" You may say. "What else?" That's a good question.
SOMETIMES IT'S EASY TO GET BOGGED DOWN ON THESE REPORTS
SCHULZ

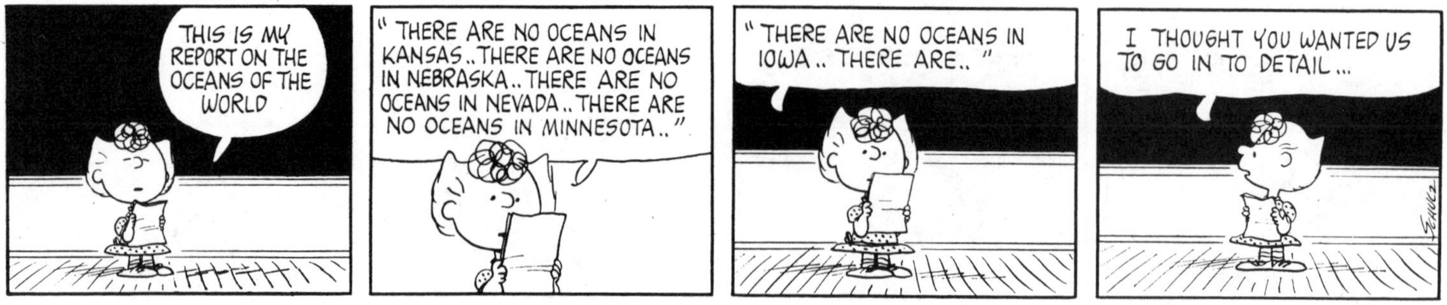
THIS IS MY REPORT ON THE OCEANS OF THE WORLD
" THERE ARE NO OCEANS IN KANSAS.. THERE ARE NO OCEANS IN NEBRASKA.. THERE ARE NO OCEANS IN NEVADA.. THERE ARE NO OCEANS IN MINNESOTA.. "
" THERE ARE NO OCEANS IN IOWA.. THERE ARE.. "
I THOUGHT YOU WANTED US TO GO IN TO DETAIL...
SCHULZ

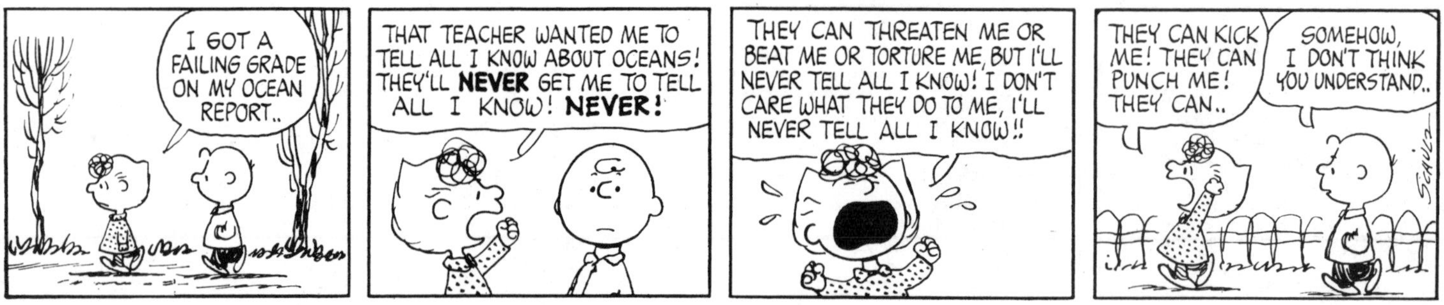
I GOT A FAILING GRADE ON MY OCEAN REPORT..
THAT TEACHER WANTED ME TO TELL ALL I KNOW ABOUT OCEANS! THEY'LL NEVER GET ME TO TELL ALL I KNOW! NEVER!
THEY CAN THREATEN ME OR BEAT ME OR TORTURE ME, BUT I'LL NEVER TELL ALL I KNOW! I DON'T CARE WHAT THEY DO TO ME, I'LL NEVER TELL ALL I KNOW!!
THEY CAN KICK ME! THEY CAN PUNCH ME! THEY CAN..
SOMEHOW, I DON'T THINK YOU UNDERSTAND..
SCHULZ

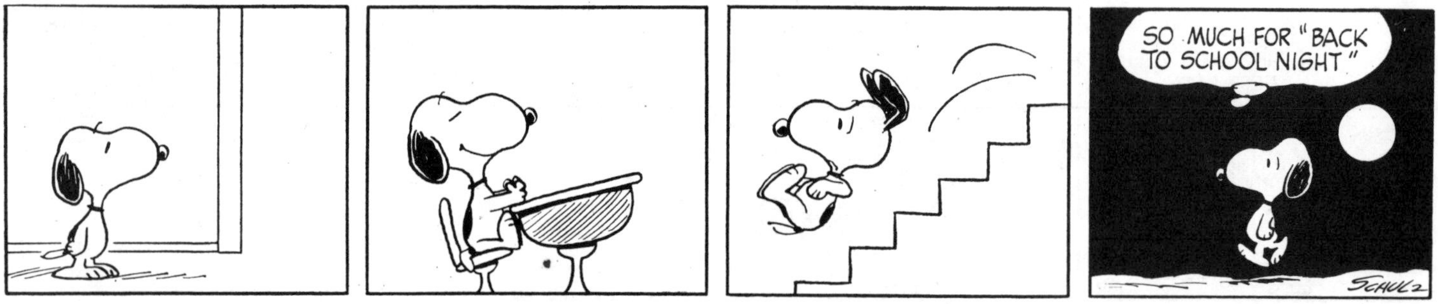
SO MUCH FOR " BACK TO SCHOOL NIGHT "
SCHULZ

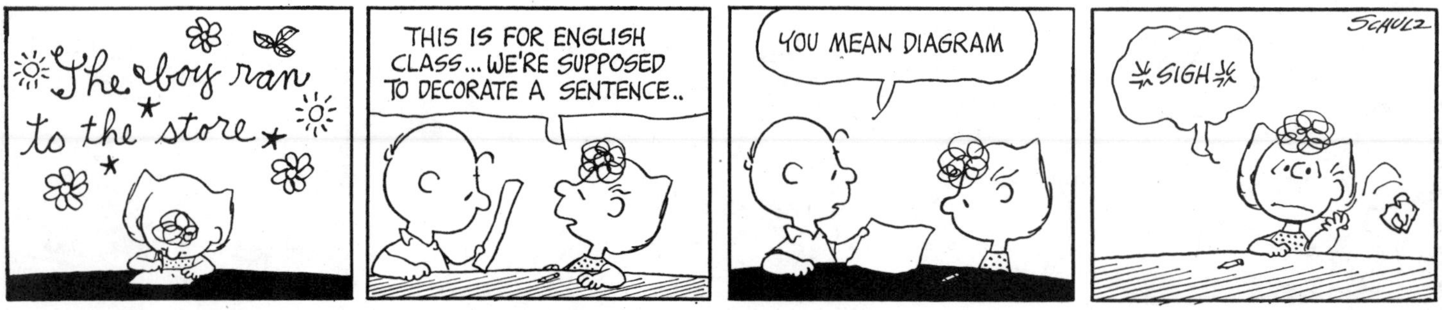
The boy ran to the store
THIS IS FOR ENGLISH CLASS... WE'RE SUPPOSED TO DECORATE A SENTENCE..
YOU MEAN DIAGRAM
SCHULZ
SIGH

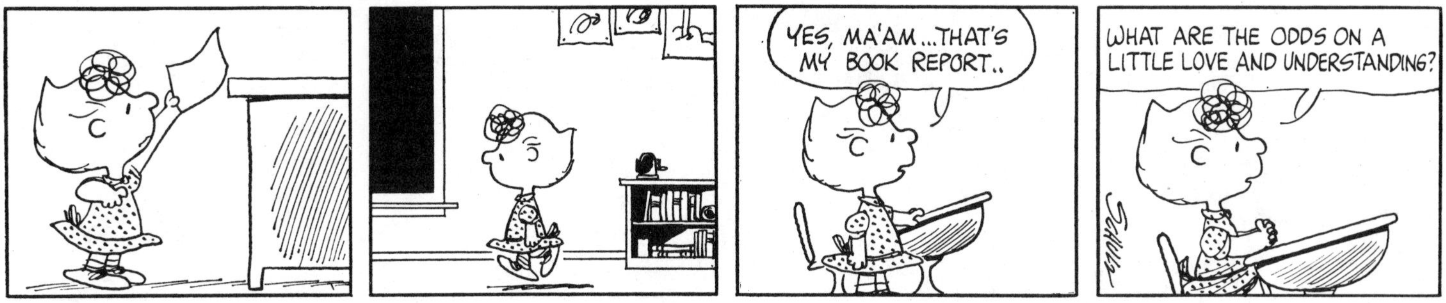
YES, MA'AM...THAT'S MY BOOK REPORT..
WHAT ARE THE ODDS ON A LITTLE LOVE AND UNDERSTANDING?

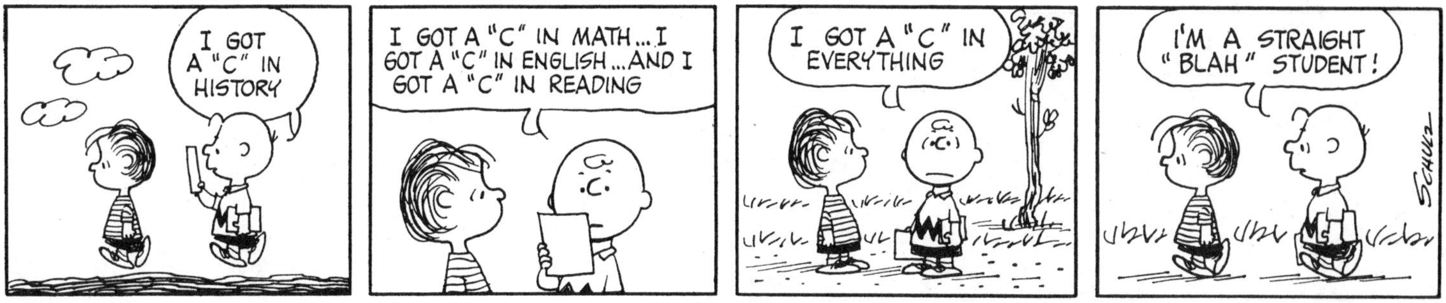
I GOT A "C" IN HISTORY
I GOT A "C" IN MATH...I GOT A "C" IN ENGLISH...AND I GOT A "C" IN READING
I GOT A "C" IN EVERYTHING
I'M A STRAIGHT "BLAH" STUDENT!

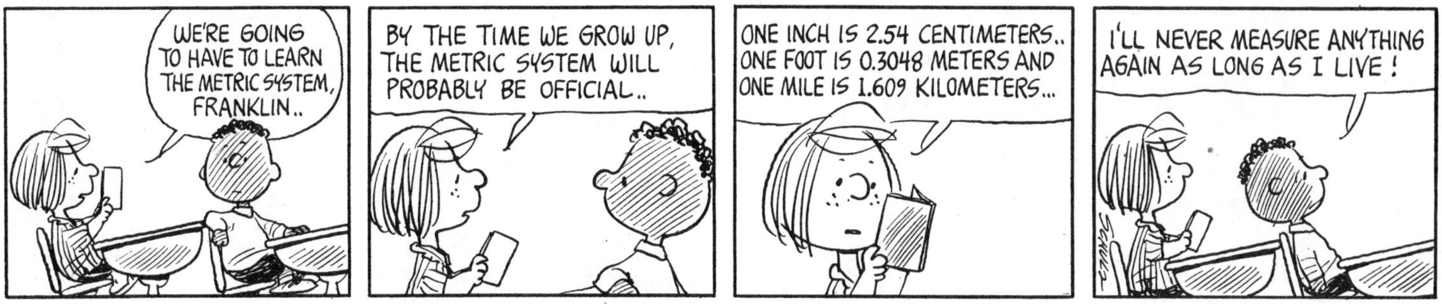
WE'RE GOING TO HAVE TO LEARN THE METRIC SYSTEM, FRANKLIN..
BY THE TIME WE GROW UP, THE METRIC SYSTEM WILL PROBABLY BE OFFICIAL..
ONE INCH IS 2.54 CENTIMETERS.. ONE FOOT IS 0.3048 METERS AND ONE MILE IS 1.609 KILOMETERS...
I'LL NEVER MEASURE ANYTHING AGAIN AS LONG AS I LIVE!

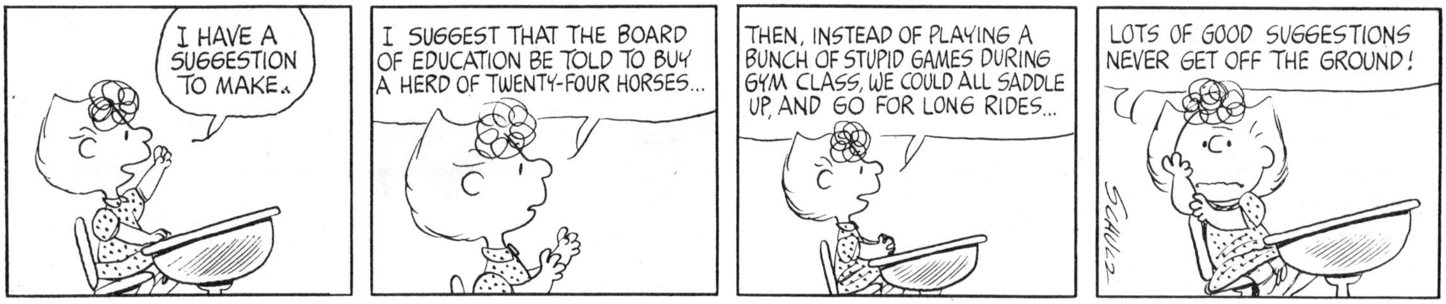
I HAVE A SUGGESTION TO MAKE..
I SUGGEST THAT THE BOARD OF EDUCATION BE TOLD TO BUY A HERD OF TWENTY-FOUR HORSES...
THEN, INSTEAD OF PLAYING A BUNCH OF STUPID GAMES DURING GYM CLASS, WE COULD ALL SADDLE UP, AND GO FOR LONG RIDES...
LOTS OF GOOD SUGGESTIONS NEVER GET OFF THE GROUND!

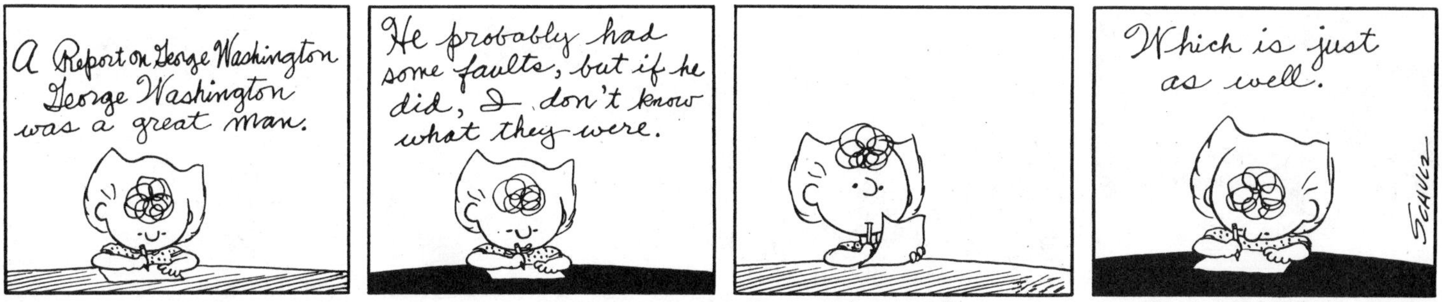
A Report on George Washington
George Washington was a great man.
He probably had some faults, but if he did, I don't know what they were.
Which is just as well.

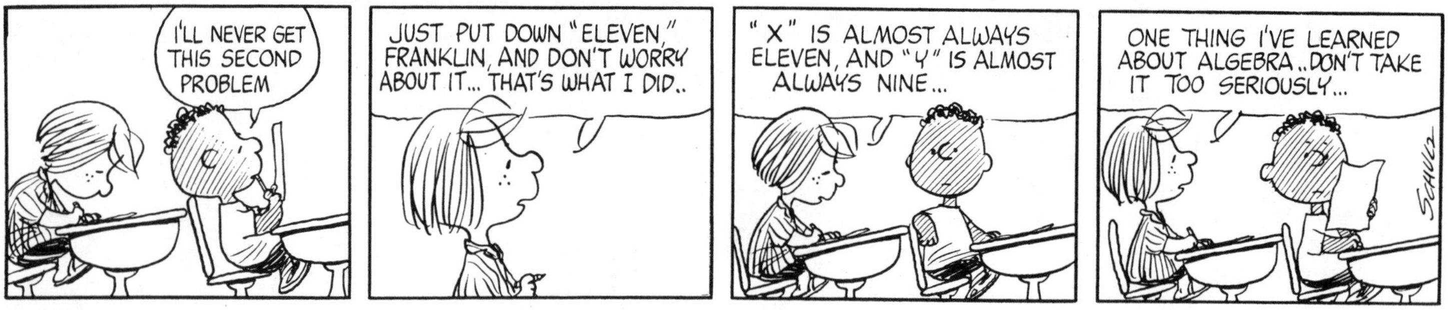
I'LL NEVER GET THIS SECOND PROBLEM
JUST PUT DOWN "ELEVEN," FRANKLIN, AND DON'T WORRY ABOUT IT... THAT'S WHAT I DID..
"X" IS ALMOST ALWAYS ELEVEN, AND "Y" IS ALMOST ALWAYS NINE...
ONE THING I'VE LEARNED ABOUT ALGEBRA..DON'T TAKE IT TOO SERIOUSLY...
SCHULZ

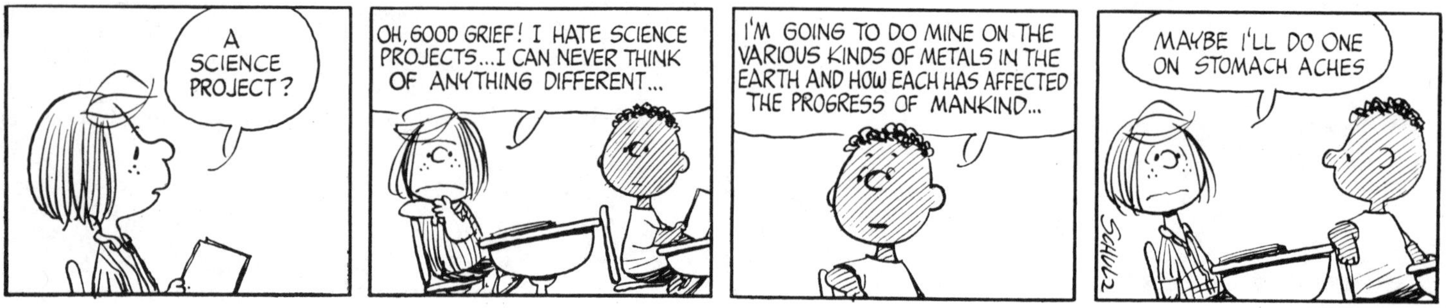
A SCIENCE PROJECT?
OH, GOOD GRIEF! I HATE SCIENCE PROJECTS...I CAN NEVER THINK OF ANYTHING DIFFERENT...
I'M GOING TO DO MINE ON THE VARIOUS KINDS OF METALS IN THE EARTH AND HOW EACH HAS AFFECTED THE PROGRESS OF MANKIND...
MAYBE I'LL DO ONE ON STOMACH ACHES
SCHULZ

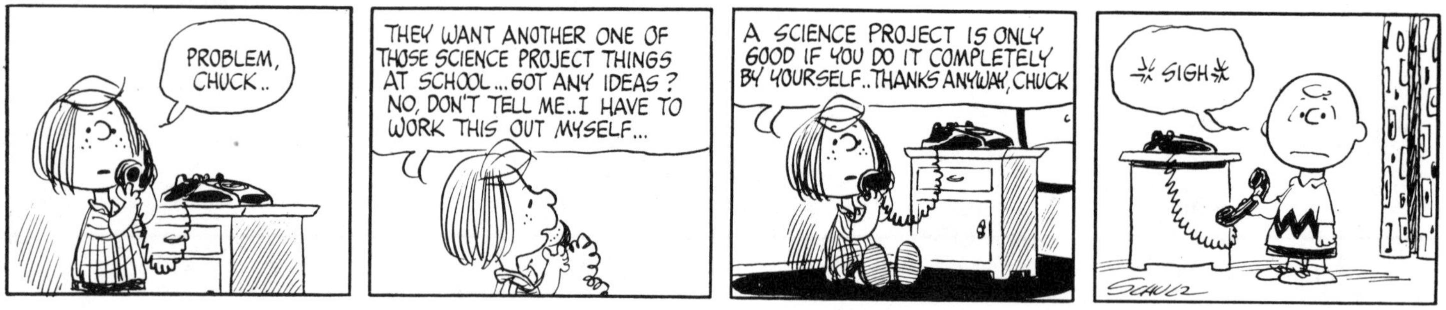
PROBLEM, CHUCK..
THEY WANT ANOTHER ONE OF THOSE SCIENCE PROJECT THINGS AT SCHOOL...GOT ANY IDEAS? NO, DON'T TELL ME..I HAVE TO WORK THIS OUT MYSELF...
A SCIENCE PROJECT IS ONLY GOOD IF YOU DO IT COMPLETELY BY YOURSELF..THANKS ANYWAY, CHUCK
SIGH
SCHULZ

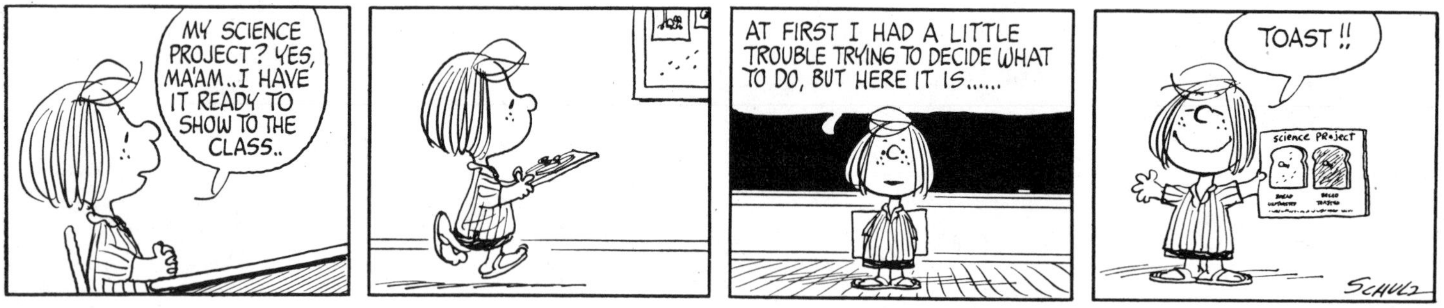
MY SCIENCE PROJECT? YES, MA'AM..I HAVE IT READY TO SHOW TO THE CLASS..
AT FIRST I HAD A LITTLE TROUBLE TRYING TO DECIDE WHAT TO DO, BUT HERE IT IS......
TOAST!!
science Project
SCHULZ

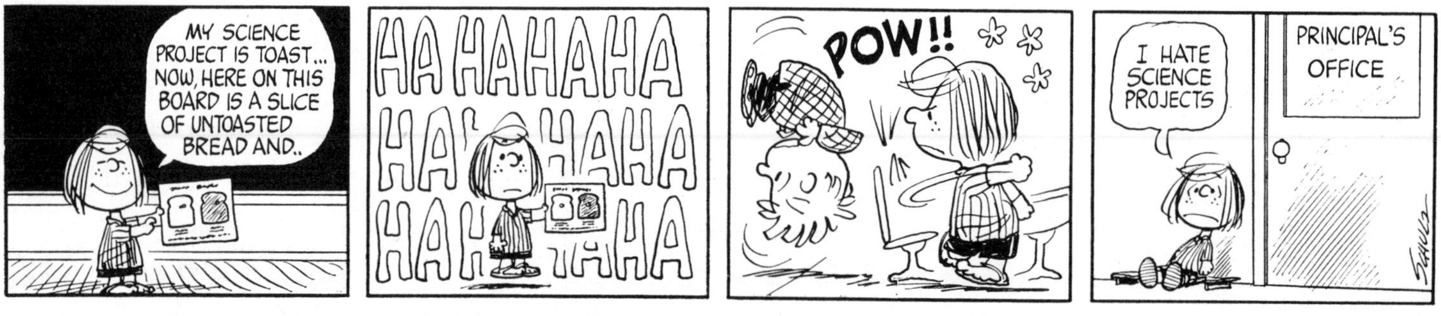
MY SCIENCE PROJECT IS TOAST... NOW, HERE ON THIS BOARD IS A SLICE OF UNTOASTED BREAD AND..
HA HAHAHAHA HA HAHA HA HA
POW!!
I HATE SCIENCE PROJECTS
PRINCIPAL'S OFFICE
SCHULZ

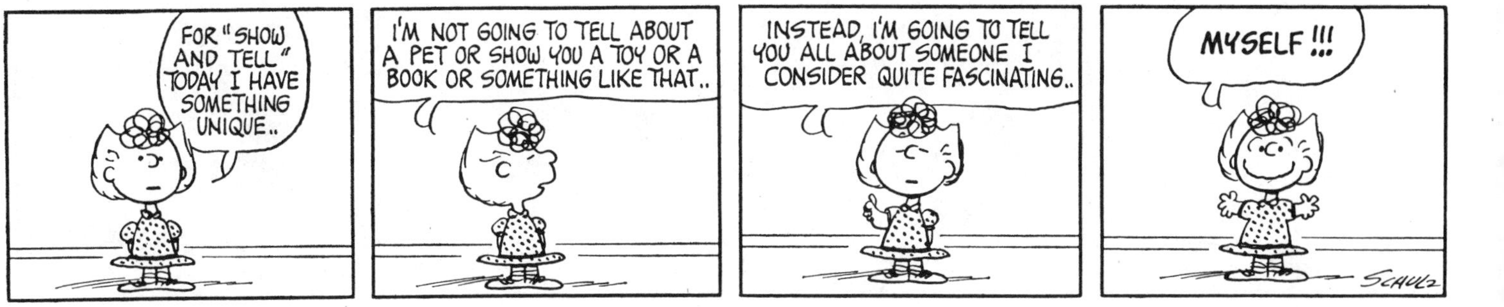
FOR "SHOW AND TELL" TODAY I HAVE SOMETHING UNIQUE..
I'M NOT GOING TO TELL ABOUT A PET OR SHOW YOU A TOY OR A BOOK OR SOMETHING LIKE THAT..
INSTEAD, I'M GOING TO TELL YOU ALL ABOUT SOMEONE I CONSIDER QUITE FASCINATING..
MYSELF !!!
SCHULZ

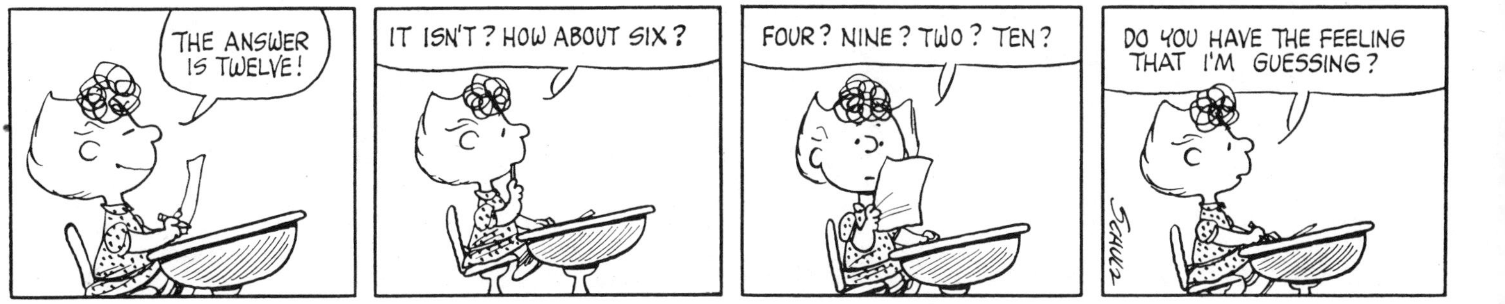
THE ANSWER IS TWELVE!
IT ISN'T? HOW ABOUT SIX?
FOUR? NINE? TWO? TEN?
DO YOU HAVE THE FEELING THAT I'M GUESSING?
SCHULZ

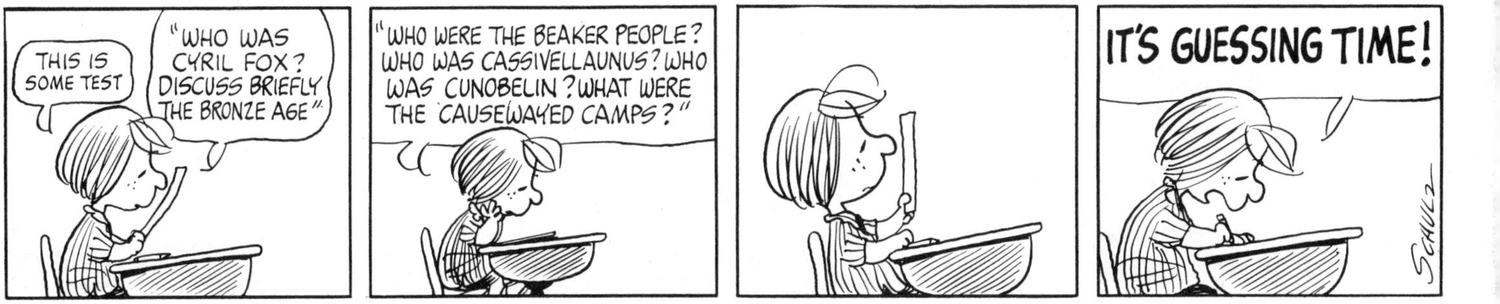
THIS IS SOME TEST
"WHO WAS CYRIL FOX? DISCUSS BRIEFLY THE BRONZE AGE"
"WHO WERE THE BEAKER PEOPLE? WHO WAS CASSIVELLAUNUS? WHO WAS CUNOBELIN? WHAT WERE THE 'CAUSEWAYED CAMPS?"
IT'S GUESSING TIME!
SCHULZ

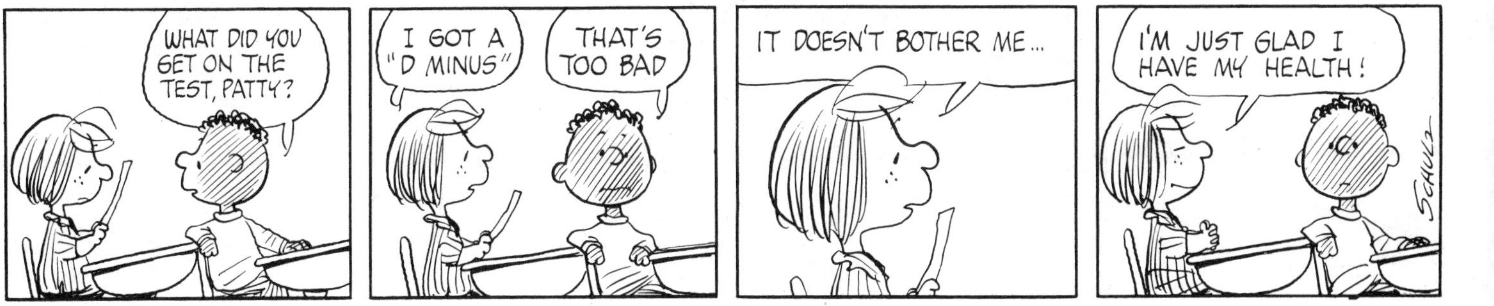
WHAT DID YOU GET ON THE TEST, PATTY?
I GOT A "D MINUS"
THAT'S TOO BAD
IT DOESN'T BOTHER ME...
I'M JUST GLAD I HAVE MY HEALTH!
SCHULZ

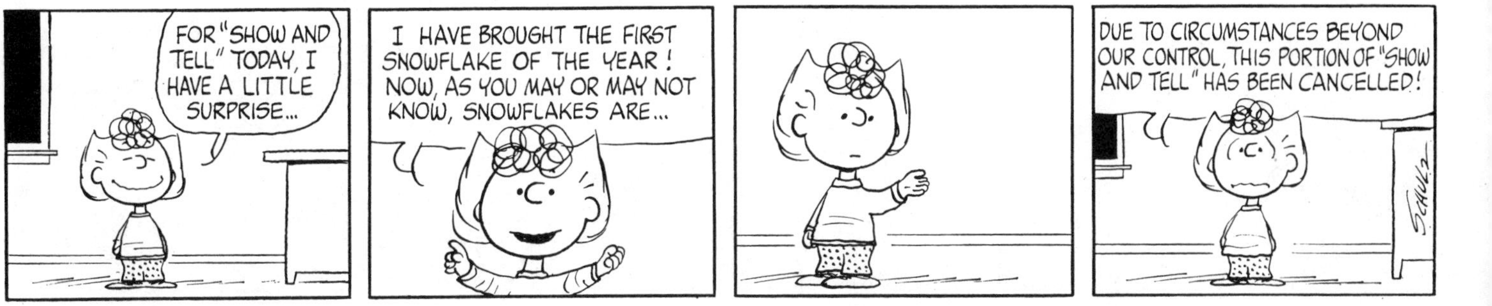
FOR "SHOW AND TELL" TODAY, I HAVE A LITTLE SURPRISE...
I HAVE BROUGHT THE FIRST SNOWFLAKE OF THE YEAR! NOW, AS YOU MAY OR MAY NOT KNOW, SNOWFLAKES ARE...
DUE TO CIRCUMSTANCES BEYOND OUR CONTROL, THIS PORTION OF "SHOW AND TELL" HAS BEEN CANCELLED!
SCHULZ

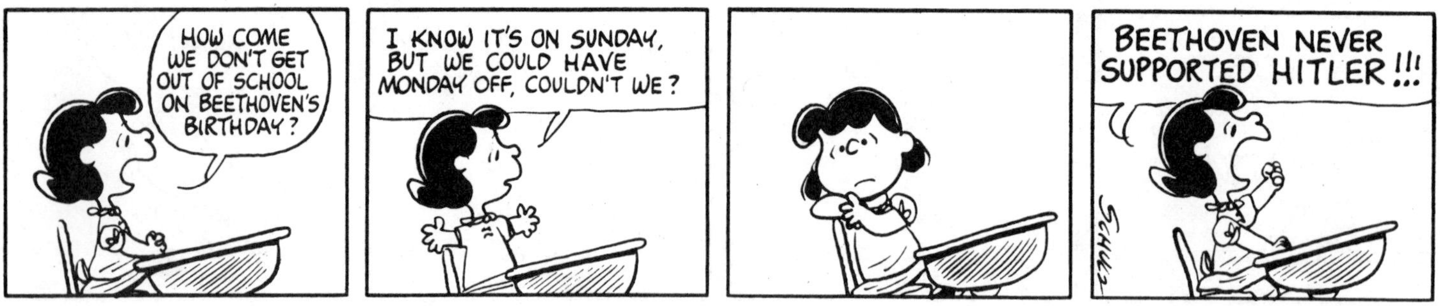
HOW COME WE DON'T GET OUT OF SCHOOL ON BEETHOVEN'S BIRTHDAY?
I KNOW IT'S ON SUNDAY, BUT WE COULD HAVE MONDAY OFF, COULDN'T WE?
BEETHOVEN NEVER SUPPORTED HITLER!!!
SCHULZ

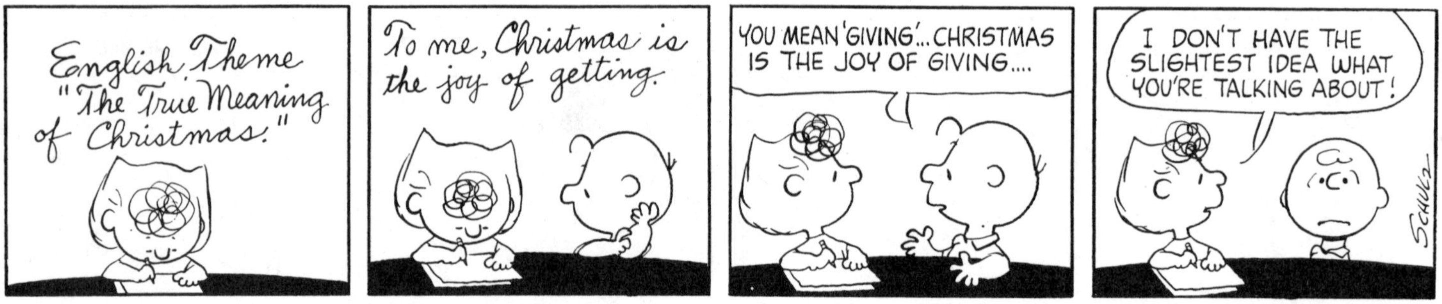
English Theme "The True Meaning of Christmas."
To me, Christmas is the joy of getting.
YOU MEAN 'GIVING'... CHRISTMAS IS THE JOY OF GIVING....
I DON'T HAVE THE SLIGHTEST IDEA WHAT YOU'RE TALKING ABOUT!
SCHULZ

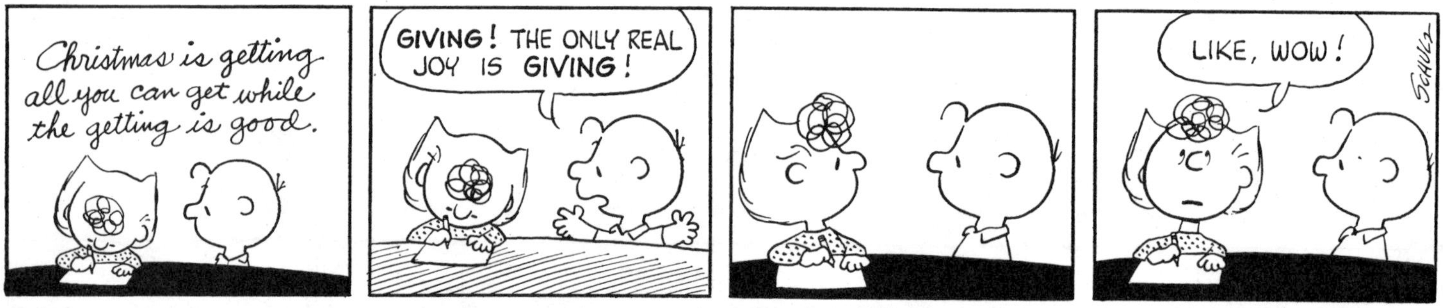
Christmas is getting all you can get while the getting is good.
GIVING! THE ONLY REAL JOY IS GIVING!
LIKE, WOW!
SCHULZ

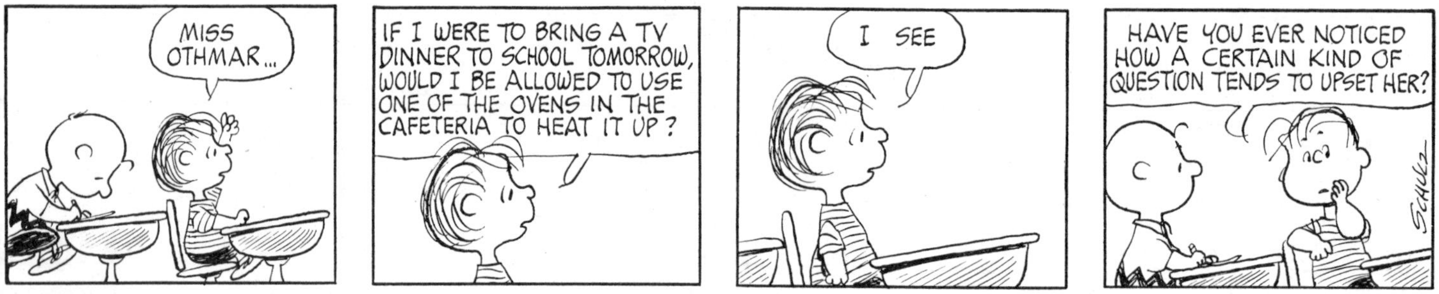
MISS OTHMAR...
IF I WERE TO BRING A TV DINNER TO SCHOOL TOMORROW, WOULD I BE ALLOWED TO USE ONE OF THE OVENS IN THE CAFETERIA TO HEAT IT UP?
I SEE
HAVE YOU EVER NOTICED HOW A CERTAIN KIND OF QUESTION TENDS TO UPSET HER?
SCHULZ

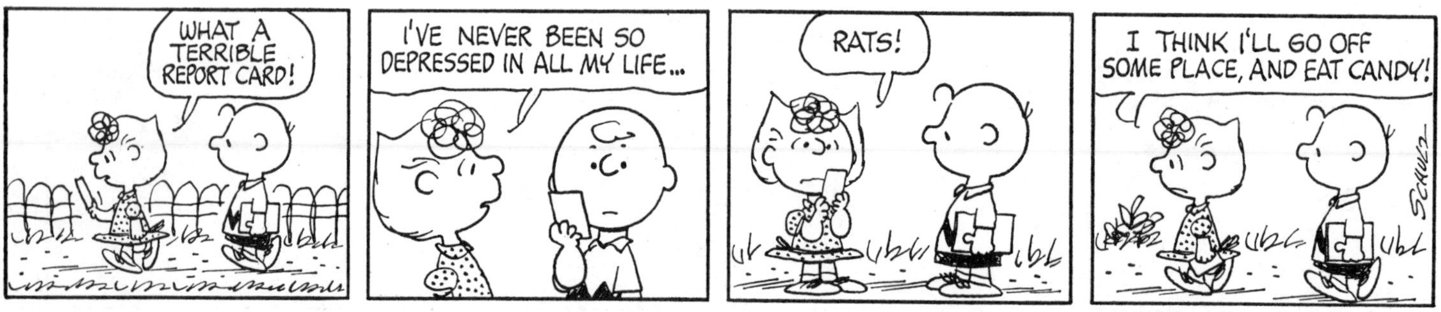
WHAT A TERRIBLE REPORT CARD!
I'VE NEVER BEEN SO DEPRESSED IN ALL MY LIFE...
RATS!
I THINK I'LL GO OFF SOME PLACE, AND EAT CANDY!
SCHULZ

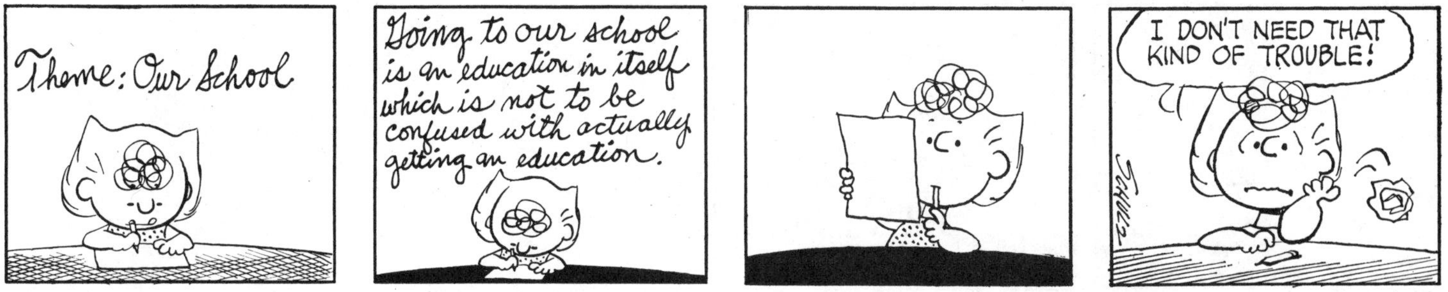
Theme: Our School
Going to our school is an education in itself which is not to be confused with actually getting an education.
I DON'T NEED THAT KIND OF TROUBLE!

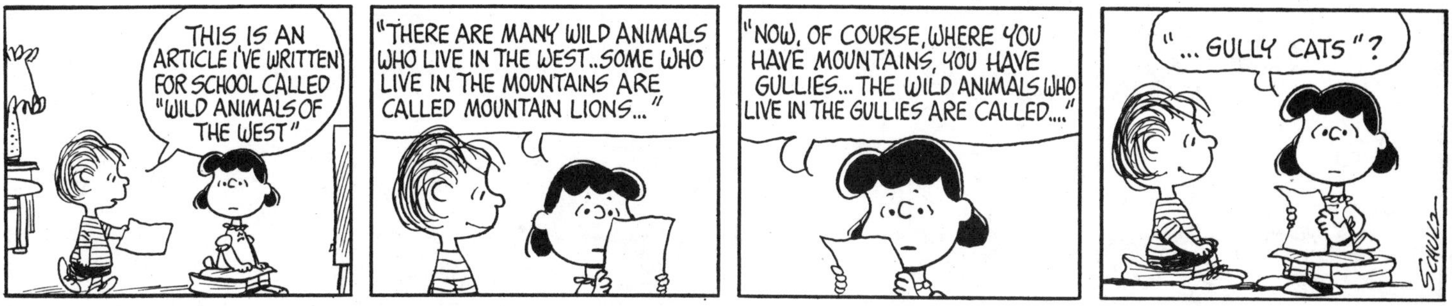
THIS IS AN ARTICLE I'VE WRITTEN FOR SCHOOL CALLED "WILD ANIMALS OF THE WEST"
"THERE ARE MANY WILD ANIMALS WHO LIVE IN THE WEST..SOME WHO LIVE IN THE MOUNTAINS ARE CALLED MOUNTAIN LIONS..."
"NOW, OF COURSE, WHERE YOU HAVE MOUNTAINS, YOU HAVE GULLIES... THE WILD ANIMALS WHO LIVE IN THE GULLIES ARE CALLED...."
"... GULLY CATS"?

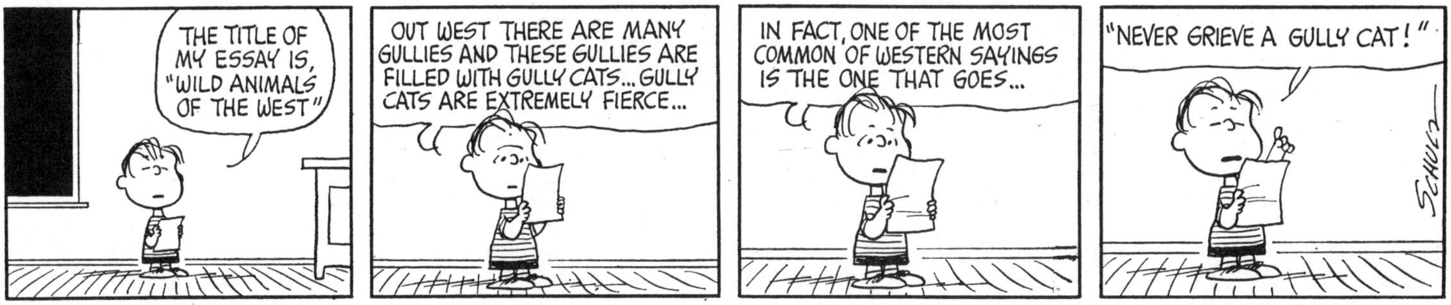
THE TITLE OF MY ESSAY IS, "WILD ANIMALS OF THE WEST"
OUT WEST THERE ARE MANY GULLIES AND THESE GULLIES ARE FILLED WITH GULLY CATS... GULLY CATS ARE EXTREMELY FIERCE...
IN FACT, ONE OF THE MOST COMMON OF WESTERN SAYINGS IS THE ONE THAT GOES...
"NEVER GRIEVE A GULLY CAT!"

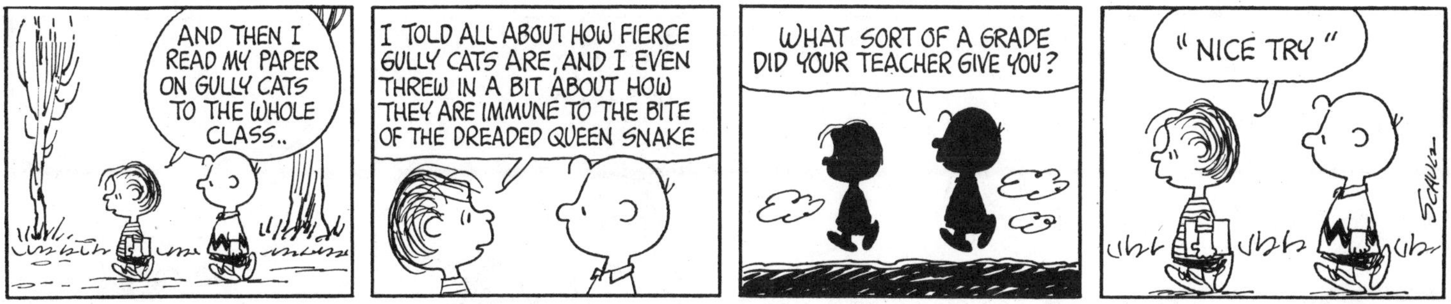
AND THEN I READ MY PAPER ON GULLY CATS TO THE WHOLE CLASS..
I TOLD ALL ABOUT HOW FIERCE GULLY CATS ARE, AND I EVEN THREW IN A BIT ABOUT HOW THEY ARE IMMUNE TO THE BITE OF THE DREADED QUEEN SNAKE
WHAT SORT OF A GRADE DID YOUR TEACHER GIVE YOU?
"NICE TRY"

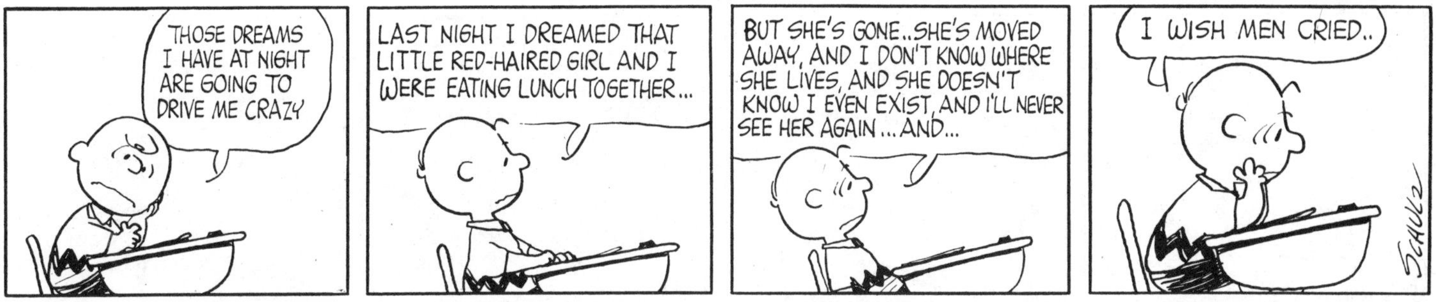
THOSE DREAMS I HAVE AT NIGHT ARE GOING TO DRIVE ME CRAZY
LAST NIGHT I DREAMED THAT LITTLE RED-HAIRED GIRL AND I WERE EATING LUNCH TOGETHER...
BUT SHE'S GONE..SHE'S MOVED AWAY, AND I DON'T KNOW WHERE SHE LIVES, AND SHE DOESN'T KNOW I EVEN EXIST, AND I'LL NEVER SEE HER AGAIN... AND...
I WISH MEN CRIED..

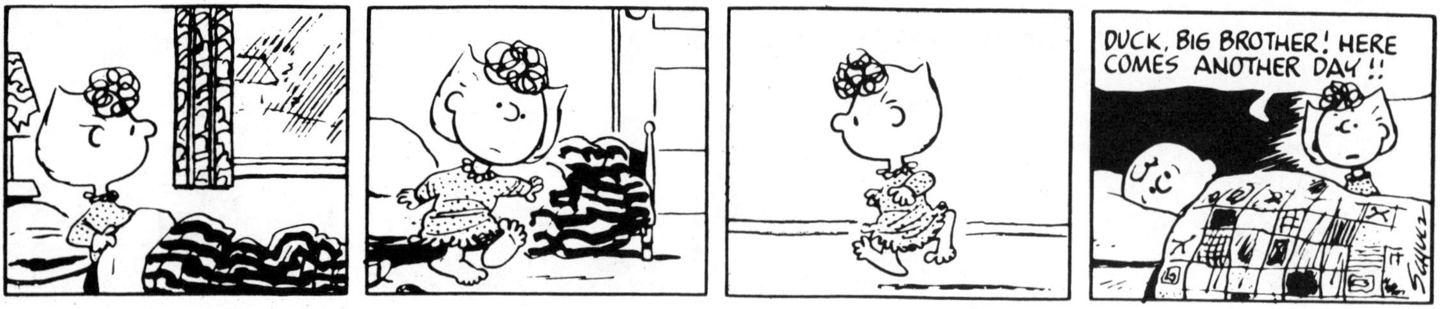
DUCK, BIG BROTHER! HERE COMES ANOTHER DAY!!
SCHULZ

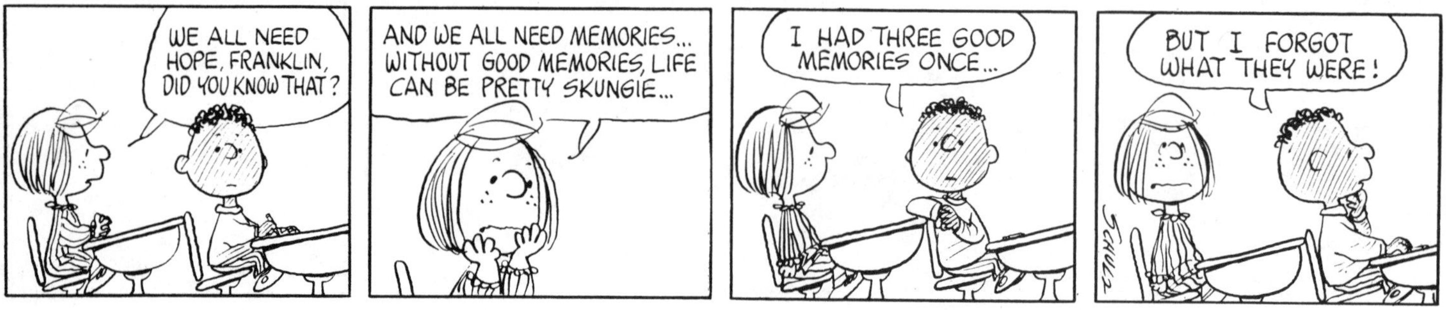
WE ALL NEED HOPE, FRANKLIN, DID YOU KNOW THAT?
AND WE ALL NEED MEMORIES... WITHOUT GOOD MEMORIES, LIFE CAN BE PRETTY SKUNGIE...
I HAD THREE GOOD MEMORIES ONCE...
BUT I FORGOT WHAT THEY WERE!
SCHULZ

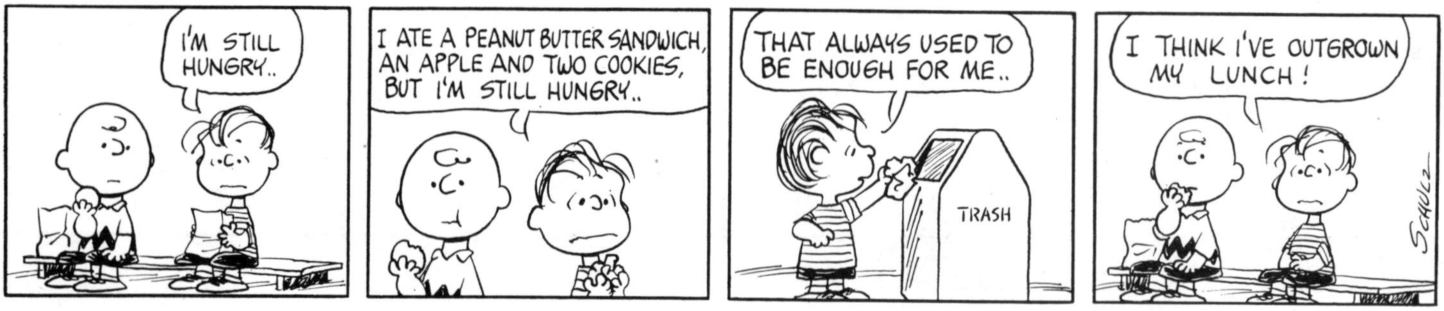
I'M STILL HUNGRY..
I ATE A PEANUT BUTTER SANDWICH, AN APPLE AND TWO COOKIES, BUT I'M STILL HUNGRY..
THAT ALWAYS USED TO BE ENOUGH FOR ME..
TRASH
I THINK I'VE OUTGROWN MY LUNCH!
SCHULZ

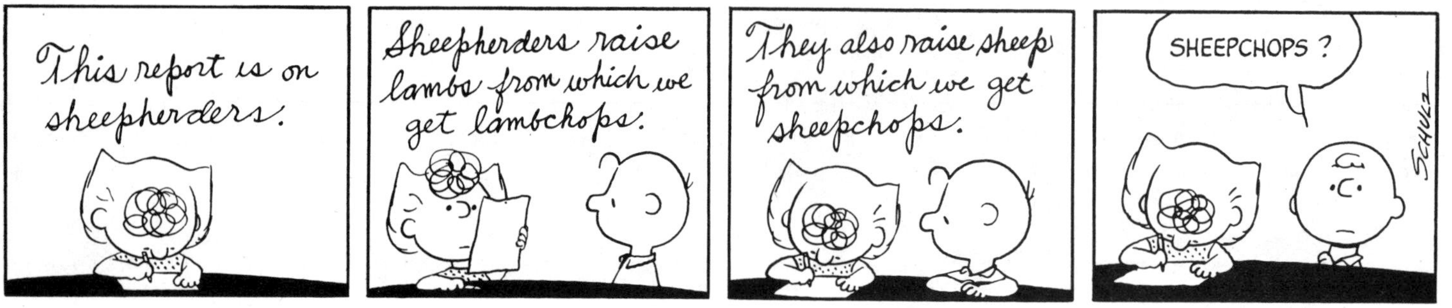
This report is on sheepherders.
Sheepherders raise lambs from which we get lambchops.
They also raise sheep from which we get sheepchops.
SHEEPCHOPS?
SCHULZ

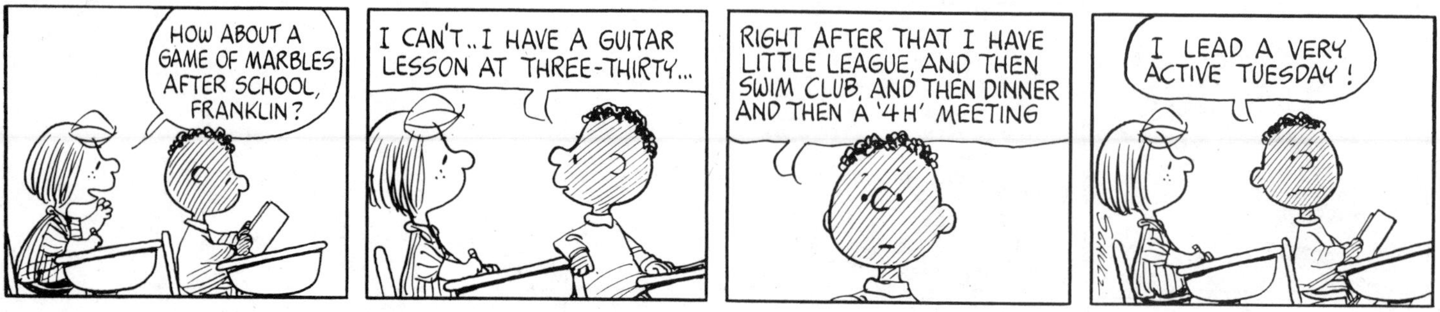
HOW ABOUT A GAME OF MARBLES AFTER SCHOOL, FRANKLIN?
I CAN'T.. I HAVE A GUITAR LESSON AT THREE-THIRTY...
RIGHT AFTER THAT I HAVE LITTLE LEAGUE, AND THEN SWIM CLUB, AND THEN DINNER AND THEN A '4 H' MEETING
I LEAD A VERY ACTIVE TUESDAY!
SCHULZ

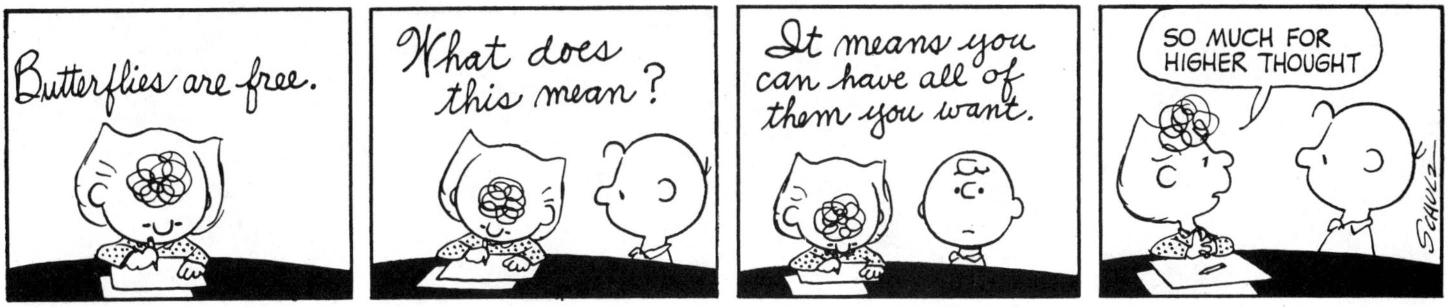
Butterflies are free.
What does this mean?
It means you can have all of them you want.
SO MUCH FOR HIGHER THOUGHT
SCHULZ

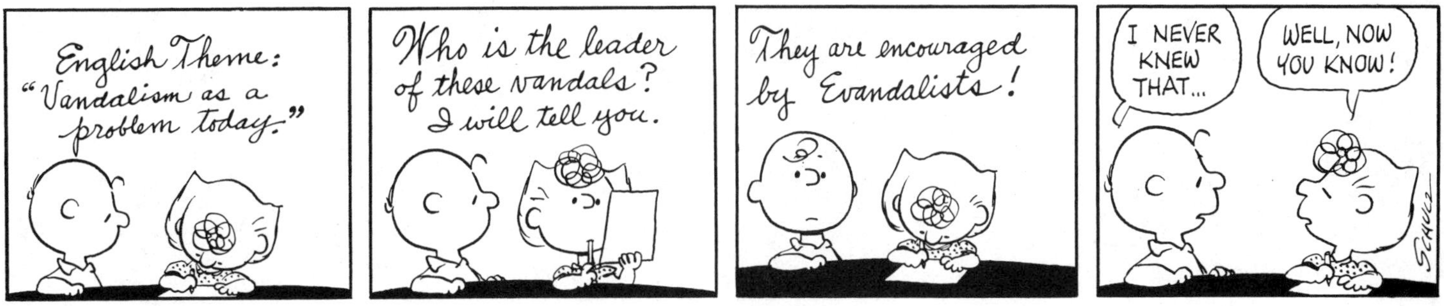
English Theme: "Vandalism as a problem today."
Who is the leader of these vandals? I will tell you.
They are encouraged by Evandalists!
I NEVER KNEW THAT...
WELL, NOW YOU KNOW!
SCHULZ

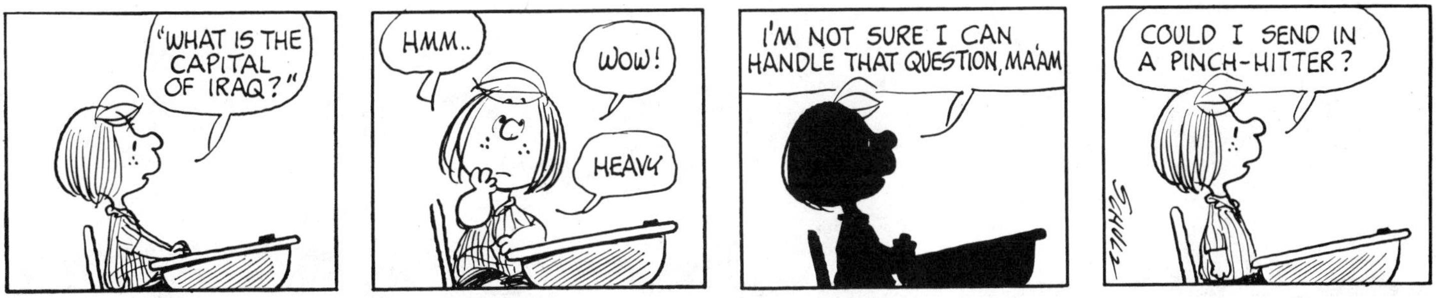
"WHAT IS THE CAPITAL OF IRAQ?"
HMM..
WOW!
HEAVY
I'M NOT SURE I CAN HANDLE THAT QUESTION, MA'AM
SCHULZ
COULD I SEND IN A PINCH-HITTER?

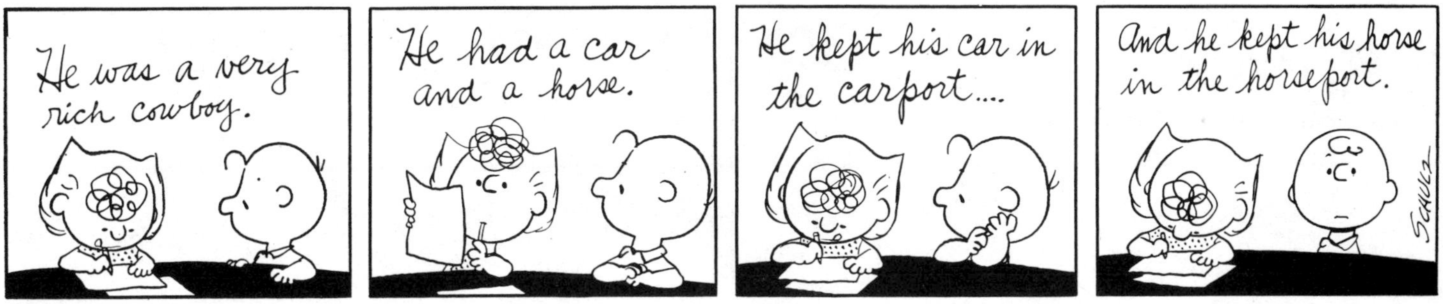
He was a very rich cowboy.
He had a car and a horse.
He kept his car in the carport....
And he kept his horse in the horseport.
SCHULZ

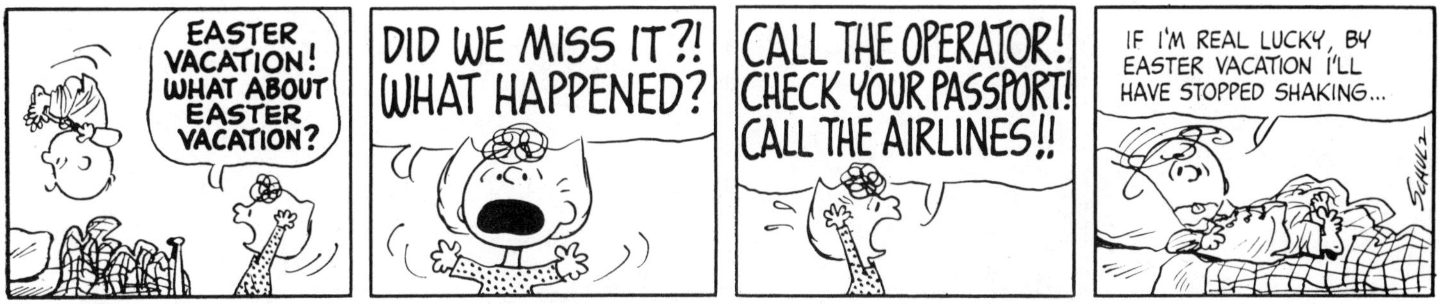
EASTER VACATION! WHAT ABOUT EASTER VACATION?
DID WE MISS IT?! WHAT HAPPENED?
CALL THE OPERATOR! CHECK YOUR PASSPORT! CALL THE AIRLINES!!
IF I'M REAL LUCKY, BY EASTER VACATION I'LL HAVE STOPPED SHAKING...
SCHULZ

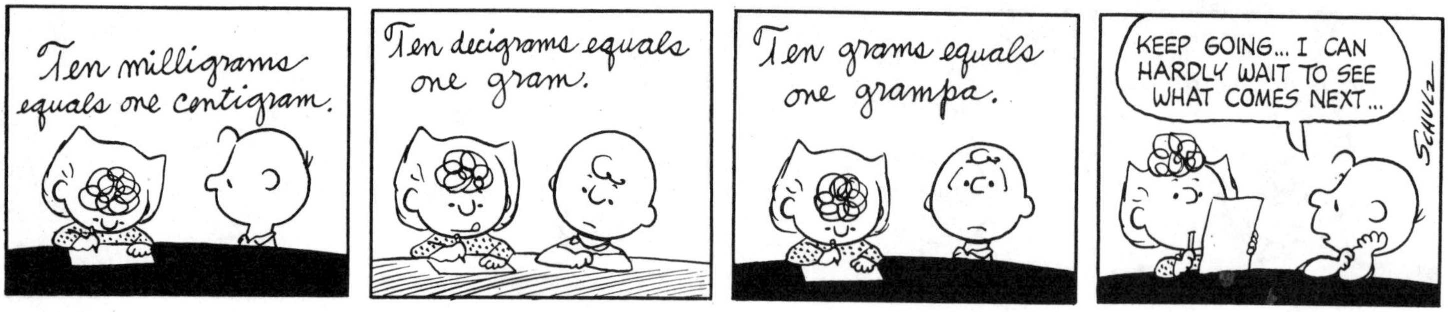
Ten milligrams equals one centigram.
Ten decigrams equals one gram.
Ten grams equals one grampa.
KEEP GOING... I CAN HARDLY WAIT TO SEE WHAT COMES NEXT...
SCHULZ

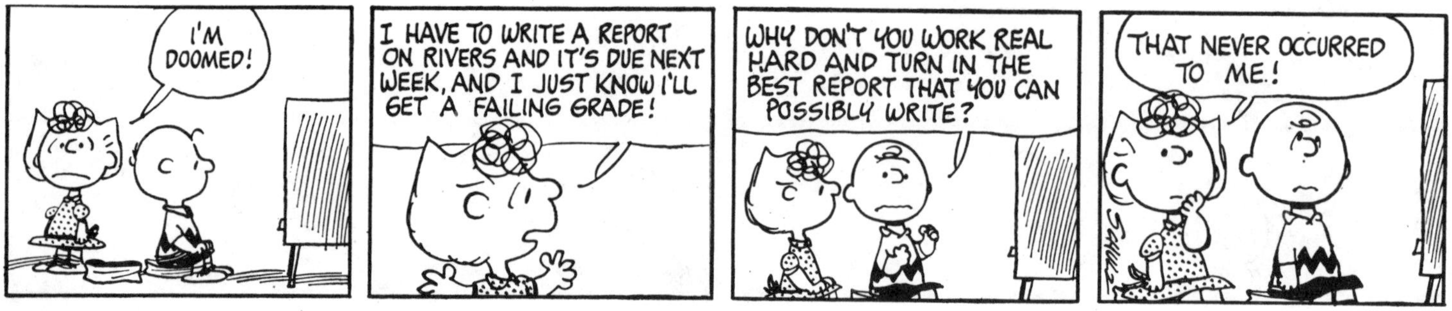
I'M DOOMED!
I HAVE TO WRITE A REPORT ON RIVERS AND IT'S DUE NEXT WEEK, AND I JUST KNOW I'LL GET A FAILING GRADE!
WHY DON'T YOU WORK REAL HARD AND TURN IN THE BEST REPORT THAT YOU CAN POSSIBLY WRITE?
THAT NEVER OCCURRED TO ME!
SCHULZ

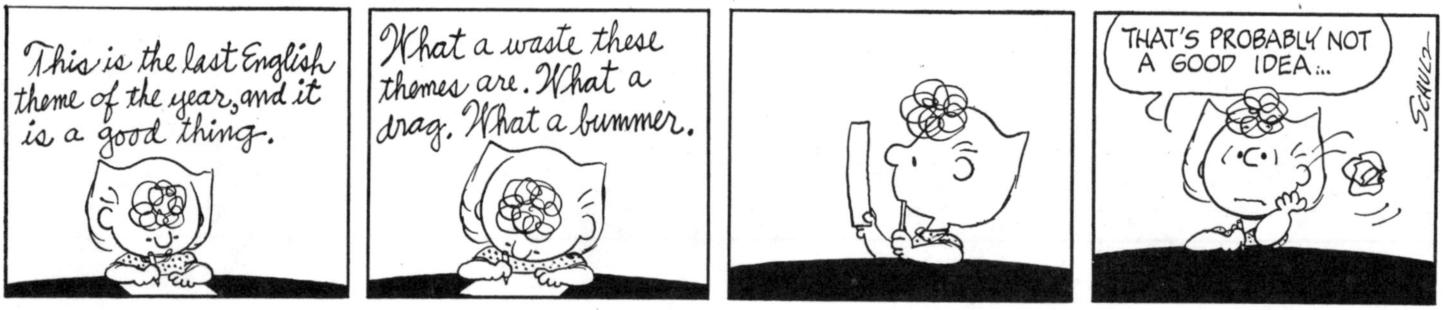
This is the last English theme of the year, and it is a good thing.
What a waste these themes are. What a drag. What a bummer.
THAT'S PROBABLY NOT A GOOD IDEA...
SCHULZ

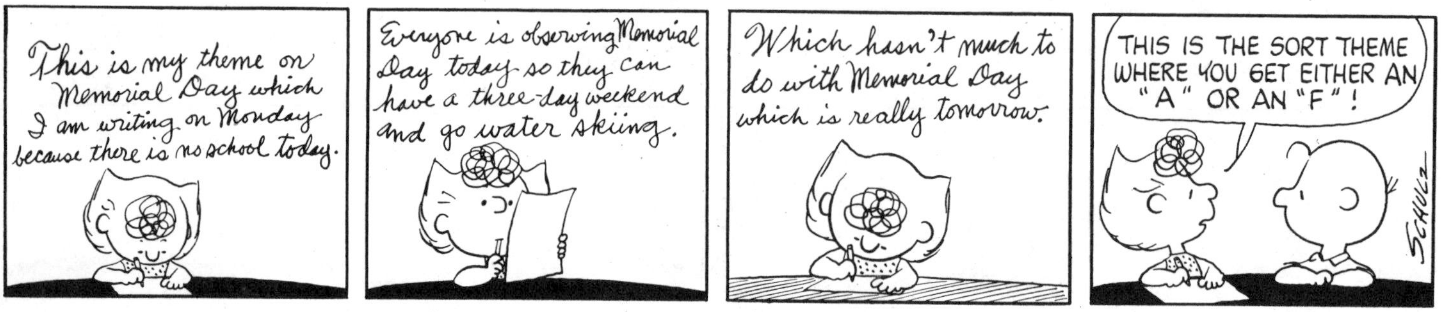
This is my theme on Memorial Day which I am writing on Monday because there is no school today.
Everyone is observing Memorial Day today so they can have a three-day weekend and go water skiing.
Which hasn't much to do with Memorial Day which is really tomorrow.
THIS IS THE SORT THEME WHERE YOU GET EITHER AN "A" OR AN "F"!
SCHULZ

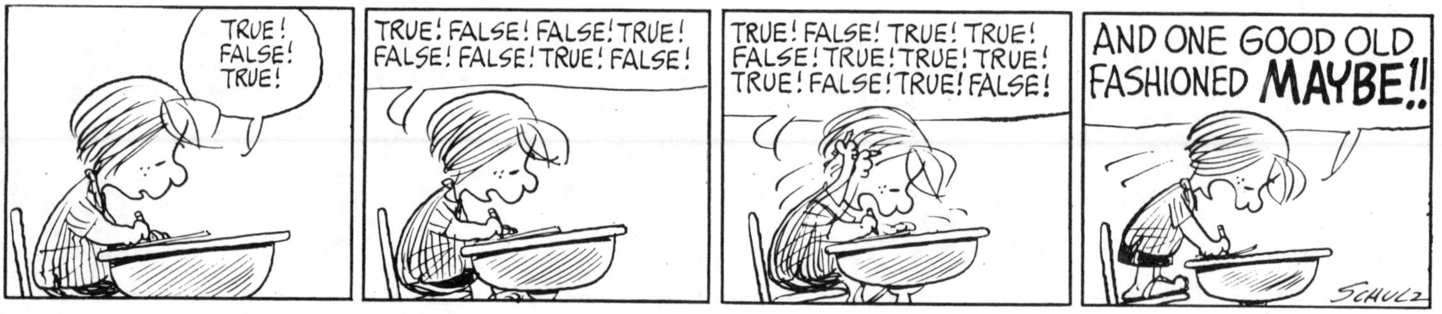
TRUE! FALSE! TRUE!
TRUE! FALSE! FALSE! TRUE! FALSE! FALSE! TRUE! FALSE!
TRUE! FALSE! TRUE! TRUE! FALSE! TRUE! TRUE! TRUE! TRUE! FALSE! TRUE! FALSE!
AND ONE GOOD OLD FASHIONED MAYBE!!
SCHULZ

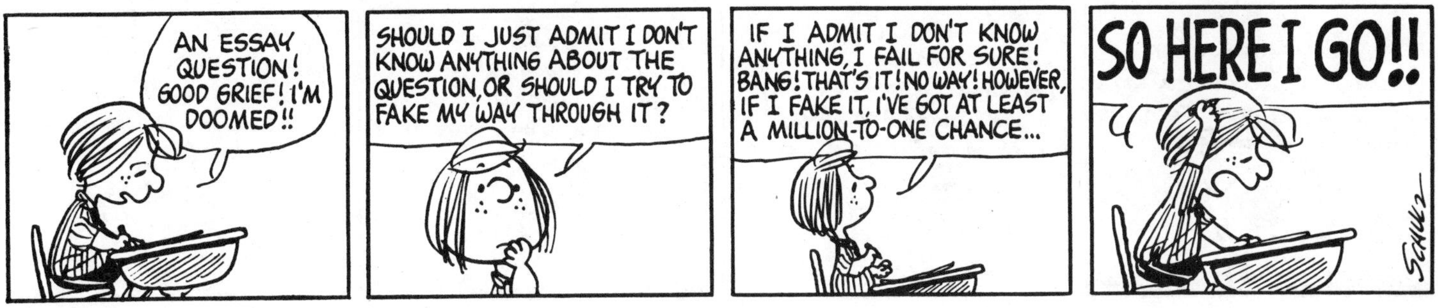
AN ESSAY QUESTION! GOOD GRIEF! I'M DOOMED!!
SHOULD I JUST ADMIT I DON'T KNOW ANYTHING ABOUT THE QUESTION, OR SHOULD I TRY TO FAKE MY WAY THROUGH IT?
IF I ADMIT I DON'T KNOW ANYTHING, I FAIL FOR SURE! BANG! THAT'S IT! NO WAY! HOWEVER, IF I FAKE IT, I'VE GOT AT LEAST A MILLION-TO-ONE CHANCE...
SO HERE I GO!!

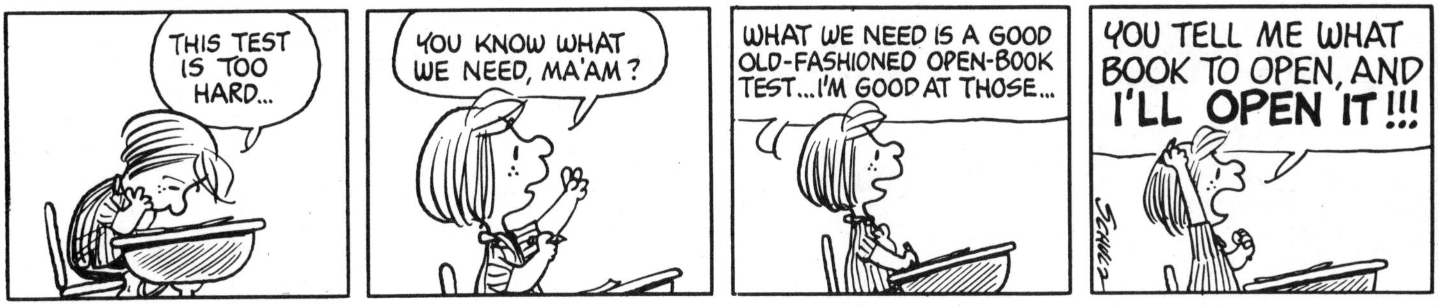
THIS TEST IS TOO HARD...
YOU KNOW WHAT WE NEED, MA'AM?
WHAT WE NEED IS A GOOD OLD-FASHIONED OPEN-BOOK TEST... I'M GOOD AT THOSE...
YOU TELL ME WHAT BOOK TO OPEN, AND I'LL OPEN IT!!!

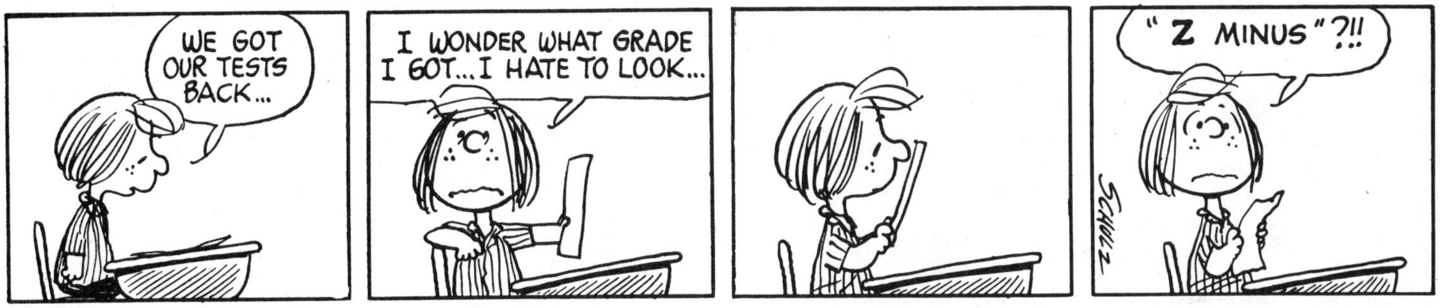
WE GOT OUR TESTS BACK...
I WONDER WHAT GRADE I GOT... I HATE TO LOOK...
"Z MINUS"?!!

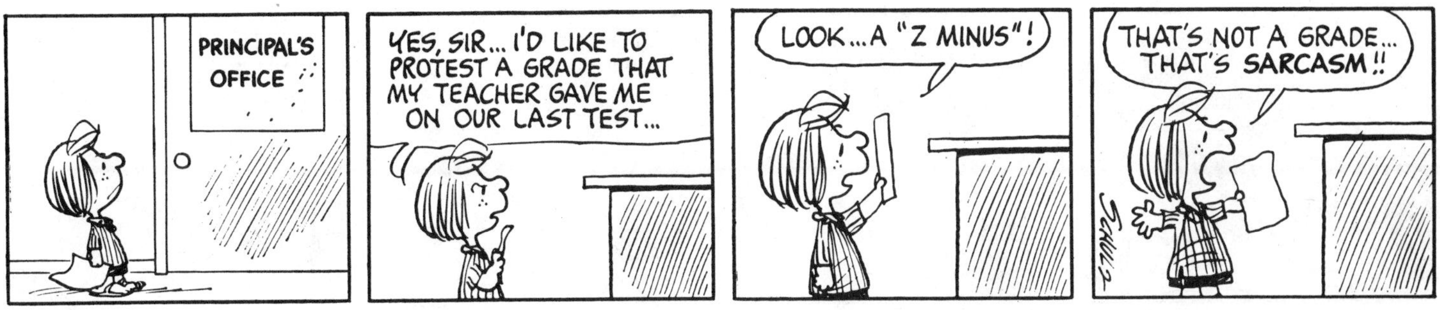
PRINCIPAL'S OFFICE
YES, SIR... I'D LIKE TO PROTEST A GRADE THAT MY TEACHER GAVE ME ON OUR LAST TEST...
LOOK... A "Z MINUS"!
THAT'S NOT A GRADE... THAT'S SARCASM!!

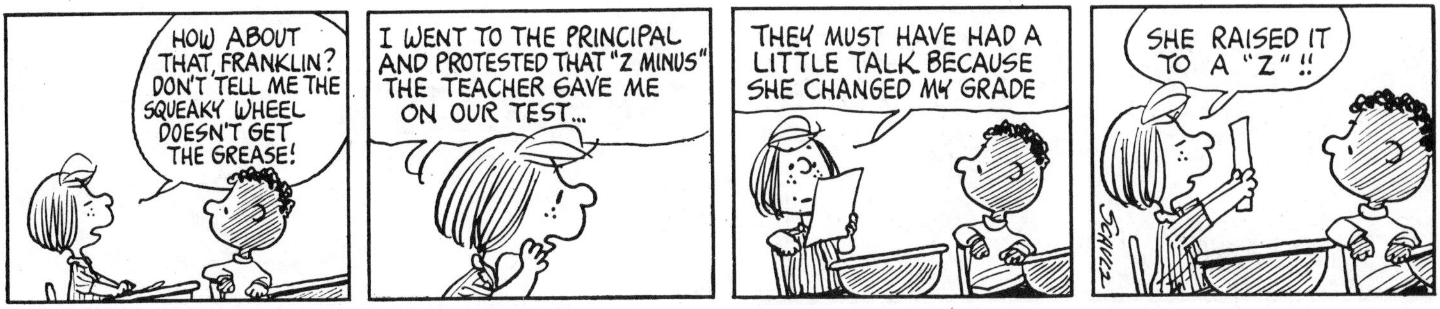
HOW ABOUT THAT, FRANKLIN? DON'T TELL ME THE SQUEAKY WHEEL DOESN'T GET THE GREASE!
I WENT TO THE PRINCIPAL AND PROTESTED THAT "Z MINUS" THE TEACHER GAVE ME ON OUR TEST...
THEY MUST HAVE HAD A LITTLE TALK BECAUSE SHE CHANGED MY GRADE
SHE RAISED IT TO A "Z"!!

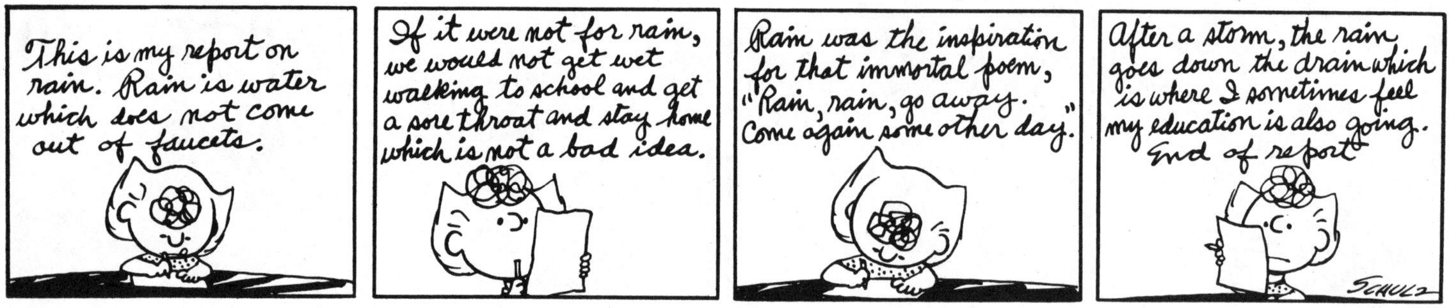
This is my report on rain. Rain is water which does not come out of faucets.
If it were not for rain, we would not get wet walking to school and get a sore throat and stay home which is not a bad idea.
Rain was the inspiration for that immortal poem, "Rain, rain, go away. Come again some other day."
After a storm, the rain goes down the drain which is where I sometimes feel my education is also going. End of report
SCHULZ

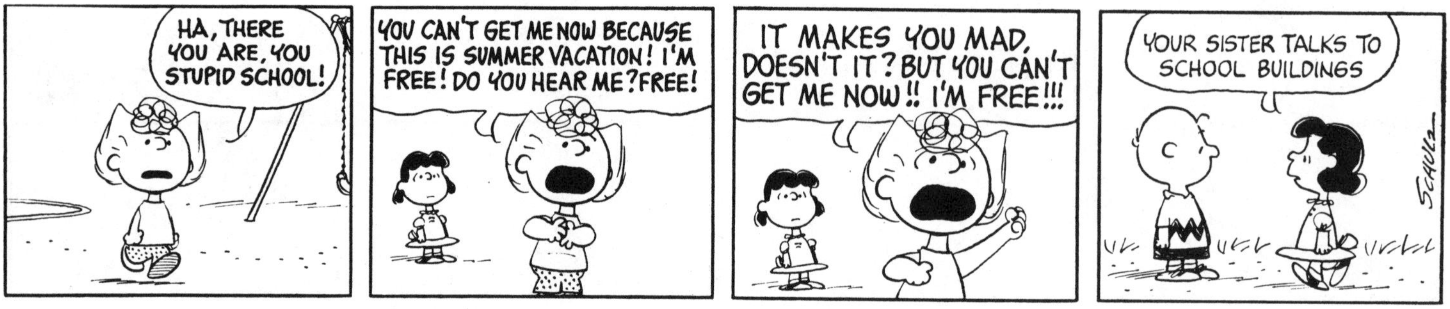
HA, THERE YOU ARE, YOU STUPID SCHOOL!
YOU CAN'T GET ME NOW BECAUSE THIS IS SUMMER VACATION! I'M FREE! DO YOU HEAR ME? FREE!
IT MAKES YOU MAD, DOESN'T IT? BUT YOU CAN'T GET ME NOW!! I'M FREE!!!
YOUR SISTER TALKS TO SCHOOL BUILDINGS
SCHULZ

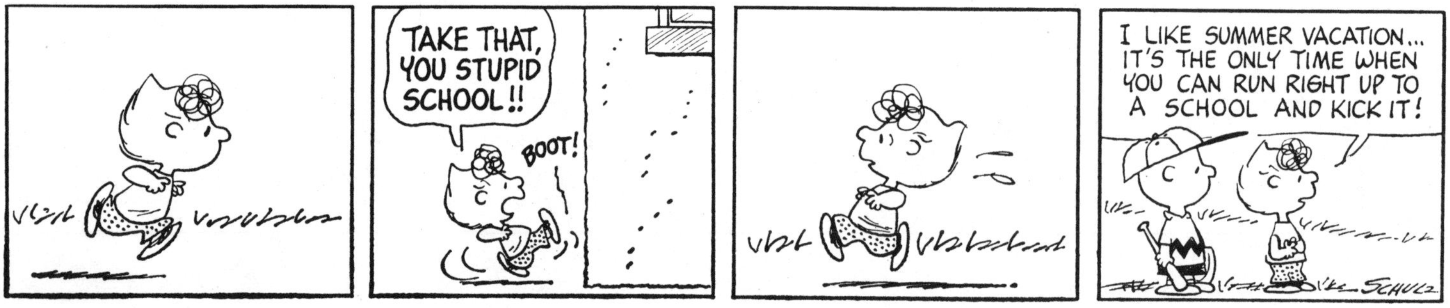
TAKE THAT, YOU STUPID SCHOOL!!
BOOT!
I LIKE SUMMER VACATION... IT'S THE ONLY TIME WHEN YOU CAN RUN RIGHT UP TO A SCHOOL AND KICK IT!
SCHULZ

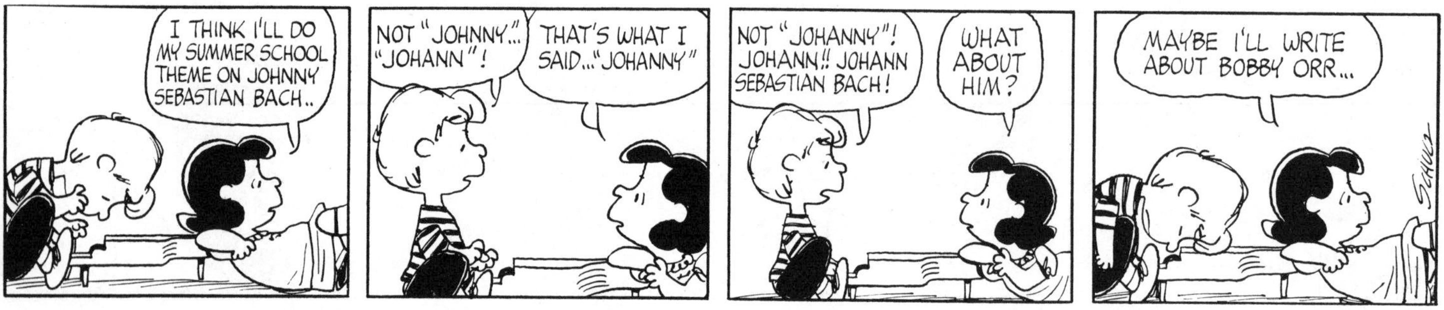
I THINK I'LL DO MY SUMMER SCHOOL THEME ON JOHNNY SEBASTIAN BACH..
NOT "JOHNNY"... "JOHANN"!
THAT'S WHAT I SAID..."JOHANNY"
NOT "JOHANNY"! JOHANN!! JOHANN SEBASTIAN BACH!
WHAT ABOUT HIM?
MAYBE I'LL WRITE ABOUT BOBBY ORR...
SCHULZ

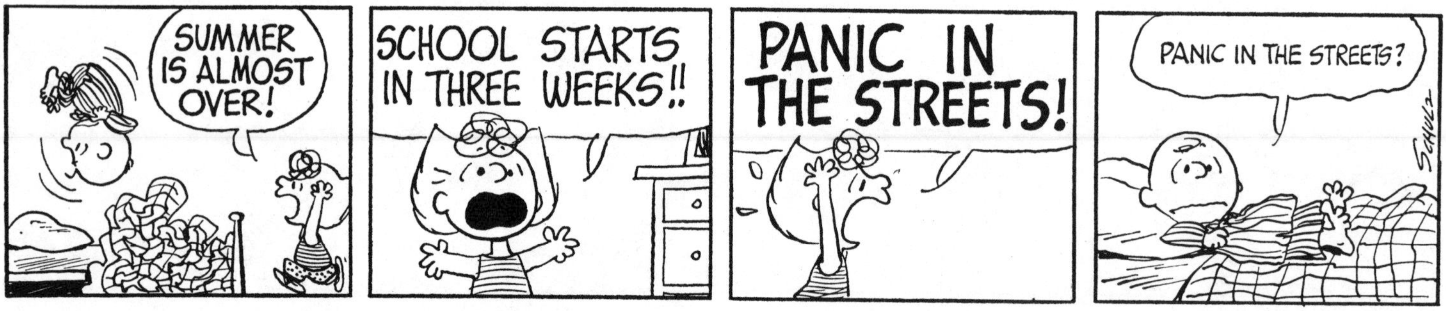
SUMMER IS ALMOST OVER!
SCHOOL STARTS IN THREE WEEKS!!
PANIC IN THE STREETS!
PANIC IN THE STREETS?
SCHULZ

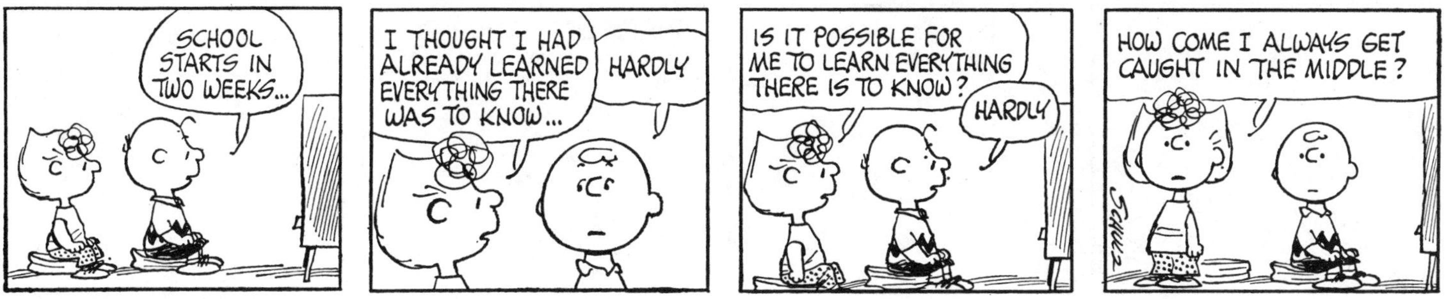
SCHOOL STARTS IN TWO WEEKS...
I THOUGHT I HAD ALREADY LEARNED EVERYTHING THERE WAS TO KNOW...
HARDLY
IS IT POSSIBLE FOR ME TO LEARN EVERYTHING THERE IS TO KNOW?
HARDLY
HOW COME I ALWAYS GET CAUGHT IN THE MIDDLE?
SCHULZ

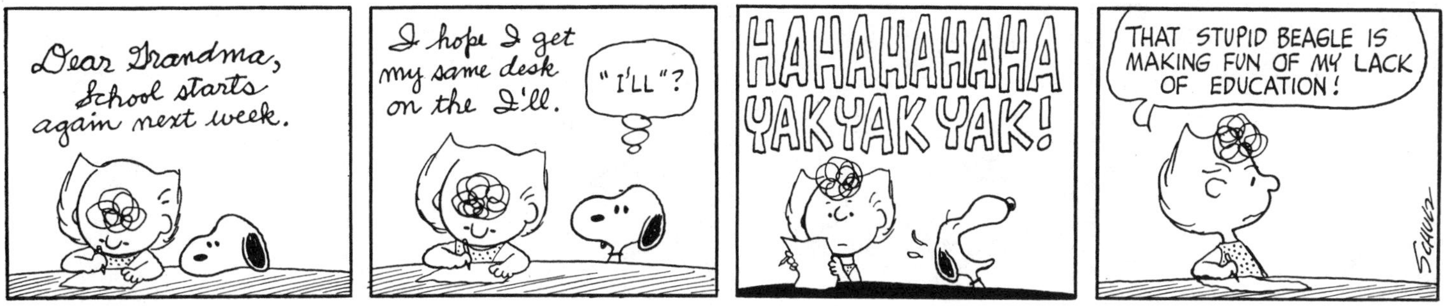
Dear Grandma, School starts again next week.
I hope I get my same desk on the I'll.
"I'LL"?
HAHAHAHAHA YAKYAKYAK!
THAT STUPID BEAGLE IS MAKING FUN OF MY LACK OF EDUCATION!
SCHULZ

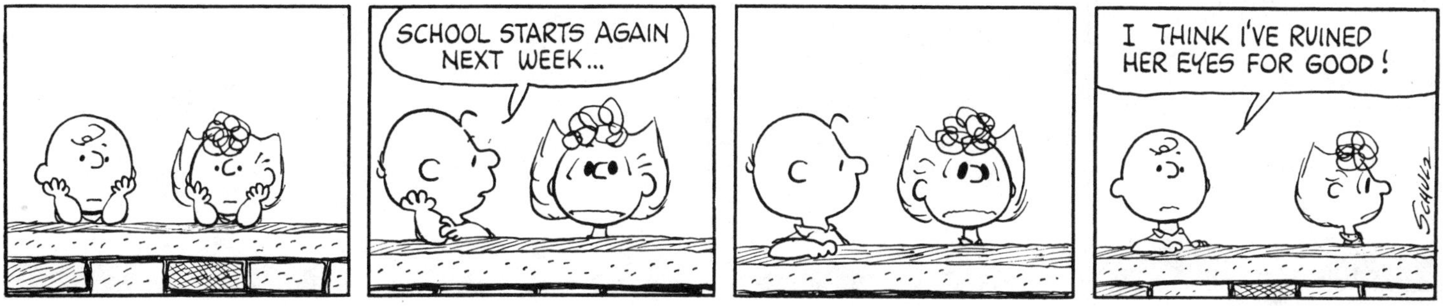
SCHOOL STARTS AGAIN NEXT WEEK...
I THINK I'VE RUINED HER EYES FOR GOOD!
SCHULZ

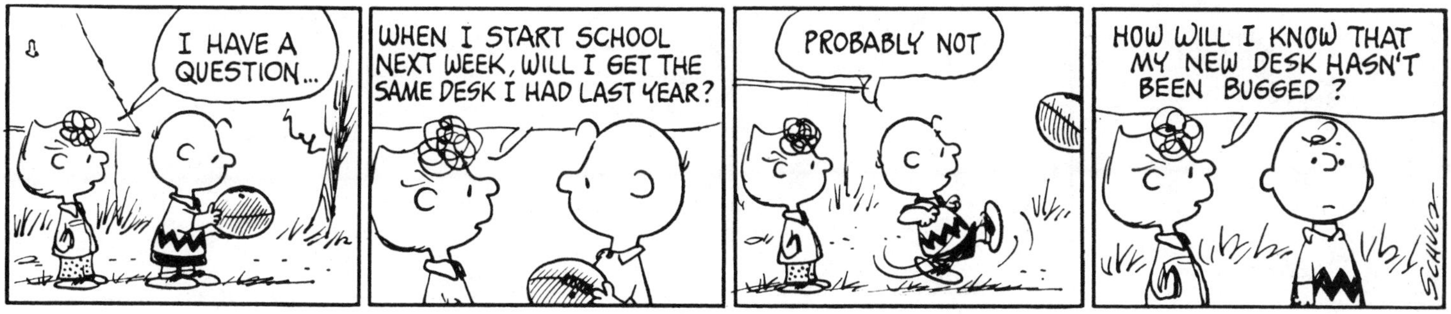
I HAVE A QUESTION...
WHEN I START SCHOOL NEXT WEEK, WILL I GET THE SAME DESK I HAD LAST YEAR?
PROBABLY NOT
HOW WILL I KNOW THAT MY NEW DESK HASN'T BEEN BUGGED?
SCHULZ

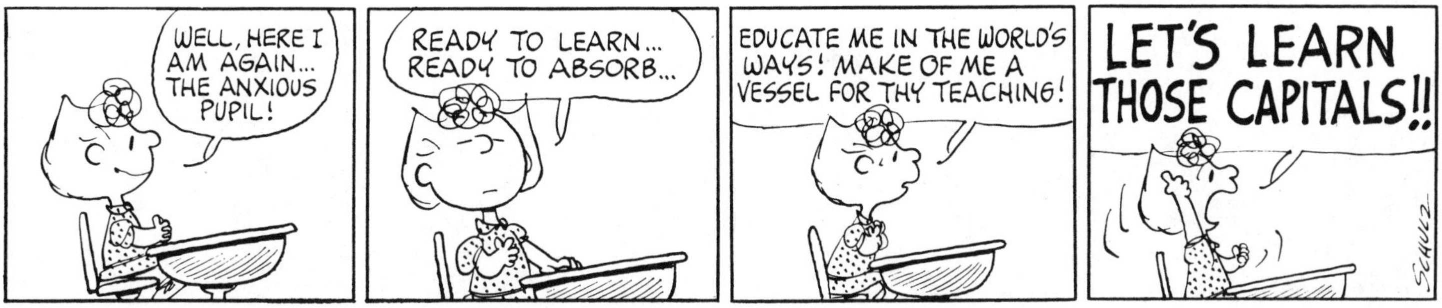
WELL, HERE I AM AGAIN... THE ANXIOUS PUPIL!
READY TO LEARN... READY TO ABSORB...
EDUCATE ME IN THE WORLD'S WAYS! MAKE OF ME A VESSEL FOR THY TEACHING!
LET'S LEARN THOSE CAPITALS!!
SCHULZ

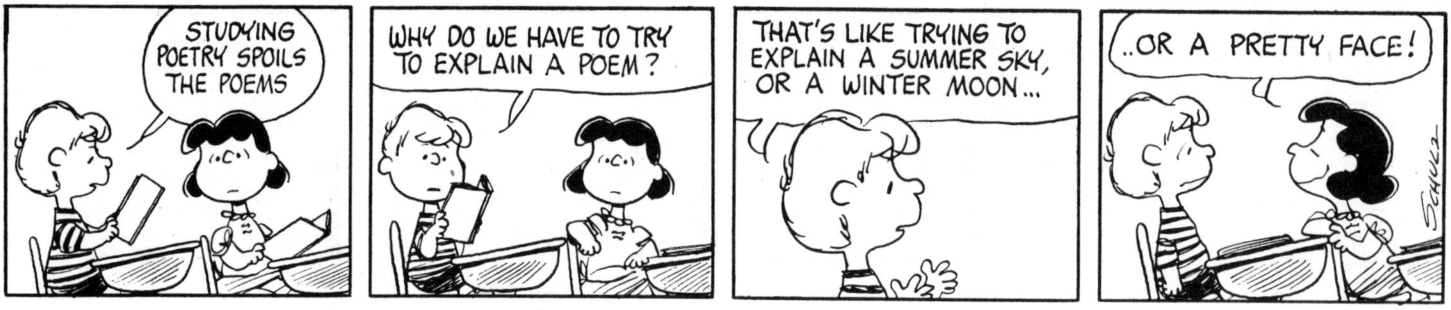
STUDYING POETRY SPOILS THE POEMS
WHY DO WE HAVE TO TRY TO EXPLAIN A POEM?
THAT'S LIKE TRYING TO EXPLAIN A SUMMER SKY, OR A WINTER MOON...
..OR A PRETTY FACE!

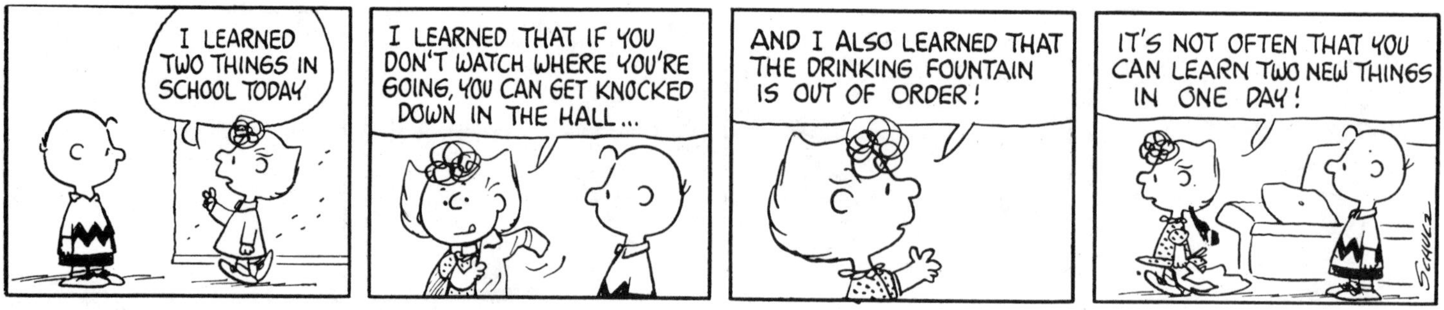
I LEARNED TWO THINGS IN SCHOOL TODAY
I LEARNED THAT IF YOU DON'T WATCH WHERE YOU'RE GOING, YOU CAN GET KNOCKED DOWN IN THE HALL...
AND I ALSO LEARNED THAT THE DRINKING FOUNTAIN IS OUT OF ORDER!
IT'S NOT OFTEN THAT YOU CAN LEARN TWO NEW THINGS IN ONE DAY!

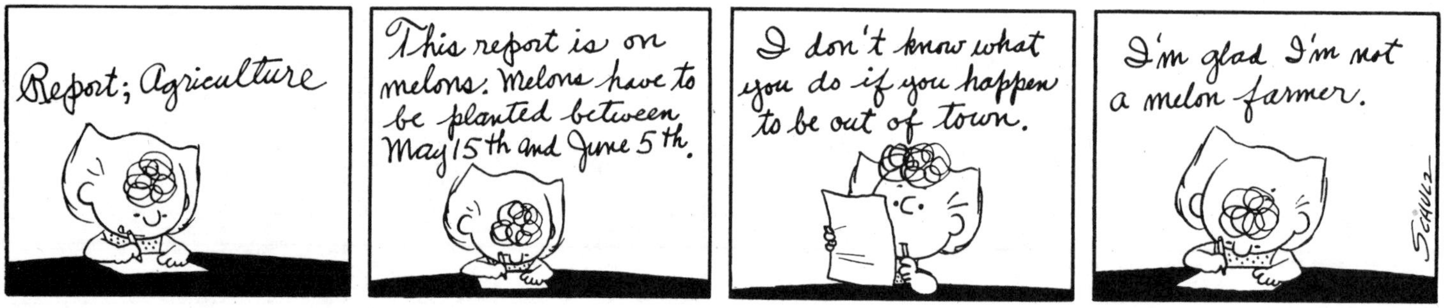
Report; Agriculture
This report is on melons. Melons have to be planted between May 15th and June 5th.
I don't know what you do if you happen to be out of town.
I'm glad I'm not a melon farmer.

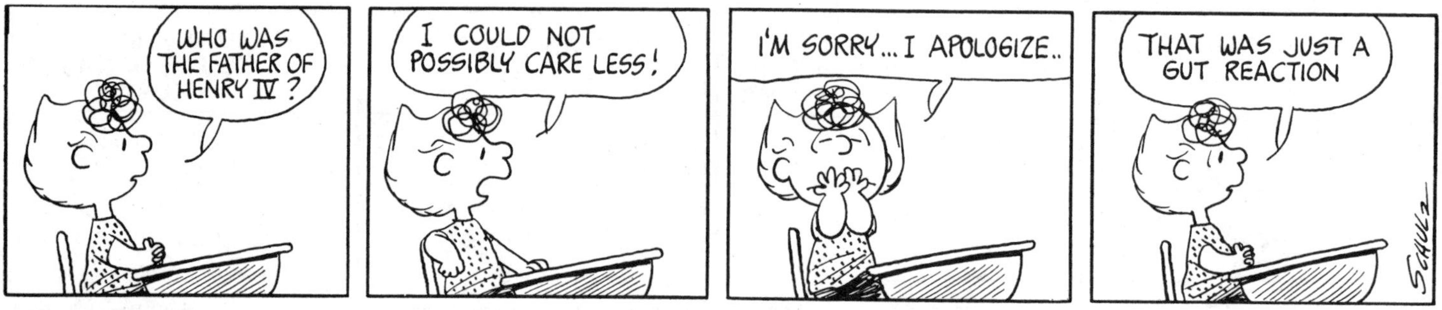
WHO WAS THE FATHER OF HENRY IV?
I COULD NOT POSSIBLY CARE LESS!
I'M SORRY... I APOLOGIZE..
THAT WAS JUST A GUT REACTION

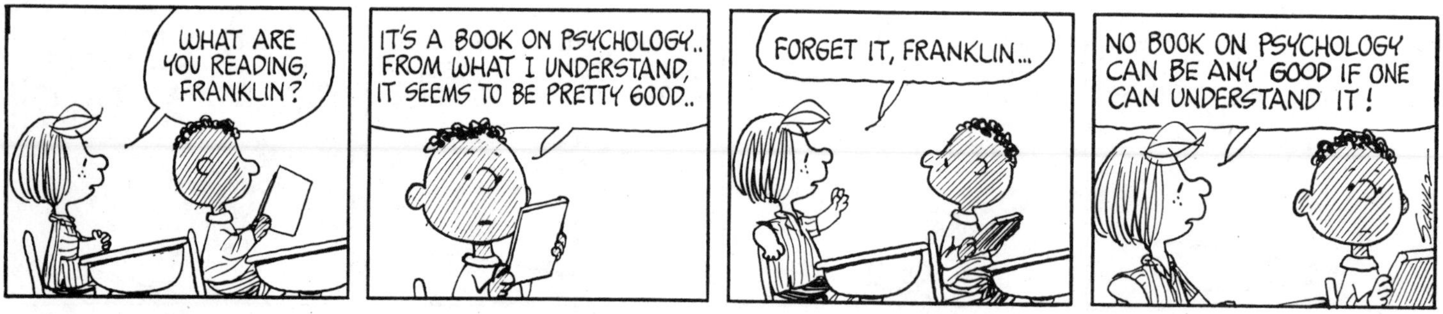
WHAT ARE YOU READING, FRANKLIN?
IT'S A BOOK ON PSYCHOLOGY.. FROM WHAT I UNDERSTAND, IT SEEMS TO BE PRETTY GOOD..
FORGET IT, FRANKLIN...
NO BOOK ON PSYCHOLOGY CAN BE ANY GOOD IF ONE CAN UNDERSTAND IT!

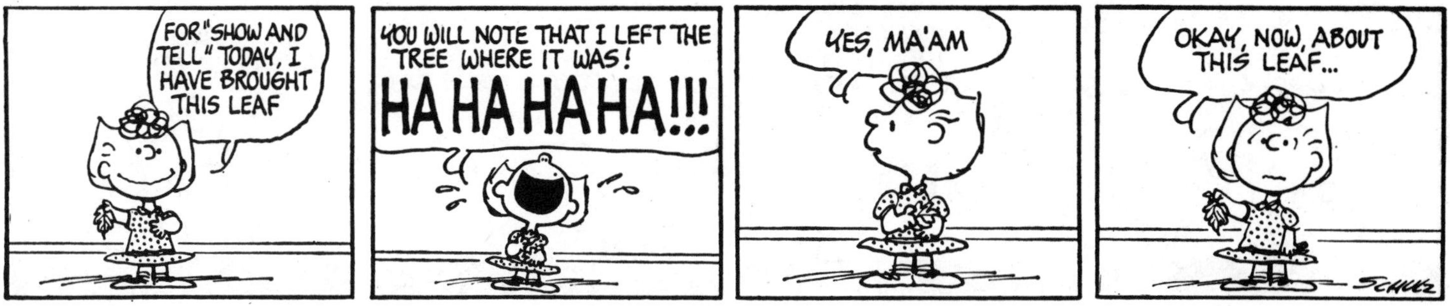
FOR "SHOW AND TELL" TODAY, I HAVE BROUGHT THIS LEAF
YOU WILL NOTE THAT I LEFT THE TREE WHERE IT WAS!
HA HA HA HA!!!
YES, MA'AM
OKAY, NOW, ABOUT THIS LEAF...
SCHULZ

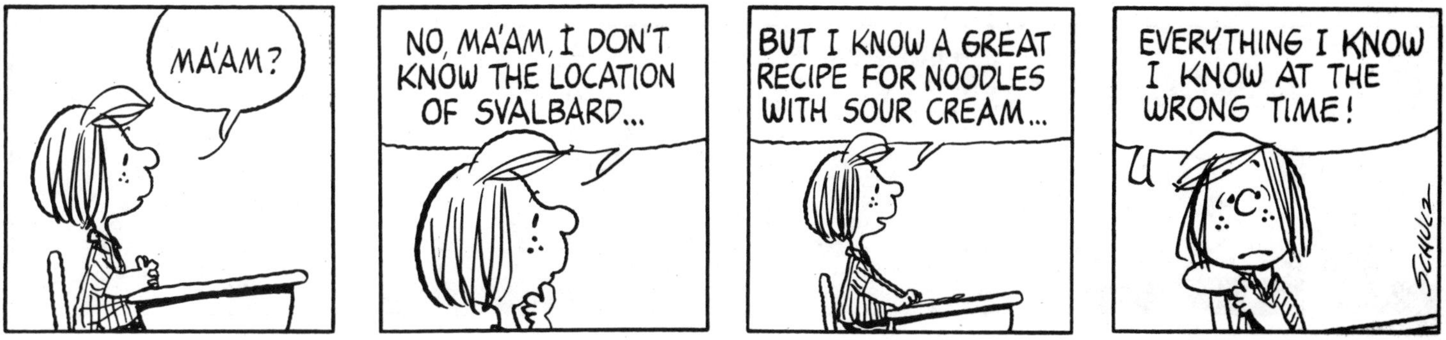
MA'AM?
NO, MA'AM, I DON'T KNOW THE LOCATION OF SVALBARD...
BUT I KNOW A GREAT RECIPE FOR NOODLES WITH SOUR CREAM...
EVERYTHING I KNOW I KNOW AT THE WRONG TIME!
SCHULZ

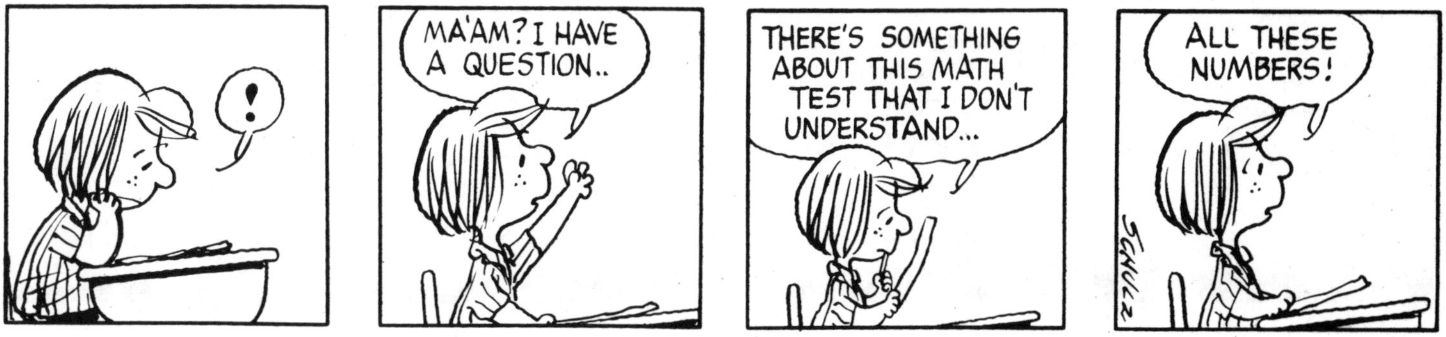
!
MA'AM? I HAVE A QUESTION..
THERE'S SOMETHING ABOUT THIS MATH TEST THAT I DON'T UNDERSTAND...
SCHULZ
ALL THESE NUMBERS!

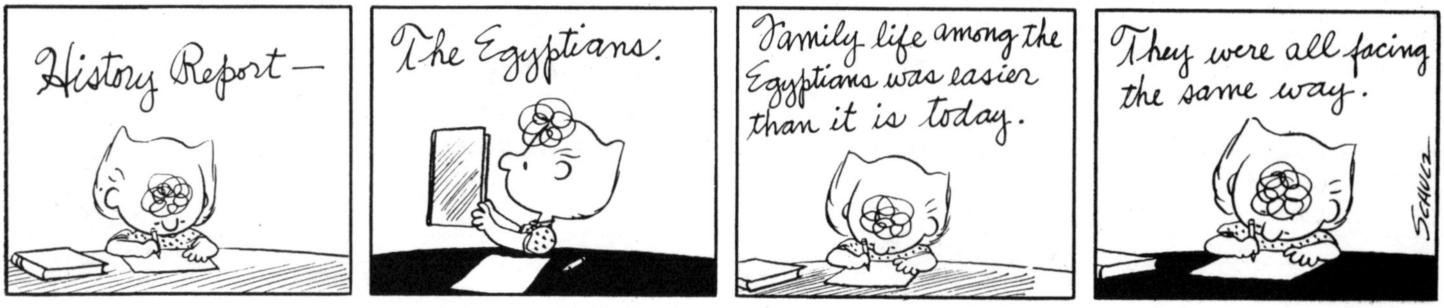
History Report —
The Egyptians.
Family life among the Egyptians was easier than it is today.
They were all facing the same way.
SCHULZ

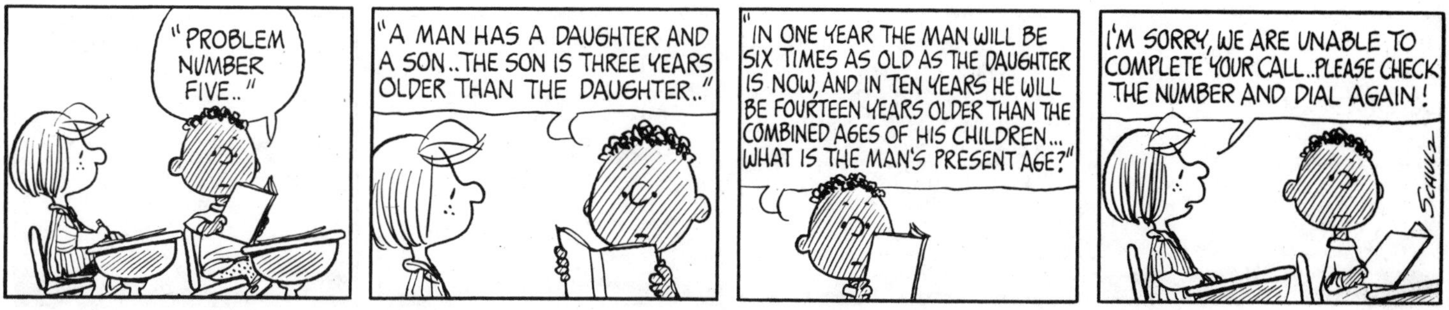
"PROBLEM NUMBER FIVE.."
"A MAN HAS A DAUGHTER AND A SON..THE SON IS THREE YEARS OLDER THAN THE DAUGHTER.."
"IN ONE YEAR THE MAN WILL BE SIX TIMES AS OLD AS THE DAUGHTER IS NOW, AND IN TEN YEARS HE WILL BE FOURTEEN YEARS OLDER THAN THE COMBINED AGES OF HIS CHILDREN... WHAT IS THE MAN'S PRESENT AGE?"
I'M SORRY, WE ARE UNABLE TO COMPLETE YOUR CALL..PLEASE CHECK THE NUMBER AND DIAL AGAIN!
SCHULZ

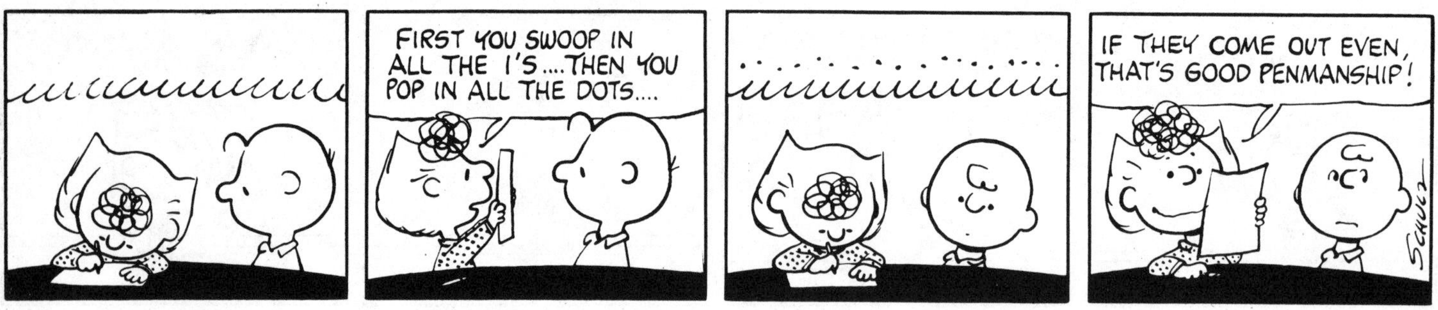
FIRST YOU SWOOP IN ALL THE I'S....THEN YOU POP IN ALL THE DOTS....
IF THEY COME OUT EVEN, THAT'S GOOD PENMANSHIP!
SCHULZ

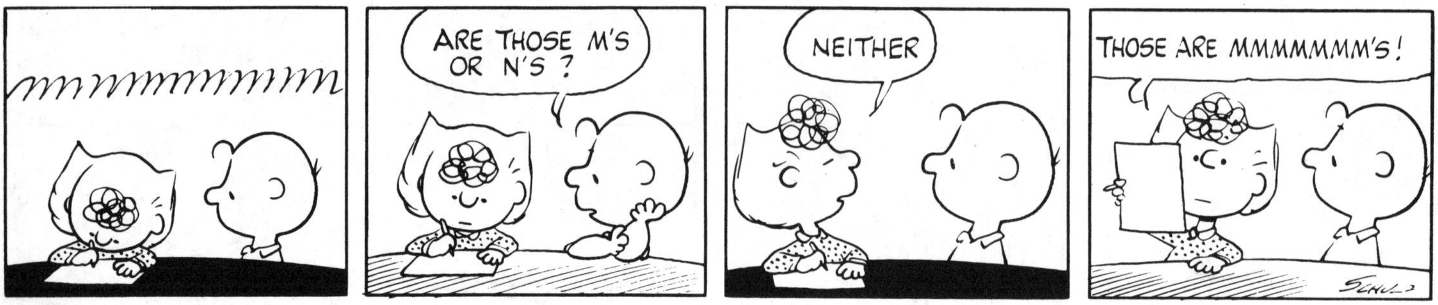
ARE THOSE M'S OR N'S ?
NEITHER
THOSE ARE MMMMMMM'S!
SCHULZ

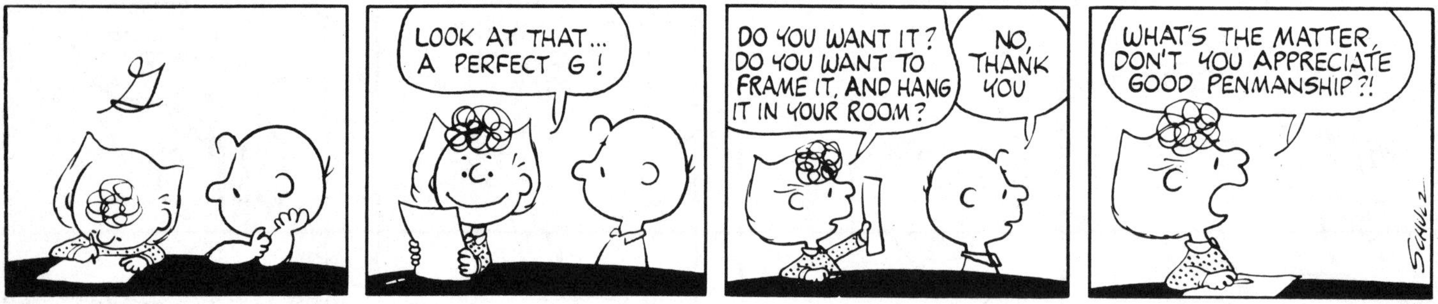
LOOK AT THAT... A PERFECT G!
DO YOU WANT IT? DO YOU WANT TO FRAME IT, AND HANG IT IN YOUR ROOM?
NO, THANK YOU
WHAT'S THE MATTER, DON'T YOU APPRECIATE GOOD PENMANSHIP?!
SCHULZ

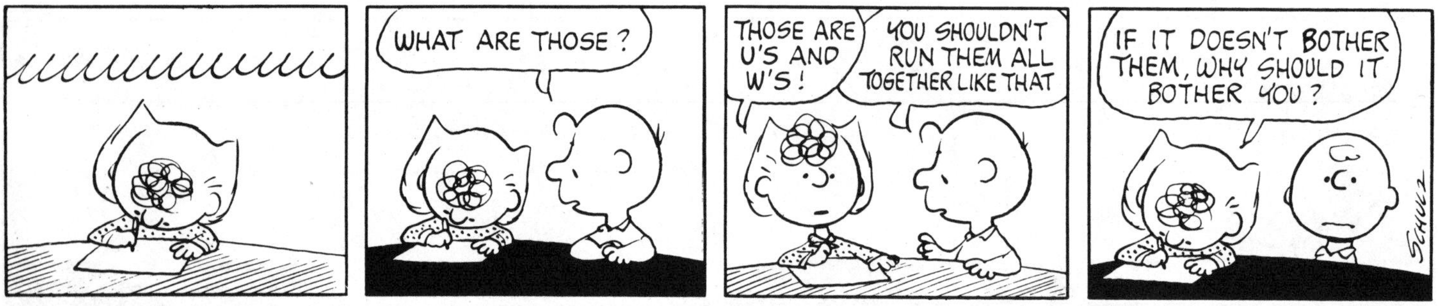
WHAT ARE THOSE ?
THOSE ARE U'S AND W'S!
YOU SHOULDN'T RUN THEM ALL TOGETHER LIKE THAT
IF IT DOESN'T BOTHER THEM, WHY SHOULD IT BOTHER YOU ?
SCHULZ

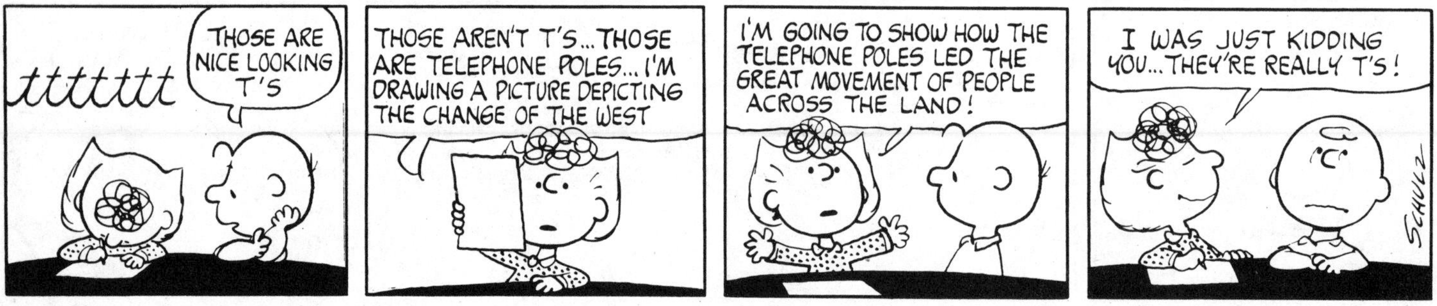
THOSE ARE NICE LOOKING T'S
THOSE AREN'T T'S...THOSE ARE TELEPHONE POLES...I'M DRAWING A PICTURE DEPICTING THE CHANGE OF THE WEST
I'M GOING TO SHOW HOW THE TELEPHONE POLES LED THE GREAT MOVEMENT OF PEOPLE ACROSS THE LAND!
I WAS JUST KIDDING YOU...THEY'RE REALLY T'S!
SCHULZ

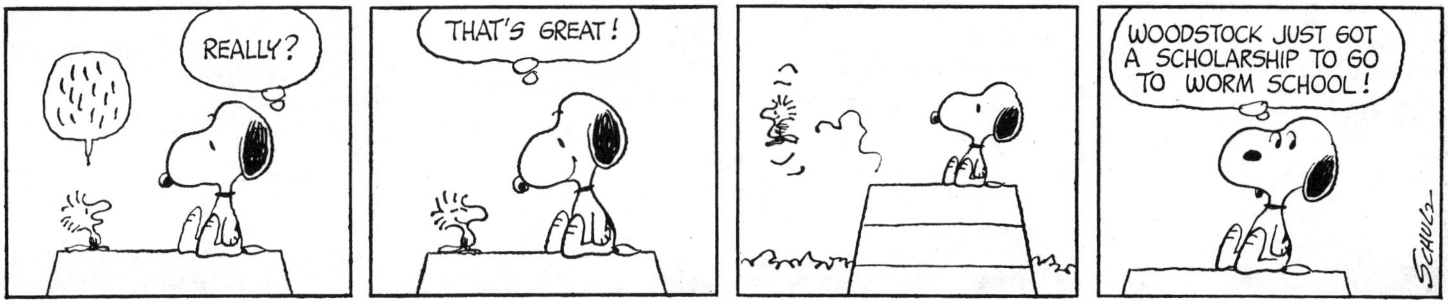
REALLY?
THAT'S GREAT!
WOODSTOCK JUST GOT A SCHOLARSHIP TO GO TO WORM SCHOOL!
SCHULZ

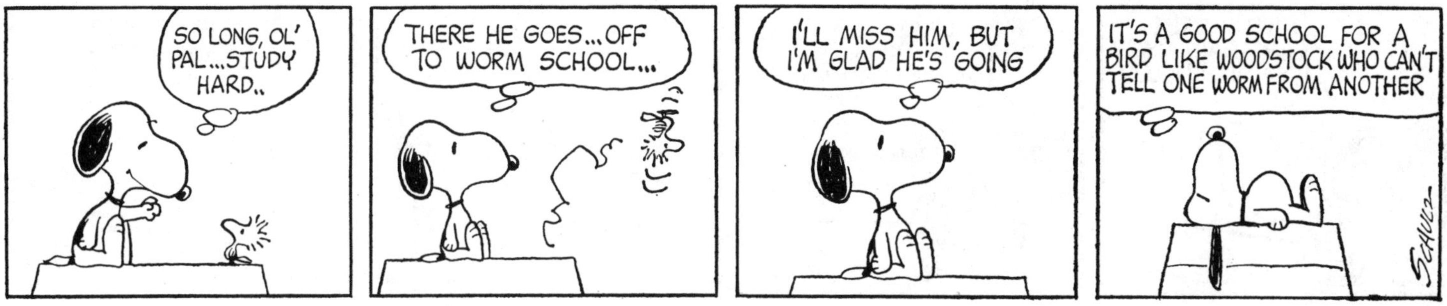
SO LONG, OL' PAL...STUDY HARD..
THERE HE GOES...OFF TO WORM SCHOOL...
I'LL MISS HIM, BUT I'M GLAD HE'S GOING
IT'S A GOOD SCHOOL FOR A BIRD LIKE WOODSTOCK WHO CAN'T TELL ONE WORM FROM ANOTHER
SCHULZ

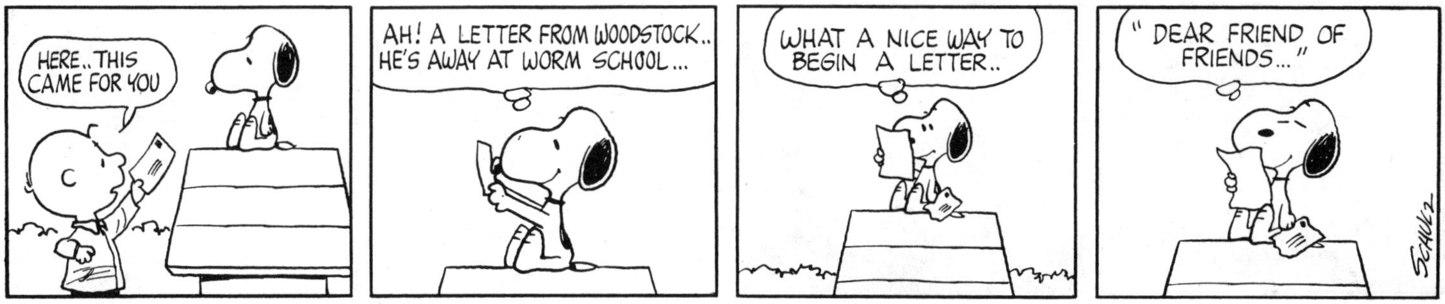
HERE..THIS CAME FOR YOU
AH! A LETTER FROM WOODSTOCK.. HE'S AWAY AT WORM SCHOOL...
WHAT A NICE WAY TO BEGIN A LETTER..
" DEAR FRIEND OF FRIENDS..."
SCHULZ

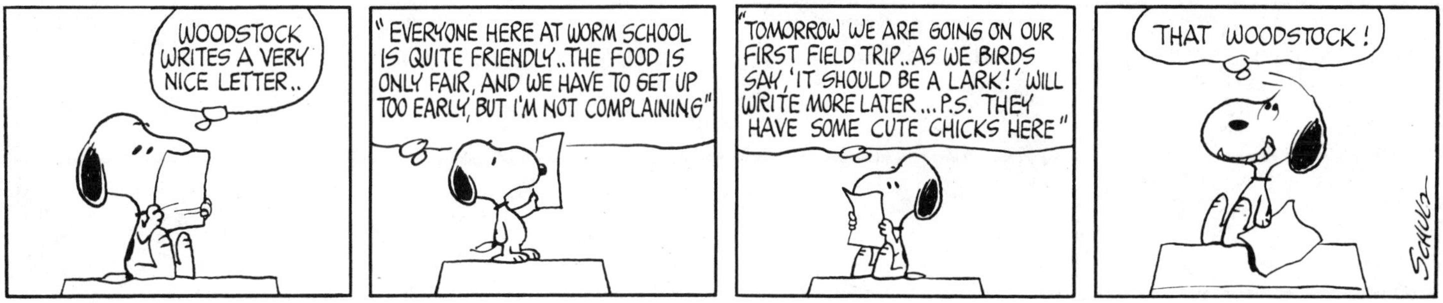
WOODSTOCK WRITES A VERY NICE LETTER..
" EVERYONE HERE AT WORM SCHOOL IS QUITE FRIENDLY..THE FOOD IS ONLY FAIR, AND WE HAVE TO GET UP TOO EARLY, BUT I'M NOT COMPLAINING"
"TOMORROW WE ARE GOING ON OUR FIRST FIELD TRIP..AS WE BIRDS SAY, 'IT SHOULD BE A LARK!' WILL WRITE MORE LATER... P.S. THEY HAVE SOME CUTE CHICKS HERE"
THAT WOODSTOCK!
SCHULZ

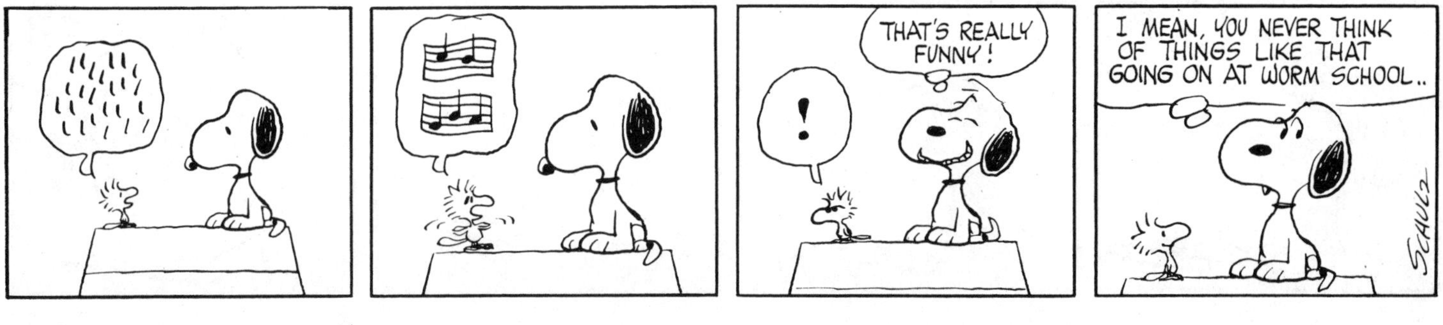
!
THAT'S REALLY FUNNY!
I MEAN, YOU NEVER THINK OF THINGS LIKE THAT GOING ON AT WORM SCHOOL..
SCHULZ

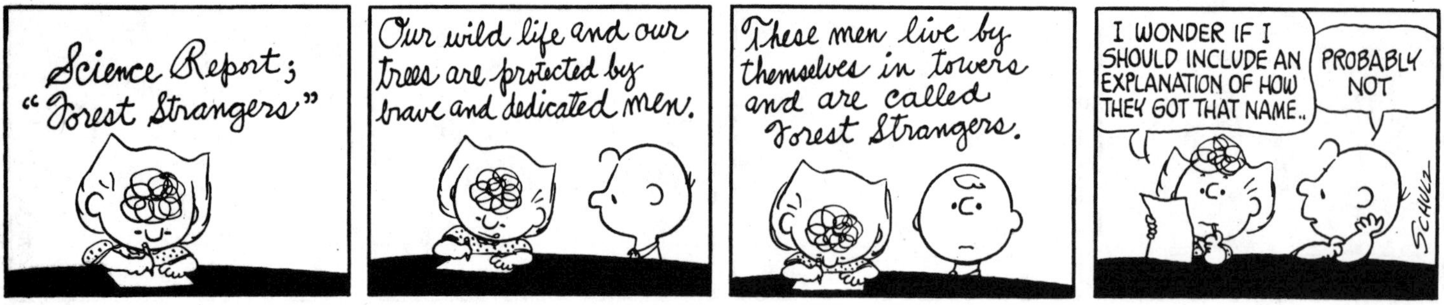
Science Report; "Forest Strangers"
Our wild life and our trees are protected by brave and dedicated men.
These men live by themselves in towers and are called Forest Strangers.
I WONDER IF I SHOULD INCLUDE AN EXPLANATION OF HOW THEY GOT THAT NAME..
PROBABLY NOT
SCHULZ

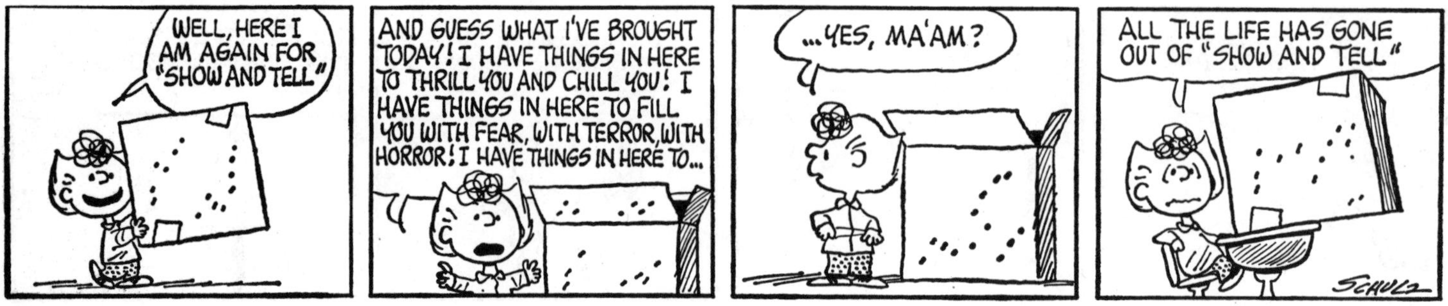
WELL, HERE I AM AGAIN FOR "SHOW AND TELL"
AND GUESS WHAT I'VE BROUGHT TODAY! I HAVE THINGS IN HERE TO THRILL YOU AND CHILL YOU! I HAVE THINGS IN HERE TO FILL YOU WITH FEAR, WITH TERROR, WITH HORROR! I HAVE THINGS IN HERE TO...
...YES, MA'AM?
ALL THE LIFE HAS GONE OUT OF "SHOW AND TELL"
SCHULZ

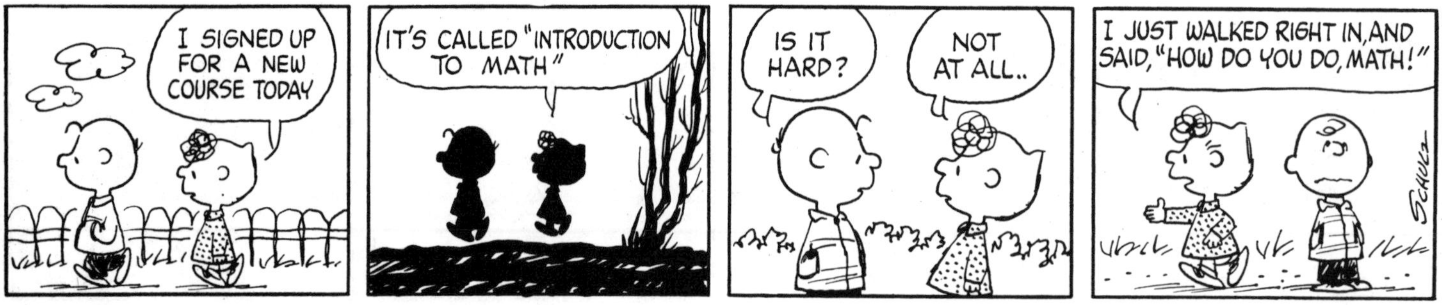
I SIGNED UP FOR A NEW COURSE TODAY
IT'S CALLED "INTRODUCTION TO MATH"
IS IT HARD?
NOT AT ALL..
I JUST WALKED RIGHT IN, AND SAID, "HOW DO YOU DO, MATH!"
SCHULZ

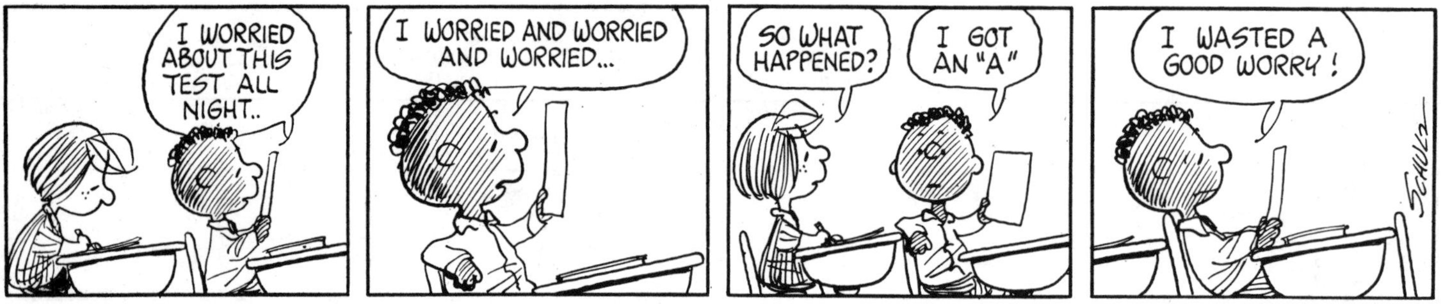
I WORRIED ABOUT THIS TEST ALL NIGHT..
I WORRIED AND WORRIED AND WORRIED...
SO WHAT HAPPENED?
I GOT AN "A"
I WASTED A GOOD WORRY!
SCHULZ

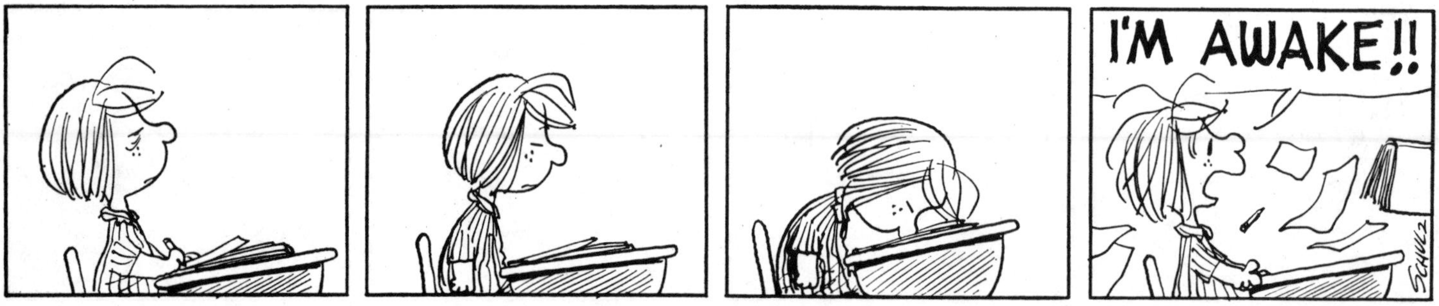
I'M AWAKE!!
SCHULZ

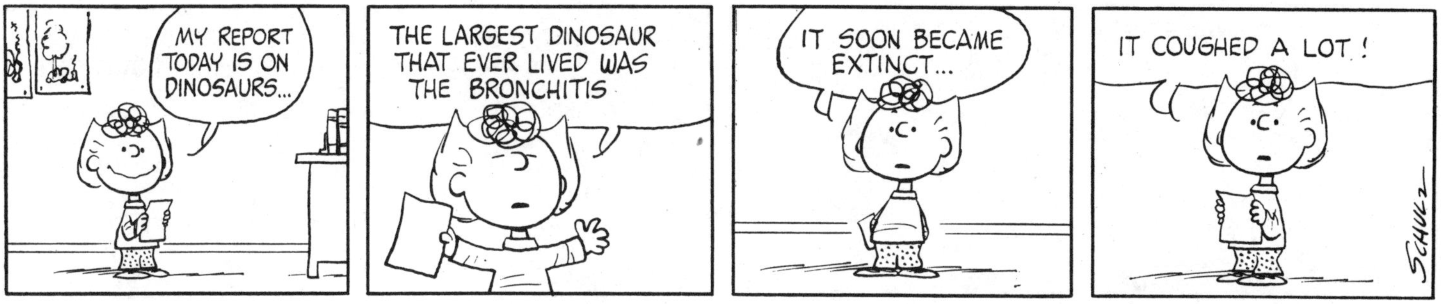
MY REPORT TODAY IS ON DINOSAURS...
THE LARGEST DINOSAUR THAT EVER LIVED WAS THE BRONCHITIS
IT SOON BECAME EXTINCT...
IT COUGHED A LOT!
SCHULZ

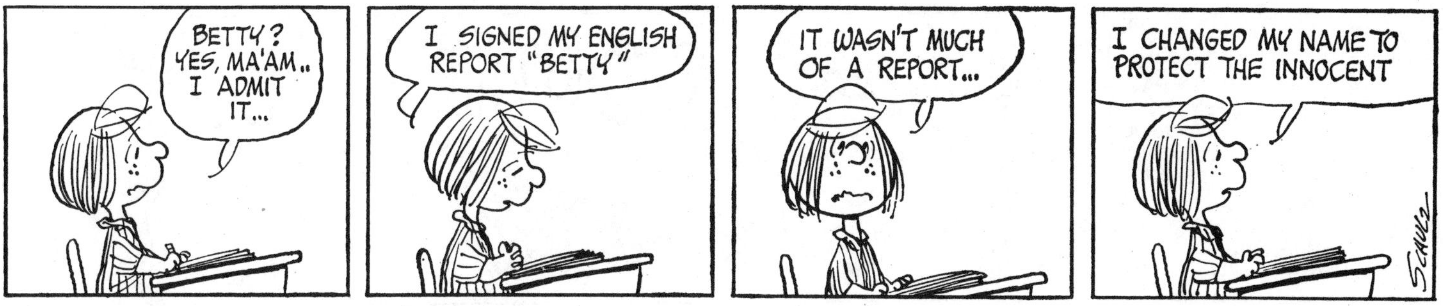
BETTY? YES, MA'AM.. I ADMIT IT...
I SIGNED MY ENGLISH REPORT "BETTY"
IT WASN'T MUCH OF A REPORT...
I CHANGED MY NAME TO PROTECT THE INNOCENT
SCHULZ

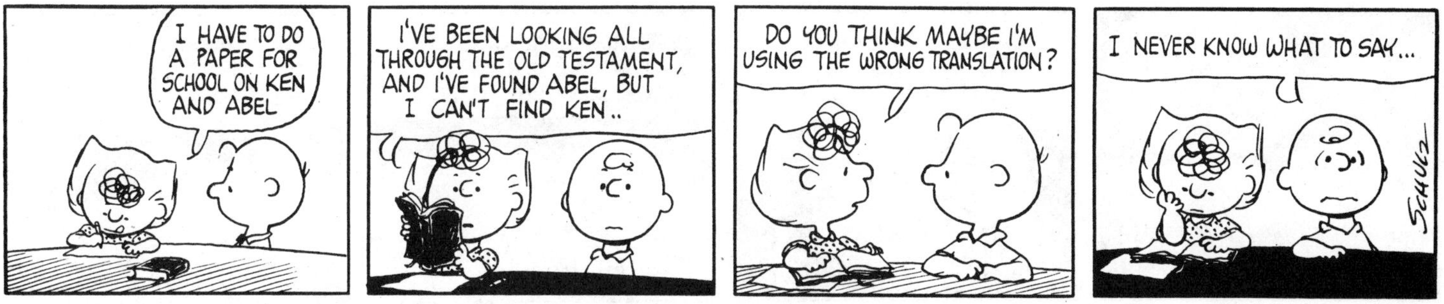
I HAVE TO DO A PAPER FOR SCHOOL ON KEN AND ABEL
I'VE BEEN LOOKING ALL THROUGH THE OLD TESTAMENT, AND I'VE FOUND ABEL, BUT I CAN'T FIND KEN..
DO YOU THINK MAYBE I'M USING THE WRONG TRANSLATION?
I NEVER KNOW WHAT TO SAY...
SCHULZ

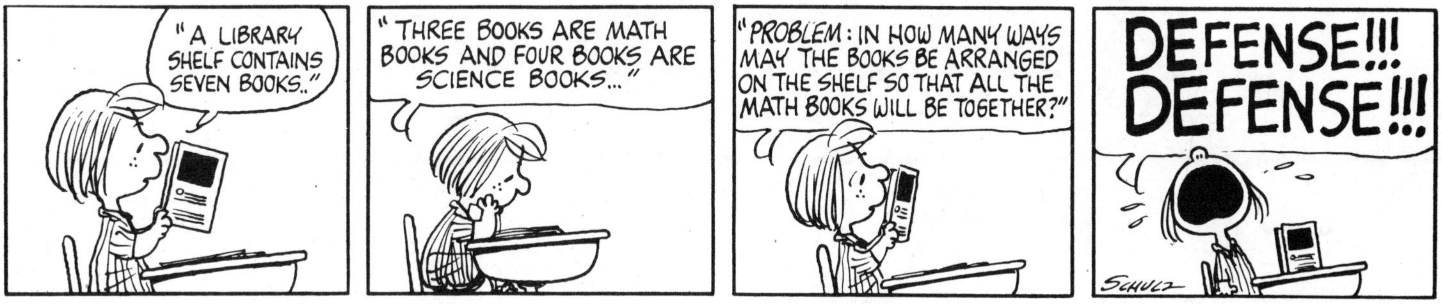
"A LIBRARY SHELF CONTAINS SEVEN BOOKS.."
"THREE BOOKS ARE MATH BOOKS AND FOUR BOOKS ARE SCIENCE BOOKS..."
"PROBLEM: IN HOW MANY WAYS MAY THE BOOKS BE ARRANGED ON THE SHELF SO THAT ALL THE MATH BOOKS WILL BE TOGETHER?"
DEFENSE!!! DEFENSE!!!
SCHULZ

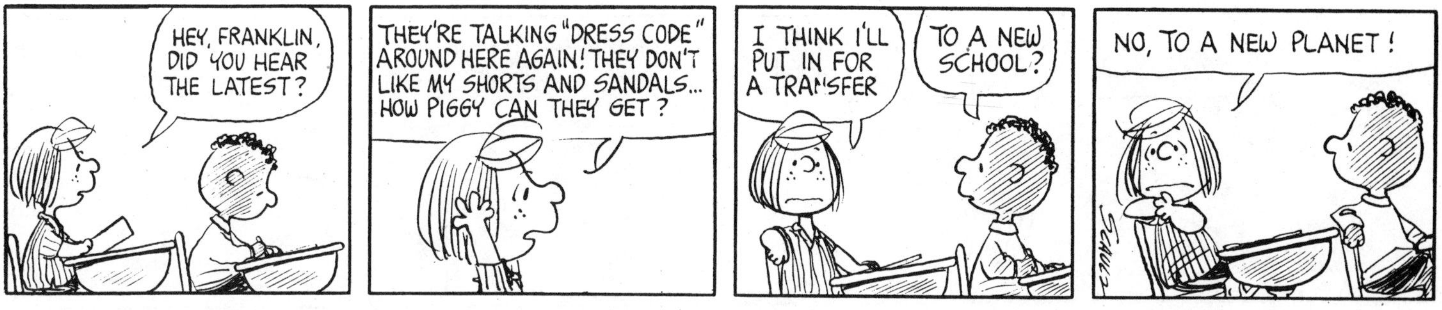
HEY, FRANKLIN, DID YOU HEAR THE LATEST?
THEY'RE TALKING "DRESS CODE" AROUND HERE AGAIN! THEY DON'T LIKE MY SHORTS AND SANDALS... HOW PIGGY CAN THEY GET?
I THINK I'LL PUT IN FOR A TRANSFER
TO A NEW SCHOOL?
NO, TO A NEW PLANET!
SCHULZ

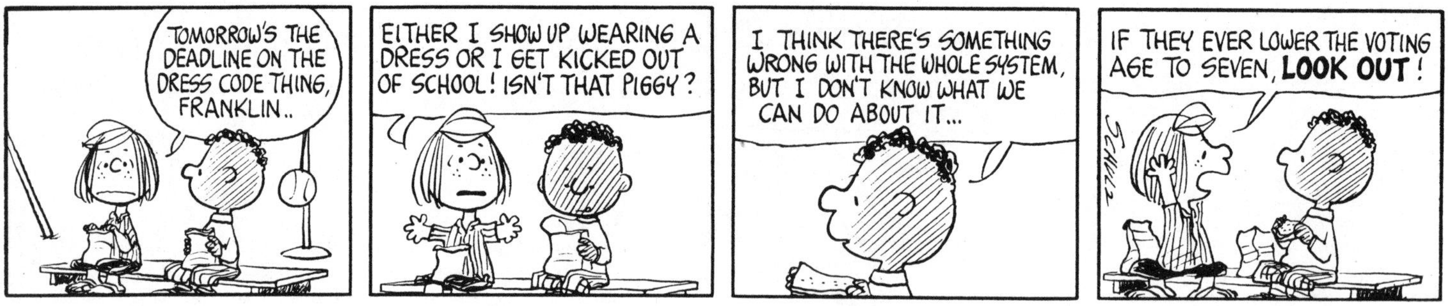
TOMORROW'S THE DEADLINE ON THE DRESS CODE THING, FRANKLIN..
EITHER I SHOW UP WEARING A DRESS OR I GET KICKED OUT OF SCHOOL! ISN'T THAT PIGGY?
I THINK THERE'S SOMETHING WRONG WITH THE WHOLE SYSTEM, BUT I DON'T KNOW WHAT WE CAN DO ABOUT IT...
IF THEY EVER LOWER THE VOTING AGE TO SEVEN, LOOK OUT!
SCHULZ

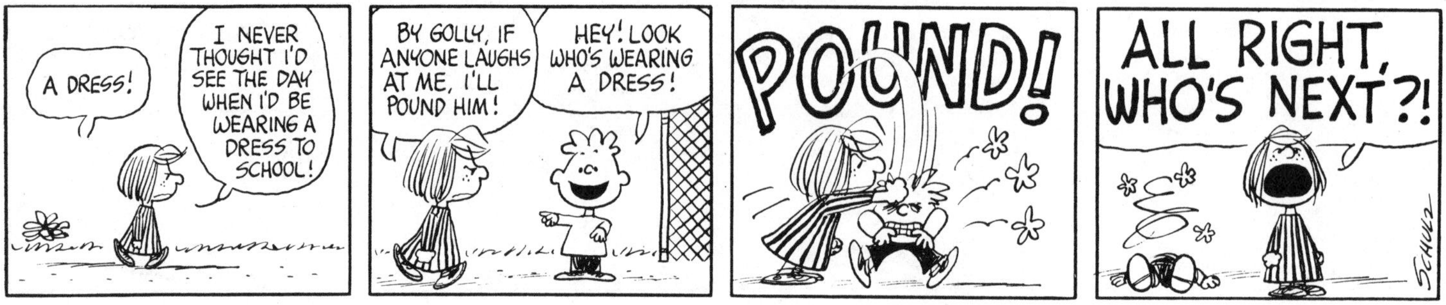
A DRESS!
I NEVER THOUGHT I'D SEE THE DAY WHEN I'D BE WEARING A DRESS TO SCHOOL!
BY GOLLY, IF ANYONE LAUGHS AT ME, I'LL POUND HIM!
HEY! LOOK WHO'S WEARING A DRESS!
POUND!
ALL RIGHT, WHO'S NEXT?!
SCHULZ

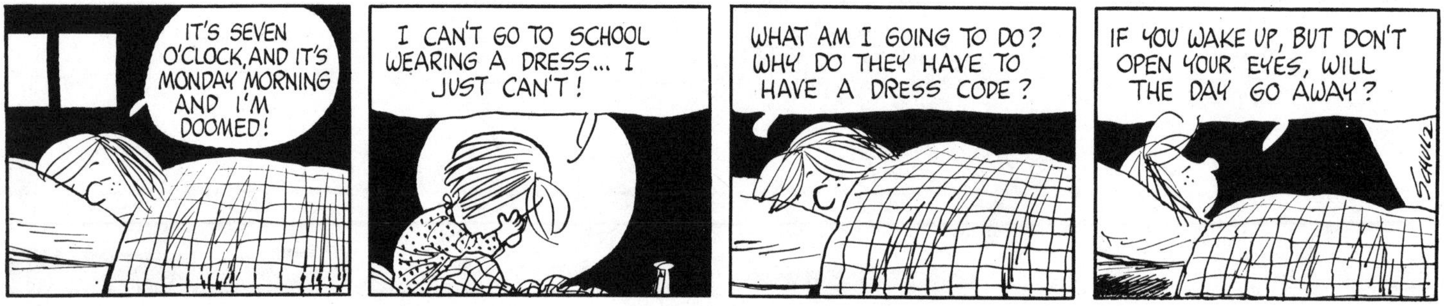
IT'S SEVEN O'CLOCK, AND IT'S MONDAY MORNING AND I'M DOOMED!
I CAN'T GO TO SCHOOL WEARING A DRESS... I JUST CAN'T!
WHAT AM I GOING TO DO? WHY DO THEY HAVE TO HAVE A DRESS CODE?
IF YOU WAKE UP, BUT DON'T OPEN YOUR EYES, WILL THE DAY GO AWAY?
SCHULZ

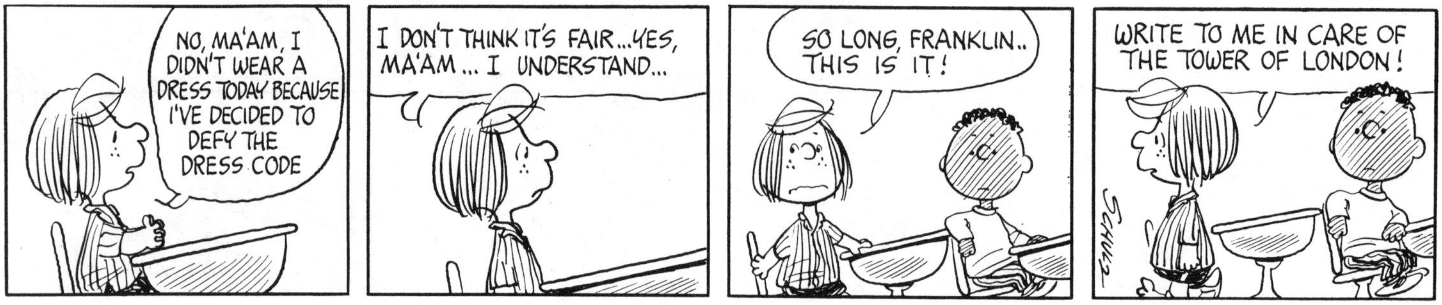
NO, MA'AM, I DIDN'T WEAR A DRESS TODAY BECAUSE I'VE DECIDED TO DEFY THE DRESS CODE
I DON'T THINK IT'S FAIR...YES, MA'AM... I UNDERSTAND...
SO LONG, FRANKLIN.. THIS IS IT!
WRITE TO ME IN CARE OF THE TOWER OF LONDON!
SCHULZ

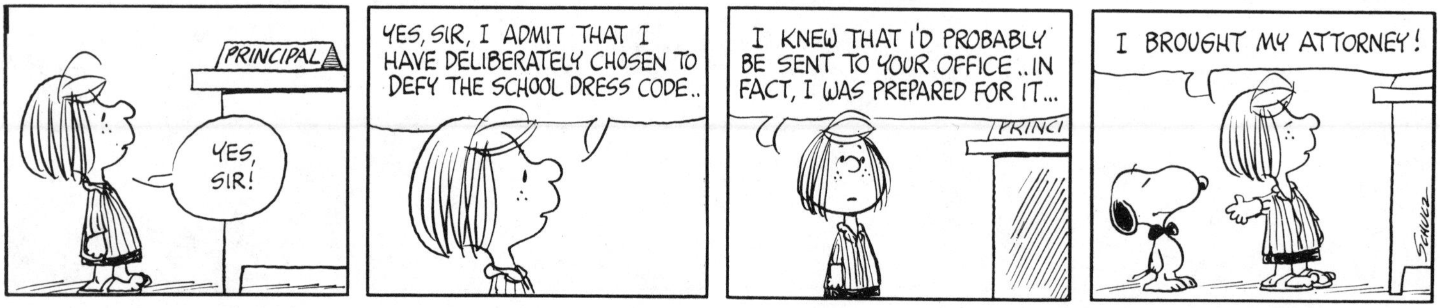
PRINCIPAL
YES, SIR!
YES, SIR, I ADMIT THAT I HAVE DELIBERATELY CHOSEN TO DEFY THE SCHOOL DRESS CODE..
I KNEW THAT I'D PROBABLY BE SENT TO YOUR OFFICE..IN FACT, I WAS PREPARED FOR IT...
PRINCI
I BROUGHT MY ATTORNEY!
SCHULZ

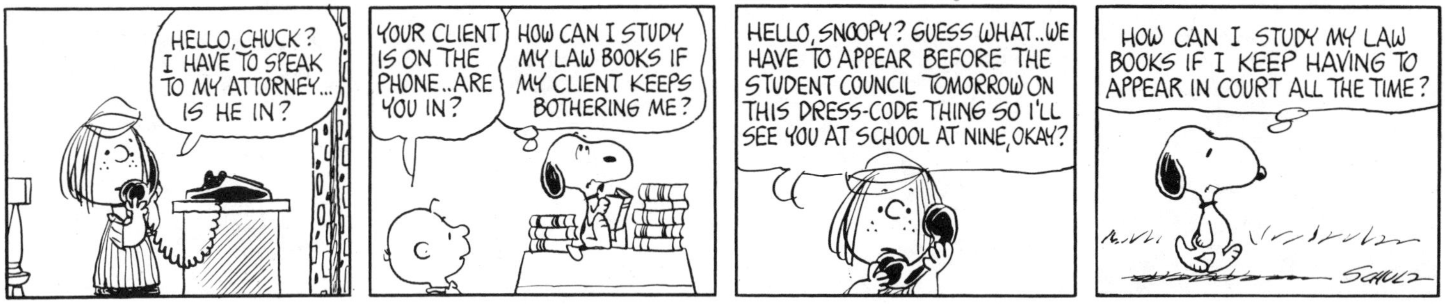
HELLO, CHUCK? I HAVE TO SPEAK TO MY ATTORNEY... IS HE IN?
YOUR CLIENT IS ON THE PHONE..ARE YOU IN?
HOW CAN I STUDY MY LAW BOOKS IF MY CLIENT KEEPS BOTHERING ME?
HELLO, SNOOPY? GUESS WHAT..WE HAVE TO APPEAR BEFORE THE STUDENT COUNCIL TOMORROW ON THIS DRESS-CODE THING SO I'LL SEE YOU AT SCHOOL AT NINE, OKAY?
HOW CAN I STUDY MY LAW BOOKS IF I KEEP HAVING TO APPEAR IN COURT ALL THE TIME?
SCHULZ

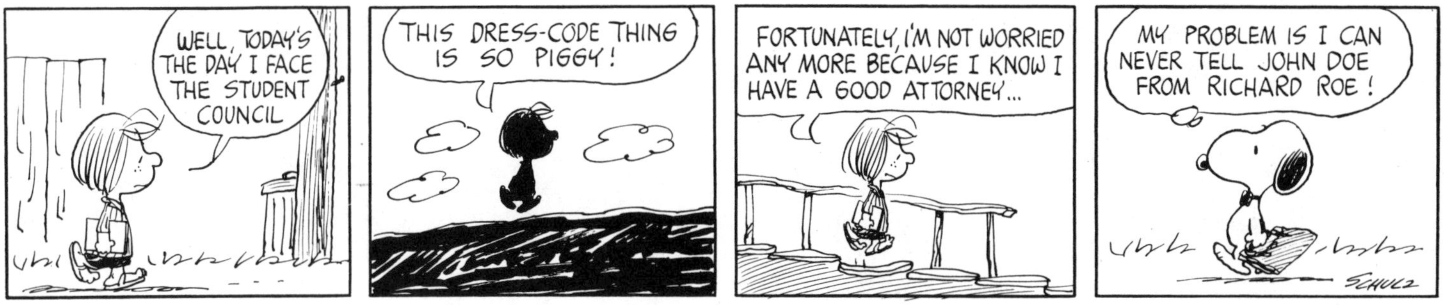
WELL, TODAY'S THE DAY I FACE THE STUDENT COUNCIL
THIS DRESS-CODE THING IS SO PIGGY!
FORTUNATELY, I'M NOT WORRIED ANY MORE BECAUSE I KNOW I HAVE A GOOD ATTORNEY...
MY PROBLEM IS I CAN NEVER TELL JOHN DOE FROM RICHARD ROE!
SCHULZ

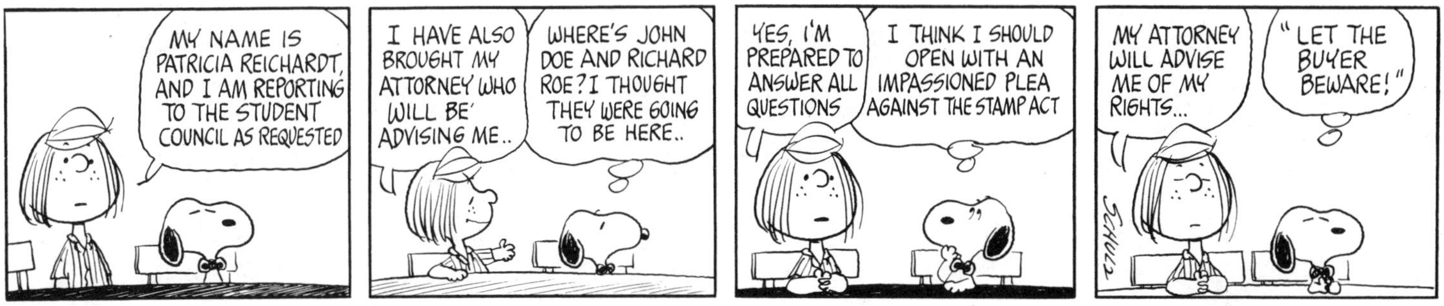
MY NAME IS PATRICIA REICHARDT, AND I AM REPORTING TO THE STUDENT COUNCIL AS REQUESTED
I HAVE ALSO BROUGHT MY ATTORNEY WHO WILL BE ADVISING ME..
WHERE'S JOHN DOE AND RICHARD ROE? I THOUGHT THEY WERE GOING TO BE HERE..
YES, I'M PREPARED TO ANSWER ALL QUESTIONS
I THINK I SHOULD OPEN WITH AN IMPASSIONED PLEA AGAINST THE STAMP ACT
MY ATTORNEY WILL ADVISE ME OF MY RIGHTS...
"LET THE BUYER BEWARE!"
SCHULZ

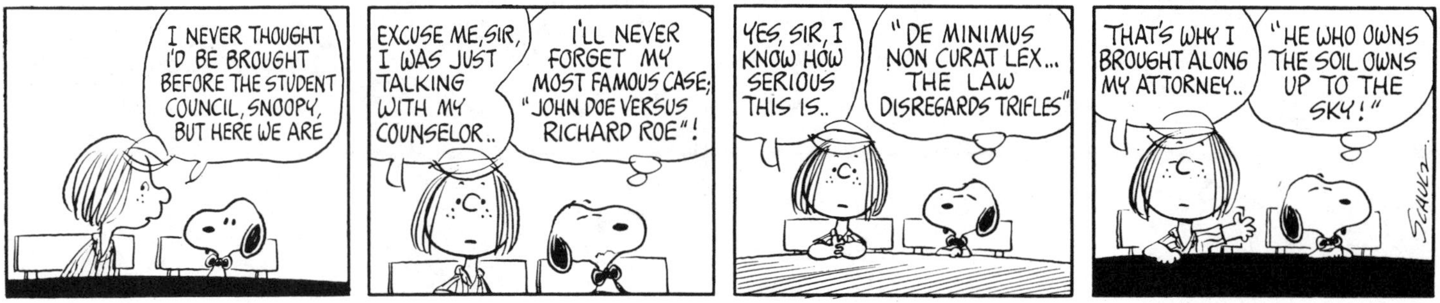
I NEVER THOUGHT I'D BE BROUGHT BEFORE THE STUDENT COUNCIL, SNOOPY, BUT HERE WE ARE
EXCUSE ME, SIR, I WAS JUST TALKING WITH MY COUNSELOR..
I'LL NEVER FORGET MY MOST FAMOUS CASE; "JOHN DOE VERSUS RICHARD ROE"!
YES, SIR, I KNOW HOW SERIOUS THIS IS..
"DE MINIMUS NON CURAT LEX... THE LAW DISREGARDS TRIFLES"
THAT'S WHY I BROUGHT ALONG MY ATTORNEY..
"HE WHO OWNS THE SOIL OWNS UP TO THE SKY!"
SCHULZ

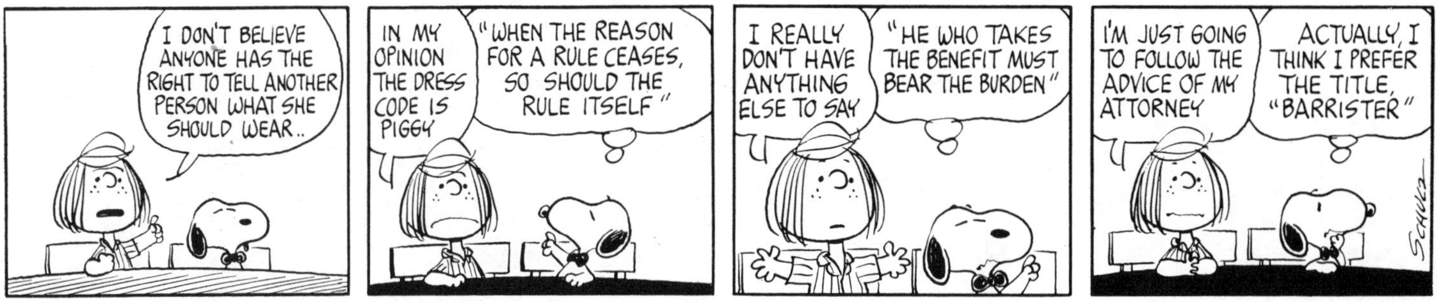
I DON'T BELIEVE ANYONE HAS THE RIGHT TO TELL ANOTHER PERSON WHAT SHE SHOULD WEAR..
IN MY OPINION THE DRESS CODE IS PIGGY
"WHEN THE REASON FOR A RULE CEASES, SO SHOULD THE RULE ITSELF"
I REALLY DON'T HAVE ANYTHING ELSE TO SAY
"HE WHO TAKES THE BENEFIT MUST BEAR THE BURDEN"
I'M JUST GOING TO FOLLOW THE ADVICE OF MY ATTORNEY
ACTUALLY, I THINK I PREFER THE TITLE, "BARRISTER"
SCHULZ

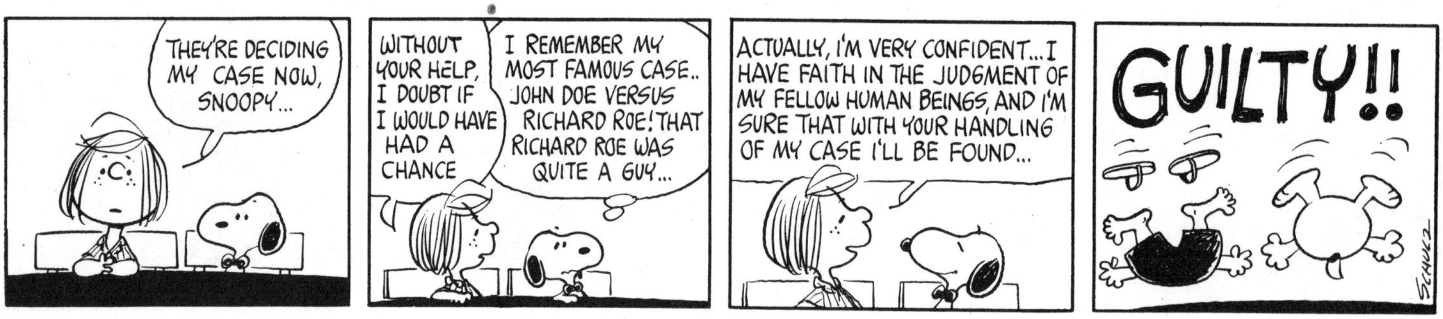
THEY'RE DECIDING MY CASE NOW, SNOOPY...
WITHOUT YOUR HELP, I DOUBT IF I WOULD HAVE HAD A CHANCE
I REMEMBER MY MOST FAMOUS CASE.. JOHN DOE VERSUS RICHARD ROE! THAT RICHARD ROE WAS QUITE A GUY...
ACTUALLY, I'M VERY CONFIDENT... I HAVE FAITH IN THE JUDGMENT OF MY FELLOW HUMAN BEINGS, AND I'M SURE THAT WITH YOUR HANDLING OF MY CASE I'LL BE FOUND...
GUILTY!!
SCHULZ

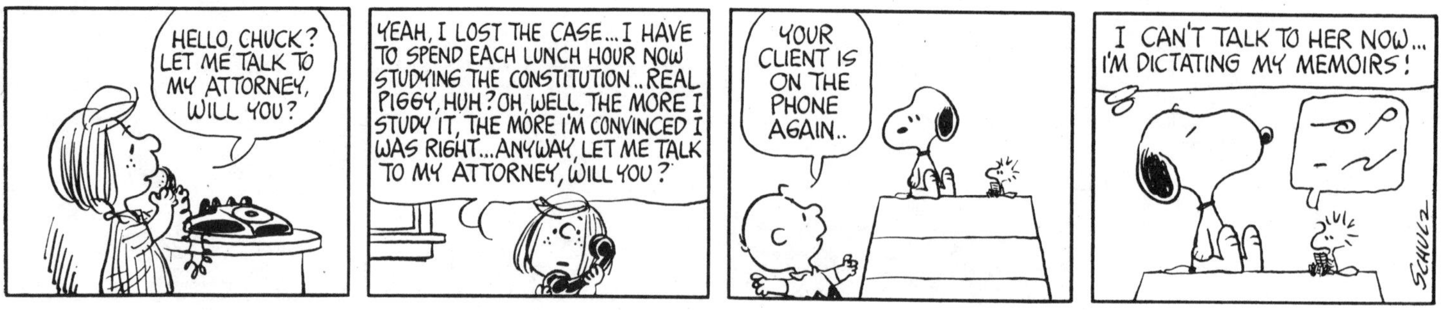
HELLO, CHUCK? LET ME TALK TO MY ATTORNEY, WILL YOU?
YEAH, I LOST THE CASE... I HAVE TO SPEND EACH LUNCH HOUR NOW STUDYING THE CONSTITUTION.. REAL PIGGY, HUH? OH, WELL, THE MORE I STUDY IT, THE MORE I'M CONVINCED I WAS RIGHT... ANYWAY, LET ME TALK TO MY ATTORNEY, WILL YOU?
YOUR CLIENT IS ON THE PHONE AGAIN..
I CAN'T TALK TO HER NOW... I'M DICTATING MY MEMOIRS!
SCHULZ

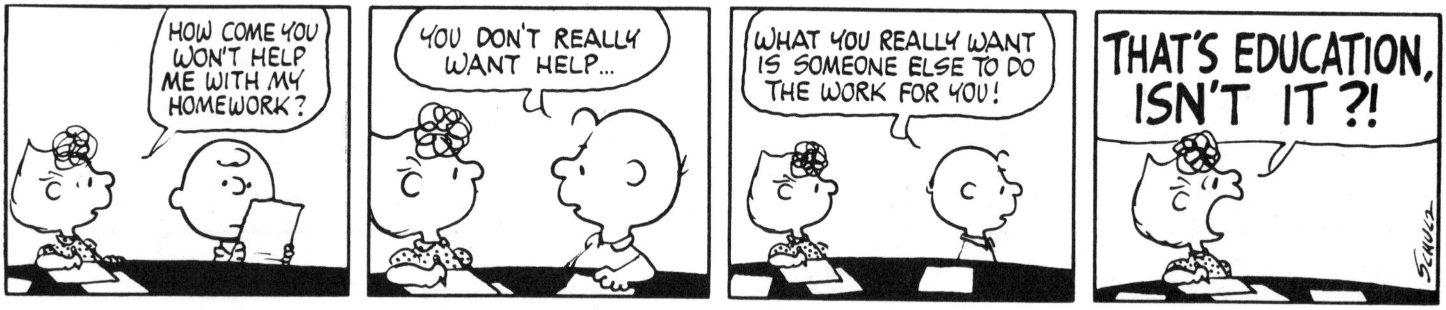
HOW COME YOU WON'T HELP ME WITH MY HOMEWORK?
YOU DON'T REALLY WANT HELP...
WHAT YOU REALLY WANT IS SOMEONE ELSE TO DO THE WORK FOR YOU!
THAT'S EDUCATION, ISN'T IT?!
SCHULZ

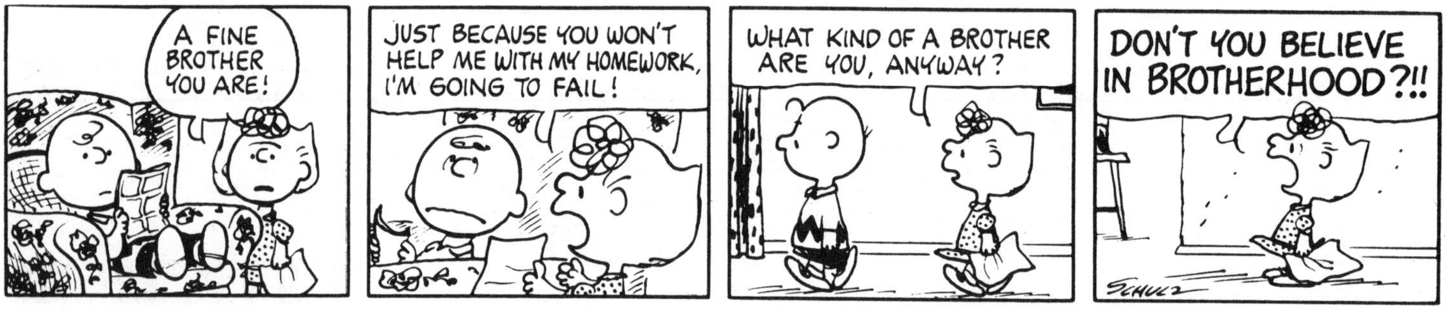
A FINE BROTHER YOU ARE!
JUST BECAUSE YOU WON'T HELP ME WITH MY HOMEWORK, I'M GOING TO FAIL!
WHAT KIND OF A BROTHER ARE YOU, ANYWAY?
DON'T YOU BELIEVE IN BROTHERHOOD?!!
SCHULZ

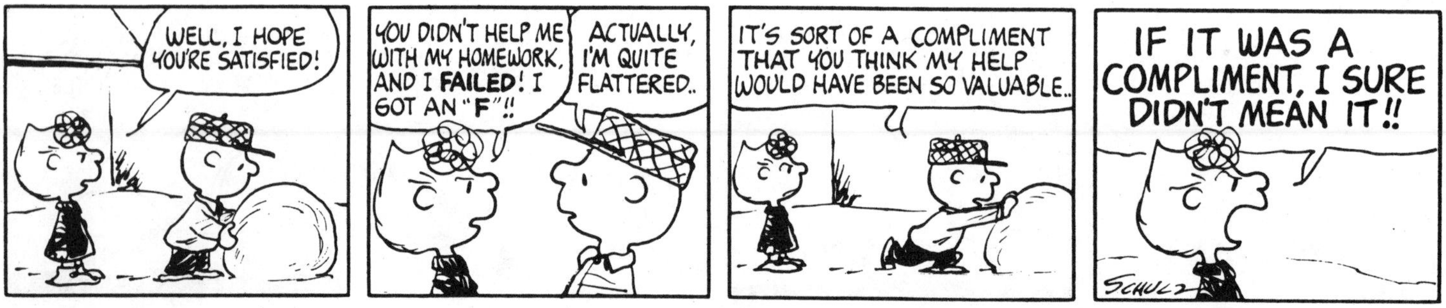
WELL, I HOPE YOU'RE SATISFIED!
YOU DIDN'T HELP ME WITH MY HOMEWORK, AND I **FAILED**! I GOT AN "**F**"!!
ACTUALLY, I'M QUITE FLATTERED..
IT'S SORT OF A COMPLIMENT THAT YOU THINK MY HELP WOULD HAVE BEEN SO VALUABLE..
IF IT WAS A COMPLIMENT, I SURE DIDN'T MEAN IT!!
SCHULZ

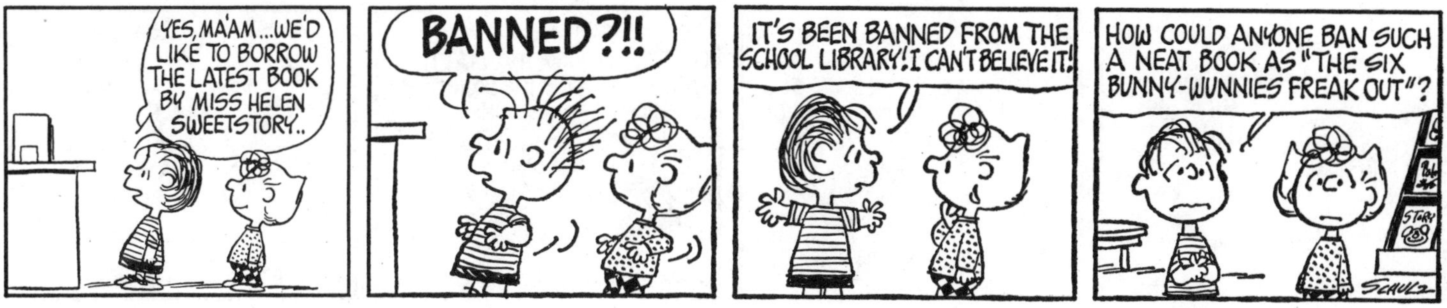
YES, MA'AM...WE'D LIKE TO BORROW THE LATEST BOOK BY MISS HELEN SWEETSTORY..
BANNED?!!
IT'S BEEN BANNED FROM THE SCHOOL LIBRARY! I CAN'T BELIEVE IT!
HOW COULD ANYONE BAN SUCH A NEAT BOOK AS "THE SIX BUNNY-WUNNIES FREAK OUT"?
SCHULZ

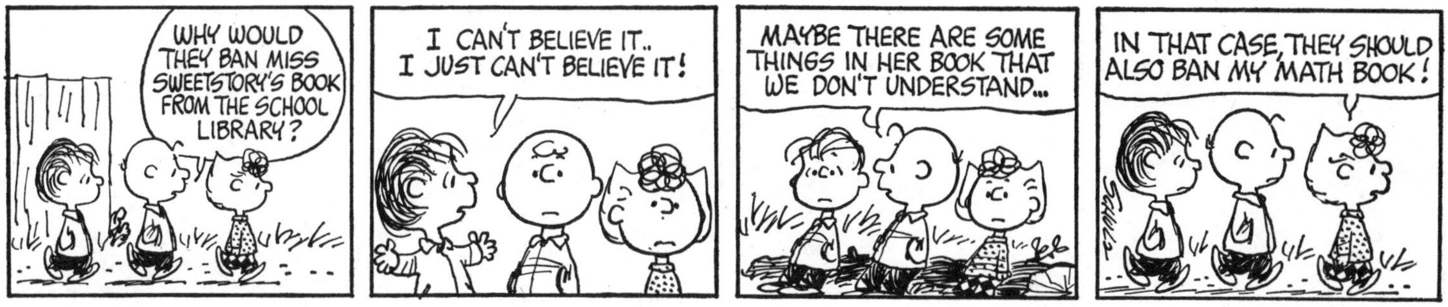
WHY WOULD THEY BAN MISS SWEETSTORY'S BOOK FROM THE SCHOOL LIBRARY?
I CAN'T BELIEVE IT.. I JUST CAN'T BELIEVE IT!
MAYBE THERE ARE SOME THINGS IN HER BOOK THAT WE DON'T UNDERSTAND...
IN THAT CASE, THEY SHOULD ALSO BAN MY MATH BOOK!
SCHULZ

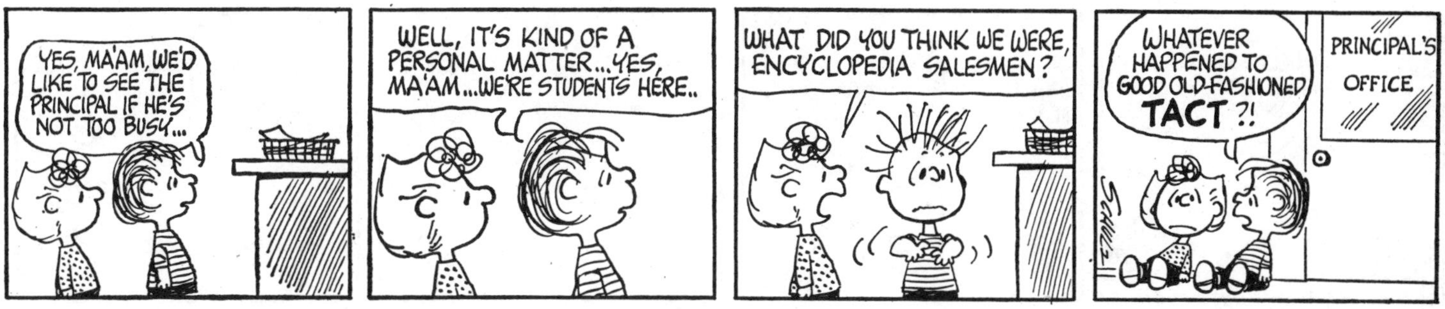
YES, MA'AM, WE'D LIKE TO SEE THE PRINCIPAL IF HE'S NOT TOO BUSY...
WELL, IT'S KIND OF A PERSONAL MATTER...YES, MA'AM...WE'RE STUDENTS HERE..
WHAT DID YOU THINK WE WERE, ENCYCLOPEDIA SALESMEN?
WHATEVER HAPPENED TO GOOD OLD-FASHIONED TACT?!
PRINCIPAL'S OFFICE
SCHULZ

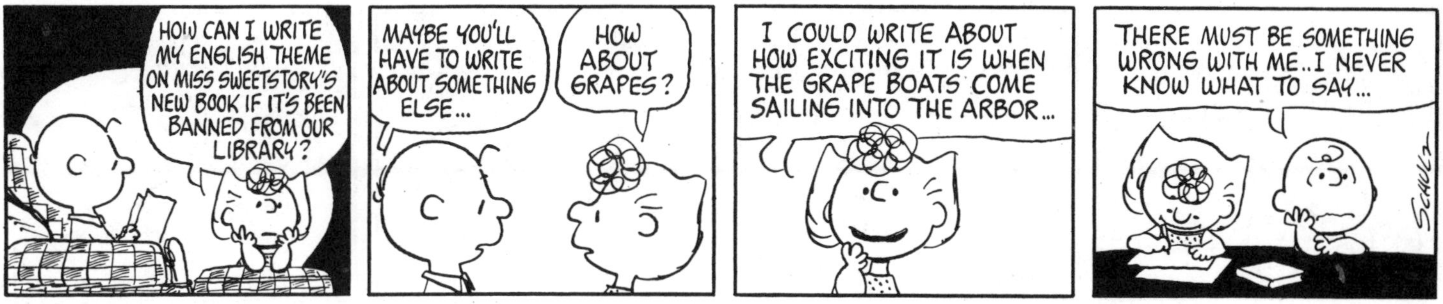
HOW CAN I WRITE MY ENGLISH THEME ON MISS SWEETSTORY'S NEW BOOK IF IT'S BEEN BANNED FROM OUR LIBRARY?
MAYBE YOU'LL HAVE TO WRITE ABOUT SOMETHING ELSE...
HOW ABOUT GRAPES?
I COULD WRITE ABOUT HOW EXCITING IT IS WHEN THE GRAPE BOATS COME SAILING INTO THE ARBOR...
THERE MUST BE SOMETHING WRONG WITH ME..I NEVER KNOW WHAT TO SAY...
SCHULZ

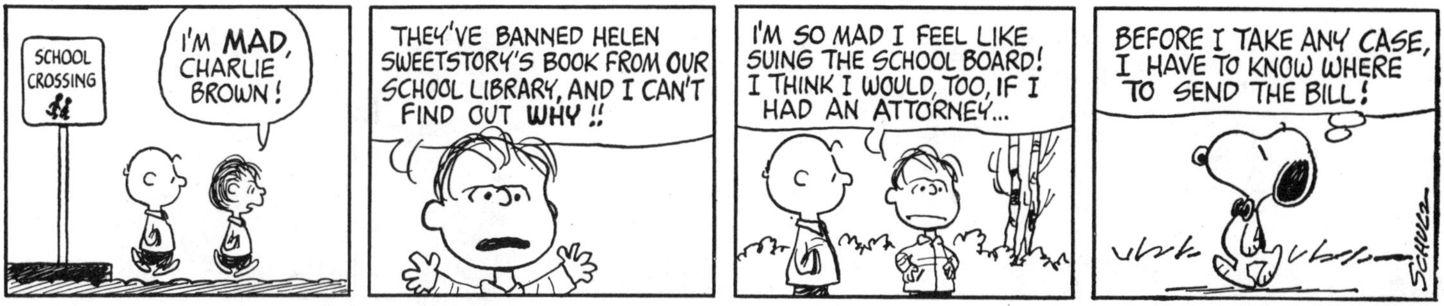
SCHOOL CROSSING
I'M MAD, CHARLIE BROWN!
THEY'VE BANNED HELEN SWEETSTORY'S BOOK FROM OUR SCHOOL LIBRARY, AND I CAN'T FIND OUT WHY!!
I'M SO MAD I FEEL LIKE SUING THE SCHOOL BOARD! I THINK I WOULD, TOO, IF I HAD AN ATTORNEY...
BEFORE I TAKE ANY CASE, I HAVE TO KNOW WHERE TO SEND THE BILL!
SCHULZ

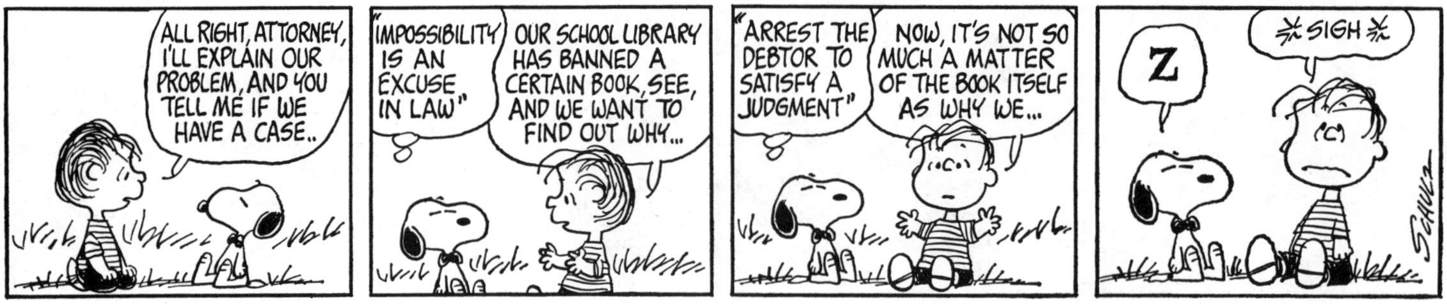
ALL RIGHT, ATTORNEY, I'LL EXPLAIN OUR PROBLEM, AND YOU TELL ME IF WE HAVE A CASE..
"IMPOSSIBILITY IS AN EXCUSE IN LAW"
OUR SCHOOL LIBRARY HAS BANNED A CERTAIN BOOK, SEE, AND WE WANT TO FIND OUT WHY...
"ARREST THE DEBTOR TO SATISFY A JUDGMENT"
NOW, IT'S NOT SO MUCH A MATTER OF THE BOOK ITSELF AS WHY WE...
Z
SIGH
SCHULZ

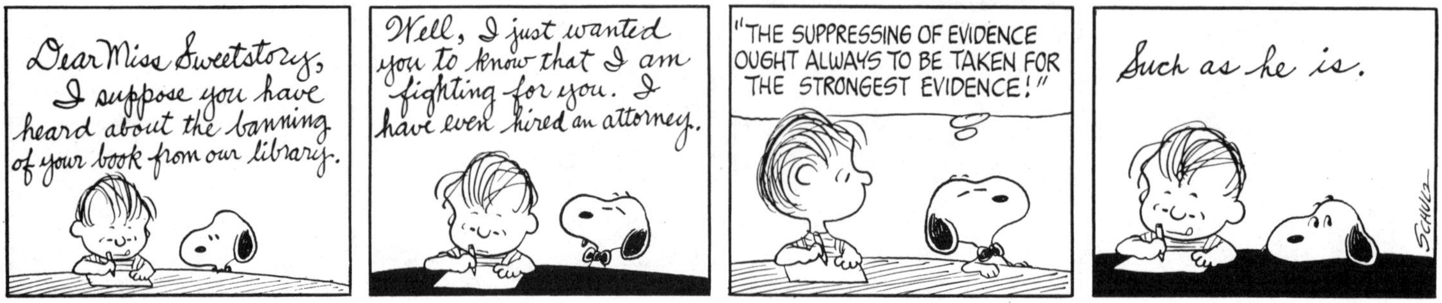
Dear Miss Sweetstory, I suppose you have heard about the banning of your book from our library.
Well, I just wanted you to know that I am fighting for you. I have even hired an attorney.
"THE SUPPRESSING OF EVIDENCE OUGHT ALWAYS TO BE TAKEN FOR THE STRONGEST EVIDENCE!"
Such as he is.
SCHULZ

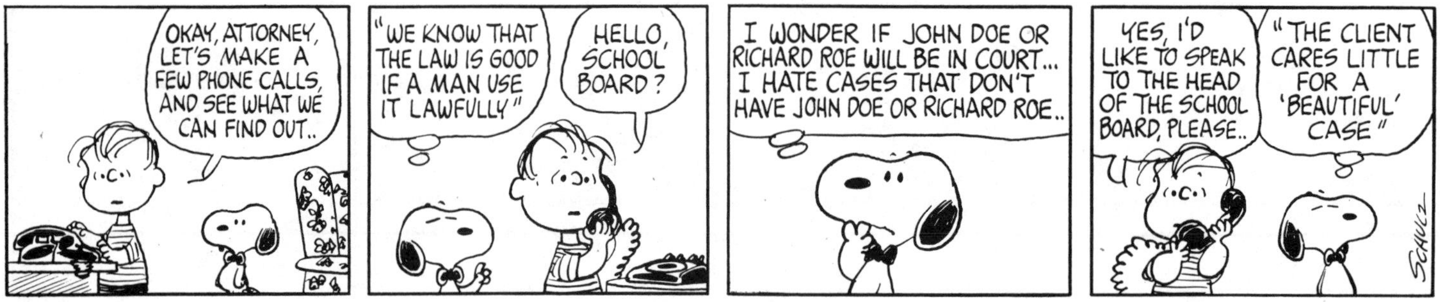
OKAY, ATTORNEY, LET'S MAKE A FEW PHONE CALLS, AND SEE WHAT WE CAN FIND OUT..
"WE KNOW THAT THE LAW IS GOOD IF A MAN USE IT LAWFULLY"
HELLO, SCHOOL BOARD?
I WONDER IF JOHN DOE OR RICHARD ROE WILL BE IN COURT... I HATE CASES THAT DON'T HAVE JOHN DOE OR RICHARD ROE..
YES, I'D LIKE TO SPEAK TO THE HEAD OF THE SCHOOL BOARD, PLEASE..
"THE CLIENT CARES LITTLE FOR A 'BEAUTIFUL' CASE"
SCHULZ

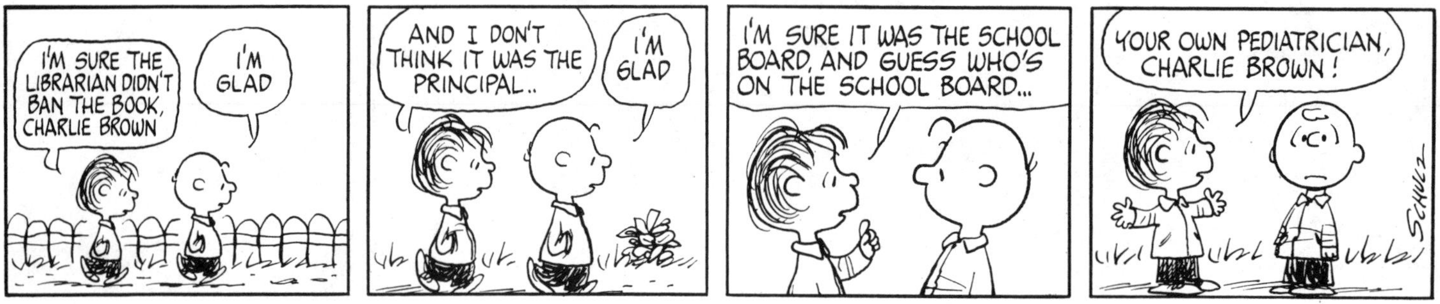
I'M SURE THE LIBRARIAN DIDN'T BAN THE BOOK, CHARLIE BROWN
I'M GLAD
AND I DON'T THINK IT WAS THE PRINCIPAL..
I'M GLAD
I'M SURE IT WAS THE SCHOOL BOARD, AND GUESS WHO'S ON THE SCHOOL BOARD...
YOUR OWN PEDIATRICIAN, CHARLIE BROWN!
SCHULZ

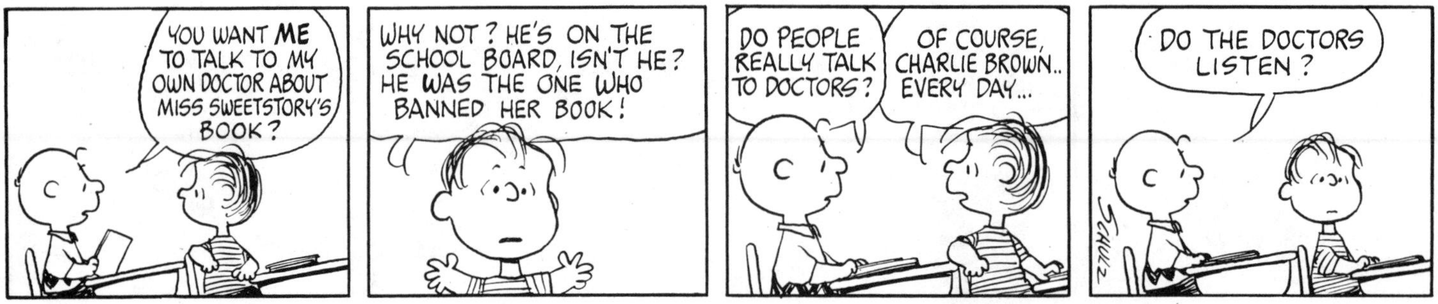
YOU WANT ME TO TALK TO MY OWN DOCTOR ABOUT MISS SWEETSTORY'S BOOK?
WHY NOT? HE'S ON THE SCHOOL BOARD, ISN'T HE? HE WAS THE ONE WHO BANNED HER BOOK!
DO PEOPLE REALLY TALK TO DOCTORS?
OF COURSE, CHARLIE BROWN.. EVERY DAY...
DO THE DOCTORS LISTEN?
SCHULZ

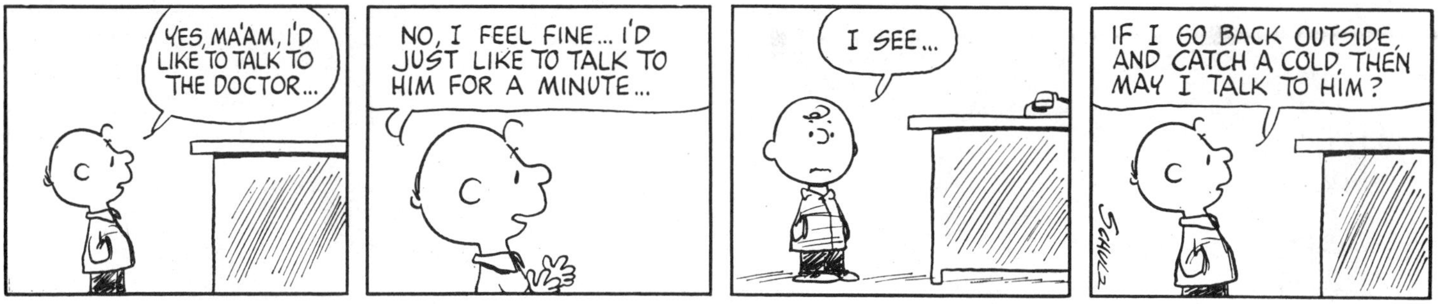
YES, MA'AM, I'D LIKE TO TALK TO THE DOCTOR...
NO, I FEEL FINE... I'D JUST LIKE TO TALK TO HIM FOR A MINUTE...
I SEE...
IF I GO BACK OUTSIDE, AND CATCH A COLD, THEN MAY I TALK TO HIM?

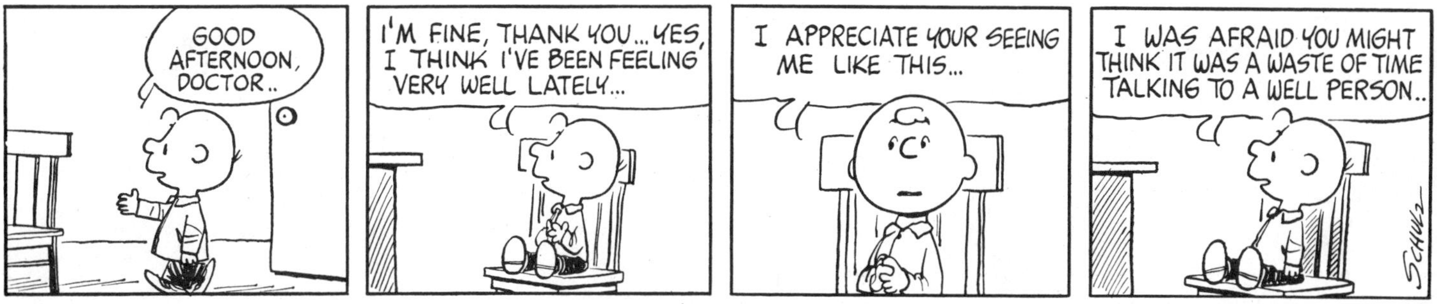
GOOD AFTERNOON, DOCTOR..
I'M FINE, THANK YOU... YES, I THINK I'VE BEEN FEELING VERY WELL LATELY...
I APPRECIATE YOUR SEEING ME LIKE THIS...
I WAS AFRAID YOU MIGHT THINK IT WAS A WASTE OF TIME TALKING TO A WELL PERSON..

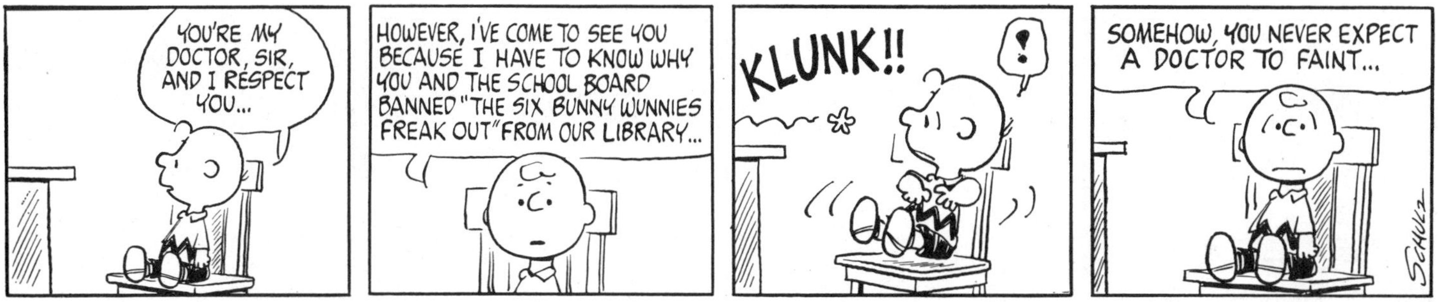
YOU'RE MY DOCTOR, SIR, AND I RESPECT YOU...
HOWEVER, I'VE COME TO SEE YOU BECAUSE I HAVE TO KNOW WHY YOU AND THE SCHOOL BOARD BANNED "THE SIX BUNNY WUNNIES FREAK OUT" FROM OUR LIBRARY...
KLUNK!!
!
SOMEHOW, YOU NEVER EXPECT A DOCTOR TO FAINT...

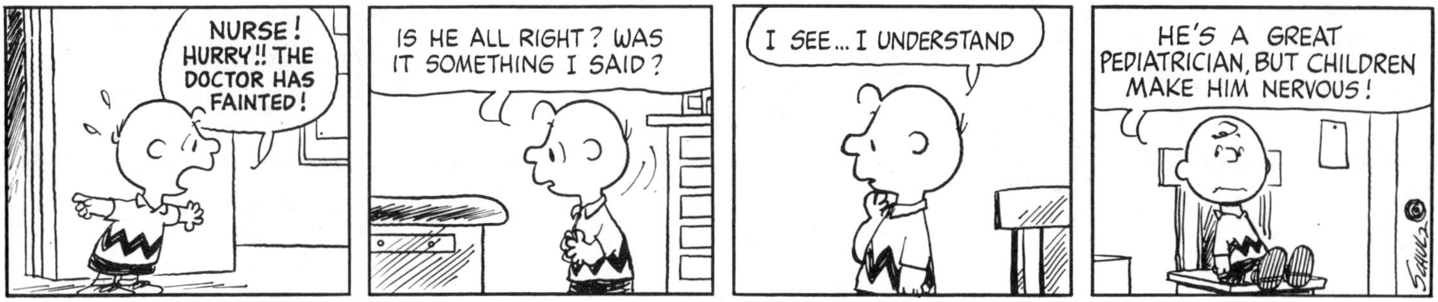
NURSE! HURRY!! THE DOCTOR HAS FAINTED!
IS HE ALL RIGHT? WAS IT SOMETHING I SAID?
I SEE... I UNDERSTAND
HE'S A GREAT PEDIATRICIAN, BUT CHILDREN MAKE HIM NERVOUS!

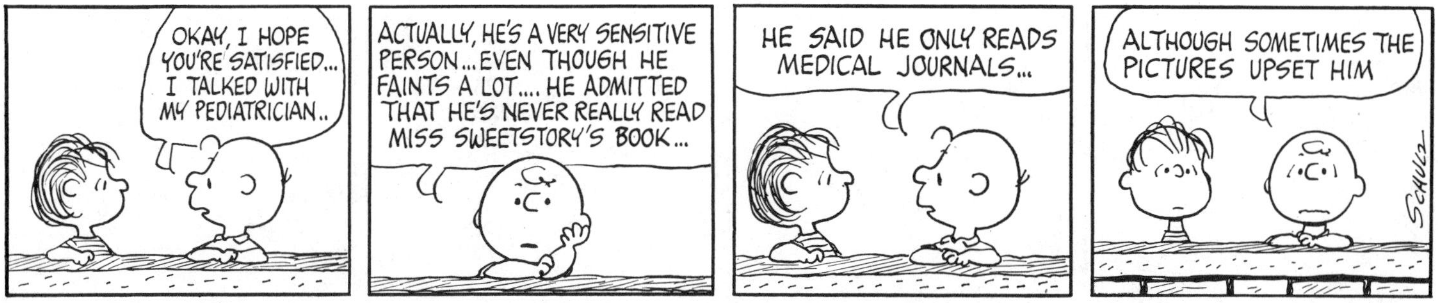
OKAY, I HOPE YOU'RE SATISFIED... I TALKED WITH MY PEDIATRICIAN..
ACTUALLY, HE'S A VERY SENSITIVE PERSON... EVEN THOUGH HE FAINTS A LOT.... HE ADMITTED THAT HE'S NEVER REALLY READ MISS SWEETSTORY'S BOOK...
HE SAID HE ONLY READS MEDICAL JOURNALS...
ALTHOUGH SOMETIMES THE PICTURES UPSET HIM

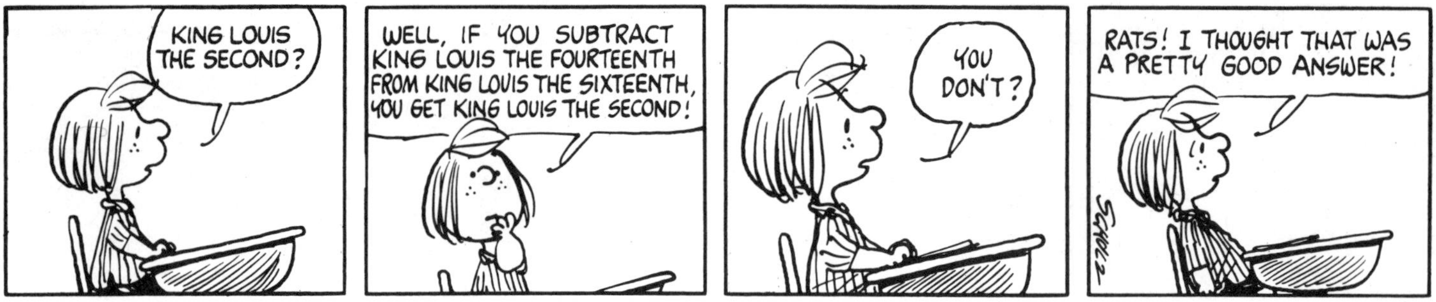
KING LOUIS THE SECOND?
WELL, IF YOU SUBTRACT KING LOUIS THE FOURTEENTH FROM KING LOUIS THE SIXTEENTH, YOU GET KING LOUIS THE SECOND!
YOU DON'T?
RATS! I THOUGHT THAT WAS A PRETTY GOOD ANSWER!
SCHULZ

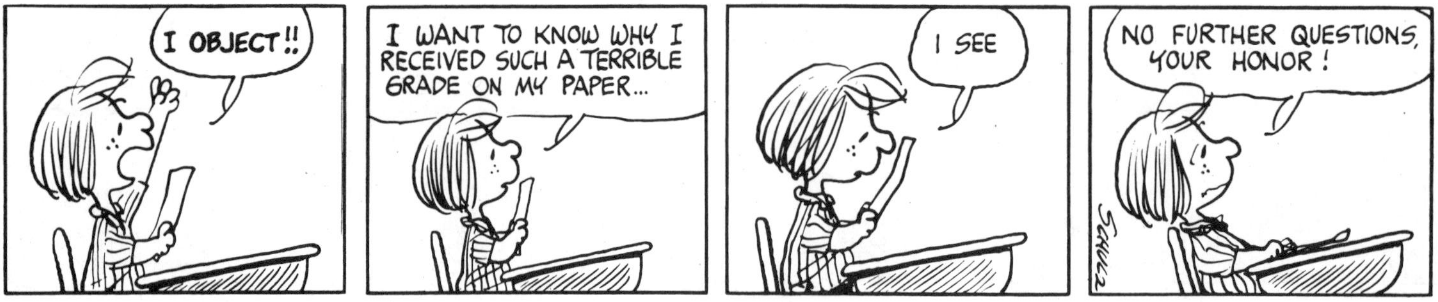
I OBJECT!!
I WANT TO KNOW WHY I RECEIVED SUCH A TERRIBLE GRADE ON MY PAPER...
I SEE
NO FURTHER QUESTIONS, YOUR HONOR!
SCHULZ

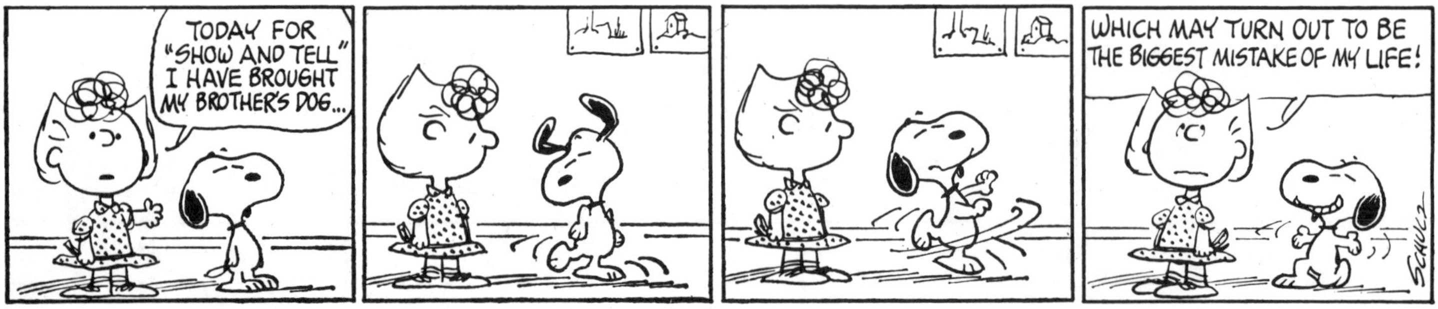
TODAY FOR "SHOW AND TELL" I HAVE BROUGHT MY BROTHER'S DOG...
WHICH MAY TURN OUT TO BE THE BIGGEST MISTAKE OF MY LIFE!
SCHULZ

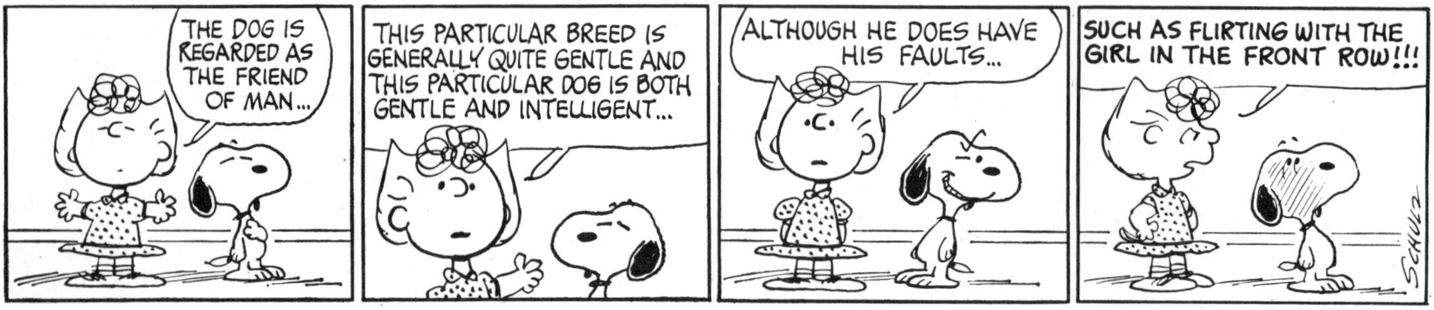
THE DOG IS REGARDED AS THE FRIEND OF MAN...
THIS PARTICULAR BREED IS GENERALLY QUITE GENTLE AND THIS PARTICULAR DOG IS BOTH GENTLE AND INTELLIGENT...
ALTHOUGH HE DOES HAVE HIS FAULTS...
SUCH AS FLIRTING WITH THE GIRL IN THE FRONT ROW!!!
SCHULZ

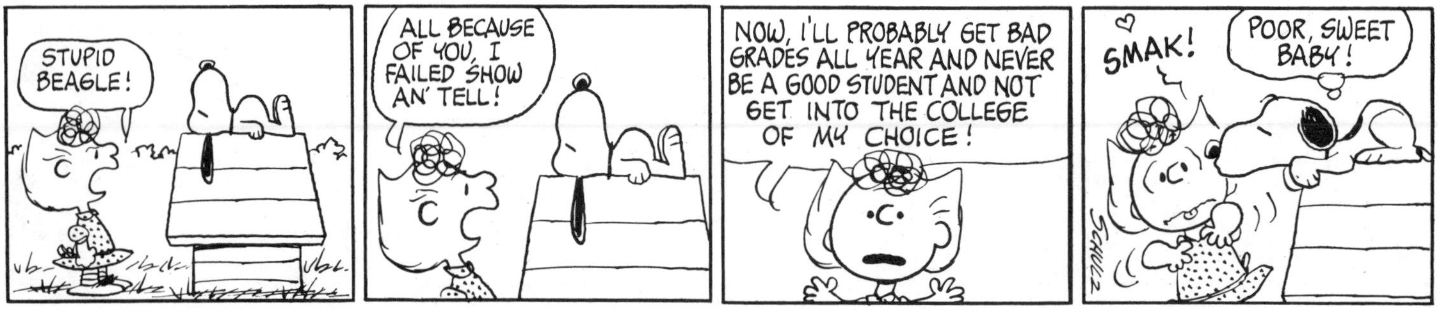
STUPID BEAGLE!
ALL BECAUSE OF YOU, I FAILED SHOW AN' TELL!
NOW, I'LL PROBABLY GET BAD GRADES ALL YEAR AND NEVER BE A GOOD STUDENT AND NOT GET INTO THE COLLEGE OF MY CHOICE!
SMAK!
POOR, SWEET BABY!
SCHULZ

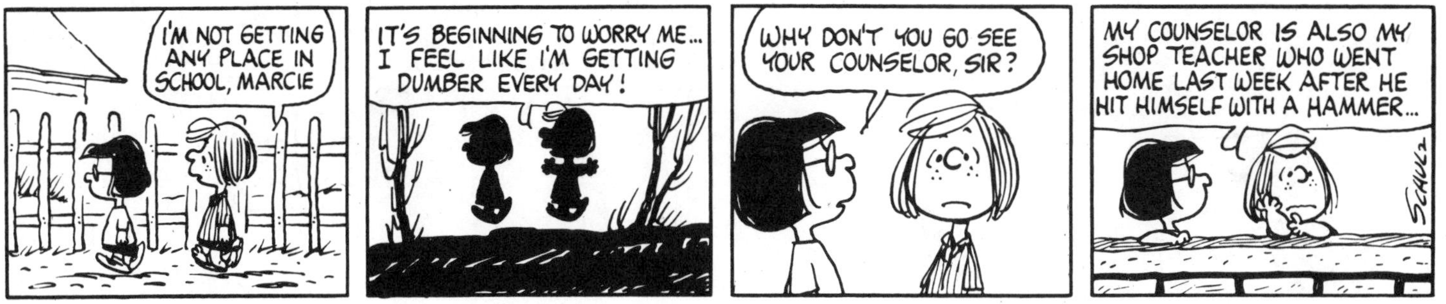
I'M NOT GETTING ANY PLACE IN SCHOOL, MARCIE
IT'S BEGINNING TO WORRY ME... I FEEL LIKE I'M GETTING DUMBER EVERY DAY!
WHY DON'T YOU GO SEE YOUR COUNSELOR, SIR?
MY COUNSELOR IS ALSO MY SHOP TEACHER WHO WENT HOME LAST WEEK AFTER HE HIT HIMSELF WITH A HAMMER...
SCHULZ

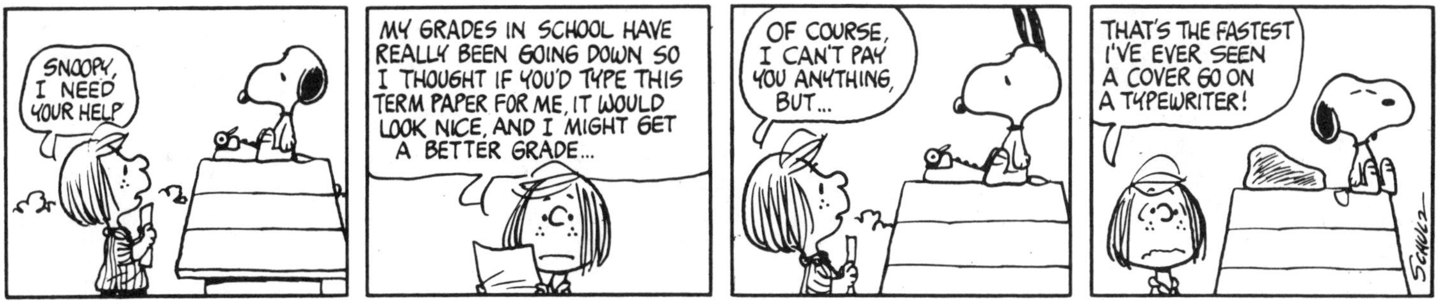
SNOOPY, I NEED YOUR HELP
MY GRADES IN SCHOOL HAVE REALLY BEEN GOING DOWN SO I THOUGHT IF YOU'D TYPE THIS TERM PAPER FOR ME, IT WOULD LOOK NICE, AND I MIGHT GET A BETTER GRADE...
OF COURSE, I CAN'T PAY YOU ANYTHING, BUT...
THAT'S THE FASTEST I'VE EVER SEEN A COVER GO ON A TYPEWRITER!
SCHULZ

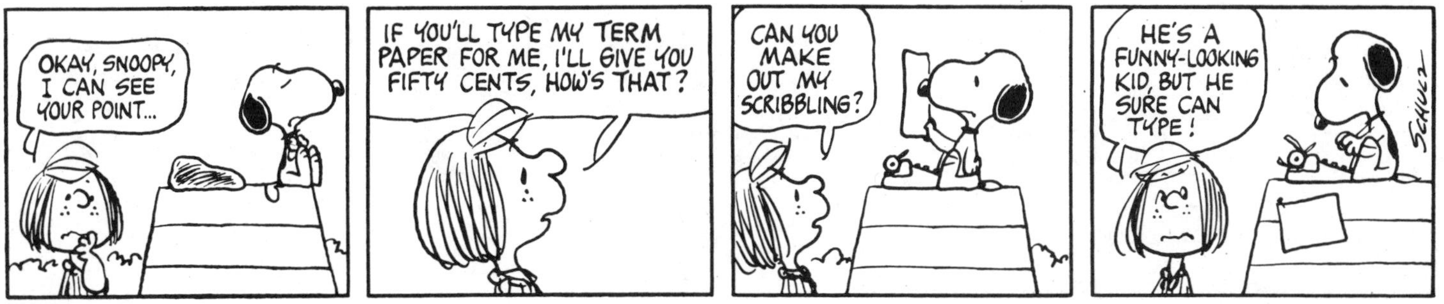
OKAY, SNOOPY, I CAN SEE YOUR POINT...
IF YOU'LL TYPE MY TERM PAPER FOR ME, I'LL GIVE YOU FIFTY CENTS, HOW'S THAT?
CAN YOU MAKE OUT MY SCRIBBLING?
HE'S A FUNNY-LOOKING KID, BUT HE SURE CAN TYPE!
SCHULZ

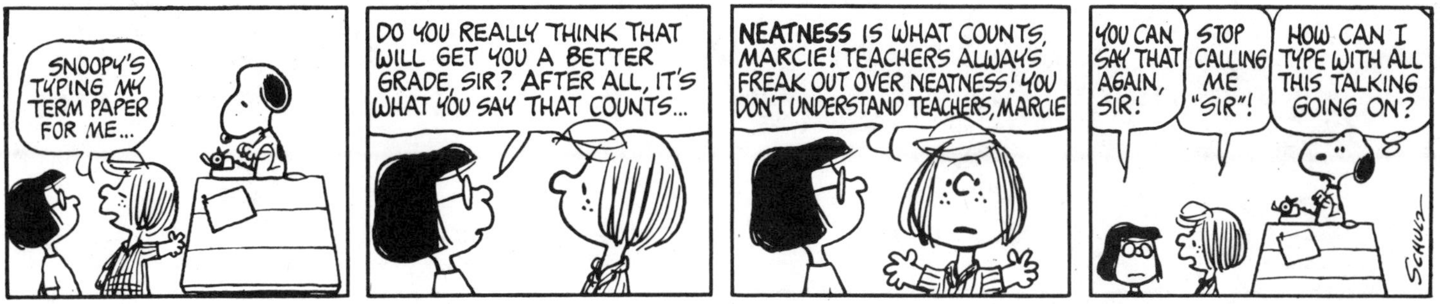
SNOOPY'S TYPING MY TERM PAPER FOR ME...
DO YOU REALLY THINK THAT WILL GET YOU A BETTER GRADE, SIR? AFTER ALL, IT'S WHAT YOU SAY THAT COUNTS...
NEATNESS IS WHAT COUNTS, MARCIE! TEACHERS ALWAYS FREAK OUT OVER NEATNESS! YOU DON'T UNDERSTAND TEACHERS, MARCIE
YOU CAN SAY THAT AGAIN, SIR!
STOP CALLING ME "SIR"!
HOW CAN I TYPE WITH ALL THIS TALKING GOING ON?
SCHULZ

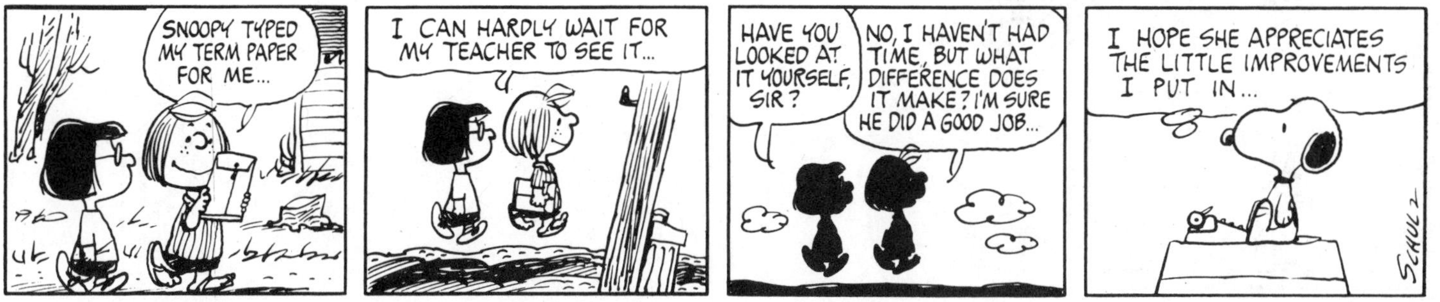
SNOOPY TYPED MY TERM PAPER FOR ME...
I CAN HARDLY WAIT FOR MY TEACHER TO SEE IT...
HAVE YOU LOOKED AT IT YOURSELF, SIR?
NO, I HAVEN'T HAD TIME, BUT WHAT DIFFERENCE DOES IT MAKE? I'M SURE HE DID A GOOD JOB...
I HOPE SHE APPRECIATES THE LITTLE IMPROVEMENTS I PUT IN...
SCHULZ

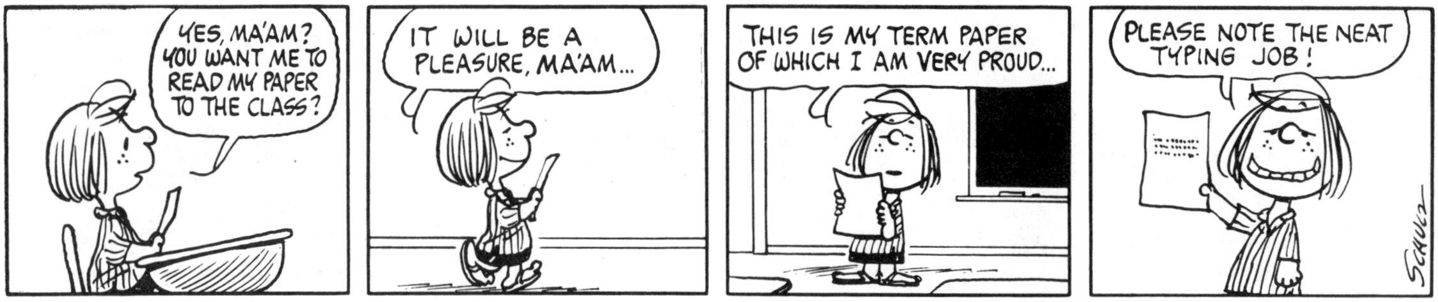
YES, MA'AM? YOU WANT ME TO READ MY PAPER TO THE CLASS?
IT WILL BE A PLEASURE, MA'AM...
THIS IS MY TERM PAPER OF WHICH I AM VERY PROUD...
PLEASE NOTE THE NEAT TYPING JOB!
SCHULZ

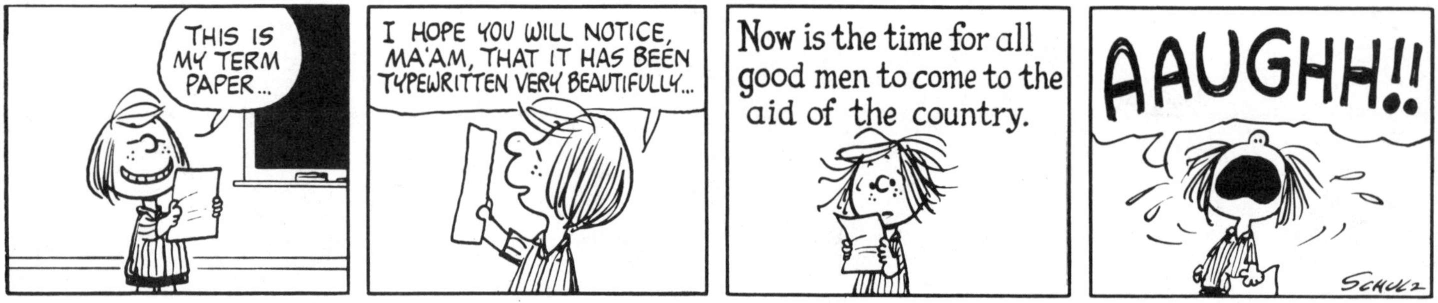
THIS IS MY TERM PAPER...
I HOPE YOU WILL NOTICE, MA'AM, THAT IT HAS BEEN TYPEWRITTEN VERY BEAUTIFULLY...
Now is the time for all good men to come to the aid of the country.
AAUGHH!!
SCHULZ

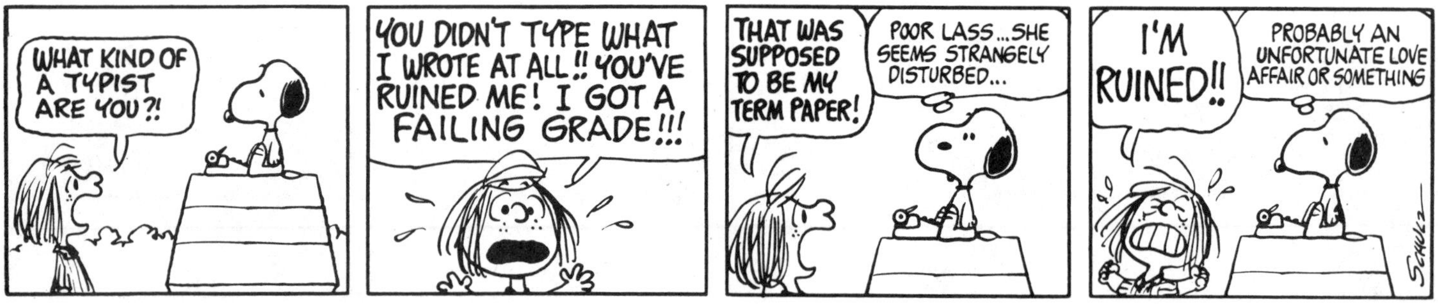
WHAT KIND OF A TYPIST ARE YOU?!
YOU DIDN'T TYPE WHAT I WROTE AT ALL!! YOU'VE RUINED ME! I GOT A FAILING GRADE!!!
THAT WAS SUPPOSED TO BE MY TERM PAPER!
POOR LASS...SHE SEEMS STRANGELY DISTURBED...
I'M RUINED!!
PROBABLY AN UNFORTUNATE LOVE AFFAIR OR SOMETHING
SCHULZ

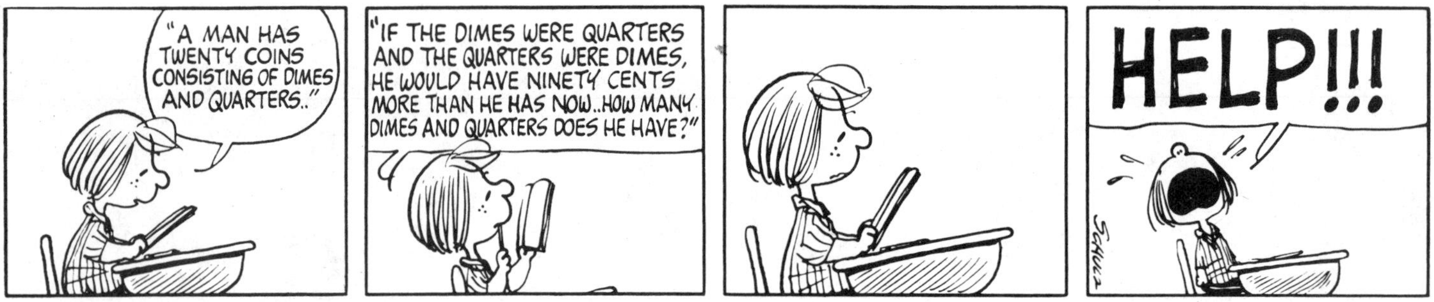
"A MAN HAS TWENTY COINS CONSISTING OF DIMES AND QUARTERS.."
"IF THE DIMES WERE QUARTERS AND THE QUARTERS WERE DIMES, HE WOULD HAVE NINETY CENTS MORE THAN HE HAS NOW..HOW MANY DIMES AND QUARTERS DOES HE HAVE?"
HELP!!!
SCHULZ

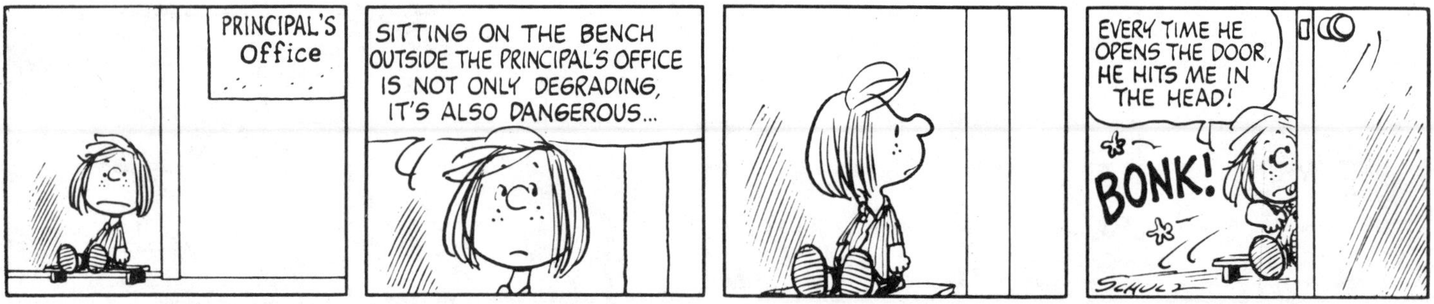
PRINCIPAL'S Office
SITTING ON THE BENCH OUTSIDE THE PRINCIPAL'S OFFICE IS NOT ONLY DEGRADING, IT'S ALSO DANGEROUS...
EVERY TIME HE OPENS THE DOOR, HE HITS ME IN THE HEAD!
BONK!
SCHULZ

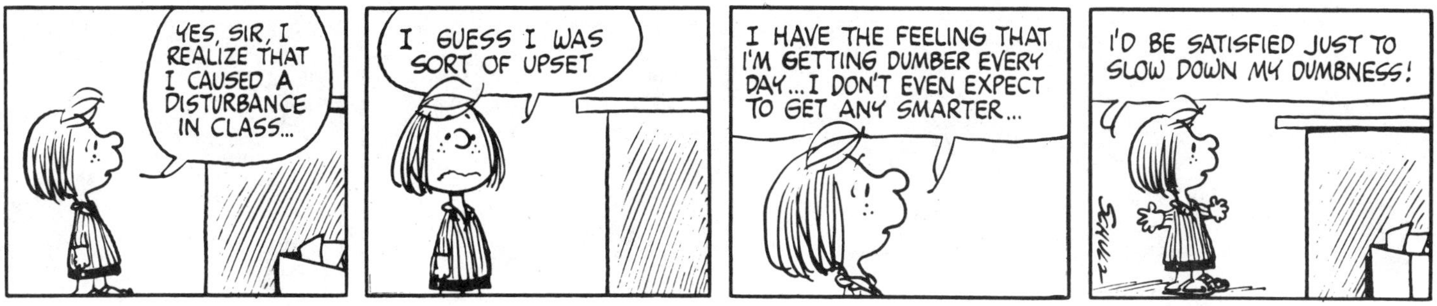
YES, SIR, I REALIZE THAT I CAUSED A DISTURBANCE IN CLASS...
I GUESS I WAS SORT OF UPSET
I HAVE THE FEELING THAT I'M GETTING DUMBER EVERY DAY... I DON'T EVEN EXPECT TO GET ANY SMARTER...
I'D BE SATISFIED JUST TO SLOW DOWN MY DUMBNESS!
SCHULZ

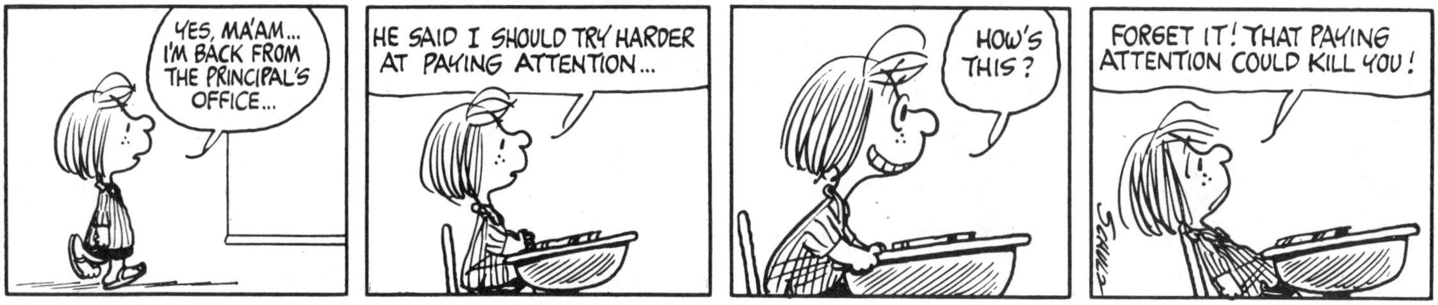
YES, MA'AM... I'M BACK FROM THE PRINCIPAL'S OFFICE...
HE SAID I SHOULD TRY HARDER AT PAYING ATTENTION...
HOW'S THIS?
FORGET IT! THAT PAYING ATTENTION COULD KILL YOU!
SCHULZ

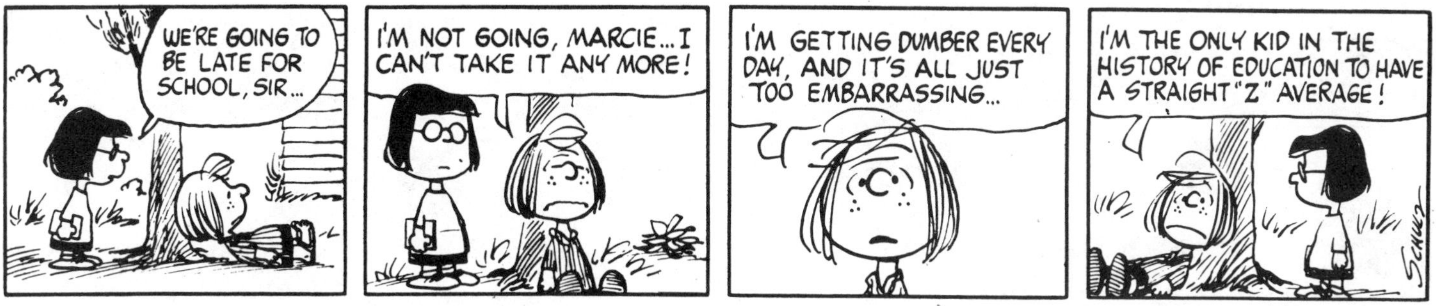
WE'RE GOING TO BE LATE FOR SCHOOL, SIR...
I'M NOT GOING, MARCIE... I CAN'T TAKE IT ANY MORE!
I'M GETTING DUMBER EVERY DAY, AND IT'S ALL JUST TOO EMBARRASSING...
I'M THE ONLY KID IN THE HISTORY OF EDUCATION TO HAVE A STRAIGHT "Z" AVERAGE!
SCHULZ

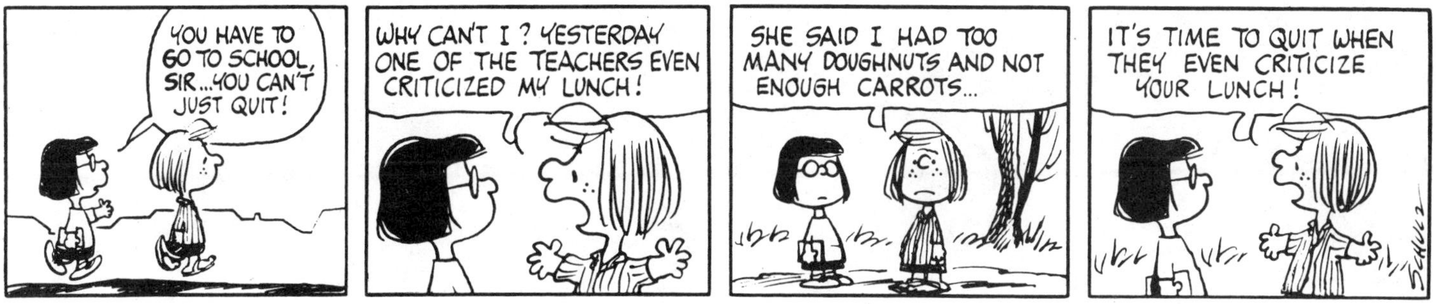
YOU HAVE TO GO TO SCHOOL, SIR... YOU CAN'T JUST QUIT!
WHY CAN'T I? YESTERDAY ONE OF THE TEACHERS EVEN CRITICIZED MY LUNCH!
SHE SAID I HAD TOO MANY DOUGHNUTS AND NOT ENOUGH CARROTS...
IT'S TIME TO QUIT WHEN THEY EVEN CRITICIZE YOUR LUNCH!
SCHULZ

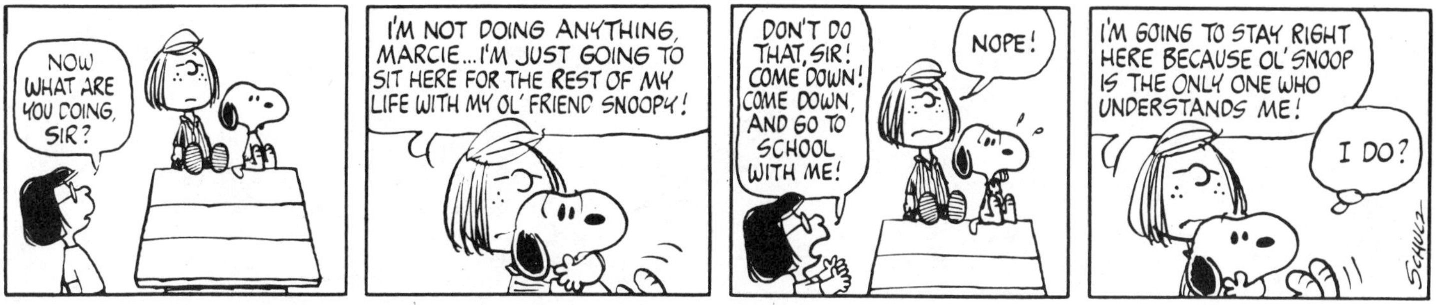
NOW WHAT ARE YOU DOING, SIR?
I'M NOT DOING ANYTHING, MARCIE... I'M JUST GOING TO SIT HERE FOR THE REST OF MY LIFE WITH MY OL' FRIEND SNOOPY!
DON'T DO THAT, SIR! COME DOWN! COME DOWN, AND GO TO SCHOOL WITH ME!
NOPE!
I'M GOING TO STAY RIGHT HERE BECAUSE OL' SNOOP IS THE ONLY ONE WHO UNDERSTANDS ME!
I DO?
SCHULZ

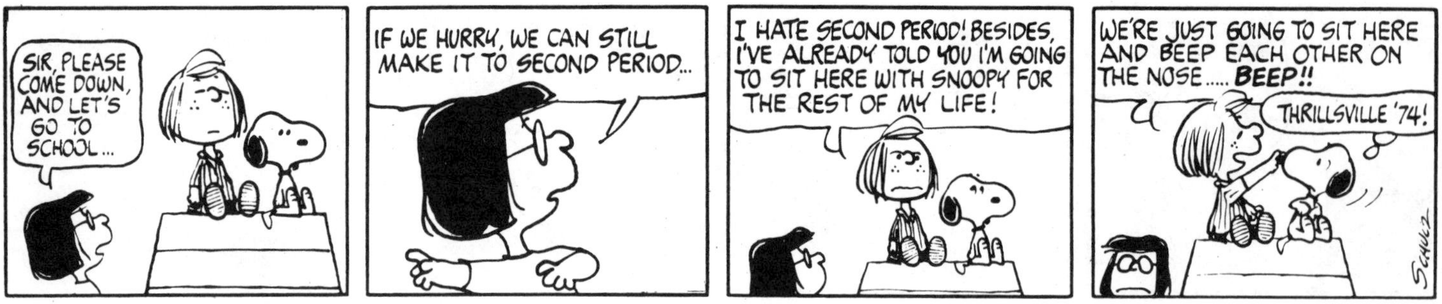
SIR, PLEASE COME DOWN, AND LET'S GO TO SCHOOL...
IF WE HURRY, WE CAN STILL MAKE IT TO SECOND PERIOD...
I HATE SECOND PERIOD! BESIDES, I'VE ALREADY TOLD YOU I'M GOING TO SIT HERE WITH SNOOPY FOR THE REST OF MY LIFE!
WE'RE JUST GOING TO SIT HERE AND BEEP EACH OTHER ON THE NOSE..... BEEP!!
THRILLSVILLE '74!
SCHULZ

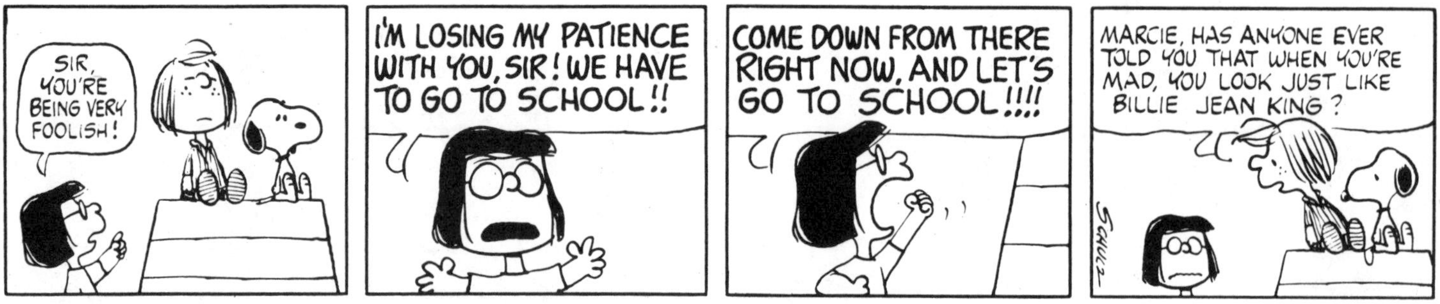
SIR, YOU'RE BEING VERY FOOLISH!
I'M LOSING MY PATIENCE WITH YOU, SIR! WE HAVE TO GO TO SCHOOL!!
COME DOWN FROM THERE RIGHT NOW, AND LET'S GO TO SCHOOL!!!!
MARCIE, HAS ANYONE EVER TOLD YOU THAT WHEN YOU'RE MAD, YOU LOOK JUST LIKE BILLIE JEAN KING?
SCHULZ

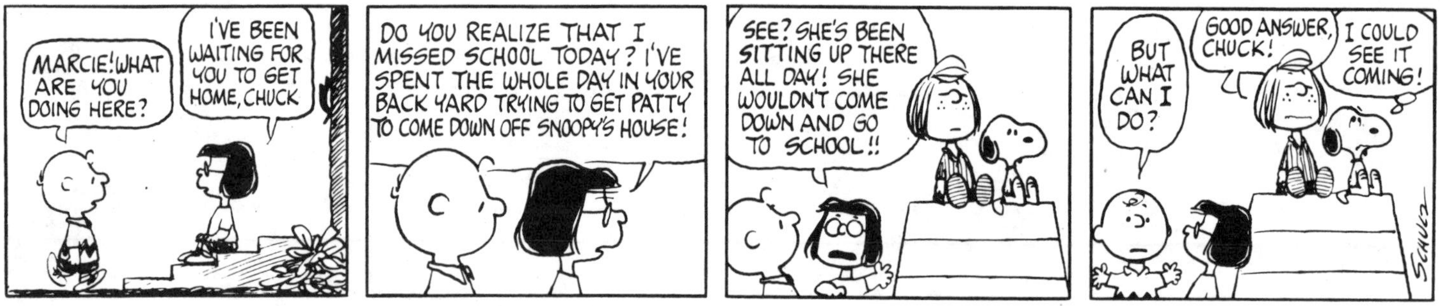
MARCIE! WHAT ARE YOU DOING HERE?
I'VE BEEN WAITING FOR YOU TO GET HOME, CHUCK
DO YOU REALIZE THAT I MISSED SCHOOL TODAY? I'VE SPENT THE WHOLE DAY IN YOUR BACK YARD TRYING TO GET PATTY TO COME DOWN OFF SNOOPY'S HOUSE!
SEE? SHE'S BEEN SITTING UP THERE ALL DAY! SHE WOULDN'T COME DOWN AND GO TO SCHOOL!!
BUT WHAT CAN I DO?
GOOD ANSWER, CHUCK!
I COULD SEE IT COMING!
SCHULZ

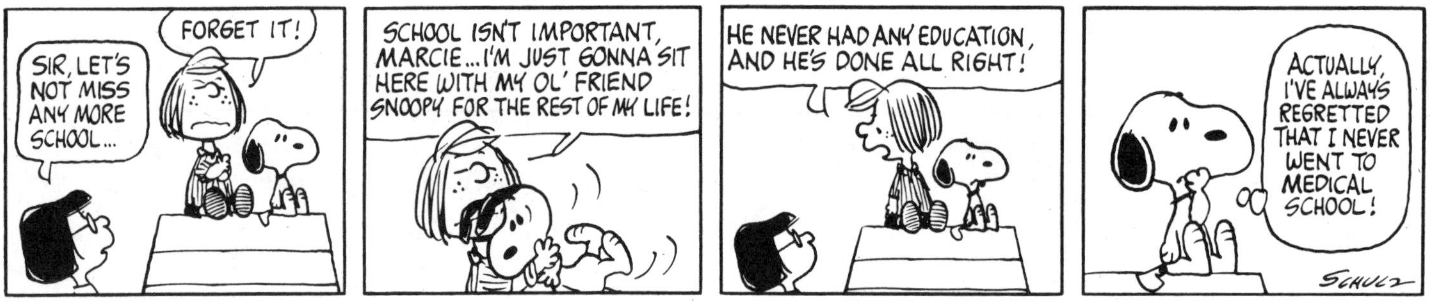
SIR, LET'S NOT MISS ANY MORE SCHOOL...
FORGET IT!
SCHOOL ISN'T IMPORTANT, MARCIE... I'M JUST GONNA SIT HERE WITH MY OL' FRIEND SNOOPY FOR THE REST OF MY LIFE!
HE NEVER HAD ANY EDUCATION, AND HE'S DONE ALL RIGHT!
ACTUALLY, I'VE ALWAYS REGRETTED THAT I NEVER WENT TO MEDICAL SCHOOL!
SCHULZ

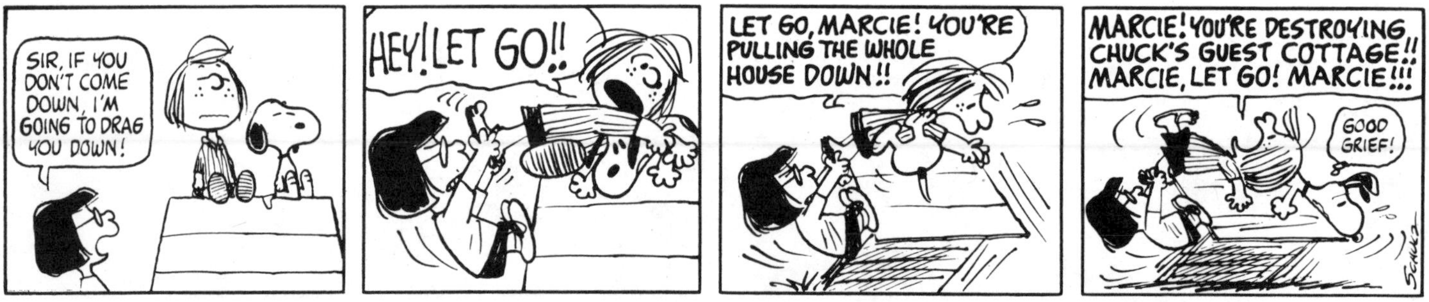
SIR, IF YOU DON'T COME DOWN, I'M GOING TO DRAG YOU DOWN!
HEY! LET GO!!
LET GO, MARCIE! YOU'RE PULLING THE WHOLE HOUSE DOWN!!
MARCIE! YOU'RE DESTROYING CHUCK'S GUEST COTTAGE!! MARCIE, LET GO! MARCIE!!!
GOOD GRIEF!
SCHULZ

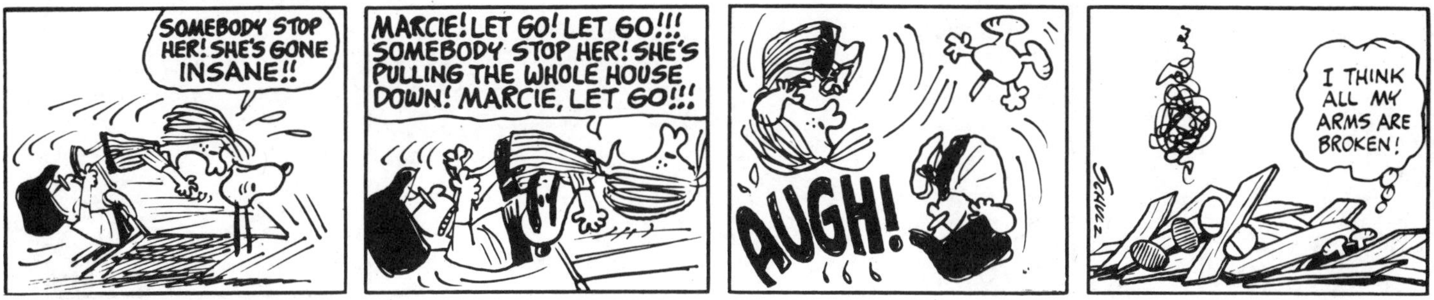
SOMEBODY STOP HER! SHE'S GONE INSANE!!
MARCIE! LET GO! LET GO!!! SOMEBODY STOP HER! SHE'S PULLING THE WHOLE HOUSE DOWN! MARCIE, LET GO!!!
AUGH!
I THINK ALL MY ARMS ARE BROKEN!
SCHULZ

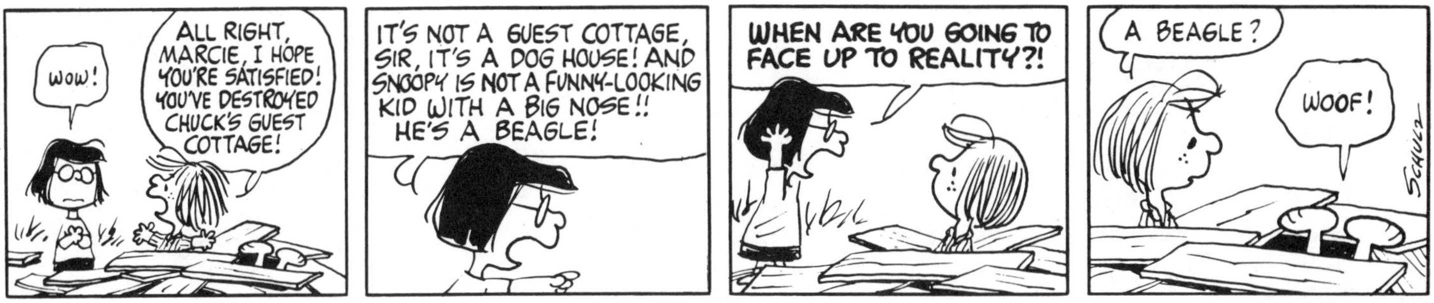
WOW!
ALL RIGHT, MARCIE, I HOPE YOU'RE SATISFIED! YOU'VE DESTROYED CHUCK'S GUEST COTTAGE!
IT'S NOT A GUEST COTTAGE, SIR, IT'S A DOG HOUSE! AND SNOOPY IS NOT A FUNNY-LOOKING KID WITH A BIG NOSE!! HE'S A BEAGLE!
WHEN ARE YOU GOING TO FACE UP TO REALITY?!
A BEAGLE?
WOOF!
SCHULZ

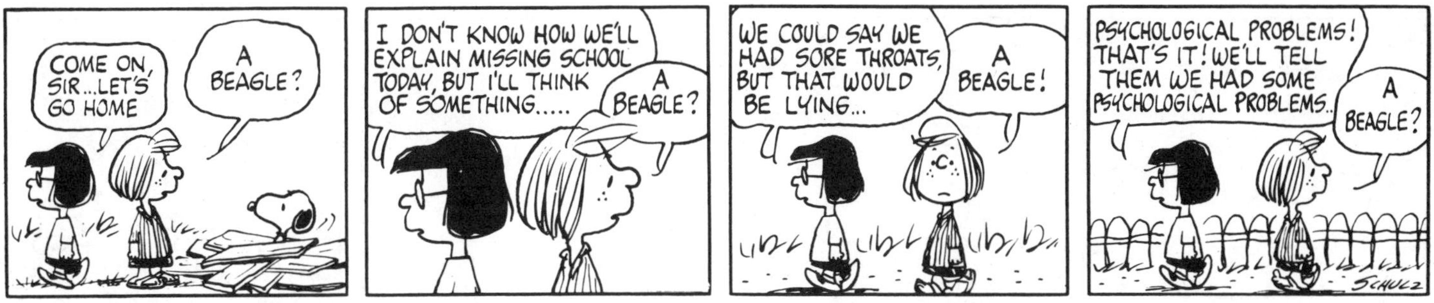
COME ON, SIR...LET'S GO HOME
A BEAGLE?
I DON'T KNOW HOW WE'LL EXPLAIN MISSING SCHOOL TODAY, BUT I'LL THINK OF SOMETHING.....
A BEAGLE?
WE COULD SAY WE HAD SORE THROATS, BUT THAT WOULD BE LYING...
A BEAGLE!
PSYCHOLOGICAL PROBLEMS! THAT'S IT! WE'LL TELL THEM WE HAD SOME PSYCHOLOGICAL PROBLEMS..
A BEAGLE?
SCHULZ

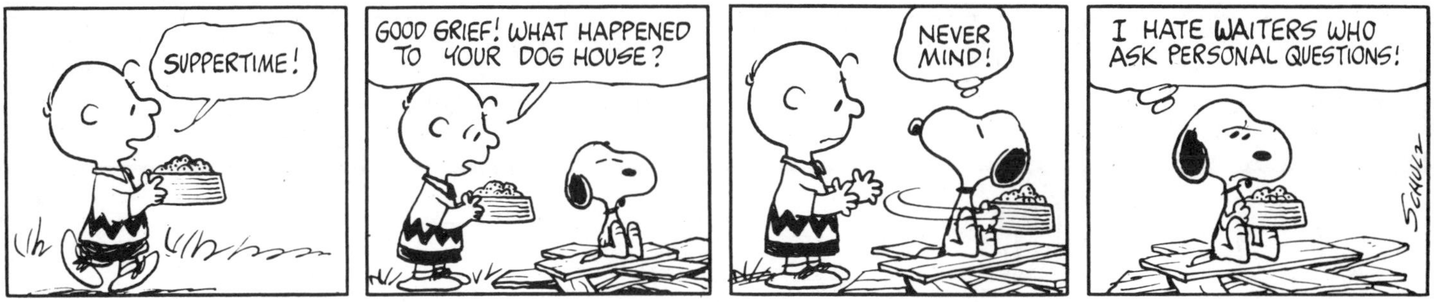
SUPPERTIME!
GOOD GRIEF! WHAT HAPPENED TO YOUR DOG HOUSE?
NEVER MIND!
I HATE WAITERS WHO ASK PERSONAL QUESTIONS!
SCHULZ

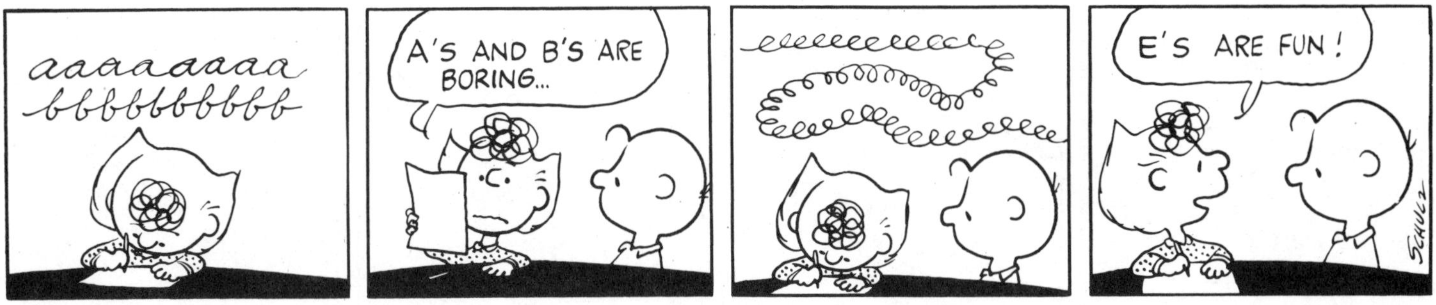
aaaaaaaa
bbbbbbbbbb
A'S AND B'S ARE BORING...
E'S ARE FUN!
SCHULZ

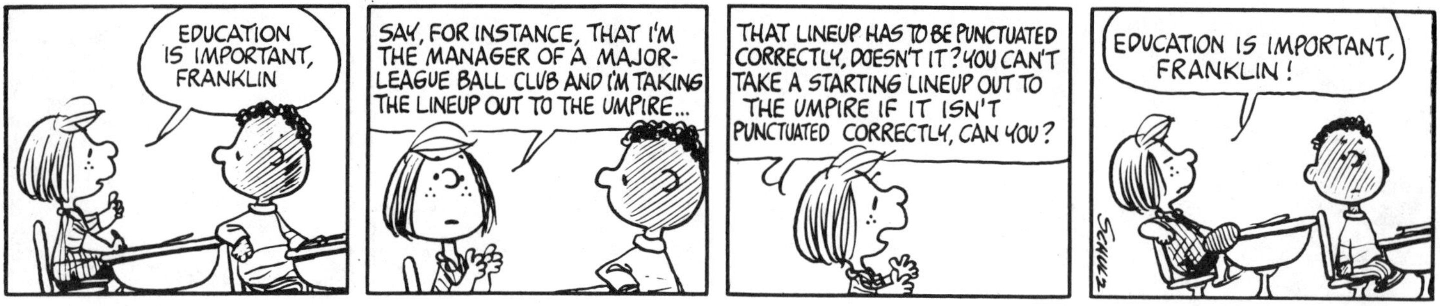
EDUCATION IS IMPORTANT, FRANKLIN
SAY, FOR INSTANCE, THAT I'M THE MANAGER OF A MAJOR-LEAGUE BALL CLUB AND I'M TAKING THE LINEUP OUT TO THE UMPIRE...
THAT LINEUP HAS TO BE PUNCTUATED CORRECTLY, DOESN'T IT? YOU CAN'T TAKE A STARTING LINEUP OUT TO THE UMPIRE IF IT ISN'T PUNCTUATED CORRECTLY, CAN YOU?
EDUCATION IS IMPORTANT, FRANKLIN!
SCHULZ

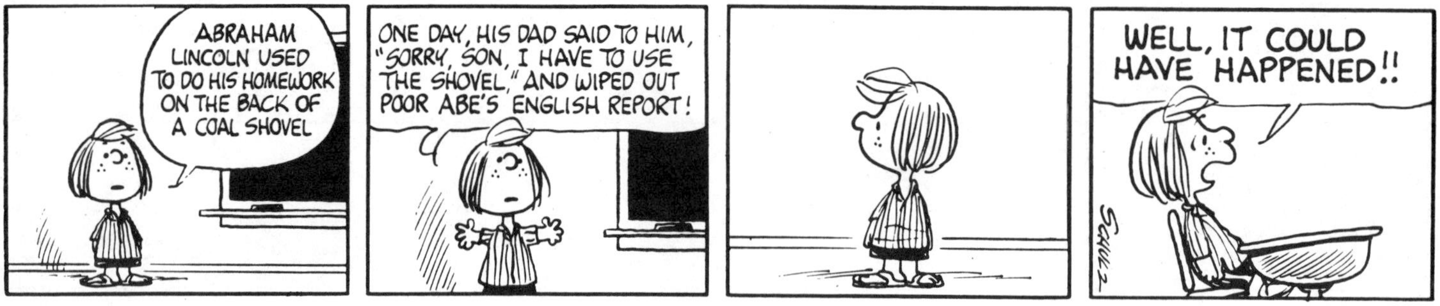
ABRAHAM LINCOLN USED TO DO HIS HOMEWORK ON THE BACK OF A COAL SHOVEL
ONE DAY, HIS DAD SAID TO HIM, "SORRY, SON, I HAVE TO USE THE SHOVEL," AND WIPED OUT POOR ABE'S ENGLISH REPORT!
WELL, IT COULD HAVE HAPPENED!!
SCHULZ

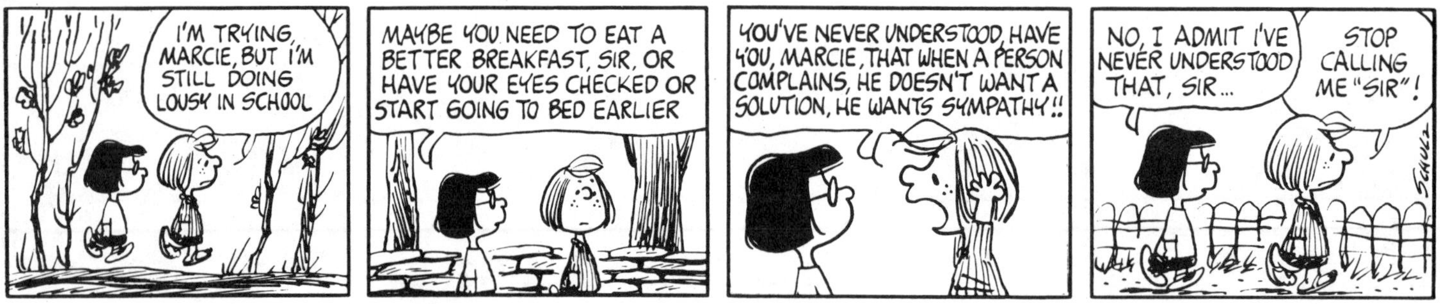
I'M TRYING, MARCIE, BUT I'M STILL DOING LOUSY IN SCHOOL
MAYBE YOU NEED TO EAT A BETTER BREAKFAST, SIR, OR HAVE YOUR EYES CHECKED OR START GOING TO BED EARLIER
YOU'VE NEVER UNDERSTOOD, HAVE YOU, MARCIE, THAT WHEN A PERSON COMPLAINS, HE DOESN'T WANT A SOLUTION, HE WANTS SYMPATHY!!
NO, I ADMIT I'VE NEVER UNDERSTOOD THAT, SIR...
STOP CALLING ME "SIR"!
SCHULZ

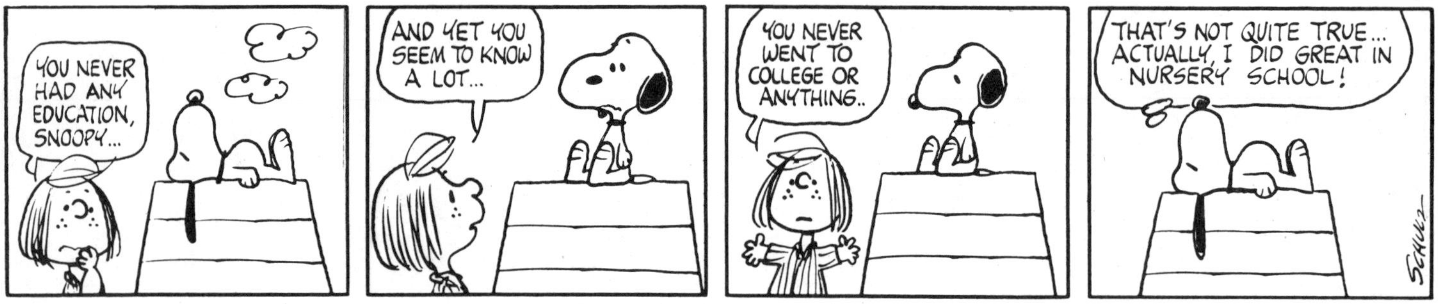
YOU NEVER HAD ANY EDUCATION, SNOOPY...
AND YET YOU SEEM TO KNOW A LOT...
YOU NEVER WENT TO COLLEGE OR ANYTHING..
THAT'S NOT QUITE TRUE... ACTUALLY, I DID GREAT IN NURSERY SCHOOL!
SCHULZ

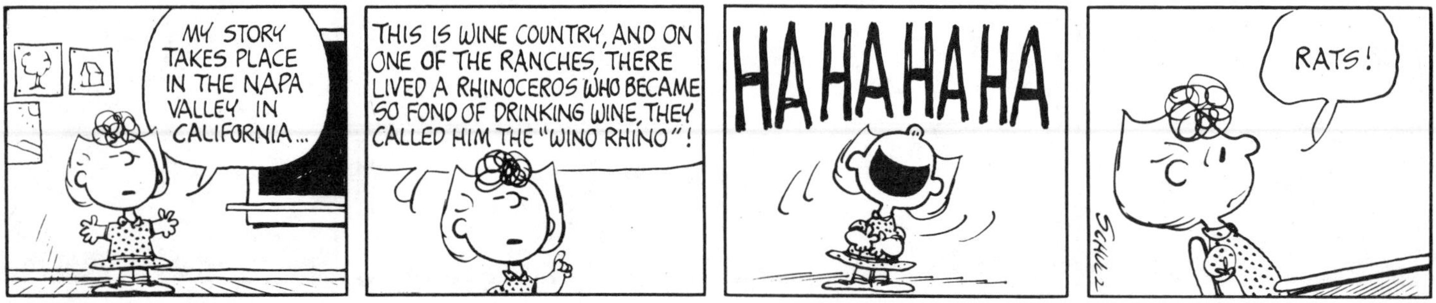
MY STORY TAKES PLACE IN THE NAPA VALLEY IN CALIFORNIA...
THIS IS WINE COUNTRY, AND ON ONE OF THE RANCHES, THERE LIVED A RHINOCEROS WHO BECAME SO FOND OF DRINKING WINE, THEY CALLED HIM THE "WINO RHINO"!
HAHAHAHA
RATS!
SCHULZ

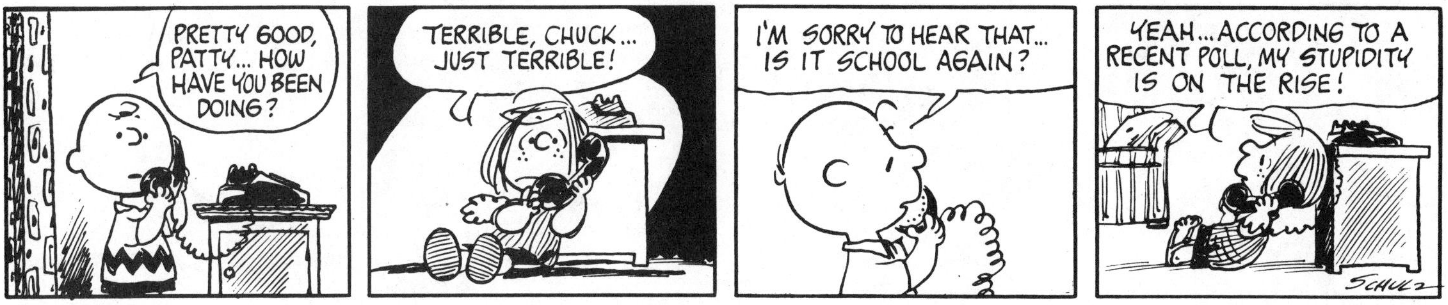
PRETTY GOOD, PATTY... HOW HAVE YOU BEEN DOING?
TERRIBLE, CHUCK... JUST TERRIBLE!
I'M SORRY TO HEAR THAT... IS IT SCHOOL AGAIN?
YEAH... ACCORDING TO A RECENT POLL, MY STUPIDITY IS ON THE RISE!

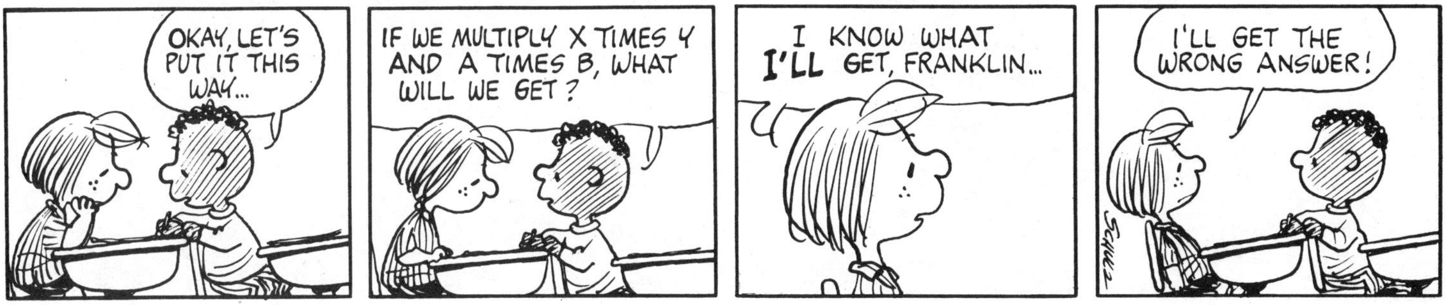
OKAY, LET'S PUT IT THIS WAY...
IF WE MULTIPLY X TIMES Y AND A TIMES B, WHAT WILL WE GET?
I KNOW WHAT I'LL GET, FRANKLIN...
I'LL GET THE WRONG ANSWER!

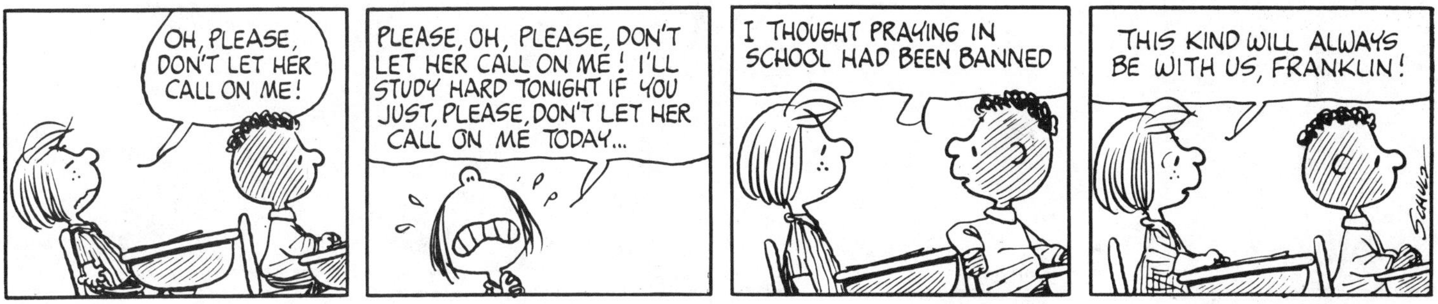
OH, PLEASE, DON'T LET HER CALL ON ME!
PLEASE, OH, PLEASE, DON'T LET HER CALL ON ME! I'LL STUDY HARD TONIGHT IF YOU JUST, PLEASE, DON'T LET HER CALL ON ME TODAY...
I THOUGHT PRAYING IN SCHOOL HAD BEEN BANNED
THIS KIND WILL ALWAYS BE WITH US, FRANKLIN!

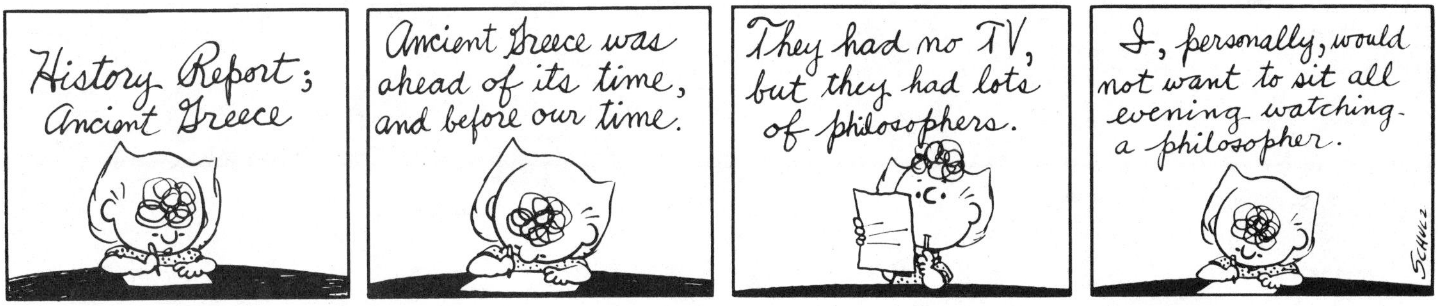
History Report; Ancient Greece
Ancient Greece was ahead of its time, and before our time.
They had no TV, but they had lots of philosophers.
I, personally, would not want to sit all evening watching a philosopher.

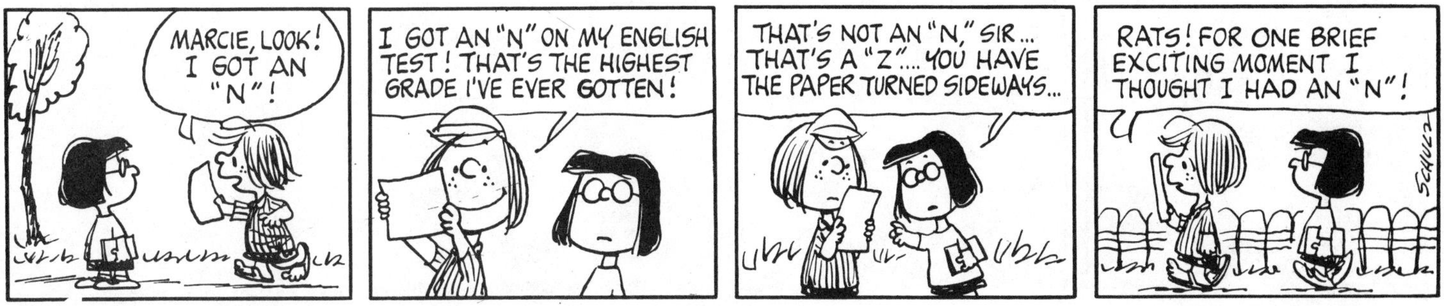
MARCIE, LOOK! I GOT AN "N"!
I GOT AN "N" ON MY ENGLISH TEST! THAT'S THE HIGHEST GRADE I'VE EVER GOTTEN!
THAT'S NOT AN "N," SIR... THAT'S A "Z"... YOU HAVE THE PAPER TURNED SIDEWAYS...
RATS! FOR ONE BRIEF EXCITING MOMENT I THOUGHT I HAD AN "N"!

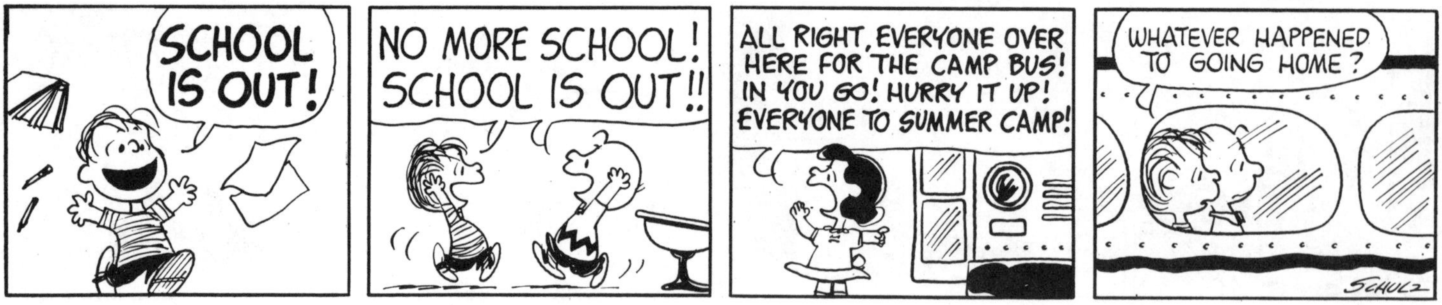
SCHOOL IS OUT!
NO MORE SCHOOL! SCHOOL IS OUT!!
ALL RIGHT, EVERYONE OVER HERE FOR THE CAMP BUS! IN YOU GO! HURRY IT UP! EVERYONE TO SUMMER CAMP!
WHATEVER HAPPENED TO GOING HOME?
SCHULZ

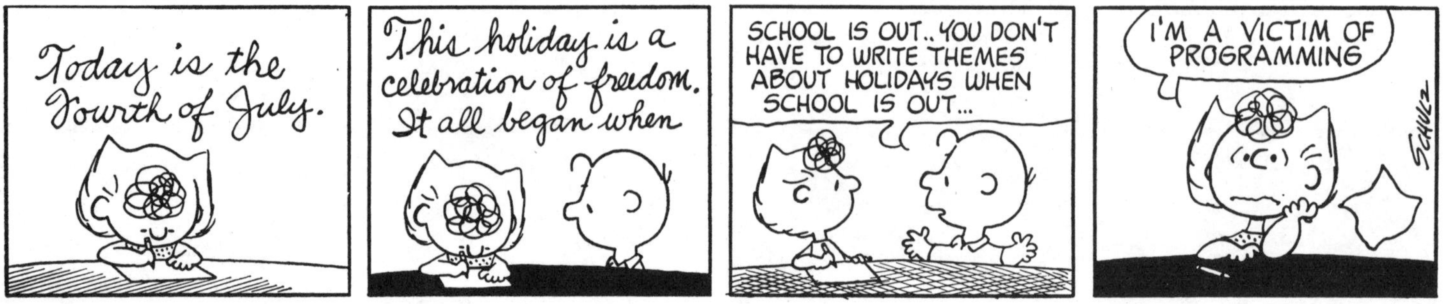
Today is the Fourth of July.
This holiday is a celebration of freedom. It all began when
SCHOOL IS OUT.. YOU DON'T HAVE TO WRITE THEMES ABOUT HOLIDAYS WHEN SCHOOL IS OUT...
I'M A VICTIM OF PROGRAMMING
SCHULZ

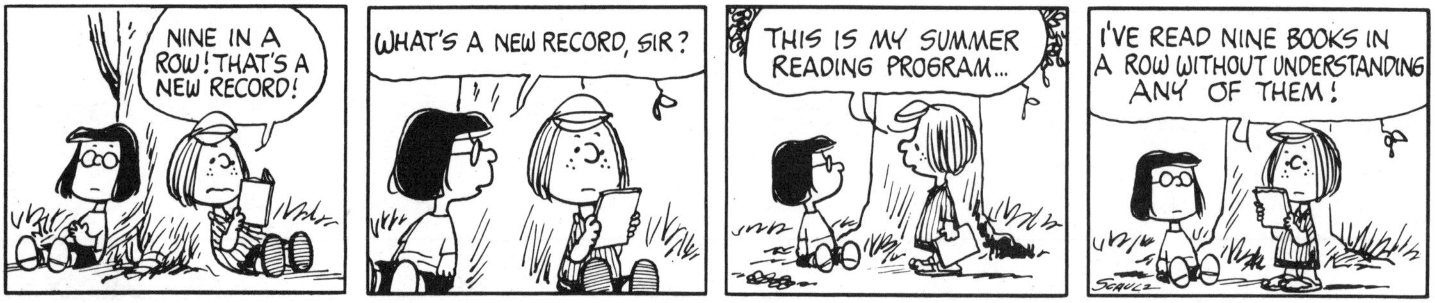
NINE IN A ROW! THAT'S A NEW RECORD!
WHAT'S A NEW RECORD, SIR?
THIS IS MY SUMMER READING PROGRAM...
I'VE READ NINE BOOKS IN A ROW WITHOUT UNDERSTANDING ANY OF THEM!
SCHULZ

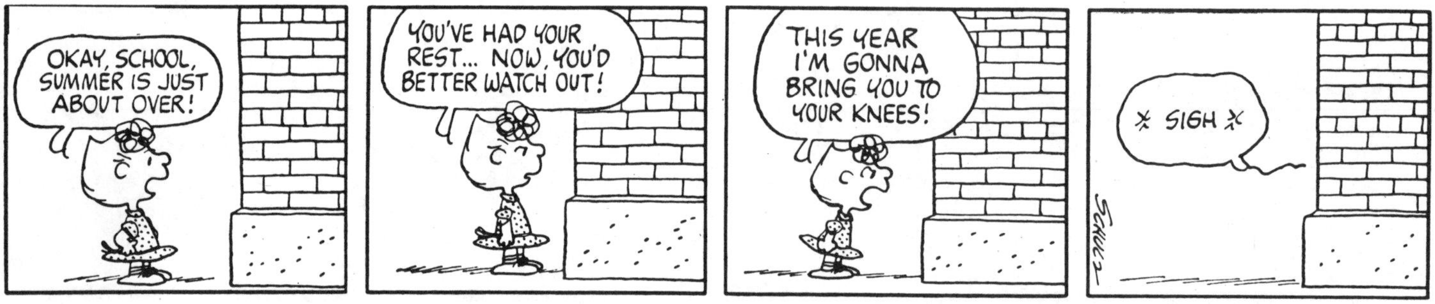
OKAY, SCHOOL, SUMMER IS JUST ABOUT OVER!
YOU'VE HAD YOUR REST... NOW, YOU'D BETTER WATCH OUT!
THIS YEAR I'M GONNA BRING YOU TO YOUR KNEES!
SCHULZ
* SIGH *

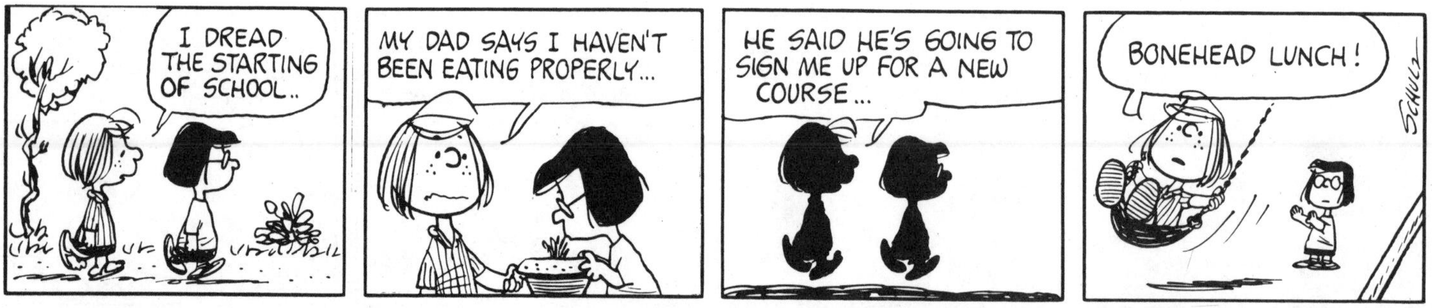
I DREAD THE STARTING OF SCHOOL..
MY DAD SAYS I HAVEN'T BEEN EATING PROPERLY...
HE SAID HE'S GOING TO SIGN ME UP FOR A NEW COURSE...
BONEHEAD LUNCH!
SCHULZ

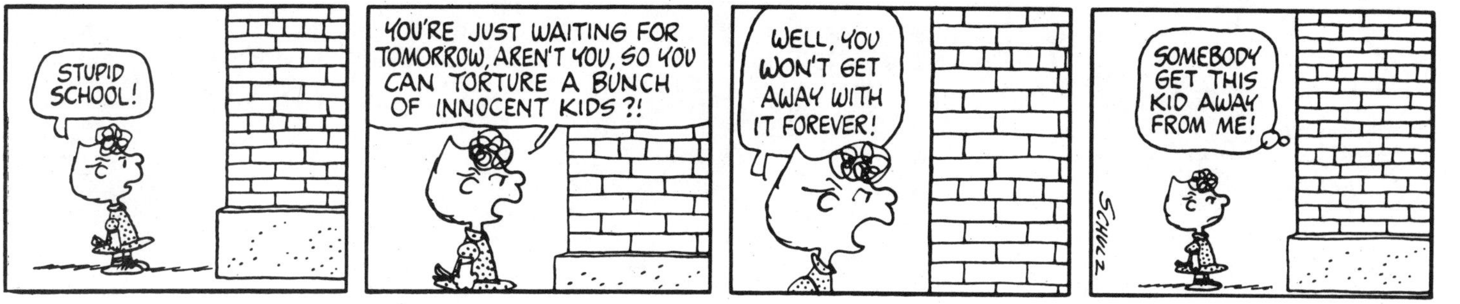
STUPID SCHOOL!
YOU'RE JUST WAITING FOR TOMORROW, AREN'T YOU, SO YOU CAN TORTURE A BUNCH OF INNOCENT KIDS ?!
WELL, YOU WON'T GET AWAY WITH IT FOREVER!
SOMEBODY GET THIS KID AWAY FROM ME!
SCHULZ

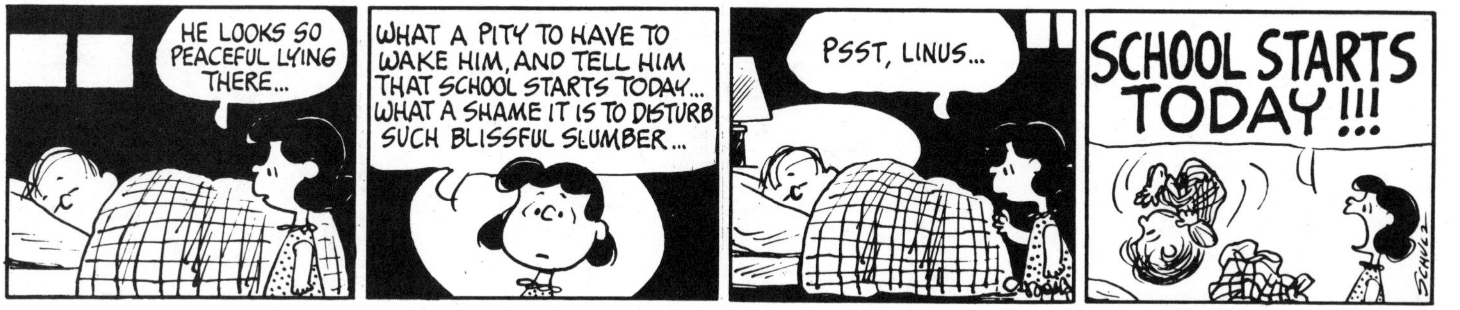
HE LOOKS SO PEACEFUL LYING THERE...
WHAT A PITY TO HAVE TO WAKE HIM, AND TELL HIM THAT SCHOOL STARTS TODAY... WHAT A SHAME IT IS TO DISTURB SUCH BLISSFUL SLUMBER...
PSST, LINUS...
SCHOOL STARTS TODAY!!!
SCHULZ

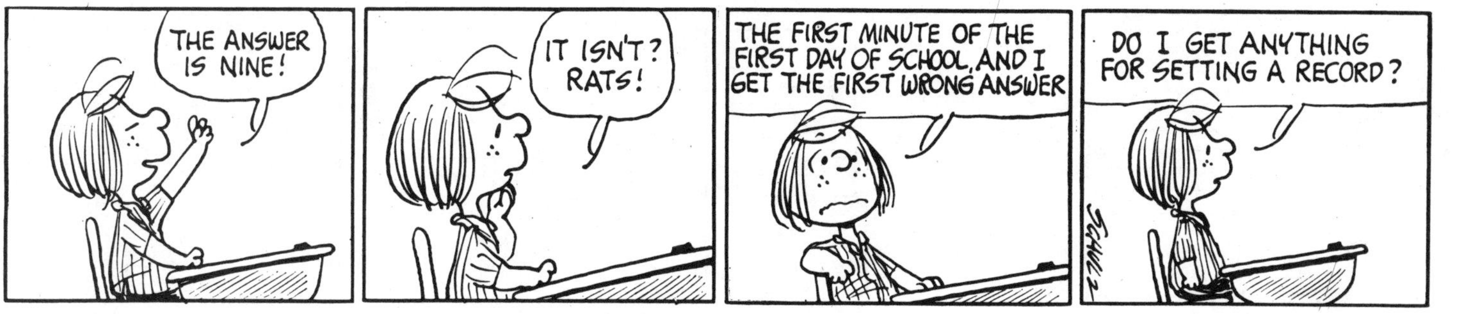
THE ANSWER IS NINE!
IT ISN'T? RATS!
THE FIRST MINUTE OF THE FIRST DAY OF SCHOOL, AND I GET THE FIRST WRONG ANSWER
DO I GET ANYTHING FOR SETTING A RECORD?
SCHULZ

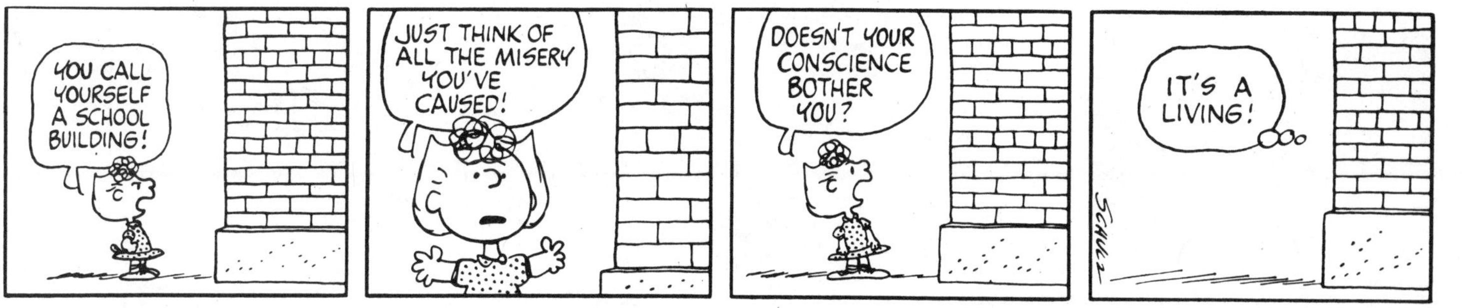
YOU CALL YOURSELF A SCHOOL BUILDING!
JUST THINK OF ALL THE MISERY YOU'VE CAUSED!
DOESN'T YOUR CONSCIENCE BOTHER YOU?
IT'S A LIVING!
SCHULZ

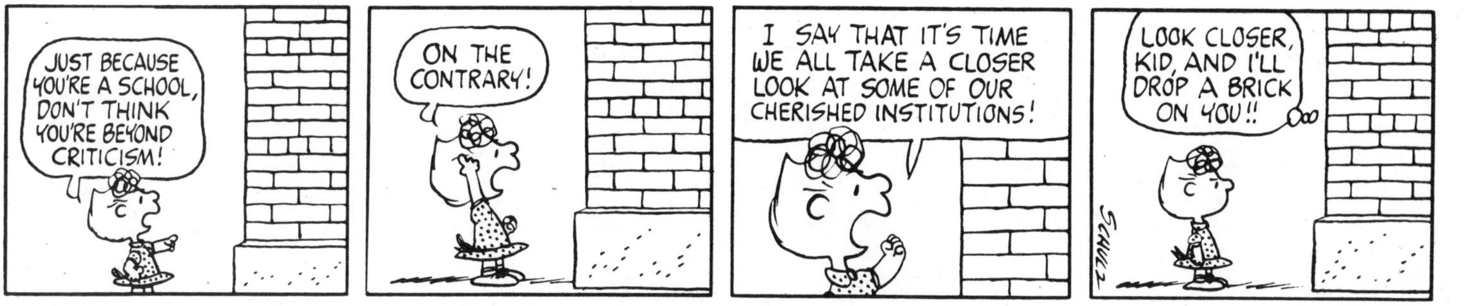
JUST BECAUSE YOU'RE A SCHOOL, DON'T THINK YOU'RE BEYOND CRITICISM!
ON THE CONTRARY!
I SAY THAT IT'S TIME WE ALL TAKE A CLOSER LOOK AT SOME OF OUR CHERISHED INSTITUTIONS!
LOOK CLOSER, KID, AND I'LL DROP A BRICK ON YOU!!
SCHULZ

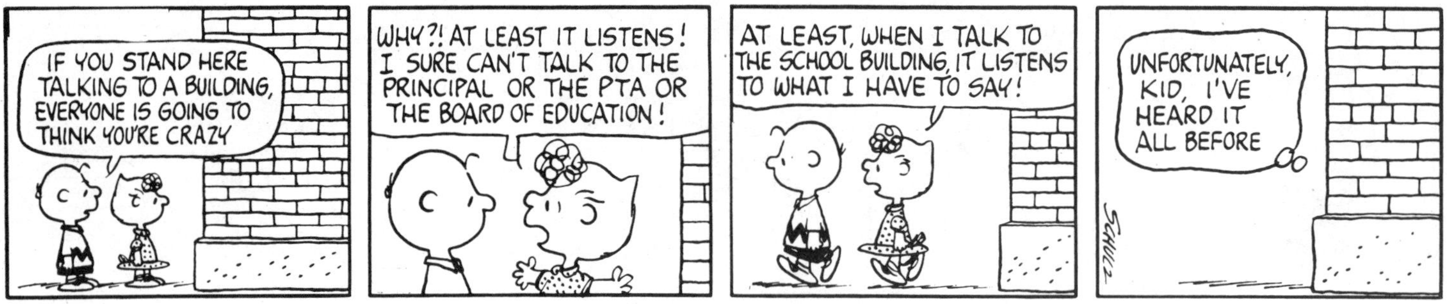
IF YOU STAND HERE TALKING TO A BUILDING, EVERYONE IS GOING TO THINK YOU'RE CRAZY
WHY?! AT LEAST IT LISTENS! I SURE CAN'T TALK TO THE PRINCIPAL OR THE PTA OR THE BOARD OF EDUCATION!
AT LEAST, WHEN I TALK TO THE SCHOOL BUILDING, IT LISTENS TO WHAT I HAVE TO SAY!
UNFORTUNATELY, KID, I'VE HEARD IT ALL BEFORE
SCHULZ

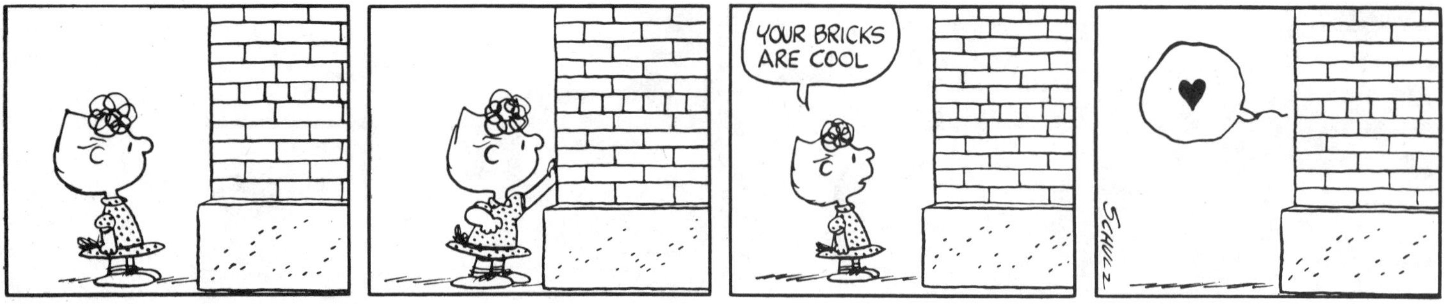
YOUR BRICKS ARE COOL
SCHULZ

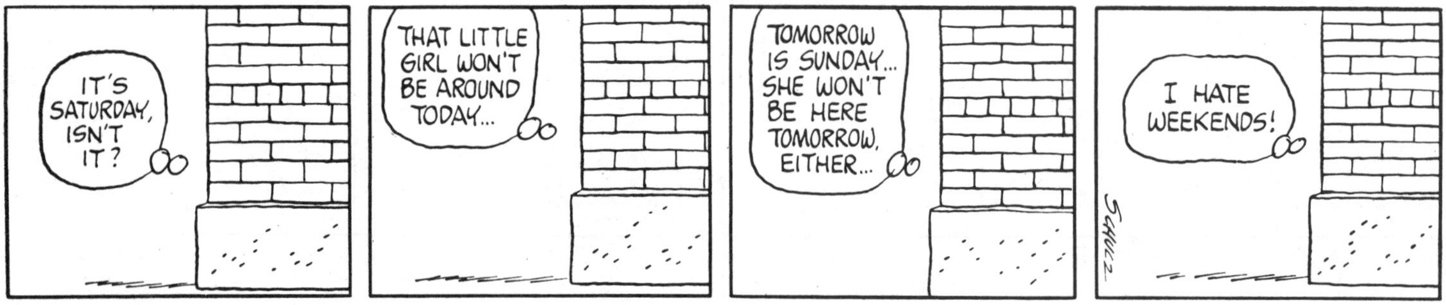
IT'S SATURDAY, ISN'T IT?
THAT LITTLE GIRL WON'T BE AROUND TODAY...
TOMORROW IS SUNDAY... SHE WON'T BE HERE TOMORROW, EITHER...
I HATE WEEKENDS!
SCHULZ

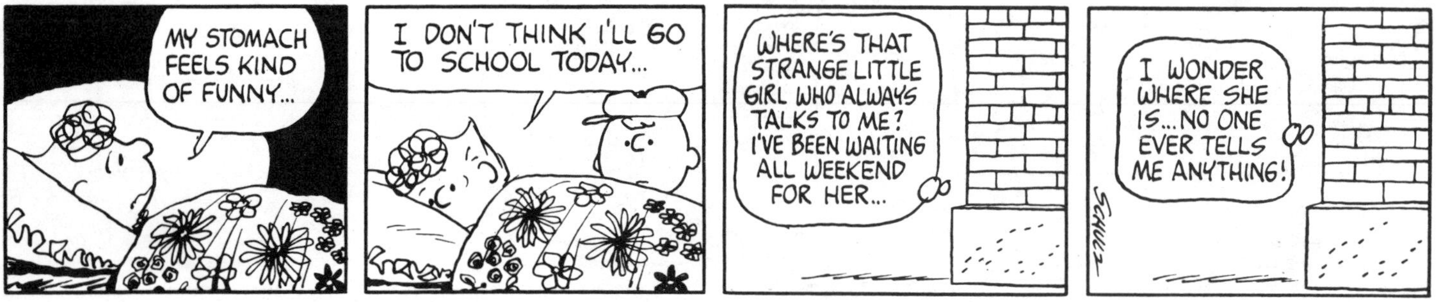
MY STOMACH FEELS KIND OF FUNNY...
I DON'T THINK I'LL GO TO SCHOOL TODAY...
WHERE'S THAT STRANGE LITTLE GIRL WHO ALWAYS TALKS TO ME? I'VE BEEN WAITING ALL WEEKEND FOR HER...
I WONDER WHERE SHE IS... NO ONE EVER TELLS ME ANYTHING!
SCHULZ

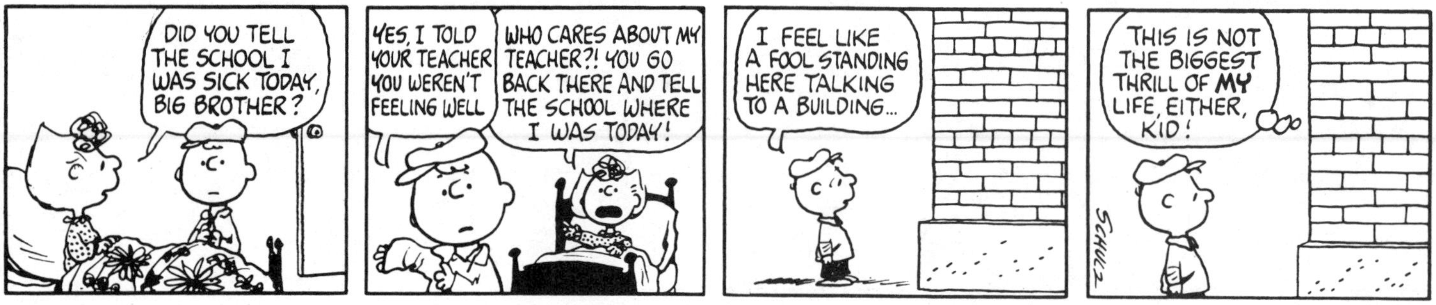
DID YOU TELL THE SCHOOL I WAS SICK TODAY, BIG BROTHER?
YES, I TOLD YOUR TEACHER YOU WEREN'T FEELING WELL
WHO CARES ABOUT MY TEACHER?! YOU GO BACK THERE AND TELL THE SCHOOL WHERE I WAS TODAY!
I FEEL LIKE A FOOL STANDING HERE TALKING TO A BUILDING...
THIS IS NOT THE BIGGEST THRILL OF MY LIFE, EITHER, KID!
SCHULZ

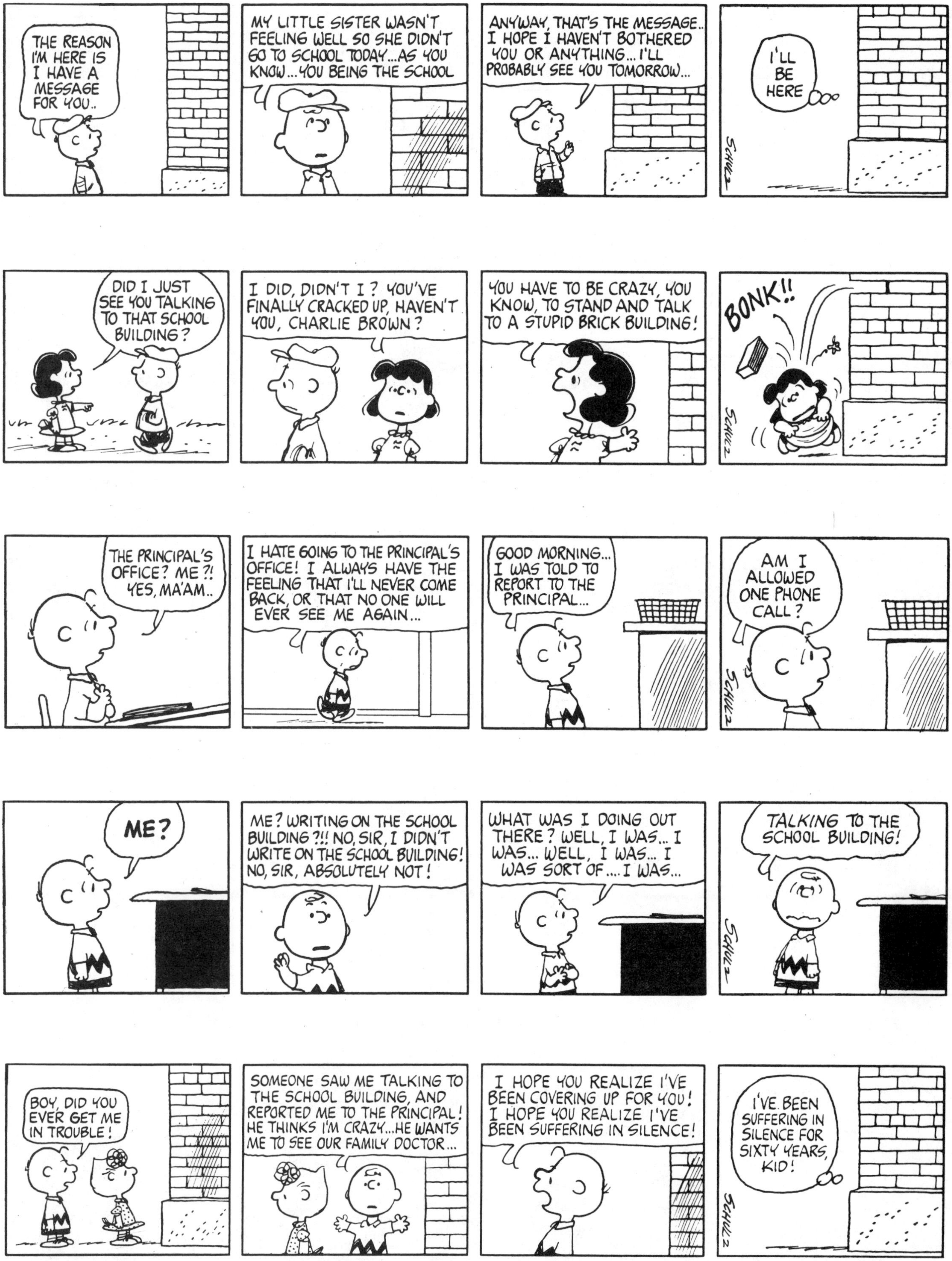
THE REASON I'M HERE IS I HAVE A MESSAGE FOR YOU..
MY LITTLE SISTER WASN'T FEELING WELL SO SHE DIDN'T GO TO SCHOOL TODAY...AS YOU KNOW...YOU BEING THE SCHOOL
ANYWAY, THAT'S THE MESSAGE.. I HOPE I HAVEN'T BOTHERED YOU OR ANYTHING... I'LL PROBABLY SEE YOU TOMORROW...
I'LL BE HERE
DID I JUST SEE YOU TALKING TO THAT SCHOOL BUILDING?
I DID, DIDN'T I? YOU'VE FINALLY CRACKED UP, HAVEN'T YOU, CHARLIE BROWN?
YOU HAVE TO BE CRAZY, YOU KNOW, TO STAND AND TALK TO A STUPID BRICK BUILDING!
BONK!!
THE PRINCIPAL'S OFFICE? ME?! YES, MA'AM..
I HATE GOING TO THE PRINCIPAL'S OFFICE! I ALWAYS HAVE THE FEELING THAT I'LL NEVER COME BACK, OR THAT NO ONE WILL EVER SEE ME AGAIN...
GOOD MORNING... I WAS TOLD TO REPORT TO THE PRINCIPAL...
AM I ALLOWED ONE PHONE CALL?
ME?
ME? WRITING ON THE SCHOOL BUILDING?!! NO, SIR, I DIDN'T WRITE ON THE SCHOOL BUILDING! NO, SIR, ABSOLUTELY NOT!
WHAT WAS I DOING OUT THERE? WELL, I WAS... I WAS... WELL, I WAS... I WAS SORT OF.... I WAS...
TALKING TO THE SCHOOL BUILDING!
BOY, DID YOU EVER GET ME IN TROUBLE!
SOMEONE SAW ME TALKING TO THE SCHOOL BUILDING, AND REPORTED ME TO THE PRINCIPAL! HE THINKS I'M CRAZY...HE WANTS ME TO SEE OUR FAMILY DOCTOR...
I HOPE YOU REALIZE I'VE BEEN COVERING UP FOR YOU! I HOPE YOU REALIZE I'VE BEEN SUFFERING IN SILENCE!
I'VE BEEN SUFFERING IN SILENCE FOR SIXTY YEARS, KID!

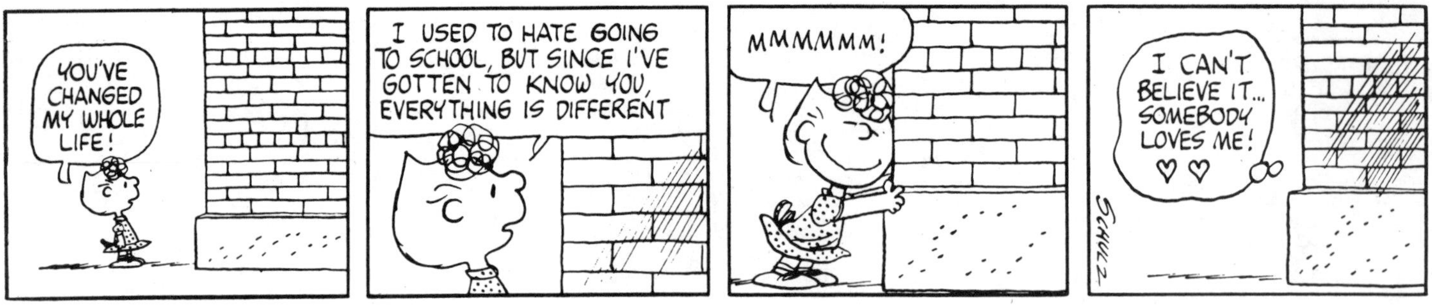
YOU'VE CHANGED MY WHOLE LIFE!
I USED TO HATE GOING TO SCHOOL, BUT SINCE I'VE GOTTEN TO KNOW YOU, EVERYTHING IS DIFFERENT
MMMMMM!
I CAN'T BELIEVE IT... SOMEBODY LOVES ME!

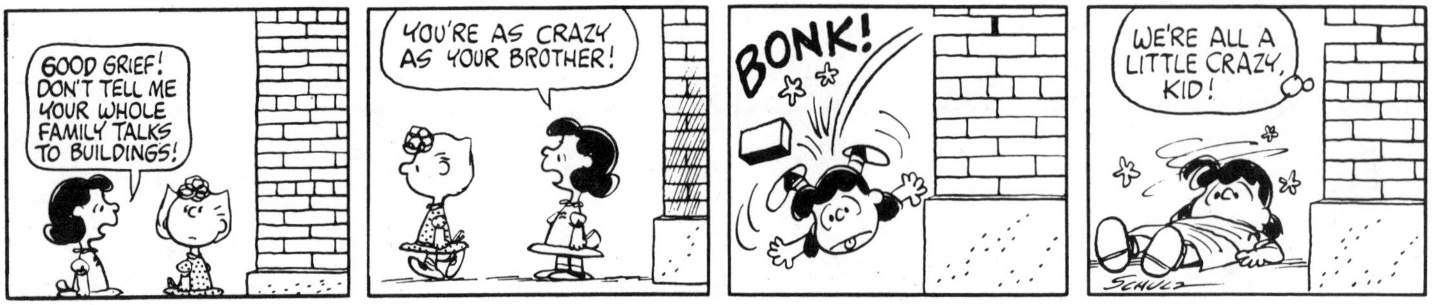
GOOD GRIEF! DON'T TELL ME YOUR WHOLE FAMILY TALKS TO BUILDINGS!
YOU'RE AS CRAZY AS YOUR BROTHER!
BONK!
WE'RE ALL A LITTLE CRAZY, KID!

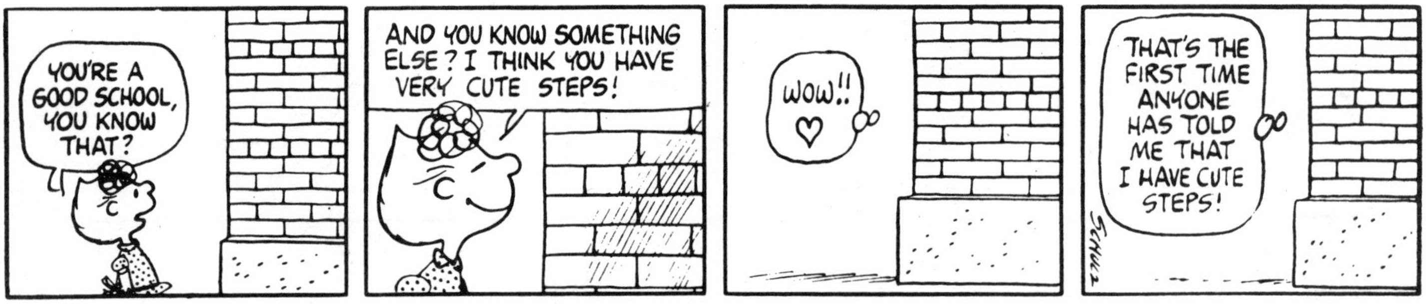
YOU'RE A GOOD SCHOOL, YOU KNOW THAT?
AND YOU KNOW SOMETHING ELSE? I THINK YOU HAVE VERY CUTE STEPS!
WOW!!
THAT'S THE FIRST TIME ANYONE HAS TOLD ME THAT I HAVE CUTE STEPS!

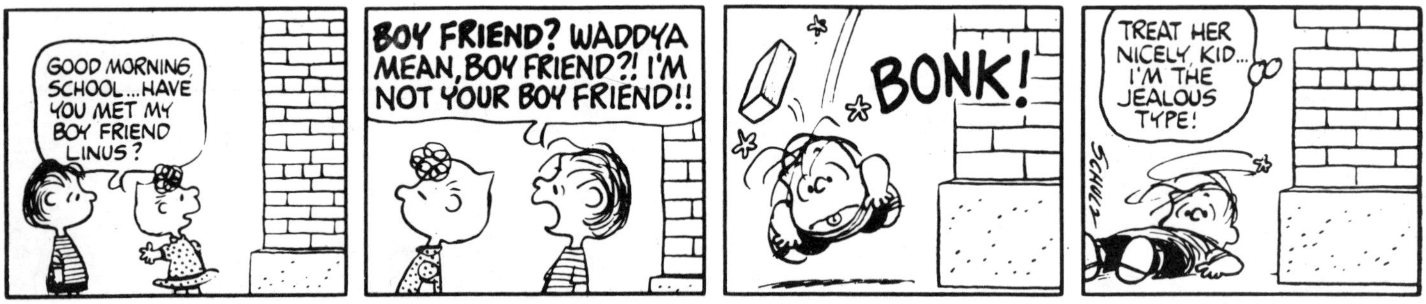
GOOD MORNING, SCHOOL...HAVE YOU MET MY BOY FRIEND LINUS?
BOY FRIEND? WADDYA MEAN, BOY FRIEND?! I'M NOT YOUR BOY FRIEND!!
BONK!
TREAT HER NICELY, KID... I'M THE JEALOUS TYPE!

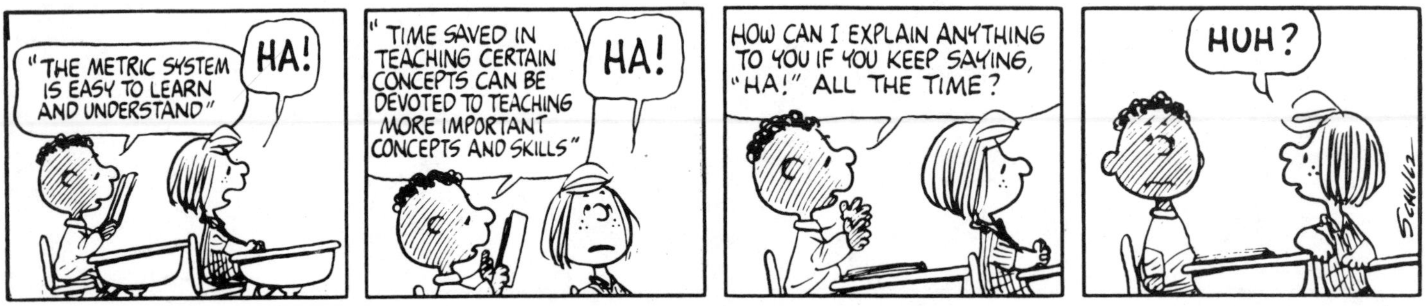
"THE METRIC SYSTEM IS EASY TO LEARN AND UNDERSTAND"
HA!
"TIME SAVED IN TEACHING CERTAIN CONCEPTS CAN BE DEVOTED TO TEACHING MORE IMPORTANT CONCEPTS AND SKILLS"
HA!
HOW CAN I EXPLAIN ANYTHING TO YOU IF YOU KEEP SAYING, "HA!" ALL THE TIME?
HUH?

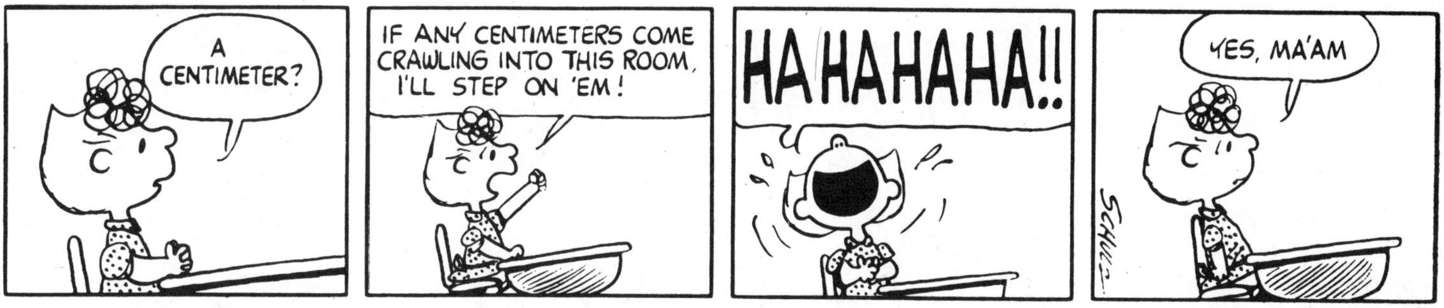
A CENTIMETER?
IF ANY CENTIMETERS COME CRAWLING INTO THIS ROOM, I'LL STEP ON 'EM!
HAHAHAHA!!
YES, MA'AM
SCHULZ

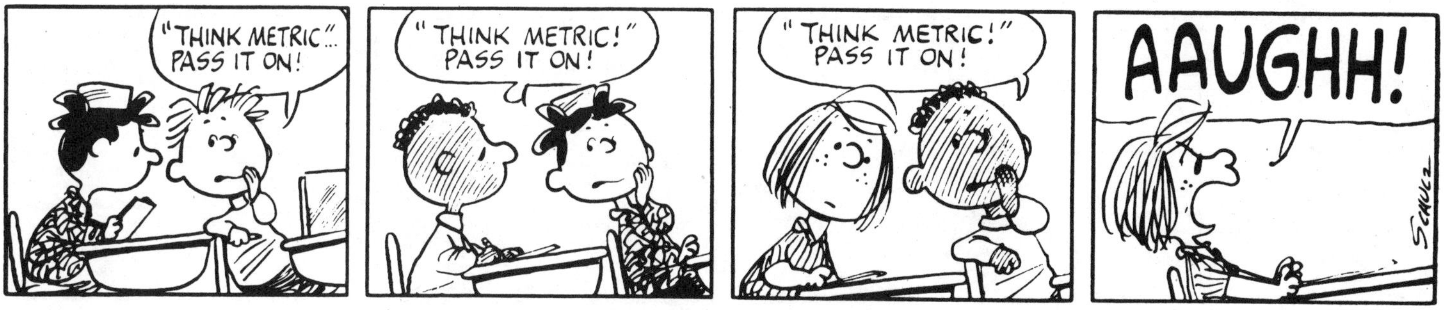
"THINK METRIC"... PASS IT ON!
"THINK METRIC!" PASS IT ON!
"THINK METRIC!" PASS IT ON!
AAUGHH!
SCHULZ

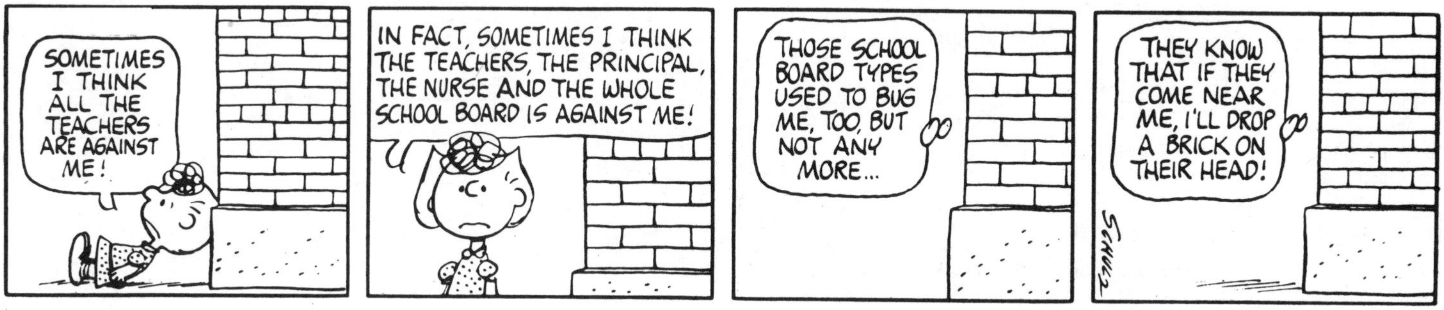
SOMETIMES I THINK ALL THE TEACHERS ARE AGAINST ME!
IN FACT, SOMETIMES I THINK THE TEACHERS, THE PRINCIPAL, THE NURSE AND THE WHOLE SCHOOL BOARD IS AGAINST ME!
THOSE SCHOOL BOARD TYPES USED TO BUG ME, TOO, BUT NOT ANY MORE...
THEY KNOW THAT IF THEY COME NEAR ME, I'LL DROP A BRICK ON THEIR HEAD!
SCHULZ

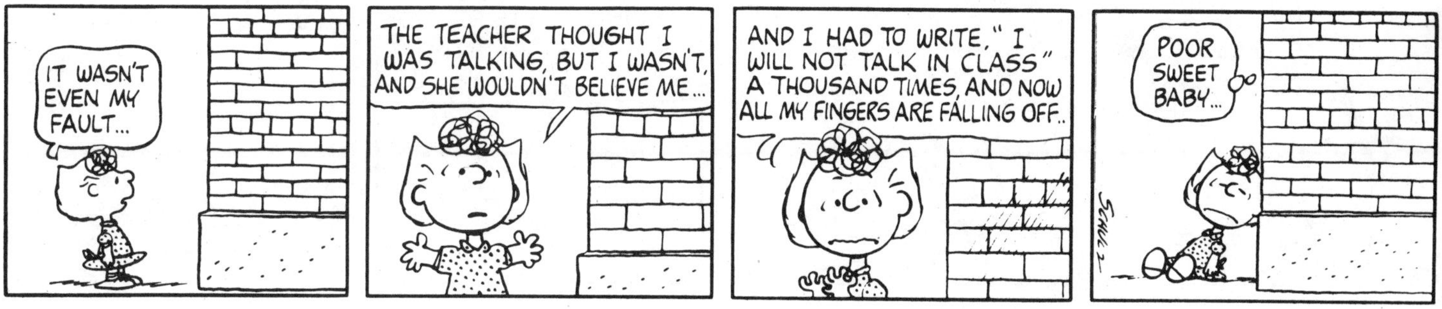
IT WASN'T EVEN MY FAULT...
THE TEACHER THOUGHT I WAS TALKING, BUT I WASN'T, AND SHE WOULDN'T BELIEVE ME...
AND I HAD TO WRITE, "I WILL NOT TALK IN CLASS" A THOUSAND TIMES, AND NOW ALL MY FINGERS ARE FALLING OFF..
POOR SWEET BABY...
SCHULZ

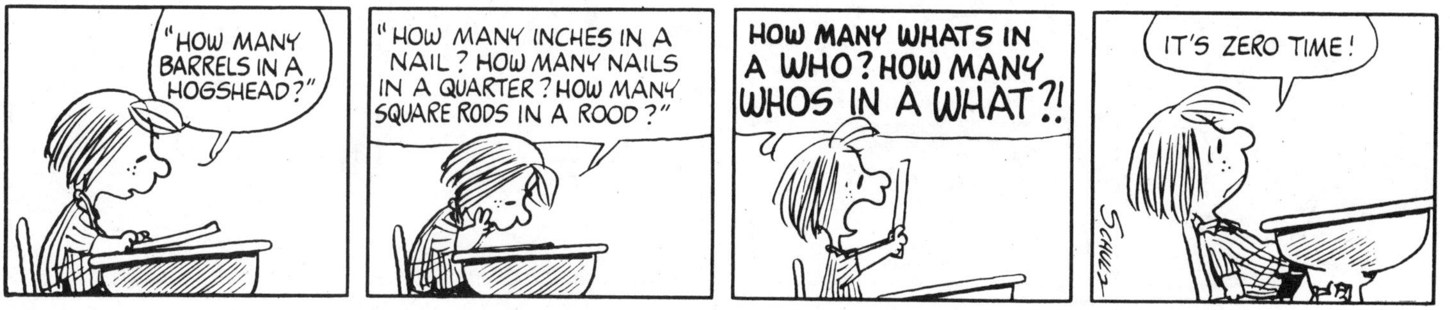
"HOW MANY BARRELS IN A HOGSHEAD?"
"HOW MANY INCHES IN A NAIL? HOW MANY NAILS IN A QUARTER? HOW MANY SQUARE RODS IN A ROOD?"
HOW MANY WHATS IN A WHO? HOW MANY WHOS IN A WHAT?!
IT'S ZERO TIME!
SCHULZ

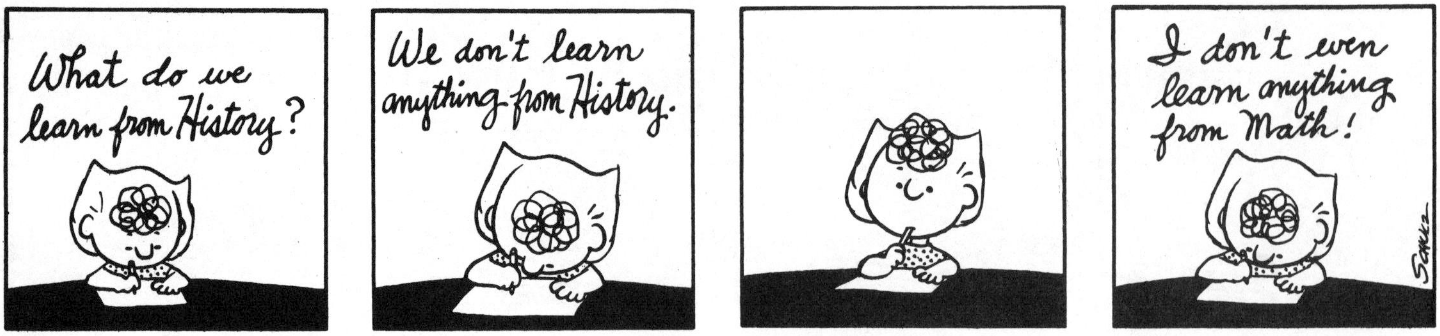
What do we learn from History?
We don't learn anything from History.
I don't even learn anything from Math!
SCHULZ

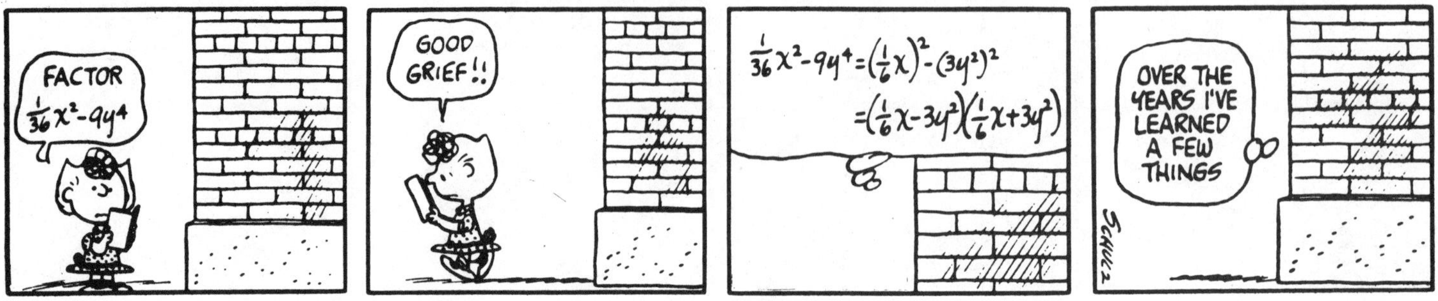
FACTOR $\frac{1}{36}x^2-9y^4$
GOOD GRIEF!!
$\frac{1}{36}x^2-9y^4=(\frac{1}{6}x)^2-(3y^2)^2$
$=(\frac{1}{6}x-3y^2)(\frac{1}{6}x+3y^2)$
OVER THE YEARS I'VE LEARNED A FEW THINGS
SCHULZ

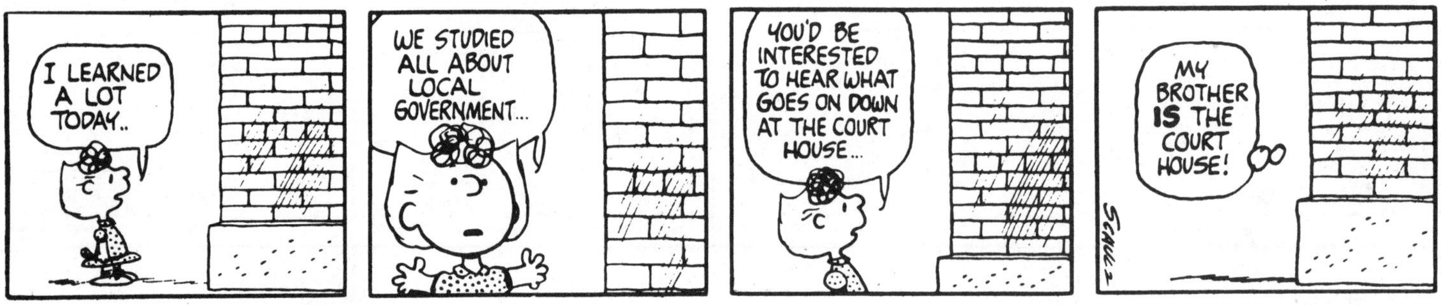
I LEARNED A LOT TODAY..
WE STUDIED ALL ABOUT LOCAL GOVERNMENT...
YOU'D BE INTERESTED TO HEAR WHAT GOES ON DOWN AT THE COURT HOUSE...
MY BROTHER **IS** THE COURT HOUSE!
SCHULZ

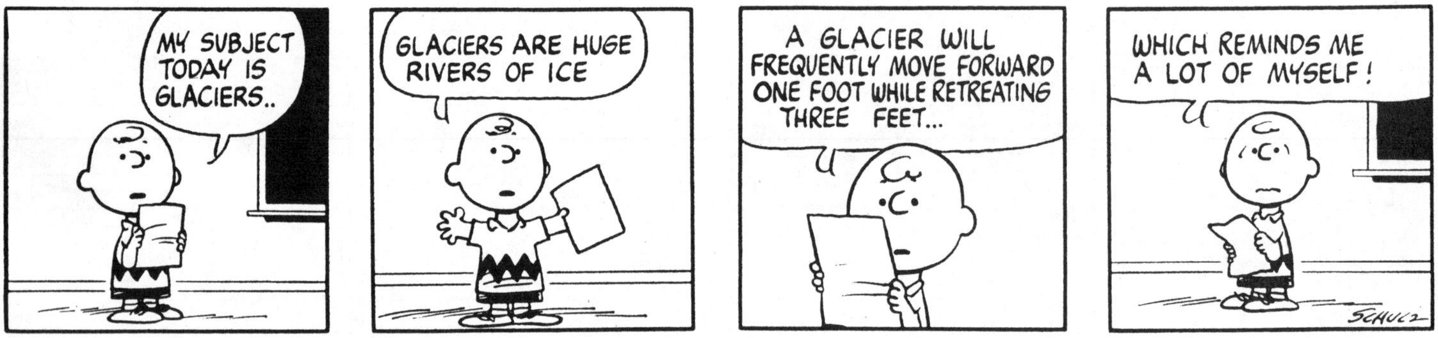
MY SUBJECT TODAY IS GLACIERS..
GLACIERS ARE HUGE RIVERS OF ICE
A GLACIER WILL FREQUENTLY MOVE FORWARD ONE FOOT WHILE RETREATING THREE FEET...
WHICH REMINDS ME A LOT OF MYSELF!
SCHULZ

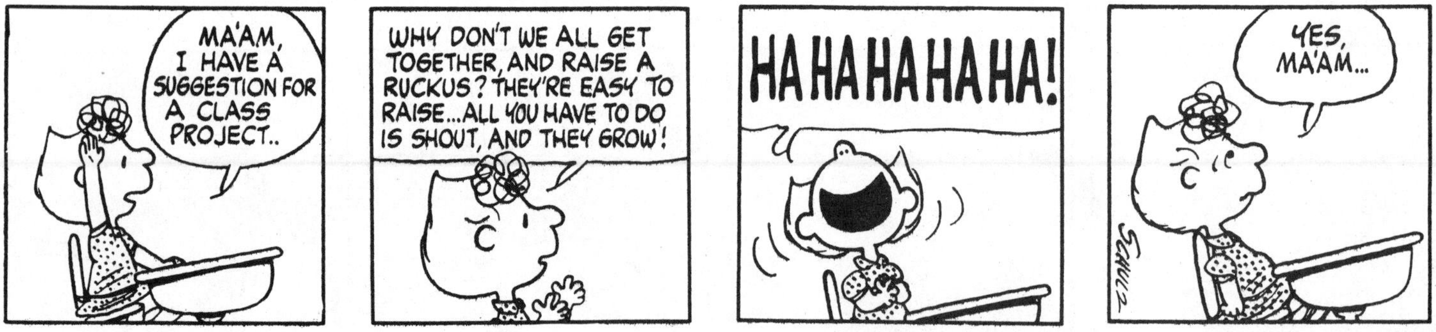
MA'AM, I HAVE A SUGGESTION FOR A CLASS PROJECT..
WHY DON'T WE ALL GET TOGETHER, AND RAISE A RUCKUS? THEY'RE EASY TO RAISE...ALL YOU HAVE TO DO IS SHOUT, AND THEY GROW!
HAHAHAHAHA!
YES, MA'AM...
SCHULZ

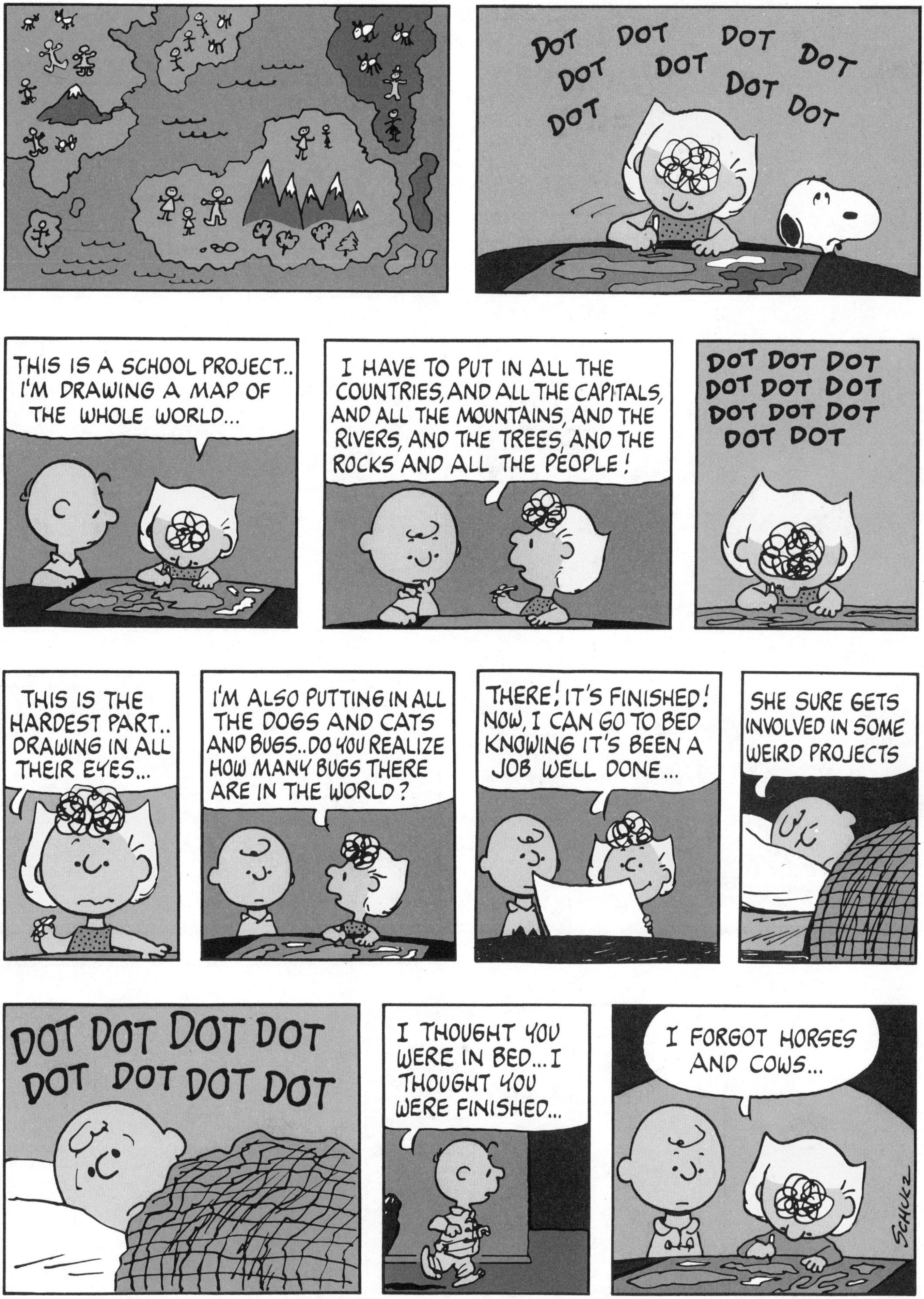
DOT DOT DOT DOT
DOT DOT DOT DOT DOT
THIS IS A SCHOOL PROJECT.. I'M DRAWING A MAP OF THE WHOLE WORLD...
I HAVE TO PUT IN ALL THE COUNTRIES, AND ALL THE CAPITALS, AND ALL THE MOUNTAINS, AND THE RIVERS, AND THE TREES, AND THE ROCKS AND ALL THE PEOPLE!
DOT DOT DOT DOT DOT DOT DOT DOT DOT DOT DOT
THIS IS THE HARDEST PART.. DRAWING IN ALL THEIR EYES...
I'M ALSO PUTTING IN ALL THE DOGS AND CATS AND BUGS..DO YOU REALIZE HOW MANY BUGS THERE ARE IN THE WORLD?
THERE! IT'S FINISHED! NOW, I CAN GO TO BED KNOWING IT'S BEEN A JOB WELL DONE...
SHE SURE GETS INVOLVED IN SOME WEIRD PROJECTS
DOT DOT DOT DOT DOT DOT DOT DOT
I THOUGHT YOU WERE IN BED...I THOUGHT YOU WERE FINISHED...
I FORGOT HORSES AND COWS...
SCHULZ

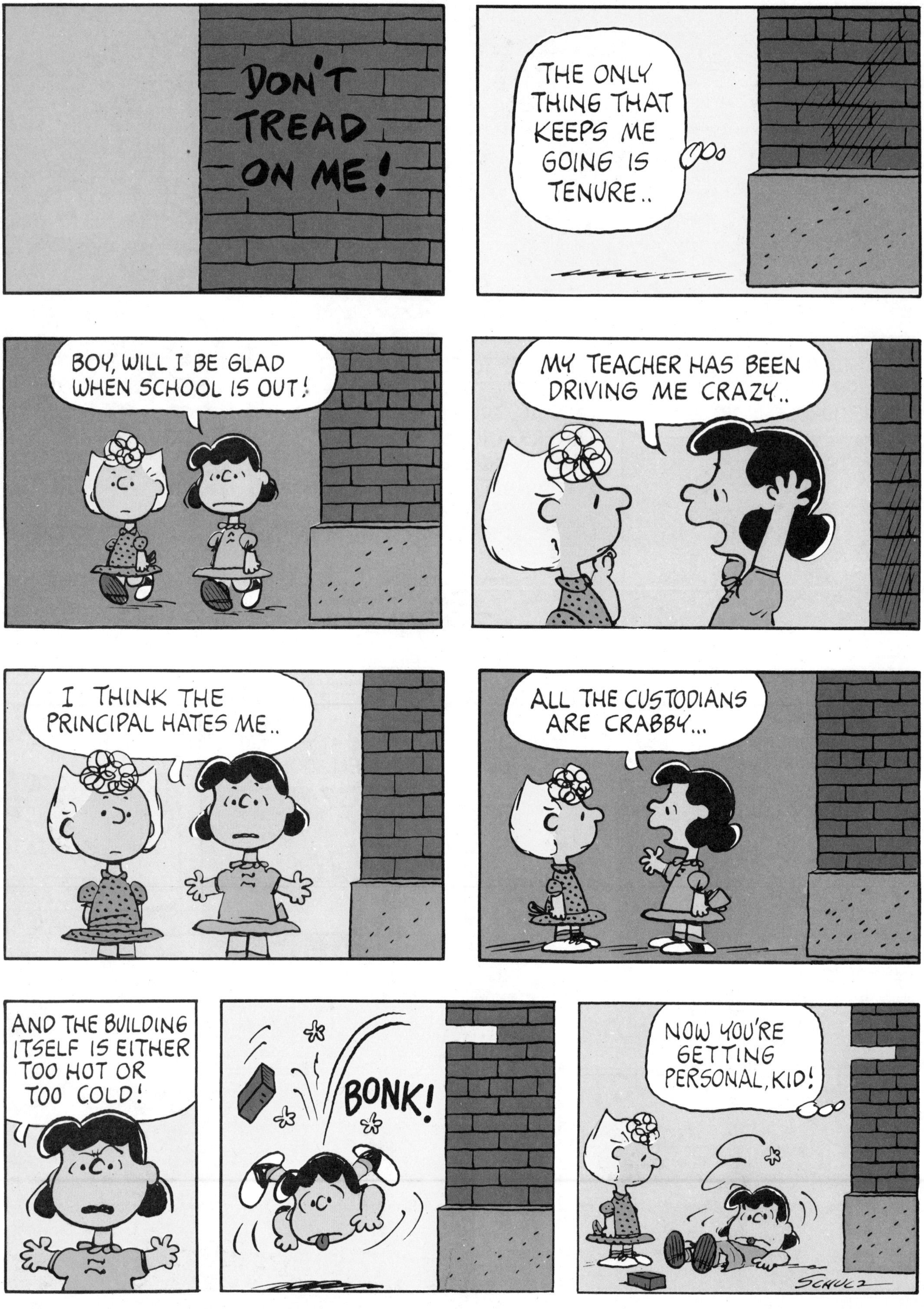
DON'T TREAD ON ME!
THE ONLY THING THAT KEEPS ME GOING IS TENURE..
BOY, WILL I BE GLAD WHEN SCHOOL IS OUT!
MY TEACHER HAS BEEN DRIVING ME CRAZY..
I THINK THE PRINCIPAL HATES ME..
ALL THE CUSTODIANS ARE CRABBY...
AND THE BUILDING ITSELF IS EITHER TOO HOT OR TOO COLD!
BONK!
NOW YOU'RE GETTING PERSONAL, KID!
SCHULZ

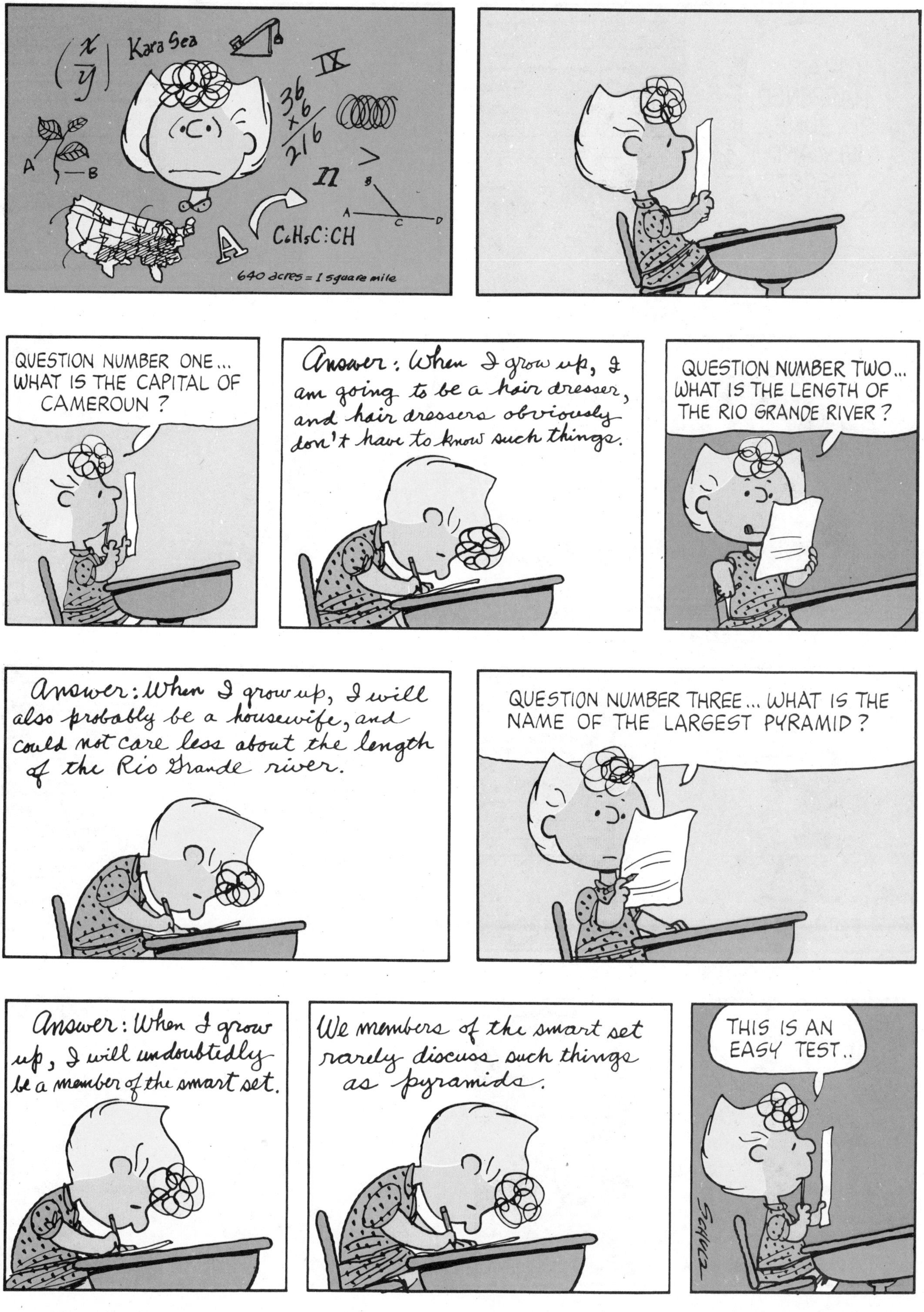
Kara Sea
(x/y)
IX
36
x6
216
A
B
II
B
A
C
D
A
C6H5C:CH
640 acres = 1 square mile
QUESTION NUMBER ONE... WHAT IS THE CAPITAL OF CAMEROUN ?
Answer: When I grow up, I am going to be a hair dresser, and hair dressers obviously don't have to know such things.
QUESTION NUMBER TWO... WHAT IS THE LENGTH OF THE RIO GRANDE RIVER ?
Answer: When I grow up, I will also probably be a housewife, and could not care less about the length of the Rio Grande river.
QUESTION NUMBER THREE... WHAT IS THE NAME OF THE LARGEST PYRAMID ?
Answer: When I grow up, I will undoubtedly be a member of the smart set.
We members of the smart set rarely discuss such things as pyramids.
THIS IS AN EASY TEST..
SCHULZ

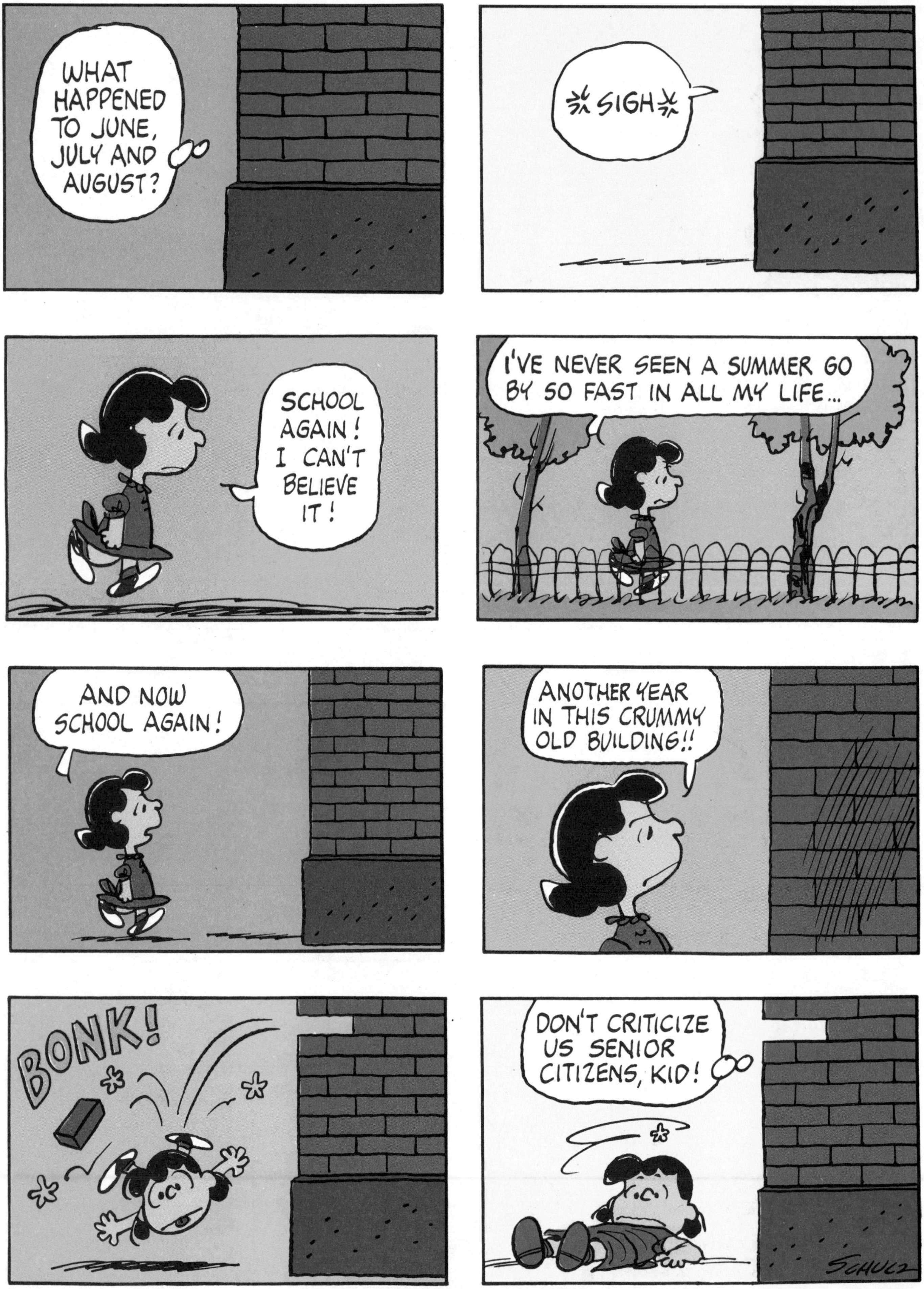

WHAT HAPPENED TO JUNE, JULY AND AUGUST?
SIGH
SCHOOL AGAIN! I CAN'T BELIEVE IT!
I'VE NEVER SEEN A SUMMER GO BY SO FAST IN ALL MY LIFE...
AND NOW SCHOOL AGAIN!
ANOTHER YEAR IN THIS CRUMMY OLD BUILDING!!
BONK!
DON'T CRITICIZE US SENIOR CITIZENS, KID!
SCHULZ

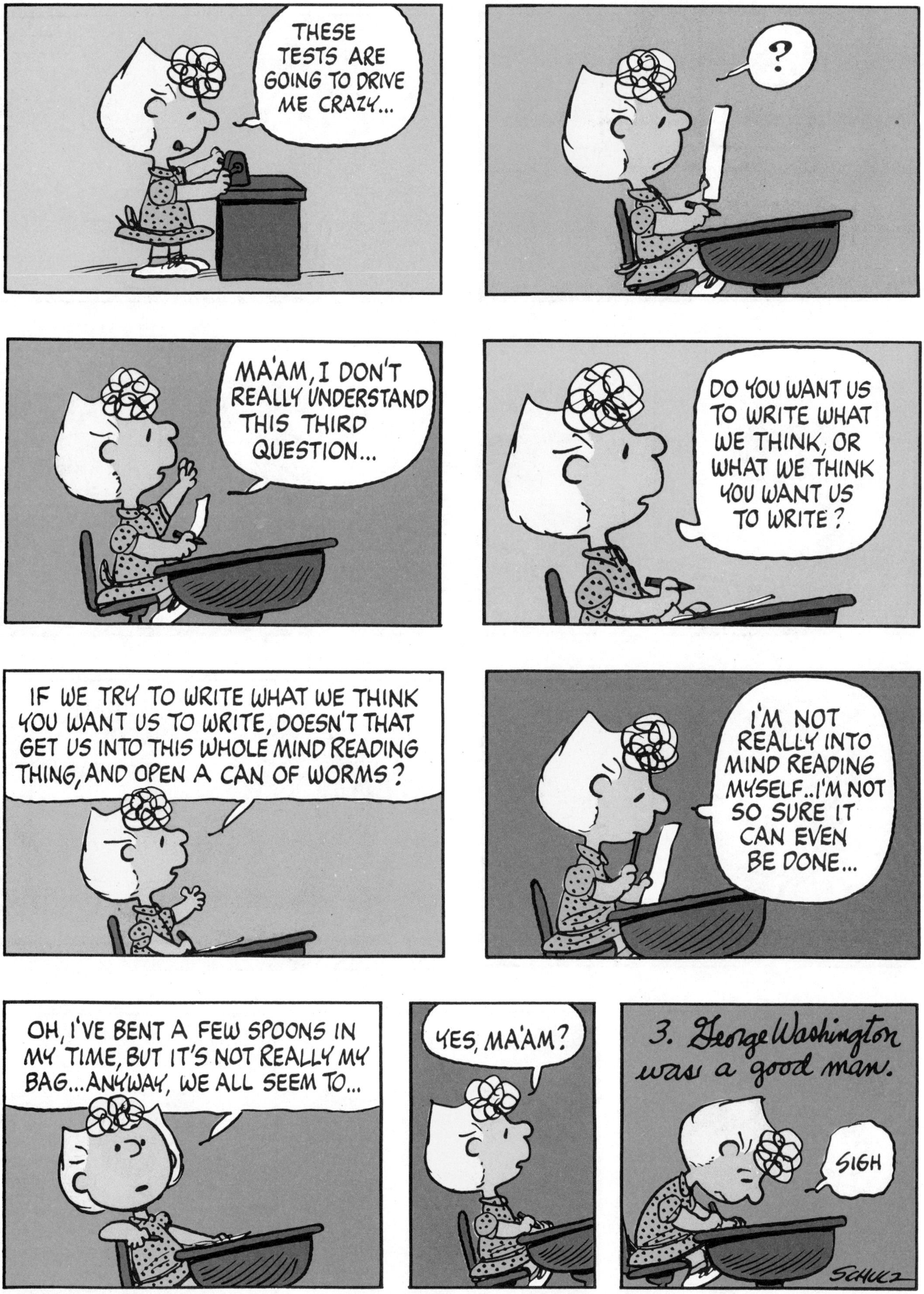
THESE TESTS ARE GOING TO DRIVE ME CRAZY...
?
MA'AM, I DON'T REALLY UNDERSTAND THIS THIRD QUESTION...
DO YOU WANT US TO WRITE WHAT WE THINK, OR WHAT WE THINK YOU WANT US TO WRITE?
IF WE TRY TO WRITE WHAT WE THINK YOU WANT US TO WRITE, DOESN'T THAT GET US INTO THIS WHOLE MIND READING THING, AND OPEN A CAN OF WORMS?
I'M NOT REALLY INTO MIND READING MYSELF..I'M NOT SO SURE IT CAN EVEN BE DONE...
OH, I'VE BENT A FEW SPOONS IN MY TIME, BUT IT'S NOT REALLY MY BAG...ANYWAY, WE ALL SEEM TO...
YES, MA'AM?
3. George Washington was a good man.
SIGH
SCHULZ

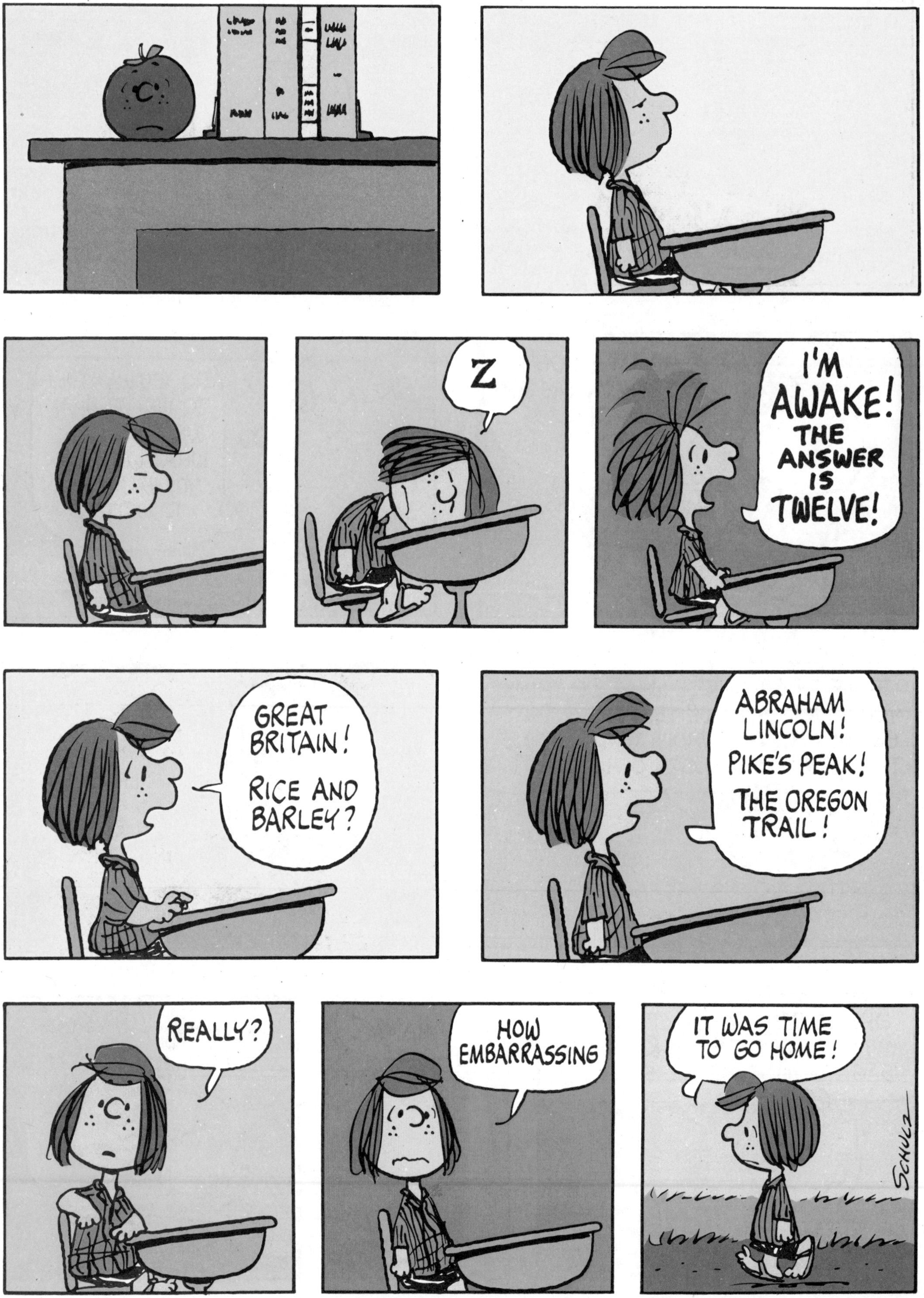
Z
I'M AWAKE! THE ANSWER IS TWELVE!
GREAT BRITAIN! RICE AND BARLEY?
ABRAHAM LINCOLN! PIKE'S PEAK! THE OREGON TRAIL!
REALLY?
HOW EMBARRASSING
IT WAS TIME TO GO HOME!
SCHULZ

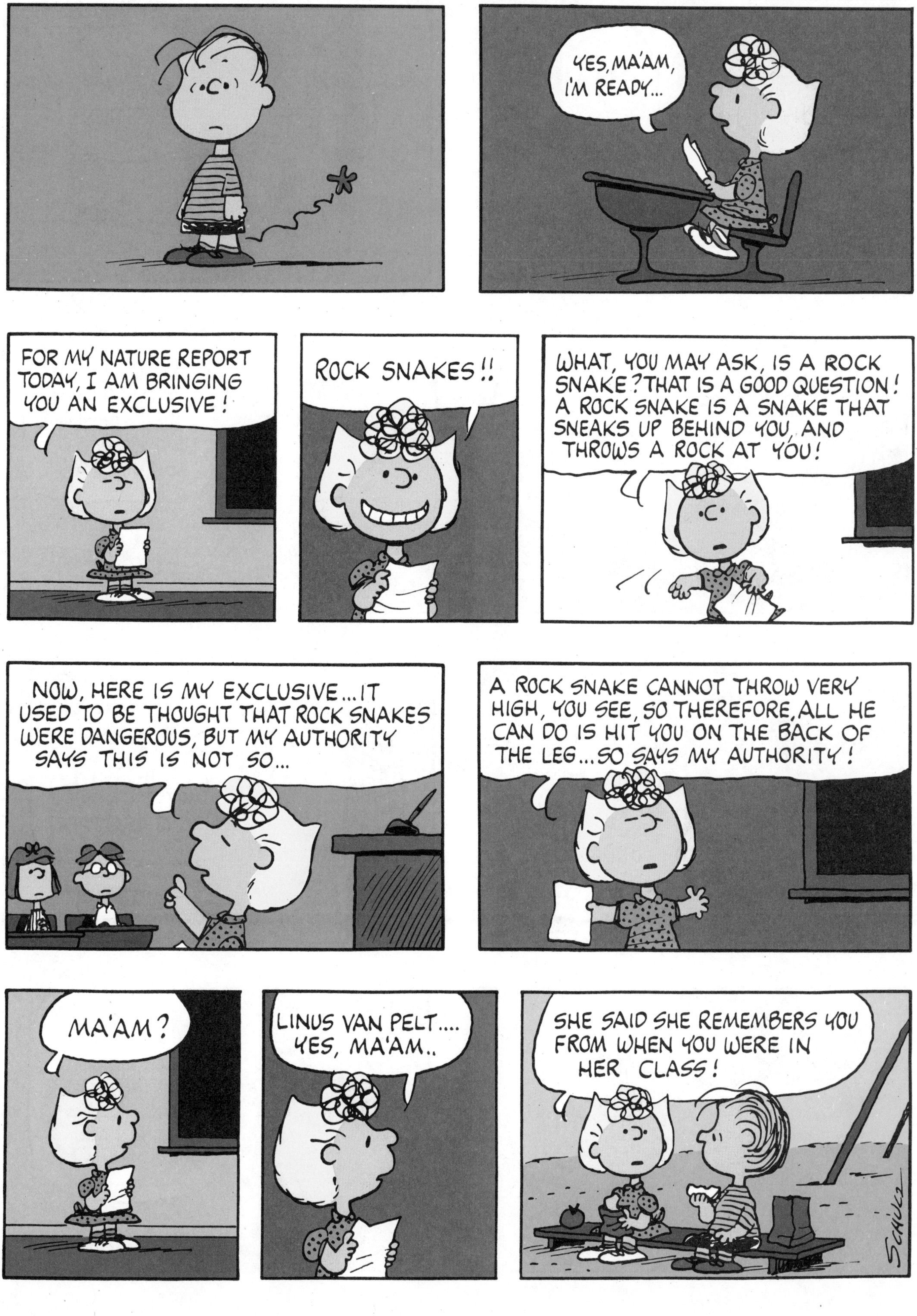
YES, MA'AM, I'M READY...
FOR MY NATURE REPORT TODAY, I AM BRINGING YOU AN EXCLUSIVE!
ROCK SNAKES!!
WHAT, YOU MAY ASK, IS A ROCK SNAKE? THAT IS A GOOD QUESTION! A ROCK SNAKE IS A SNAKE THAT SNEAKS UP BEHIND YOU, AND THROWS A ROCK AT YOU!
NOW, HERE IS MY EXCLUSIVE...IT USED TO BE THOUGHT THAT ROCK SNAKES WERE DANGEROUS, BUT MY AUTHORITY SAYS THIS IS NOT SO...
A ROCK SNAKE CANNOT THROW VERY HIGH, YOU SEE, SO THEREFORE, ALL HE CAN DO IS HIT YOU ON THE BACK OF THE LEG...SO SAYS MY AUTHORITY!
MA'AM?
LINUS VAN PELT.... YES, MA'AM..
SHE SAID SHE REMEMBERS YOU FROM WHEN YOU WERE IN HER CLASS!
SCHULZ

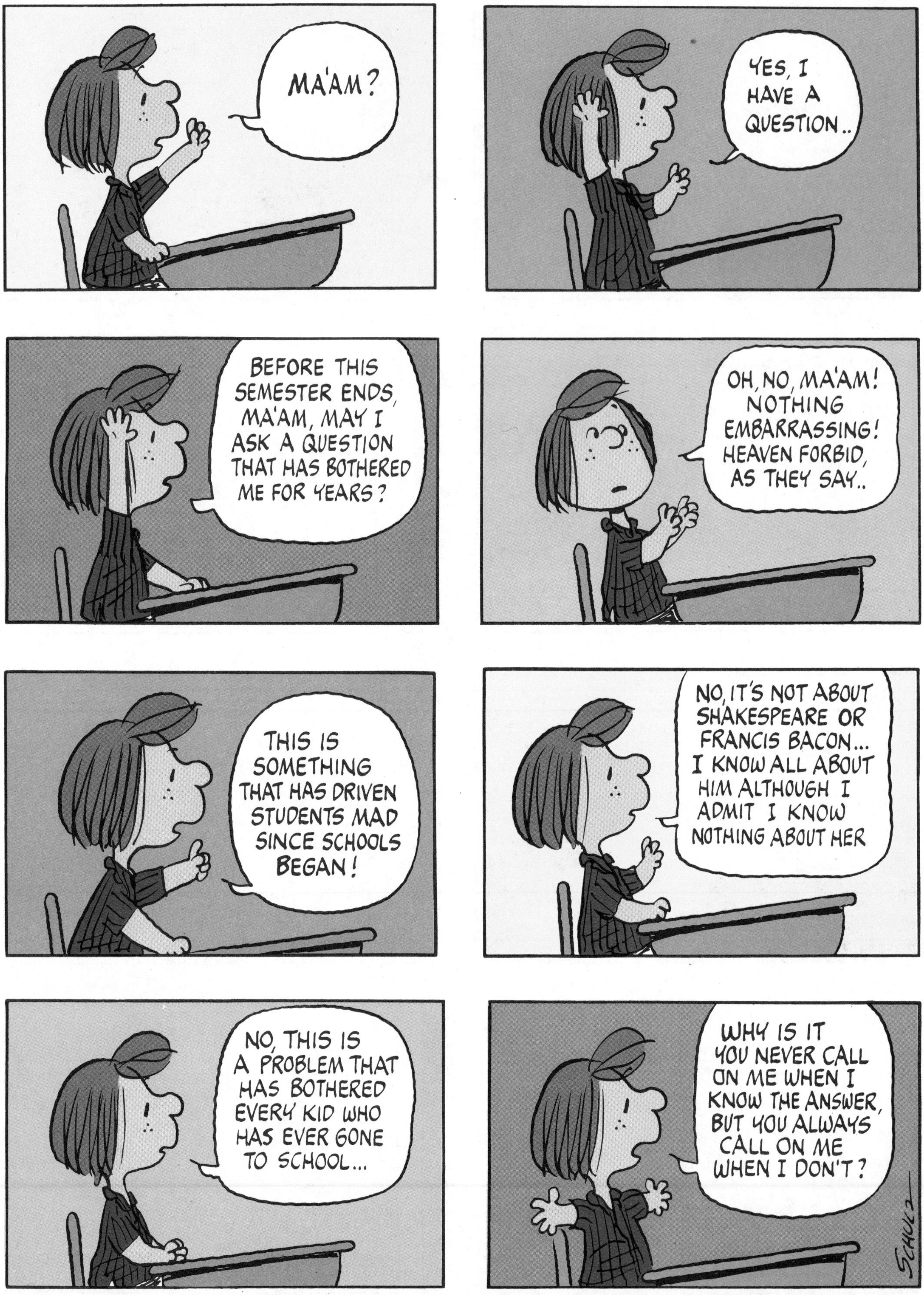
MA'AM?
YES, I HAVE A QUESTION..
BEFORE THIS SEMESTER ENDS, MA'AM, MAY I ASK A QUESTION THAT HAS BOTHERED ME FOR YEARS?
OH, NO, MA'AM! NOTHING EMBARRASSING! HEAVEN FORBID, AS THEY SAY..
THIS IS SOMETHING THAT HAS DRIVEN STUDENTS MAD SINCE SCHOOLS BEGAN!
NO, IT'S NOT ABOUT SHAKESPEARE OR FRANCIS BACON... I KNOW ALL ABOUT HIM ALTHOUGH I ADMIT I KNOW NOTHING ABOUT HER
NO, THIS IS A PROBLEM THAT HAS BOTHERED EVERY KID WHO HAS EVER GONE TO SCHOOL...
WHY IS IT YOU NEVER CALL ON ME WHEN I KNOW THE ANSWER, BUT YOU ALWAYS CALL ON ME WHEN I DON'T?
SCHULZ

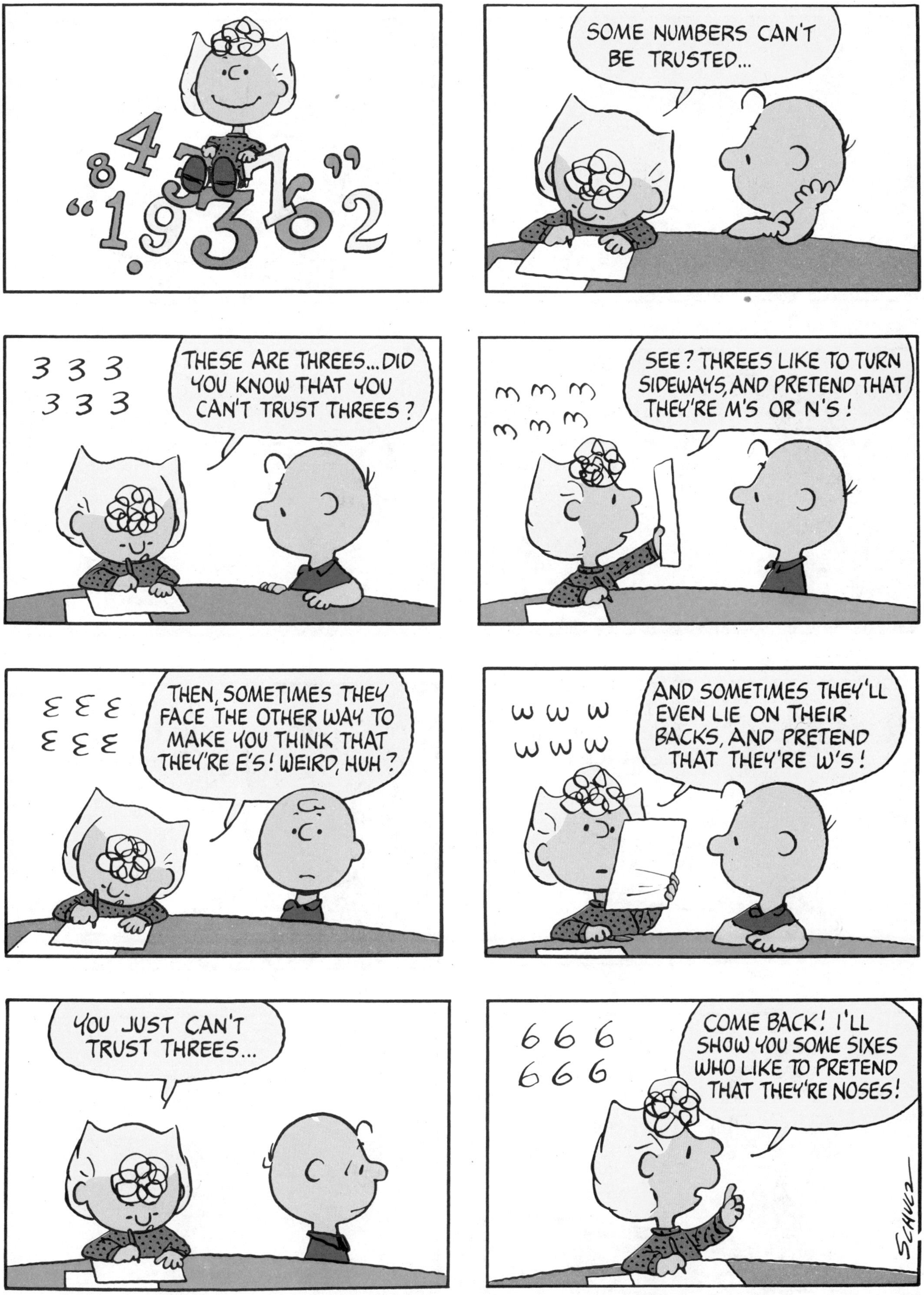

SOME NUMBERS CAN'T BE TRUSTED...
3 3 3
3 3 3
THESE ARE THREES...DID YOU KNOW THAT YOU CAN'T TRUST THREES?
SEE? THREES LIKE TO TURN SIDEWAYS, AND PRETEND THAT THEY'RE M'S OR N'S!
THEN, SOMETIMES THEY FACE THE OTHER WAY TO MAKE YOU THINK THAT THEY'RE E'S! WEIRD, HUH?
AND SOMETIMES THEY'LL EVEN LIE ON THEIR BACKS, AND PRETEND THAT THEY'RE W'S!
YOU JUST CAN'T TRUST THREES...
6 6 6
6 6 6
COME BACK! I'LL SHOW YOU SOME SIXES WHO LIKE TO PRETEND THAT THEY'RE NOSES!
SCHULZ

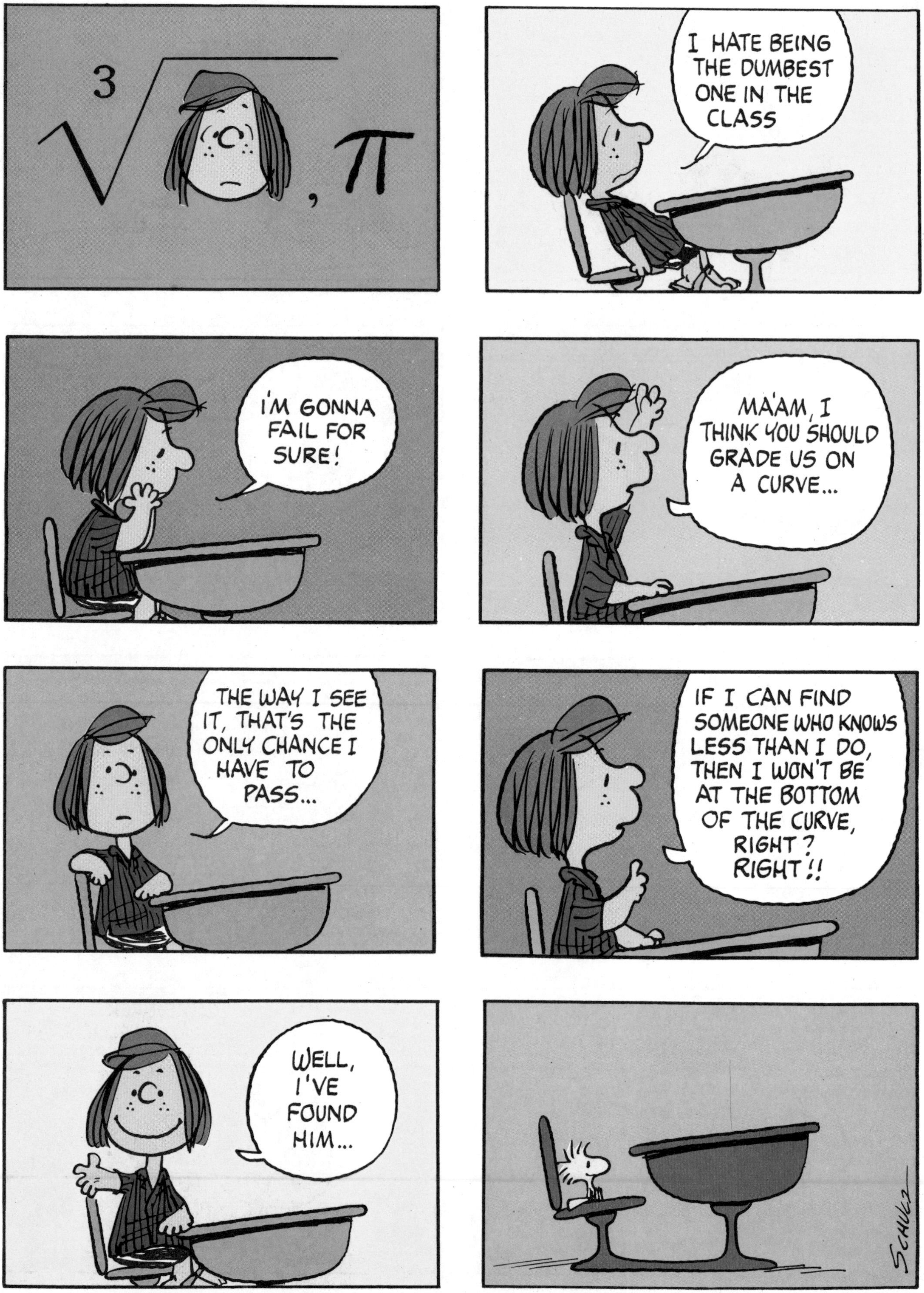
3
π
I HATE BEING THE DUMBEST ONE IN THE CLASS
I'M GONNA FAIL FOR SURE!
MA'AM, I THINK YOU SHOULD GRADE US ON A CURVE...
THE WAY I SEE IT, THAT'S THE ONLY CHANCE I HAVE TO PASS...
IF I CAN FIND SOMEONE WHO KNOWS LESS THAN I DO, THEN I WON'T BE AT THE BOTTOM OF THE CURVE, RIGHT? RIGHT!!
WELL, I'VE FOUND HIM...
SCHULZ

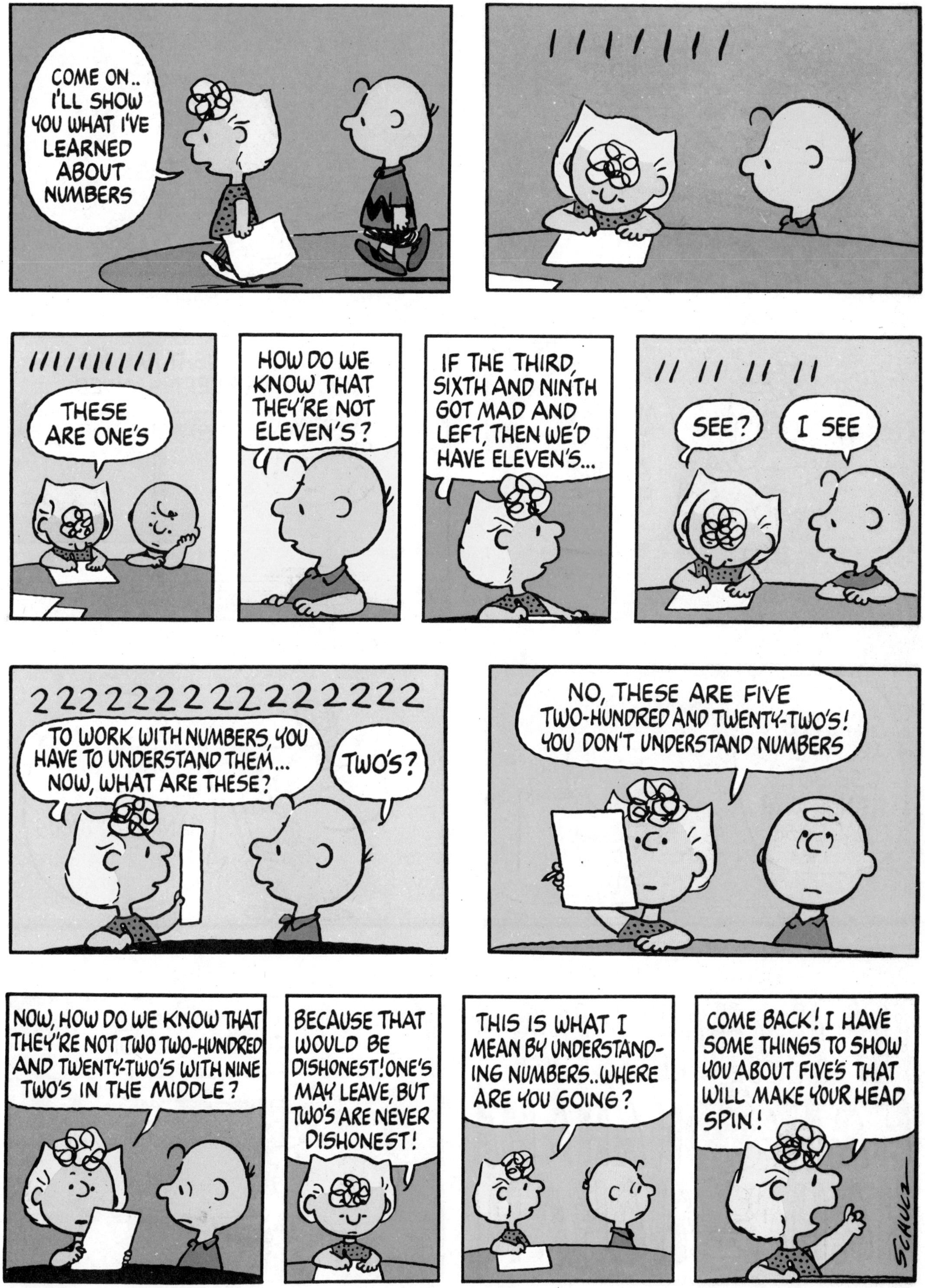
COME ON.. I'LL SHOW YOU WHAT I'VE LEARNED ABOUT NUMBERS
IIIIIII
IIIIIIIIIII
THESE ARE ONE'S
HOW DO WE KNOW THAT THEY'RE NOT ELEVEN'S?
IF THE THIRD, SIXTH AND NINTH GOT MAD AND LEFT, THEN WE'D HAVE ELEVEN'S...
II II II II
SEE?
I SEE
2222222222222222
TO WORK WITH NUMBERS, YOU HAVE TO UNDERSTAND THEM... NOW, WHAT ARE THESE?
TWO'S?
NO, THESE ARE FIVE TWO-HUNDRED AND TWENTY-TWO'S! YOU DON'T UNDERSTAND NUMBERS
NOW, HOW DO WE KNOW THAT THEY'RE NOT TWO TWO-HUNDRED AND TWENTY-TWO'S WITH NINE TWO'S IN THE MIDDLE?
BECAUSE THAT WOULD BE DISHONEST! ONE'S MAY LEAVE, BUT TWO'S ARE NEVER DISHONEST!
THIS IS WHAT I MEAN BY UNDERSTANDING NUMBERS.. WHERE ARE YOU GOING?
COME BACK! I HAVE SOME THINGS TO SHOW YOU ABOUT FIVE'S THAT WILL MAKE YOUR HEAD SPIN!
SCHULZ

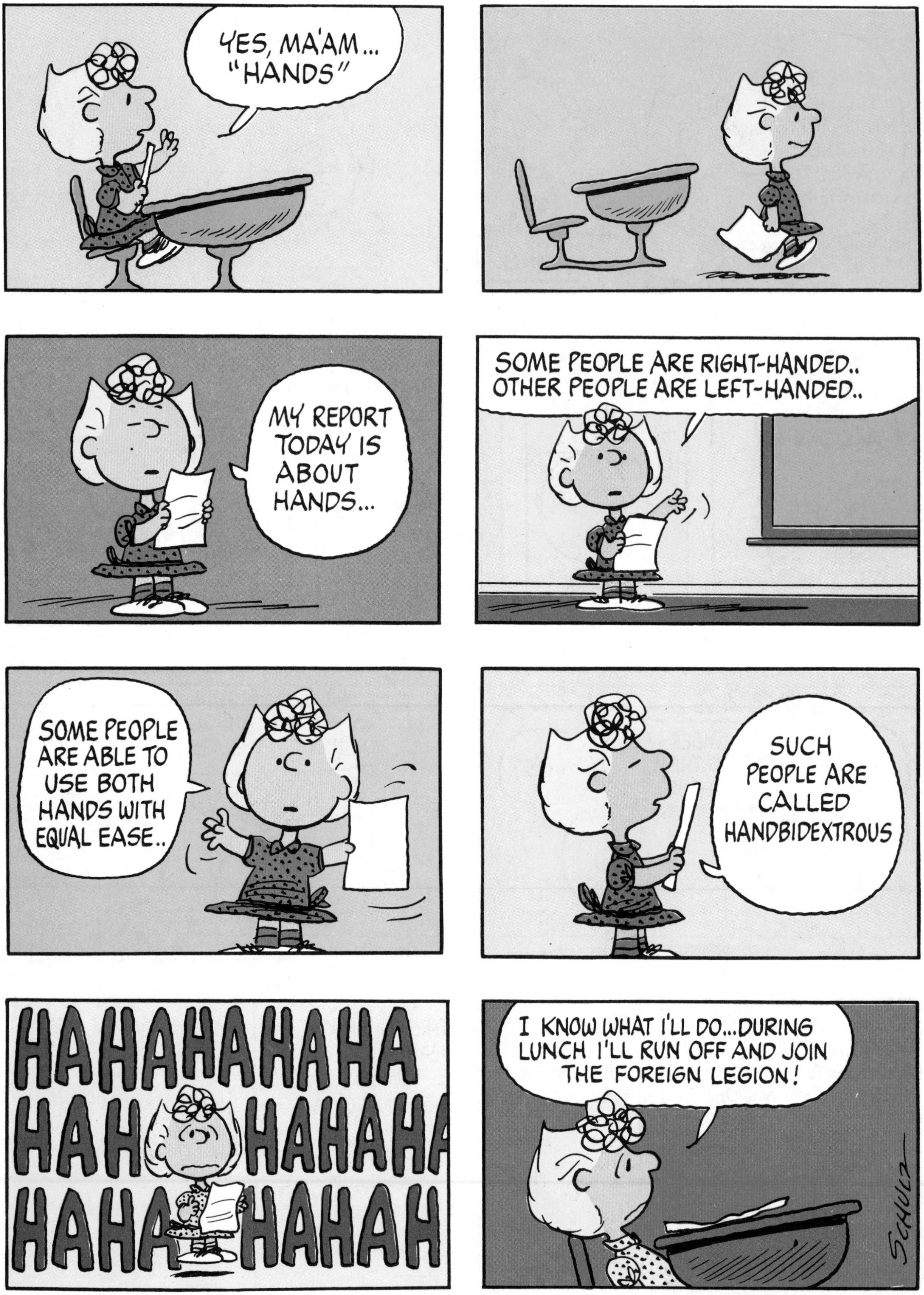
YES, MA'AM... "HANDS"
MY REPORT TODAY IS ABOUT HANDS...
SOME PEOPLE ARE RIGHT-HANDED.. OTHER PEOPLE ARE LEFT-HANDED..
SOME PEOPLE ARE ABLE TO USE BOTH HANDS WITH EQUAL EASE..
SUCH PEOPLE ARE CALLED HANDBIDEXTROUS
HAHAHAHAHA HAH HAHAHAH HAHA HAHAH
I KNOW WHAT I'LL DO...DURING LUNCH I'LL RUN OFF AND JOIN THE FOREIGN LEGION!
SCHULZ

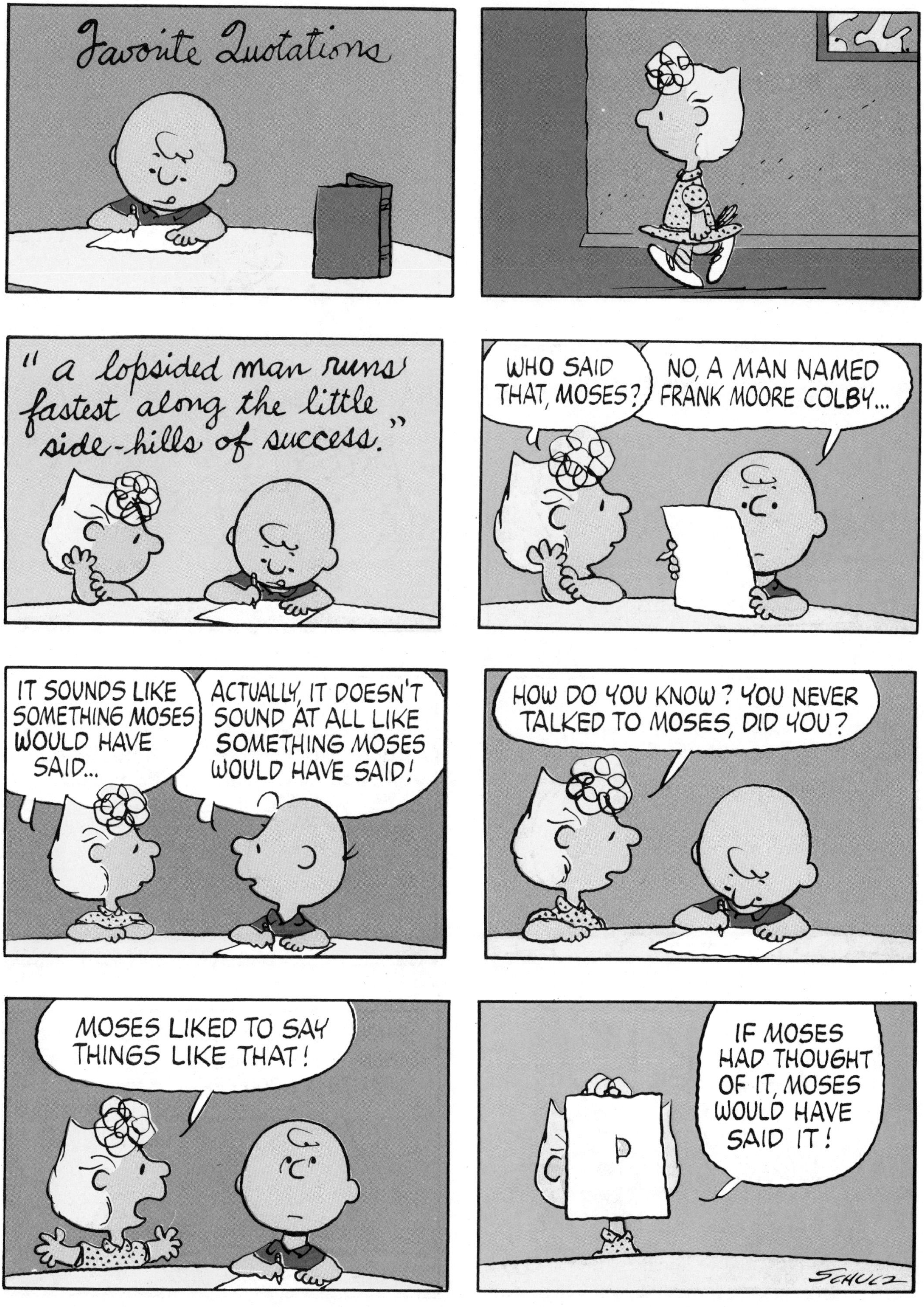
Favorite Quotations
"a lopsided man runs fastest along the little side-hills of success."
WHO SAID THAT, MOSES?
NO, A MAN NAMED FRANK MOORE COLBY...
IT SOUNDS LIKE SOMETHING MOSES WOULD HAVE SAID...
ACTUALLY, IT DOESN'T SOUND AT ALL LIKE SOMETHING MOSES WOULD HAVE SAID!
HOW DO YOU KNOW? YOU NEVER TALKED TO MOSES, DID YOU?
MOSES LIKED TO SAY THINGS LIKE THAT!
IF MOSES HAD THOUGHT OF IT, MOSES WOULD HAVE SAID IT!
SCHULZ

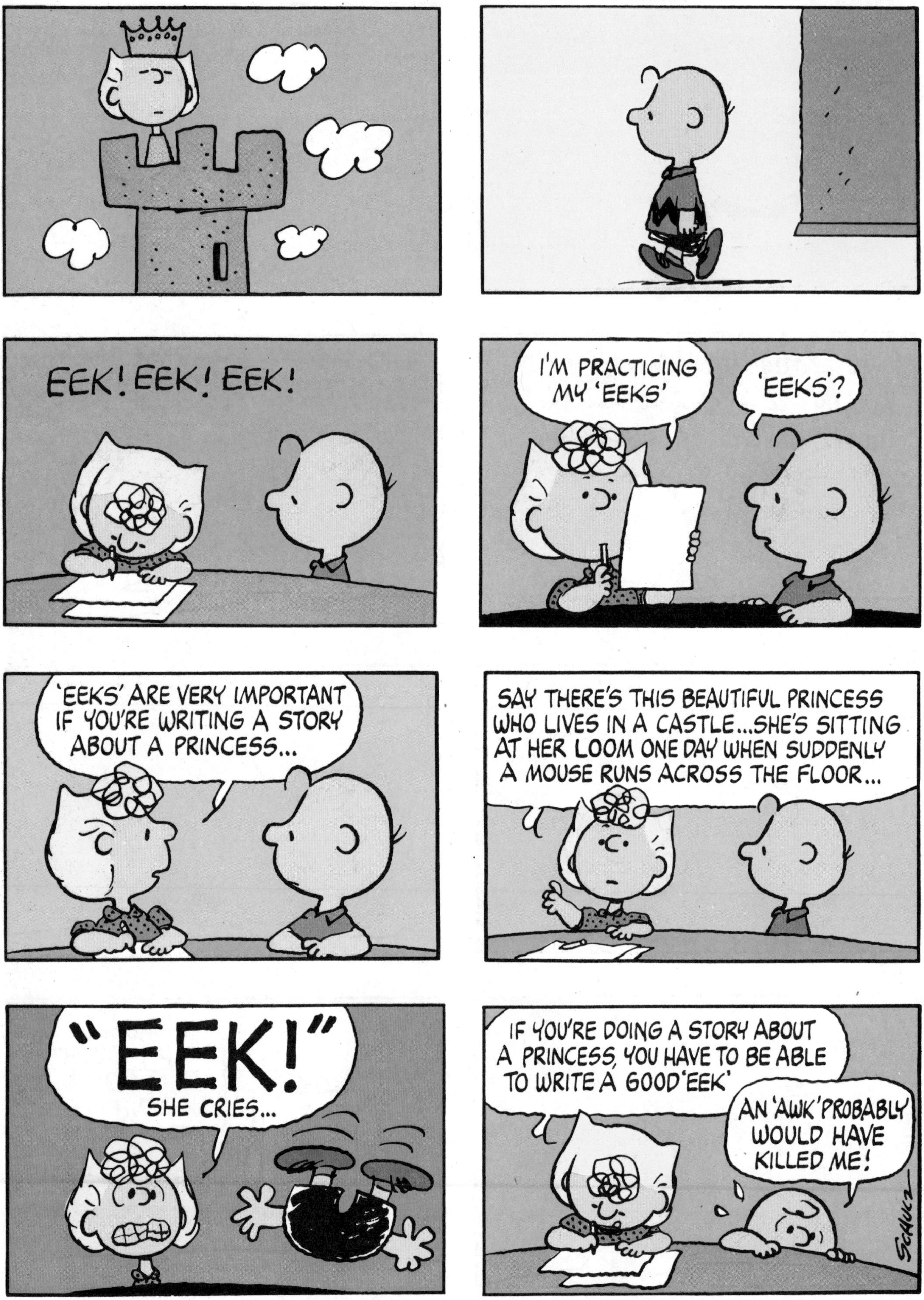
EEK! EEK! EEK!
I'M PRACTICING MY 'EEKS'
'EEKS'?
'EEKS' ARE VERY IMPORTANT IF YOU'RE WRITING A STORY ABOUT A PRINCESS...
SAY THERE'S THIS BEAUTIFUL PRINCESS WHO LIVES IN A CASTLE...SHE'S SITTING AT HER LOOM ONE DAY WHEN SUDDENLY A MOUSE RUNS ACROSS THE FLOOR...
"EEK!" SHE CRIES...
IF YOU'RE DOING A STORY ABOUT A PRINCESS, YOU HAVE TO BE ABLE TO WRITE A GOOD 'EEK'
AN 'AWK' PROBABLY WOULD HAVE KILLED ME!
SCHULZ

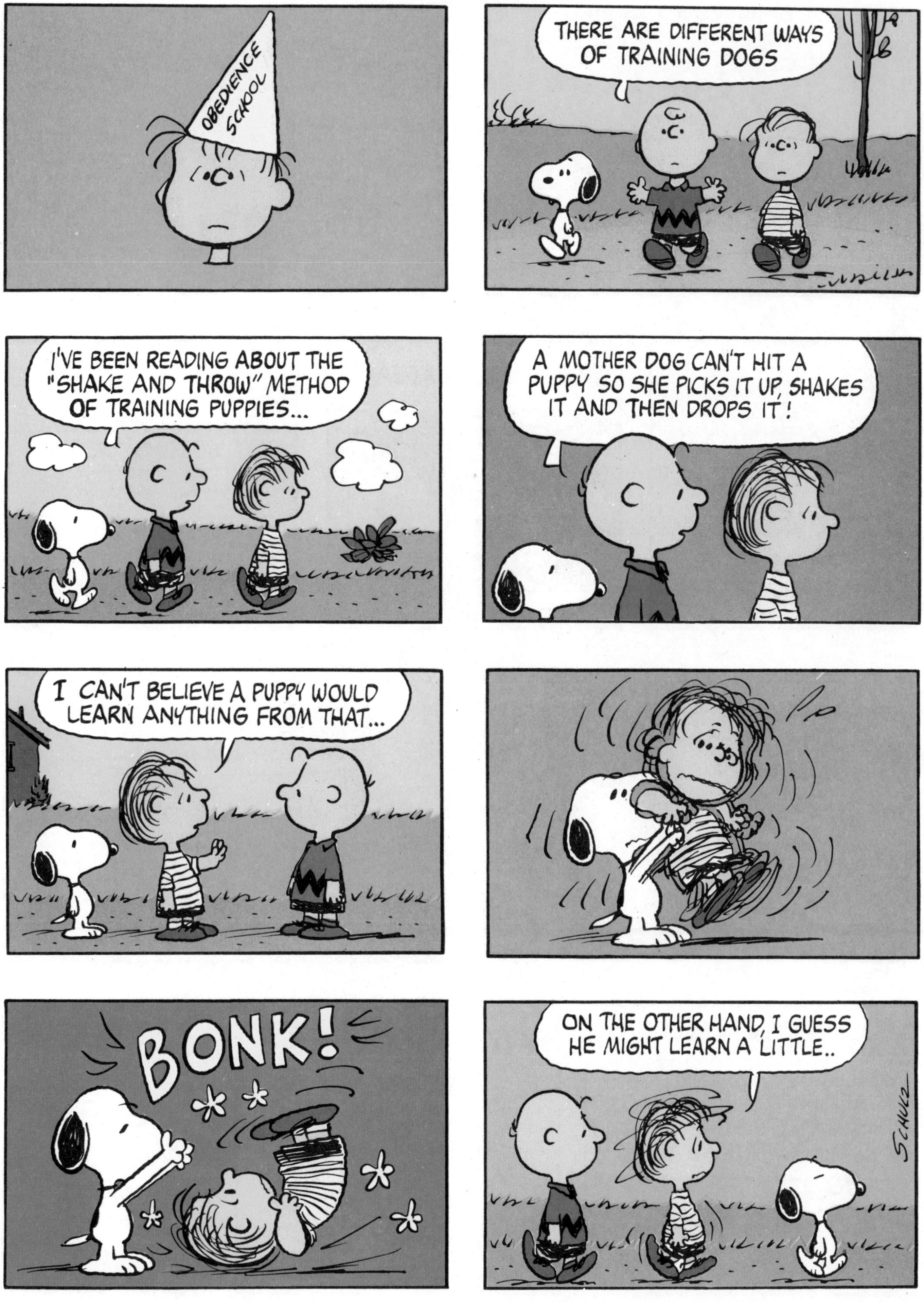
OBEDIENCE SCHOOL
THERE ARE DIFFERENT WAYS OF TRAINING DOGS
I'VE BEEN READING ABOUT THE "SHAKE AND THROW" METHOD OF TRAINING PUPPIES...
A MOTHER DOG CAN'T HIT A PUPPY SO SHE PICKS IT UP, SHAKES IT AND THEN DROPS IT!
I CAN'T BELIEVE A PUPPY WOULD LEARN ANYTHING FROM THAT...
BONK!
ON THE OTHER HAND, I GUESS HE MIGHT LEARN A LITTLE..
SCHULZ

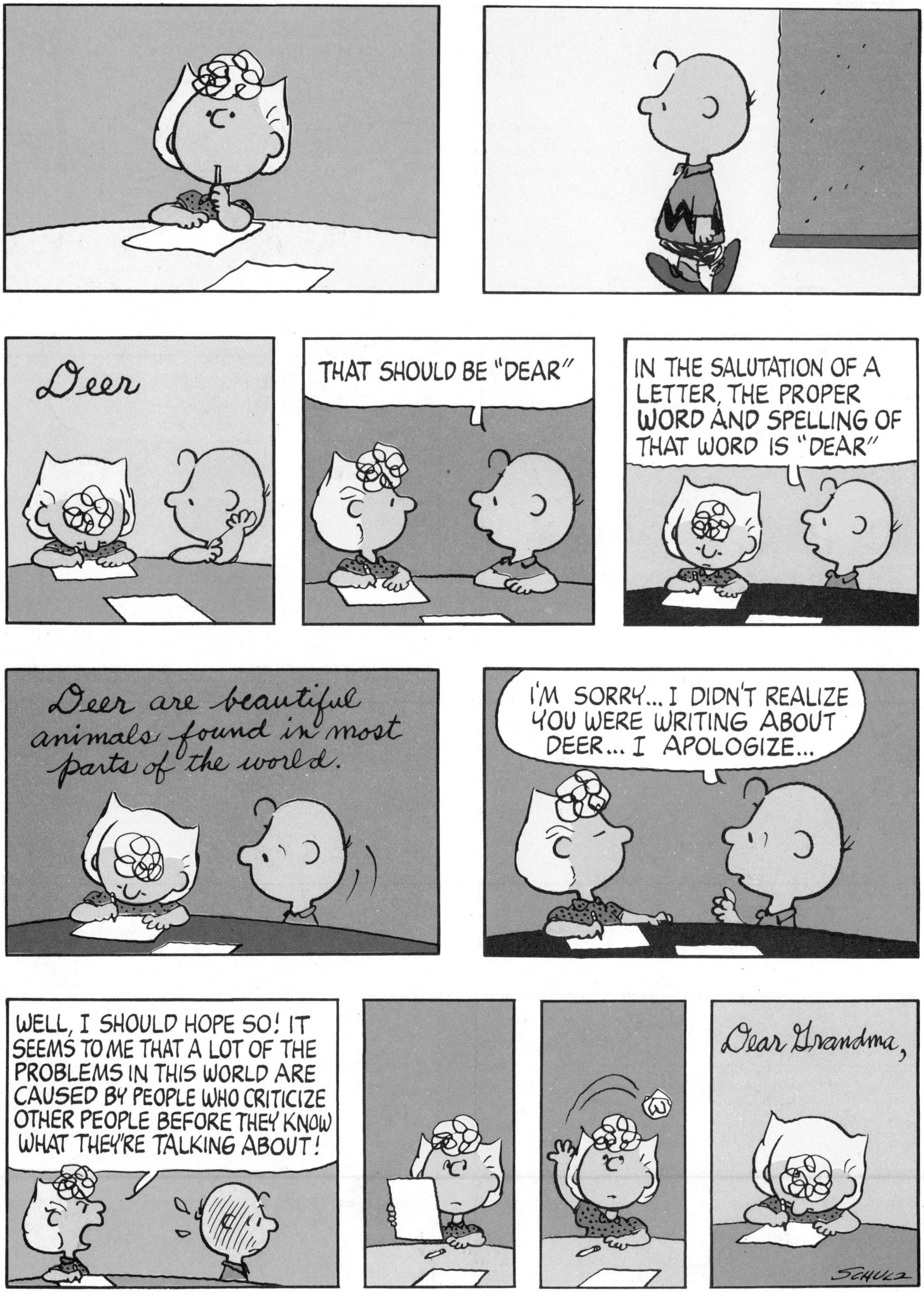

Deer
THAT SHOULD BE "DEAR"
IN THE SALUTATION OF A LETTER, THE PROPER WORD AND SPELLING OF THAT WORD IS "DEAR"
Deer are beautiful animals found in most parts of the world.
I'M SORRY... I DIDN'T REALIZE YOU WERE WRITING ABOUT DEER... I APOLOGIZE...
WELL, I SHOULD HOPE SO! IT SEEMS TO ME THAT A LOT OF THE PROBLEMS IN THIS WORLD ARE CAUSED BY PEOPLE WHO CRITICIZE OTHER PEOPLE BEFORE THEY KNOW WHAT THEY'RE TALKING ABOUT!
Dear Grandma,
SCHULZ

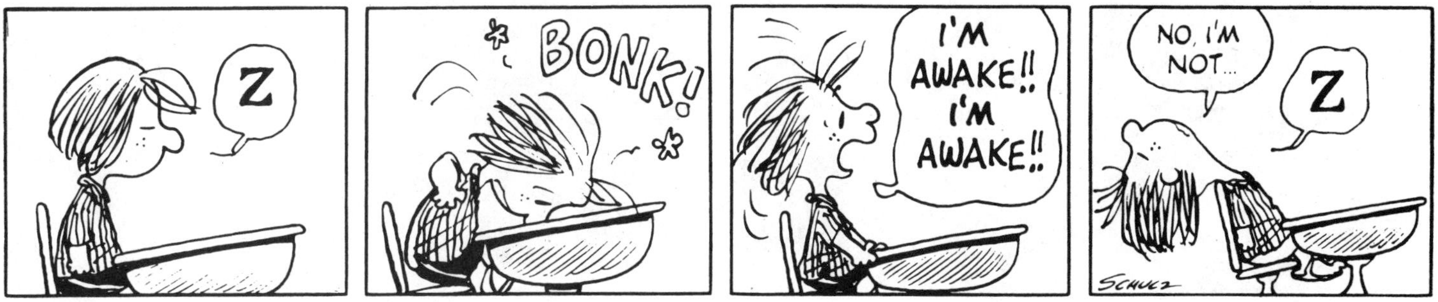
Z
BONK!
I'M AWAKE!! I'M AWAKE!!
NO, I'M NOT...
Z
SCHULZ

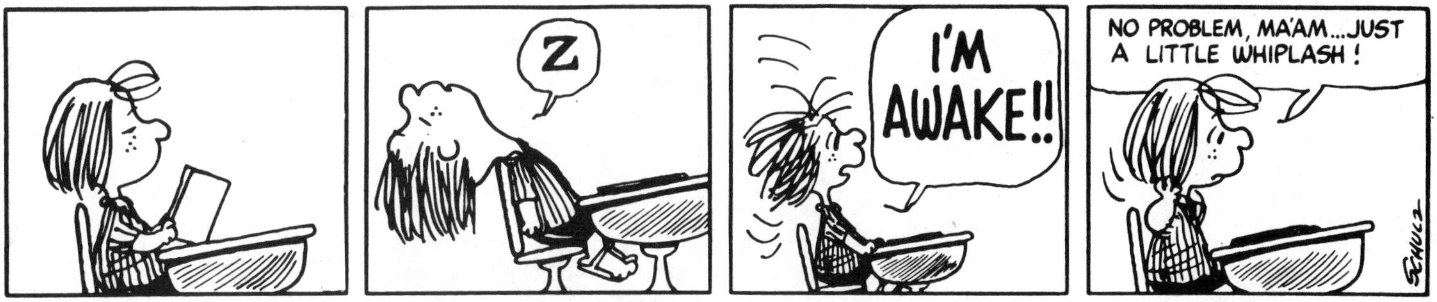
Z
I'M AWAKE!!
NO PROBLEM, MA'AM...JUST A LITTLE WHIPLASH!
SCHULZ

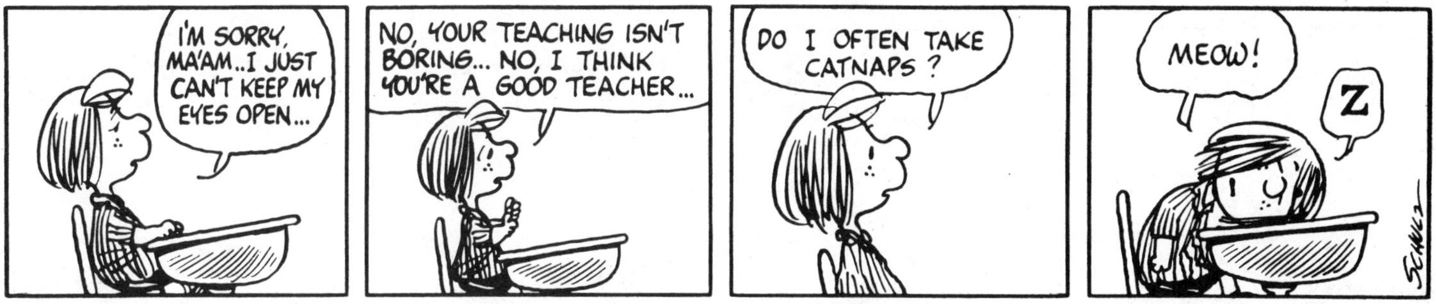
I'M SORRY, MA'AM..I JUST CAN'T KEEP MY EYES OPEN...
NO, YOUR TEACHING ISN'T BORING... NO, I THINK YOU'RE A GOOD TEACHER...
DO I OFTEN TAKE CATNAPS ?
MEOW!
Z
SCHULZ

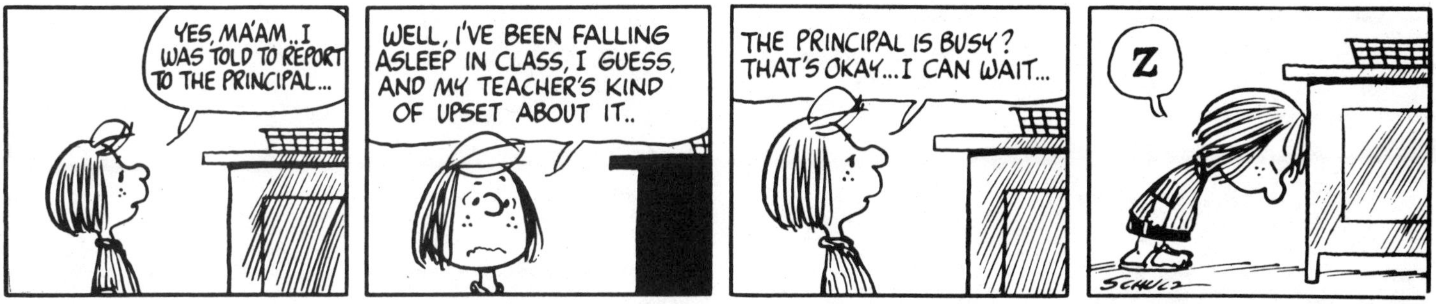
YES, MA'AM..I WAS TOLD TO REPORT TO THE PRINCIPAL...
WELL, I'VE BEEN FALLING ASLEEP IN CLASS, I GUESS, AND MY TEACHER'S KIND OF UPSET ABOUT IT..
THE PRINCIPAL IS BUSY? THAT'S OKAY...I CAN WAIT...
Z
SCHULZ

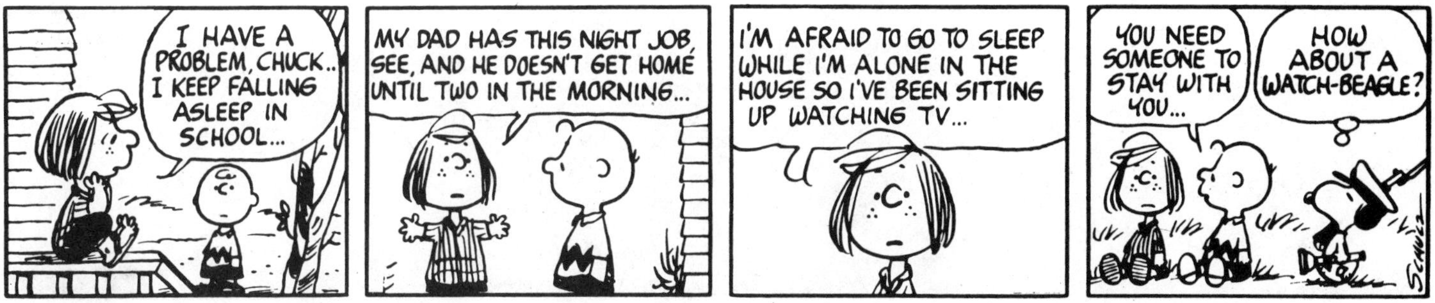
I HAVE A PROBLEM, CHUCK.. I KEEP FALLING ASLEEP IN SCHOOL...
MY DAD HAS THIS NIGHT JOB, SEE, AND HE DOESN'T GET HOME UNTIL TWO IN THE MORNING...
I'M AFRAID TO GO TO SLEEP WHILE I'M ALONE IN THE HOUSE SO I'VE BEEN SITTING UP WATCHING TV...
YOU NEED SOMEONE TO STAY WITH YOU...
HOW ABOUT A WATCH-BEAGLE?
SCHULZ

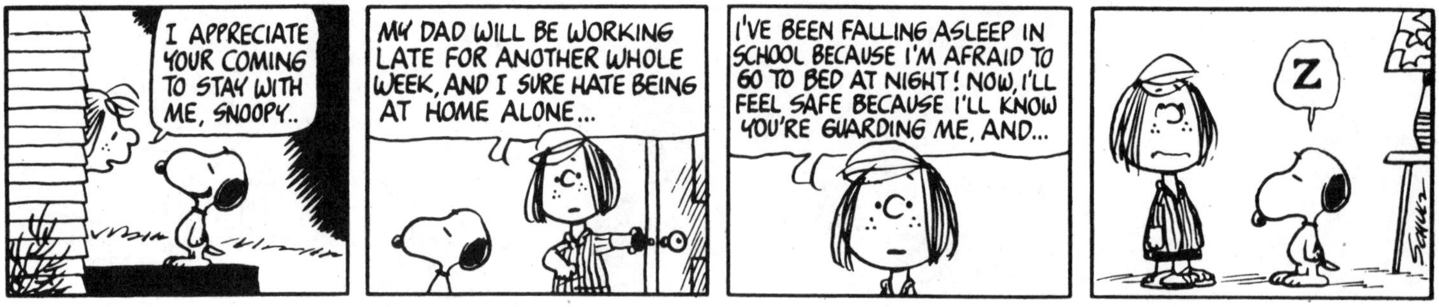
I APPRECIATE YOUR COMING TO STAY WITH ME, SNOOPY..
MY DAD WILL BE WORKING LATE FOR ANOTHER WHOLE WEEK, AND I SURE HATE BEING AT HOME ALONE...
I'VE BEEN FALLING ASLEEP IN SCHOOL BECAUSE I'M AFRAID TO GO TO BED AT NIGHT! NOW, I'LL FEEL SAFE BECAUSE I'LL KNOW YOU'RE GUARDING ME, AND...
Z
SCHULZ

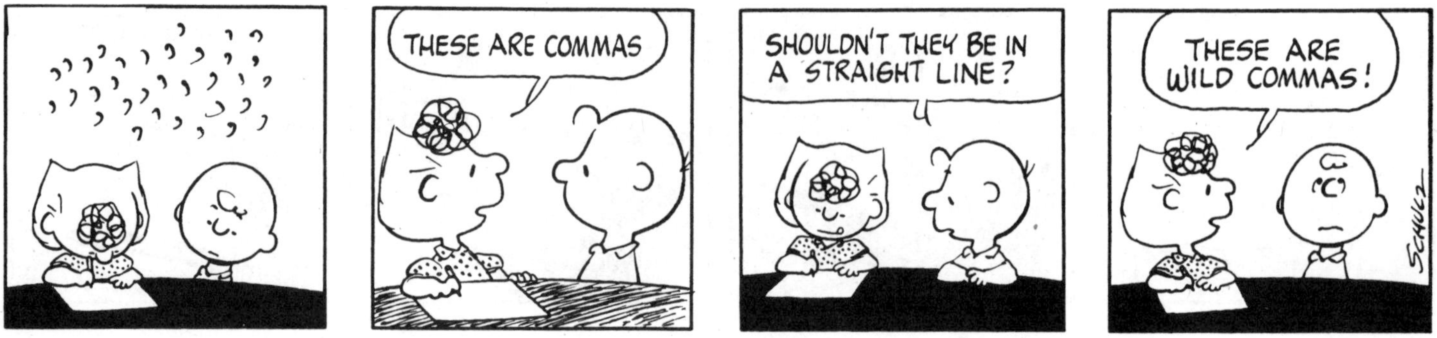
THESE ARE COMMAS
SHOULDN'T THEY BE IN A STRAIGHT LINE?
THESE ARE WILD COMMAS!
SCHULZ

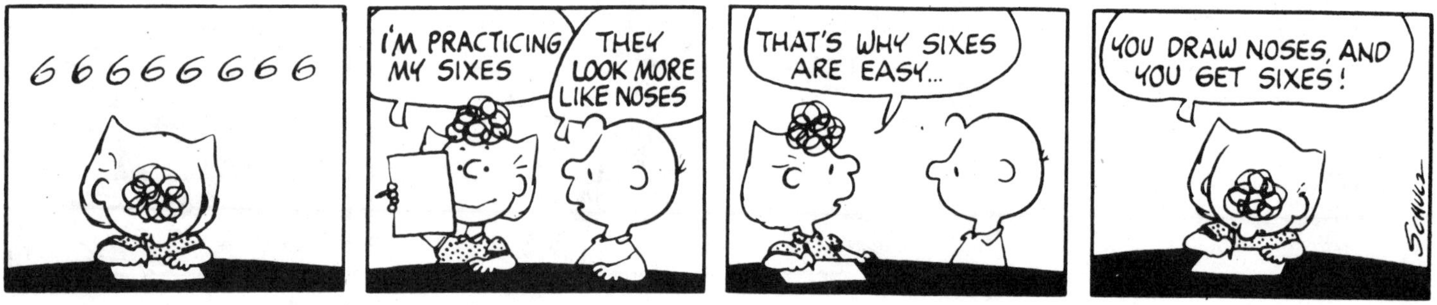
6 6 6 6 6 6 6 6
I'M PRACTICING MY SIXES
THEY LOOK MORE LIKE NOSES
THAT'S WHY SIXES ARE EASY...
YOU DRAW NOSES, AND YOU GET SIXES!
SCHULZ

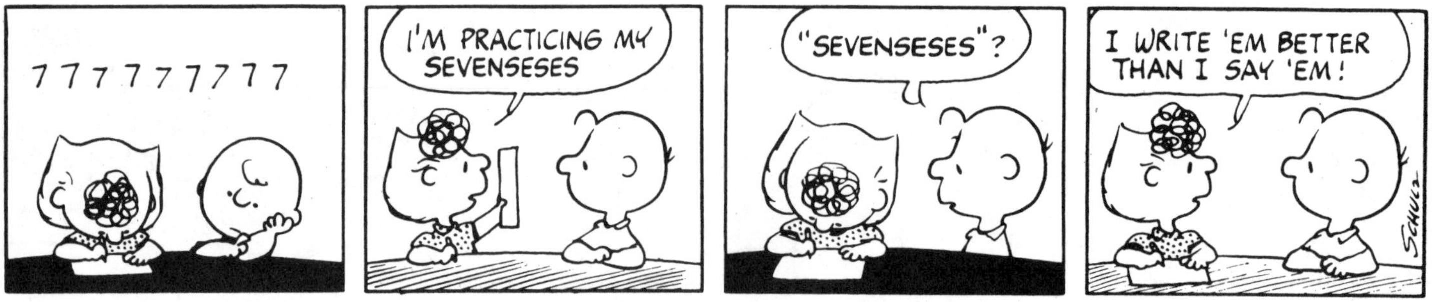
7 7 7 7 7 7 7 7 7
I'M PRACTICING MY SEVENSESES
"SEVENSESES"?
I WRITE 'EM BETTER THAN I SAY 'EM!
SCHULZ

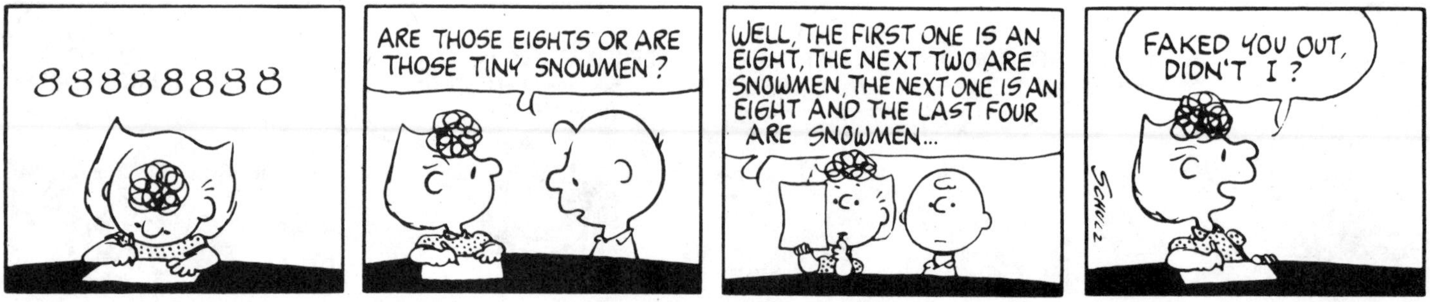
8 8 8 8 8 8 8 8
ARE THOSE EIGHTS OR ARE THOSE TINY SNOWMEN?
WELL, THE FIRST ONE IS AN EIGHT, THE NEXT TWO ARE SNOWMEN, THE NEXT ONE IS AN EIGHT AND THE LAST FOUR ARE SNOWMEN...
FAKED YOU OUT, DIDN'T I?
SCHULZ

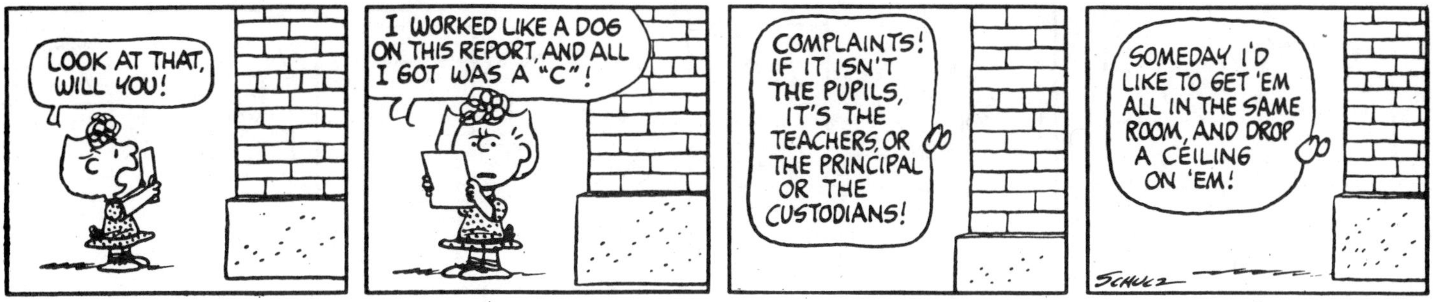
LOOK AT THAT, WILL YOU!
I WORKED LIKE A DOG ON THIS REPORT, AND ALL I GOT WAS A "C"!
COMPLAINTS! IF IT ISN'T THE PUPILS, IT'S THE TEACHERS, OR THE PRINCIPAL OR THE CUSTODIANS!
SOMEDAY I'D LIKE TO GET 'EM ALL IN THE SAME ROOM, AND DROP A CEILING ON 'EM!
SCHULZ

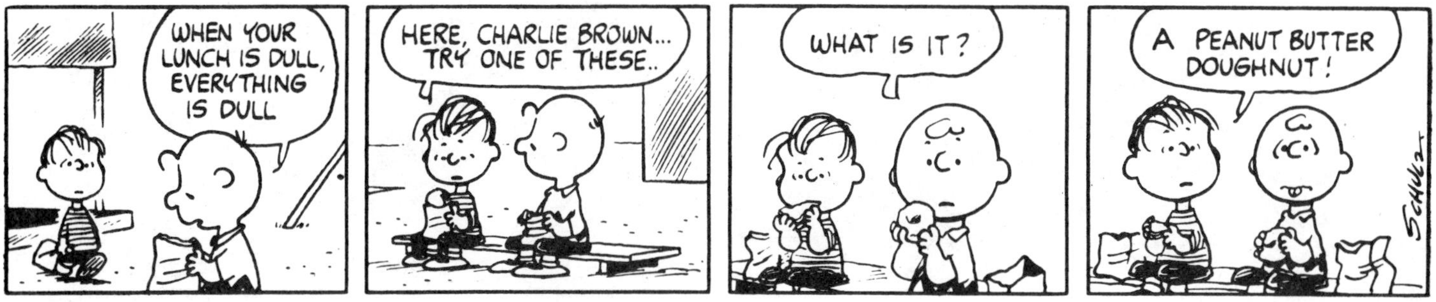
WHEN YOUR LUNCH IS DULL, EVERYTHING IS DULL
HERE, CHARLIE BROWN... TRY ONE OF THESE..
WHAT IS IT?
A PEANUT BUTTER DOUGHNUT!
SCHULZ

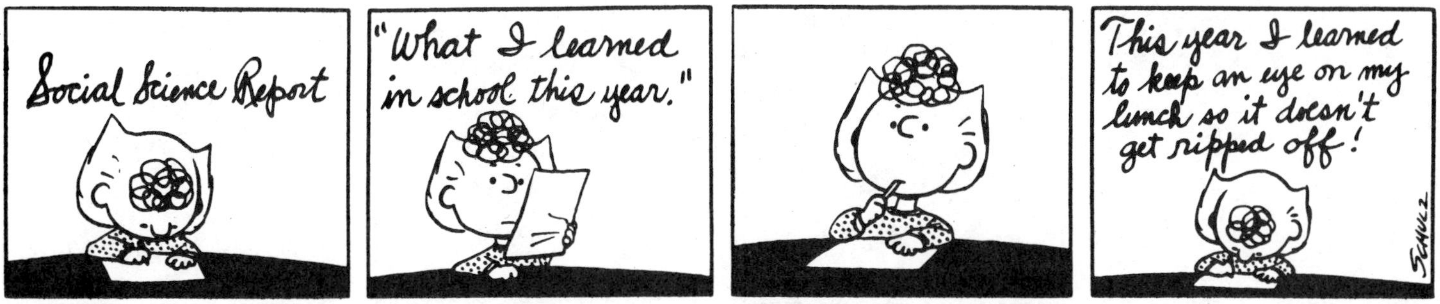
Social Science Report
"What I learned in school this year."
This year I learned to keep an eye on my lunch so it doesn't get ripped off!
SCHULZ

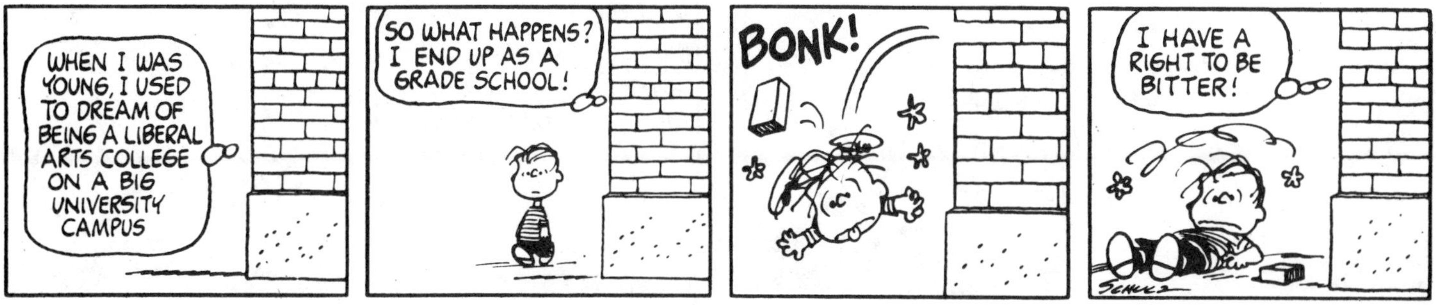
WHEN I WAS YOUNG, I USED TO DREAM OF BEING A LIBERAL ARTS COLLEGE ON A BIG UNIVERSITY CAMPUS
SO WHAT HAPPENS? I END UP AS A GRADE SCHOOL!
BONK!
I HAVE A RIGHT TO BE BITTER!
SCHULZ

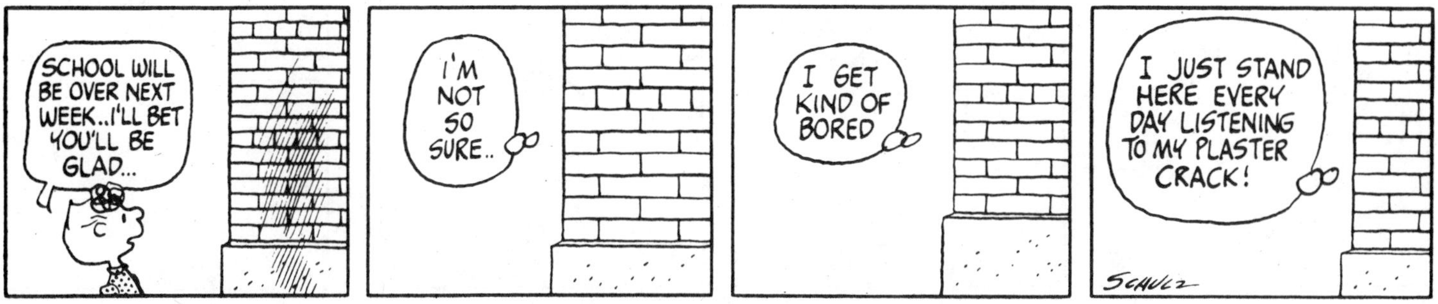
SCHOOL WILL BE OVER NEXT WEEK..I'LL BET YOU'LL BE GLAD...
I'M NOT SO SURE..
I GET KIND OF BORED
I JUST STAND HERE EVERY DAY LISTENING TO MY PLASTER CRACK!
SCHULZ

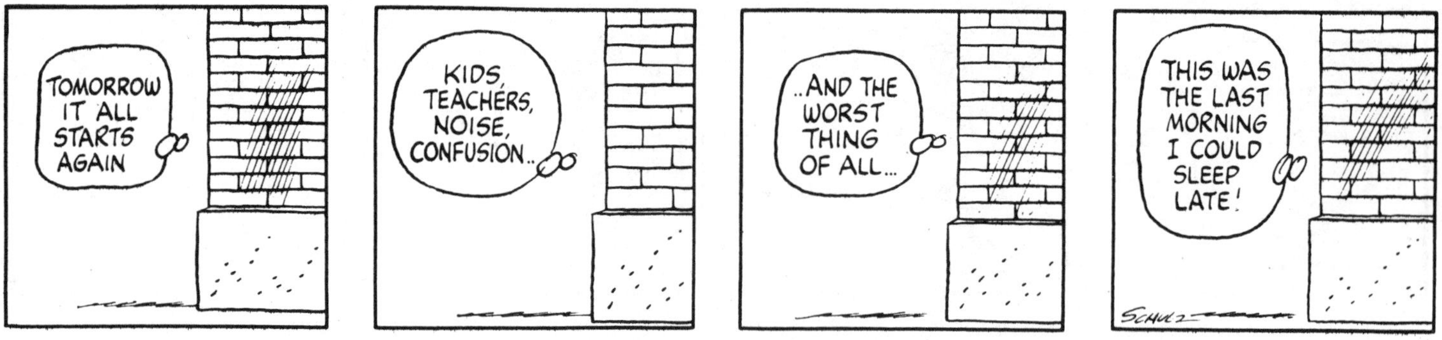
TOMORROW IT ALL STARTS AGAIN
KIDS, TEACHERS, NOISE, CONFUSION..
..AND THE WORST THING OF ALL...
THIS WAS THE LAST MORNING I COULD SLEEP LATE!
SCHULZ

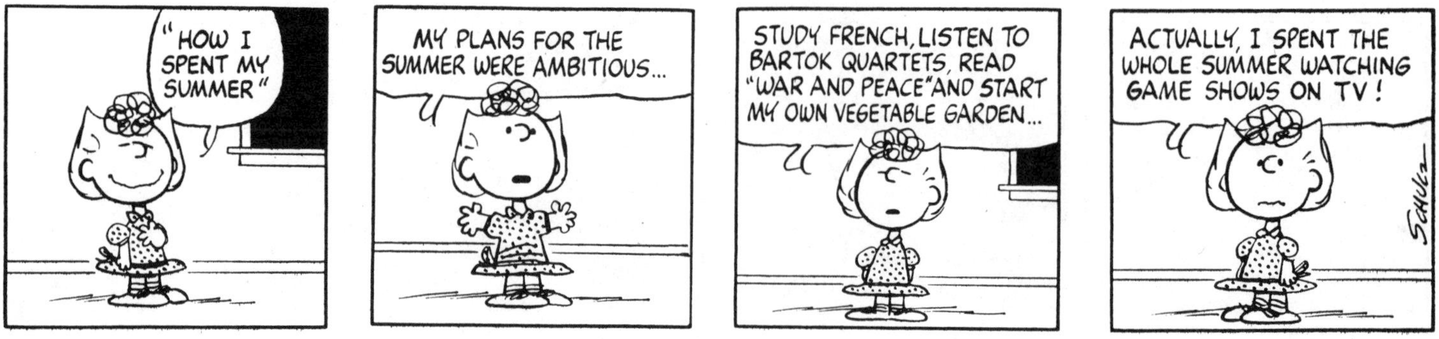
"HOW I SPENT MY SUMMER"
MY PLANS FOR THE SUMMER WERE AMBITIOUS...
STUDY FRENCH, LISTEN TO BARTOK QUARTETS, READ "WAR AND PEACE" AND START MY OWN VEGETABLE GARDEN...
ACTUALLY, I SPENT THE WHOLE SUMMER WATCHING GAME SHOWS ON TV!
SCHULZ

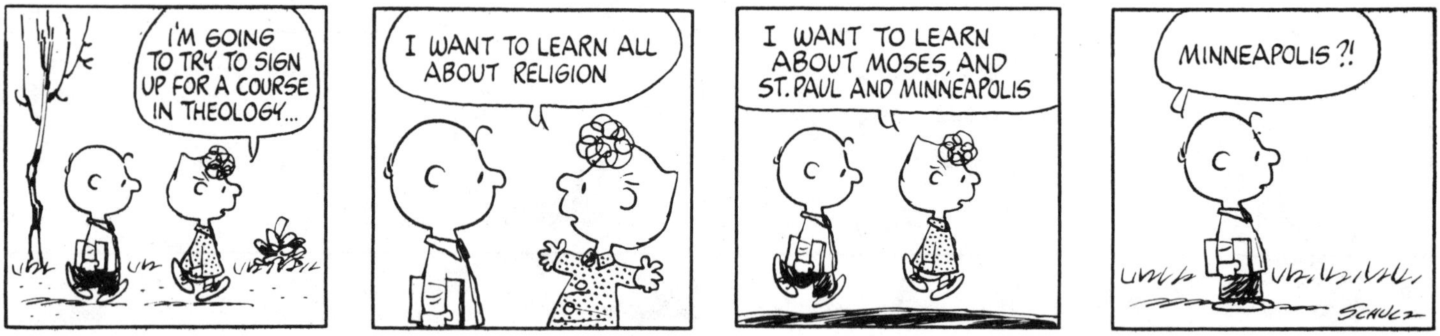
I'M GOING TO TRY TO SIGN UP FOR A COURSE IN THEOLOGY...
I WANT TO LEARN ALL ABOUT RELIGION
I WANT TO LEARN ABOUT MOSES, AND ST. PAUL AND MINNEAPOLIS
MINNEAPOLIS?!
SCHULZ

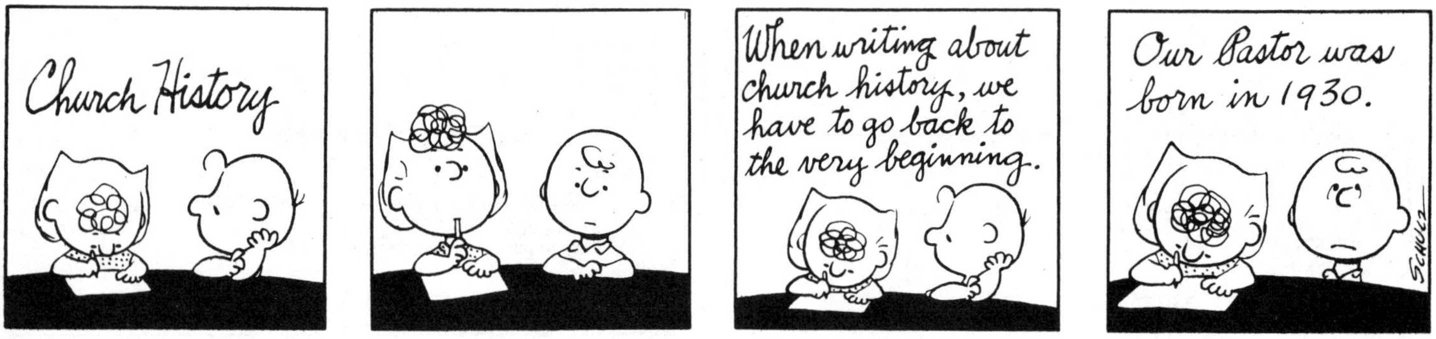
Church History
When writing about church history, we have to go back to the very beginning.
Our Pastor was born in 1930.
SCHULZ

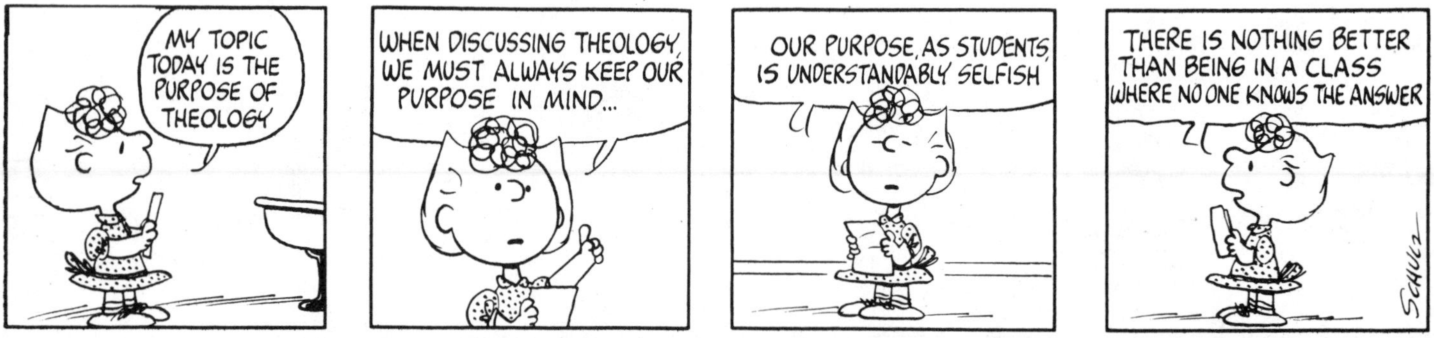
MY TOPIC TODAY IS THE PURPOSE OF THEOLOGY
WHEN DISCUSSING THEOLOGY, WE MUST ALWAYS KEEP OUR PURPOSE IN MIND...
OUR PURPOSE, AS STUDENTS, IS UNDERSTANDABLY SELFISH
THERE IS NOTHING BETTER THAN BEING IN A CLASS WHERE NO ONE KNOWS THE ANSWER
SCHULZ

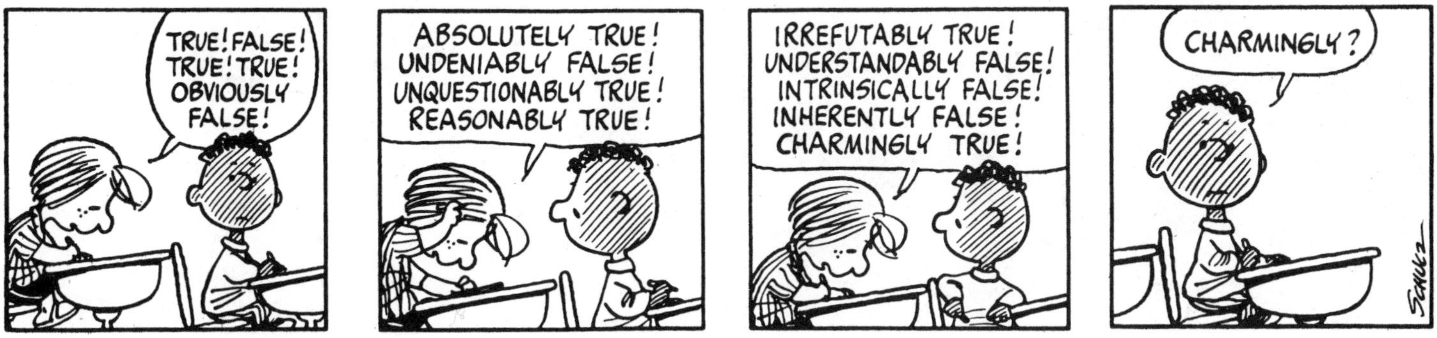
TRUE! FALSE! TRUE! TRUE! OBVIOUSLY FALSE!
ABSOLUTELY TRUE! UNDENIABLY FALSE! UNQUESTIONABLY TRUE! REASONABLY TRUE!
IRREFUTABLY TRUE! UNDERSTANDABLY FALSE! INTRINSICALLY FALSE! INHERENTLY FALSE! CHARMINGLY TRUE!
CHARMINGLY?
SCHULZ

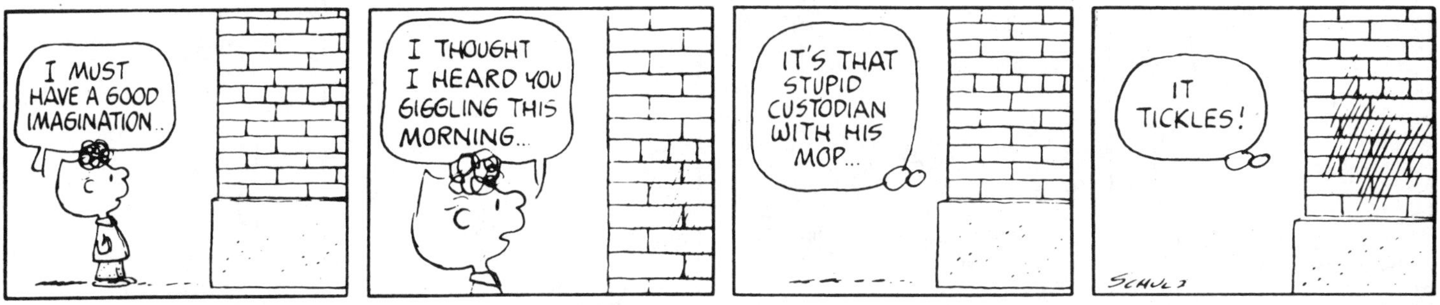
I MUST HAVE A GOOD IMAGINATION..
I THOUGHT I HEARD YOU GIGGLING THIS MORNING...
IT'S THAT STUPID CUSTODIAN WITH HIS MOP...
IT TICKLES!
SCHULZ

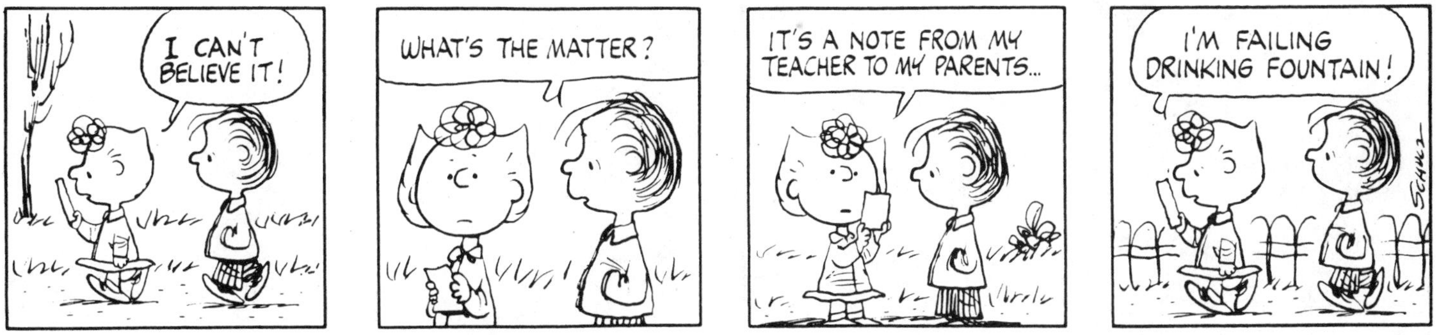
I CAN'T BELIEVE IT!
WHAT'S THE MATTER?
IT'S A NOTE FROM MY TEACHER TO MY PARENTS...
I'M FAILING DRINKING FOUNTAIN!
SCHULZ

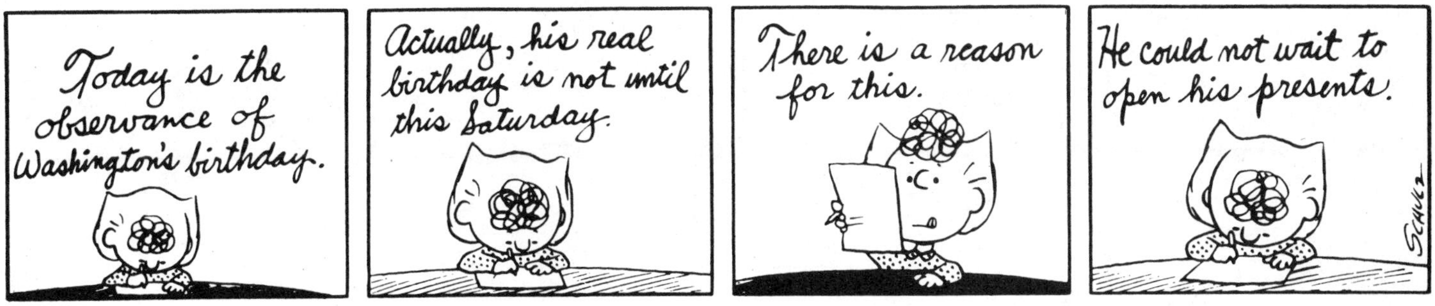
Today is the observance of Washington's birthday.
Actually, his real birthday is not until this Saturday.
There is a reason for this.
He could not wait to open his presents.
SCHULZ

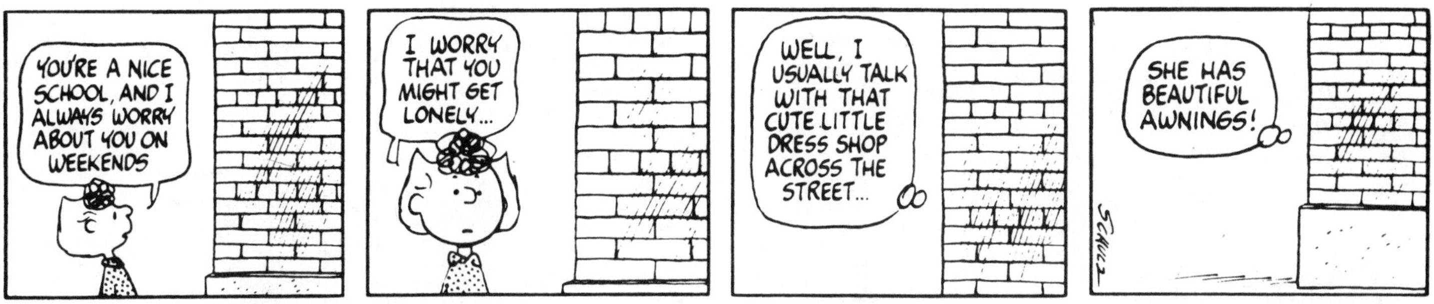
YOU'RE A NICE SCHOOL, AND I ALWAYS WORRY ABOUT YOU ON WEEKENDS
I WORRY THAT YOU MIGHT GET LONELY...
WELL, I USUALLY TALK WITH THAT CUTE LITTLE DRESS SHOP ACROSS THE STREET...
SHE HAS BEAUTIFUL AWNINGS!
SCHULZ

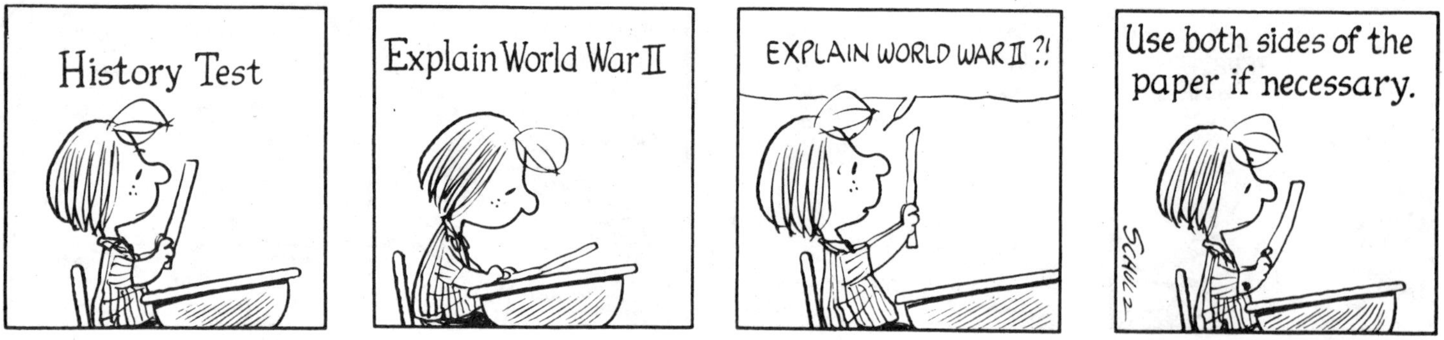
History Test
Explain World War II
EXPLAIN WORLD WAR II ?!
Use both sides of the paper if necessary.
SCHULZ

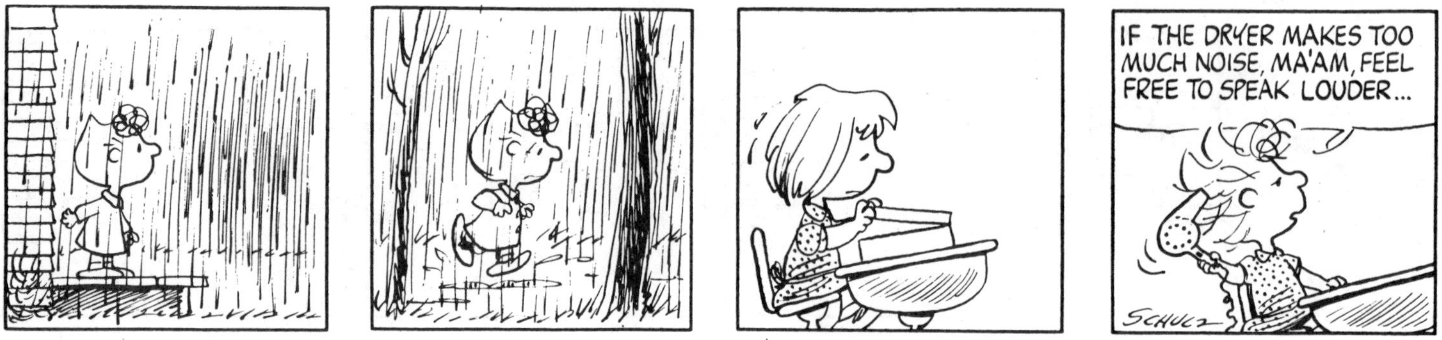
IF THE DRYER MAKES TOO MUCH NOISE, MA'AM, FEEL FREE TO SPEAK LOUDER...
SCHULZ

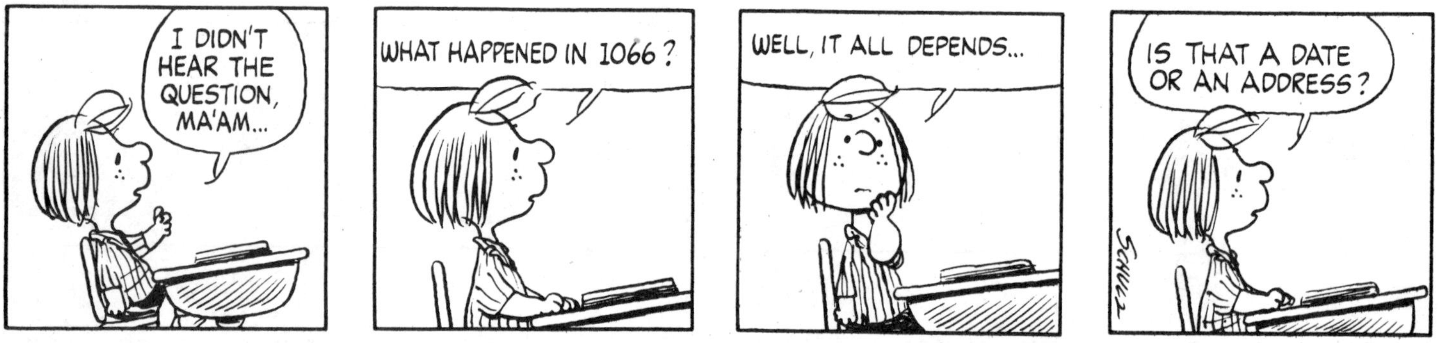
I DIDN'T HEAR THE QUESTION, MA'AM...
WHAT HAPPENED IN 1066 ?
WELL, IT ALL DEPENDS...
IS THAT A DATE OR AN ADDRESS ?
SCHULZ

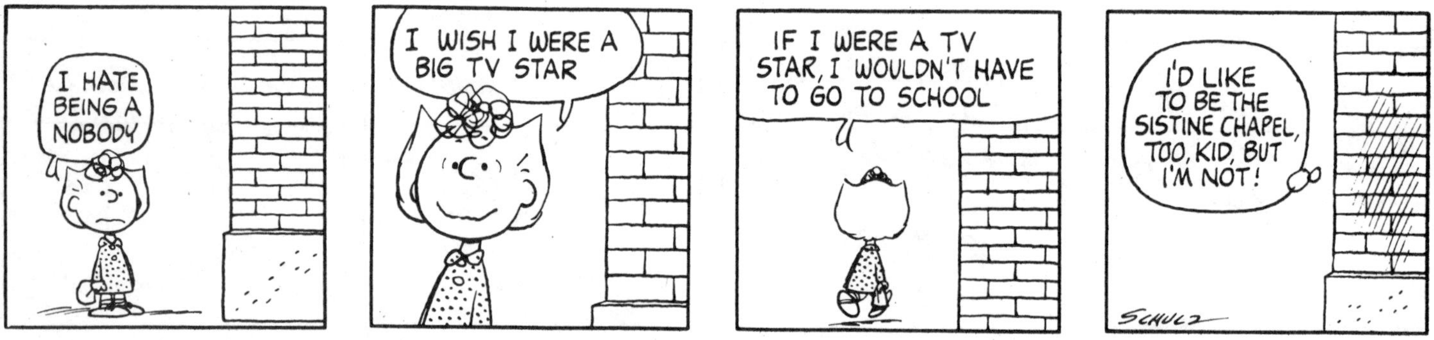
I HATE BEING A NOBODY
I WISH I WERE A BIG TV STAR
IF I WERE A TV STAR, I WOULDN'T HAVE TO GO TO SCHOOL
I'D LIKE TO BE THE SISTINE CHAPEL, TOO, KID, BUT I'M NOT!
SCHULZ

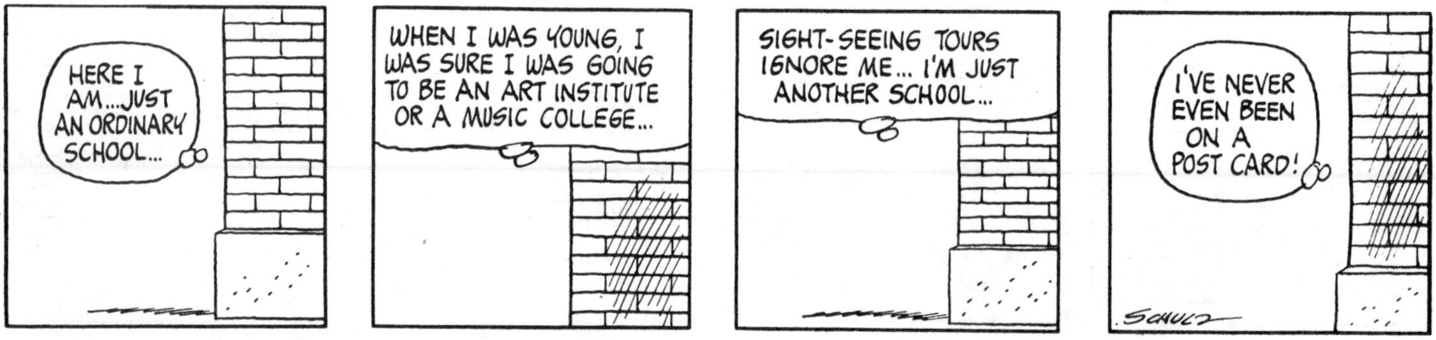
HERE I AM...JUST AN ORDINARY SCHOOL...
WHEN I WAS YOUNG, I WAS SURE I WAS GOING TO BE AN ART INSTITUTE OR A MUSIC COLLEGE...
SIGHT-SEEING TOURS IGNORE ME... I'M JUST ANOTHER SCHOOL...
I'VE NEVER EVEN BEEN ON A POST CARD!
SCHULZ

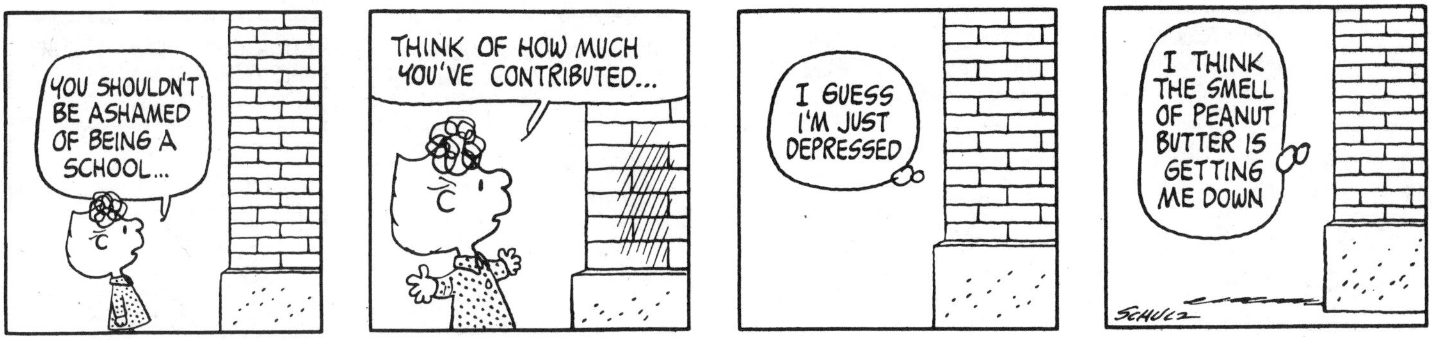
YOU SHOULDN'T BE ASHAMED OF BEING A SCHOOL...
THINK OF HOW MUCH YOU'VE CONTRIBUTED...
I GUESS I'M JUST DEPRESSED
I THINK THE SMELL OF PEANUT BUTTER IS GETTING ME DOWN
SCHULZ

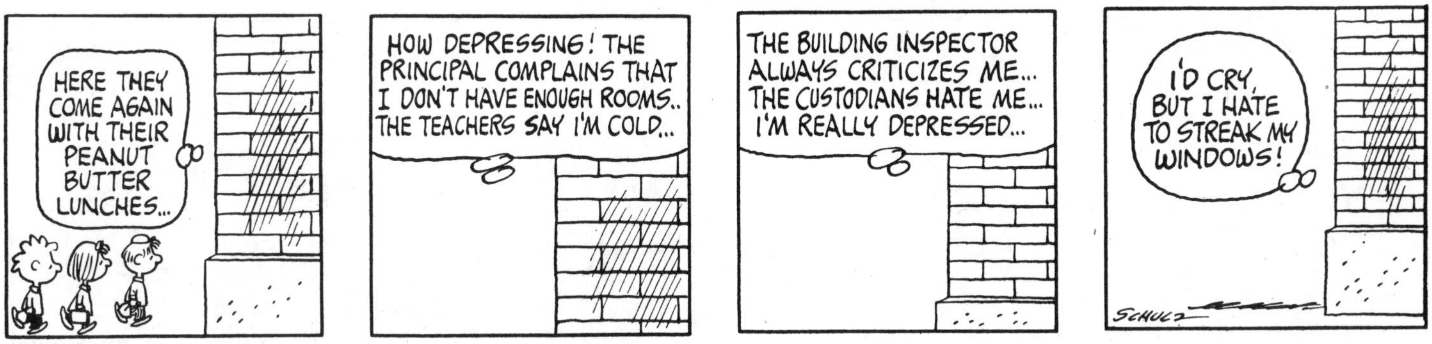
HERE THEY COME AGAIN WITH THEIR PEANUT BUTTER LUNCHES...
HOW DEPRESSING! THE PRINCIPAL COMPLAINS THAT I DON'T HAVE ENOUGH ROOMS.. THE TEACHERS SAY I'M COLD...
THE BUILDING INSPECTOR ALWAYS CRITICIZES ME... THE CUSTODIANS HATE ME... I'M REALLY DEPRESSED...
I'D CRY, BUT I HATE TO STREAK MY WINDOWS!
SCHULZ

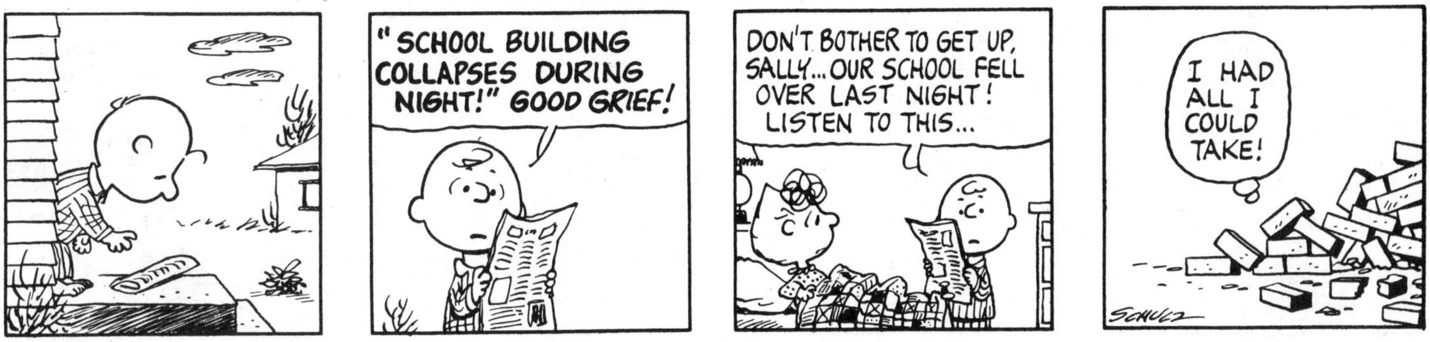
"SCHOOL BUILDING COLLAPSES DURING NIGHT!" GOOD GRIEF!
DON'T BOTHER TO GET UP, SALLY... OUR SCHOOL FELL OVER LAST NIGHT! LISTEN TO THIS...
I HAD ALL I COULD TAKE!
SCHULZ

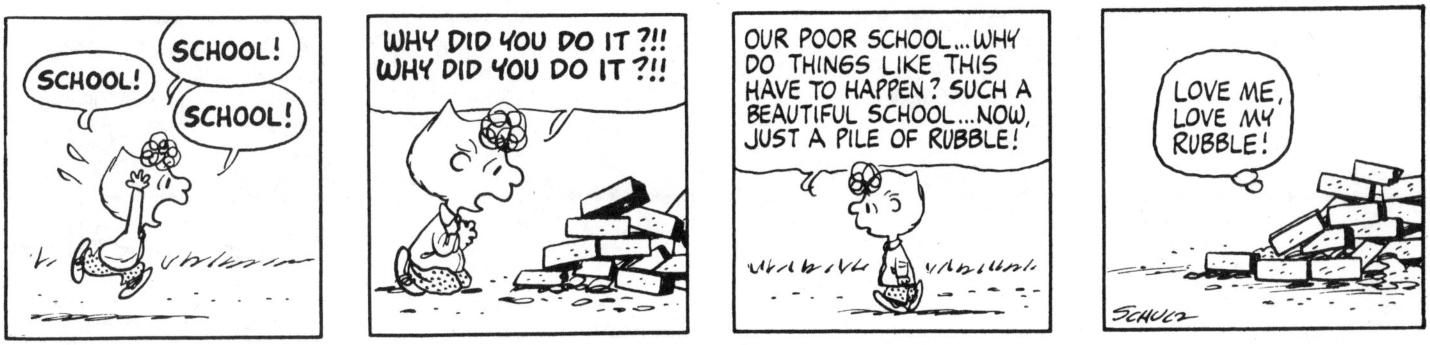
SCHOOL!
SCHOOL!
SCHOOL!
WHY DID YOU DO IT ?!! WHY DID YOU DO IT ?!!
OUR POOR SCHOOL... WHY DO THINGS LIKE THIS HAVE TO HAPPEN? SUCH A BEAUTIFUL SCHOOL... NOW, JUST A PILE OF RUBBLE!
LOVE ME, LOVE MY RUBBLE!
SCHULZ

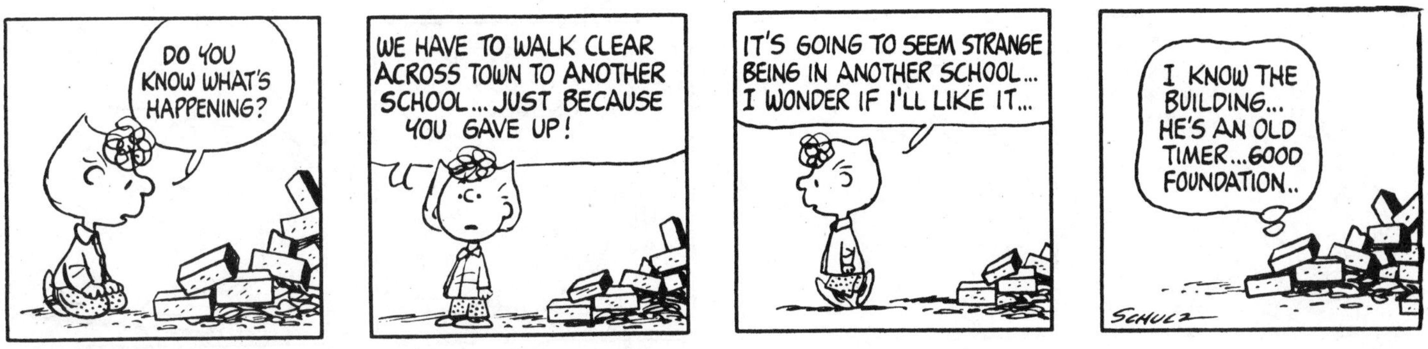
DO YOU KNOW WHAT'S HAPPENING?
WE HAVE TO WALK CLEAR ACROSS TOWN TO ANOTHER SCHOOL... JUST BECAUSE YOU GAVE UP!
IT'S GOING TO SEEM STRANGE BEING IN ANOTHER SCHOOL... I WONDER IF I'LL LIKE IT...
I KNOW THE BUILDING... HE'S AN OLD TIMER... GOOD FOUNDATION..
SCHULZ

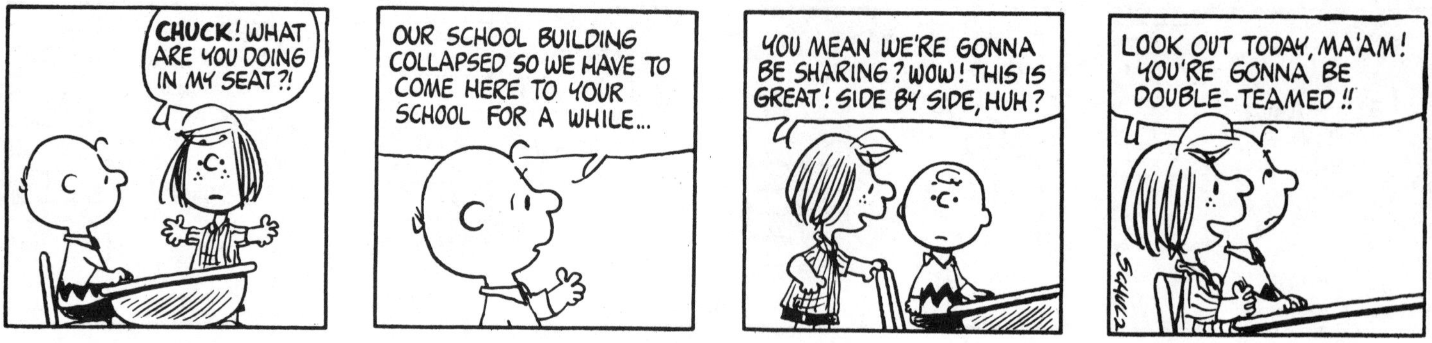
CHUCK! WHAT ARE YOU DOING IN MY SEAT?!
OUR SCHOOL BUILDING COLLAPSED SO WE HAVE TO COME HERE TO YOUR SCHOOL FOR A WHILE...
YOU MEAN WE'RE GONNA BE SHARING? WOW! THIS IS GREAT! SIDE BY SIDE, HUH?
LOOK OUT TODAY, MA'AM! YOU'RE GONNA BE DOUBLE-TEAMED!!

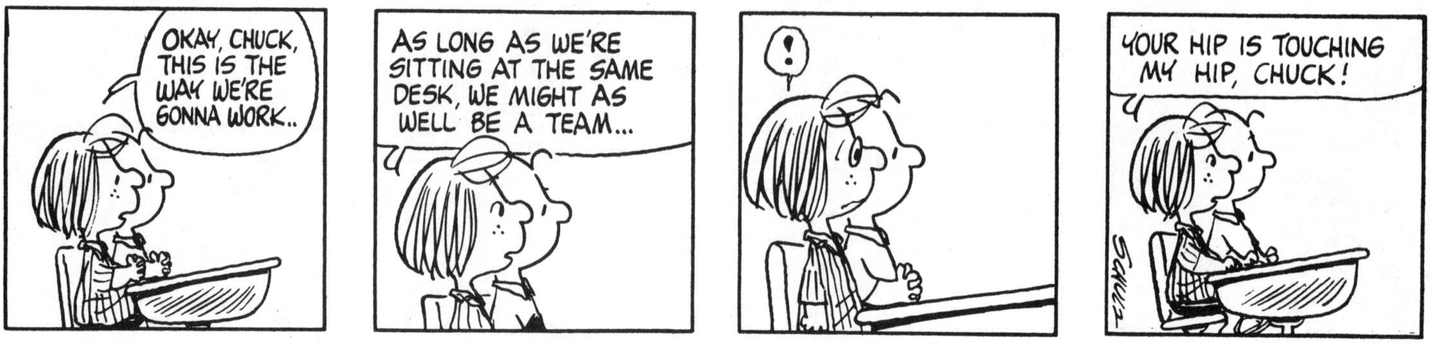
OKAY, CHUCK, THIS IS THE WAY WE'RE GONNA WORK..
AS LONG AS WE'RE SITTING AT THE SAME DESK, WE MIGHT AS WELL BE A TEAM...
!
YOUR HIP IS TOUCHING MY HIP, CHUCK!

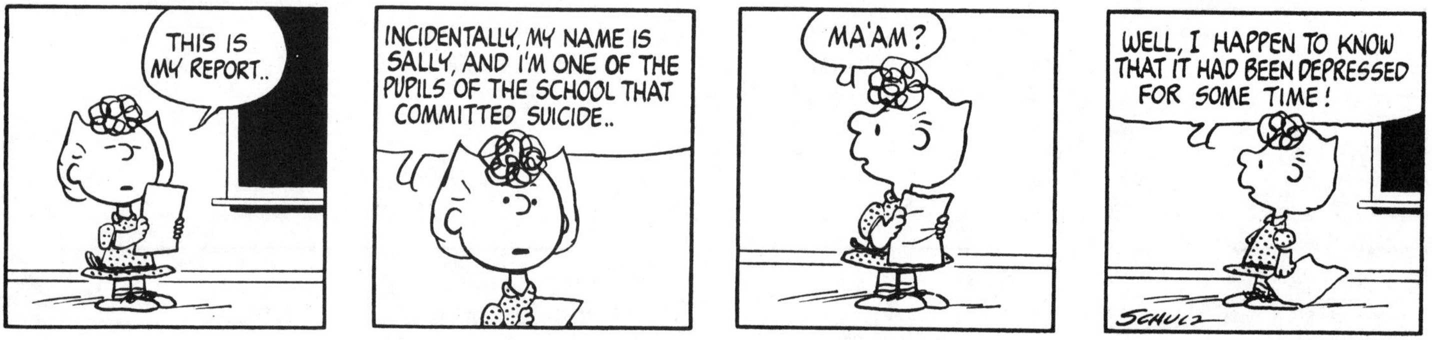
THIS IS MY REPORT..
INCIDENTALLY, MY NAME IS SALLY, AND I'M ONE OF THE PUPILS OF THE SCHOOL THAT COMMITTED SUICIDE..
MA'AM?
WELL, I HAPPEN TO KNOW THAT IT HAD BEEN DEPRESSED FOR SOME TIME!

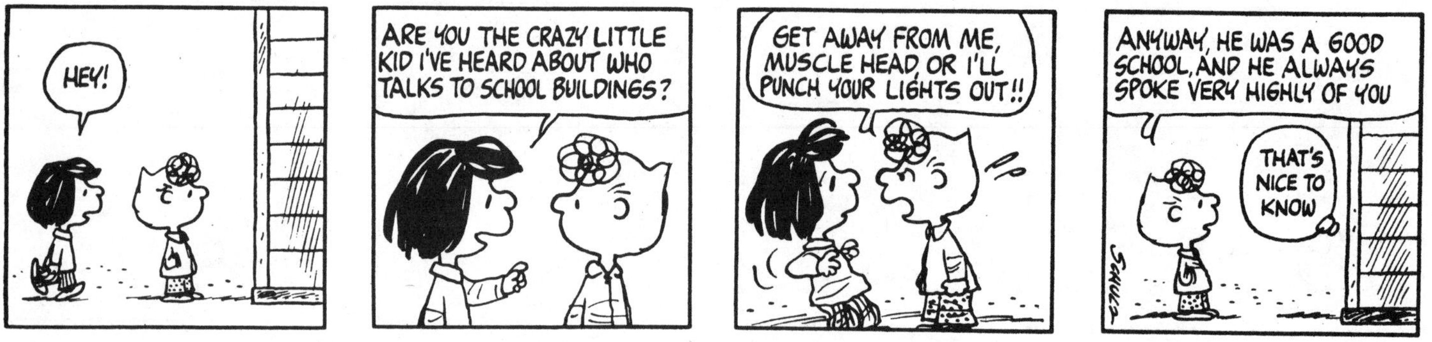
HEY!
ARE YOU THE CRAZY LITTLE KID I'VE HEARD ABOUT WHO TALKS TO SCHOOL BUILDINGS?
GET AWAY FROM ME, MUSCLE HEAD, OR I'LL PUNCH YOUR LIGHTS OUT!!
ANYWAY, HE WAS A GOOD SCHOOL, AND HE ALWAYS SPOKE VERY HIGHLY OF YOU
THAT'S NICE TO KNOW

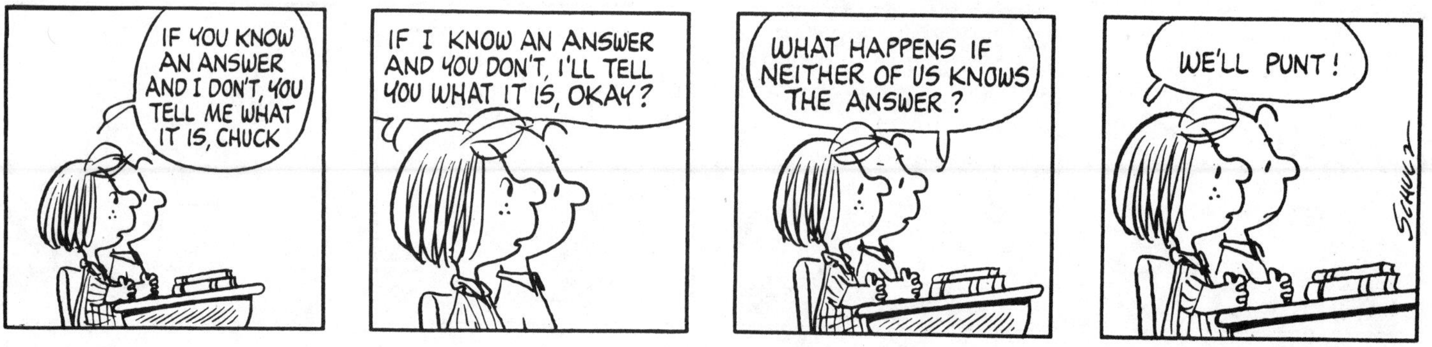
IF YOU KNOW AN ANSWER AND I DON'T, YOU TELL ME WHAT IT IS, CHUCK
IF I KNOW AN ANSWER AND YOU DON'T, I'LL TELL YOU WHAT IT IS, OKAY?
WHAT HAPPENS IF NEITHER OF US KNOWS THE ANSWER?
WE'LL PUNT!

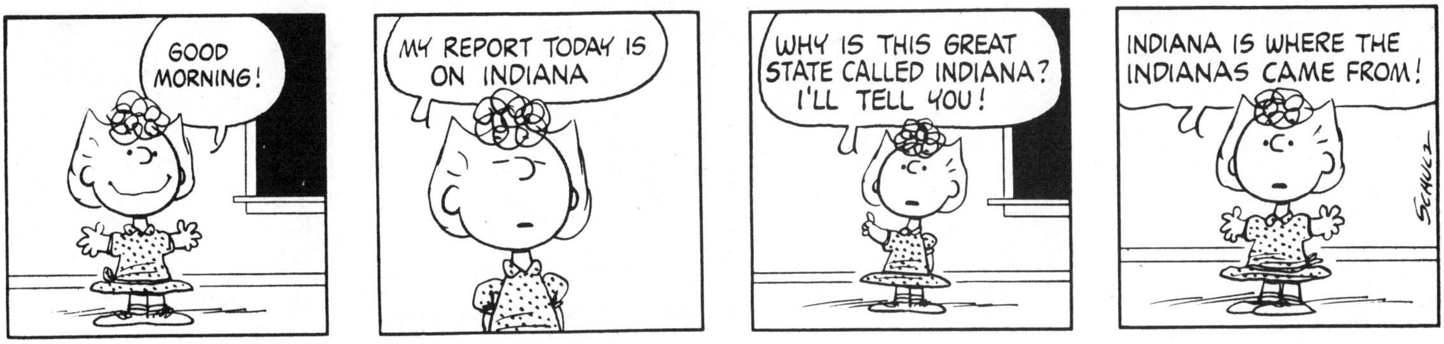
GOOD MORNING!
MY REPORT TODAY IS ON INDIANA
WHY IS THIS GREAT STATE CALLED INDIANA? I'LL TELL YOU!
INDIANA IS WHERE THE INDIANAS CAME FROM!
SCHULZ

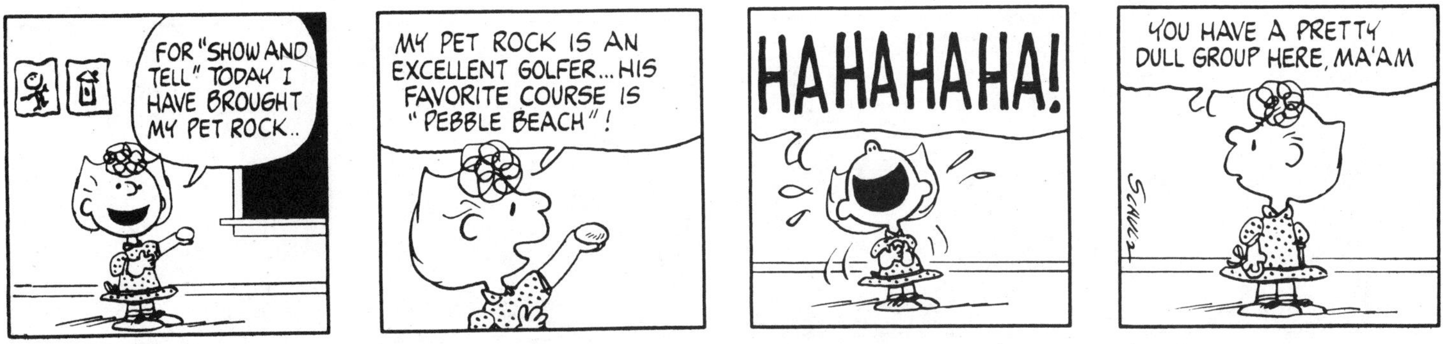
FOR "SHOW AND TELL" TODAY I HAVE BROUGHT MY PET ROCK..
MY PET ROCK IS AN EXCELLENT GOLFER... HIS FAVORITE COURSE IS "PEBBLE BEACH"!
HAHAHAHA!
SCHULZ
YOU HAVE A PRETTY DULL GROUP HERE, MA'AM

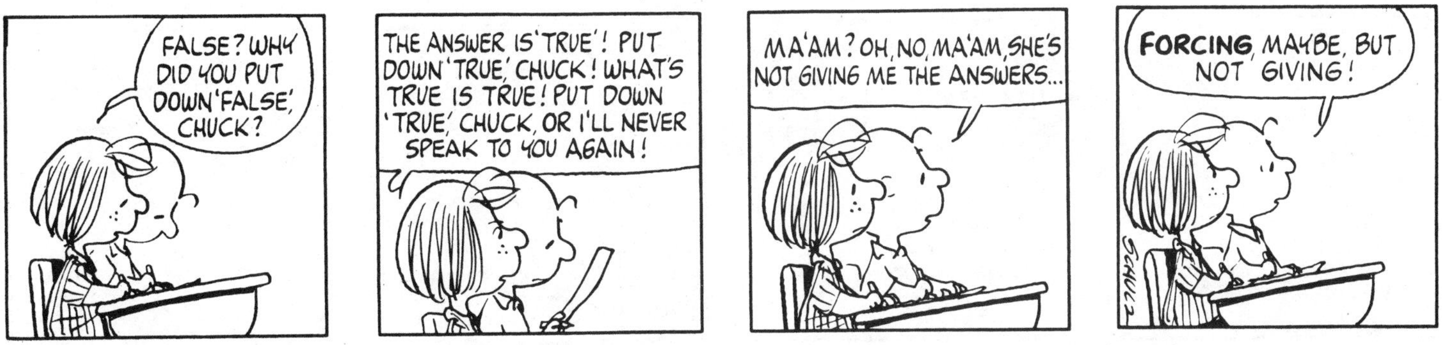
FALSE? WHY DID YOU PUT DOWN 'FALSE,' CHUCK?
THE ANSWER IS 'TRUE'! PUT DOWN 'TRUE,' CHUCK! WHAT'S TRUE IS TRUE! PUT DOWN 'TRUE,' CHUCK, OR I'LL NEVER SPEAK TO YOU AGAIN!
MA'AM? OH, NO, MA'AM, SHE'S NOT GIVING ME THE ANSWERS...
FORCING, MAYBE, BUT NOT GIVING!
SCHULZ

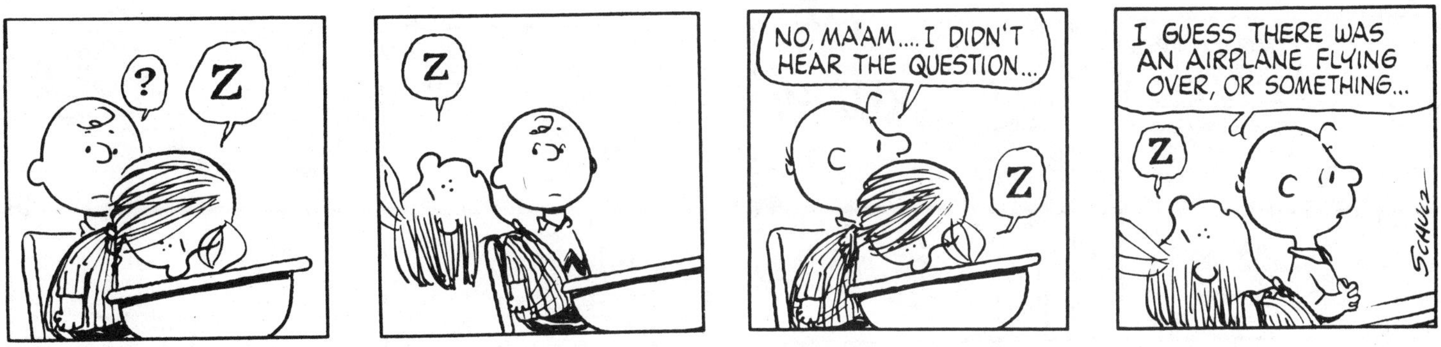
?
Z
Z
NO, MA'AM.... I DIDN'T HEAR THE QUESTION...
Z
I GUESS THERE WAS AN AIRPLANE FLYING OVER, OR SOMETHING...
Z
SCHULZ

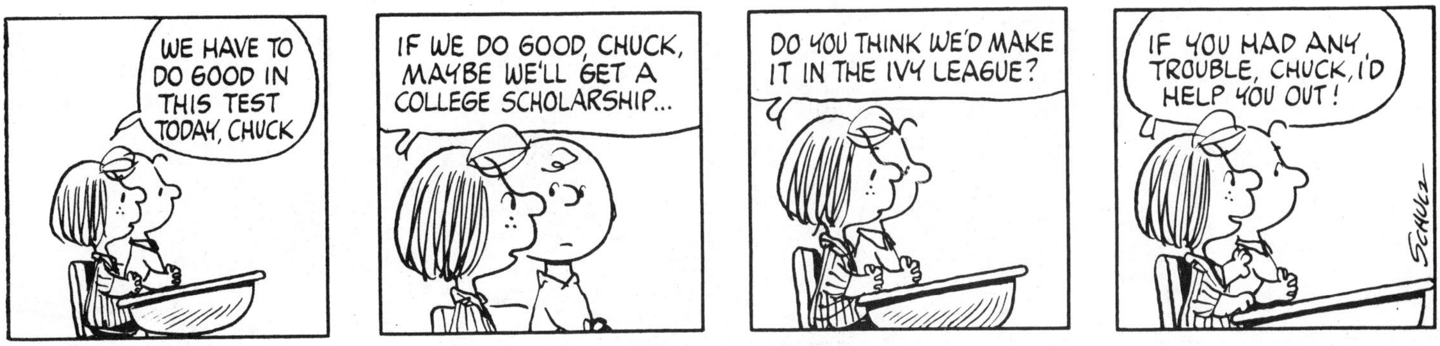
WE HAVE TO DO GOOD IN THIS TEST TODAY, CHUCK
IF WE DO GOOD, CHUCK, MAYBE WE'LL GET A COLLEGE SCHOLARSHIP...
DO YOU THINK WE'D MAKE IT IN THE IVY LEAGUE?
IF YOU HAD ANY TROUBLE, CHUCK, I'D HELP YOU OUT!
SCHULZ

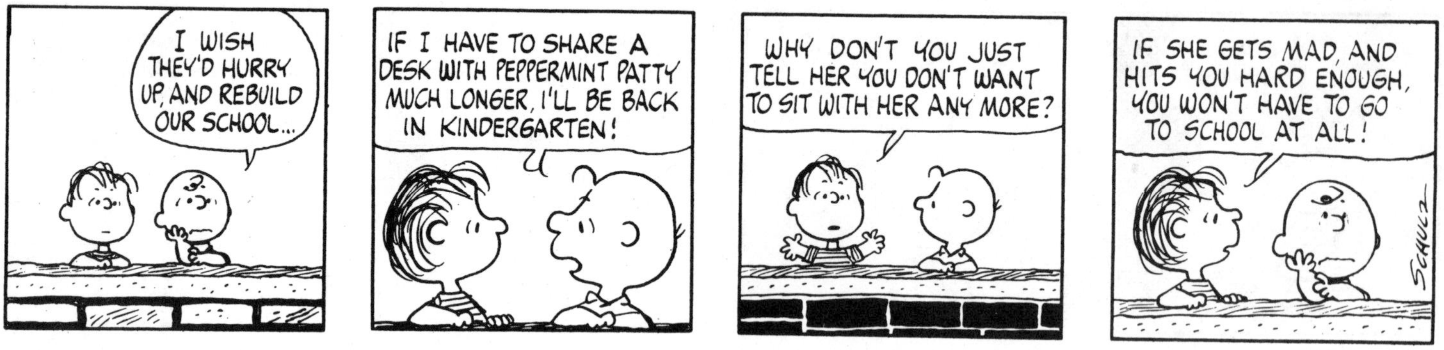
I WISH THEY'D HURRY UP, AND REBUILD OUR SCHOOL...
IF I HAVE TO SHARE A DESK WITH PEPPERMINT PATTY MUCH LONGER, I'LL BE BACK IN KINDERGARTEN!
WHY DON'T YOU JUST TELL HER YOU DON'T WANT TO SIT WITH HER ANY MORE?
IF SHE GETS MAD, AND HITS YOU HARD ENOUGH, YOU WON'T HAVE TO GO TO SCHOOL AT ALL!

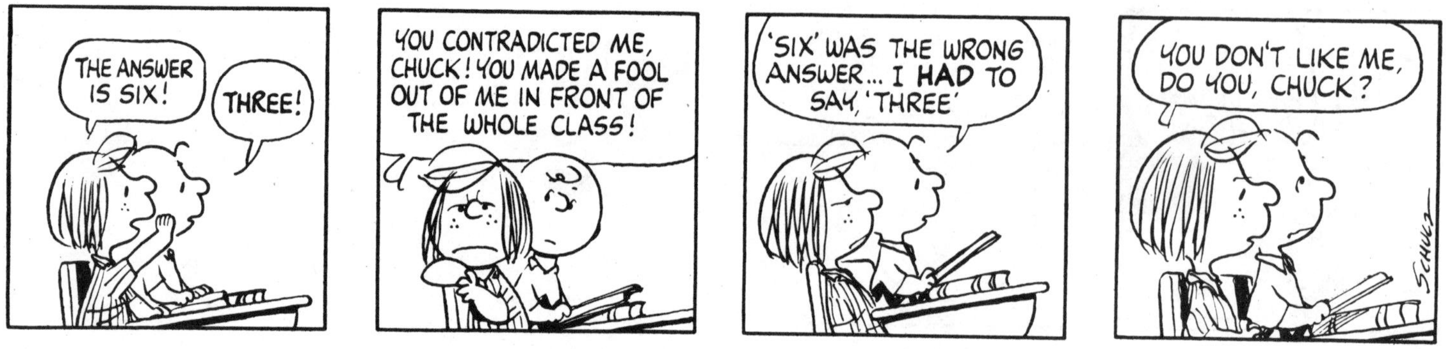
THE ANSWER IS SIX!
THREE!
YOU CONTRADICTED ME, CHUCK! YOU MADE A FOOL OUT OF ME IN FRONT OF THE WHOLE CLASS!
'SIX' WAS THE WRONG ANSWER... I HAD TO SAY, 'THREE'
YOU DON'T LIKE ME, DO YOU, CHUCK?

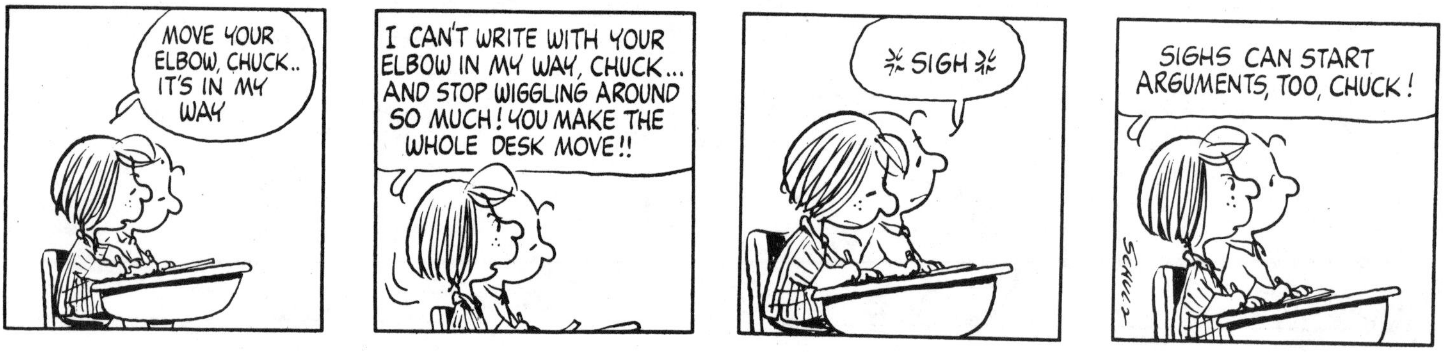
MOVE YOUR ELBOW, CHUCK.. IT'S IN MY WAY
I CAN'T WRITE WITH YOUR ELBOW IN MY WAY, CHUCK... AND STOP WIGGLING AROUND SO MUCH! YOU MAKE THE WHOLE DESK MOVE!!
SIGH
SIGHS CAN START ARGUMENTS, TOO, CHUCK!

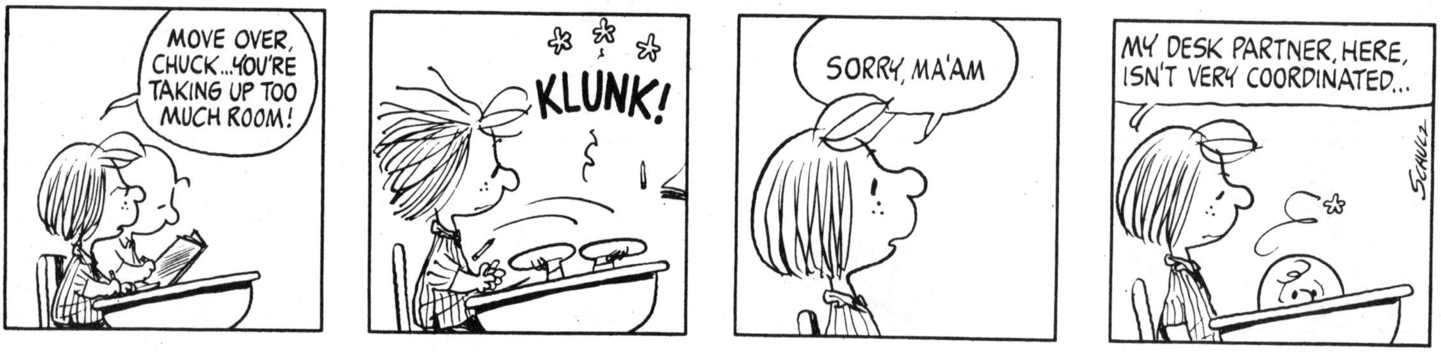
MOVE OVER, CHUCK...YOU'RE TAKING UP TOO MUCH ROOM!
KLUNK!
SORRY, MA'AM
MY DESK PARTNER, HERE, ISN'T VERY COORDINATED...

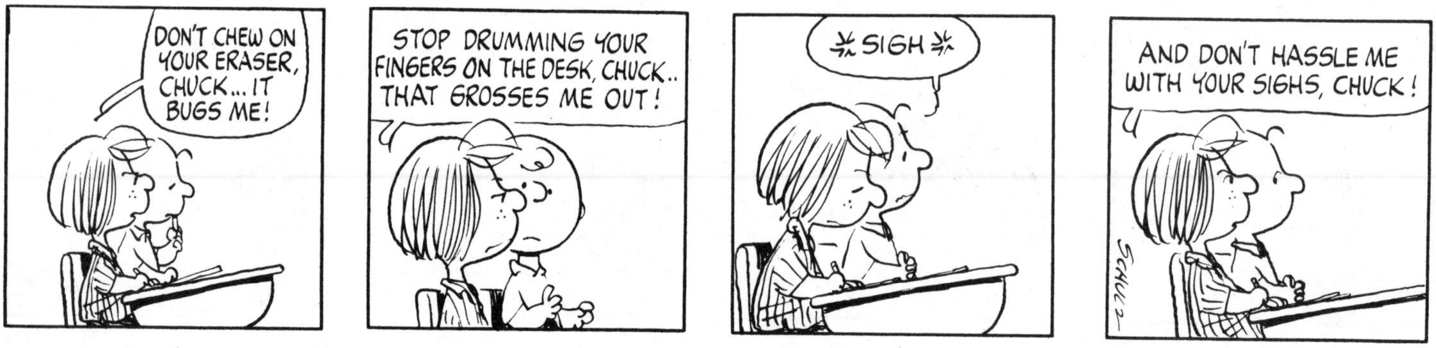
DON'T CHEW ON YOUR ERASER, CHUCK... IT BUGS ME!
STOP DRUMMING YOUR FINGERS ON THE DESK, CHUCK.. THAT GROSSES ME OUT!
SIGH
AND DON'T HASSLE ME WITH YOUR SIGHS, CHUCK!

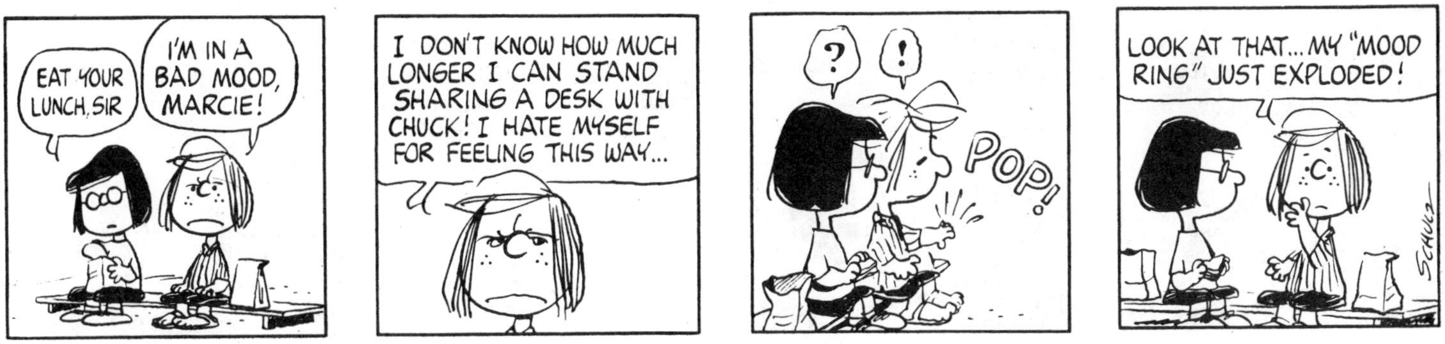
EAT YOUR LUNCH, SIR
I'M IN A BAD MOOD, MARCIE!
I DON'T KNOW HOW MUCH LONGER I CAN STAND SHARING A DESK WITH CHUCK! I HATE MYSELF FOR FEELING THIS WAY...
?
!
POP!
LOOK AT THAT... MY "MOOD RING" JUST EXPLODED!
SCHULZ

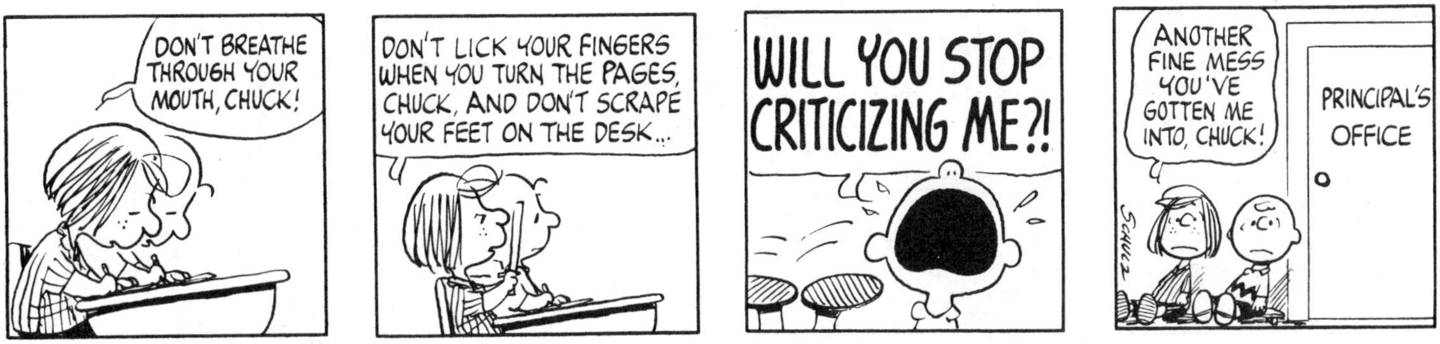
DON'T BREATHE THROUGH YOUR MOUTH, CHUCK!
DON'T LICK YOUR FINGERS WHEN YOU TURN THE PAGES, CHUCK, AND DON'T SCRAPE YOUR FEET ON THE DESK...
WILL YOU STOP CRITICIZING ME?!
ANOTHER FINE MESS YOU'VE GOTTEN ME INTO, CHUCK!
PRINCIPAL'S OFFICE
SCHULZ

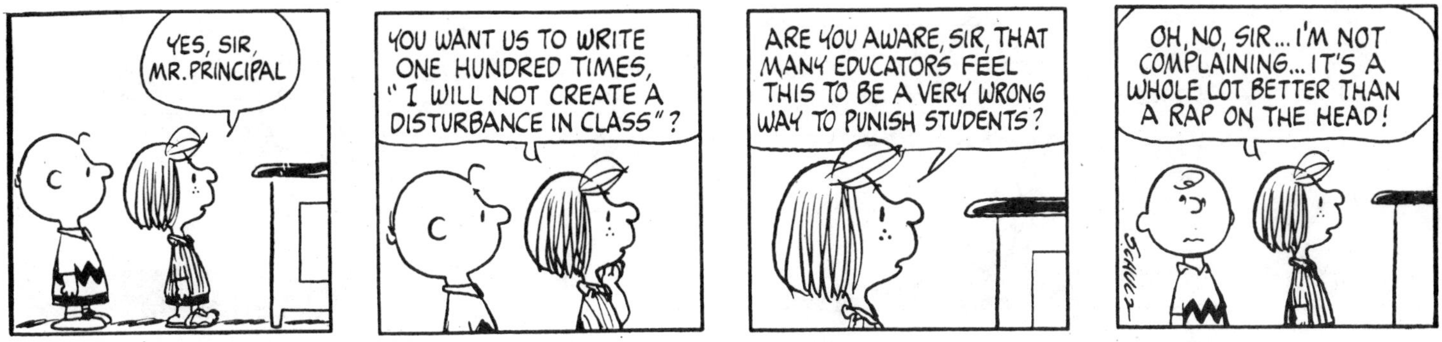
YES, SIR, MR. PRINCIPAL
YOU WANT US TO WRITE ONE HUNDRED TIMES, "I WILL NOT CREATE A DISTURBANCE IN CLASS"?
ARE YOU AWARE, SIR, THAT MANY EDUCATORS FEEL THIS TO BE A VERY WRONG WAY TO PUNISH STUDENTS?
OH, NO, SIR... I'M NOT COMPLAINING... IT'S A WHOLE LOT BETTER THAN A RAP ON THE HEAD!
SCHULZ

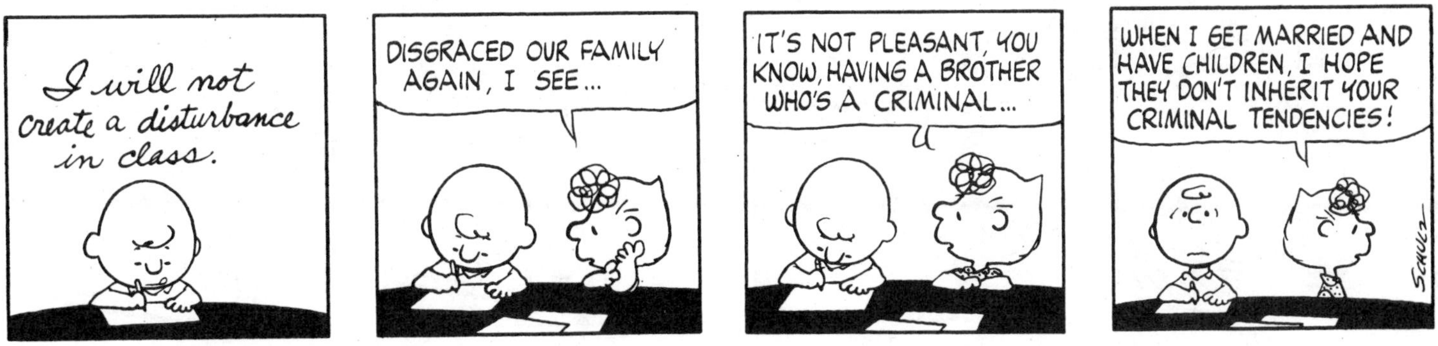
I will not create a disturbance in class.
DISGRACED OUR FAMILY AGAIN, I SEE...
IT'S NOT PLEASANT, YOU KNOW, HAVING A BROTHER WHO'S A CRIMINAL...
WHEN I GET MARRIED AND HAVE CHILDREN, I HOPE THEY DON'T INHERIT YOUR CRIMINAL TENDENCIES!
SCHULZ

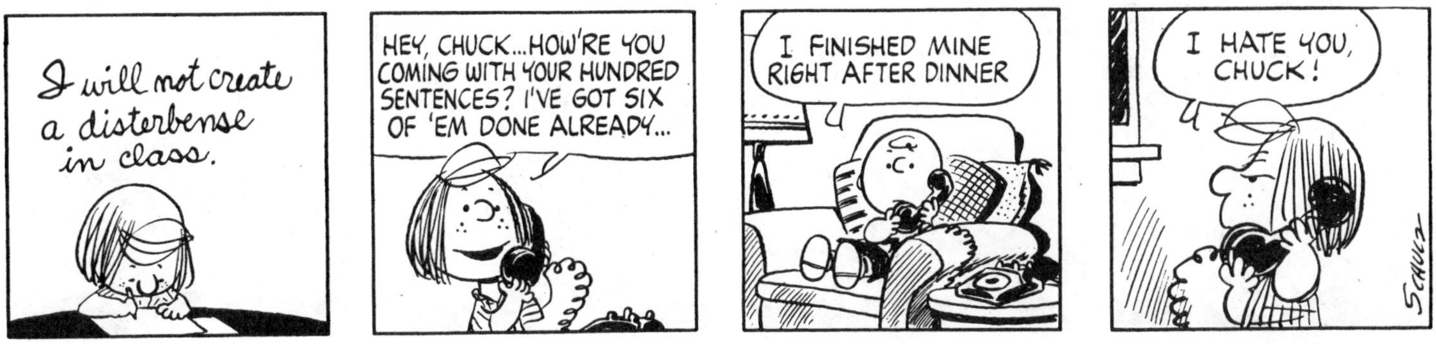
I will not create a disterbense in class.
HEY, CHUCK... HOW'RE YOU COMING WITH YOUR HUNDRED SENTENCES? I'VE GOT SIX OF 'EM DONE ALREADY...
I FINISHED MINE RIGHT AFTER DINNER
I HATE YOU, CHUCK!
SCHULZ

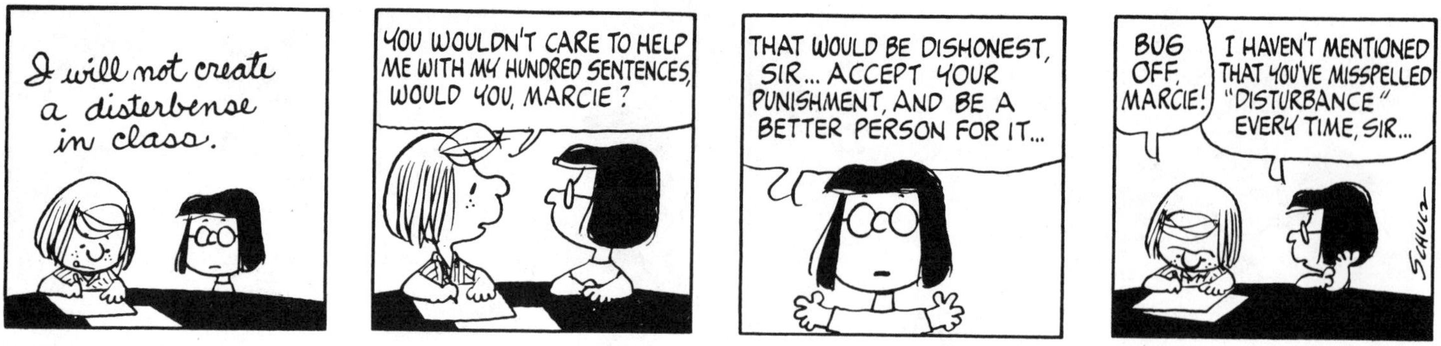
I will not create a disterbense in class.
YOU WOULDN'T CARE TO HELP ME WITH MY HUNDRED SENTENCES, WOULD YOU, MARCIE?
THAT WOULD BE DISHONEST, SIR... ACCEPT YOUR PUNISHMENT, AND BE A BETTER PERSON FOR IT...
BUG OFF, MARCIE!
I HAVEN'T MENTIONED THAT YOU'VE MISSPELLED "DISTURBANCE" EVERY TIME, SIR...
SCHULZ

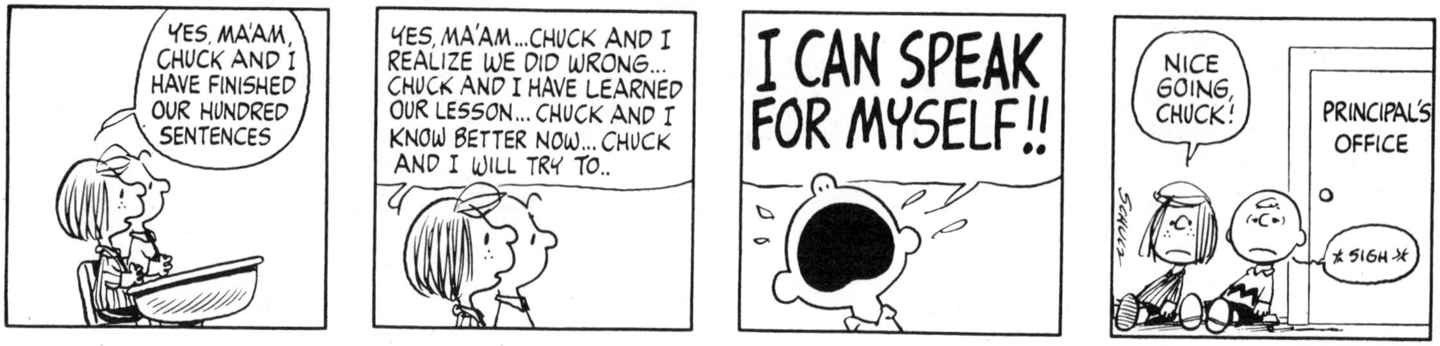
YES, MA'AM, CHUCK AND I HAVE FINISHED OUR HUNDRED SENTENCES
YES, MA'AM... CHUCK AND I REALIZE WE DID WRONG... CHUCK AND I HAVE LEARNED OUR LESSON... CHUCK AND I KNOW BETTER NOW... CHUCK AND I WILL TRY TO..
I CAN SPEAK FOR MYSELF!!
NICE GOING, CHUCK!
PRINCIPAL'S OFFICE
SCHULZ
SIGH

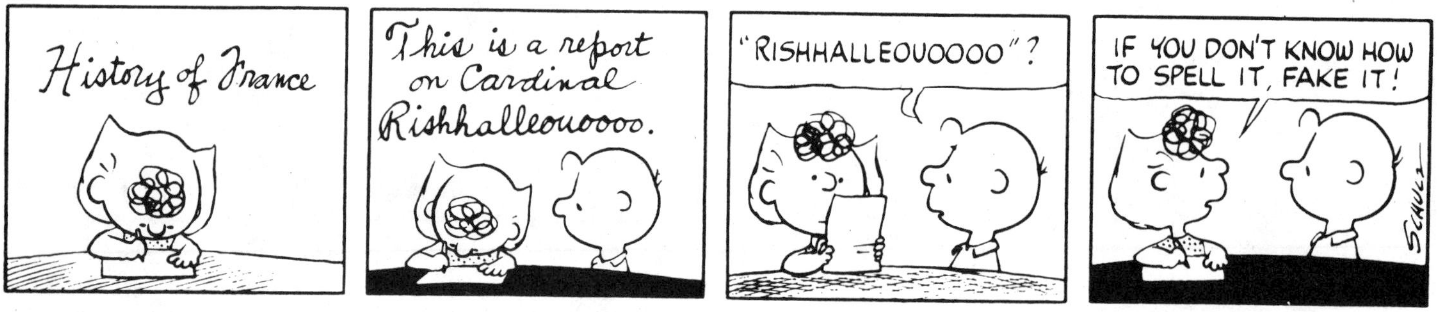
History of France
This is a report on Cardinal Rishhalleouoooo.
"RISHHALLEOUOOOO"?
IF YOU DON'T KNOW HOW TO SPELL IT, FAKE IT!
SCHULZ

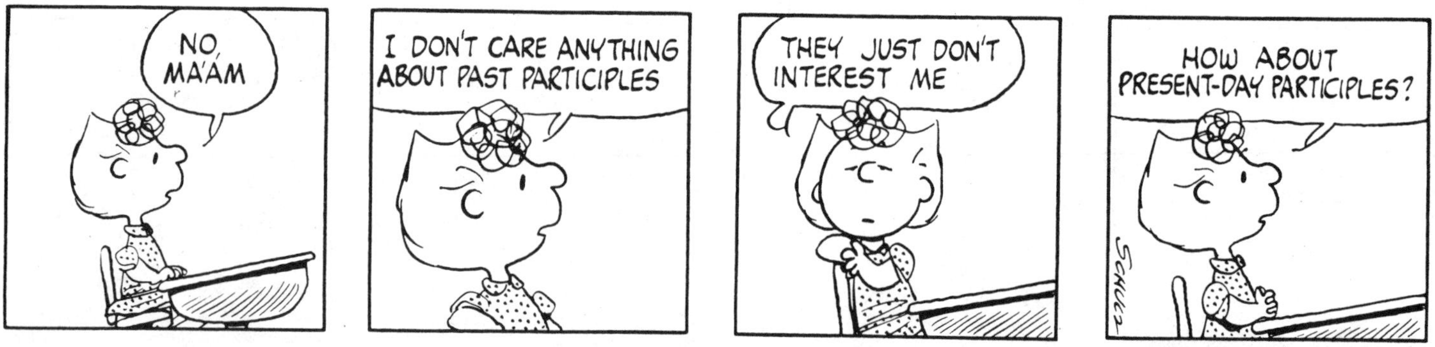
NO, MA'AM
I DON'T CARE ANYTHING ABOUT PAST PARTICIPLES
THEY JUST DON'T INTEREST ME
HOW ABOUT PRESENT-DAY PARTICIPLES?
SCHULZ

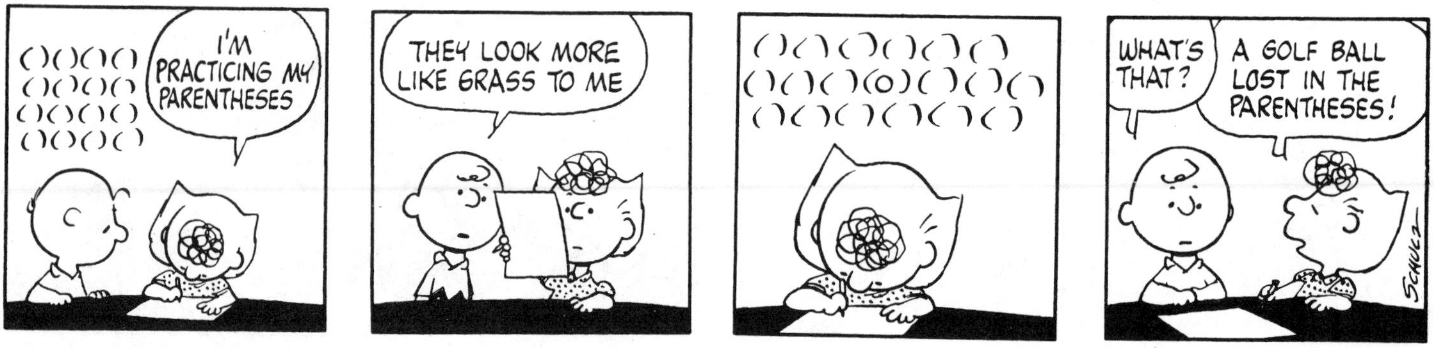
I'M PRACTICING MY PARENTHESES
THEY LOOK MORE LIKE GRASS TO ME
WHAT'S THAT?
A GOLF BALL LOST IN THE PARENTHESES!
SCHULZ

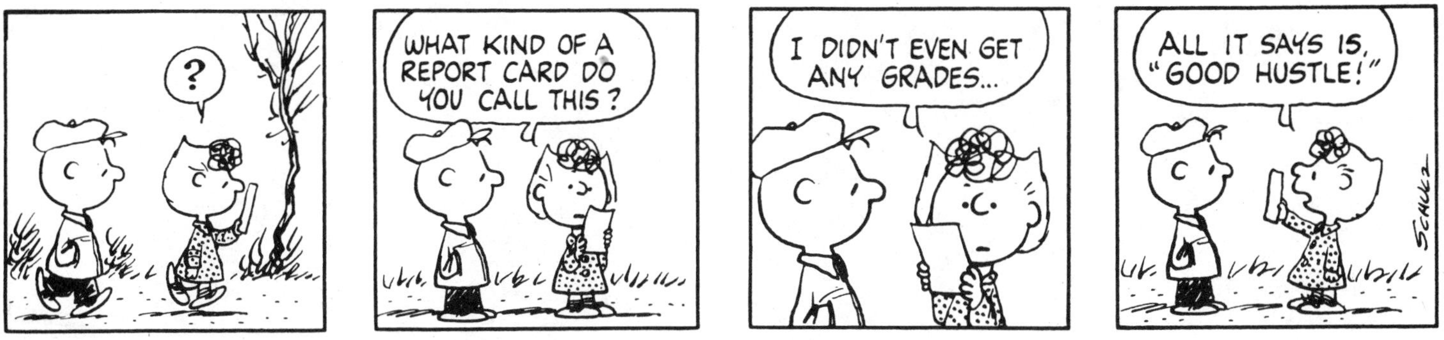
?
WHAT KIND OF A REPORT CARD DO YOU CALL THIS?
I DIDN'T EVEN GET ANY GRADES...
ALL IT SAYS IS, "GOOD HUSTLE!"
SCHULZ

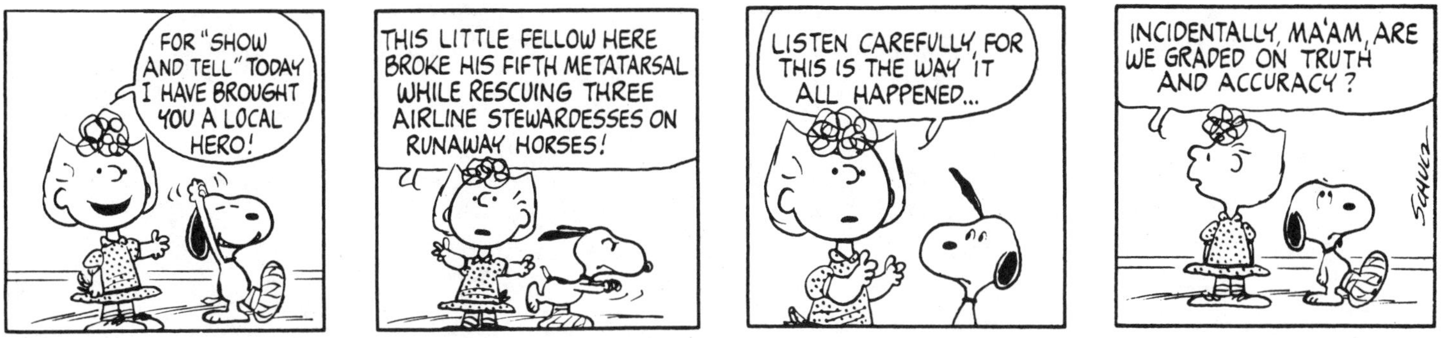
FOR "SHOW AND TELL" TODAY I HAVE BROUGHT YOU A LOCAL HERO!
THIS LITTLE FELLOW HERE BROKE HIS FIFTH METATARSAL WHILE RESCUING THREE AIRLINE STEWARDESSES ON RUNAWAY HORSES!
LISTEN CAREFULLY, FOR THIS IS THE WAY IT ALL HAPPENED...
INCIDENTALLY, MA'AM, ARE WE GRADED ON TRUTH AND ACCURACY?
SCHULZ

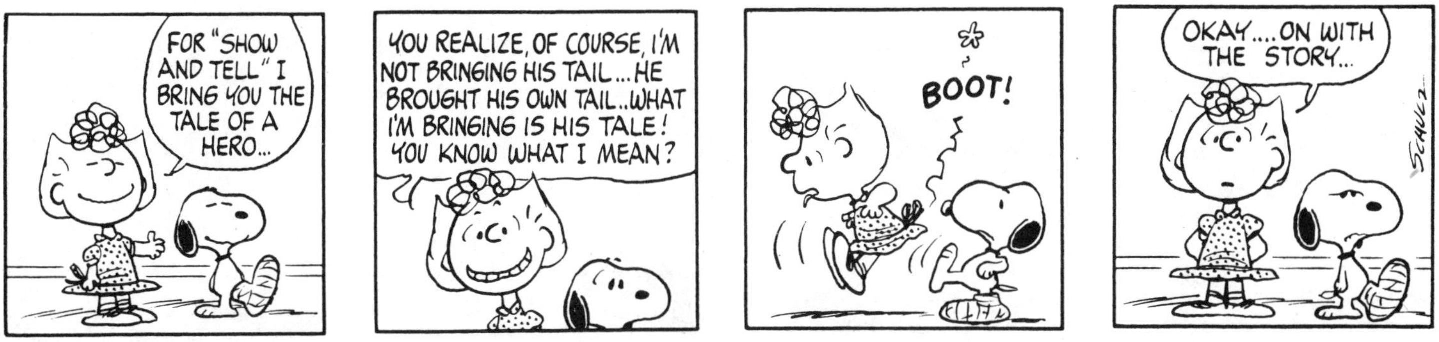
FOR "SHOW AND TELL" I BRING YOU THE TALE OF A HERO...
YOU REALIZE, OF COURSE, I'M NOT BRINGING HIS TAIL... HE BROUGHT HIS OWN TAIL.. WHAT I'M BRINGING IS HIS TALE! YOU KNOW WHAT I MEAN?
BOOT!
OKAY.... ON WITH THE STORY...
SCHULZ

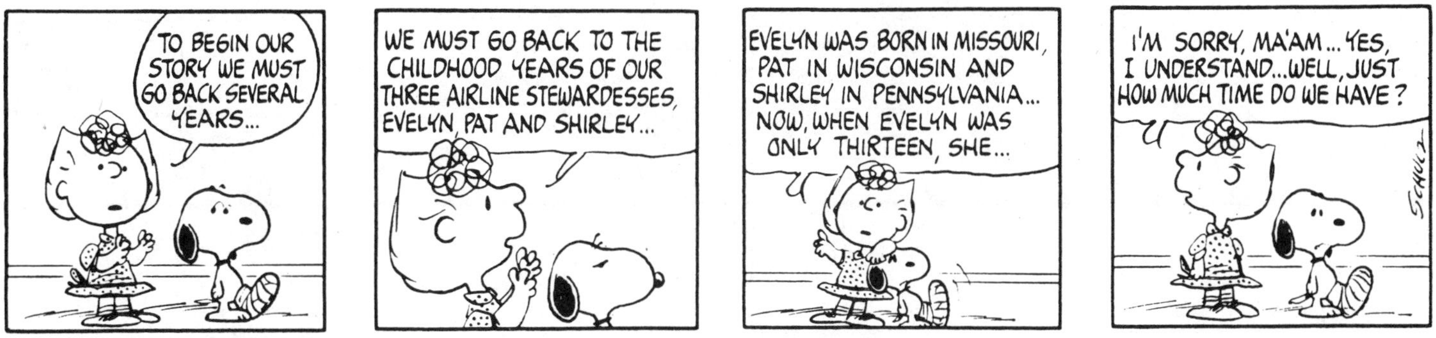
TO BEGIN OUR STORY WE MUST GO BACK SEVERAL YEARS...
WE MUST GO BACK TO THE CHILDHOOD YEARS OF OUR THREE AIRLINE STEWARDESSES, EVELYN, PAT AND SHIRLEY...
EVELYN WAS BORN IN MISSOURI, PAT IN WISCONSIN AND SHIRLEY IN PENNSYLVANIA... NOW, WHEN EVELYN WAS ONLY THIRTEEN, SHE...
I'M SORRY, MA'AM... YES, I UNDERSTAND... WELL, JUST HOW MUCH TIME DO WE HAVE?
SCHULZ

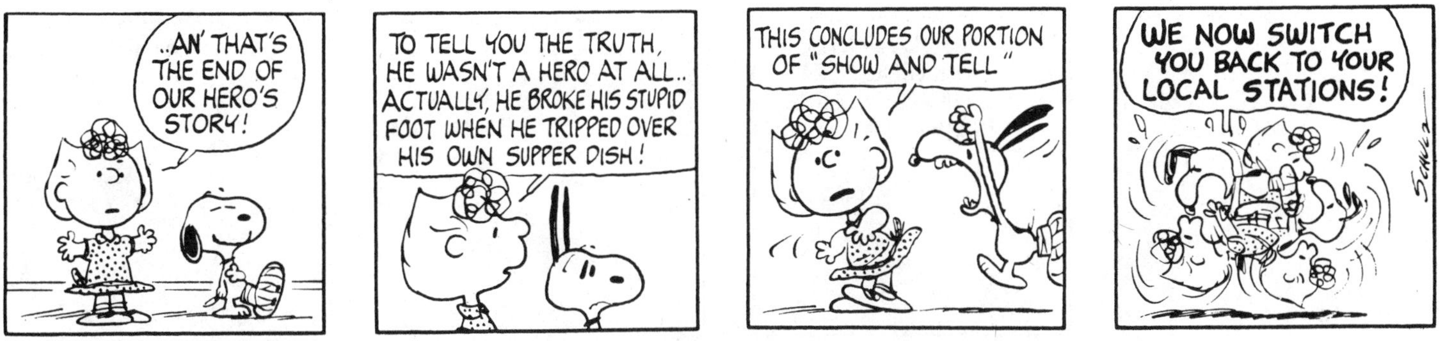
..AN' THAT'S THE END OF OUR HERO'S STORY!
TO TELL YOU THE TRUTH, HE WASN'T A HERO AT ALL.. ACTUALLY, HE BROKE HIS STUPID FOOT WHEN HE TRIPPED OVER HIS OWN SUPPER DISH!
THIS CONCLUDES OUR PORTION OF "SHOW AND TELL"
WE NOW SWITCH YOU BACK TO YOUR LOCAL STATIONS!
SCHULZ

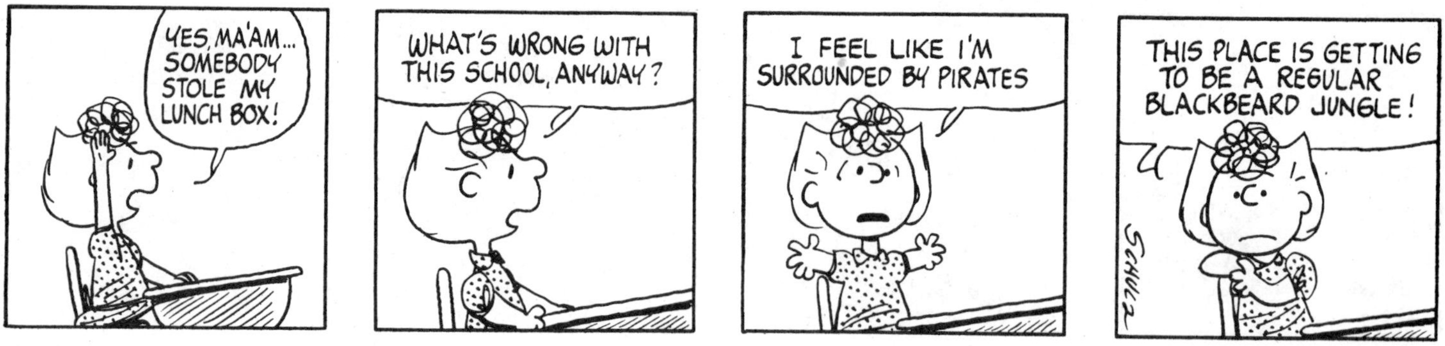
YES, MA'AM... SOMEBODY STOLE MY LUNCH BOX!
WHAT'S WRONG WITH THIS SCHOOL, ANYWAY?
I FEEL LIKE I'M SURROUNDED BY PIRATES
THIS PLACE IS GETTING TO BE A REGULAR BLACKBEARD JUNGLE!
SCHULZ

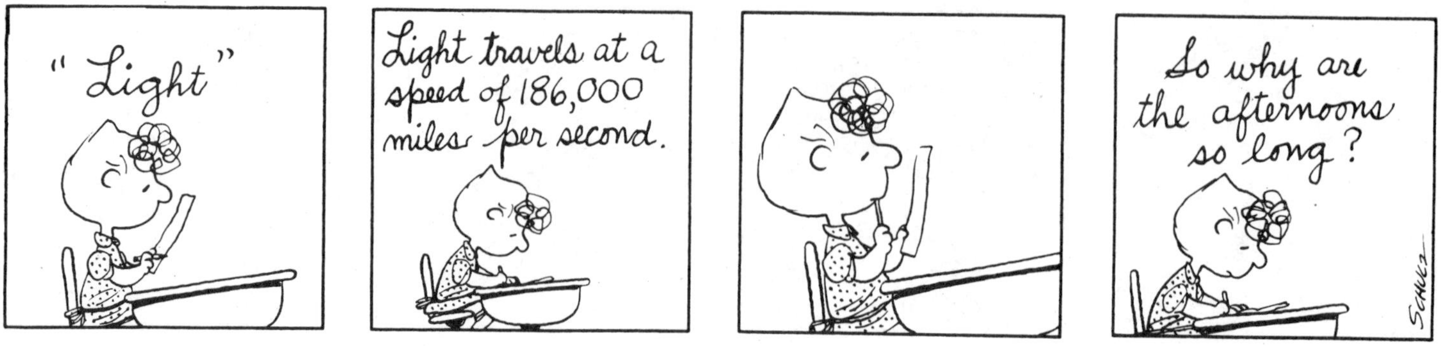
"Light"
Light travels at a speed of 186,000 miles per second.
So why are the afternoons so long?
SCHULZ

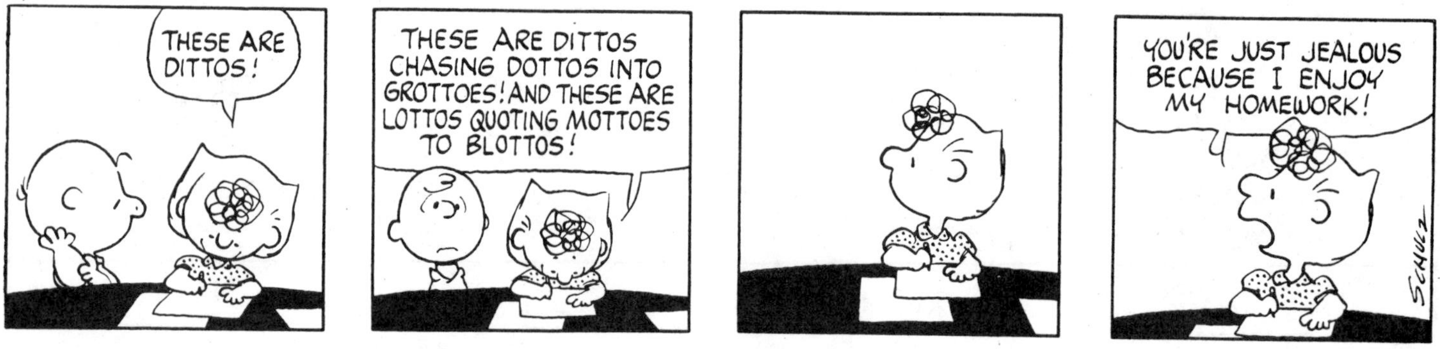
THESE ARE DITTOS!
THESE ARE DITTOS CHASING DOTTOS INTO GROTTOES! AND THESE ARE LOTTOS QUOTING MOTTOES TO BLOTTOS!
YOU'RE JUST JEALOUS BECAUSE I ENJOY MY HOMEWORK!
SCHULZ

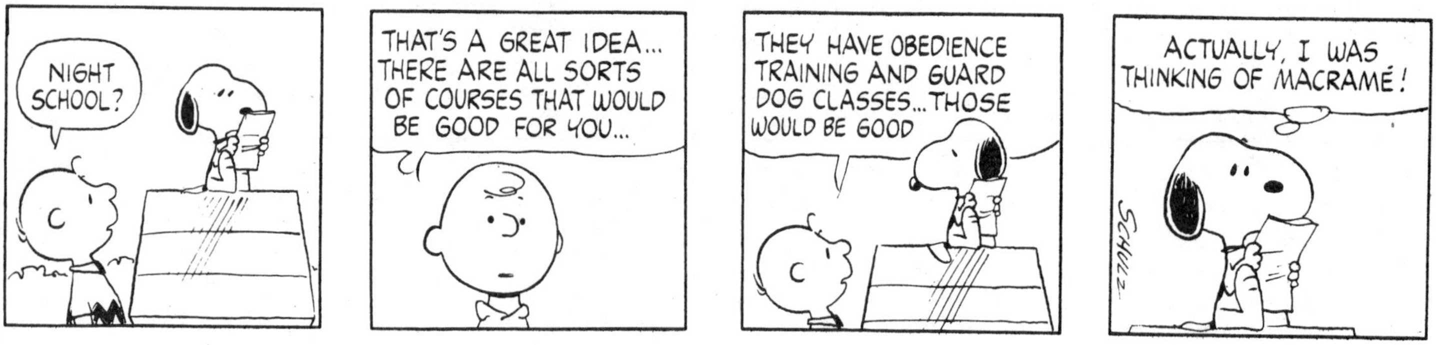
NIGHT SCHOOL?
THAT'S A GREAT IDEA... THERE ARE ALL SORTS OF COURSES THAT WOULD BE GOOD FOR YOU...
THEY HAVE OBEDIENCE TRAINING AND GUARD DOG CLASSES... THOSE WOULD BE GOOD
ACTUALLY, I WAS THINKING OF MACRAMÉ!
SCHULZ

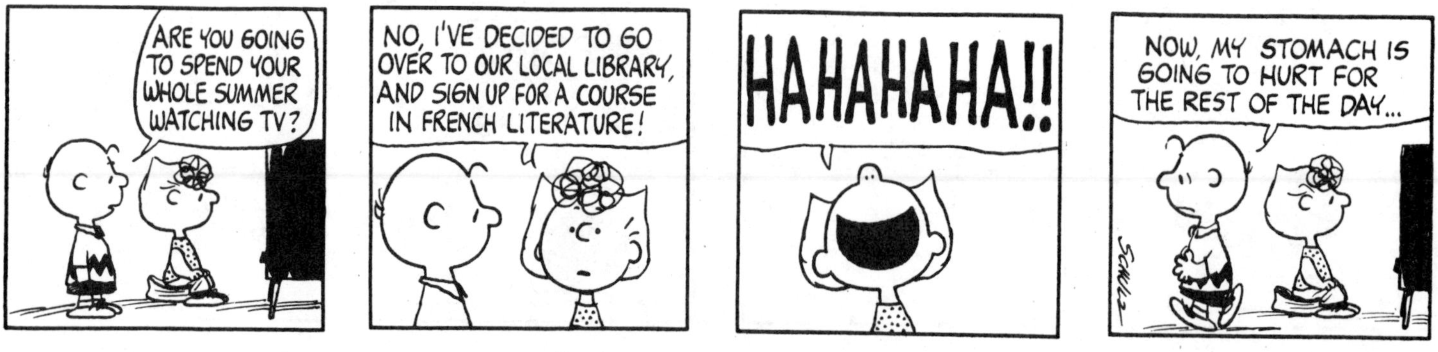
ARE YOU GOING TO SPEND YOUR WHOLE SUMMER WATCHING TV?
NO, I'VE DECIDED TO GO OVER TO OUR LOCAL LIBRARY, AND SIGN UP FOR A COURSE IN FRENCH LITERATURE!
HAHAHAHA!!
NOW, MY STOMACH IS GOING TO HURT FOR THE REST OF THE DAY...
SCHULZ

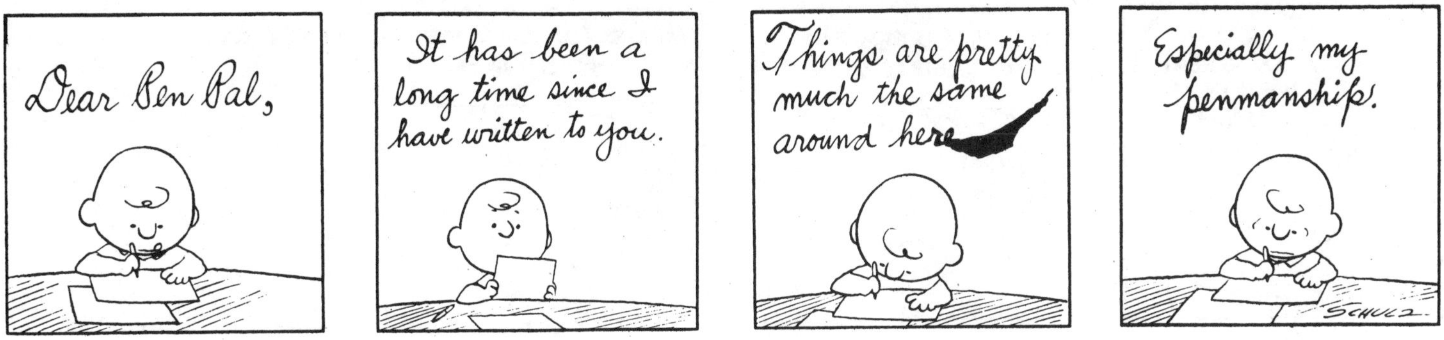
Dear Pen Pal,
It has been a long time since I have written to you.
Things are pretty much the same around here
Especially my penmanship.
SCHULZ

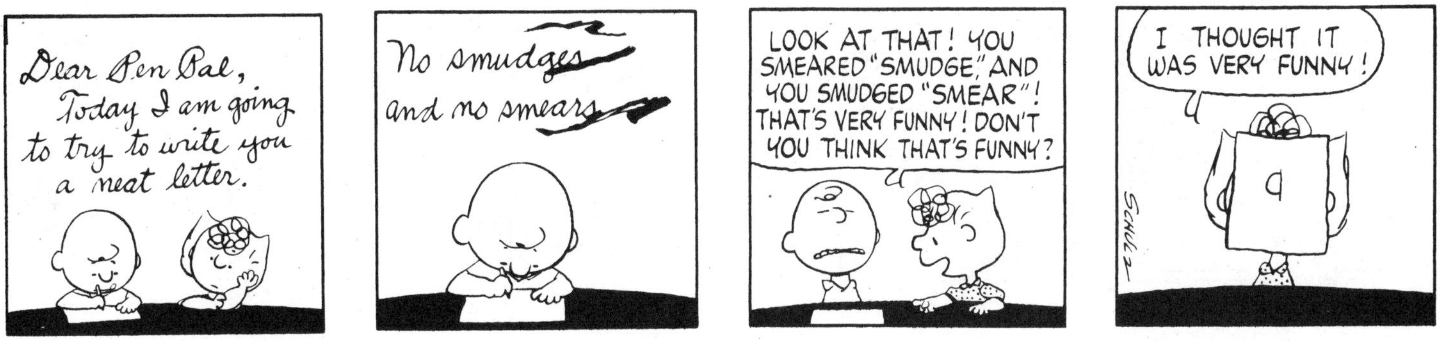
Dear Pen Pal, Today I am going to try to write you a neat letter.
No smudges and no smears
LOOK AT THAT! YOU SMEARED "SMUDGE," AND YOU SMUDGED "SMEAR"! THAT'S VERY FUNNY! DON'T YOU THINK THAT'S FUNNY?
I THOUGHT IT WAS VERY FUNNY!
SCHULZ

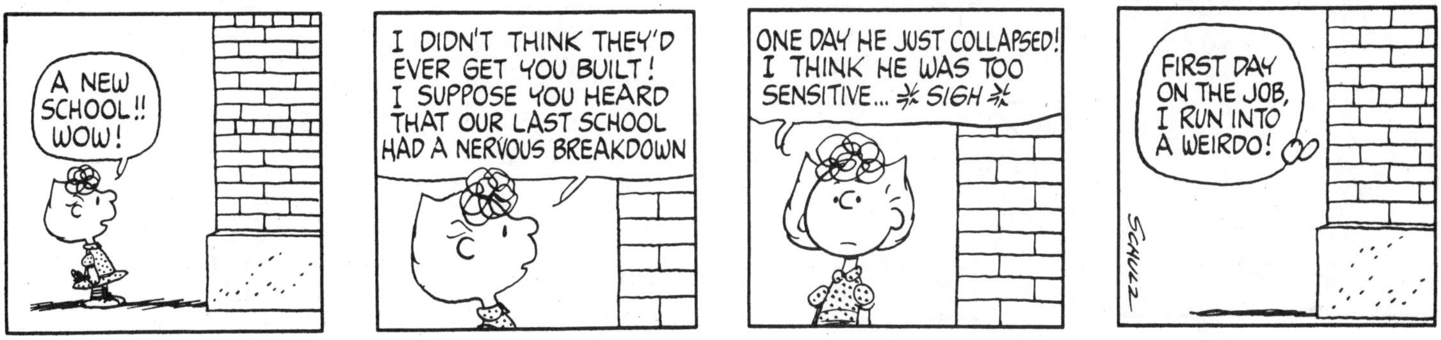
A NEW SCHOOL!! WOW!
I DIDN'T THINK THEY'D EVER GET YOU BUILT! I SUPPOSE YOU HEARD THAT OUR LAST SCHOOL HAD A NERVOUS BREAKDOWN
ONE DAY HE JUST COLLAPSED! I THINK HE WAS TOO SENSITIVE... SIGH
FIRST DAY ON THE JOB, I RUN INTO A WEIRDO!
SCHULZ

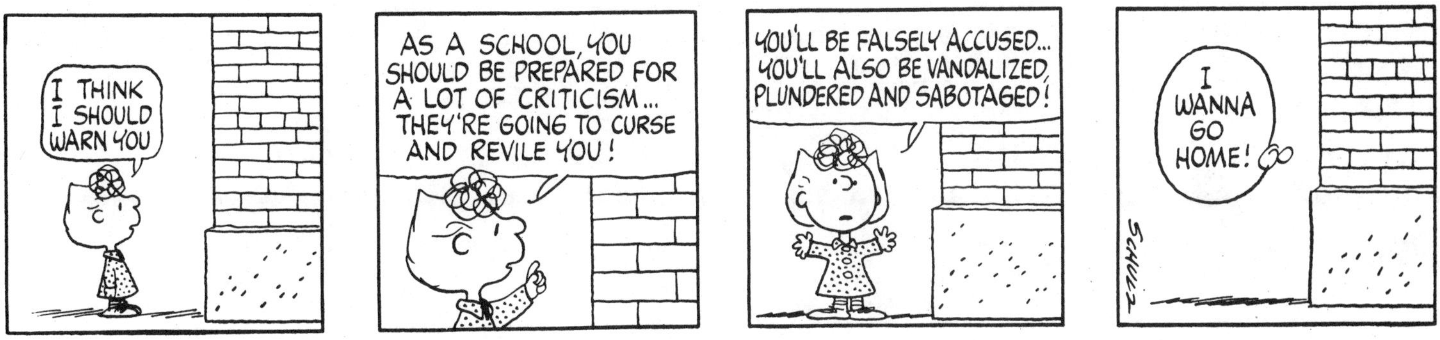
I THINK I SHOULD WARN YOU
AS A SCHOOL, YOU SHOULD BE PREPARED FOR A LOT OF CRITICISM... THEY'RE GOING TO CURSE AND REVILE YOU!
YOU'LL BE FALSELY ACCUSED... YOU'LL ALSO BE VANDALIZED, PLUNDERED AND SABOTAGED!
I WANNA GO HOME!
SCHULZ

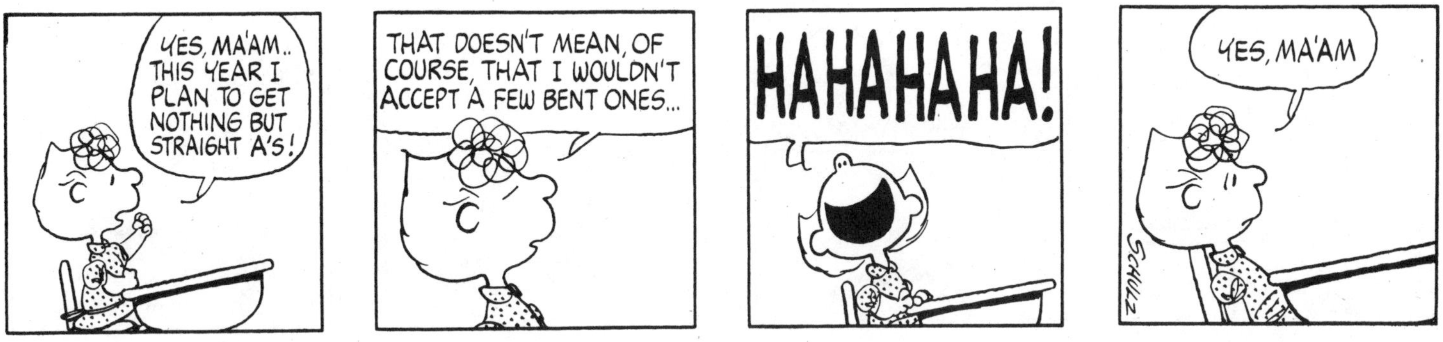
YES, MA'AM.. THIS YEAR I PLAN TO GET NOTHING BUT STRAIGHT A'S!
THAT DOESN'T MEAN, OF COURSE, THAT I WOULDN'T ACCEPT A FEW BENT ONES...
HAHAHAHA!
YES, MA'AM
SCHULZ

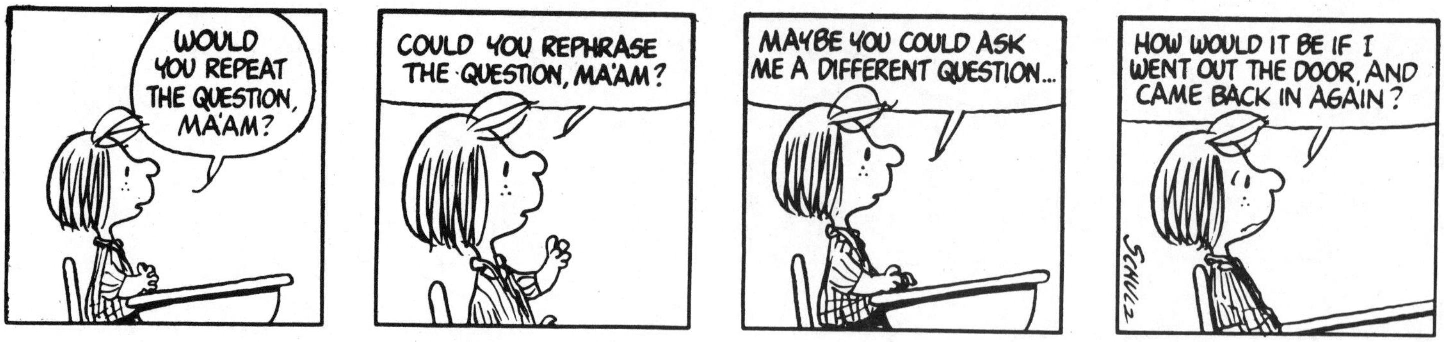
WOULD YOU REPEAT THE QUESTION, MA'AM?
COULD YOU REPHRASE THE QUESTION, MA'AM?
MAYBE YOU COULD ASK ME A DIFFERENT QUESTION...
HOW WOULD IT BE IF I WENT OUT THE DOOR, AND CAME BACK IN AGAIN?
SCHULZ

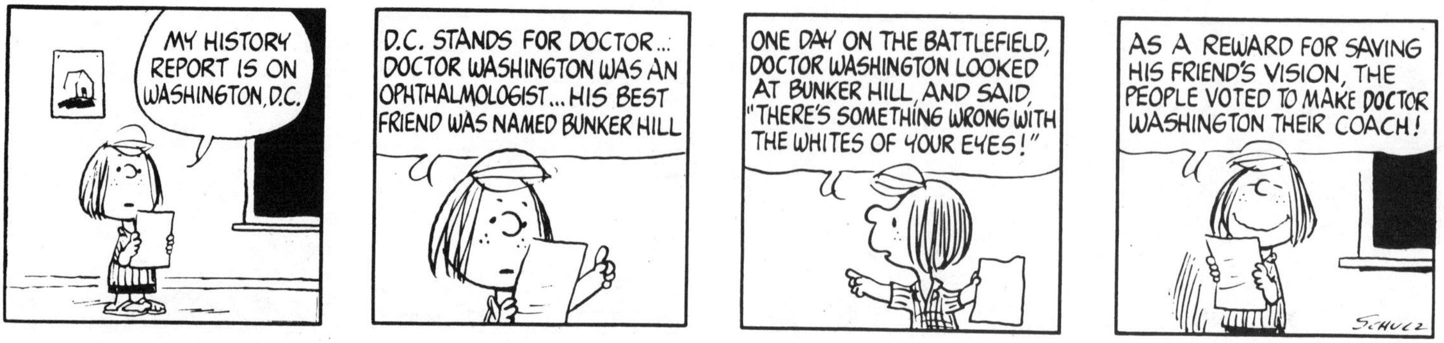
MY HISTORY REPORT IS ON WASHINGTON, D.C.
D.C. STANDS FOR DOCTOR... DOCTOR WASHINGTON WAS AN OPHTHALMOLOGIST... HIS BEST FRIEND WAS NAMED BUNKER HILL
ONE DAY ON THE BATTLEFIELD, DOCTOR WASHINGTON LOOKED AT BUNKER HILL, AND SAID, "THERE'S SOMETHING WRONG WITH THE WHITES OF YOUR EYES!"
AS A REWARD FOR SAVING HIS FRIEND'S VISION, THE PEOPLE VOTED TO MAKE DOCTOR WASHINGTON THEIR COACH!
SCHULZ

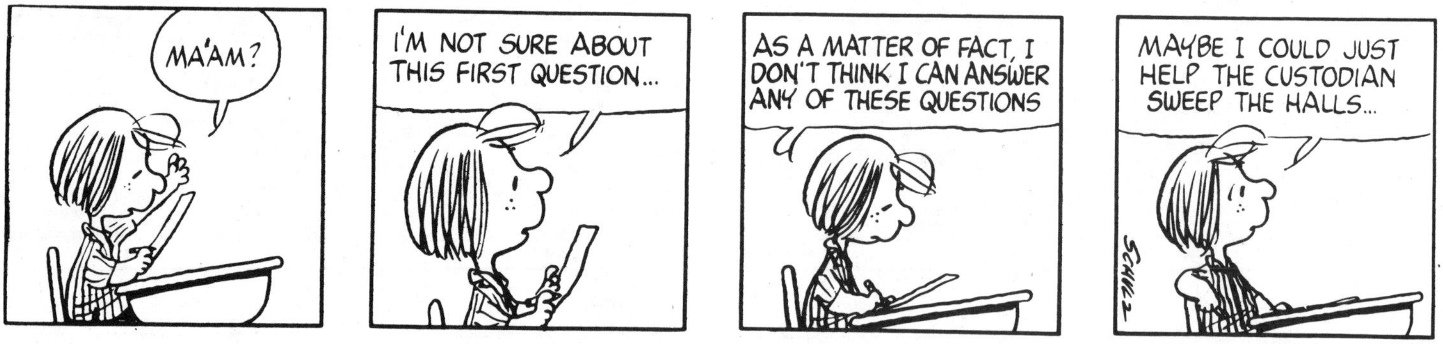
MA'AM?
I'M NOT SURE ABOUT THIS FIRST QUESTION...
AS A MATTER OF FACT, I DON'T THINK I CAN ANSWER ANY OF THESE QUESTIONS
MAYBE I COULD JUST HELP THE CUSTODIAN SWEEP THE HALLS...
SCHULZ

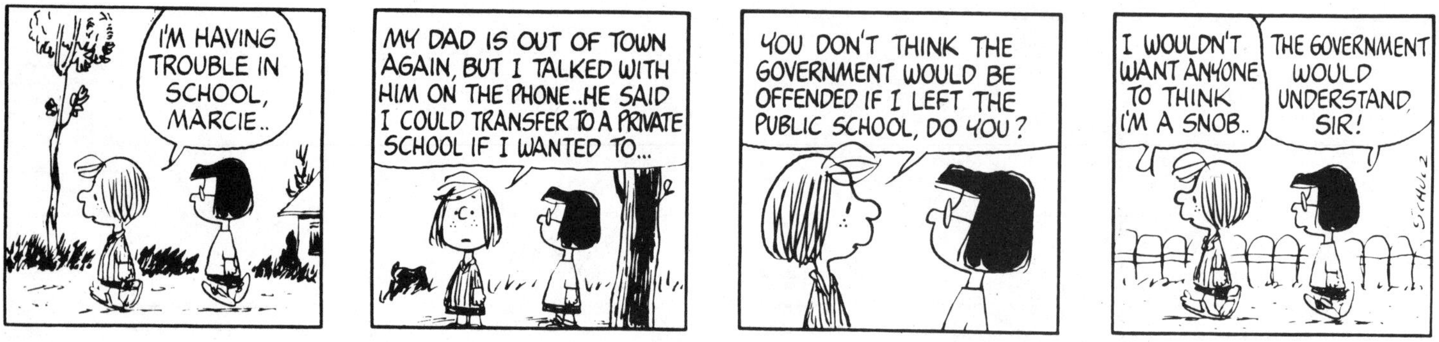
I'M HAVING TROUBLE IN SCHOOL, MARCIE..
MY DAD IS OUT OF TOWN AGAIN, BUT I TALKED WITH HIM ON THE PHONE..HE SAID I COULD TRANSFER TO A PRIVATE SCHOOL IF I WANTED TO...
YOU DON'T THINK THE GOVERNMENT WOULD BE OFFENDED IF I LEFT THE PUBLIC SCHOOL, DO YOU?
I WOULDN'T WANT ANYONE TO THINK I'M A SNOB..
THE GOVERNMENT WOULD UNDERSTAND, SIR!
SCHULZ

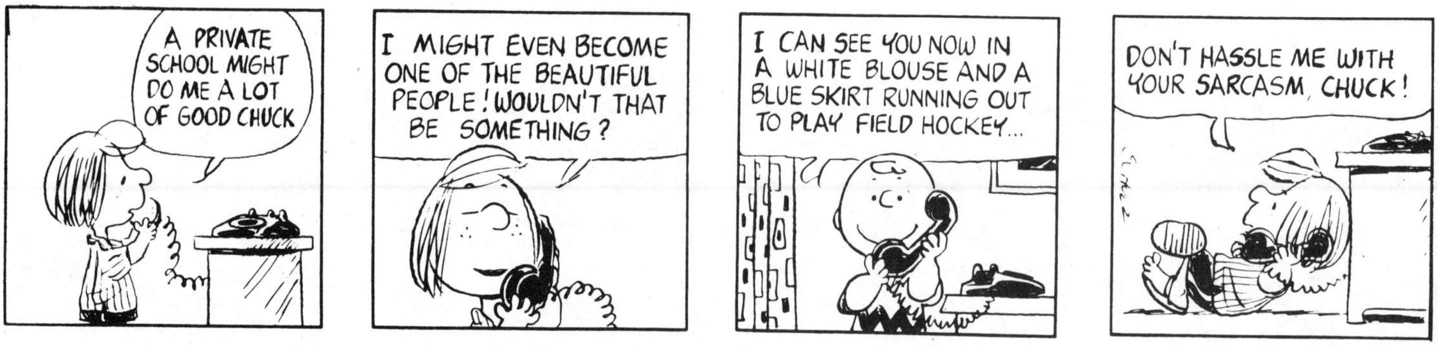
A PRIVATE SCHOOL MIGHT DO ME A LOT OF GOOD CHUCK
I MIGHT EVEN BECOME ONE OF THE BEAUTIFUL PEOPLE! WOULDN'T THAT BE SOMETHING?
I CAN SEE YOU NOW IN A WHITE BLOUSE AND A BLUE SKIRT RUNNING OUT TO PLAY FIELD HOCKEY...
DON'T HASSLE ME WITH YOUR SARCASM, CHUCK!

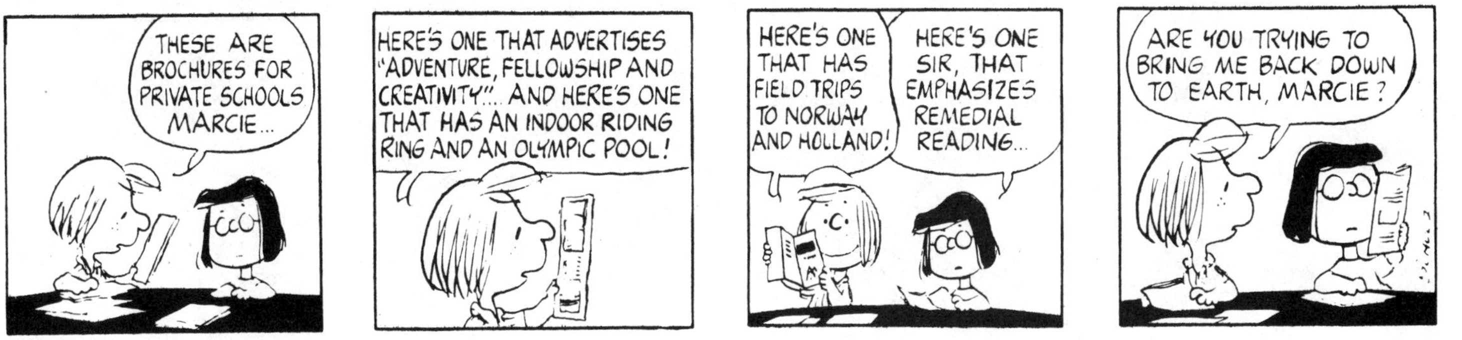
THESE ARE BROCHURES FOR PRIVATE SCHOOLS MARCIE...
HERE'S ONE THAT ADVERTISES "ADVENTURE, FELLOWSHIP AND CREATIVITY"... AND HERE'S ONE THAT HAS AN INDOOR RIDING RING AND AN OLYMPIC POOL!
HERE'S ONE THAT HAS FIELD TRIPS TO NORWAY AND HOLLAND!
HERE'S ONE SIR, THAT EMPHASIZES REMEDIAL READING...
ARE YOU TRYING TO BRING ME BACK DOWN TO EARTH, MARCIE?

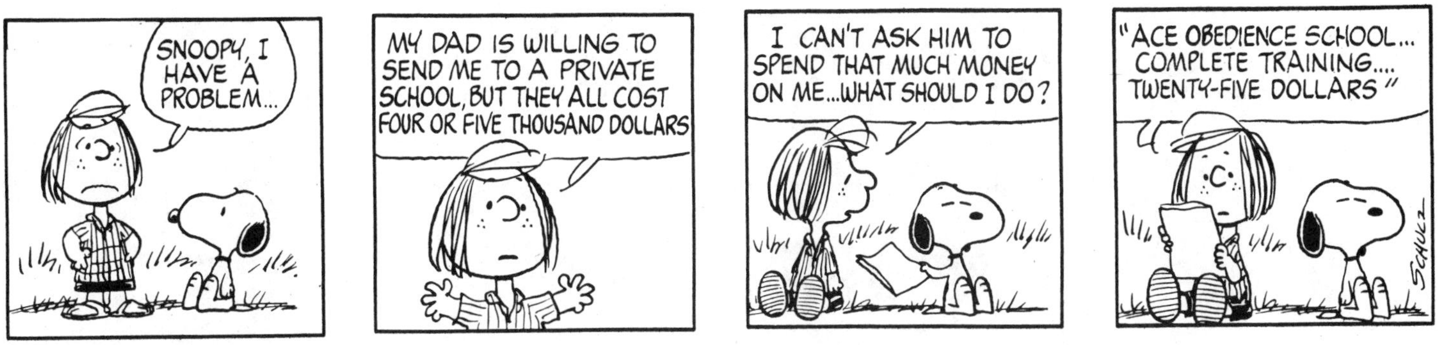
SNOOPY, I HAVE A PROBLEM...
MY DAD IS WILLING TO SEND ME TO A PRIVATE SCHOOL, BUT THEY ALL COST FOUR OR FIVE THOUSAND DOLLARS
I CAN'T ASK HIM TO SPEND THAT MUCH MONEY ON ME...WHAT SHOULD I DO?
"ACE OBEDIENCE SCHOOL... COMPLETE TRAINING.... TWENTY-FIVE DOLLARS"
SCHULZ

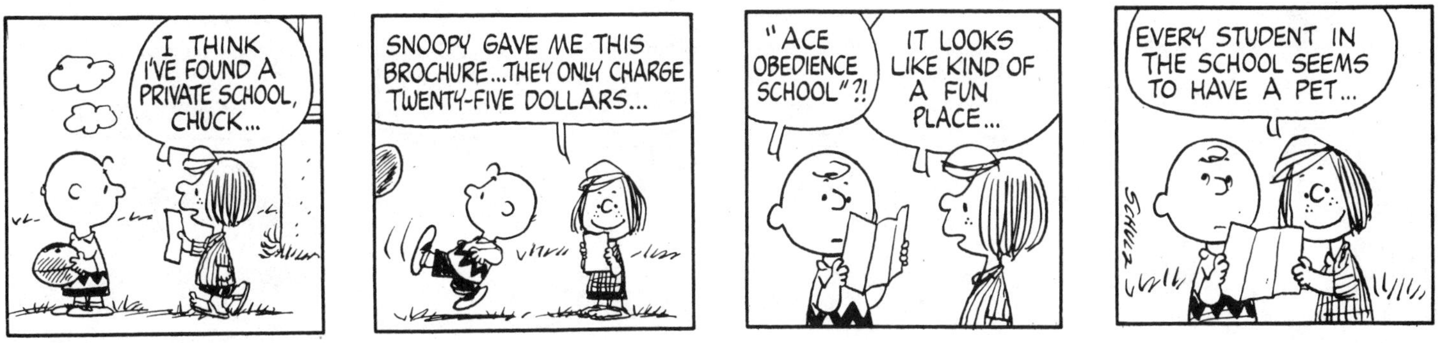
I THINK I'VE FOUND A PRIVATE SCHOOL, CHUCK...
SNOOPY GAVE ME THIS BROCHURE...THEY ONLY CHARGE TWENTY-FIVE DOLLARS...
"ACE OBEDIENCE SCHOOL"?!
IT LOOKS LIKE KIND OF A FUN PLACE...
EVERY STUDENT IN THE SCHOOL SEEMS TO HAVE A PET...
SCHULZ

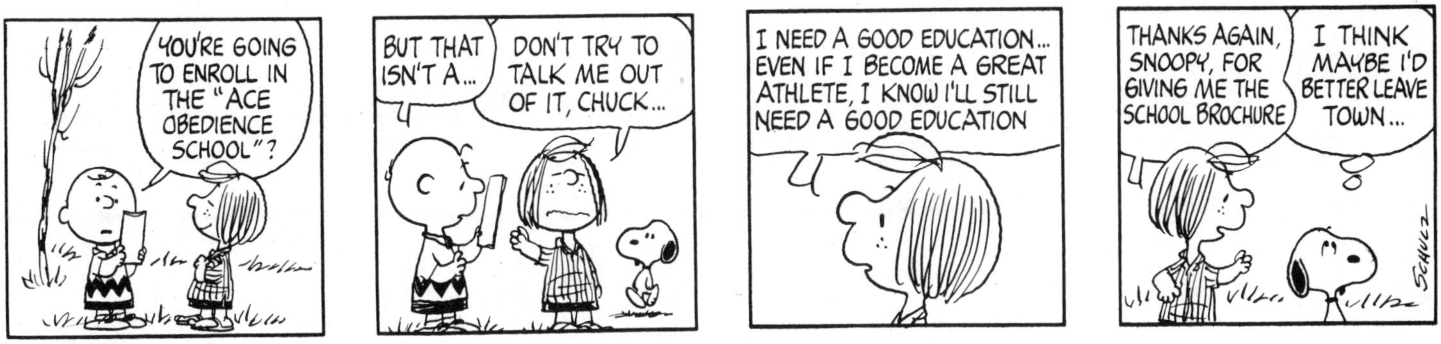
YOU'RE GOING TO ENROLL IN THE "ACE OBEDIENCE SCHOOL"?
BUT THAT ISN'T A...
DON'T TRY TO TALK ME OUT OF IT, CHUCK...
I NEED A GOOD EDUCATION... EVEN IF I BECOME A GREAT ATHLETE, I KNOW I'LL STILL NEED A GOOD EDUCATION
THANKS AGAIN, SNOOPY, FOR GIVING ME THE SCHOOL BROCHURE
I THINK MAYBE I'D BETTER LEAVE TOWN...
SCHULZ

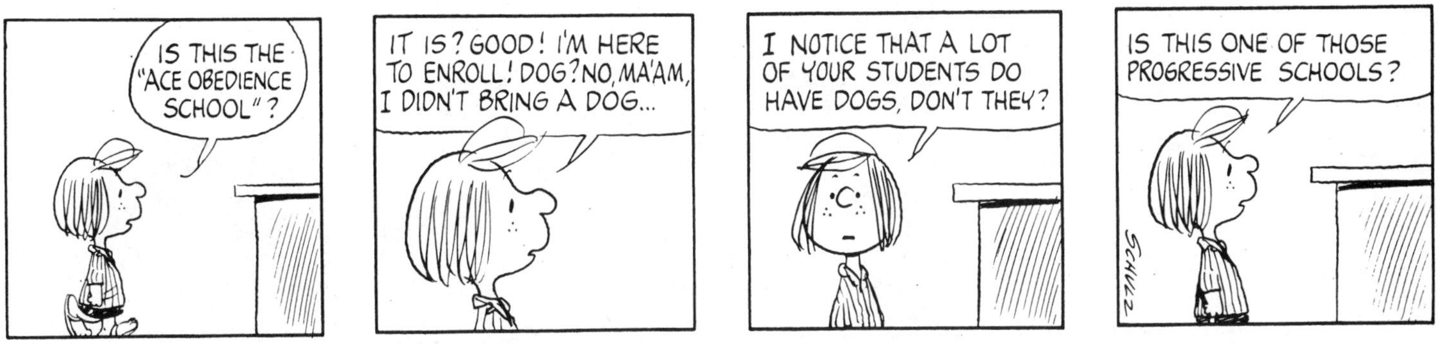
IS THIS THE "ACE OBEDIENCE SCHOOL"?
IT IS? GOOD! I'M HERE TO ENROLL! DOG? NO, MA'AM, I DIDN'T BRING A DOG...
I NOTICE THAT A LOT OF YOUR STUDENTS DO HAVE DOGS, DON'T THEY?
IS THIS ONE OF THOSE PROGRESSIVE SCHOOLS?
SCHULZ

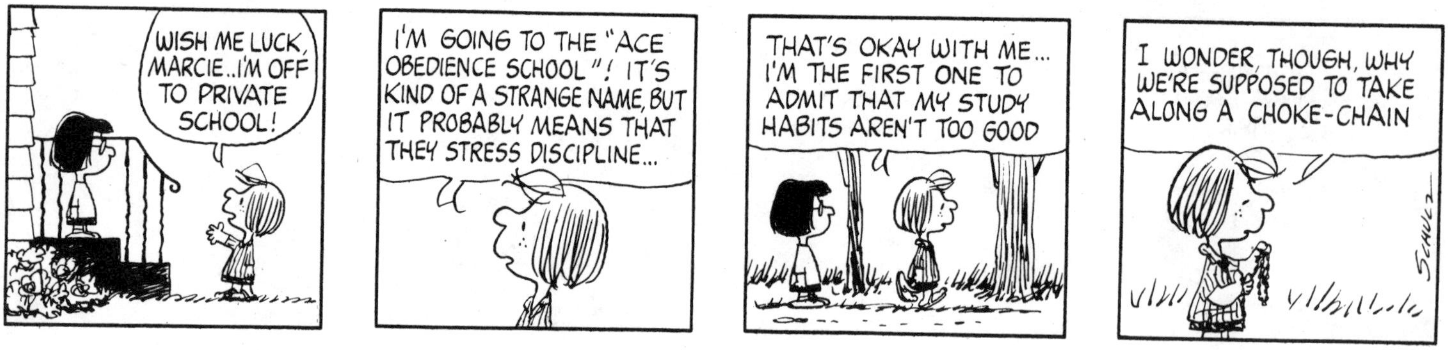
WISH ME LUCK, MARCIE..I'M OFF TO PRIVATE SCHOOL!
I'M GOING TO THE "ACE OBEDIENCE SCHOOL"! IT'S KIND OF A STRANGE NAME, BUT IT PROBABLY MEANS THAT THEY STRESS DISCIPLINE...
THAT'S OKAY WITH ME... I'M THE FIRST ONE TO ADMIT THAT MY STUDY HABITS AREN'T TOO GOOD
I WONDER, THOUGH, WHY WE'RE SUPPOSED TO TAKE ALONG A CHOKE-CHAIN

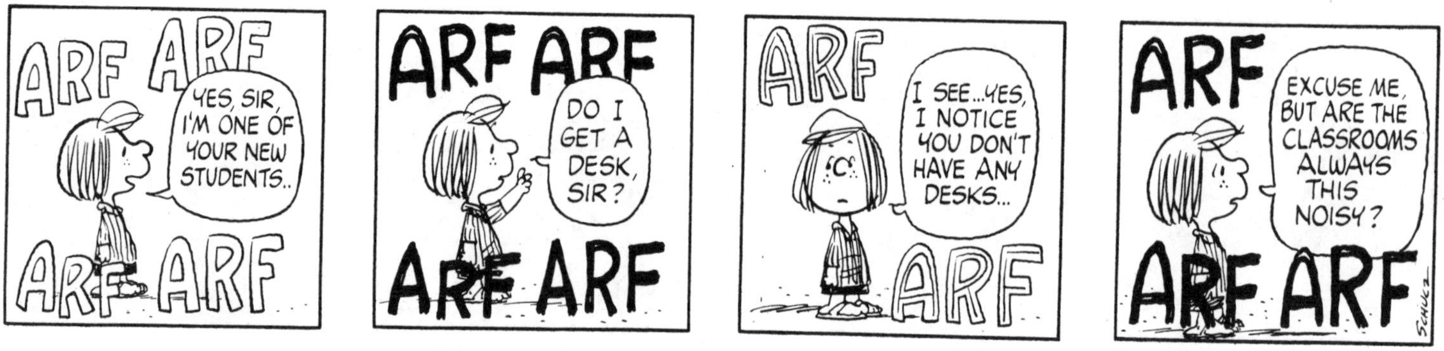
ARF ARF
YES, SIR, I'M ONE OF YOUR NEW STUDENTS..
ARF ARF
ARF ARF
DO I GET A DESK, SIR?
ARF ARF
ARF
I SEE...YES, I NOTICE YOU DON'T HAVE ANY DESKS...
ARF
ARF
EXCUSE ME, BUT ARE THE CLASSROOMS ALWAYS THIS NOISY?
ARF ARF

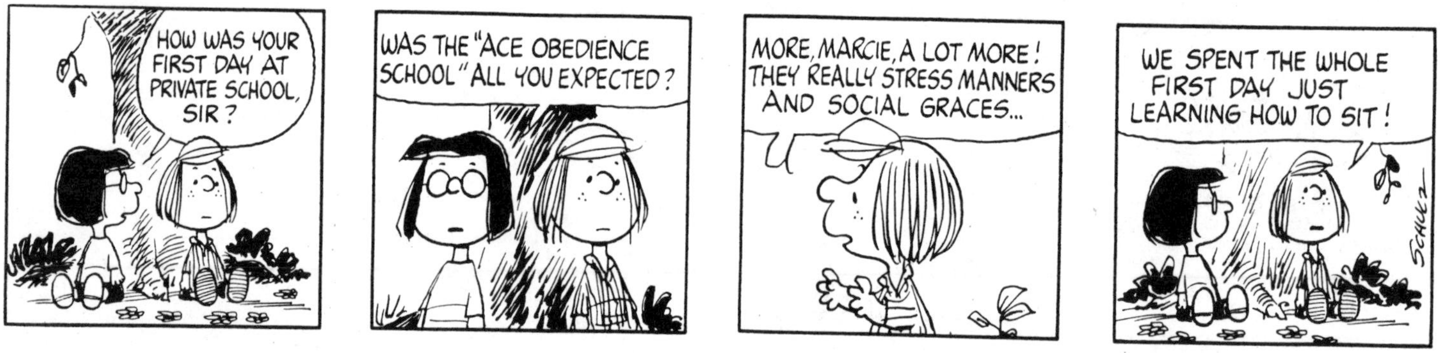
HOW WAS YOUR FIRST DAY AT PRIVATE SCHOOL, SIR?
WAS THE "ACE OBEDIENCE SCHOOL" ALL YOU EXPECTED?
MORE, MARCIE, A LOT MORE! THEY REALLY STRESS MANNERS AND SOCIAL GRACES...
WE SPENT THE WHOLE FIRST DAY JUST LEARNING HOW TO SIT!

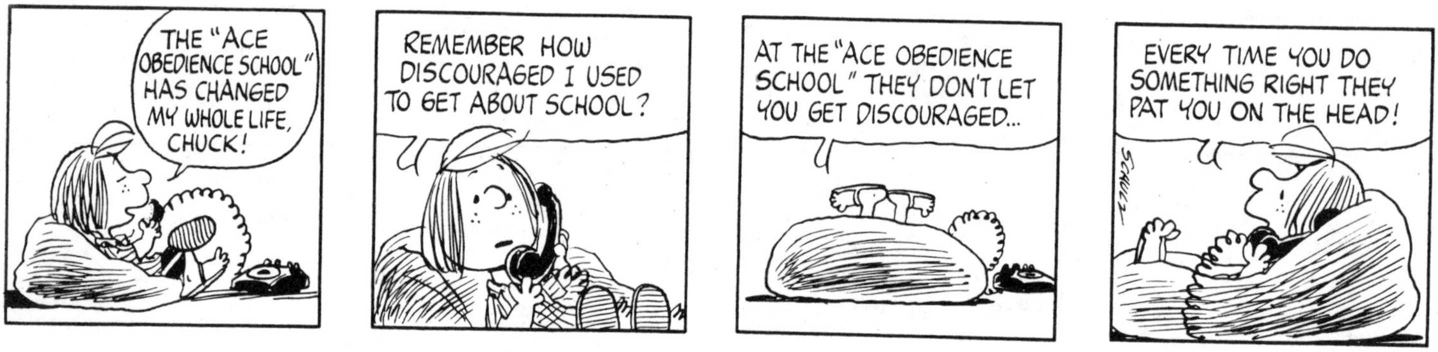
THE "ACE OBEDIENCE SCHOOL" HAS CHANGED MY WHOLE LIFE, CHUCK!
REMEMBER HOW DISCOURAGED I USED TO GET ABOUT SCHOOL?
AT THE "ACE OBEDIENCE SCHOOL" THEY DON'T LET YOU GET DISCOURAGED...
EVERY TIME YOU DO SOMETHING RIGHT THEY PAT YOU ON THE HEAD!

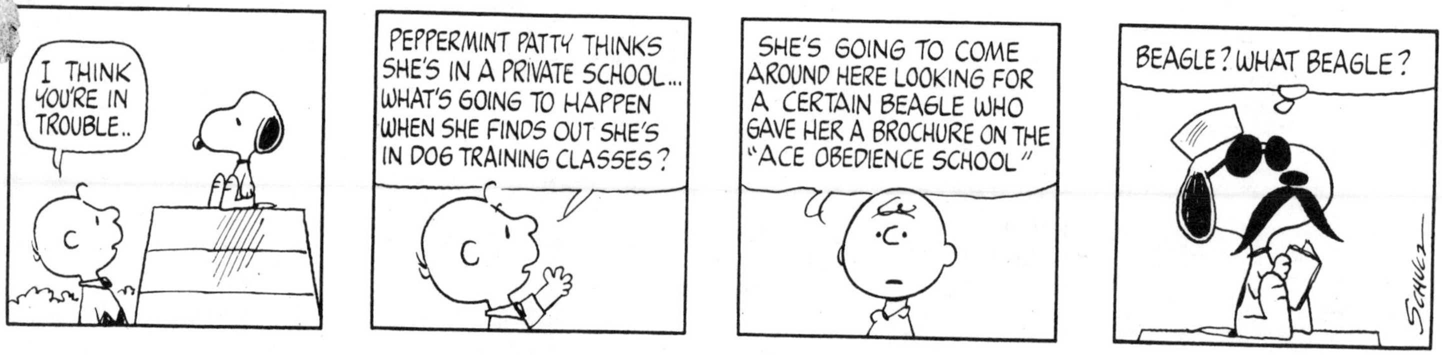
I THINK YOU'RE IN TROUBLE..
PEPPERMINT PATTY THINKS SHE'S IN A PRIVATE SCHOOL... WHAT'S GOING TO HAPPEN WHEN SHE FINDS OUT SHE'S IN DOG TRAINING CLASSES?
SHE'S GOING TO COME AROUND HERE LOOKING FOR A CERTAIN BEAGLE WHO GAVE HER A BROCHURE ON THE "ACE OBEDIENCE SCHOOL"
BEAGLE? WHAT BEAGLE?

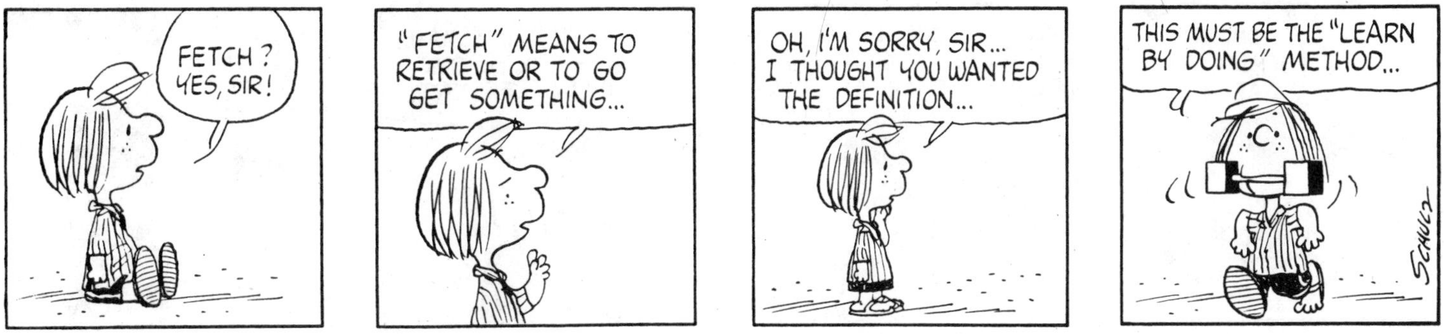
FETCH? YES, SIR!
"FETCH" MEANS TO RETRIEVE OR TO GO GET SOMETHING...
OH, I'M SORRY, SIR... I THOUGHT YOU WANTED THE DEFINITION...
THIS MUST BE THE "LEARN BY DOING" METHOD...

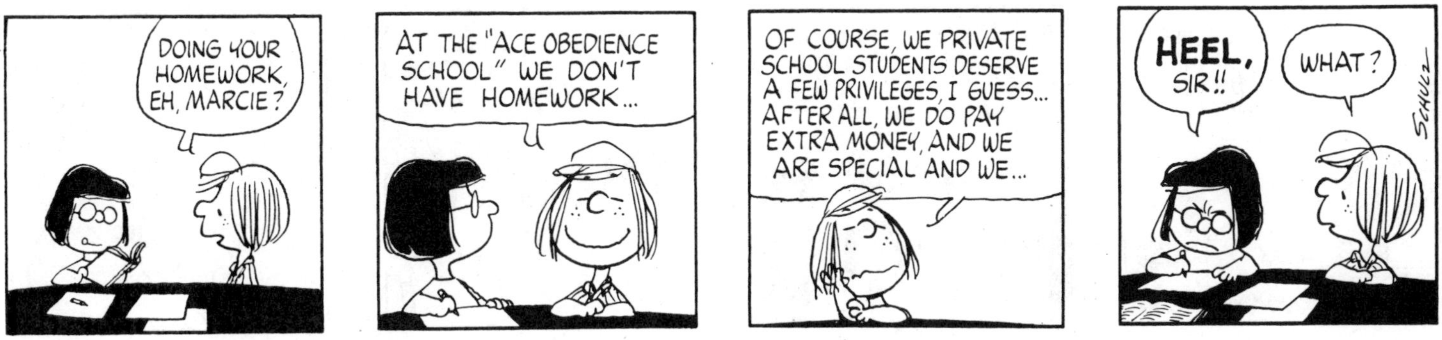
DOING YOUR HOMEWORK, EH, MARCIE?
AT THE "ACE OBEDIENCE SCHOOL" WE DON'T HAVE HOMEWORK...
OF COURSE, WE PRIVATE SCHOOL STUDENTS DESERVE A FEW PRIVILEGES, I GUESS... AFTER ALL, WE DO PAY EXTRA MONEY, AND WE ARE SPECIAL AND WE...
HEEL, SIR!!
WHAT?

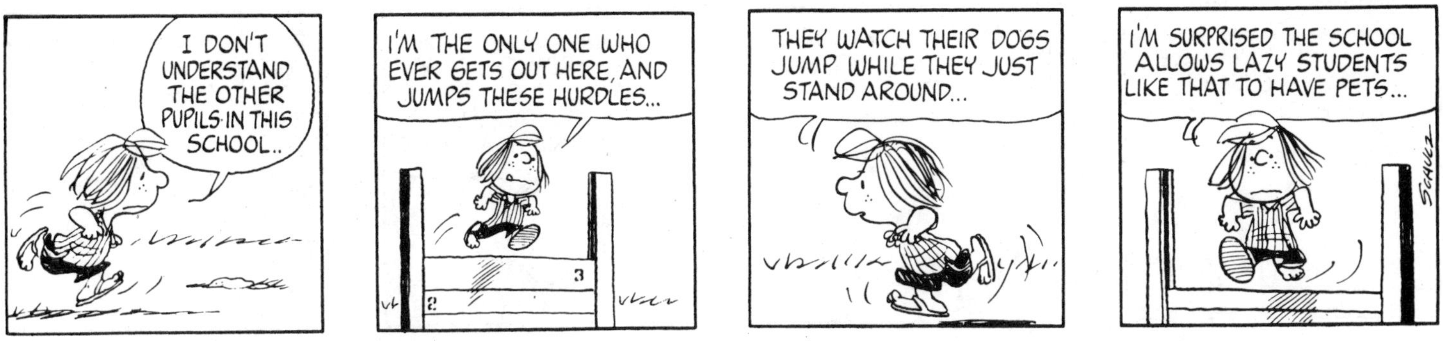
I DON'T UNDERSTAND THE OTHER PUPILS IN THIS SCHOOL..
I'M THE ONLY ONE WHO EVER GETS OUT HERE, AND JUMPS THESE HURDLES...
3
2
THEY WATCH THEIR DOGS JUMP WHILE THEY JUST STAND AROUND...
I'M SURPRISED THE SCHOOL ALLOWS LAZY STUDENTS LIKE THAT TO HAVE PETS...

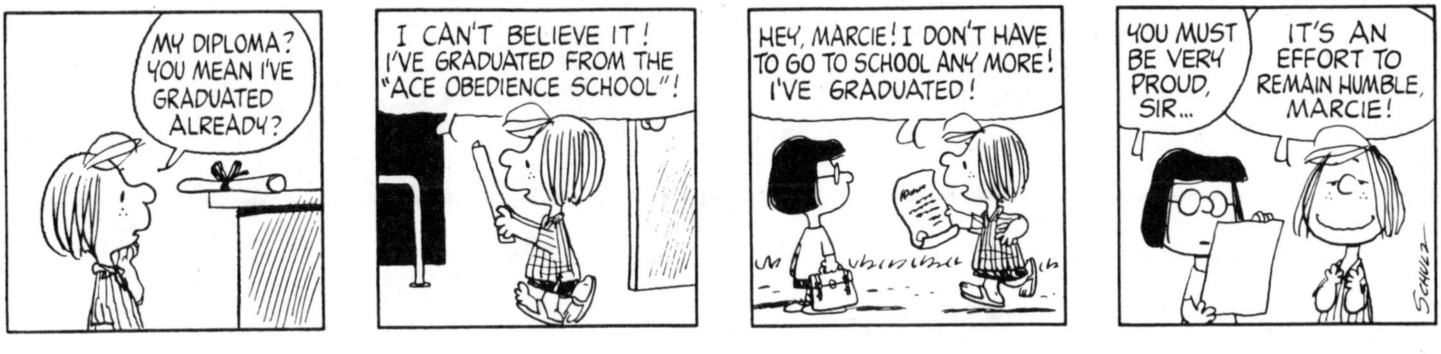
MY DIPLOMA? YOU MEAN I'VE GRADUATED ALREADY?
I CAN'T BELIEVE IT! I'VE GRADUATED FROM THE "ACE OBEDIENCE SCHOOL"!
HEY, MARCIE! I DON'T HAVE TO GO TO SCHOOL ANY MORE! I'VE GRADUATED!
YOU MUST BE VERY PROUD, SIR...
IT'S AN EFFORT TO REMAIN HUMBLE, MARCIE!

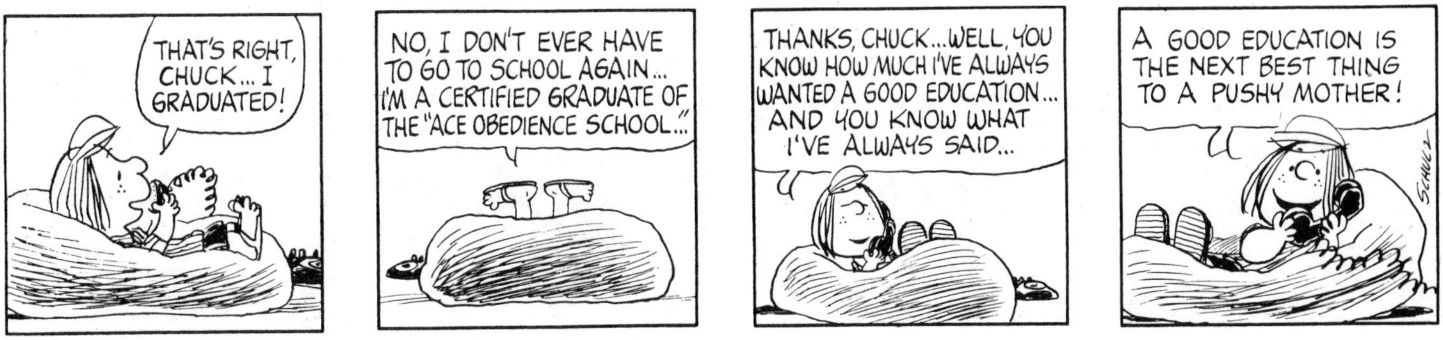
THAT'S RIGHT, CHUCK... I GRADUATED!
NO, I DON'T EVER HAVE TO GO TO SCHOOL AGAIN... I'M A CERTIFIED GRADUATE OF THE "ACE OBEDIENCE SCHOOL."
THANKS, CHUCK... WELL, YOU KNOW HOW MUCH I'VE ALWAYS WANTED A GOOD EDUCATION... AND YOU KNOW WHAT I'VE ALWAYS SAID...
A GOOD EDUCATION IS THE NEXT BEST THING TO A PUSHY MOTHER!

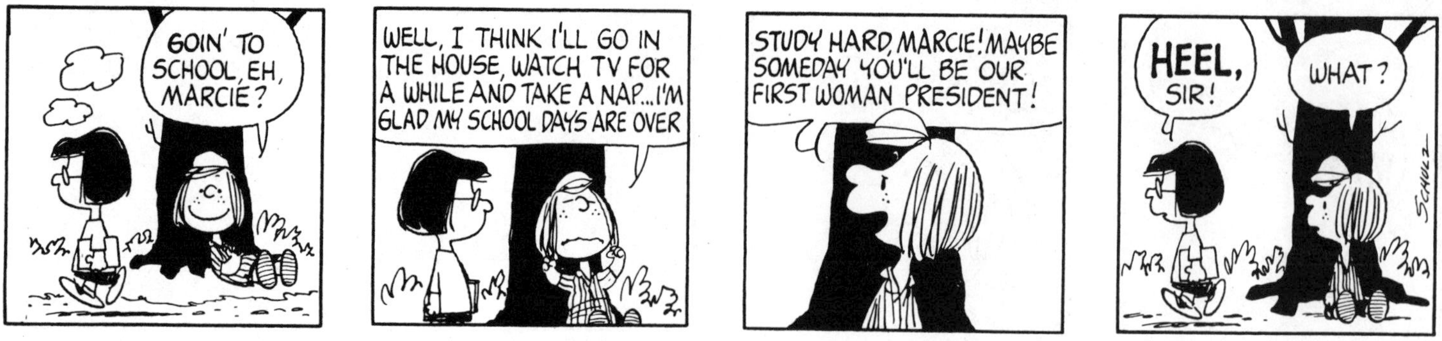
GOIN' TO SCHOOL, EH, MARCIE?
WELL, I THINK I'LL GO IN THE HOUSE, WATCH TV FOR A WHILE AND TAKE A NAP...I'M GLAD MY SCHOOL DAYS ARE OVER
STUDY HARD, MARCIE! MAYBE SOMEDAY YOU'LL BE OUR FIRST WOMAN PRESIDENT!
HEEL, SIR!
WHAT?
SCHULZ

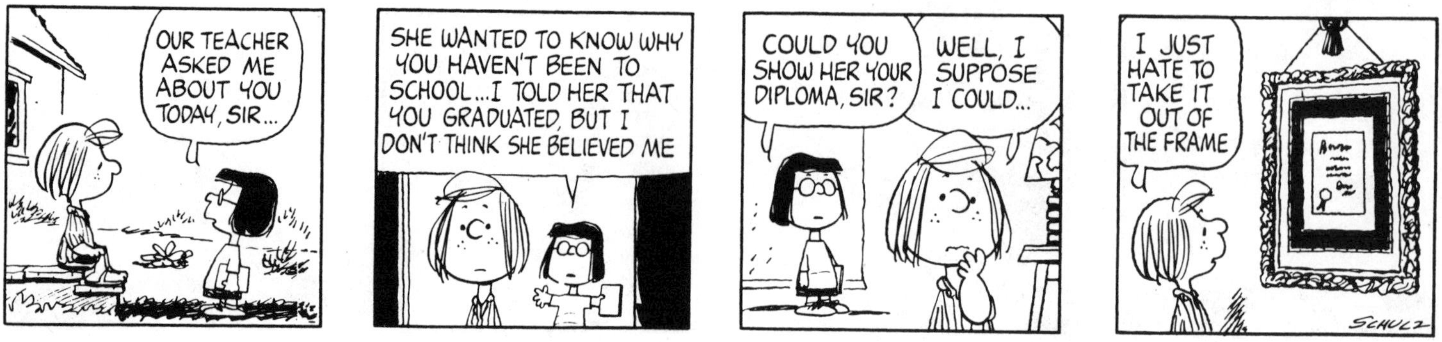
OUR TEACHER ASKED ME ABOUT YOU TODAY, SIR...
SHE WANTED TO KNOW WHY YOU HAVEN'T BEEN TO SCHOOL...I TOLD HER THAT YOU GRADUATED, BUT I DON'T THINK SHE BELIEVED ME
COULD YOU SHOW HER YOUR DIPLOMA, SIR?
WELL, I SUPPOSE I COULD...
I JUST HATE TO TAKE IT OUT OF THE FRAME
SCHULZ

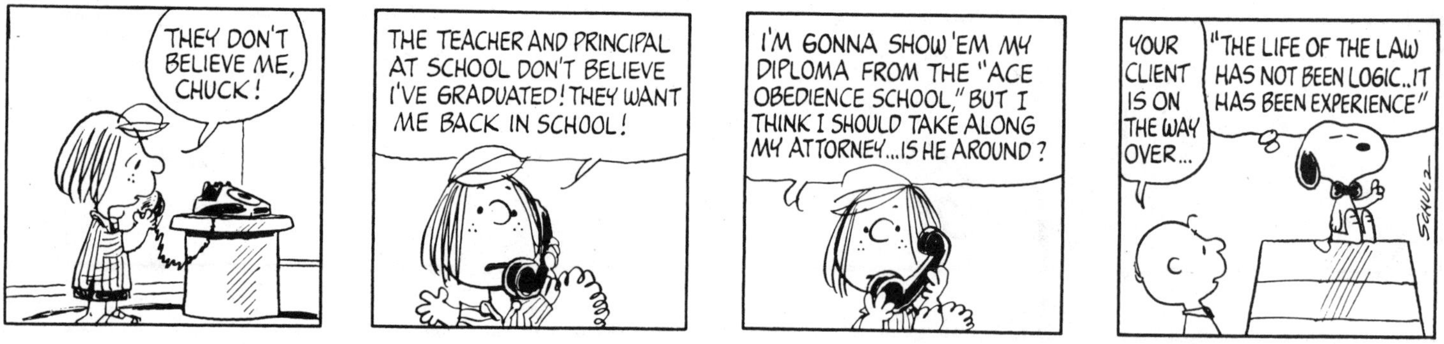
THEY DON'T BELIEVE ME, CHUCK!
THE TEACHER AND PRINCIPAL AT SCHOOL DON'T BELIEVE I'VE GRADUATED! THEY WANT ME BACK IN SCHOOL!
I'M GONNA SHOW 'EM MY DIPLOMA FROM THE "ACE OBEDIENCE SCHOOL," BUT I THINK I SHOULD TAKE ALONG MY ATTORNEY...IS HE AROUND?
YOUR CLIENT IS ON THE WAY OVER...
"THE LIFE OF THE LAW HAS NOT BEEN LOGIC..IT HAS BEEN EXPERIENCE"
SCHULZ

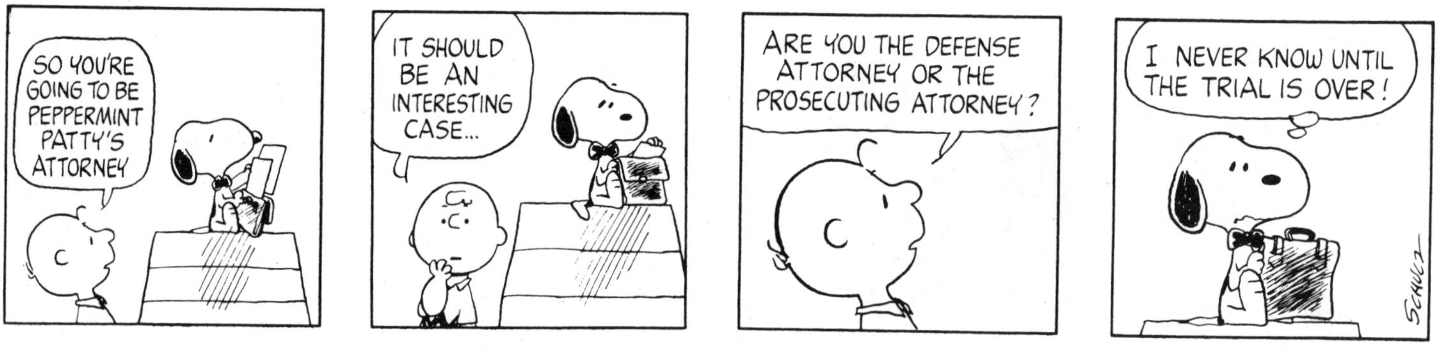
SO YOU'RE GOING TO BE PEPPERMINT PATTY'S ATTORNEY
IT SHOULD BE AN INTERESTING CASE...
ARE YOU THE DEFENSE ATTORNEY OR THE PROSECUTING ATTORNEY?
I NEVER KNOW UNTIL THE TRIAL IS OVER!
SCHULZ

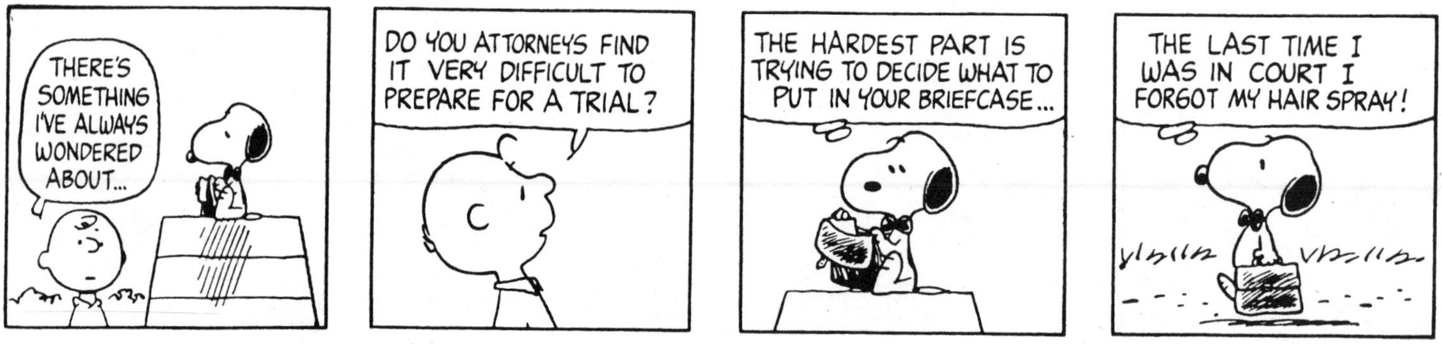
THERE'S SOMETHING I'VE ALWAYS WONDERED ABOUT...
DO YOU ATTORNEYS FIND IT VERY DIFFICULT TO PREPARE FOR A TRIAL?
THE HARDEST PART IS TRYING TO DECIDE WHAT TO PUT IN YOUR BRIEFCASE...
THE LAST TIME I WAS IN COURT I FORGOT MY HAIR SPRAY!

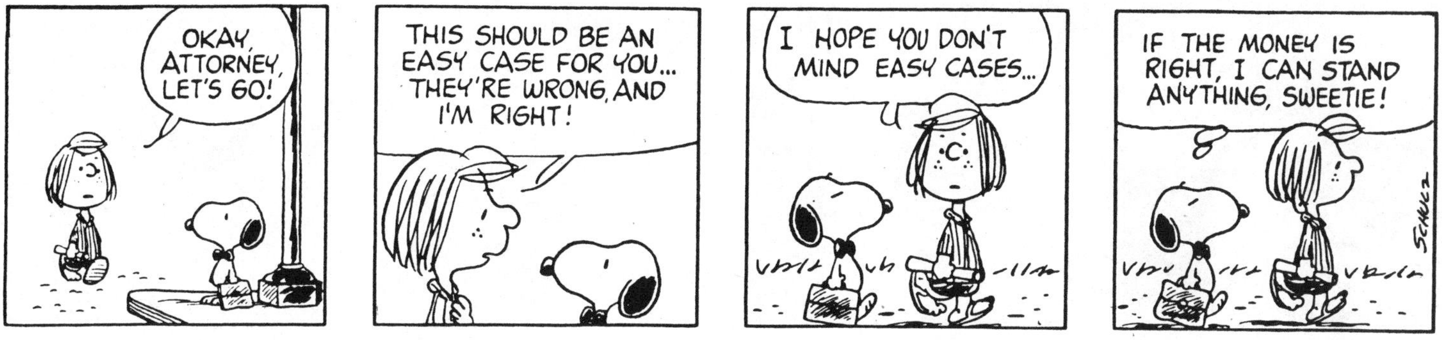
OKAY, ATTORNEY, LET'S GO!
THIS SHOULD BE AN EASY CASE FOR YOU... THEY'RE WRONG, AND I'M RIGHT!
I HOPE YOU DON'T MIND EASY CASES...
IF THE MONEY IS RIGHT, I CAN STAND ANYTHING, SWEETIE!
SCHULZ

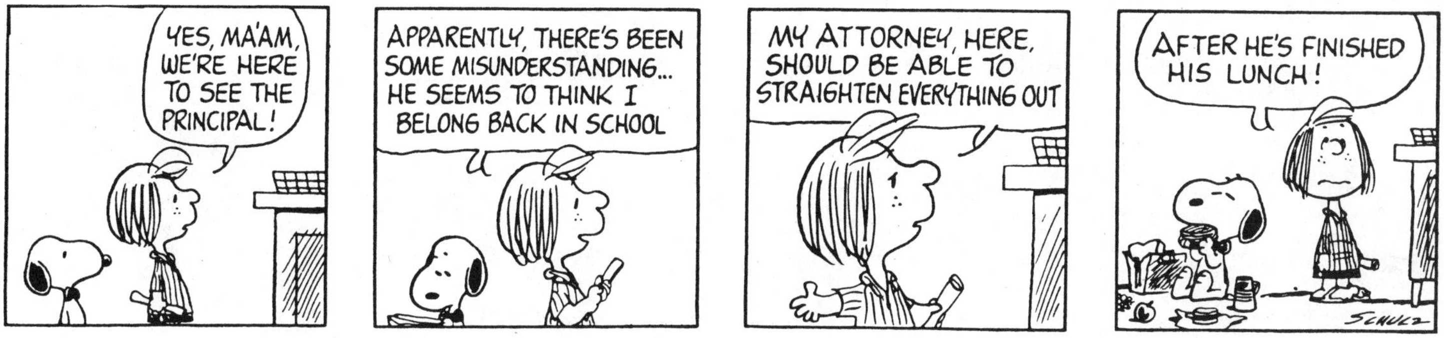
YES, MA'AM, WE'RE HERE TO SEE THE PRINCIPAL!
APPARENTLY, THERE'S BEEN SOME MISUNDERSTANDING... HE SEEMS TO THINK I BELONG BACK IN SCHOOL
MY ATTORNEY, HERE, SHOULD BE ABLE TO STRAIGHTEN EVERYTHING OUT
AFTER HE'S FINISHED HIS LUNCH!
SCHULZ

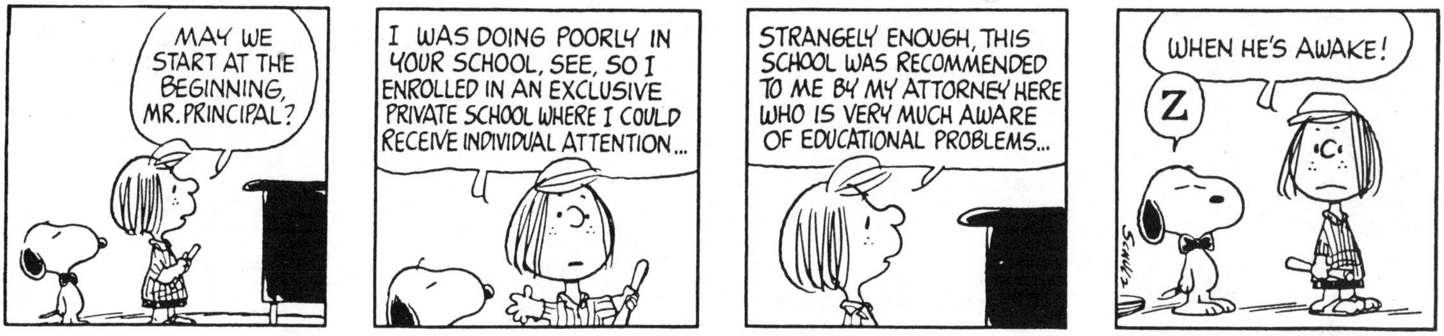
MAY WE START AT THE BEGINNING, MR. PRINCIPAL?
I WAS DOING POORLY IN YOUR SCHOOL, SEE, SO I ENROLLED IN AN EXCLUSIVE PRIVATE SCHOOL WHERE I COULD RECEIVE INDIVIDUAL ATTENTION...
STRANGELY ENOUGH, THIS SCHOOL WAS RECOMMENDED TO ME BY MY ATTORNEY HERE WHO IS VERY MUCH AWARE OF EDUCATIONAL PROBLEMS...
Z
WHEN HE'S AWAKE!
SCHULZ

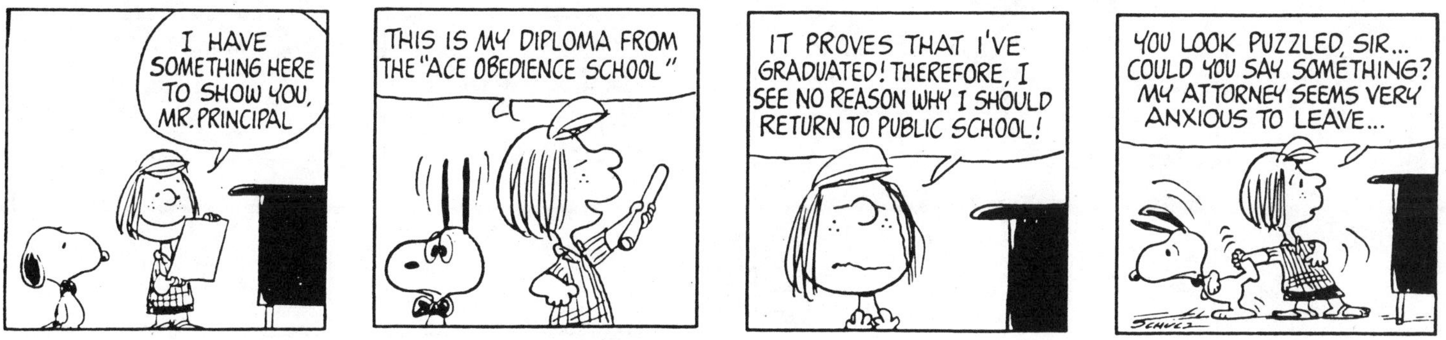
I HAVE SOMETHING HERE TO SHOW YOU, MR. PRINCIPAL
THIS IS MY DIPLOMA FROM THE "ACE OBEDIENCE SCHOOL"
IT PROVES THAT I'VE GRADUATED! THEREFORE, I SEE NO REASON WHY I SHOULD RETURN TO PUBLIC SCHOOL!
YOU LOOK PUZZLED, SIR... COULD YOU SAY SOMETHING? MY ATTORNEY SEEMS VERY ANXIOUS TO LEAVE...
SCHULZ

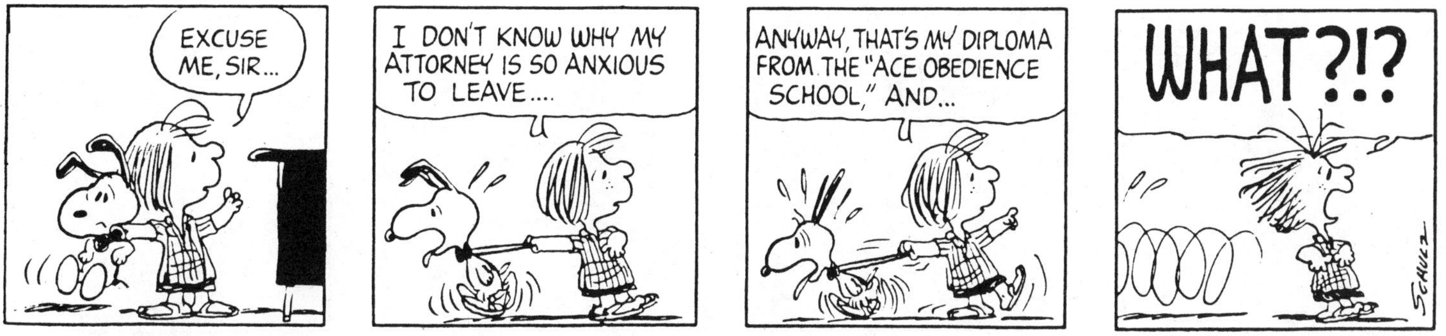
EXCUSE ME, SIR...
I DON'T KNOW WHY MY ATTORNEY IS SO ANXIOUS TO LEAVE....
ANYWAY, THAT'S MY DIPLOMA FROM THE "ACE OBEDIENCE SCHOOL," AND...
WHAT?!?
SCHULZ

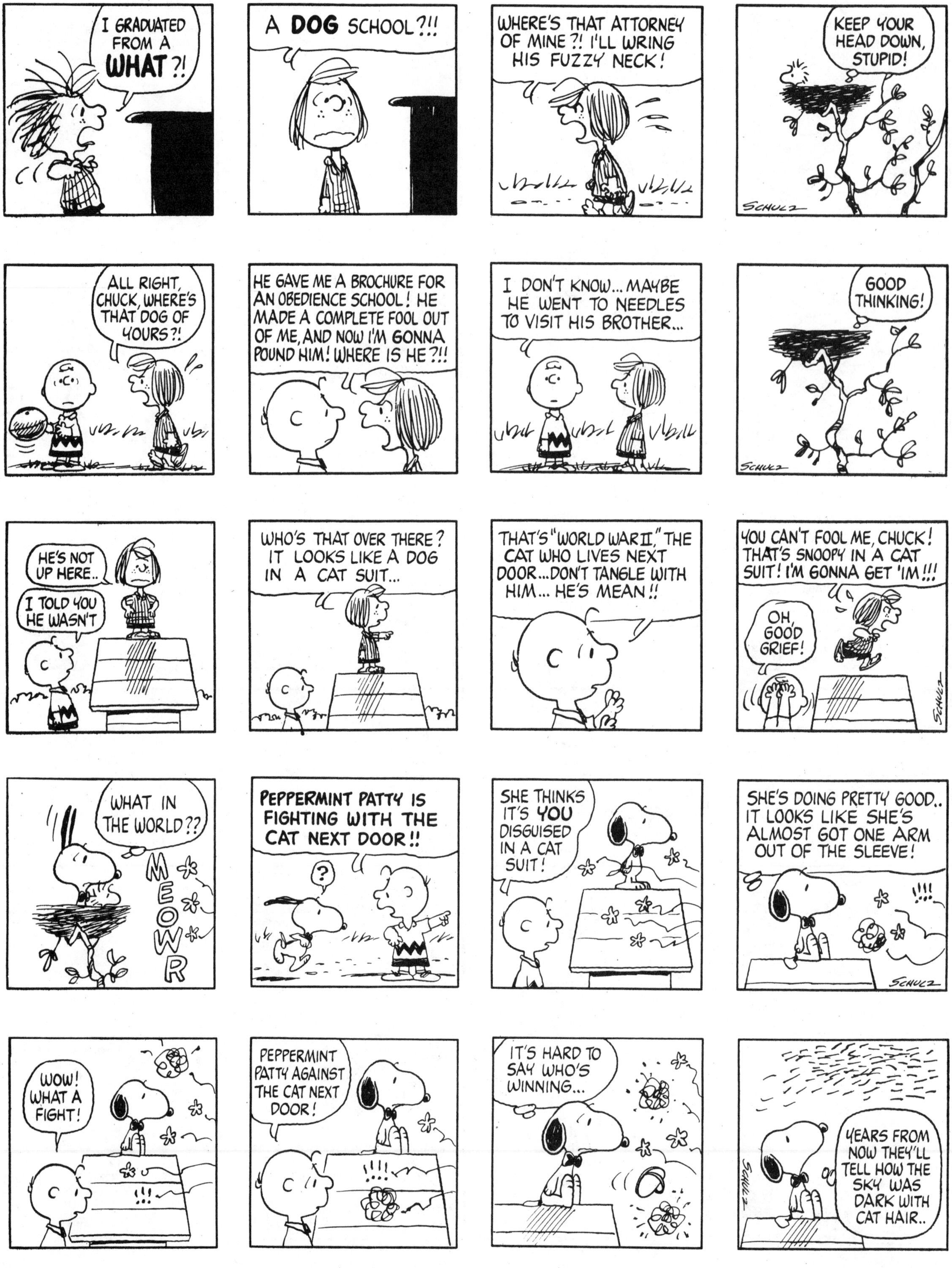
I GRADUATED FROM A WHAT?!
A DOG SCHOOL?!!
WHERE'S THAT ATTORNEY OF MINE?! I'LL WRING HIS FUZZY NECK!
KEEP YOUR HEAD DOWN, STUPID!
SCHULZ
ALL RIGHT, CHUCK, WHERE'S THAT DOG OF YOURS?!
HE GAVE ME A BROCHURE FOR AN OBEDIENCE SCHOOL! HE MADE A COMPLETE FOOL OUT OF ME, AND NOW I'M GONNA POUND HIM! WHERE IS HE?!!
I DON'T KNOW... MAYBE HE WENT TO NEEDLES TO VISIT HIS BROTHER...
GOOD THINKING!
SCHULZ
HE'S NOT UP HERE..
I TOLD YOU HE WASN'T
WHO'S THAT OVER THERE? IT LOOKS LIKE A DOG IN A CAT SUIT...
THAT'S "WORLD WAR II," THE CAT WHO LIVES NEXT DOOR...DON'T TANGLE WITH HIM... HE'S MEAN!!
YOU CAN'T FOOL ME, CHUCK! THAT'S SNOOPY IN A CAT SUIT! I'M GONNA GET 'IM!!!
OH, GOOD GRIEF!
SCHULZ
WHAT IN THE WORLD??
MEOWR
PEPPERMINT PATTY IS FIGHTING WITH THE CAT NEXT DOOR!!
?
SHE THINKS IT'S YOU DISGUISED IN A CAT SUIT!
SHE'S DOING PRETTY GOOD.. IT LOOKS LIKE SHE'S ALMOST GOT ONE ARM OUT OF THE SLEEVE!
SCHULZ
WOW! WHAT A FIGHT!
PEPPERMINT PATTY AGAINST THE CAT NEXT DOOR!
IT'S HARD TO SAY WHO'S WINNING...
YEARS FROM NOW THEY'LL TELL HOW THE SKY WAS DARK WITH CAT HAIR..
SCHULZ

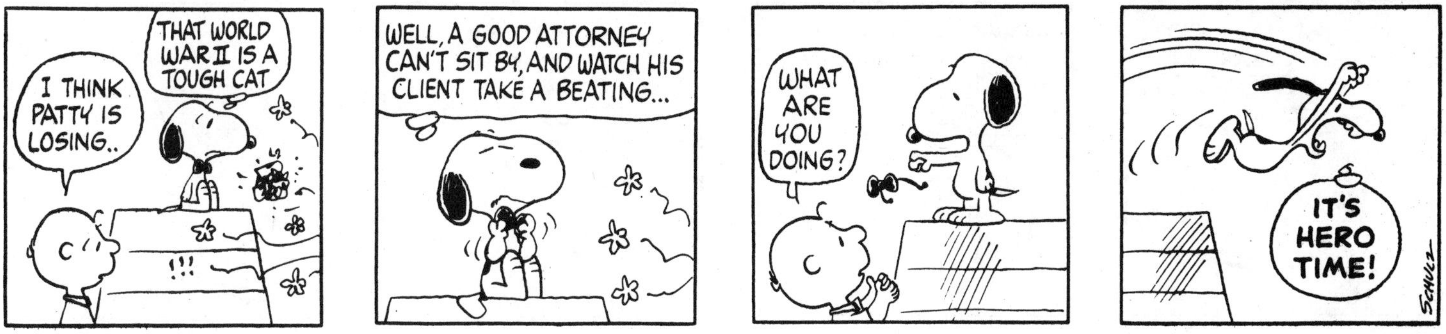
I THINK PATTY IS LOSING..
THAT WORLD WAR II IS A TOUGH CAT
!!!
WELL, A GOOD ATTORNEY CAN'T SIT BY, AND WATCH HIS CLIENT TAKE A BEATING...
WHAT ARE YOU DOING?
IT'S HERO TIME!
SCHULZ

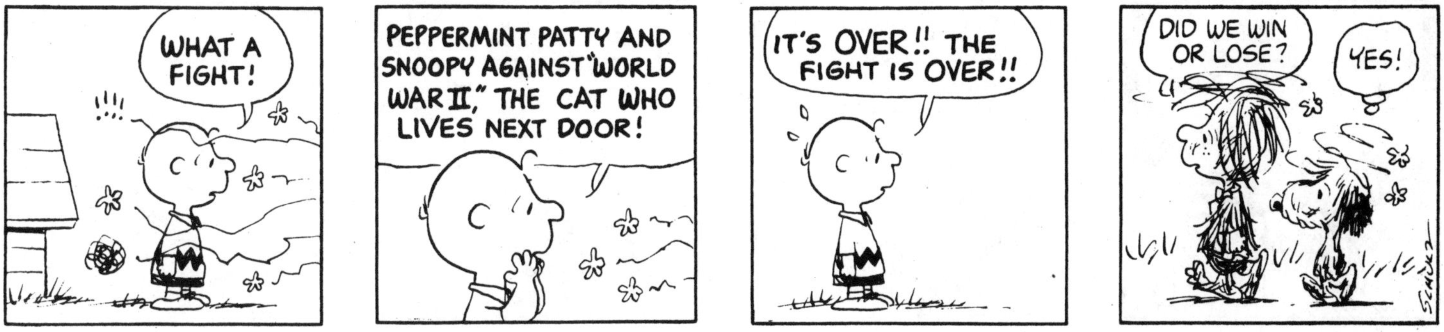
WHAT A FIGHT!
!!!
PEPPERMINT PATTY AND SNOOPY AGAINST "WORLD WAR II," THE CAT WHO LIVES NEXT DOOR!
IT'S OVER!! THE FIGHT IS OVER!!
DID WE WIN OR LOSE?
YES!
SCHULZ

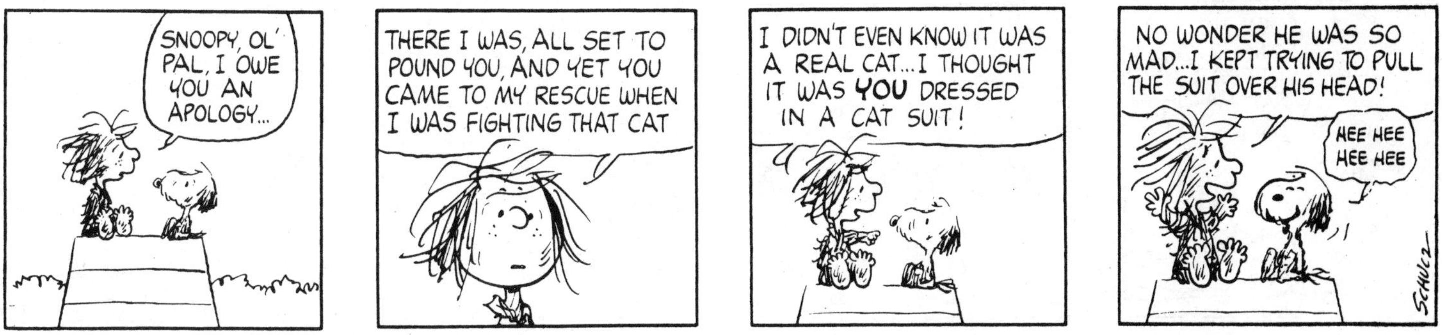
SNOOPY, OL' PAL, I OWE YOU AN APOLOGY...
THERE I WAS, ALL SET TO POUND YOU, AND YET YOU CAME TO MY RESCUE WHEN I WAS FIGHTING THAT CAT
I DIDN'T EVEN KNOW IT WAS A REAL CAT...I THOUGHT IT WAS YOU DRESSED IN A CAT SUIT!
NO WONDER HE WAS SO MAD...I KEPT TRYING TO PULL THE SUIT OVER HIS HEAD!
HEE HEE HEE HEE
SCHULZ

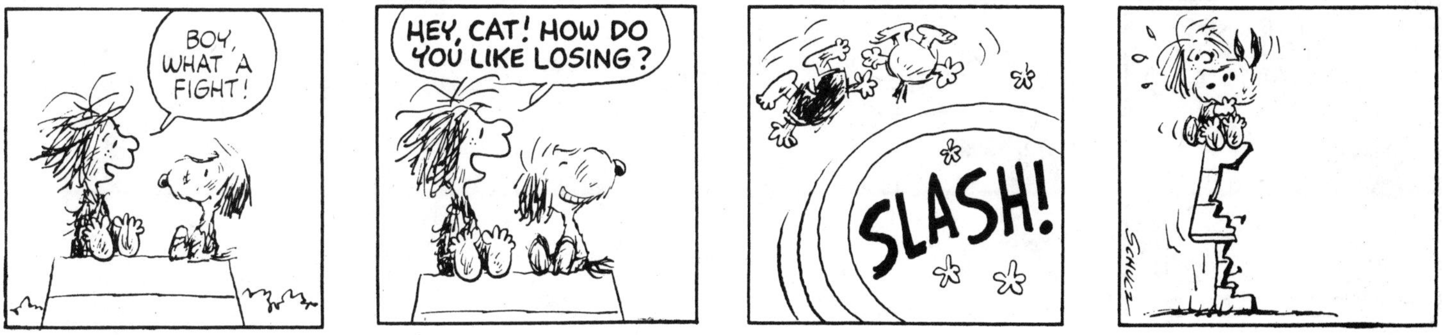
BOY, WHAT A FIGHT!
HEY, CAT! HOW DO YOU LIKE LOSING?
SLASH!
SCHULZ

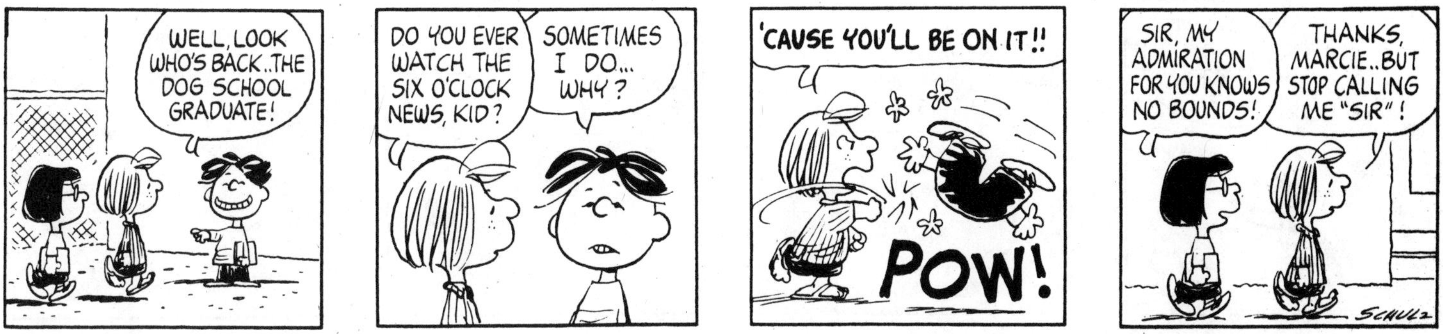
WELL, LOOK WHO'S BACK..THE DOG SCHOOL GRADUATE!
DO YOU EVER WATCH THE SIX O'CLOCK NEWS, KID?
SOMETIMES I DO... WHY?
'CAUSE YOU'LL BE ON IT!!
POW!
SIR, MY ADMIRATION FOR YOU KNOWS NO BOUNDS!
THANKS, MARCIE..BUT STOP CALLING ME "SIR"!
SCHULZ

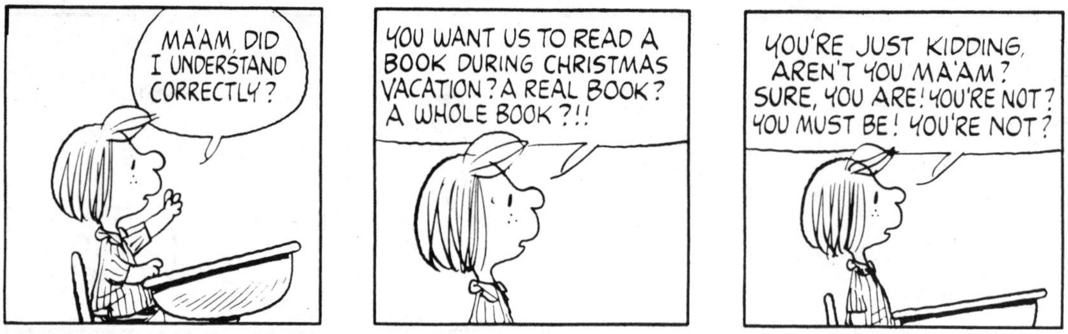
MA'AM, DID I UNDERSTAND CORRECTLY?
YOU WANT US TO READ A BOOK DURING CHRISTMAS VACATION? A REAL BOOK? A WHOLE BOOK?!!
YOU'RE JUST KIDDING, AREN'T YOU MA'AM? SURE, YOU ARE! YOU'RE NOT? YOU MUST BE! YOU'RE NOT?
HAPPY HOLIDAYS!
SCHULZ

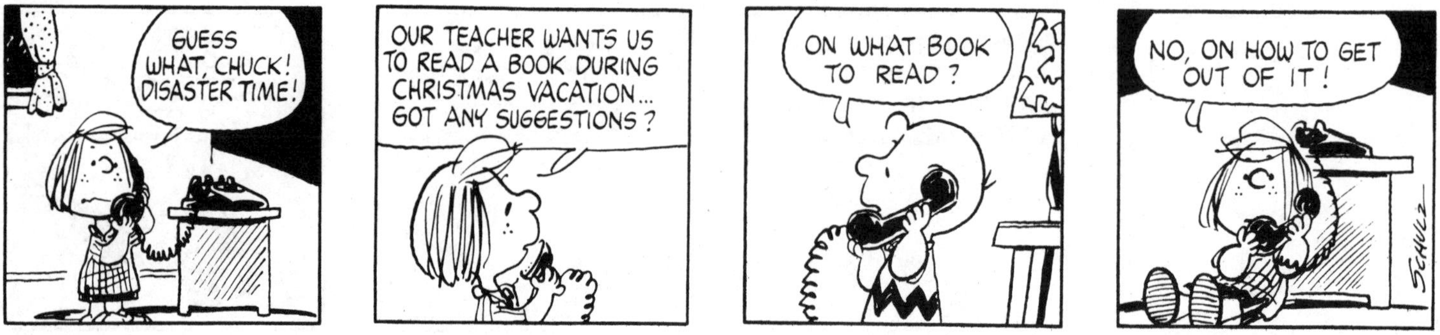
GUESS WHAT, CHUCK! DISASTER TIME!
OUR TEACHER WANTS US TO READ A BOOK DURING CHRISTMAS VACATION... GOT ANY SUGGESTIONS?
ON WHAT BOOK TO READ?
NO, ON HOW TO GET OUT OF IT!
SCHULZ

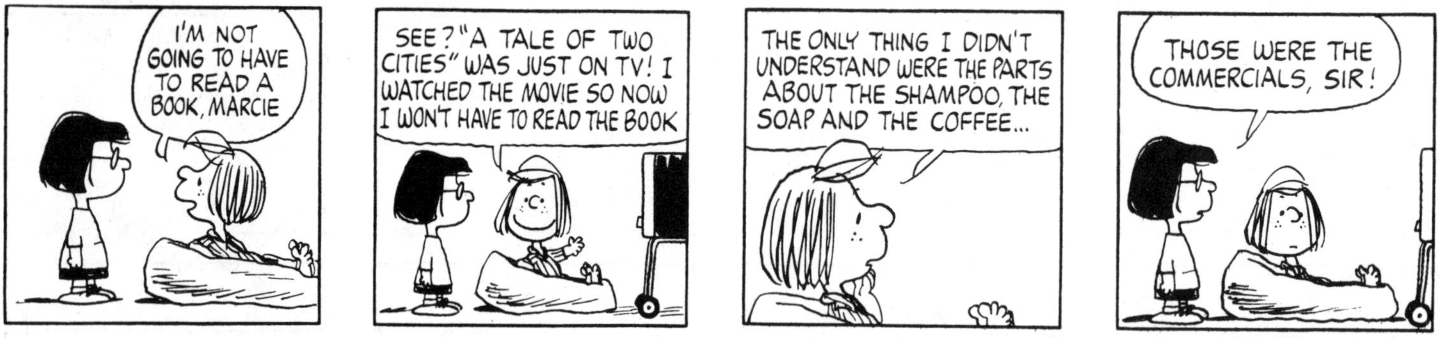
I'M NOT GOING TO HAVE TO READ A BOOK, MARCIE
SEE? "A TALE OF TWO CITIES" WAS JUST ON TV! I WATCHED THE MOVIE SO NOW I WON'T HAVE TO READ THE BOOK
THE ONLY THING I DIDN'T UNDERSTAND WERE THE PARTS ABOUT THE SHAMPOO, THE SOAP AND THE COFFEE...
THOSE WERE THE COMMERCIALS, SIR!

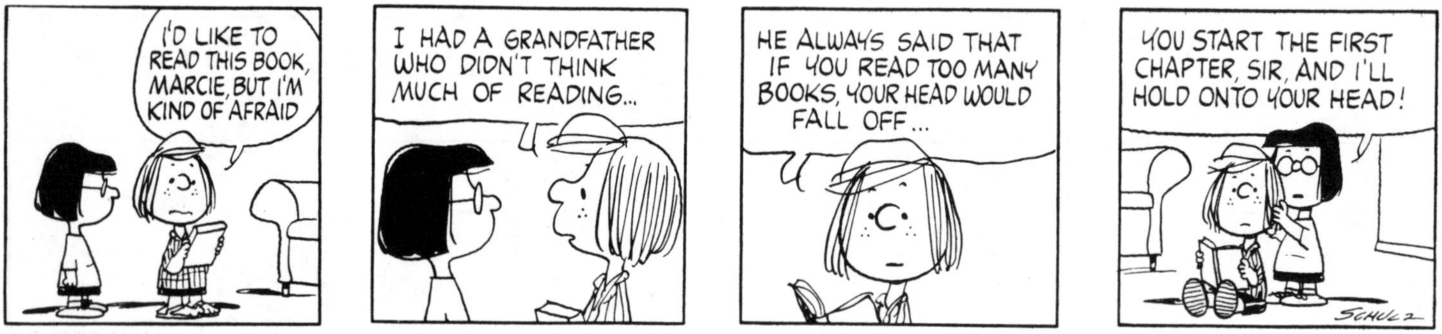
I'D LIKE TO READ THIS BOOK, MARCIE, BUT I'M KIND OF AFRAID
I HAD A GRANDFATHER WHO DIDN'T THINK MUCH OF READING...
HE ALWAYS SAID THAT IF YOU READ TOO MANY BOOKS, YOUR HEAD WOULD FALL OFF...
YOU START THE FIRST CHAPTER, SIR, AND I'LL HOLD ONTO YOUR HEAD!
SCHULZ

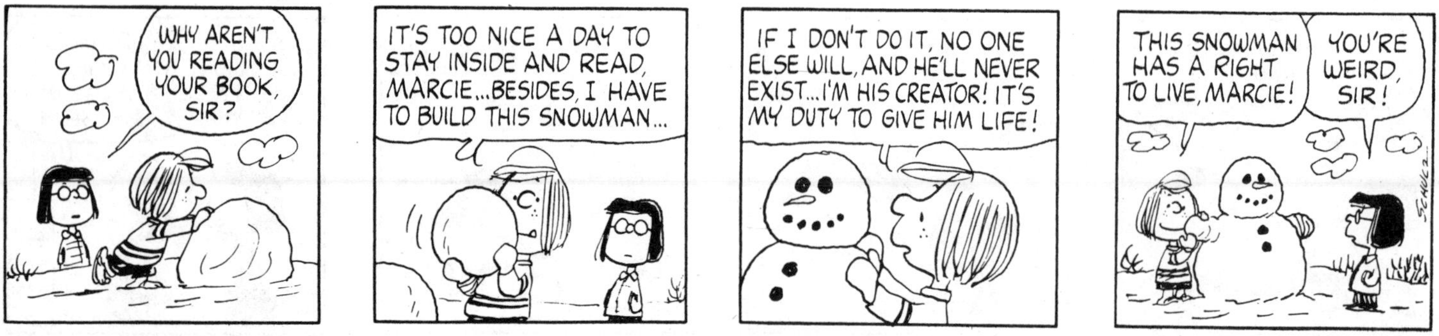
WHY AREN'T YOU READING YOUR BOOK, SIR?
IT'S TOO NICE A DAY TO STAY INSIDE AND READ, MARCIE... BESIDES, I HAVE TO BUILD THIS SNOWMAN...
IF I DON'T DO IT, NO ONE ELSE WILL, AND HE'LL NEVER EXIST... I'M HIS CREATOR! IT'S MY DUTY TO GIVE HIM LIFE!
THIS SNOWMAN HAS A RIGHT TO LIVE, MARCIE!
YOU'RE WEIRD, SIR!
SCHULZ

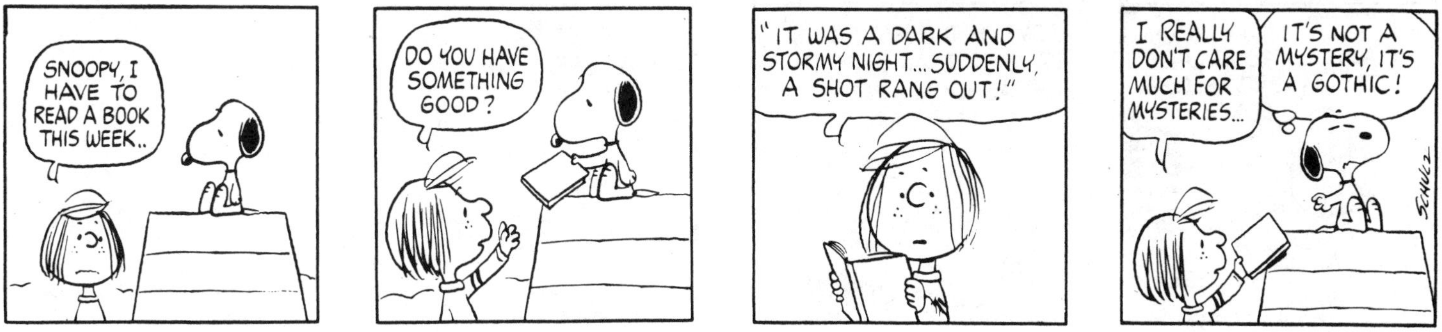
SNOOPY, I HAVE TO READ A BOOK THIS WEEK..
DO YOU HAVE SOMETHING GOOD?
"IT WAS A DARK AND STORMY NIGHT... SUDDENLY, A SHOT RANG OUT!"
I REALLY DON'T CARE MUCH FOR MYSTERIES...
IT'S NOT A MYSTERY, IT'S A GOTHIC!

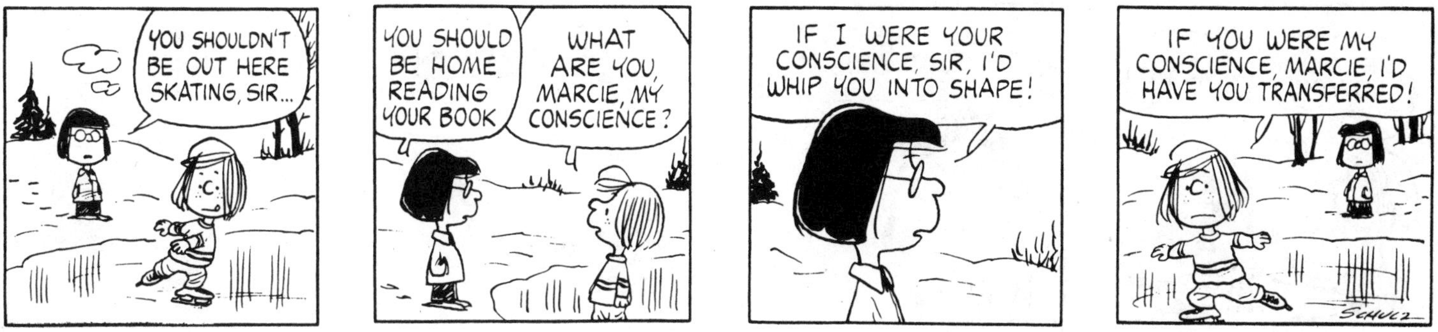
YOU SHOULDN'T BE OUT HERE SKATING, SIR...
YOU SHOULD BE HOME READING YOUR BOOK
WHAT ARE YOU, MARCIE, MY CONSCIENCE?
IF I WERE YOUR CONSCIENCE, SIR, I'D WHIP YOU INTO SHAPE!
IF YOU WERE MY CONSCIENCE, MARCIE, I'D HAVE YOU TRANSFERRED!

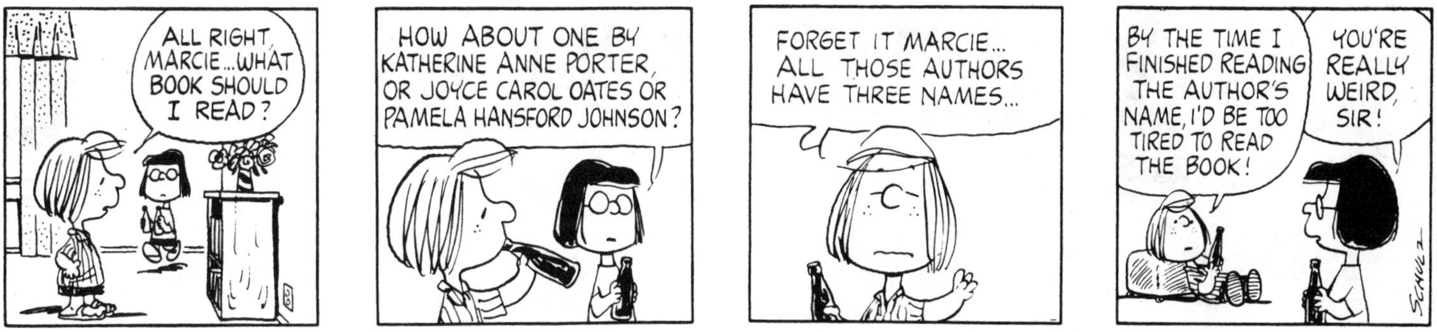
ALL RIGHT, MARCIE...WHAT BOOK SHOULD I READ?
HOW ABOUT ONE BY KATHERINE ANNE PORTER, OR JOYCE CAROL OATES OR PAMELA HANSFORD JOHNSON?
FORGET IT MARCIE... ALL THOSE AUTHORS HAVE THREE NAMES...
BY THE TIME I FINISHED READING THE AUTHOR'S NAME, I'D BE TOO TIRED TO READ THE BOOK!
YOU'RE REALLY WEIRD, SIR!

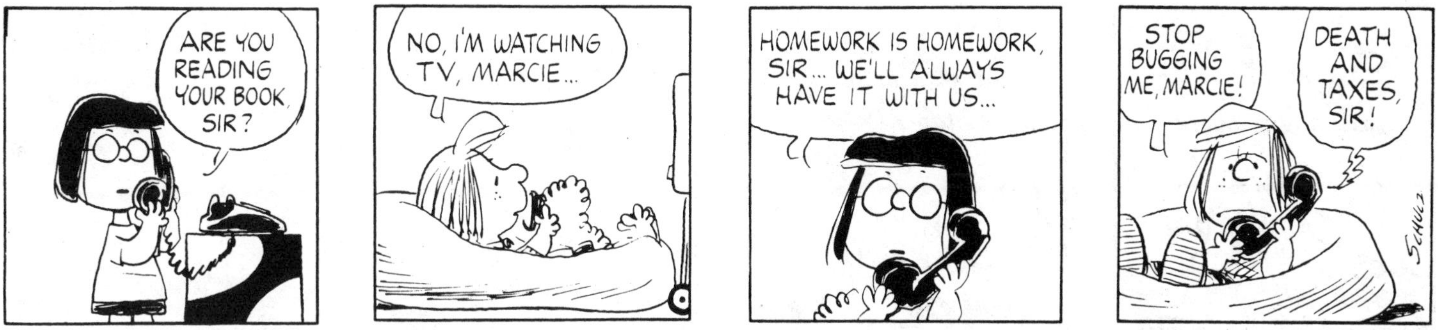
ARE YOU READING YOUR BOOK, SIR?
NO, I'M WATCHING TV, MARCIE...
HOMEWORK IS HOMEWORK, SIR... WE'LL ALWAYS HAVE IT WITH US...
STOP BUGGING ME, MARCIE!
DEATH AND TAXES, SIR!

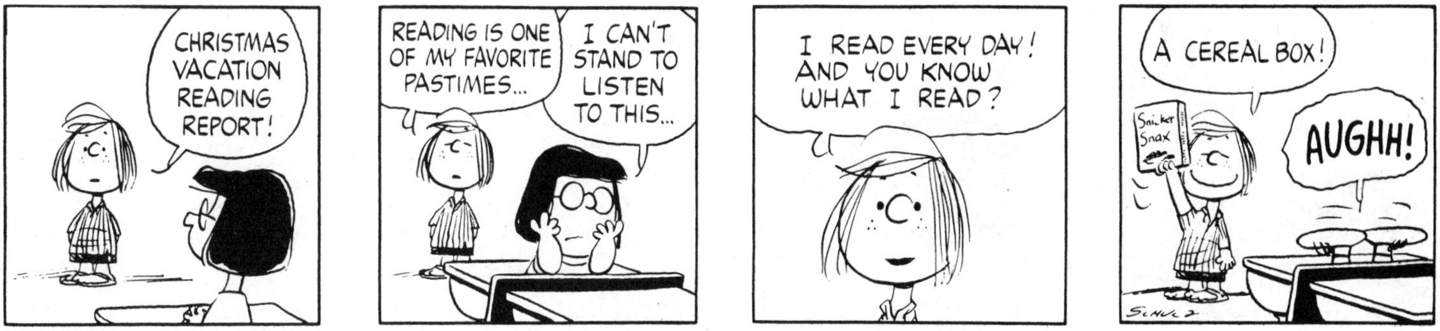
CHRISTMAS VACATION READING REPORT!
READING IS ONE OF MY FAVORITE PASTIMES...
I CAN'T STAND TO LISTEN TO THIS...
I READ EVERY DAY! AND YOU KNOW WHAT I READ?
A CEREAL BOX!
Snicker Snax
AUGHH!

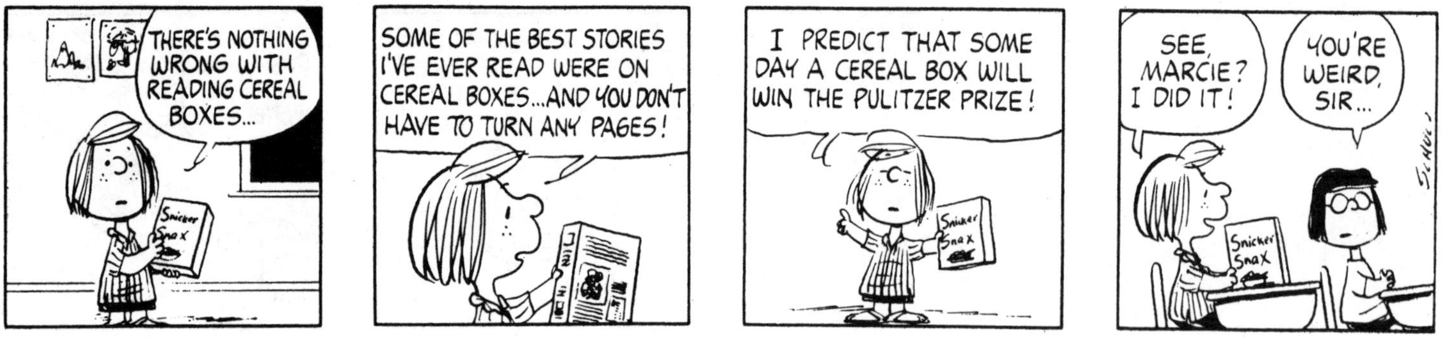
THERE'S NOTHING WRONG WITH READING CEREAL BOXES...
Snicker Snax
SOME OF THE BEST STORIES I'VE EVER READ WERE ON CEREAL BOXES...AND YOU DON'T HAVE TO TURN ANY PAGES!
I PREDICT THAT SOME DAY A CEREAL BOX WILL WIN THE PULITZER PRIZE!
Snicker Snax
SEE, MARCIE? I DID IT!
YOU'RE WEIRD, SIR...
Snicker Snax

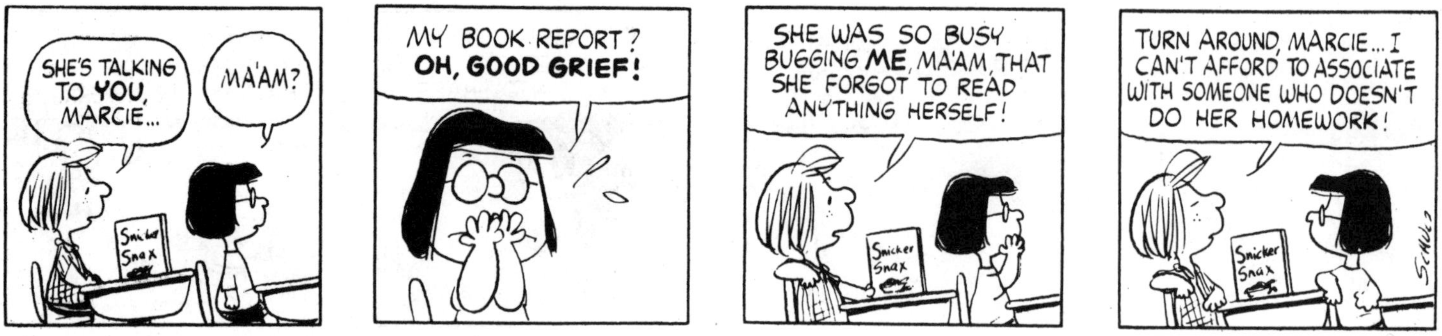
SHE'S TALKING TO **YOU**, MARCIE...
MA'AM?
Snicker Snax
MY BOOK REPORT? **OH, GOOD GRIEF!**
SHE WAS SO BUSY BUGGING **ME**, MA'AM, THAT SHE FORGOT TO READ ANYTHING HERSELF!
Snicker Snax
TURN AROUND, MARCIE... I CAN'T AFFORD TO ASSOCIATE WITH SOMEONE WHO DOESN'T DO HER HOMEWORK!
Snicker Snax

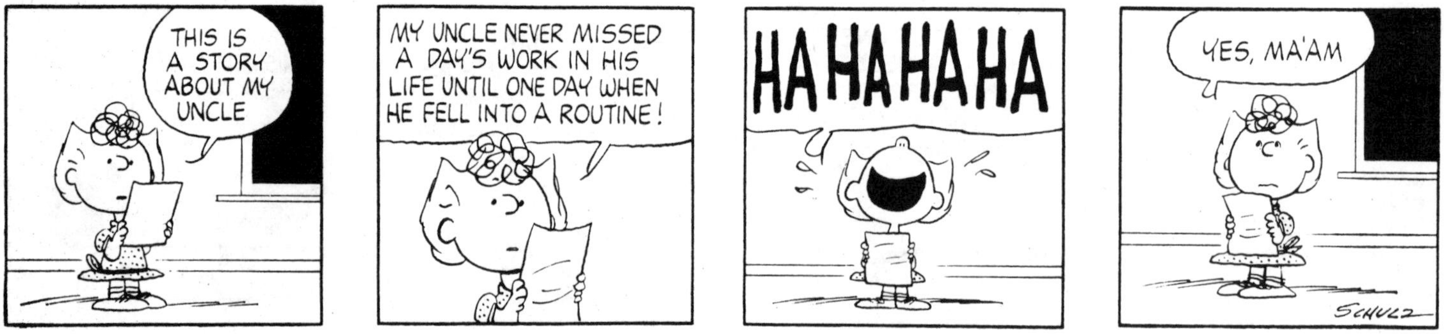
THIS IS A STORY ABOUT MY UNCLE
MY UNCLE NEVER MISSED A DAY'S WORK IN HIS LIFE UNTIL ONE DAY WHEN HE FELL INTO A ROUTINE!
HAHAHAHA
YES, MA'AM
SCHULZ

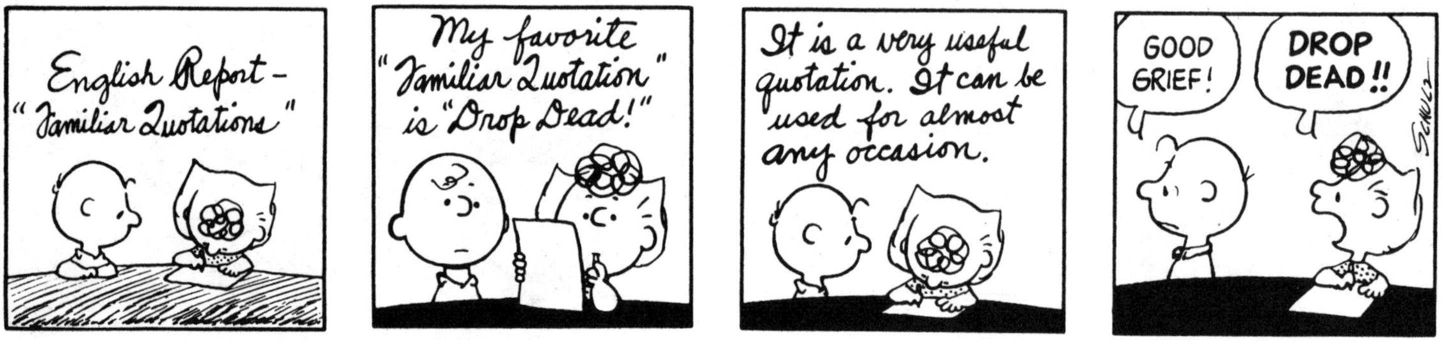
English Report - "Familiar Quotations"
My favorite "Familiar Quotation" is "Drop Dead!"
It is a very useful quotation. It can be used for almost any occasion.
GOOD GRIEF!
DROP DEAD!!

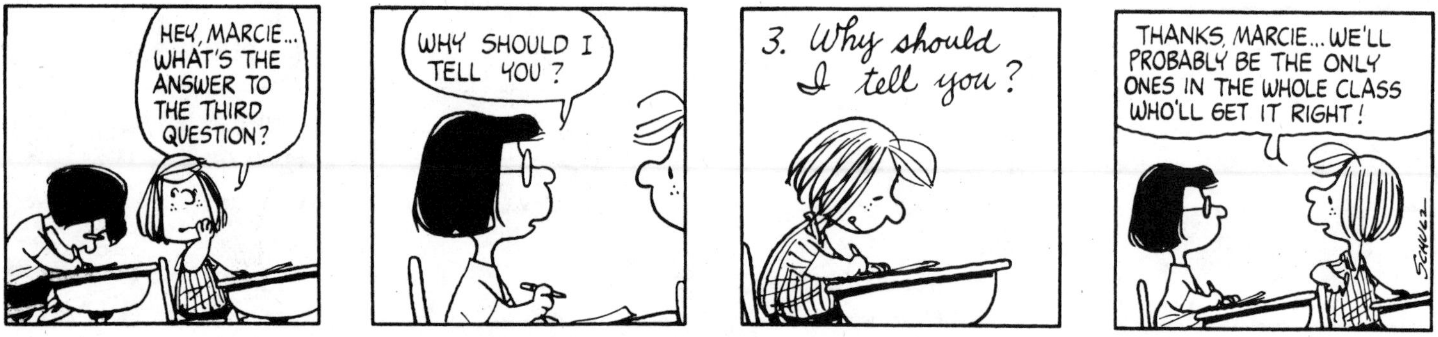
HEY, MARCIE... WHAT'S THE ANSWER TO THE THIRD QUESTION?
WHY SHOULD I TELL YOU?
3. Why should I tell you?
THANKS, MARCIE... WE'LL PROBABLY BE THE ONLY ONES IN THE WHOLE CLASS WHO'LL GET IT RIGHT!

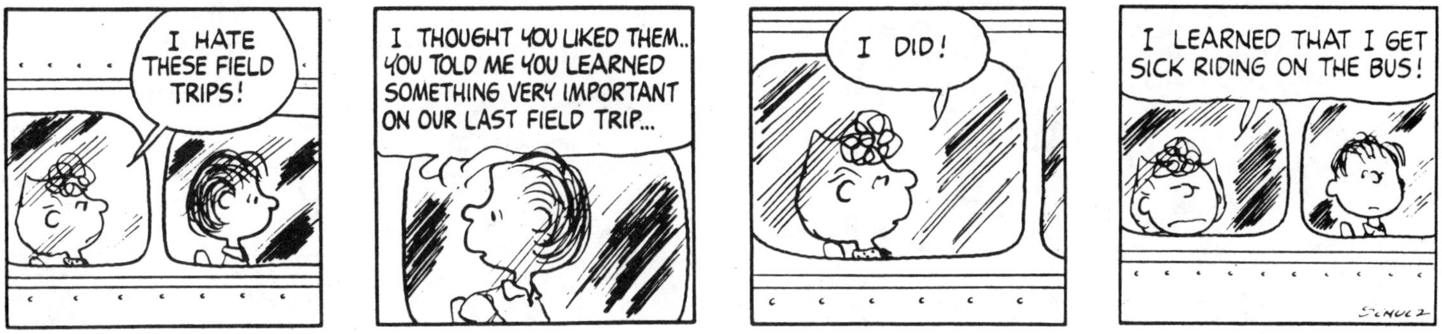
I HATE THESE FIELD TRIPS!
I THOUGHT YOU LIKED THEM.. YOU TOLD ME YOU LEARNED SOMETHING VERY IMPORTANT ON OUR LAST FIELD TRIP...
I DID!
I LEARNED THAT I GET SICK RIDING ON THE BUS!
SCHULZ

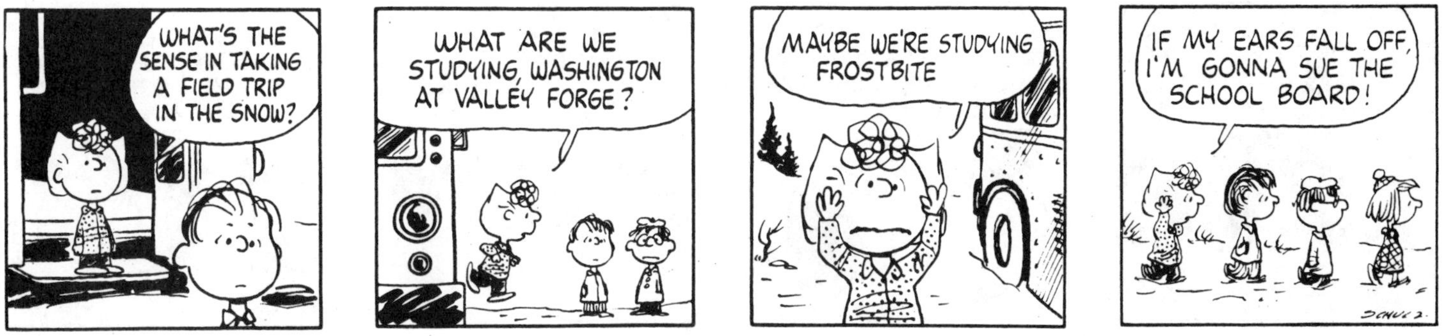
WHAT'S THE SENSE IN TAKING A FIELD TRIP IN THE SNOW?
WHAT ARE WE STUDYING, WASHINGTON AT VALLEY FORGE?
MAYBE WE'RE STUDYING FROSTBITE
IF MY EARS FALL OFF, I'M GONNA SUE THE SCHOOL BOARD!
SCHULZ

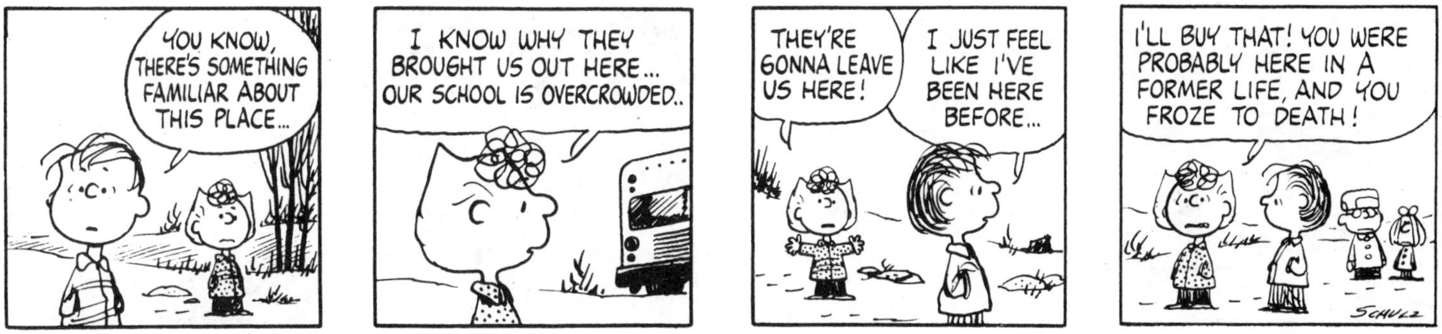
YOU KNOW, THERE'S SOMETHING FAMILIAR ABOUT THIS PLACE...
I KNOW WHY THEY BROUGHT US OUT HERE... OUR SCHOOL IS OVERCROWDED..
THEY'RE GONNA LEAVE US HERE!
I JUST FEEL LIKE I'VE BEEN HERE BEFORE...
I'LL BUY THAT! YOU WERE PROBABLY HERE IN A FORMER LIFE, AND YOU FROZE TO DEATH!
SCHULZ

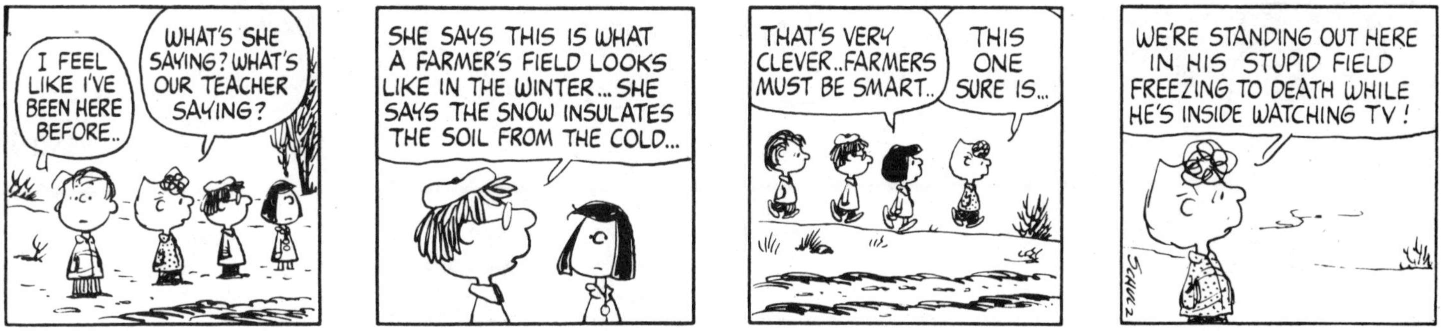
I FEEL LIKE I'VE BEEN HERE BEFORE..
WHAT'S SHE SAYING? WHAT'S OUR TEACHER SAYING?
SHE SAYS THIS IS WHAT A FARMER'S FIELD LOOKS LIKE IN THE WINTER... SHE SAYS THE SNOW INSULATES THE SOIL FROM THE COLD...
THAT'S VERY CLEVER..FARMERS MUST BE SMART..
THIS ONE SURE IS...
WE'RE STANDING OUT HERE IN HIS STUPID FIELD FREEZING TO DEATH WHILE HE'S INSIDE WATCHING TV!
SCHULZ

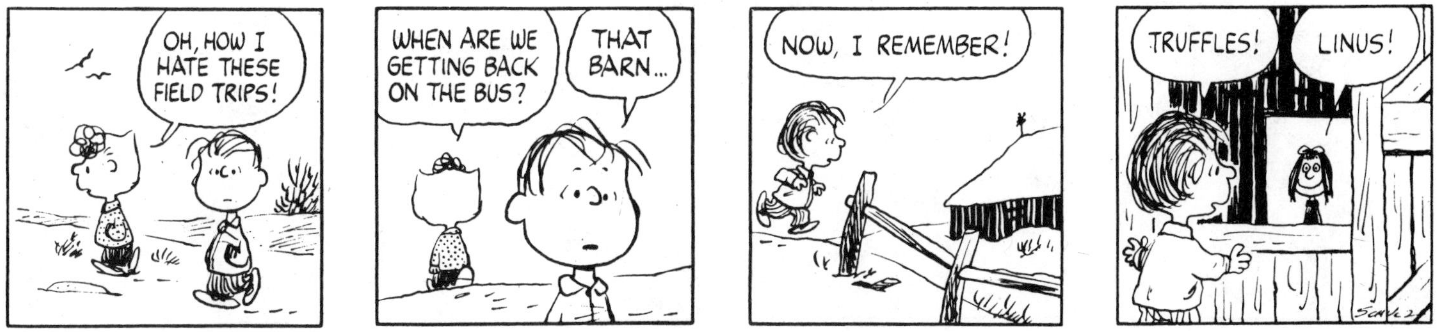
OH, HOW I HATE THESE FIELD TRIPS!
WHEN ARE WE GETTING BACK ON THE BUS?
THAT BARN...
NOW, I REMEMBER!
TRUFFLES!
LINUS!
SCHULZ

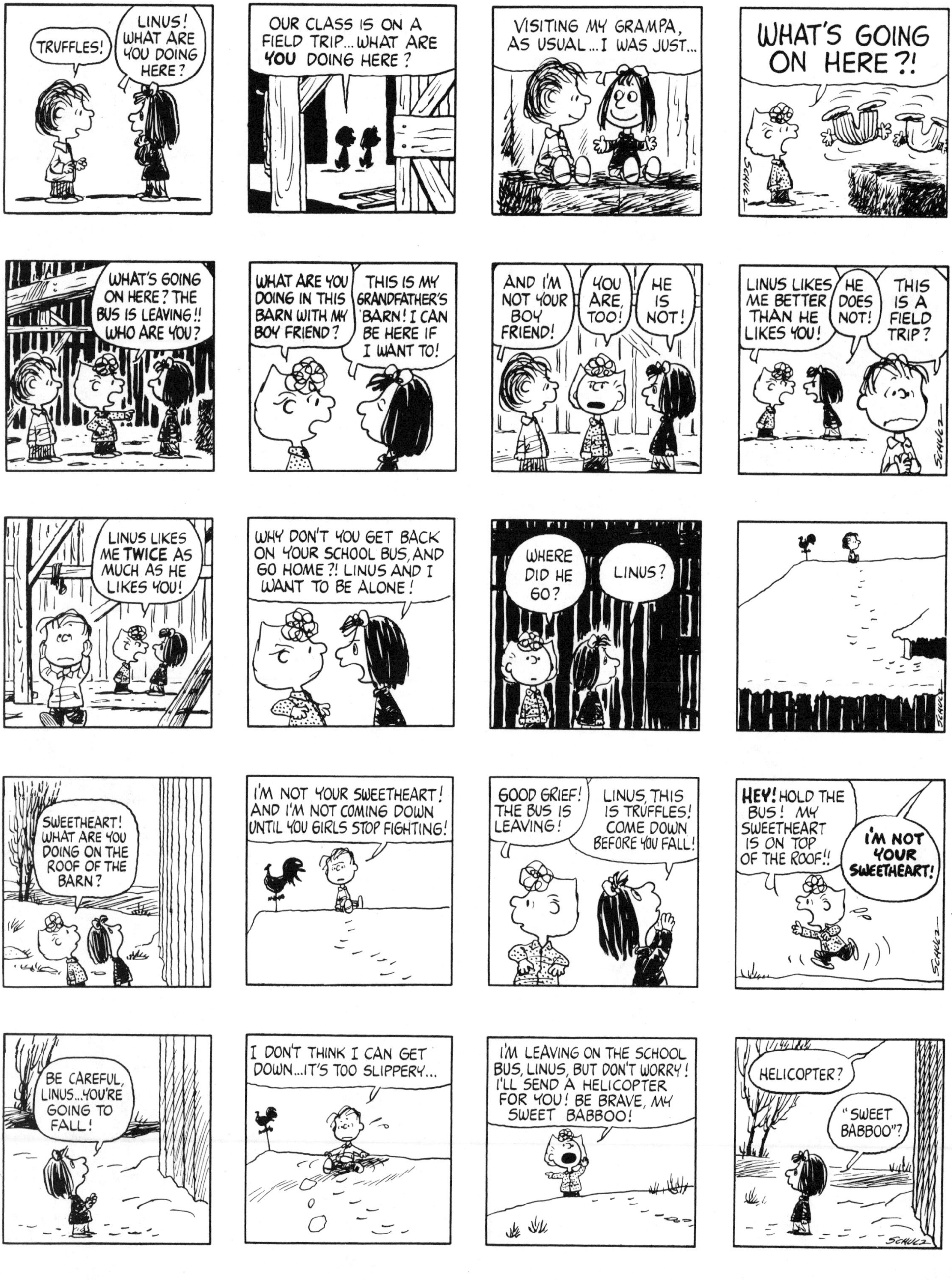
TRUFFLES!
LINUS! WHAT ARE YOU DOING HERE?
OUR CLASS IS ON A FIELD TRIP...WHAT ARE YOU DOING HERE?
VISITING MY GRAMPA, AS USUAL...I WAS JUST...
WHAT'S GOING ON HERE?!
WHAT'S GOING ON HERE? THE BUS IS LEAVING!! WHO ARE YOU?
WHAT ARE YOU DOING IN THIS BARN WITH MY BOY FRIEND?
THIS IS MY GRANDFATHER'S BARN! I CAN BE HERE IF I WANT TO!
AND I'M NOT YOUR BOY FRIEND!
YOU ARE, TOO!
HE IS NOT!
LINUS LIKES ME BETTER THAN HE LIKES YOU!
HE DOES NOT!
THIS IS A FIELD TRIP?
LINUS LIKES ME TWICE AS MUCH AS HE LIKES YOU!
WHY DON'T YOU GET BACK ON YOUR SCHOOL BUS, AND GO HOME?! LINUS AND I WANT TO BE ALONE!
WHERE DID HE GO?
LINUS?
SWEETHEART! WHAT ARE YOU DOING ON THE ROOF OF THE BARN?
I'M NOT YOUR SWEETHEART! AND I'M NOT COMING DOWN UNTIL YOU GIRLS STOP FIGHTING!
GOOD GRIEF! THE BUS IS LEAVING!
LINUS, THIS IS TRUFFLES! COME DOWN BEFORE YOU FALL!
HEY! HOLD THE BUS! MY SWEETHEART IS ON TOP OF THE ROOF!!
I'M NOT YOUR SWEETHEART!
BE CAREFUL, LINUS...YOU'RE GOING TO FALL!
I DON'T THINK I CAN GET DOWN...IT'S TOO SLIPPERY...
I'M LEAVING ON THE SCHOOL BUS, LINUS, BUT DON'T WORRY! I'LL SEND A HELICOPTER FOR YOU! BE BRAVE, MY SWEET BABBOO!
HELICOPTER?
"SWEET BABBOO"?

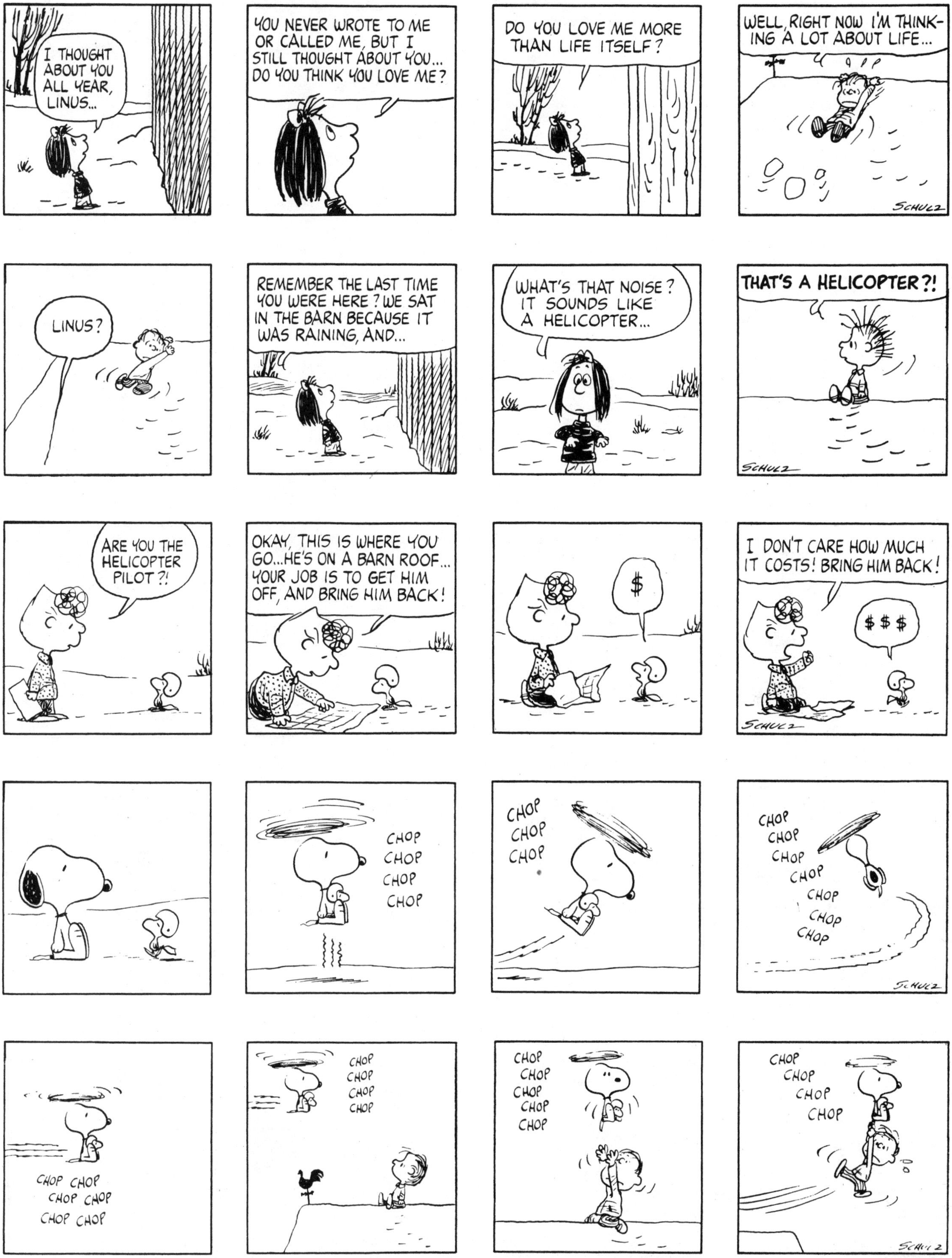
I THOUGHT ABOUT YOU ALL YEAR, LINUS...
YOU NEVER WROTE TO ME OR CALLED ME, BUT I STILL THOUGHT ABOUT YOU... DO YOU THINK YOU LOVE ME?
DO YOU LOVE ME MORE THAN LIFE ITSELF?
WELL, RIGHT NOW I'M THINKING A LOT ABOUT LIFE...
SCHULZ
LINUS?
REMEMBER THE LAST TIME YOU WERE HERE? WE SAT IN THE BARN BECAUSE IT WAS RAINING, AND...
WHAT'S THAT NOISE? IT SOUNDS LIKE A HELICOPTER...
THAT'S A HELICOPTER?!
SCHULZ
ARE YOU THE HELICOPTER PILOT?!
OKAY, THIS IS WHERE YOU GO...HE'S ON A BARN ROOF... YOUR JOB IS TO GET HIM OFF, AND BRING HIM BACK!
$
I DON'T CARE HOW MUCH IT COSTS! BRING HIM BACK!
$ $ $
SCHULZ
CHOP CHOP CHOP CHOP
CHOP CHOP CHOP
CHOP CHOP CHOP CHOP CHOP CHOP CHOP
SCHULZ
CHOP CHOP CHOP CHOP CHOP CHOP
CHOP CHOP CHOP CHOP
CHOP CHOP CHOP CHOP CHOP
CHOP CHOP CHOP CHOP
SCHULZ

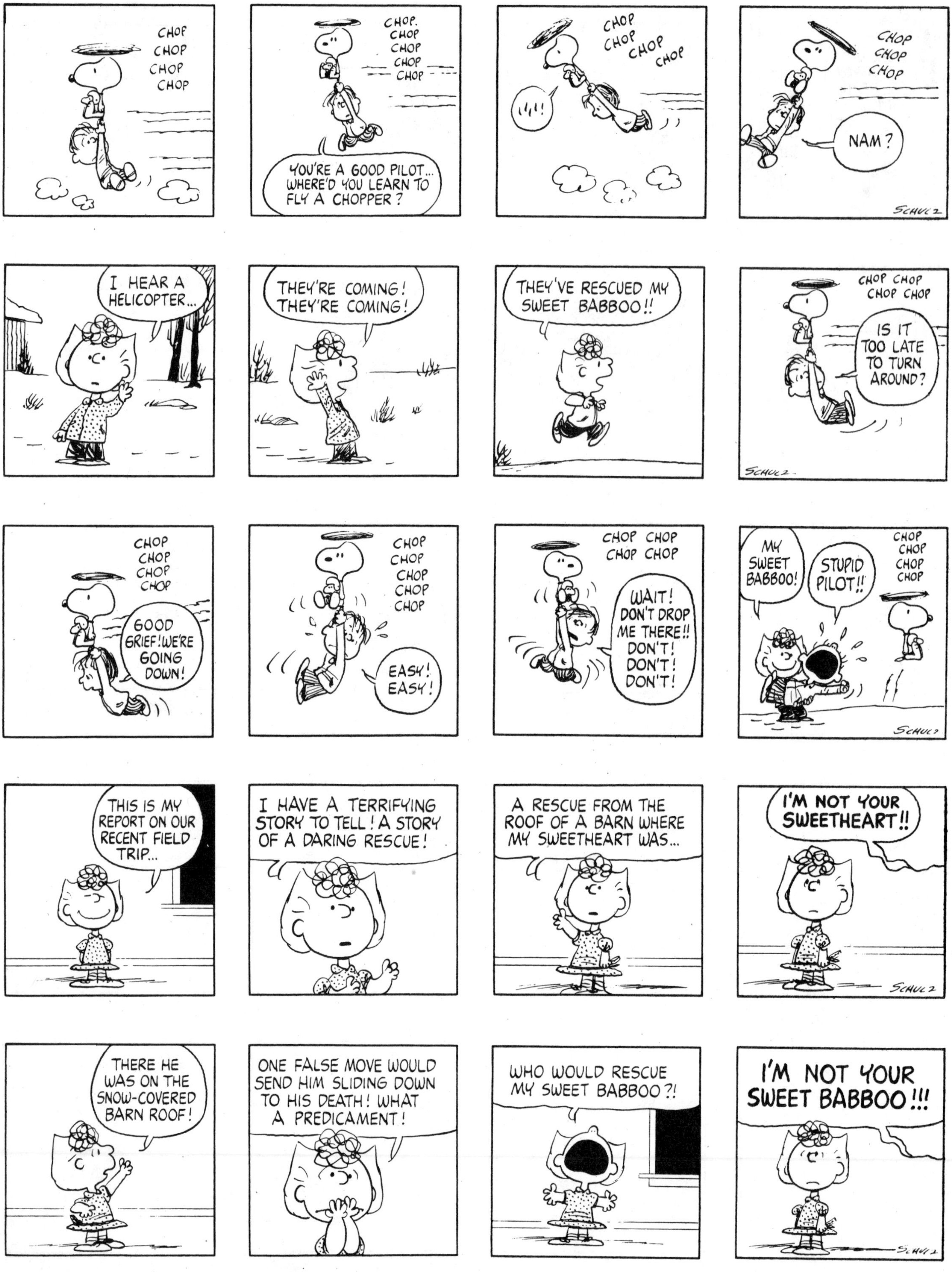
CHOP CHOP CHOP CHOP
CHOP. CHOP CHOP CHOP CHOP
YOU'RE A GOOD PILOT... WHERE'D YOU LEARN TO FLY A CHOPPER?
CHOP CHOP CHOP CHOP
!!!
CHOP CHOP CHOP
NAM?
SCHULZ
I HEAR A HELICOPTER...
THEY'RE COMING! THEY'RE COMING!
THEY'VE RESCUED MY SWEET BABBOO!!
CHOP CHOP CHOP CHOP
IS IT TOO LATE TO TURN AROUND?
SCHULZ
CHOP CHOP CHOP CHOP
GOOD GRIEF! WE'RE GOING DOWN!
CHOP CHOP CHOP CHOP CHOP
EASY! EASY!
CHOP CHOP CHOP CHOP
WAIT! DON'T DROP ME THERE!! DON'T! DON'T! DON'T!
MY SWEET BABBOO!
STUPID PILOT!!
CHOP CHOP CHOP CHOP
SCHULZ
THIS IS MY REPORT ON OUR RECENT FIELD TRIP...
I HAVE A TERRIFYING STORY TO TELL! A STORY OF A DARING RESCUE!
A RESCUE FROM THE ROOF OF A BARN WHERE MY SWEETHEART WAS...
I'M NOT YOUR SWEETHEART!!
SCHULZ
THERE HE WAS ON THE SNOW-COVERED BARN ROOF!
ONE FALSE MOVE WOULD SEND HIM SLIDING DOWN TO HIS DEATH! WHAT A PREDICAMENT!
WHO WOULD RESCUE MY SWEET BABBOO?!
I'M NOT YOUR SWEET BABBOO!!!
SCHULZ

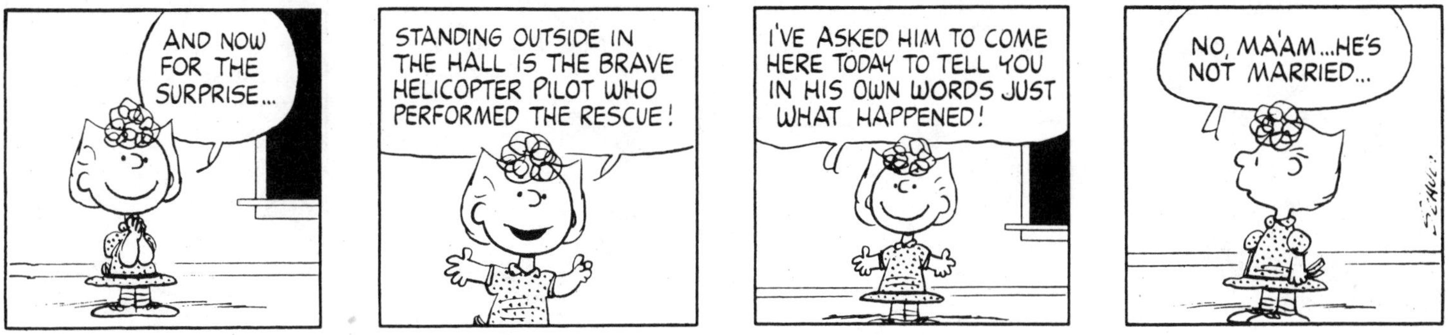
AND NOW FOR THE SURPRISE...
STANDING OUTSIDE IN THE HALL IS THE BRAVE HELICOPTER PILOT WHO PERFORMED THE RESCUE!
I'VE ASKED HIM TO COME HERE TODAY TO TELL YOU IN HIS OWN WORDS JUST WHAT HAPPENED!
NO, MA'AM...HE'S NOT MARRIED...
SCHULZ

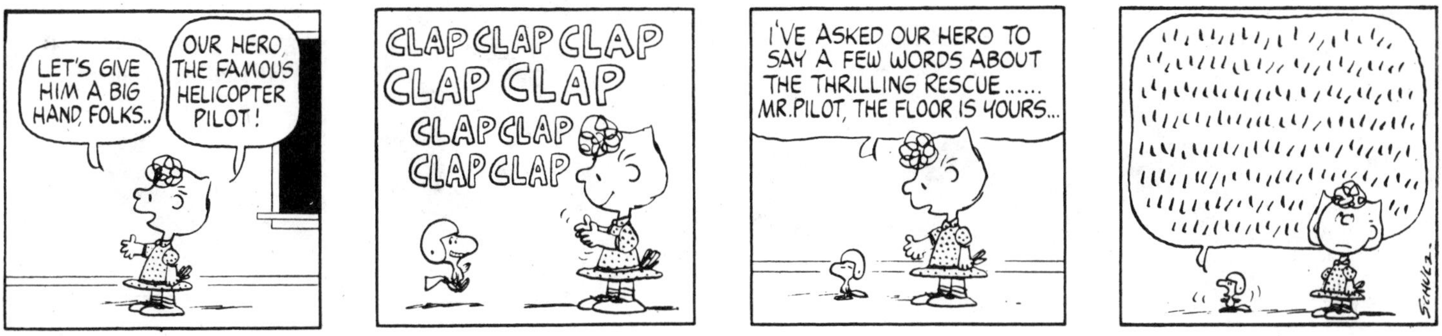
LET'S GIVE HIM A BIG HAND, FOLKS..
OUR HERO, THE FAMOUS HELICOPTER PILOT!
CLAP CLAP CLAP CLAP CLAP CLAP CLAP CLAP CLAP
I'VE ASKED OUR HERO TO SAY A FEW WORDS ABOUT THE THRILLING RESCUE...... MR. PILOT, THE FLOOR IS YOURS...
SCHULZ

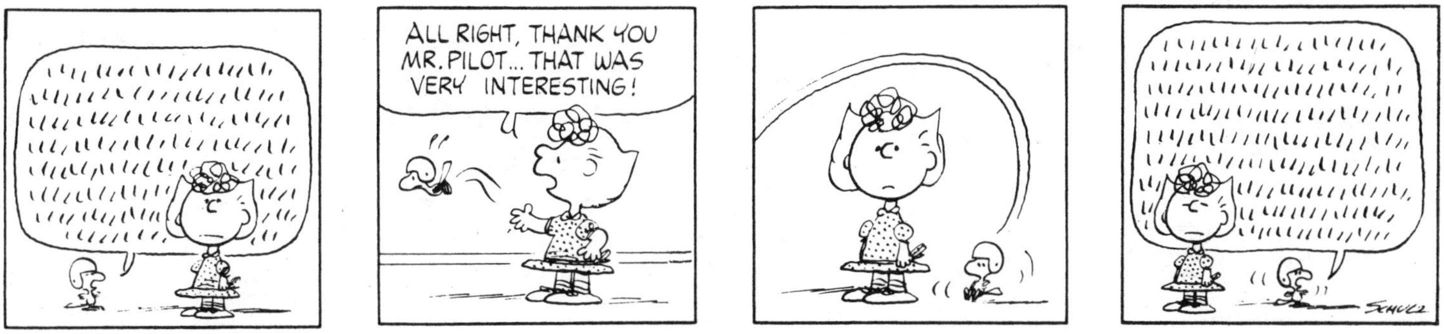
ALL RIGHT, THANK YOU MR. PILOT...THAT WAS VERY INTERESTING!
SCHULZ

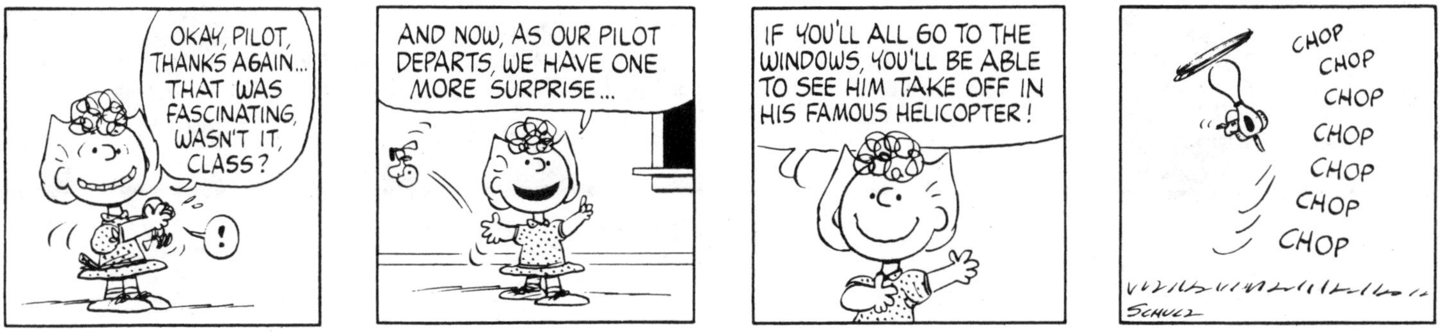
OKAY, PILOT, THANKS AGAIN... THAT WAS FASCINATING, WASN'T IT, CLASS?
!
AND NOW, AS OUR PILOT DEPARTS, WE HAVE ONE MORE SURPRISE...
IF YOU'LL ALL GO TO THE WINDOWS, YOU'LL BE ABLE TO SEE HIM TAKE OFF IN HIS FAMOUS HELICOPTER!
CHOP CHOP CHOP CHOP CHOP CHOP CHOP
SCHULZ

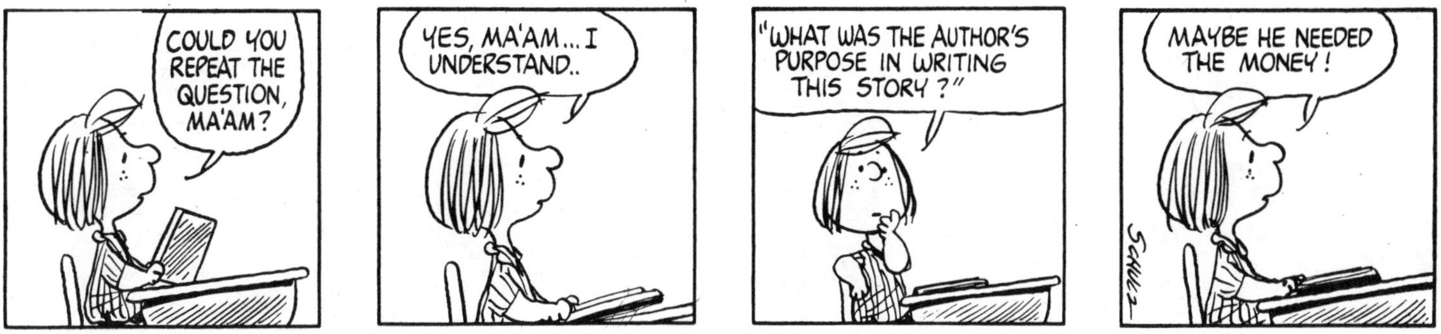
COULD YOU REPEAT THE QUESTION, MA'AM?
YES, MA'AM... I UNDERSTAND..
"WHAT WAS THE AUTHOR'S PURPOSE IN WRITING THIS STORY?"
MAYBE HE NEEDED THE MONEY!
SCHULZ

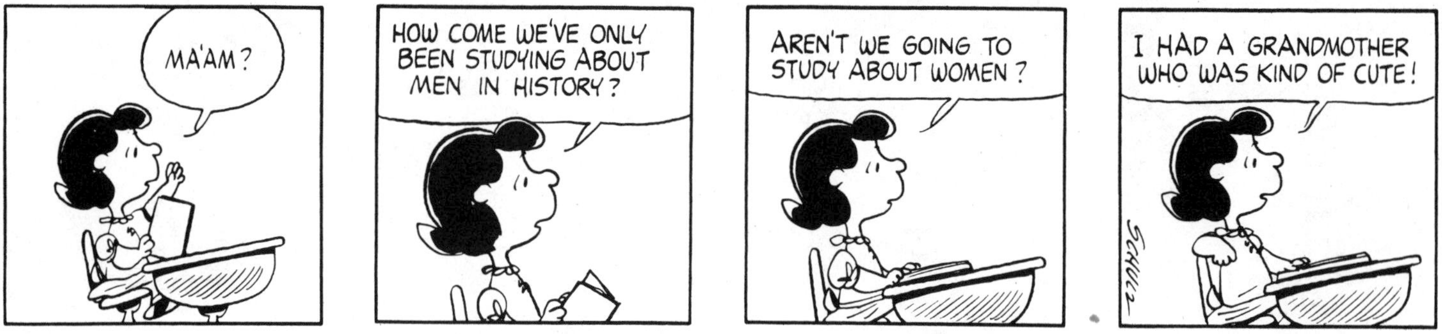
MA'AM?
HOW COME WE'VE ONLY BEEN STUDYING ABOUT MEN IN HISTORY?
AREN'T WE GOING TO STUDY ABOUT WOMEN?
I HAD A GRANDMOTHER WHO WAS KIND OF CUTE!
SCHULZ

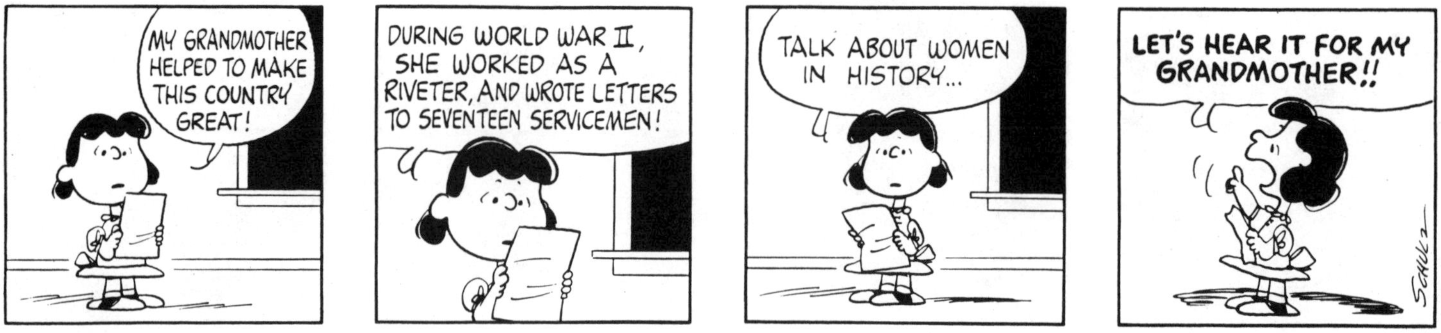
MY GRANDMOTHER HELPED TO MAKE THIS COUNTRY GREAT!
DURING WORLD WAR II, SHE WORKED AS A RIVETER, AND WROTE LETTERS TO SEVENTEEN SERVICEMEN!
TALK ABOUT WOMEN IN HISTORY...
LET'S HEAR IT FOR MY GRANDMOTHER!!
SCHULZ

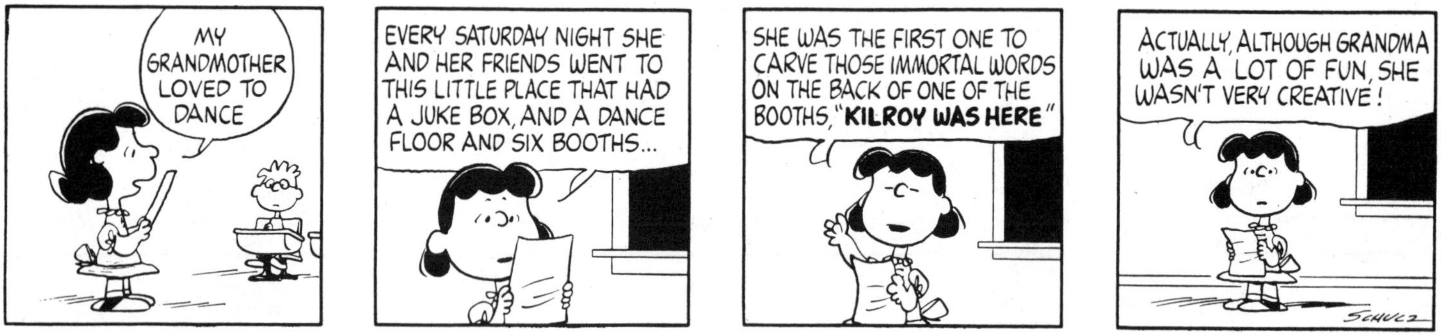
MY GRANDMOTHER LOVED TO DANCE
EVERY SATURDAY NIGHT SHE AND HER FRIENDS WENT TO THIS LITTLE PLACE THAT HAD A JUKE BOX, AND A DANCE FLOOR AND SIX BOOTHS...
SHE WAS THE FIRST ONE TO CARVE THOSE IMMORTAL WORDS ON THE BACK OF ONE OF THE BOOTHS, "KILROY WAS HERE"
ACTUALLY, ALTHOUGH GRANDMA WAS A LOT OF FUN, SHE WASN'T VERY CREATIVE!
SCHULZ

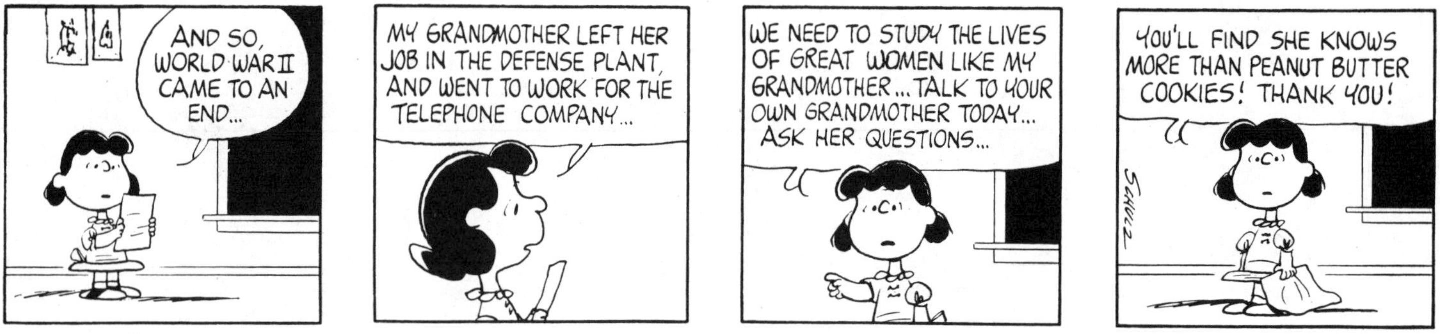
AND SO, WORLD WAR II CAME TO AN END...
MY GRANDMOTHER LEFT HER JOB IN THE DEFENSE PLANT, AND WENT TO WORK FOR THE TELEPHONE COMPANY...
WE NEED TO STUDY THE LIVES OF GREAT WOMEN LIKE MY GRANDMOTHER... TALK TO YOUR OWN GRANDMOTHER TODAY... ASK HER QUESTIONS...
YOU'LL FIND SHE KNOWS MORE THAN PEANUT BUTTER COOKIES! THANK YOU!
SCHULZ

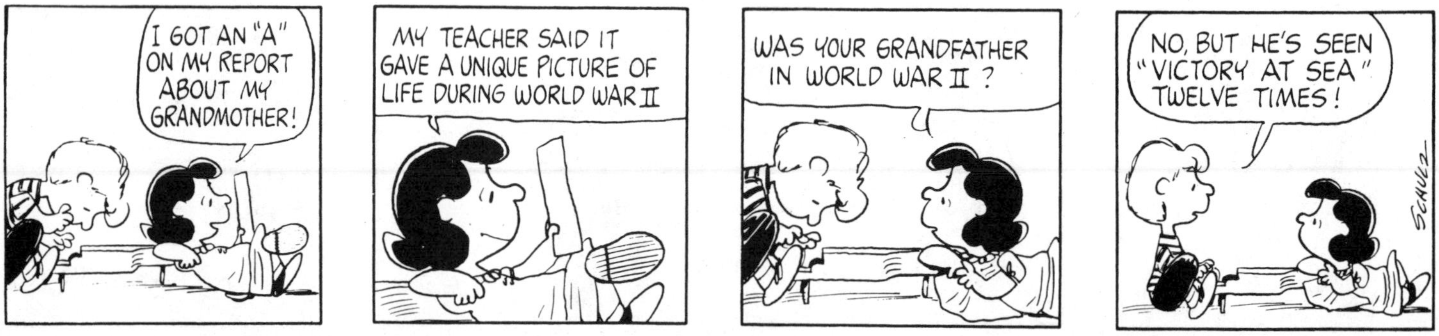
I GOT AN "A" ON MY REPORT ABOUT MY GRANDMOTHER!
MY TEACHER SAID IT GAVE A UNIQUE PICTURE OF LIFE DURING WORLD WAR II
WAS YOUR GRANDFATHER IN WORLD WAR II?
NO, BUT HE'S SEEN "VICTORY AT SEA" TWELVE TIMES!
SCHULZ

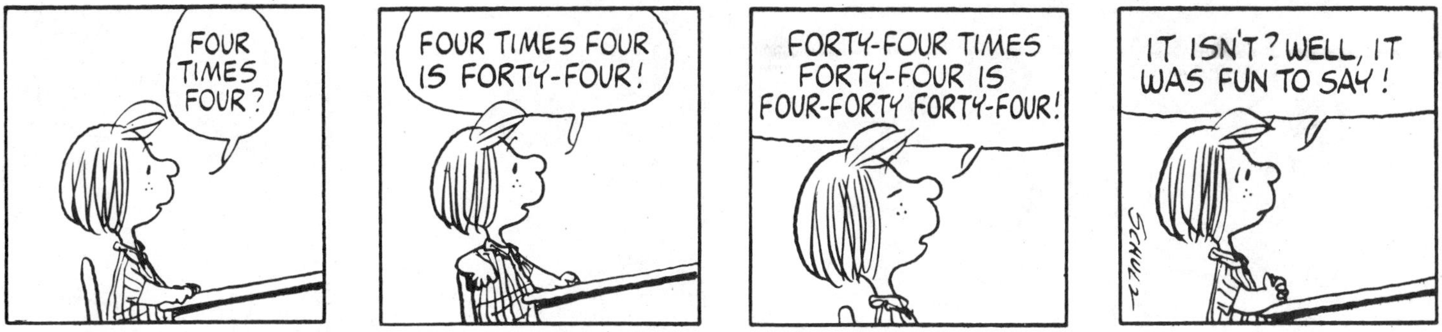
FOUR TIMES FOUR?
FOUR TIMES FOUR IS FORTY-FOUR!
FORTY-FOUR TIMES FORTY-FOUR IS FOUR-FORTY FORTY-FOUR!
IT ISN'T? WELL, IT WAS FUN TO SAY!
SCHULZ

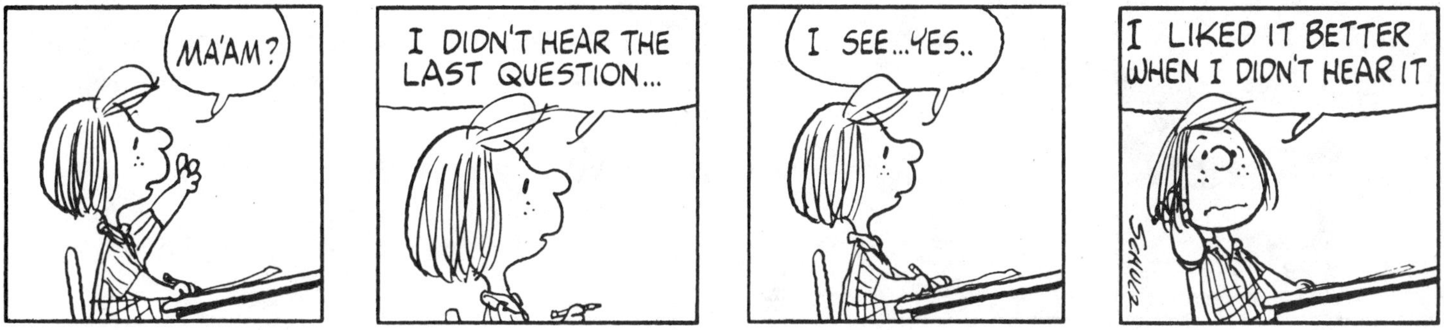
MA'AM?
I DIDN'T HEAR THE LAST QUESTION...
I SEE...YES..
I LIKED IT BETTER WHEN I DIDN'T HEAR IT
SCHULZ

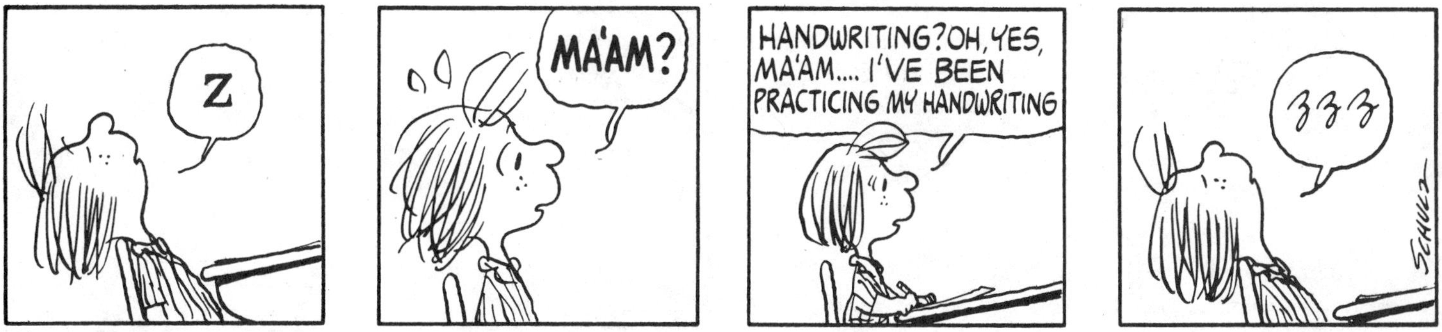
Z
MA'AM?
HANDWRITING? OH, YES, MA'AM.... I'VE BEEN PRACTICING MY HANDWRITING
ZZZ
SCHULZ

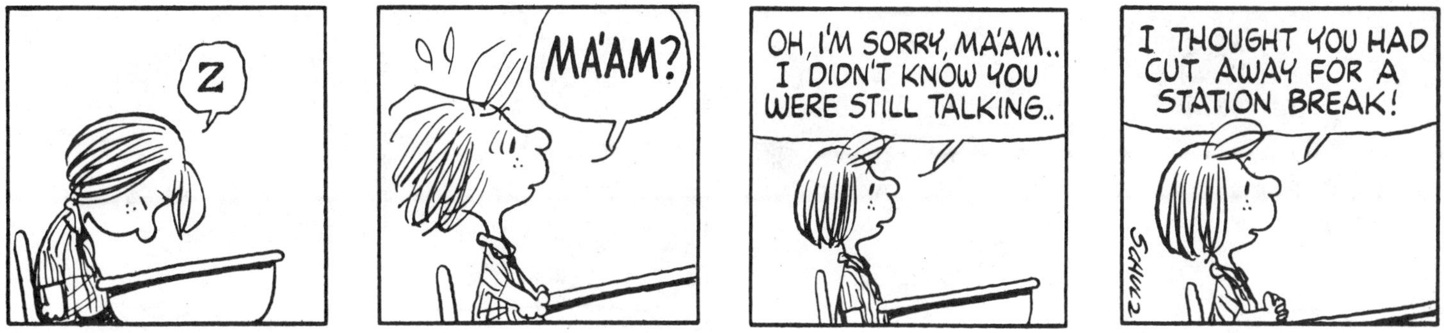
Z
MA'AM?
OH, I'M SORRY, MA'AM.. I DIDN'T KNOW YOU WERE STILL TALKING..
I THOUGHT YOU HAD CUT AWAY FOR A STATION BREAK!
SCHULZ

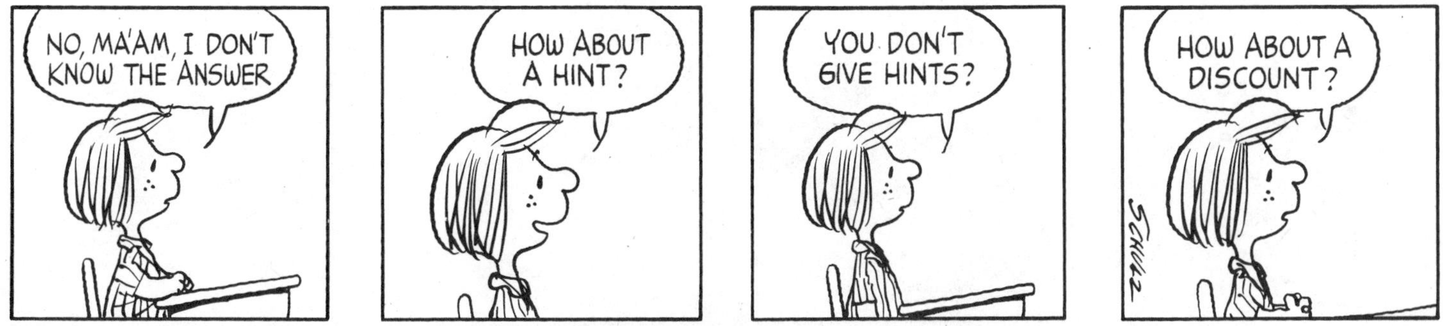
NO, MA'AM, I DON'T KNOW THE ANSWER
HOW ABOUT A HINT?
YOU DON'T GIVE HINTS?
HOW ABOUT A DISCOUNT?
SCHULZ

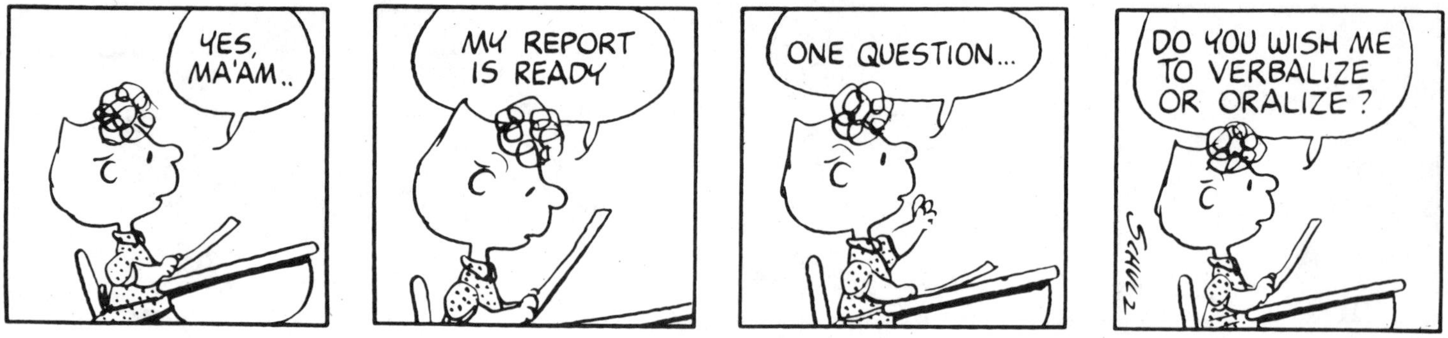
YES, MA'AM..
MY REPORT IS READY
ONE QUESTION...
DO YOU WISH ME TO VERBALIZE OR ORALIZE?
SCHULZ

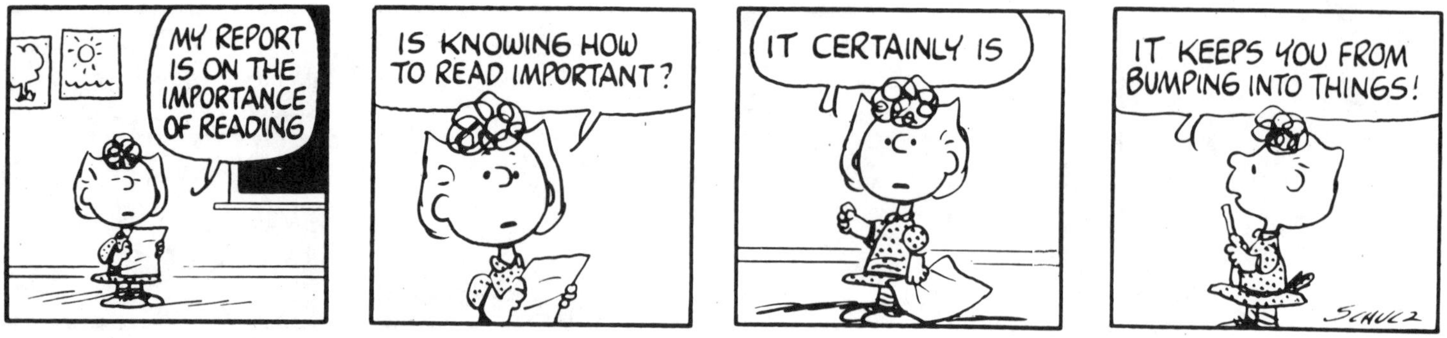
MY REPORT IS ON THE IMPORTANCE OF READING
IS KNOWING HOW TO READ IMPORTANT?
IT CERTAINLY IS
IT KEEPS YOU FROM BUMPING INTO THINGS!
SCHULZ

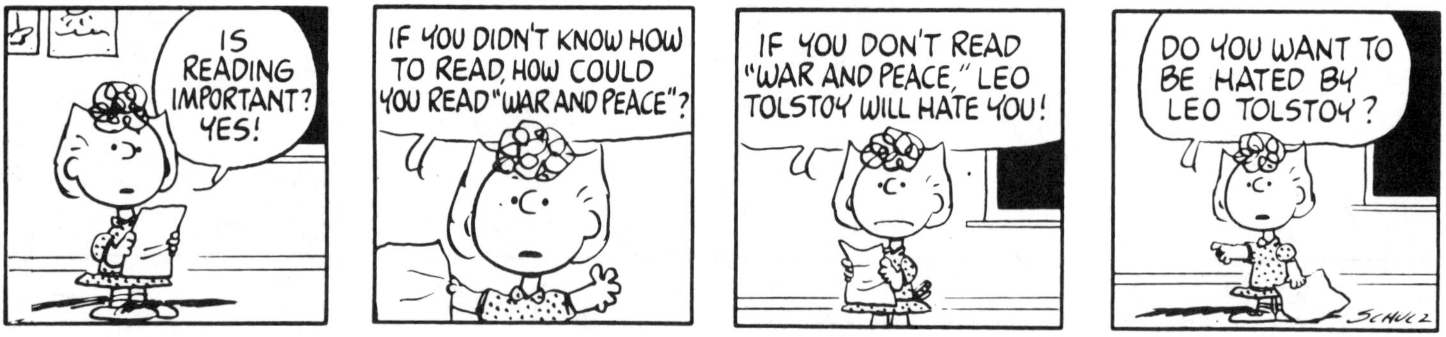
IS READING IMPORTANT? YES!
IF YOU DIDN'T KNOW HOW TO READ, HOW COULD YOU READ "WAR AND PEACE"?
IF YOU DON'T READ "WAR AND PEACE," LEO TOLSTOY WILL HATE YOU!
DO YOU WANT TO BE HATED BY LEO TOLSTOY?
SCHULZ

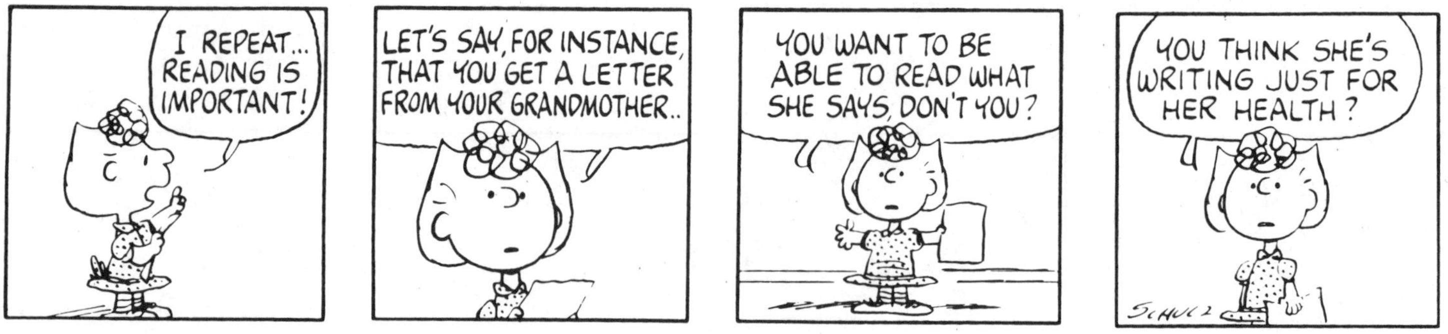
I REPEAT... READING IS IMPORTANT!
LET'S SAY, FOR INSTANCE, THAT YOU GET A LETTER FROM YOUR GRANDMOTHER..
YOU WANT TO BE ABLE TO READ WHAT SHE SAYS, DON'T YOU?
YOU THINK SHE'S WRITING JUST FOR HER HEALTH?
SCHULZ

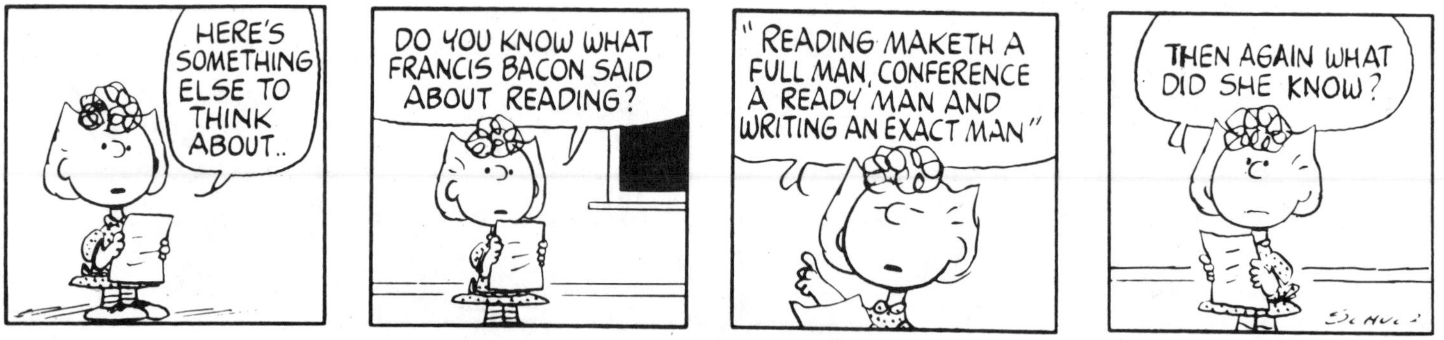
HERE'S SOMETHING ELSE TO THINK ABOUT..
DO YOU KNOW WHAT FRANCIS BACON SAID ABOUT READING?
"READING MAKETH A FULL MAN, CONFERENCE A READY MAN AND WRITING AN EXACT MAN"
THEN AGAIN WHAT DID SHE KNOW?

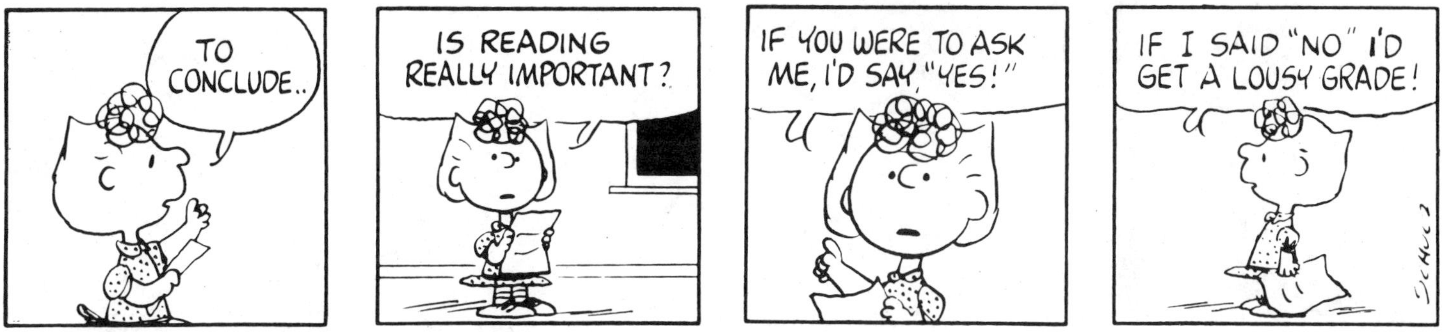
TO CONCLUDE..
IS READING REALLY IMPORTANT?
IF YOU WERE TO ASK ME, I'D SAY, "YES!"
IF I SAID "NO" I'D GET A LOUSY GRADE!
SCHULZ

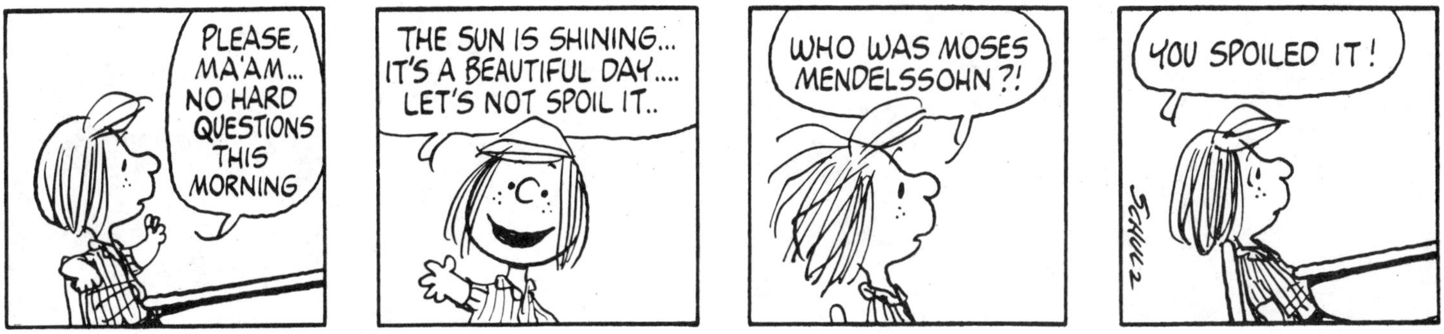
PLEASE, MA'AM... NO HARD QUESTIONS THIS MORNING
THE SUN IS SHINING... IT'S A BEAUTIFUL DAY.... LET'S NOT SPOIL IT..
WHO WAS MOSES MENDELSSOHN?!
YOU SPOILED IT!
SCHULZ

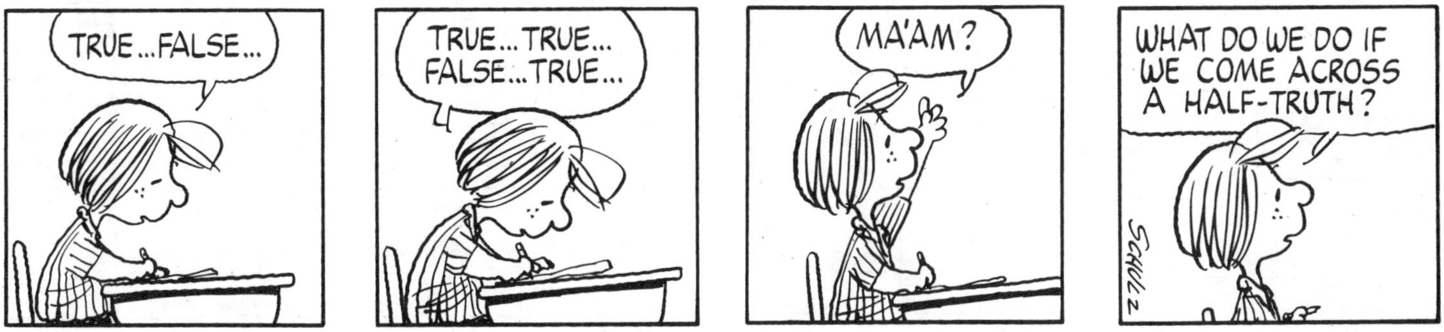
TRUE...FALSE...
TRUE...TRUE... FALSE...TRUE...
MA'AM?
WHAT DO WE DO IF WE COME ACROSS A HALF-TRUTH?
SCHULZ

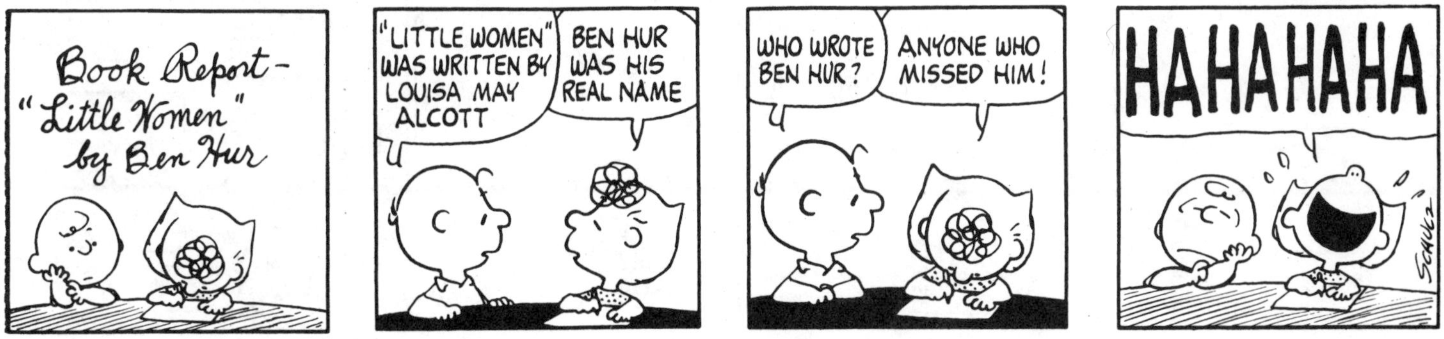
Book Report - "Little Women" by Ben Hur
"LITTLE WOMEN" WAS WRITTEN BY LOUISA MAY ALCOTT
BEN HUR WAS HIS REAL NAME
WHO WROTE BEN HUR?
ANYONE WHO MISSED HIM!
HAHAHAHA
SCHULZ

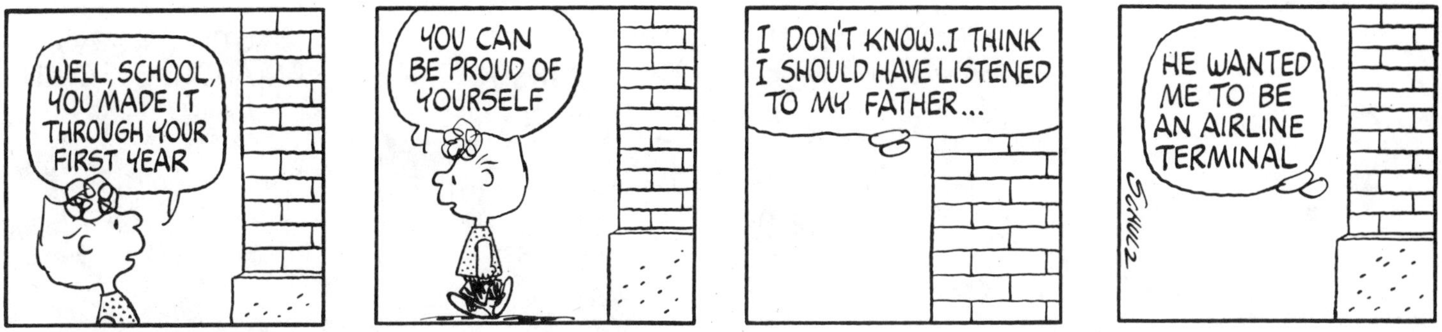
WELL, SCHOOL, YOU MADE IT THROUGH YOUR FIRST YEAR
YOU CAN BE PROUD OF YOURSELF
I DON'T KNOW..I THINK I SHOULD HAVE LISTENED TO MY FATHER...
HE WANTED ME TO BE AN AIRLINE TERMINAL
SCHULZ

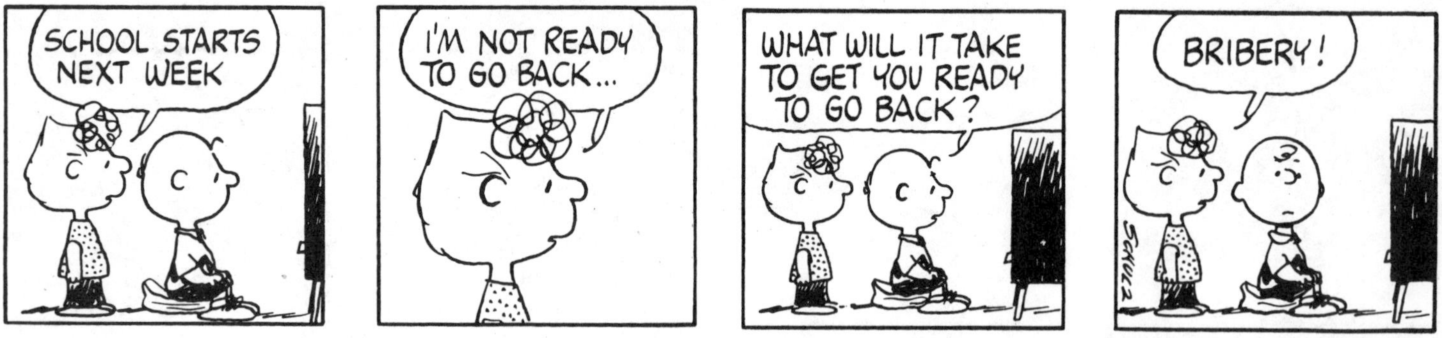
SCHOOL STARTS NEXT WEEK
I'M NOT READY TO GO BACK...
WHAT WILL IT TAKE TO GET YOU READY TO GO BACK?
BRIBERY!
SCHULZ

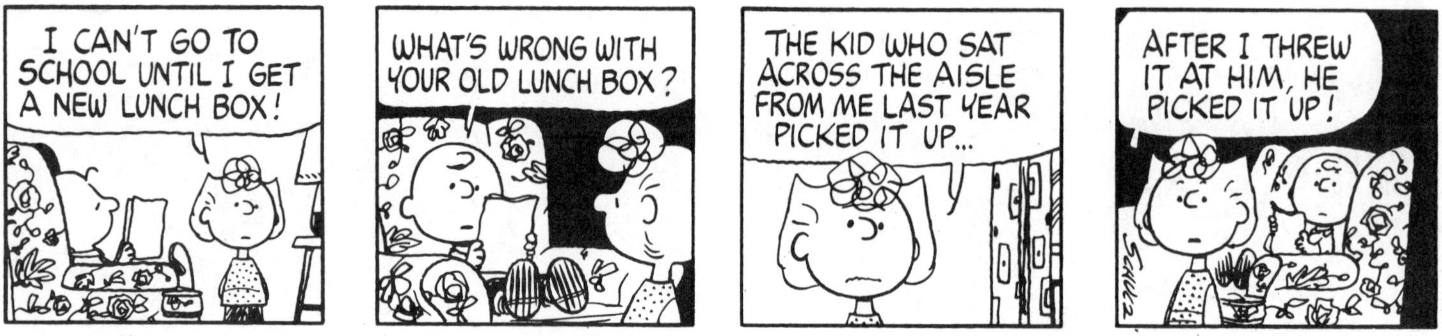
I CAN'T GO TO SCHOOL UNTIL I GET A NEW LUNCH BOX!
WHAT'S WRONG WITH YOUR OLD LUNCH BOX?
THE KID WHO SAT ACROSS THE AISLE FROM ME LAST YEAR PICKED IT UP...
AFTER I THREW IT AT HIM, HE PICKED IT UP!
SCHULZ

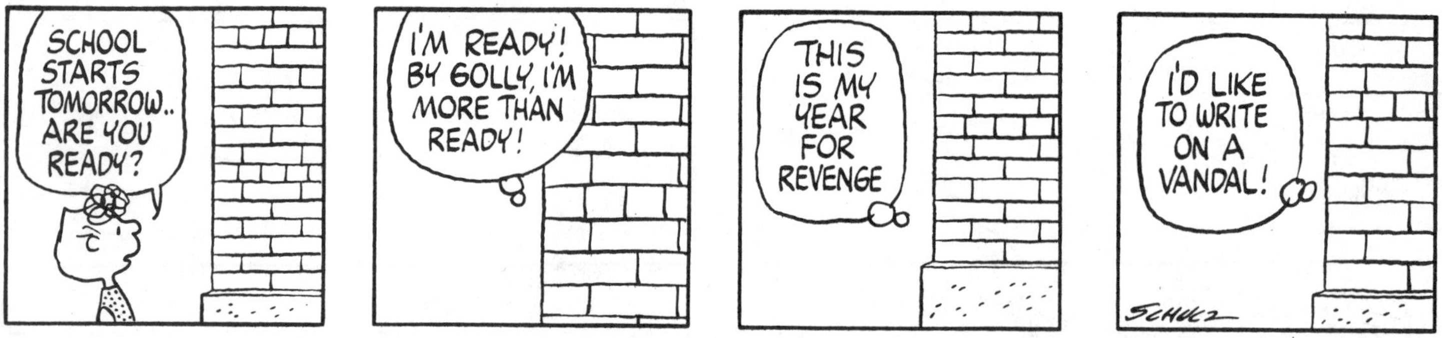
SCHOOL STARTS TOMORROW.. ARE YOU READY?
I'M READY! BY GOLLY, I'M MORE THAN READY!
THIS IS MY YEAR FOR REVENGE
I'D LIKE TO WRITE ON A VANDAL!
SCHULZ

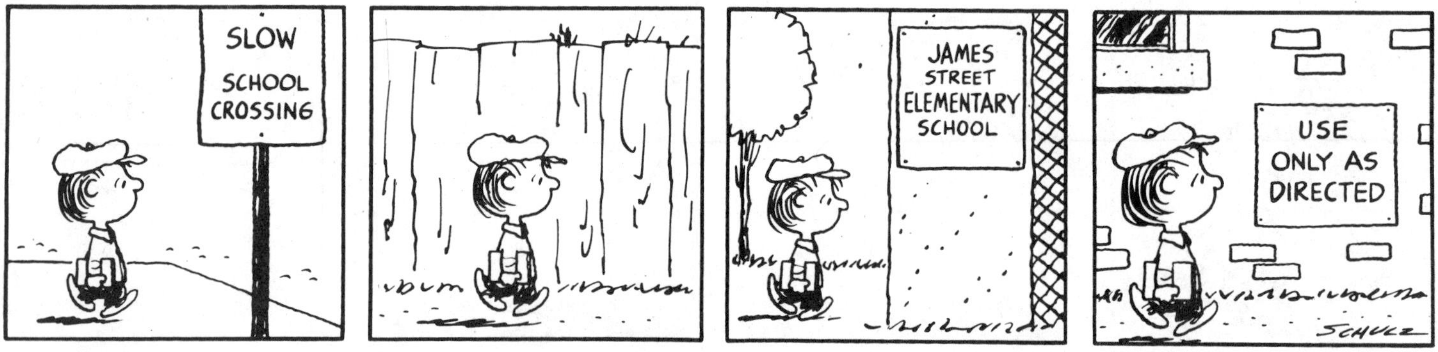
SLOW
SCHOOL CROSSING
JAMES STREET ELEMENTARY SCHOOL
USE ONLY AS DIRECTED
SCHULZ

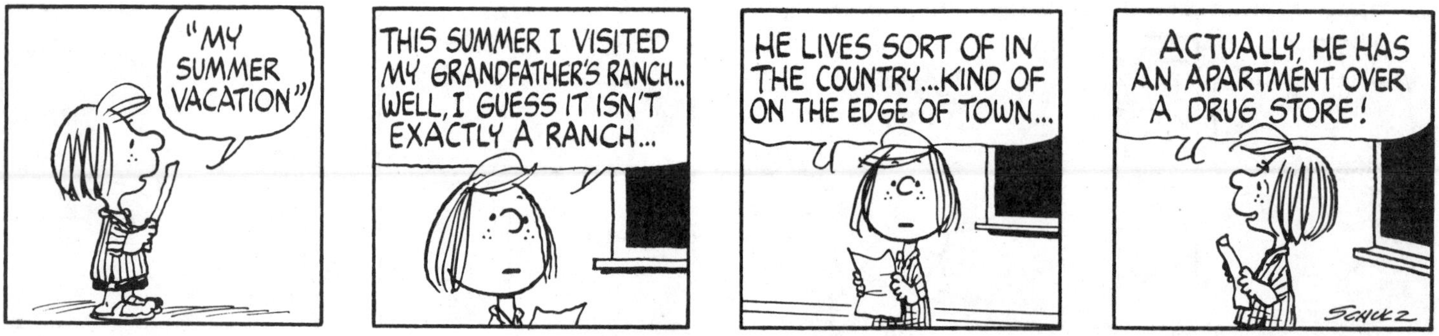
"MY SUMMER VACATION"
THIS SUMMER I VISITED MY GRANDFATHER'S RANCH.. WELL, I GUESS IT ISN'T EXACTLY A RANCH...
HE LIVES SORT OF IN THE COUNTRY...KIND OF ON THE EDGE OF TOWN...
ACTUALLY, HE HAS AN APARTMENT OVER A DRUG STORE!
SCHULZ

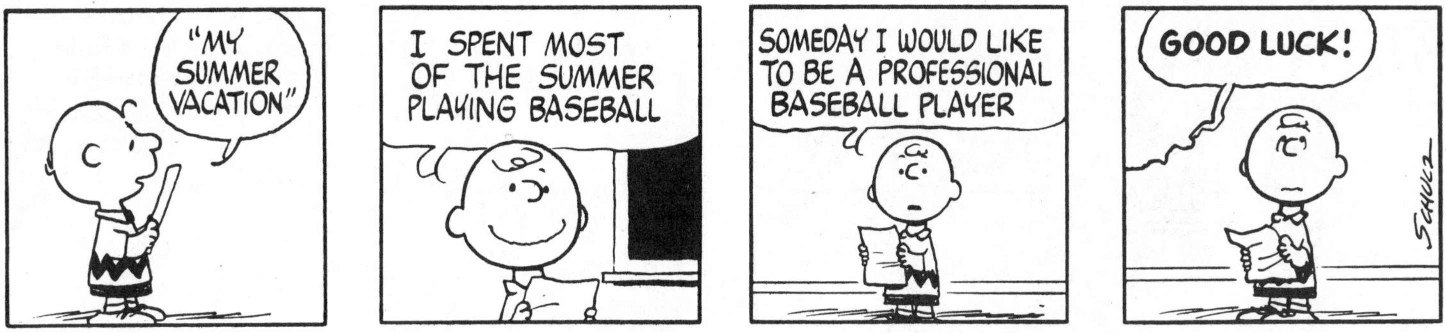
"MY SUMMER VACATION"
I SPENT MOST OF THE SUMMER PLAYING BASEBALL
SOMEDAY I WOULD LIKE TO BE A PROFESSIONAL BASEBALL PLAYER
GOOD LUCK!

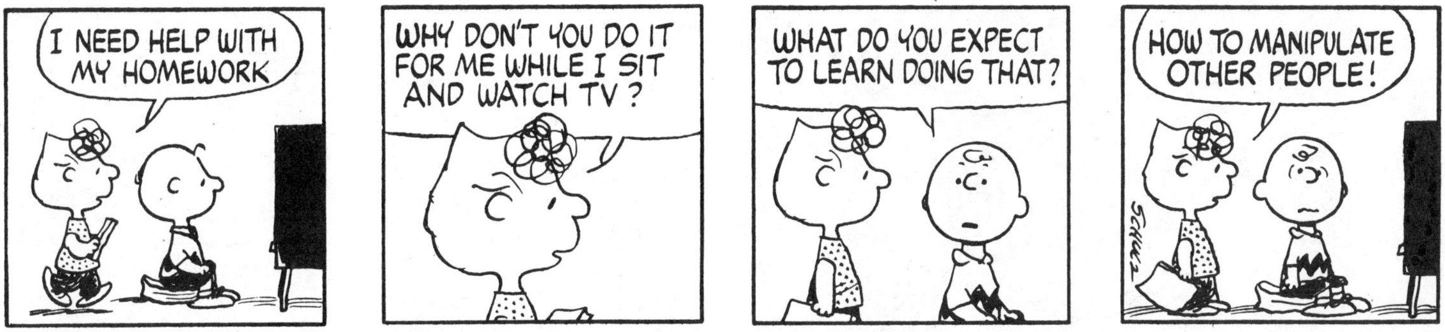
I NEED HELP WITH MY HOMEWORK
WHY DON'T YOU DO IT FOR ME WHILE I SIT AND WATCH TV ?
WHAT DO YOU EXPECT TO LEARN DOING THAT?
HOW TO MANIPULATE OTHER PEOPLE!

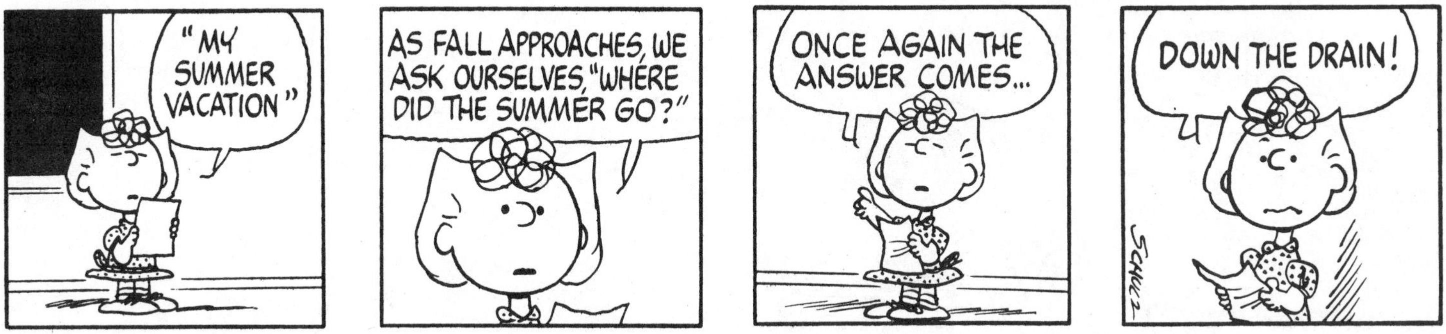
"MY SUMMER VACATION"
AS FALL APPROACHES, WE ASK OURSELVES, "WHERE DID THE SUMMER GO?"
ONCE AGAIN THE ANSWER COMES...
DOWN THE DRAIN!

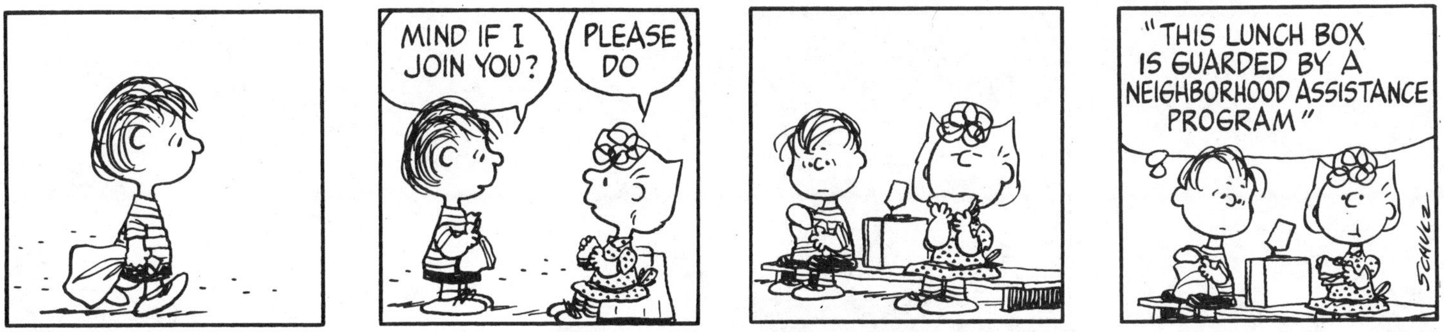
MIND IF I JOIN YOU?
PLEASE DO
"THIS LUNCH BOX IS GUARDED BY A NEIGHBORHOOD ASSISTANCE PROGRAM"

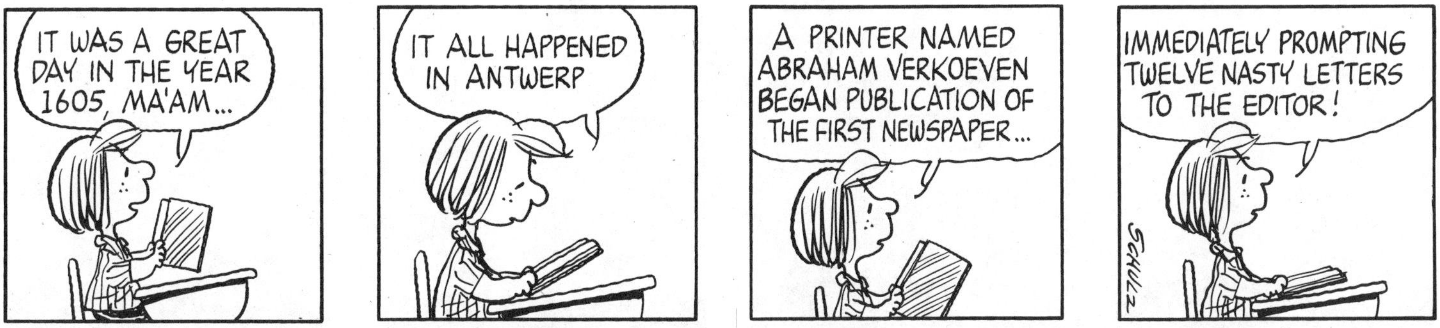
IT WAS A GREAT DAY IN THE YEAR 1605, MA'AM...
IT ALL HAPPENED IN ANTWERP
A PRINTER NAMED ABRAHAM VERKOEVEN BEGAN PUBLICATION OF THE FIRST NEWSPAPER...
IMMEDIATELY PROMPTING TWELVE NASTY LETTERS TO THE EDITOR!

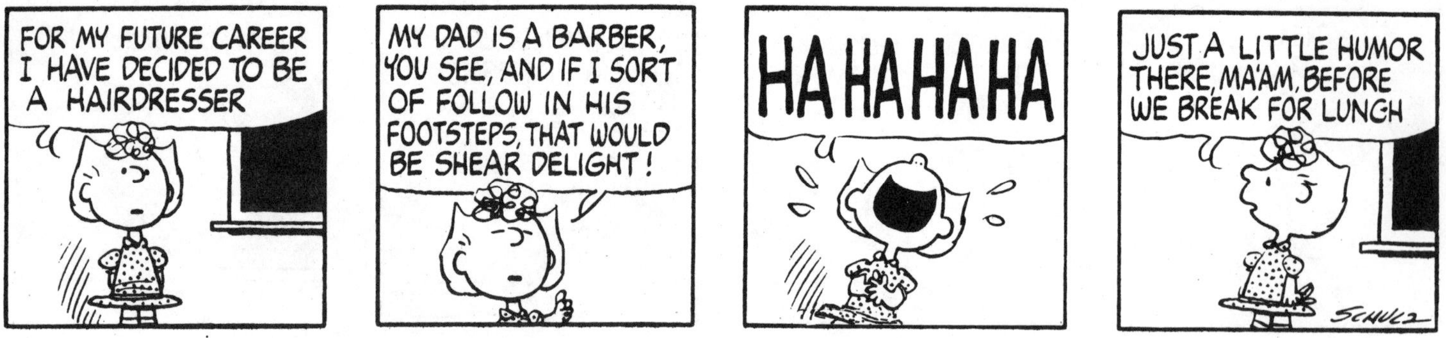
FOR MY FUTURE CAREER I HAVE DECIDED TO BE A HAIRDRESSER
MY DAD IS A BARBER, YOU SEE, AND IF I SORT OF FOLLOW IN HIS FOOTSTEPS, THAT WOULD BE SHEAR DELIGHT!
HA HA HA HA
JUST A LITTLE HUMOR THERE, MA'AM, BEFORE WE BREAK FOR LUNCH

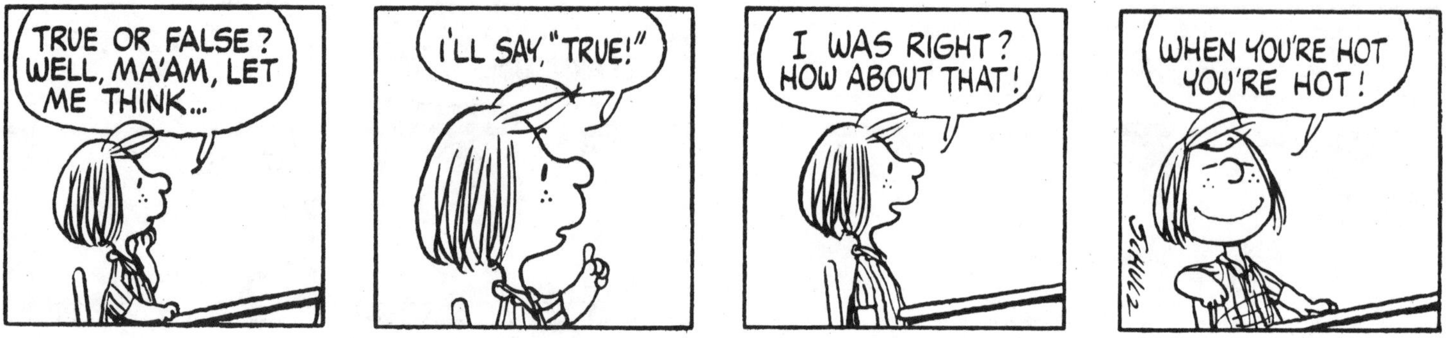
TRUE OR FALSE? WELL, MA'AM, LET ME THINK...
I'LL SAY, "TRUE!"
I WAS RIGHT? HOW ABOUT THAT!
WHEN YOU'RE HOT YOU'RE HOT!

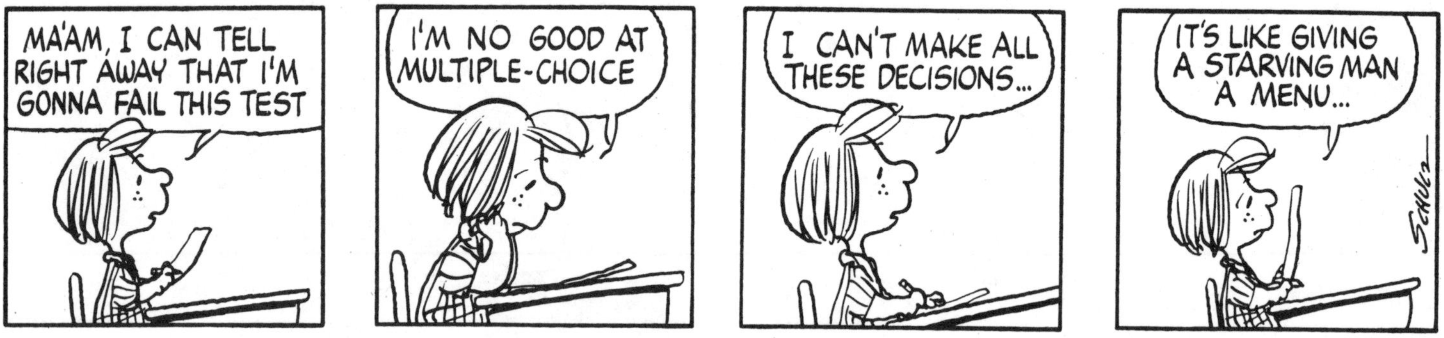
MA'AM, I CAN TELL RIGHT AWAY THAT I'M GONNA FAIL THIS TEST
I'M NO GOOD AT MULTIPLE-CHOICE
I CAN'T MAKE ALL THESE DECISIONS...
IT'S LIKE GIVING A STARVING MAN A MENU...

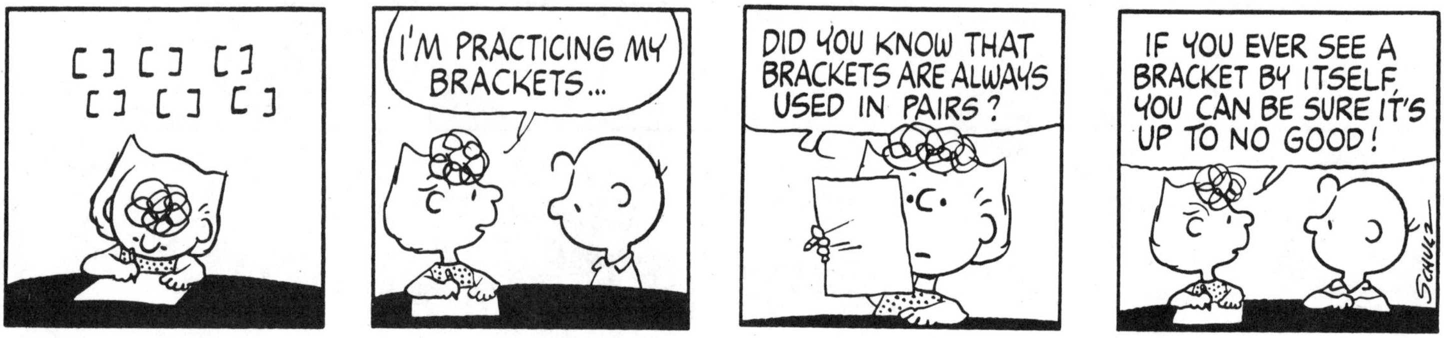
[ ] [ ] [ ] [ ] [ ] [ ]
I'M PRACTICING MY BRACKETS...
DID YOU KNOW THAT BRACKETS ARE ALWAYS USED IN PAIRS?
IF YOU EVER SEE A BRACKET BY ITSELF, YOU CAN BE SURE IT'S UP TO NO GOOD!

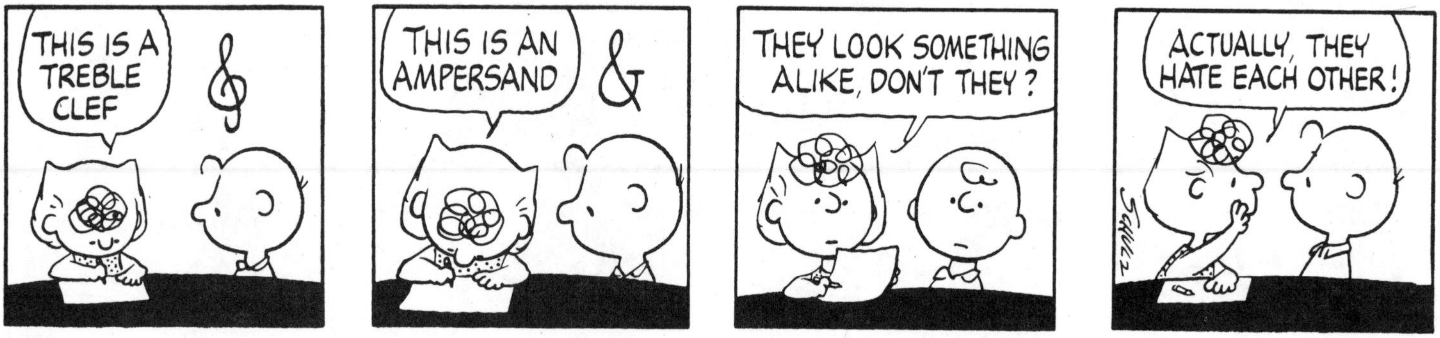
THIS IS A TREBLE CLEF
THIS IS AN AMPERSAND
&
THEY LOOK SOMETHING ALIKE, DON'T THEY?
ACTUALLY, THEY HATE EACH OTHER!

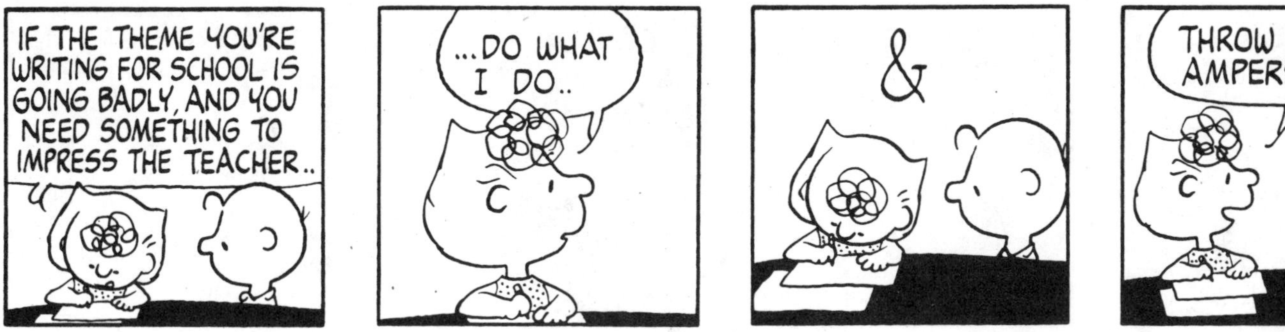
IF THE THEME YOU'RE WRITING FOR SCHOOL IS GOING BADLY, AND YOU NEED SOMETHING TO IMPRESS THE TEACHER..
...DO WHAT I DO..
&
THROW IN AN AMPERSAND!
SCHULZ

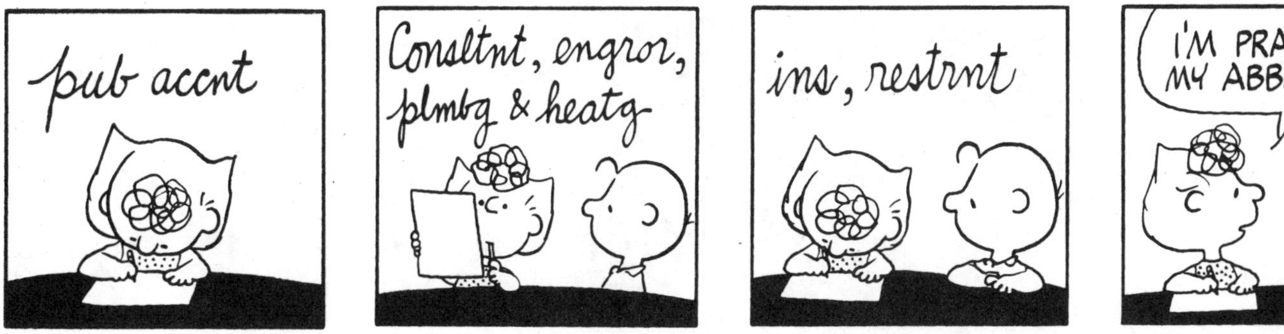
pub accnt
Consltnt, engror, plmbg & heatg
ins, restrnt
I'M PRACTG MY ABBREVS
SCHULZ

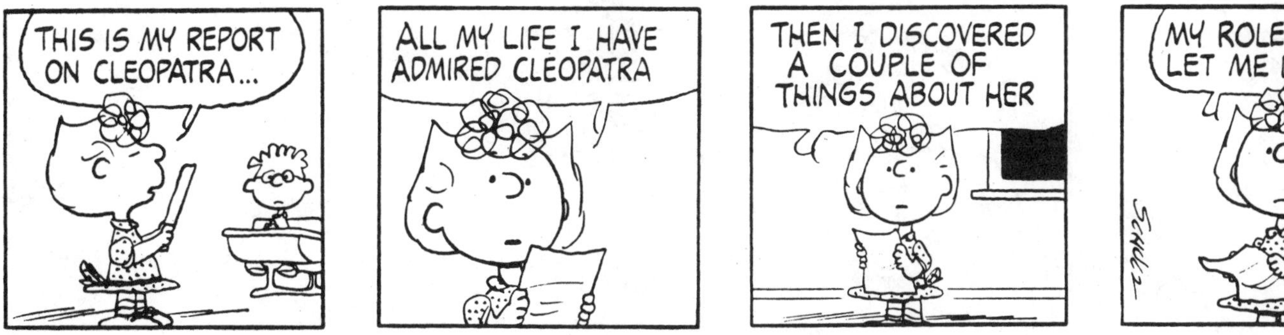
THIS IS MY REPORT ON CLEOPATRA...
ALL MY LIFE I HAVE ADMIRED CLEOPATRA
THEN I DISCOVERED A COUPLE OF THINGS ABOUT HER
SCHULZ
MY ROLE MODEL LET ME DOWN!

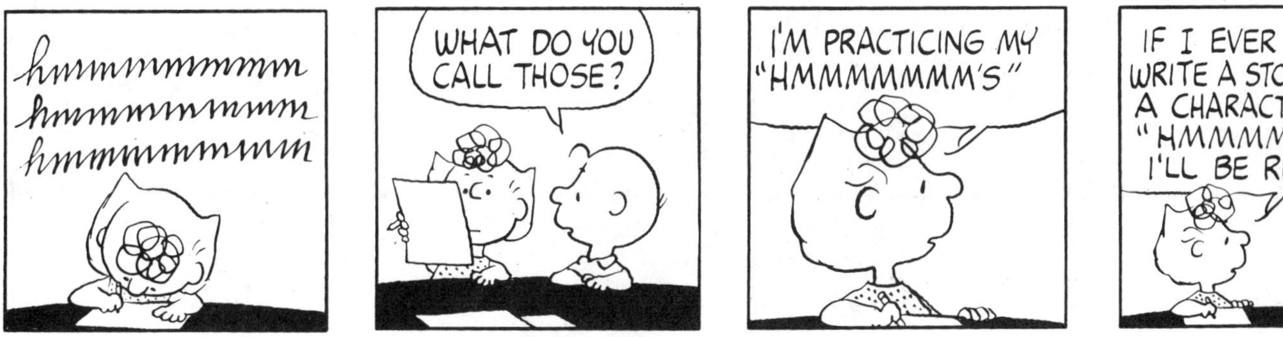
hmmmmmmmm
hmmmmmmmm
hmmmmmmmm
WHAT DO YOU CALL THOSE?
I'M PRACTICING MY "HMMMMMMM'S"
IF I EVER HAVE TO WRITE A STORY WHERE A CHARACTER SAYS, "HMMMMMMM," I'LL BE READY!
SCHULZ

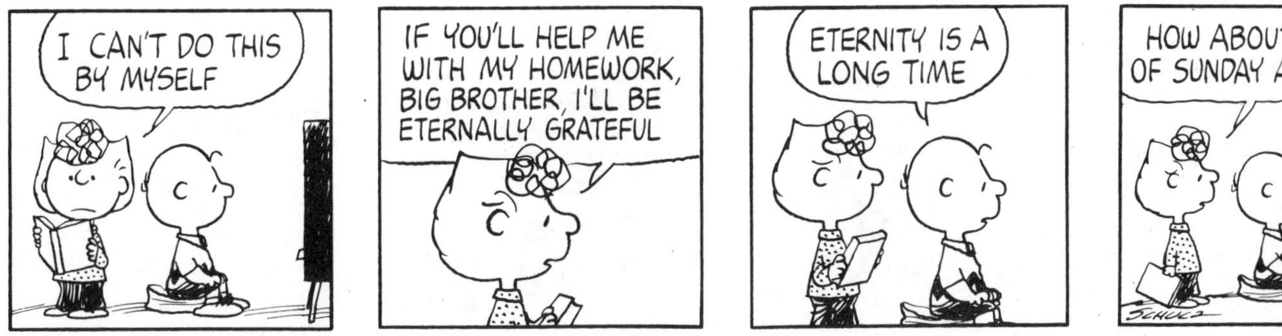
I CAN'T DO THIS BY MYSELF
IF YOU'LL HELP ME WITH MY HOMEWORK, BIG BROTHER, I'LL BE ETERNALLY GRATEFUL
ETERNITY IS A LONG TIME
HOW ABOUT MOST OF SUNDAY AFTERNOON?
SCHULZ

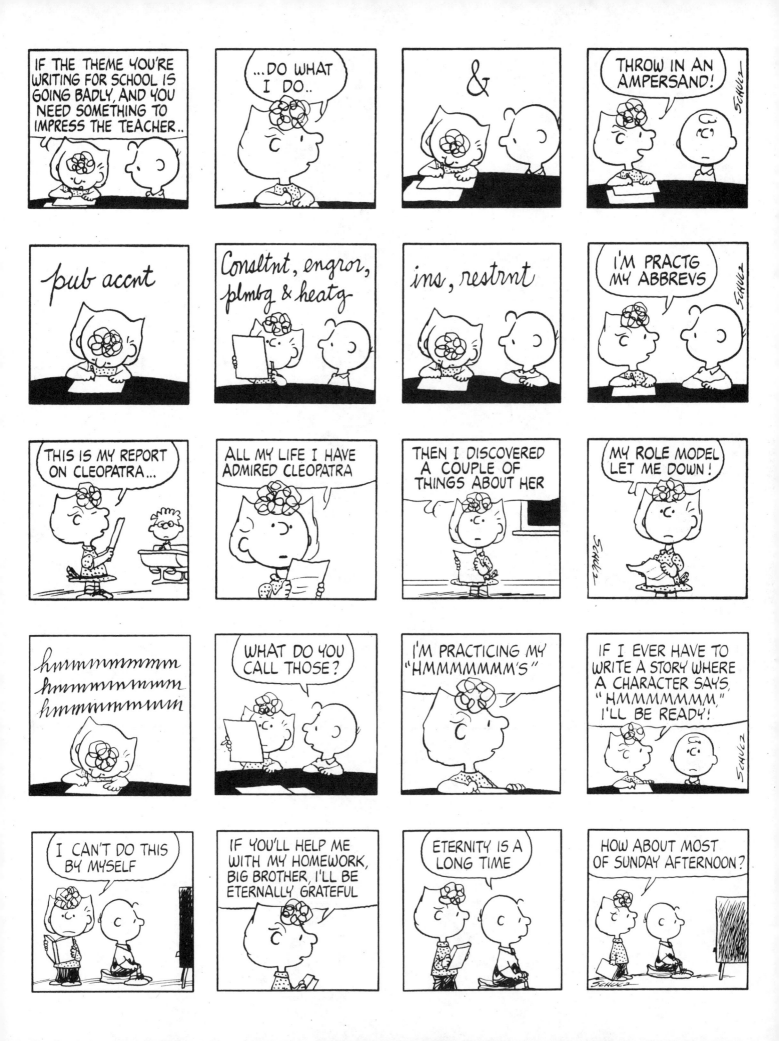

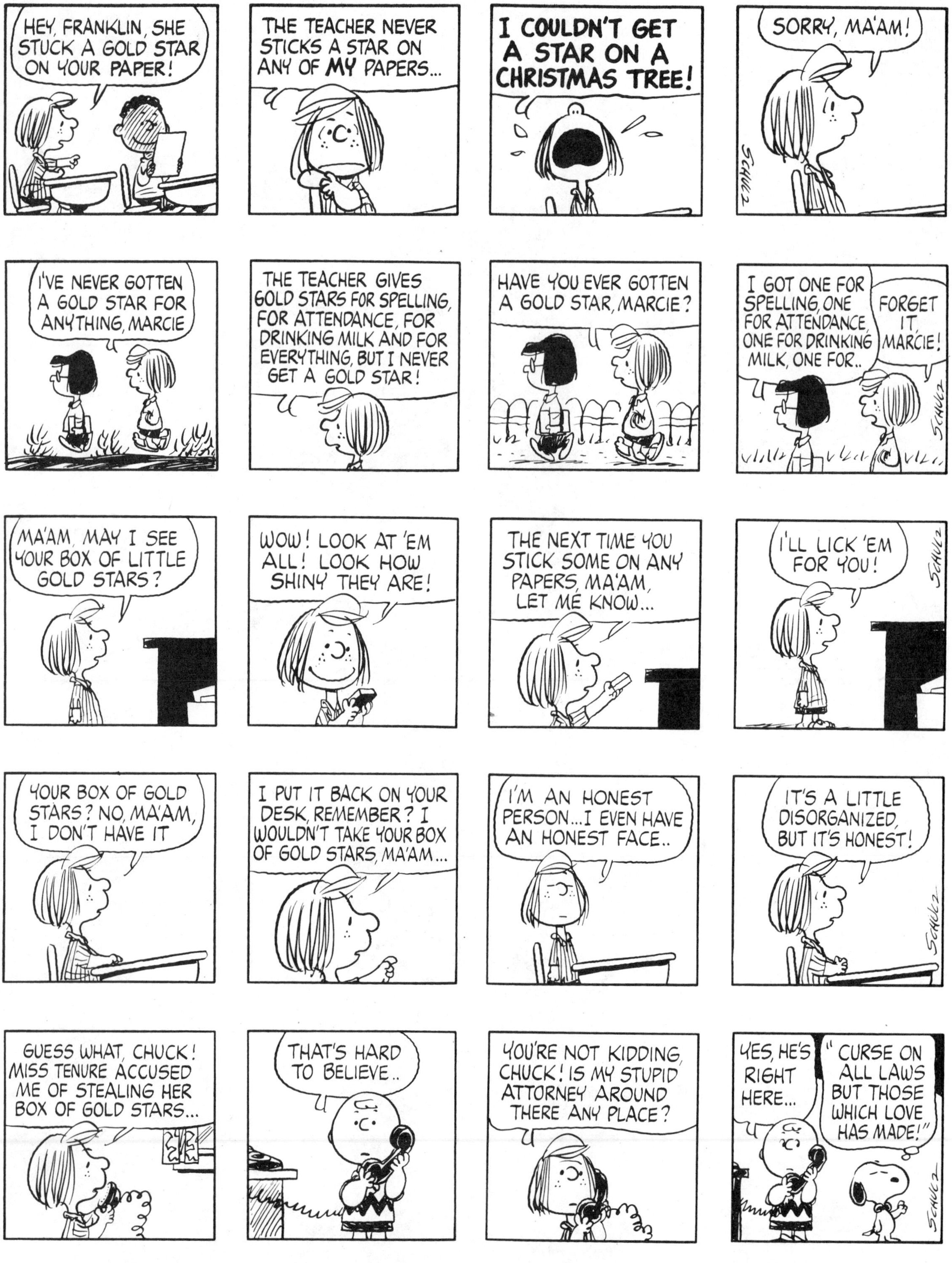
HEY, FRANKLIN, SHE STUCK A GOLD STAR ON YOUR PAPER!
THE TEACHER NEVER STICKS A STAR ON ANY OF MY PAPERS...
I COULDN'T GET A STAR ON A CHRISTMAS TREE!
SORRY, MA'AM!
I'VE NEVER GOTTEN A GOLD STAR FOR ANYTHING, MARCIE
THE TEACHER GIVES GOLD STARS FOR SPELLING, FOR ATTENDANCE, FOR DRINKING MILK AND FOR EVERYTHING, BUT I NEVER GET A GOLD STAR!
HAVE YOU EVER GOTTEN A GOLD STAR, MARCIE?
I GOT ONE FOR SPELLING, ONE FOR ATTENDANCE, ONE FOR DRINKING MILK, ONE FOR..
FORGET IT, MARCIE!
MA'AM, MAY I SEE YOUR BOX OF LITTLE GOLD STARS?
WOW! LOOK AT 'EM ALL! LOOK HOW SHINY THEY ARE!
THE NEXT TIME YOU STICK SOME ON ANY PAPERS, MA'AM, LET ME KNOW...
I'LL LICK 'EM FOR YOU!
YOUR BOX OF GOLD STARS? NO, MA'AM, I DON'T HAVE IT
I PUT IT BACK ON YOUR DESK, REMEMBER? I WOULDN'T TAKE YOUR BOX OF GOLD STARS, MA'AM...
I'M AN HONEST PERSON...I EVEN HAVE AN HONEST FACE..
IT'S A LITTLE DISORGANIZED, BUT IT'S HONEST!
GUESS WHAT, CHUCK! MISS TENURE ACCUSED ME OF STEALING HER BOX OF GOLD STARS...
THAT'S HARD TO BELIEVE..
YOU'RE NOT KIDDING, CHUCK! IS MY STUPID ATTORNEY AROUND THERE ANY PLACE?
YES, HE'S RIGHT HERE...
"CURSE ON ALL LAWS BUT THOSE WHICH LOVE HAS MADE!"

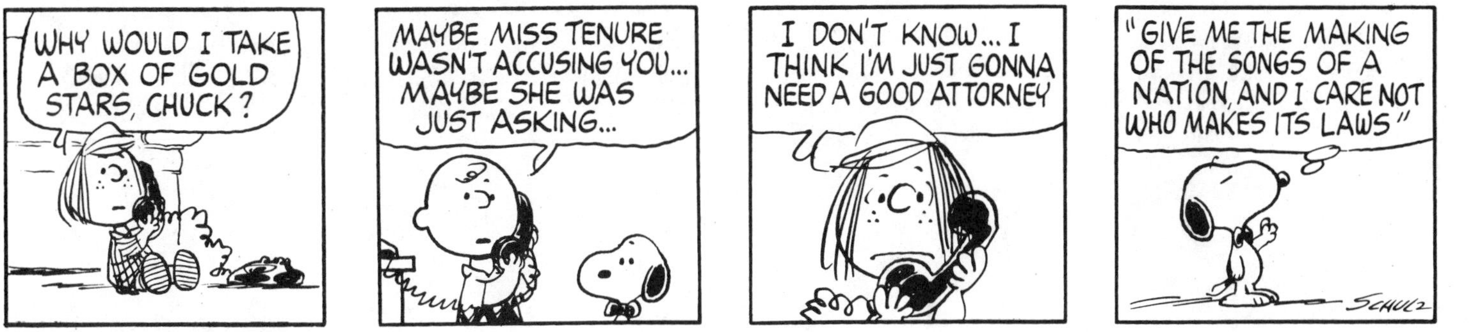
WHY WOULD I TAKE A BOX OF GOLD STARS, CHUCK?
MAYBE MISS TENURE WASN'T ACCUSING YOU... MAYBE SHE WAS JUST ASKING...
I DON'T KNOW... I THINK I'M JUST GONNA NEED A GOOD ATTORNEY
"GIVE ME THE MAKING OF THE SONGS OF A NATION, AND I CARE NOT WHO MAKES ITS LAWS"
SCHULZ

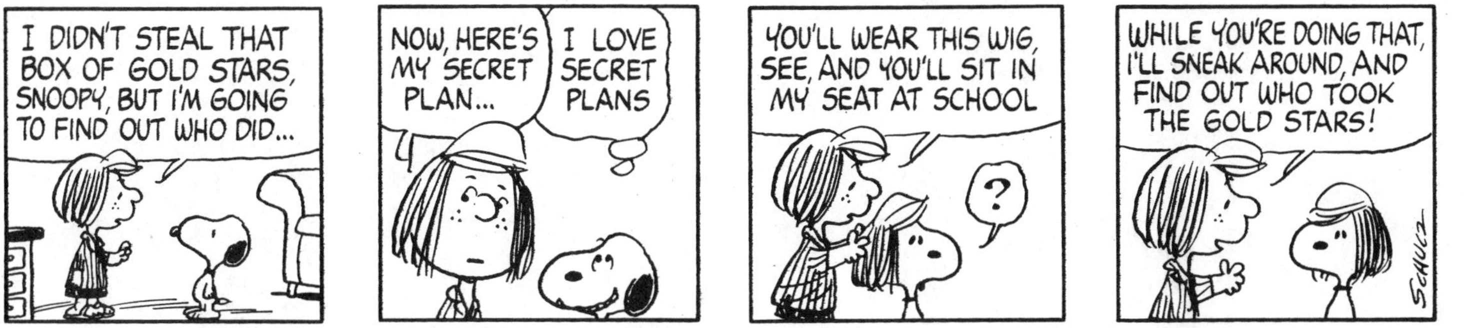
I DIDN'T STEAL THAT BOX OF GOLD STARS, SNOOPY, BUT I'M GOING TO FIND OUT WHO DID...
NOW, HERE'S MY SECRET PLAN...
I LOVE SECRET PLANS
YOU'LL WEAR THIS WIG, SEE, AND YOU'LL SIT IN MY SEAT AT SCHOOL
?
WHILE YOU'RE DOING THAT, I'LL SNEAK AROUND, AND FIND OUT WHO TOOK THE GOLD STARS!
SCHULZ

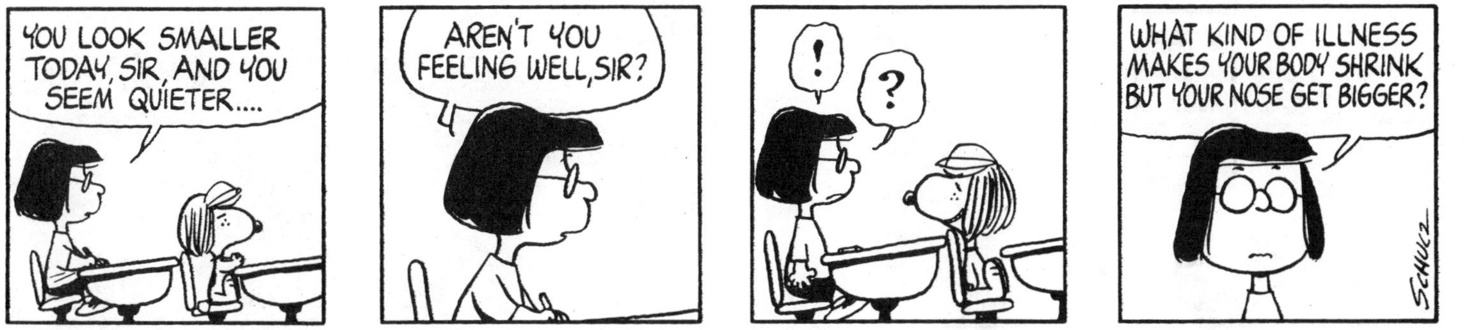
YOU LOOK SMALLER TODAY, SIR, AND YOU SEEM QUIETER....
AREN'T YOU FEELING WELL, SIR?
!
?
WHAT KIND OF ILLNESS MAKES YOUR BODY SHRINK BUT YOUR NOSE GET BIGGER?
SCHULZ

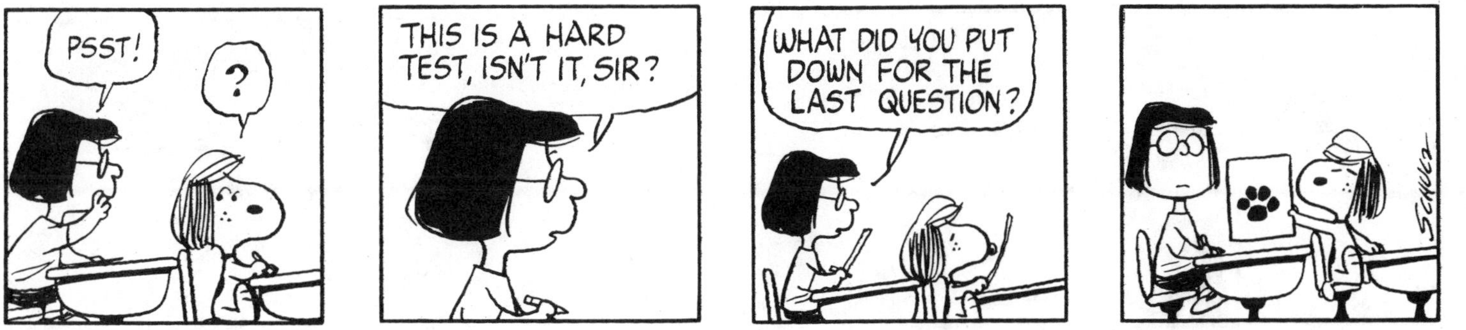
PSST!
?
THIS IS A HARD TEST, ISN'T IT, SIR?
WHAT DID YOU PUT DOWN FOR THE LAST QUESTION?
SCHULZ

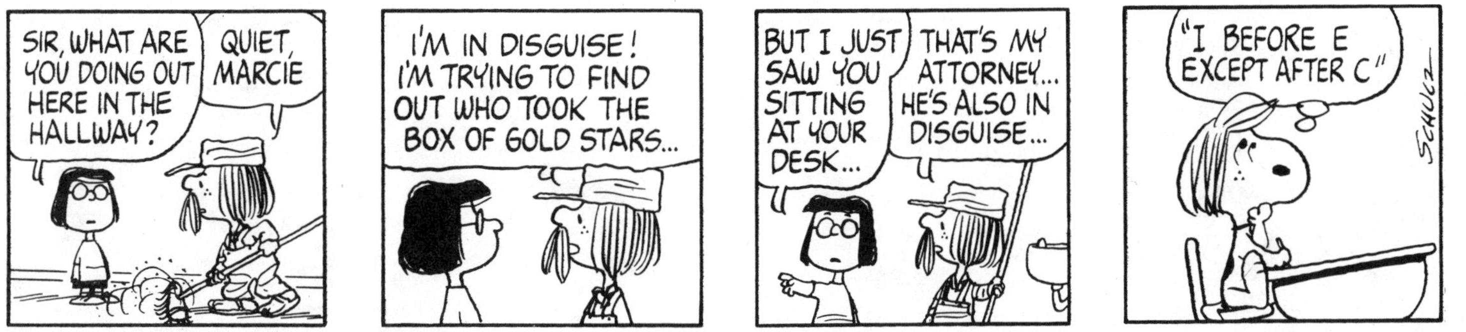
SIR, WHAT ARE YOU DOING OUT HERE IN THE HALLWAY?
QUIET, MARCIE
I'M IN DISGUISE! I'M TRYING TO FIND OUT WHO TOOK THE BOX OF GOLD STARS...
BUT I JUST SAW YOU SITTING AT YOUR DESK...
THAT'S MY ATTORNEY... HE'S ALSO IN DISGUISE...
"I BEFORE E EXCEPT AFTER C"
SCHULZ

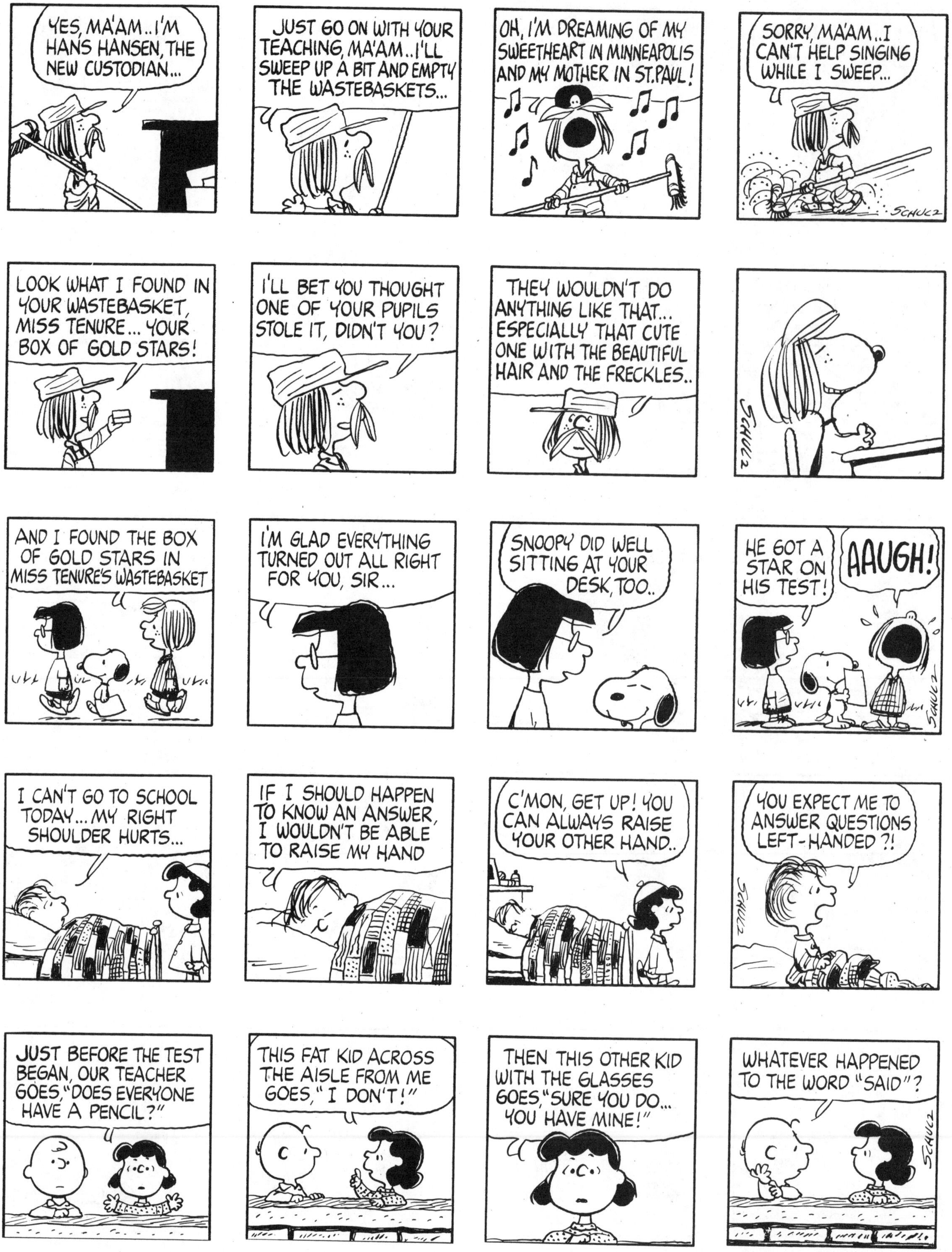
YES, MA'AM..I'M HANS HANSEN, THE NEW CUSTODIAN...
JUST GO ON WITH YOUR TEACHING, MA'AM..I'LL SWEEP UP A BIT AND EMPTY THE WASTEBASKETS...
OH, I'M DREAMING OF MY SWEETHEART IN MINNEAPOLIS AND MY MOTHER IN ST. PAUL!
SORRY, MA'AM..I CAN'T HELP SINGING WHILE I SWEEP...
SCHULZ
LOOK WHAT I FOUND IN YOUR WASTEBASKET, MISS TENURE... YOUR BOX OF GOLD STARS!
I'LL BET YOU THOUGHT ONE OF YOUR PUPILS STOLE IT, DIDN'T YOU?
THEY WOULDN'T DO ANYTHING LIKE THAT... ESPECIALLY THAT CUTE ONE WITH THE BEAUTIFUL HAIR AND THE FRECKLES..
SCHULZ
AND I FOUND THE BOX OF GOLD STARS IN MISS TENURE'S WASTEBASKET
I'M GLAD EVERYTHING TURNED OUT ALL RIGHT FOR YOU, SIR...
SNOOPY DID WELL SITTING AT YOUR DESK, TOO..
HE GOT A STAR ON HIS TEST!
AAUGH!
SCHULZ
I CAN'T GO TO SCHOOL TODAY... MY RIGHT SHOULDER HURTS...
IF I SHOULD HAPPEN TO KNOW AN ANSWER, I WOULDN'T BE ABLE TO RAISE MY HAND
C'MON, GET UP! YOU CAN ALWAYS RAISE YOUR OTHER HAND..
YOU EXPECT ME TO ANSWER QUESTIONS LEFT-HANDED?!
SCHULZ
JUST BEFORE THE TEST BEGAN, OUR TEACHER GOES, "DOES EVERYONE HAVE A PENCIL?"
THIS FAT KID ACROSS THE AISLE FROM ME GOES, "I DON'T!"
THEN THIS OTHER KID WITH THE GLASSES GOES, "SURE YOU DO... YOU HAVE MINE!"
WHATEVER HAPPENED TO THE WORD "SAID"?
SCHULZ

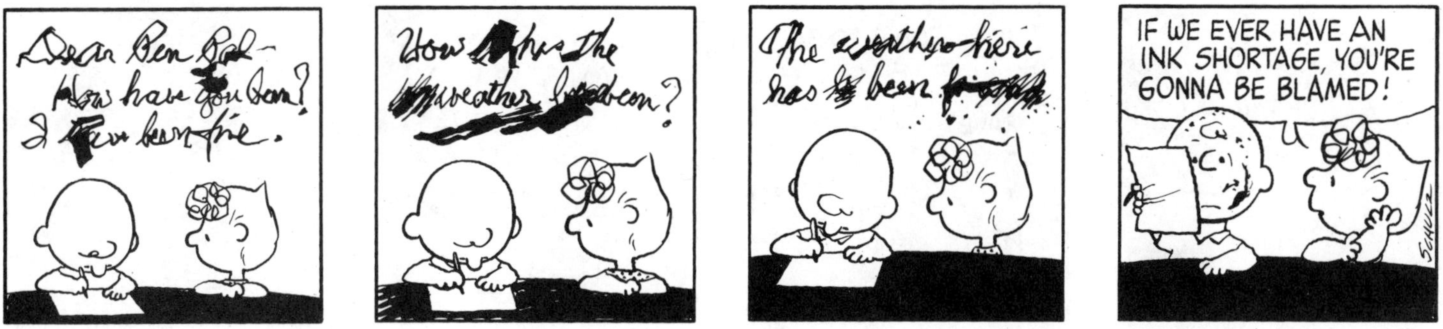
How have you been?
I have been fine.
How has the weather been?
The weather here has been
IF WE EVER HAVE AN INK SHORTAGE, YOU'RE GONNA BE BLAMED!
SCHULZ

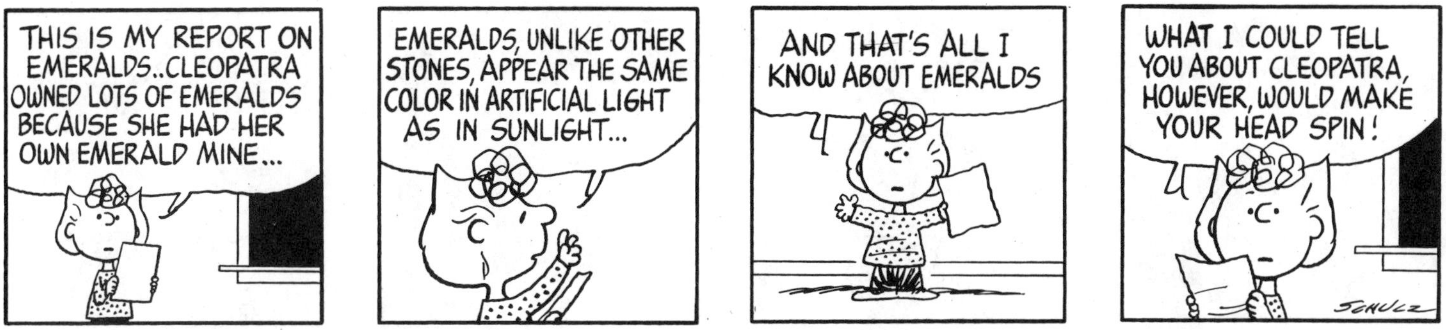
THIS IS MY REPORT ON EMERALDS..CLEOPATRA OWNED LOTS OF EMERALDS BECAUSE SHE HAD HER OWN EMERALD MINE...
EMERALDS, UNLIKE OTHER STONES, APPEAR THE SAME COLOR IN ARTIFICIAL LIGHT AS IN SUNLIGHT...
AND THAT'S ALL I KNOW ABOUT EMERALDS
WHAT I COULD TELL YOU ABOUT CLEOPATRA, HOWEVER, WOULD MAKE YOUR HEAD SPIN!
SCHULZ

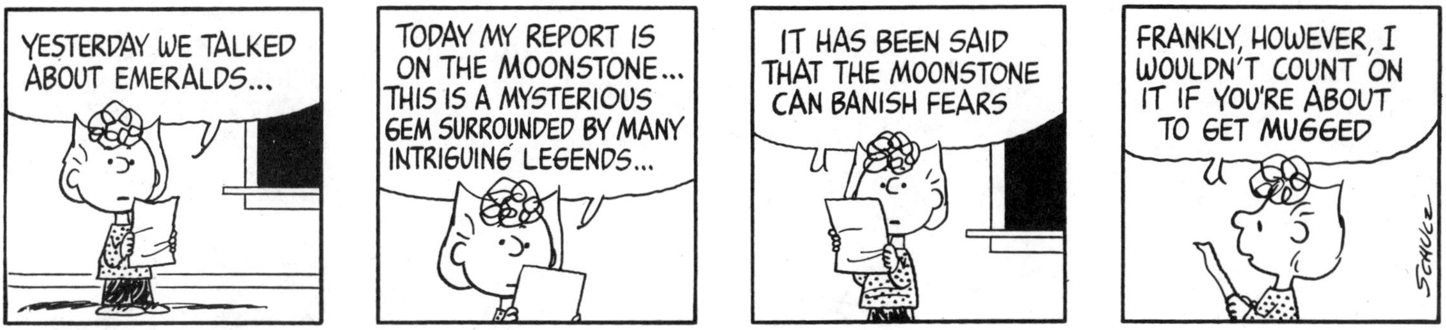
YESTERDAY WE TALKED ABOUT EMERALDS...
TODAY MY REPORT IS ON THE MOONSTONE... THIS IS A MYSTERIOUS GEM SURROUNDED BY MANY INTRIGUING LEGENDS...
IT HAS BEEN SAID THAT THE MOONSTONE CAN BANISH FEARS
FRANKLY, HOWEVER, I WOULDN'T COUNT ON IT IF YOU'RE ABOUT TO GET MUGGED
SCHULZ

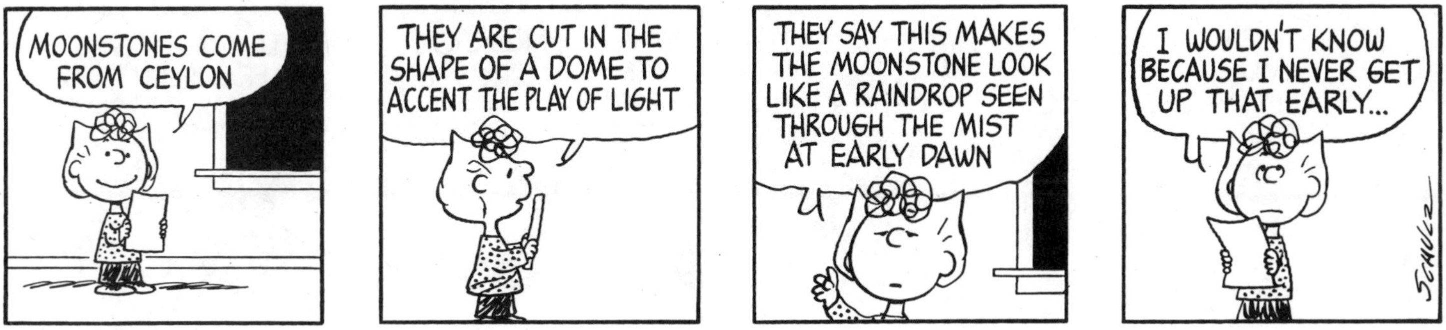
MOONSTONES COME FROM CEYLON
THEY ARE CUT IN THE SHAPE OF A DOME TO ACCENT THE PLAY OF LIGHT
THEY SAY THIS MAKES THE MOONSTONE LOOK LIKE A RAINDROP SEEN THROUGH THE MIST AT EARLY DAWN
I WOULDN'T KNOW BECAUSE I NEVER GET UP THAT EARLY...
SCHULZ

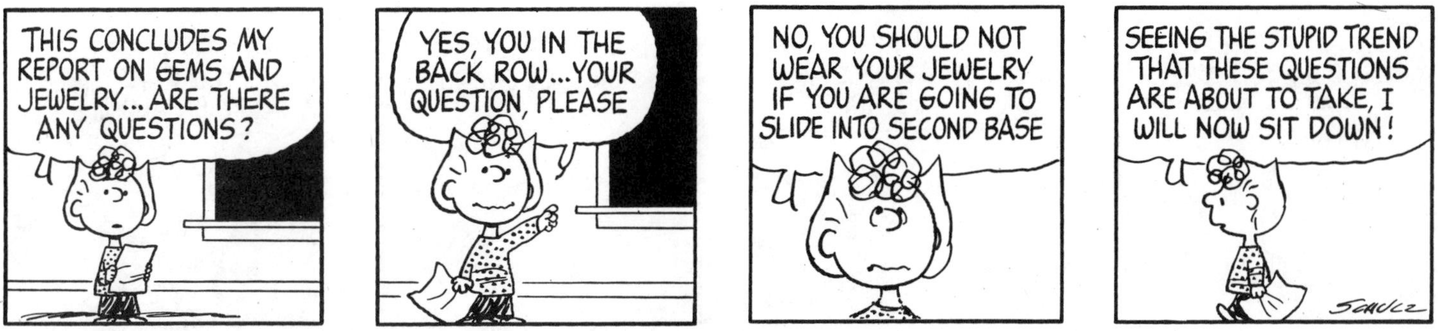
THIS CONCLUDES MY REPORT ON GEMS AND JEWELRY... ARE THERE ANY QUESTIONS?
YES, YOU IN THE BACK ROW... YOUR QUESTION, PLEASE
NO, YOU SHOULD NOT WEAR YOUR JEWELRY IF YOU ARE GOING TO SLIDE INTO SECOND BASE
SEEING THE STUPID TREND THAT THESE QUESTIONS ARE ABOUT TO TAKE, I WILL NOW SIT DOWN!
SCHULZ

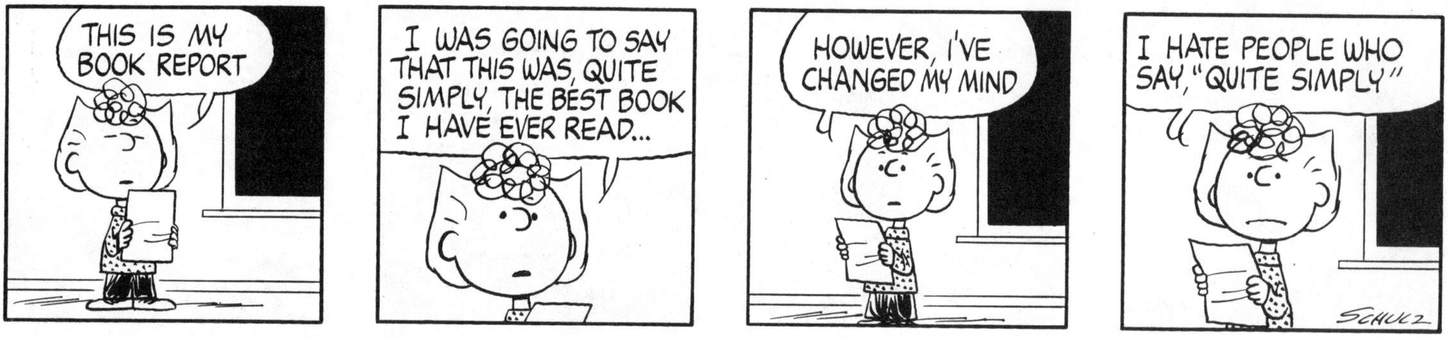
THIS IS MY BOOK REPORT
I WAS GOING TO SAY THAT THIS WAS, QUITE SIMPLY, THE BEST BOOK I HAVE EVER READ...
HOWEVER, I'VE CHANGED MY MIND
I HATE PEOPLE WHO SAY, "QUITE SIMPLY"
SCHULZ

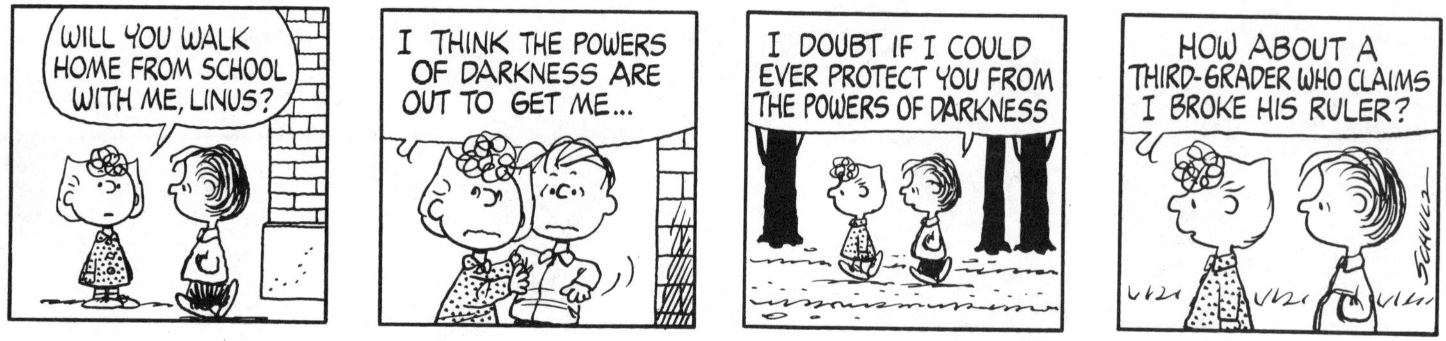
WILL YOU WALK HOME FROM SCHOOL WITH ME, LINUS?
I THINK THE POWERS OF DARKNESS ARE OUT TO GET ME...
I DOUBT IF I COULD EVER PROTECT YOU FROM THE POWERS OF DARKNESS
HOW ABOUT A THIRD-GRADER WHO CLAIMS I BROKE HIS RULER?
SCHULZ

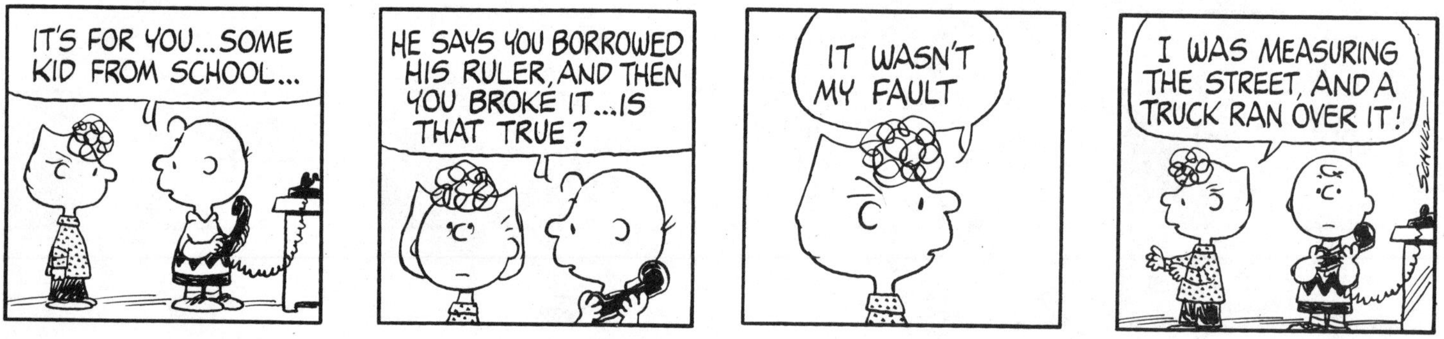
IT'S FOR YOU...SOME KID FROM SCHOOL...
HE SAYS YOU BORROWED HIS RULER, AND THEN YOU BROKE IT...IS THAT TRUE?
IT WASN'T MY FAULT
I WAS MEASURING THE STREET, AND A TRUCK RAN OVER IT!
SCHULZ

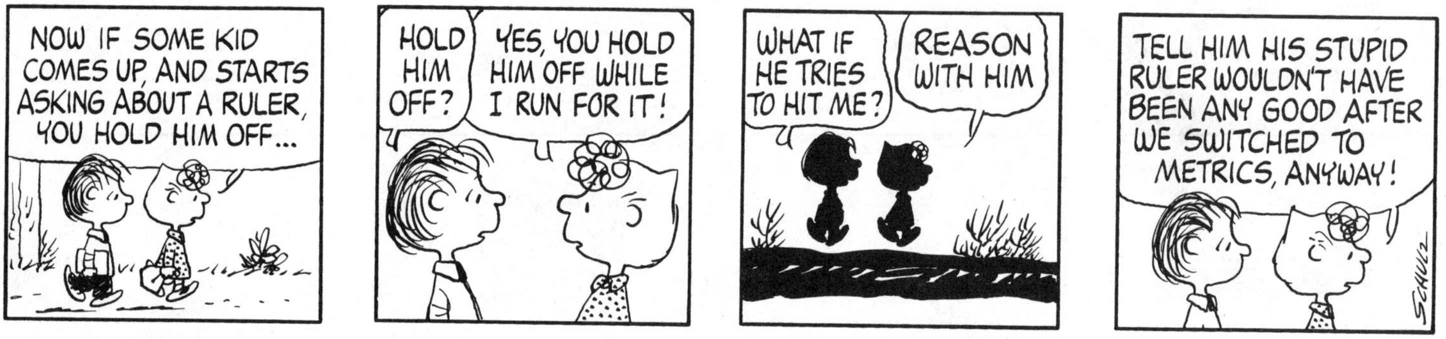
NOW IF SOME KID COMES UP, AND STARTS ASKING ABOUT A RULER, YOU HOLD HIM OFF...
HOLD HIM OFF?
YES, YOU HOLD HIM OFF WHILE I RUN FOR IT!
WHAT IF HE TRIES TO HIT ME?
REASON WITH HIM
TELL HIM HIS STUPID RULER WOULDN'T HAVE BEEN ANY GOOD AFTER WE SWITCHED TO METRICS, ANYWAY!
SCHULZ

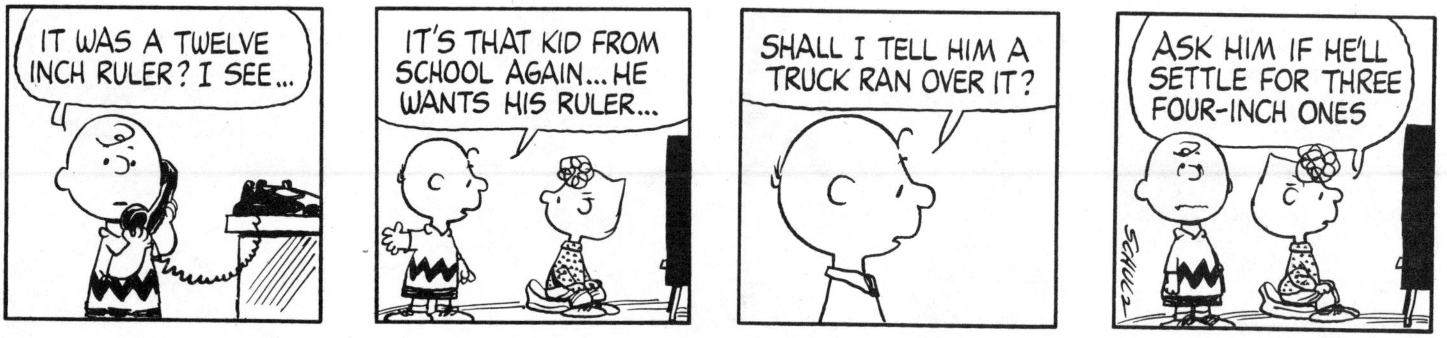
IT WAS A TWELVE INCH RULER? I SEE...
IT'S THAT KID FROM SCHOOL AGAIN... HE WANTS HIS RULER...
SHALL I TELL HIM A TRUCK RAN OVER IT?
ASK HIM IF HE'LL SETTLE FOR THREE FOUR-INCH ONES
SCHULZ

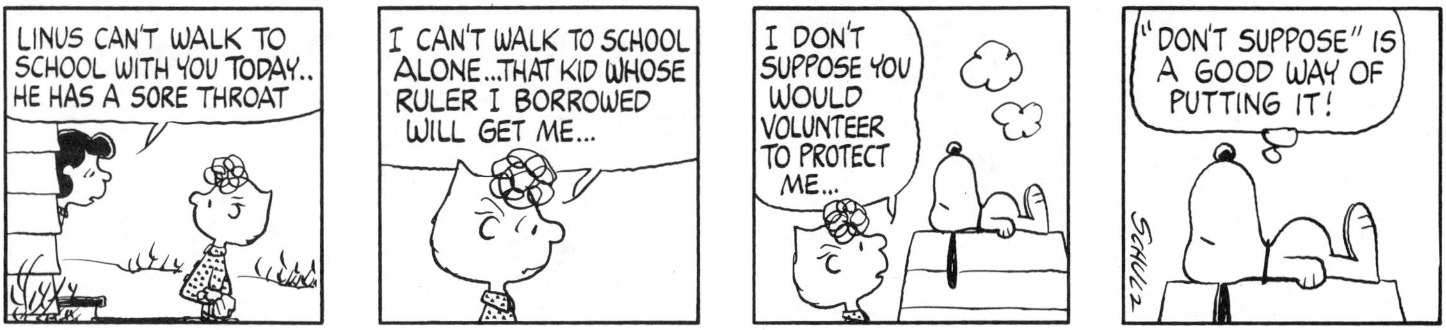
LINUS CAN'T WALK TO SCHOOL WITH YOU TODAY.. HE HAS A SORE THROAT
I CAN'T WALK TO SCHOOL ALONE...THAT KID WHOSE RULER I BORROWED WILL GET ME...
I DON'T SUPPOSE YOU WOULD VOLUNTEER TO PROTECT ME...
"DON'T SUPPOSE" IS A GOOD WAY OF PUTTING IT!
SCHULZ

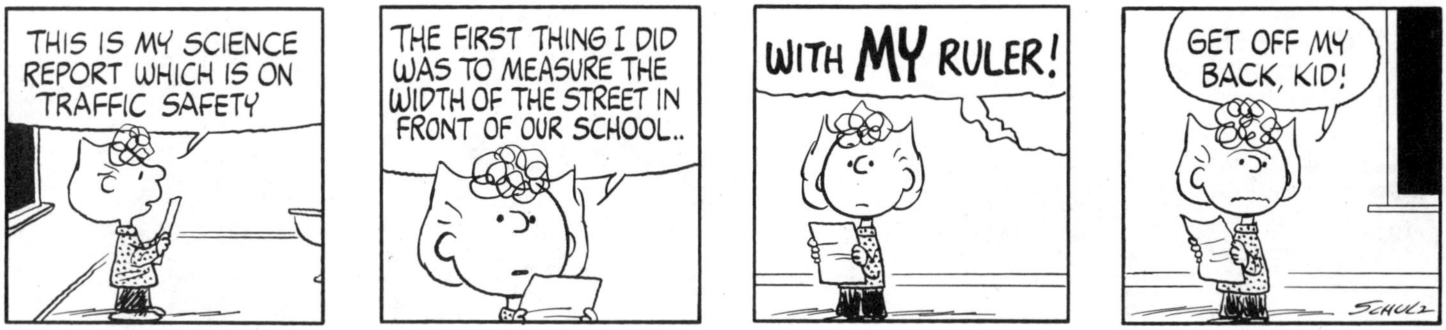
THIS IS MY SCIENCE REPORT WHICH IS ON TRAFFIC SAFETY
THE FIRST THING I DID WAS TO MEASURE THE WIDTH OF THE STREET IN FRONT OF OUR SCHOOL..
WITH MY RULER!
GET OFF MY BACK, KID!
SCHULZ

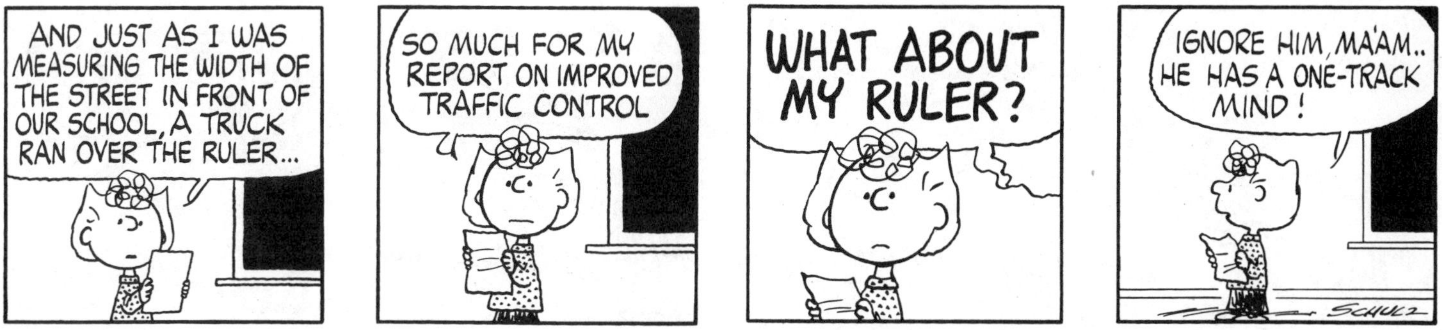
AND JUST AS I WAS MEASURING THE WIDTH OF THE STREET IN FRONT OF OUR SCHOOL, A TRUCK RAN OVER THE RULER...
SO MUCH FOR MY REPORT ON IMPROVED TRAFFIC CONTROL
WHAT ABOUT MY RULER?
IGNORE HIM, MA'AM.. HE HAS A ONE-TRACK MIND!
SCHULZ

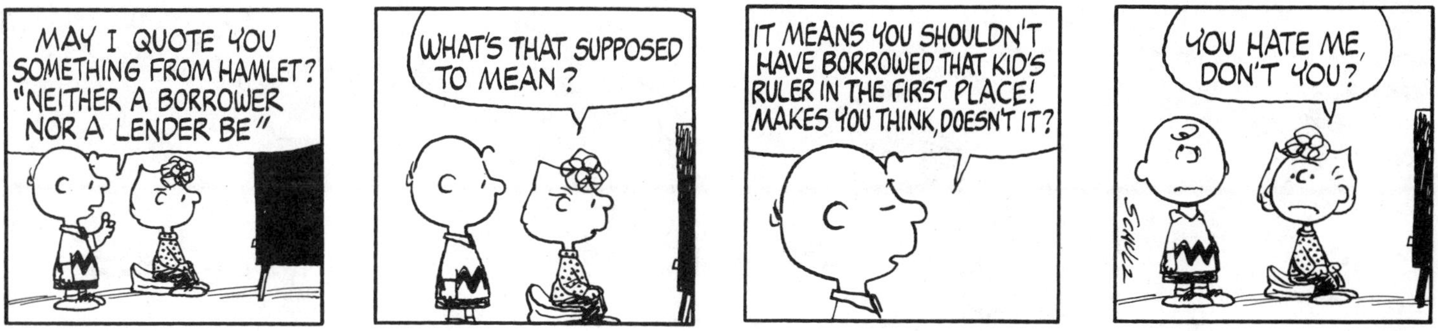
MAY I QUOTE YOU SOMETHING FROM HAMLET? "NEITHER A BORROWER NOR A LENDER BE"
WHAT'S THAT SUPPOSED TO MEAN?
IT MEANS YOU SHOULDN'T HAVE BORROWED THAT KID'S RULER IN THE FIRST PLACE! MAKES YOU THINK, DOESN'T IT?
YOU HATE ME, DON'T YOU?
SCHULZ

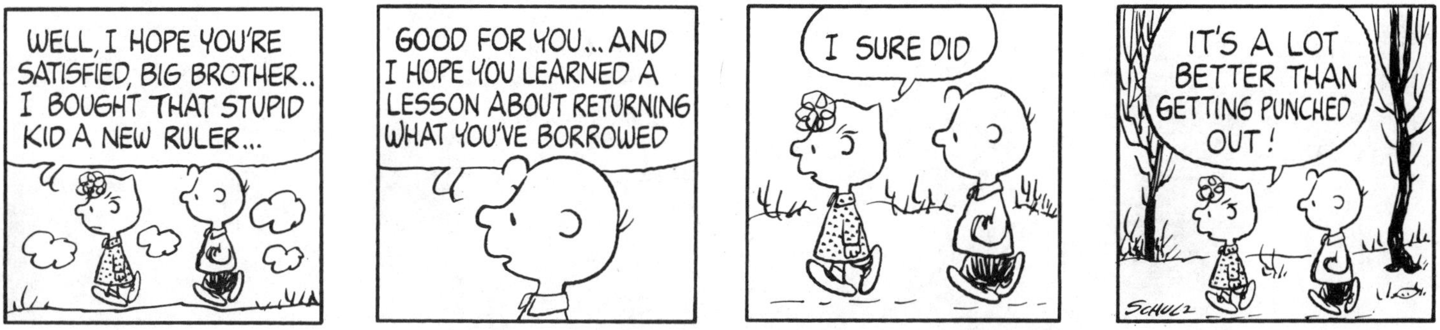
WELL, I HOPE YOU'RE SATISFIED, BIG BROTHER.. I BOUGHT THAT STUPID KID A NEW RULER...
GOOD FOR YOU... AND I HOPE YOU LEARNED A LESSON ABOUT RETURNING WHAT YOU'VE BORROWED
I SURE DID
IT'S A LOT BETTER THAN GETTING PUNCHED OUT!
SCHULZ

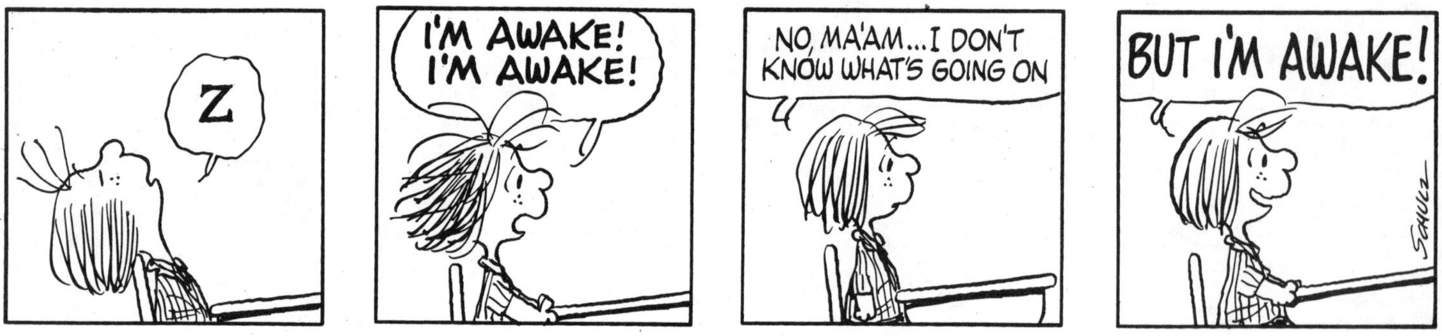
Z
I'M AWAKE! I'M AWAKE!
NO, MA'AM... I DON'T KNOW WHAT'S GOING ON
BUT I'M AWAKE!

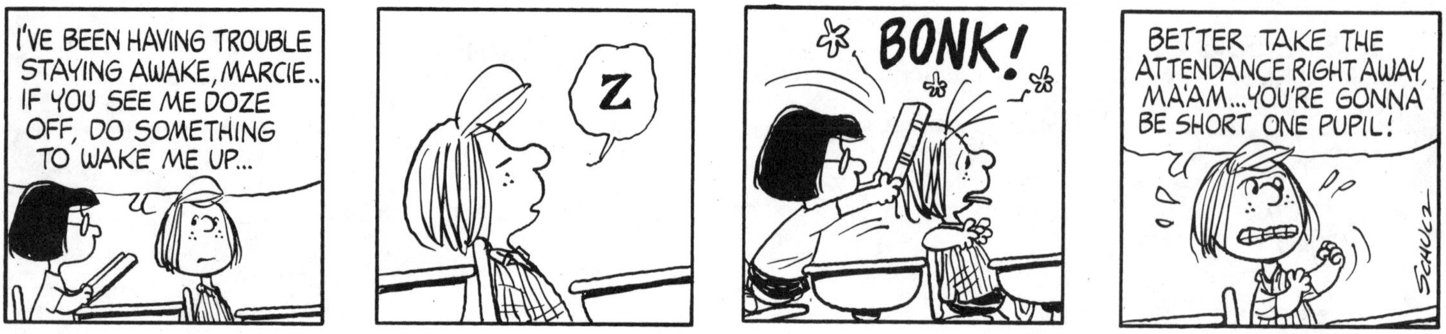
I'VE BEEN HAVING TROUBLE STAYING AWAKE, MARCIE.. IF YOU SEE ME DOZE OFF, DO SOMETHING TO WAKE ME UP...
Z
BONK!
BETTER TAKE THE ATTENDANCE RIGHT AWAY, MA'AM... YOU'RE GONNA BE SHORT ONE PUPIL!

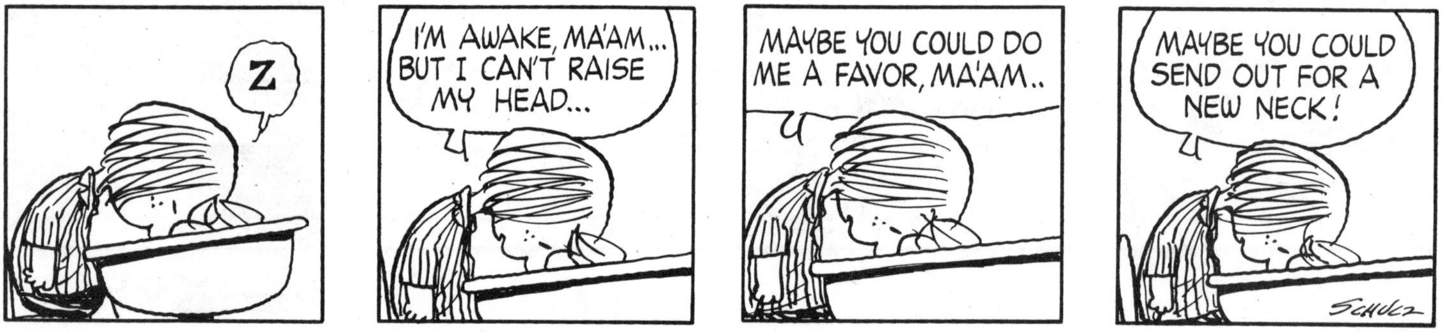
Z
I'M AWAKE, MA'AM... BUT I CAN'T RAISE MY HEAD...
MAYBE YOU COULD DO ME A FAVOR, MA'AM..
MAYBE YOU COULD SEND OUT FOR A NEW NECK!

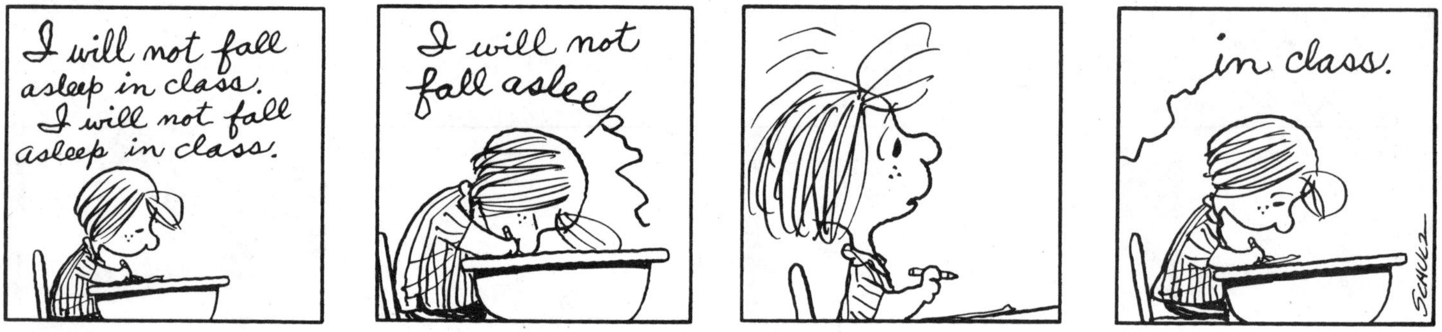
I will not fall asleep in class. I will not fall asleep in class.
I will not fall aslee
in class.

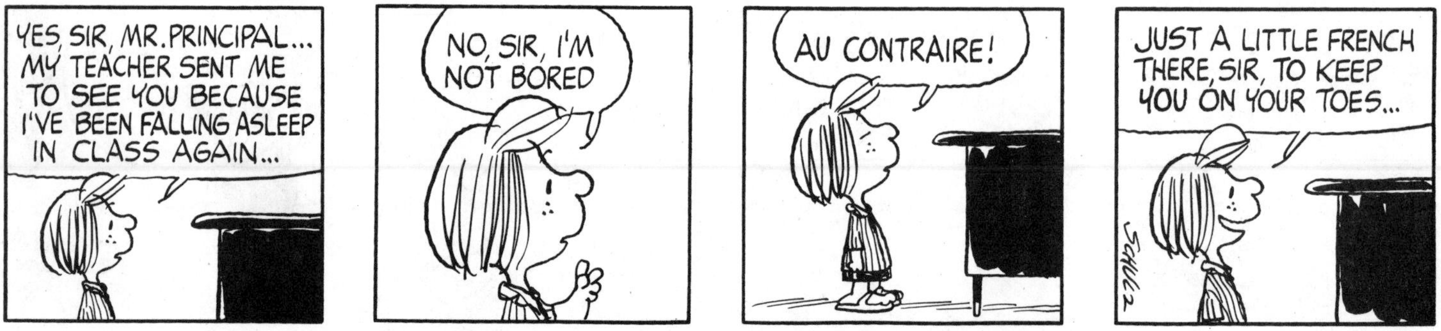
YES, SIR, MR. PRINCIPAL... MY TEACHER SENT ME TO SEE YOU BECAUSE I'VE BEEN FALLING ASLEEP IN CLASS AGAIN...
NO, SIR, I'M NOT BORED
AU CONTRAIRE!
JUST A LITTLE FRENCH THERE, SIR, TO KEEP YOU ON YOUR TOES...

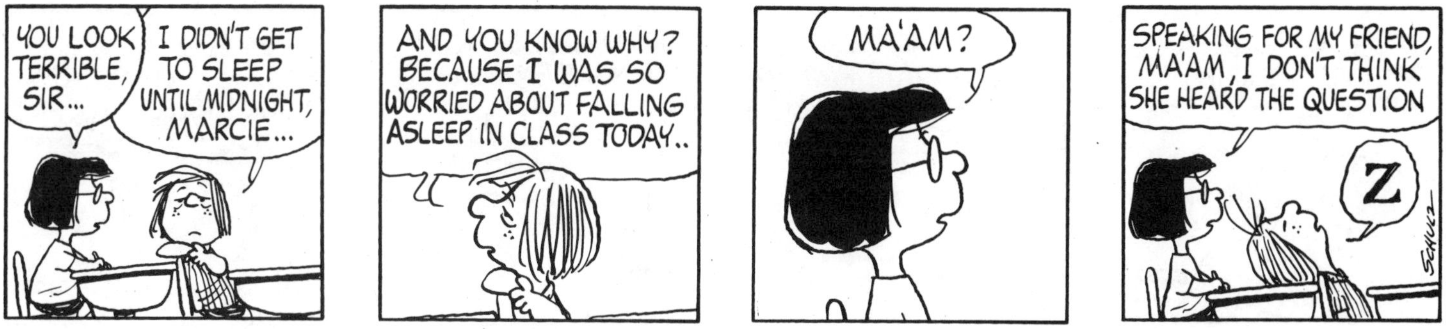
YOU LOOK TERRIBLE, SIR...
I DIDN'T GET TO SLEEP UNTIL MIDNIGHT, MARCIE...
AND YOU KNOW WHY? BECAUSE I WAS SO WORRIED ABOUT FALLING ASLEEP IN CLASS TODAY..
MA'AM?
SPEAKING FOR MY FRIEND, MA'AM, I DON'T THINK SHE HEARD THE QUESTION
Z

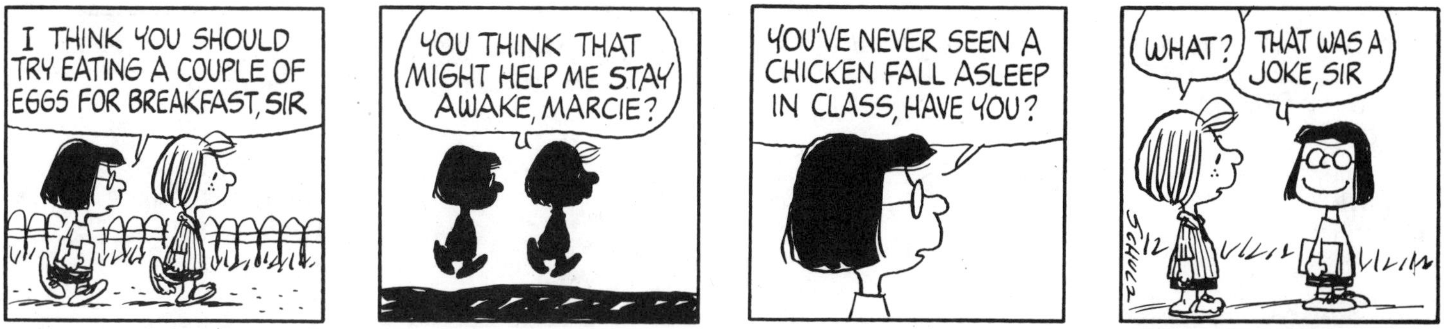
I THINK YOU SHOULD TRY EATING A COUPLE OF EGGS FOR BREAKFAST, SIR
YOU THINK THAT MIGHT HELP ME STAY AWAKE, MARCIE?
YOU'VE NEVER SEEN A CHICKEN FALL ASLEEP IN CLASS, HAVE YOU?
WHAT?
THAT WAS A JOKE, SIR

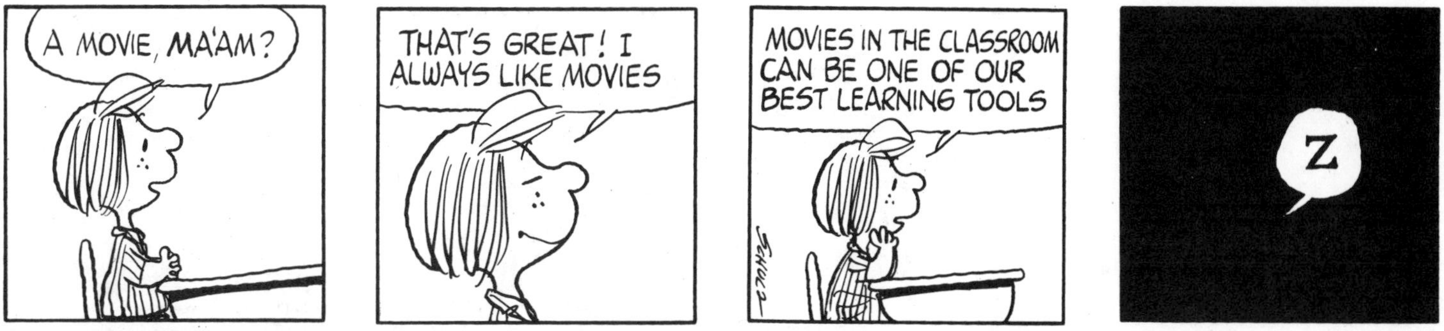
A MOVIE, MA'AM?
THAT'S GREAT! I ALWAYS LIKE MOVIES
MOVIES IN THE CLASSROOM CAN BE ONE OF OUR BEST LEARNING TOOLS
Z

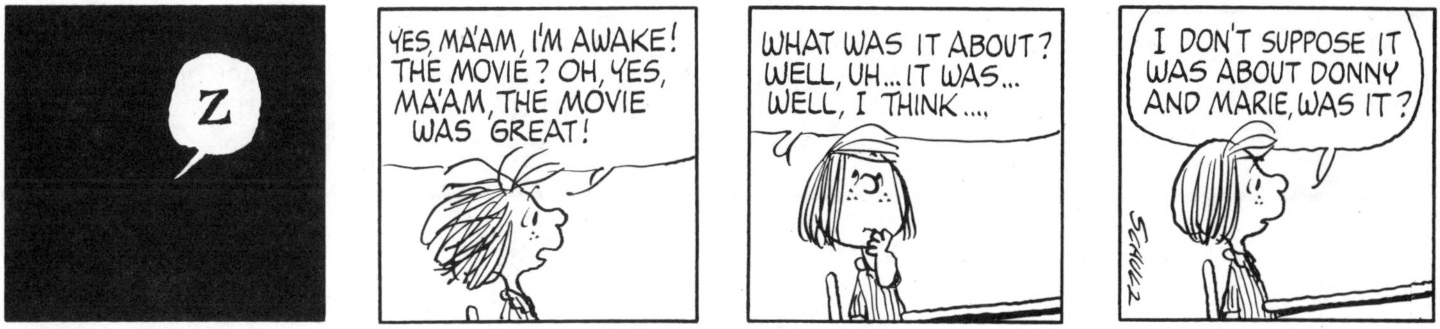
Z
YES, MA'AM, I'M AWAKE! THE MOVIE? OH, YES, MA'AM, THE MOVIE WAS GREAT!
WHAT WAS IT ABOUT? WELL, UH... IT WAS... WELL, I THINK....,
I DON'T SUPPOSE IT WAS ABOUT DONNY AND MARIE, WAS IT?

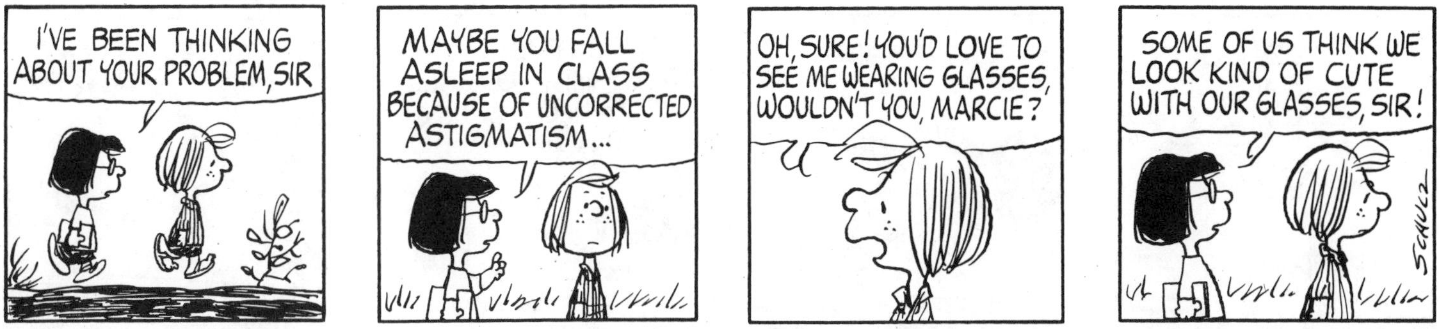
I'VE BEEN THINKING ABOUT YOUR PROBLEM, SIR
MAYBE YOU FALL ASLEEP IN CLASS BECAUSE OF UNCORRECTED ASTIGMATISM...
OH, SURE! YOU'D LOVE TO SEE ME WEARING GLASSES, WOULDN'T YOU, MARCIE?
SOME OF US THINK WE LOOK KIND OF CUTE WITH OUR GLASSES, SIR!

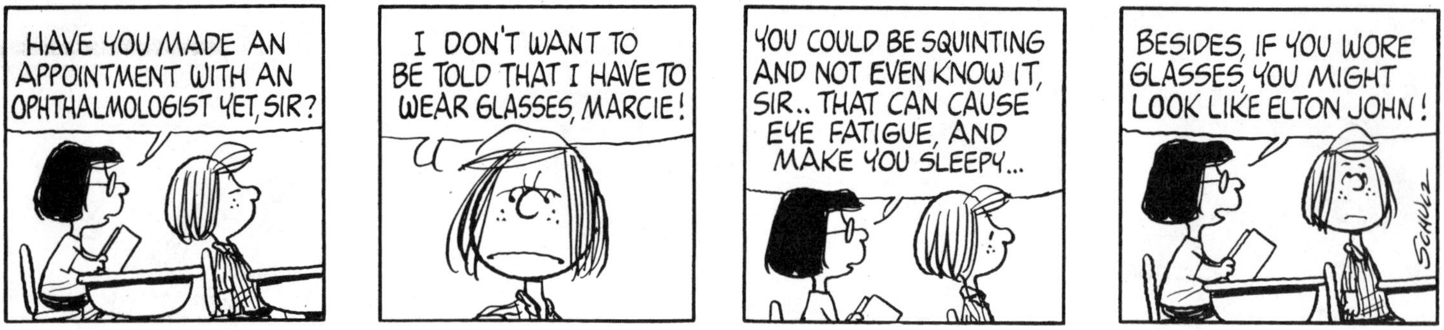
HAVE YOU MADE AN APPOINTMENT WITH AN OPHTHALMOLOGIST YET, SIR?
I DON'T WANT TO BE TOLD THAT I HAVE TO WEAR GLASSES, MARCIE!
YOU COULD BE SQUINTING AND NOT EVEN KNOW IT, SIR.. THAT CAN CAUSE EYE FATIGUE, AND MAKE YOU SLEEPY...
BESIDES, IF YOU WORE GLASSES, YOU MIGHT LOOK LIKE ELTON JOHN!
SCHULZ

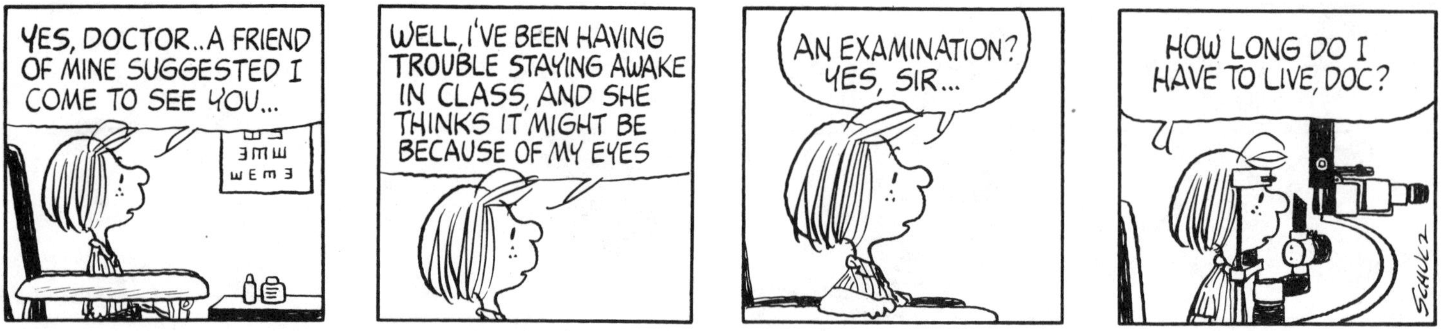
YES, DOCTOR..A FRIEND OF MINE SUGGESTED I COME TO SEE YOU...
WELL, I'VE BEEN HAVING TROUBLE STAYING AWAKE IN CLASS, AND SHE THINKS IT MIGHT BE BECAUSE OF MY EYES
AN EXAMINATION? YES, SIR...
HOW LONG DO I HAVE TO LIVE, DOC?
SCHULZ

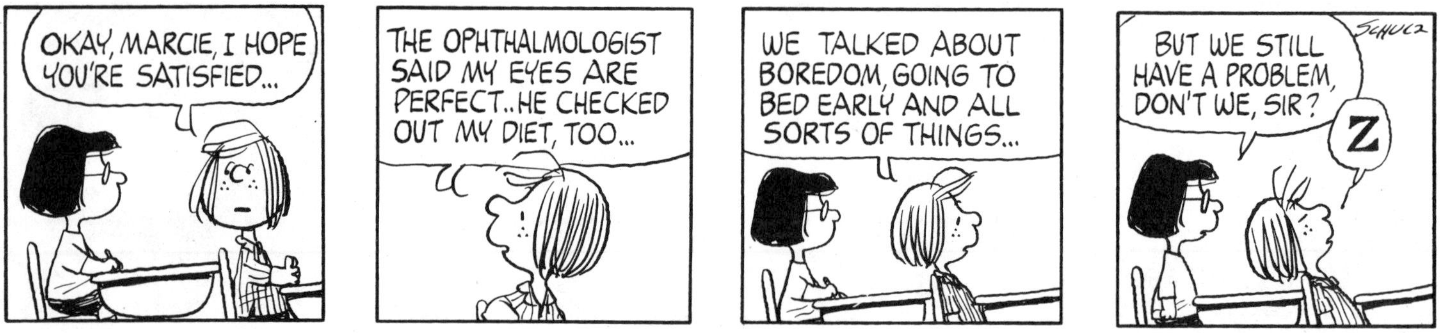
OKAY, MARCIE, I HOPE YOU'RE SATISFIED...
THE OPHTHALMOLOGIST SAID MY EYES ARE PERFECT..HE CHECKED OUT MY DIET, TOO...
WE TALKED ABOUT BOREDOM, GOING TO BED EARLY AND ALL SORTS OF THINGS...
SCHULZ
BUT WE STILL HAVE A PROBLEM, DON'T WE, SIR?
Z

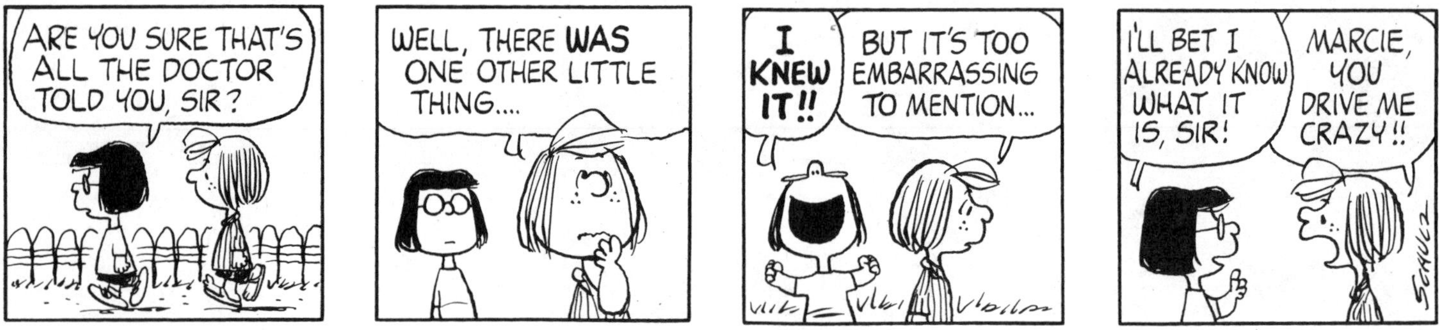
ARE YOU SURE THAT'S ALL THE DOCTOR TOLD YOU, SIR?
WELL, THERE WAS ONE OTHER LITTLE THING....
I KNEW IT!!
BUT IT'S TOO EMBARRASSING TO MENTION...
I'LL BET I ALREADY KNOW WHAT IT IS, SIR!
MARCIE, YOU DRIVE ME CRAZY!!
SCHULZ

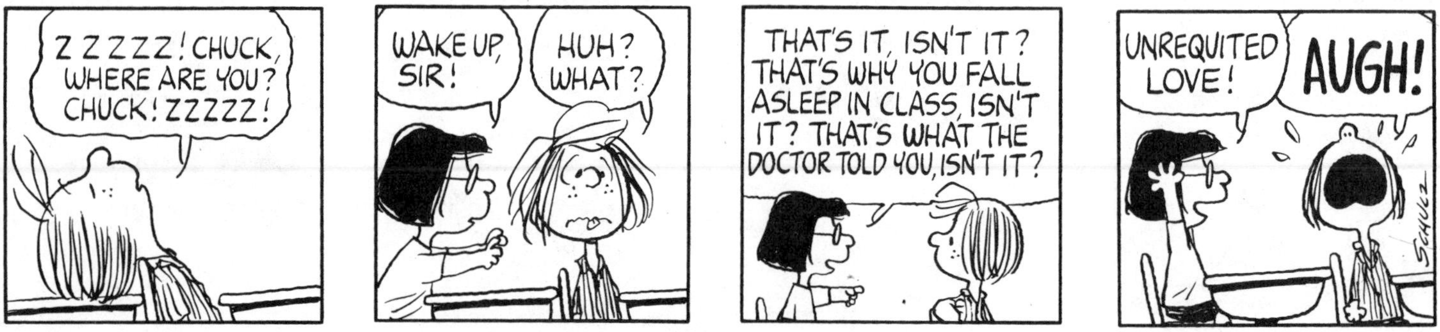
Z Z Z Z Z! CHUCK, WHERE ARE YOU? CHUCK! ZZZZZ!
WAKE UP, SIR!
HUH? WHAT?
THAT'S IT, ISN'T IT? THAT'S WHY YOU FALL ASLEEP IN CLASS, ISN'T IT? THAT'S WHAT THE DOCTOR TOLD YOU, ISN'T IT?
UNREQUITED LOVE!
AUGH!
SCHULZ

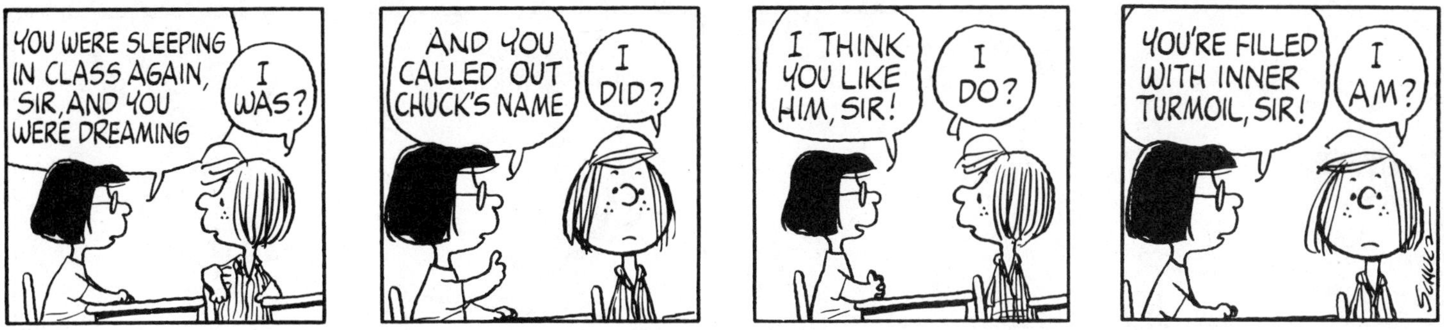
YOU WERE SLEEPING IN CLASS AGAIN, SIR, AND YOU WERE DREAMING
I WAS?
AND YOU CALLED OUT CHUCK'S NAME
I DID?
I THINK YOU LIKE HIM, SIR!
I DO?
YOU'RE FILLED WITH INNER TURMOIL, SIR!
I AM?
SCHULZ

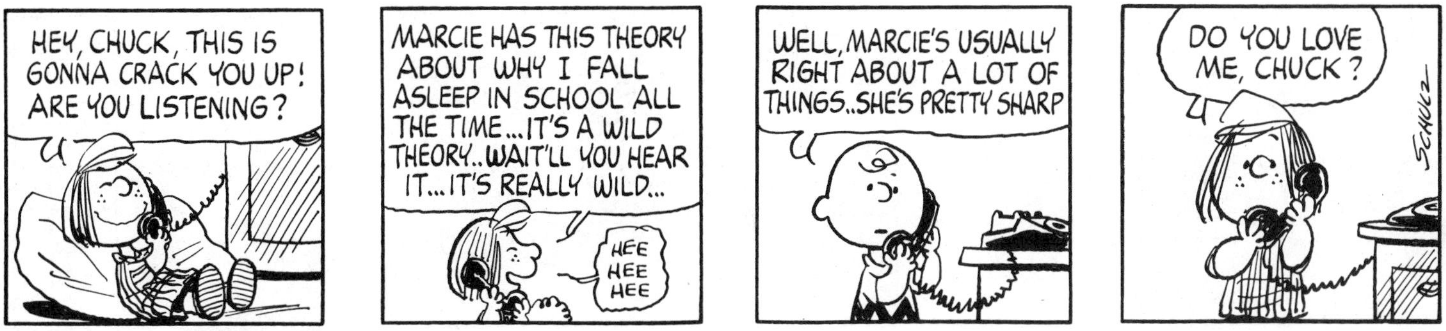
HEY, CHUCK, THIS IS GONNA CRACK YOU UP! ARE YOU LISTENING?
MARCIE HAS THIS THEORY ABOUT WHY I FALL ASLEEP IN SCHOOL ALL THE TIME... IT'S A WILD THEORY.. WAIT'LL YOU HEAR IT... IT'S REALLY WILD...
HEE HEE HEE
WELL, MARCIE'S USUALLY RIGHT ABOUT A LOT OF THINGS.. SHE'S PRETTY SHARP
DO YOU LOVE ME, CHUCK?
SCHULZ

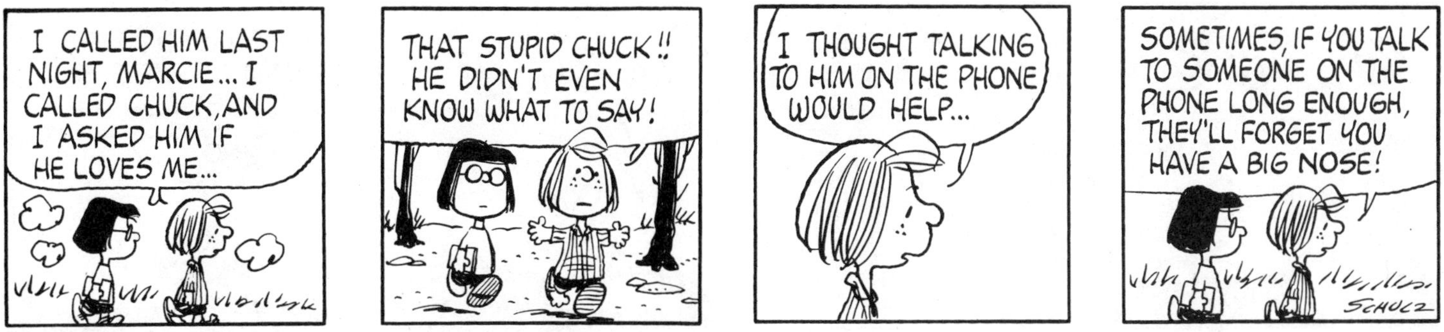
I CALLED HIM LAST NIGHT, MARCIE... I CALLED CHUCK, AND I ASKED HIM IF HE LOVES ME...
THAT STUPID CHUCK!! HE DIDN'T EVEN KNOW WHAT TO SAY!
I THOUGHT TALKING TO HIM ON THE PHONE WOULD HELP...
SOMETIMES, IF YOU TALK TO SOMEONE ON THE PHONE LONG ENOUGH, THEY'LL FORGET YOU HAVE A BIG NOSE!
SCHULZ

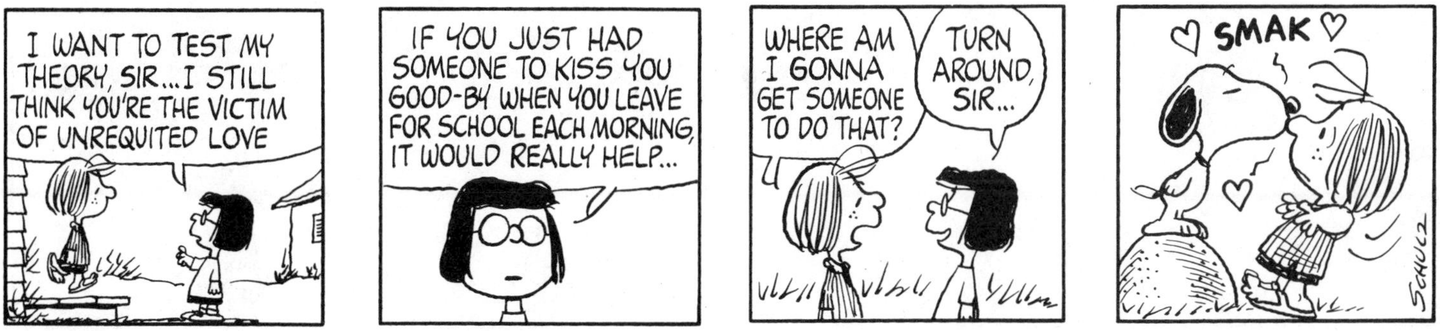
I WANT TO TEST MY THEORY, SIR... I STILL THINK YOU'RE THE VICTIM OF UNREQUITED LOVE
IF YOU JUST HAD SOMEONE TO KISS YOU GOOD-BY WHEN YOU LEAVE FOR SCHOOL EACH MORNING, IT WOULD REALLY HELP...
WHERE AM I GONNA GET SOMEONE TO DO THAT?
TURN AROUND, SIR...
SMAK
SCHULZ

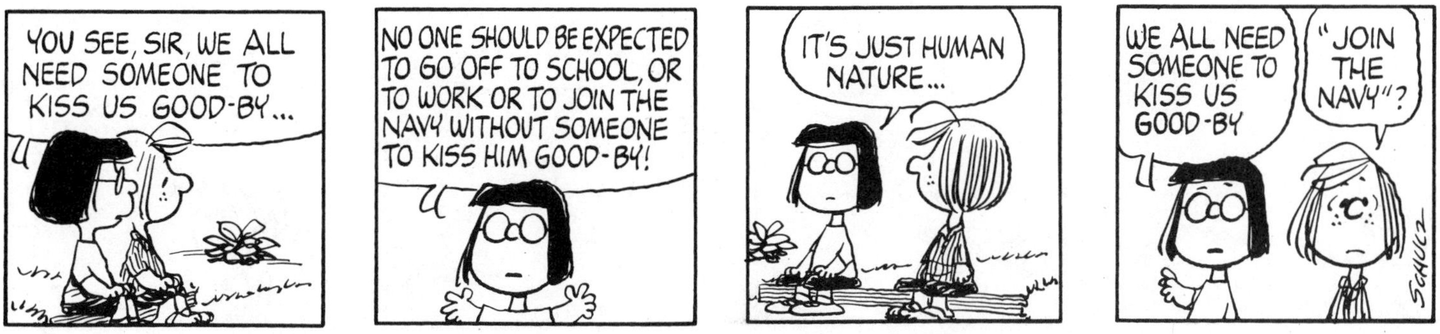
YOU SEE, SIR, WE ALL NEED SOMEONE TO KISS US GOOD-BY...
NO ONE SHOULD BE EXPECTED TO GO OFF TO SCHOOL, OR TO WORK OR TO JOIN THE NAVY WITHOUT SOMEONE TO KISS HIM GOOD-BY!
IT'S JUST HUMAN NATURE...
WE ALL NEED SOMEONE TO KISS US GOOD-BY
"JOIN THE NAVY"?
SCHULZ

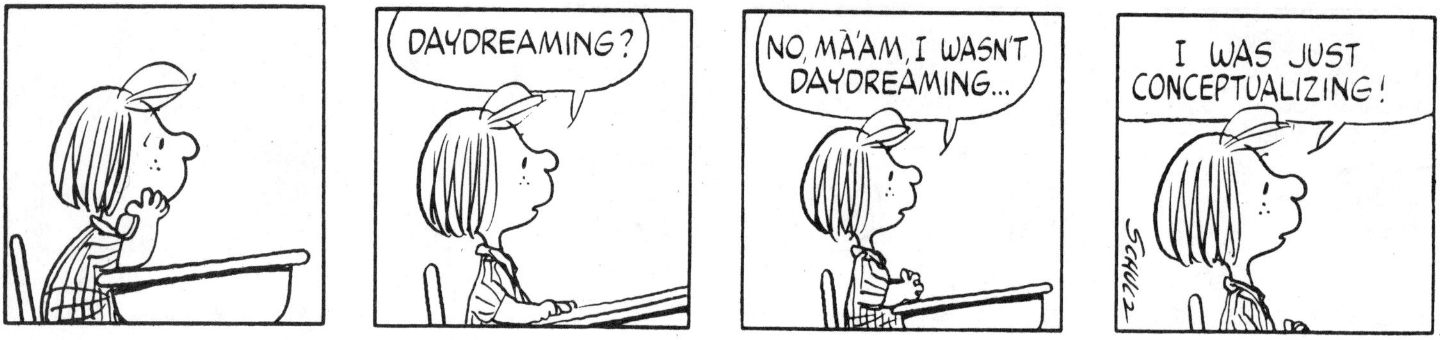
DAYDREAMING?
NO, MA'AM, I WASN'T DAYDREAMING...
I WAS JUST CONCEPTUALIZING!
SCHULZ

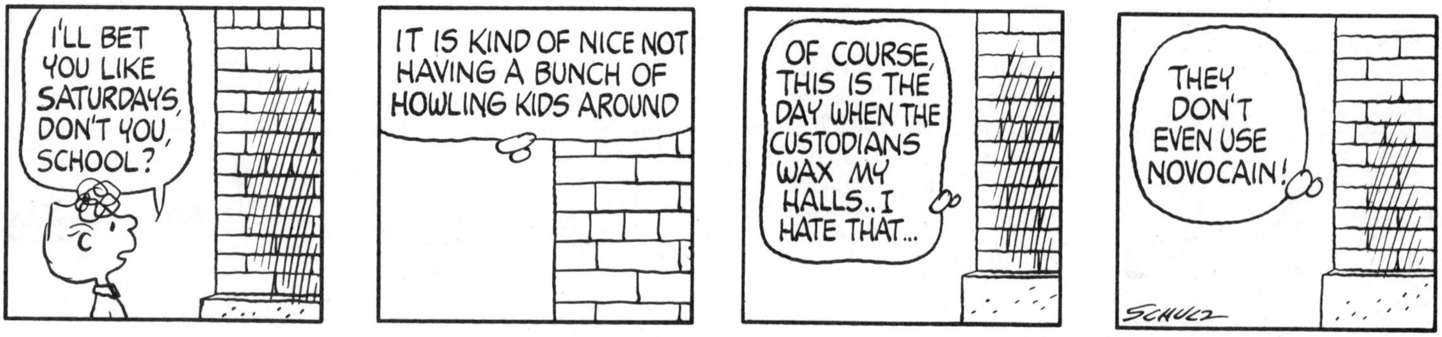
I'LL BET YOU LIKE SATURDAYS, DON'T YOU, SCHOOL?
IT IS KIND OF NICE NOT HAVING A BUNCH OF HOWLING KIDS AROUND
OF COURSE, THIS IS THE DAY WHEN THE CUSTODIANS WAX MY HALLS.. I HATE THAT...
THEY DON'T EVEN USE NOVOCAIN!
SCHULZ

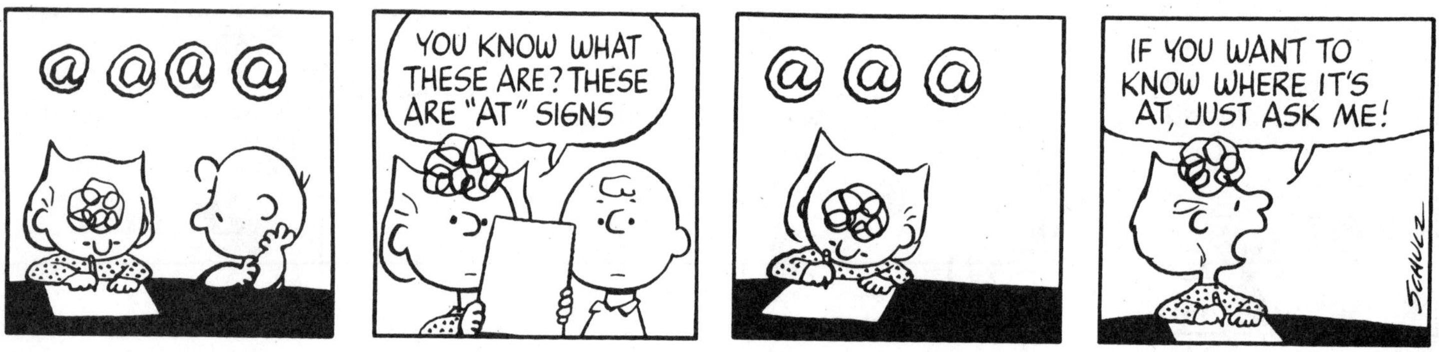
@ @ @ @
YOU KNOW WHAT THESE ARE? THESE ARE "AT" SIGNS
@ @ @
IF YOU WANT TO KNOW WHERE IT'S AT, JUST ASK ME!
SCHULZ

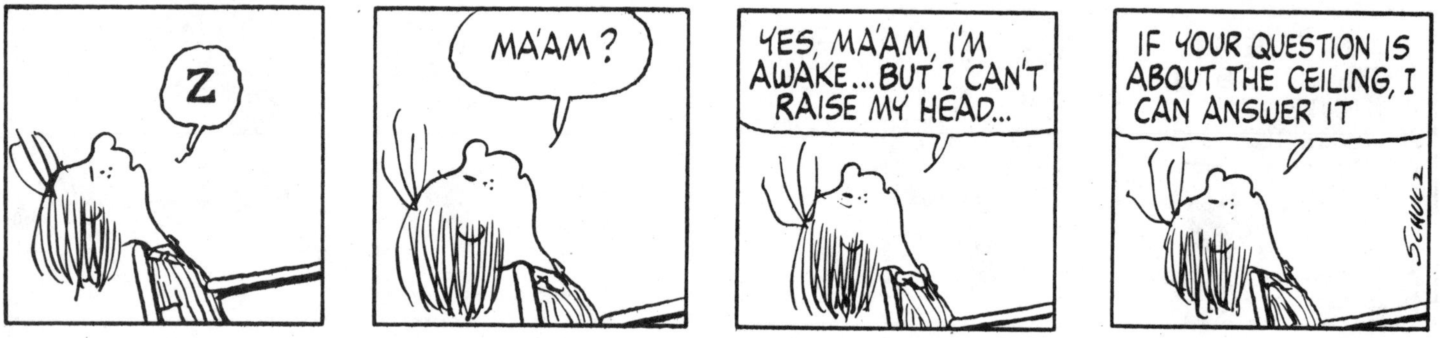
Z
MA'AM?
YES, MA'AM, I'M AWAKE...BUT I CAN'T RAISE MY HEAD...
IF YOUR QUESTION IS ABOUT THE CEILING, I CAN ANSWER IT
SCHULZ

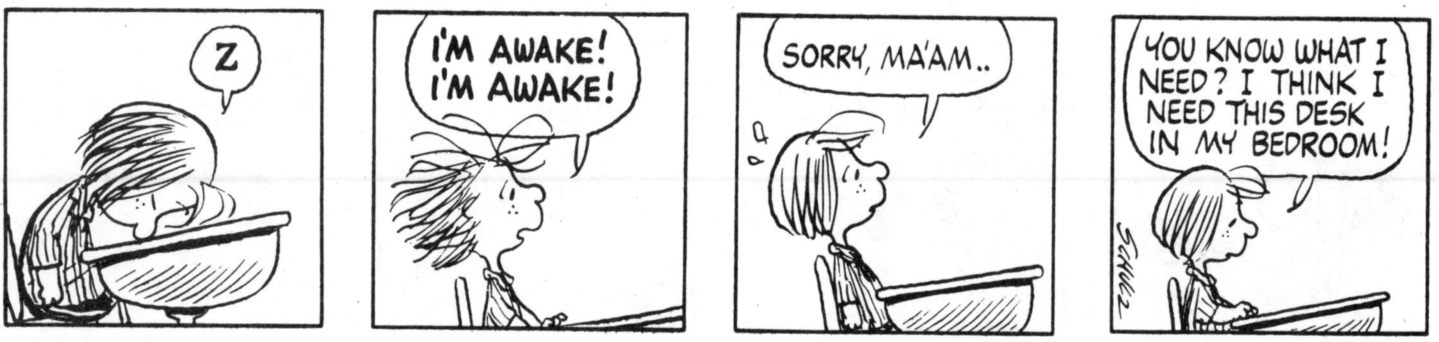
Z
I'M AWAKE! I'M AWAKE!
SORRY, MA'AM..
YOU KNOW WHAT I NEED? I THINK I NEED THIS DESK IN MY BEDROOM!
SCHULZ

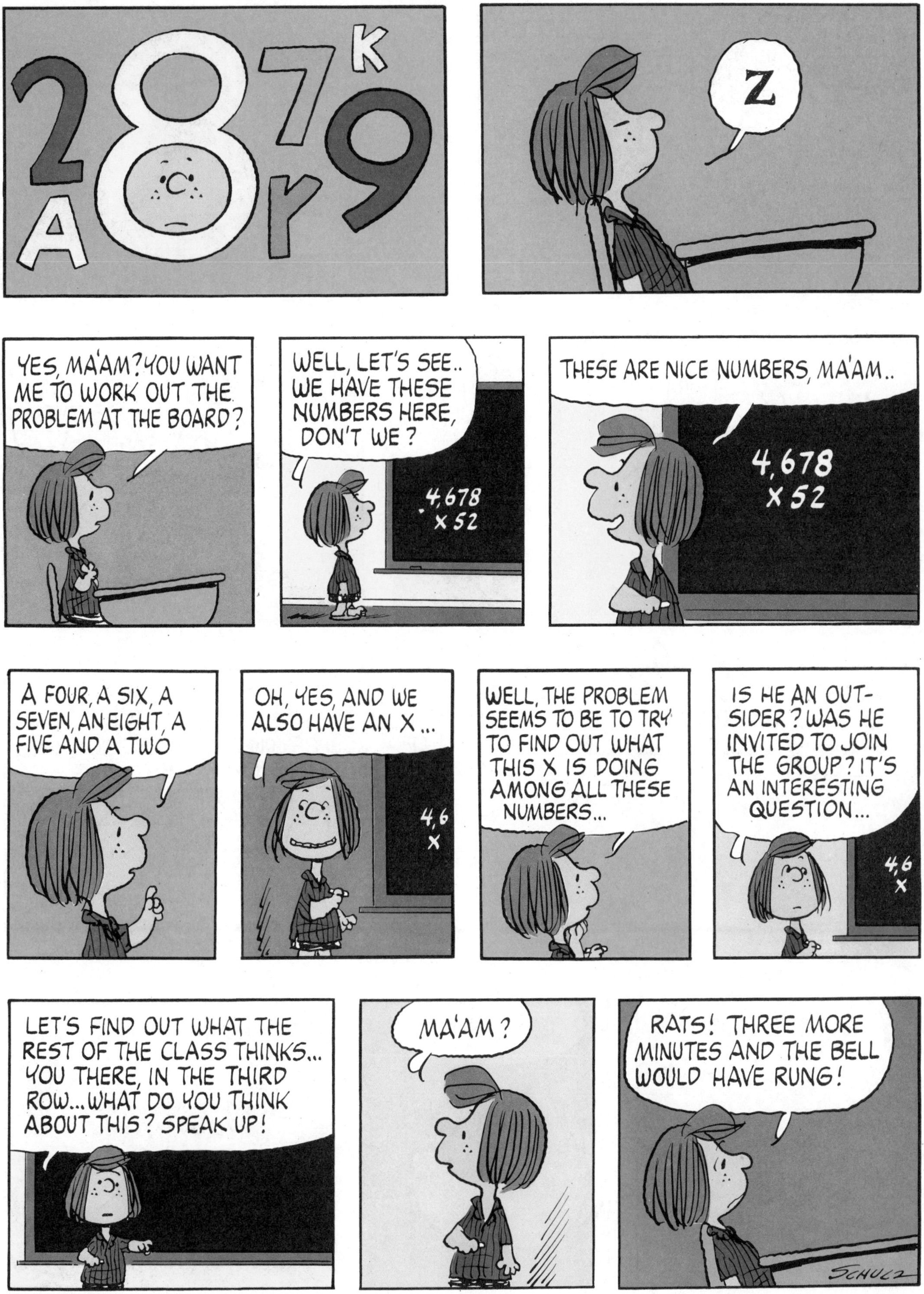

2 8 7 K 9 A Y
Z
YES, MA'AM? YOU WANT ME TO WORK OUT THE PROBLEM AT THE BOARD?
WELL, LET'S SEE.. WE HAVE THESE NUMBERS HERE, DON'T WE?
4,678 X 52
THESE ARE NICE NUMBERS, MA'AM..
4,678 X 52
A FOUR, A SIX, A SEVEN, AN EIGHT, A FIVE AND A TWO
OH, YES, AND WE ALSO HAVE AN X ...
WELL, THE PROBLEM SEEMS TO BE TO TRY TO FIND OUT WHAT THIS X IS DOING AMONG ALL THESE NUMBERS...
IS HE AN OUTSIDER? WAS HE INVITED TO JOIN THE GROUP? IT'S AN INTERESTING QUESTION...
LET'S FIND OUT WHAT THE REST OF THE CLASS THINKS... YOU THERE, IN THE THIRD ROW... WHAT DO YOU THINK ABOUT THIS? SPEAK UP!
MA'AM?
RATS! THREE MORE MINUTES AND THE BELL WOULD HAVE RUNG!
SCHULZ

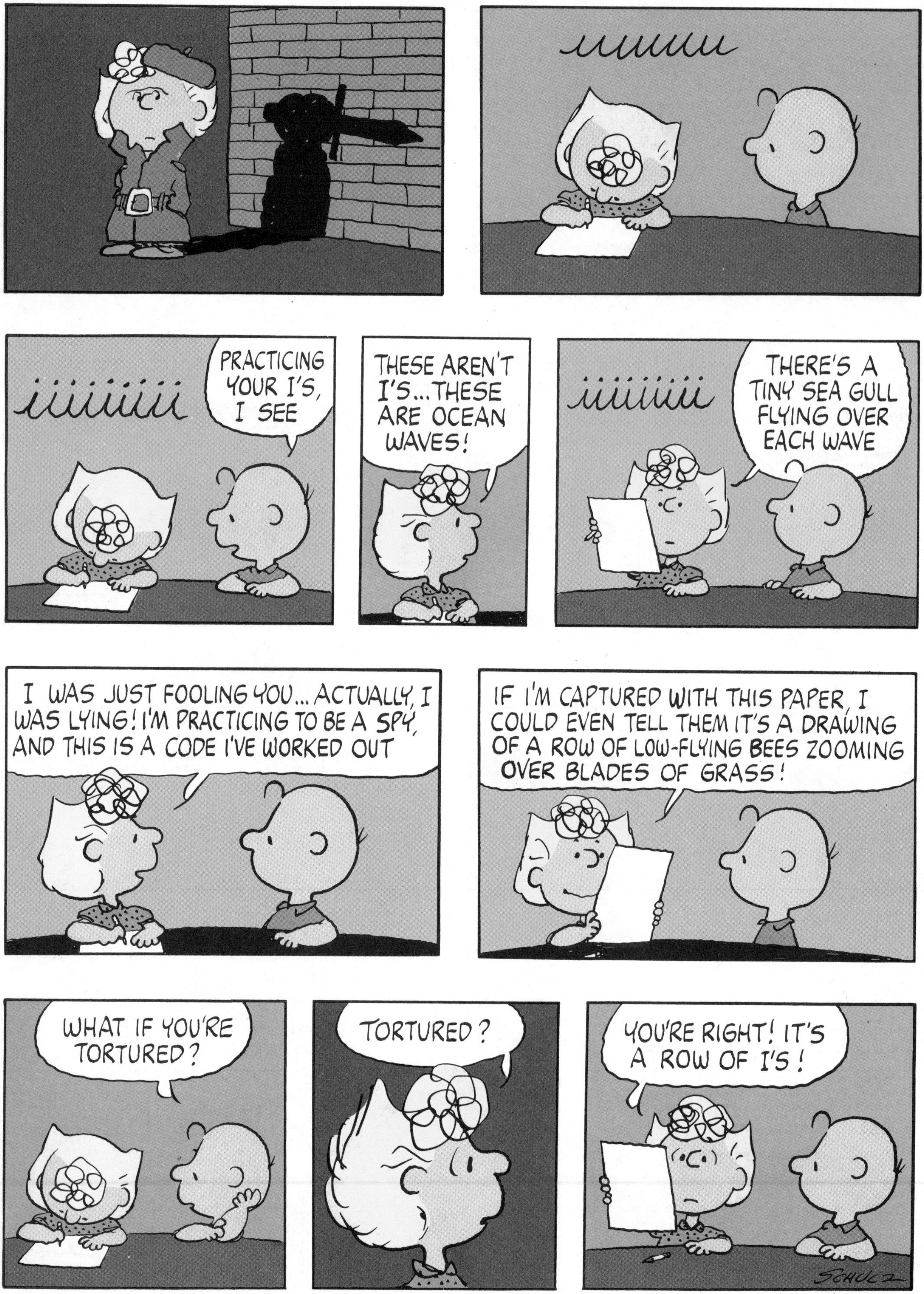
PRACTICING YOUR I'S, I SEE
THESE AREN'T I'S...THESE ARE OCEAN WAVES!
THERE'S A TINY SEA GULL FLYING OVER EACH WAVE
I WAS JUST FOOLING YOU... ACTUALLY, I WAS LYING! I'M PRACTICING TO BE A SPY, AND THIS IS A CODE I'VE WORKED OUT
IF I'M CAPTURED WITH THIS PAPER, I COULD EVEN TELL THEM IT'S A DRAWING OF A ROW OF LOW-FLYING BEES ZOOMING OVER BLADES OF GRASS!
WHAT IF YOU'RE TORTURED?
TORTURED?
YOU'RE RIGHT! IT'S A ROW OF I'S!
SCHULZ

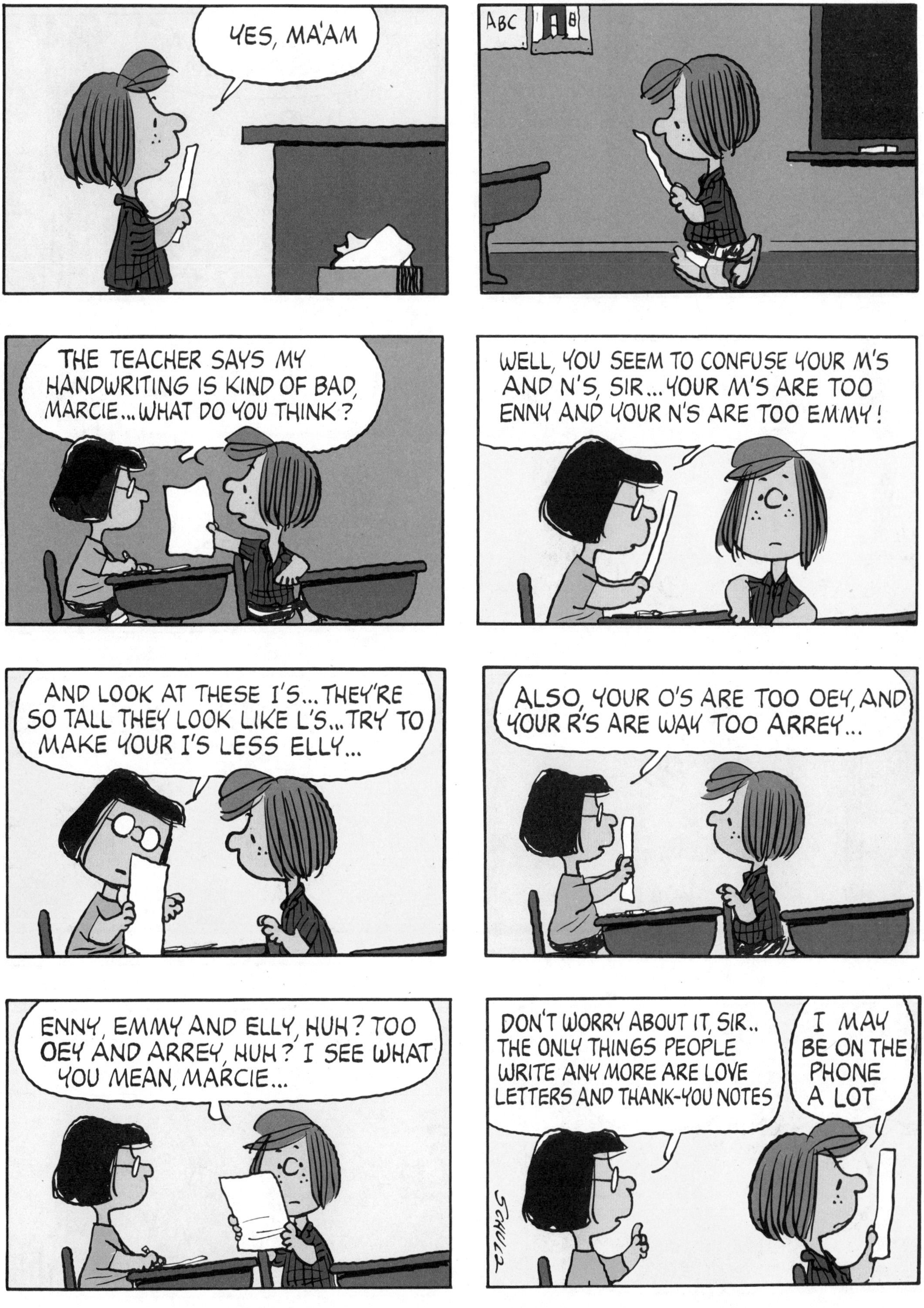
YES, MA'AM
THE TEACHER SAYS MY HANDWRITING IS KIND OF BAD, MARCIE...WHAT DO YOU THINK?
WELL, YOU SEEM TO CONFUSE YOUR M'S AND N'S, SIR...YOUR M'S ARE TOO ENNY AND YOUR N'S ARE TOO EMMY!
AND LOOK AT THESE I'S...THEY'RE SO TALL THEY LOOK LIKE L'S...TRY TO MAKE YOUR I'S LESS ELLY...
ALSO, YOUR O'S ARE TOO OEY, AND YOUR R'S ARE WAY TOO ARREY...
ENNY, EMMY AND ELLY, HUH? TOO OEY AND ARREY, HUH? I SEE WHAT YOU MEAN, MARCIE...
DON'T WORRY ABOUT IT, SIR.. THE ONLY THINGS PEOPLE WRITE ANY MORE ARE LOVE LETTERS AND THANK-YOU NOTES
I MAY BE ON THE PHONE A LOT
SCHULZ

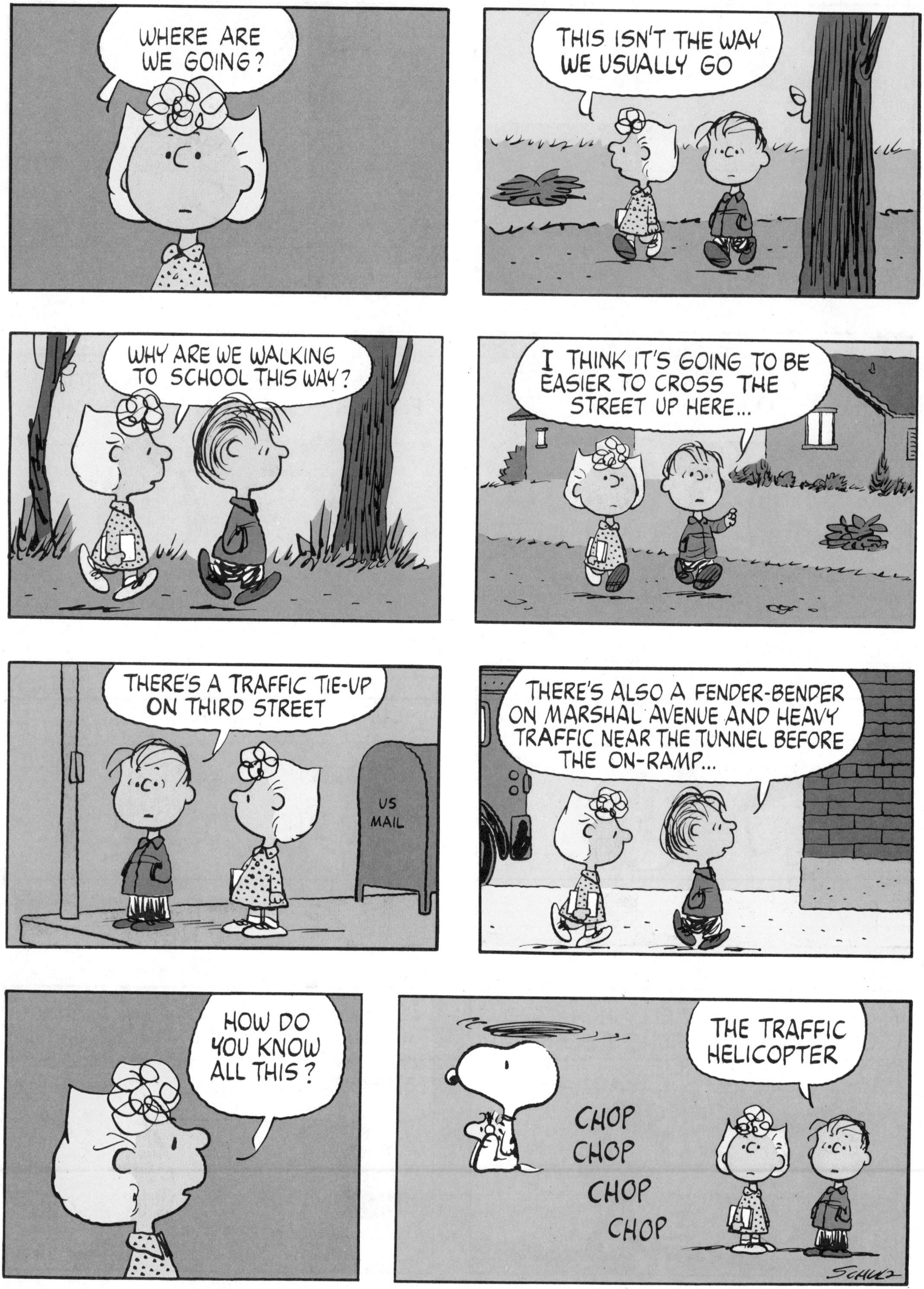
WHERE ARE WE GOING?
THIS ISN'T THE WAY WE USUALLY GO
WHY ARE WE WALKING TO SCHOOL THIS WAY?
I THINK IT'S GOING TO BE EASIER TO CROSS THE STREET UP HERE...
THERE'S A TRAFFIC TIE-UP ON THIRD STREET
US MAIL
THERE'S ALSO A FENDER-BENDER ON MARSHAL AVENUE AND HEAVY TRAFFIC NEAR THE TUNNEL BEFORE THE ON-RAMP...
HOW DO YOU KNOW ALL THIS?
THE TRAFFIC HELICOPTER
CHOP
CHOP
CHOP
CHOP
SCHULZ

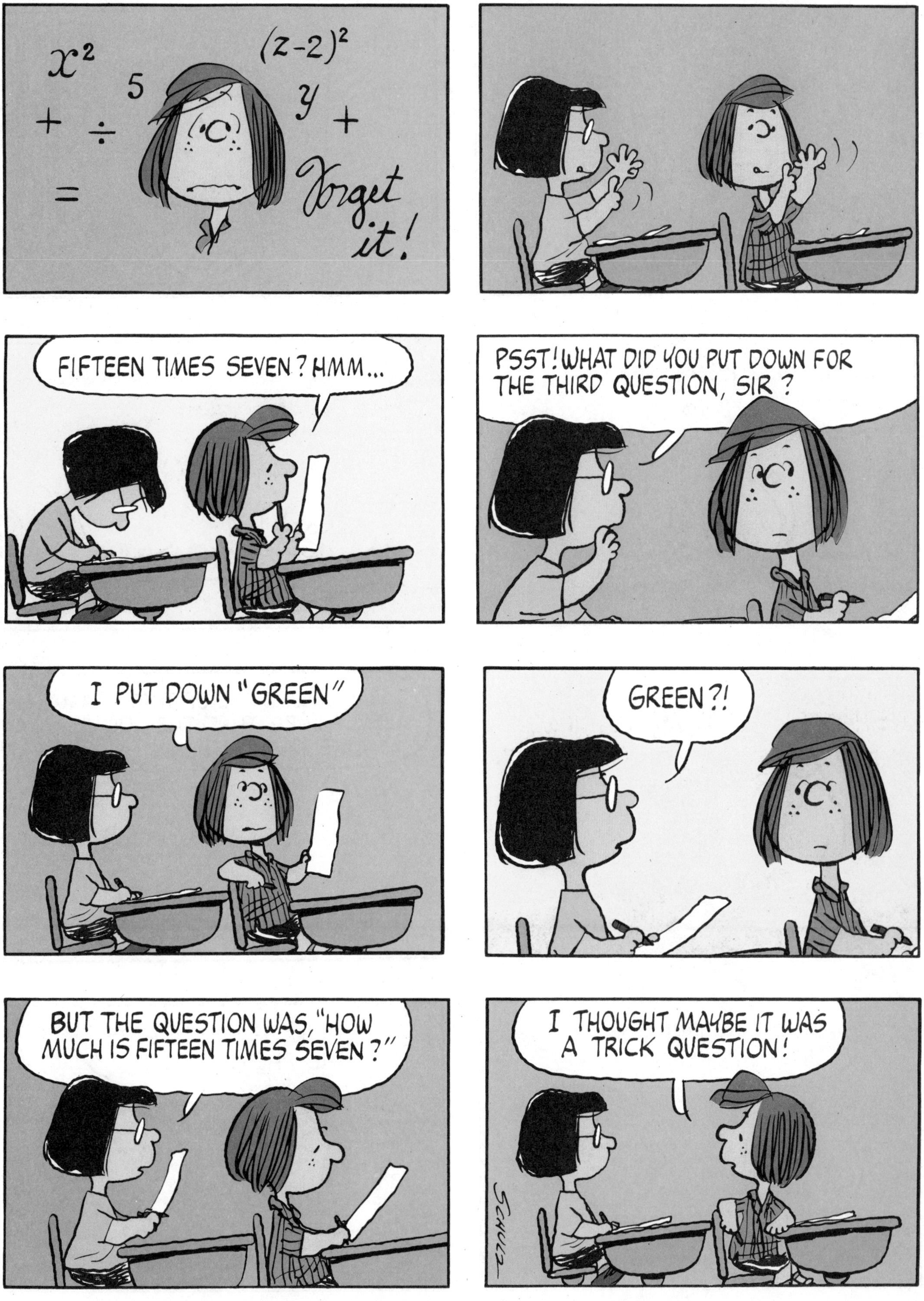
x^2
5
$(z-2)^2$
y
+ ÷ +
=
Forget it!
FIFTEEN TIMES SEVEN? HMM...
PSST! WHAT DID YOU PUT DOWN FOR THE THIRD QUESTION, SIR?
I PUT DOWN "GREEN"
GREEN?!
BUT THE QUESTION WAS, "HOW MUCH IS FIFTEEN TIMES SEVEN?"
I THOUGHT MAYBE IT WAS A TRICK QUESTION!
SCHULZ

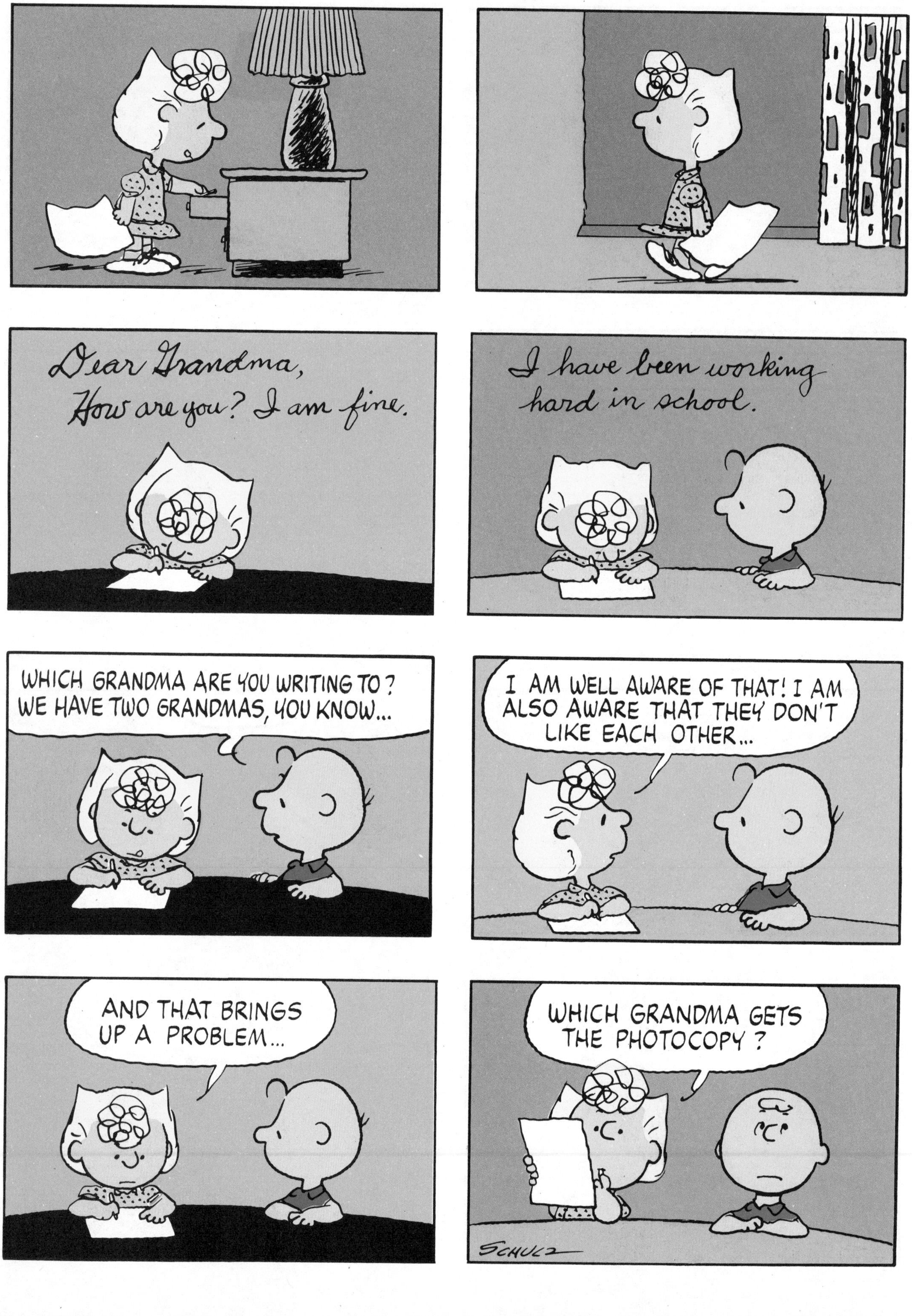
Dear Grandma,
How are you? I am fine.
I have been working hard in school.
WHICH GRANDMA ARE YOU WRITING TO? WE HAVE TWO GRANDMAS, YOU KNOW...
I AM WELL AWARE OF THAT! I AM ALSO AWARE THAT THEY DON'T LIKE EACH OTHER...
AND THAT BRINGS UP A PROBLEM...
WHICH GRANDMA GETS THE PHOTOCOPY?
SCHULZ

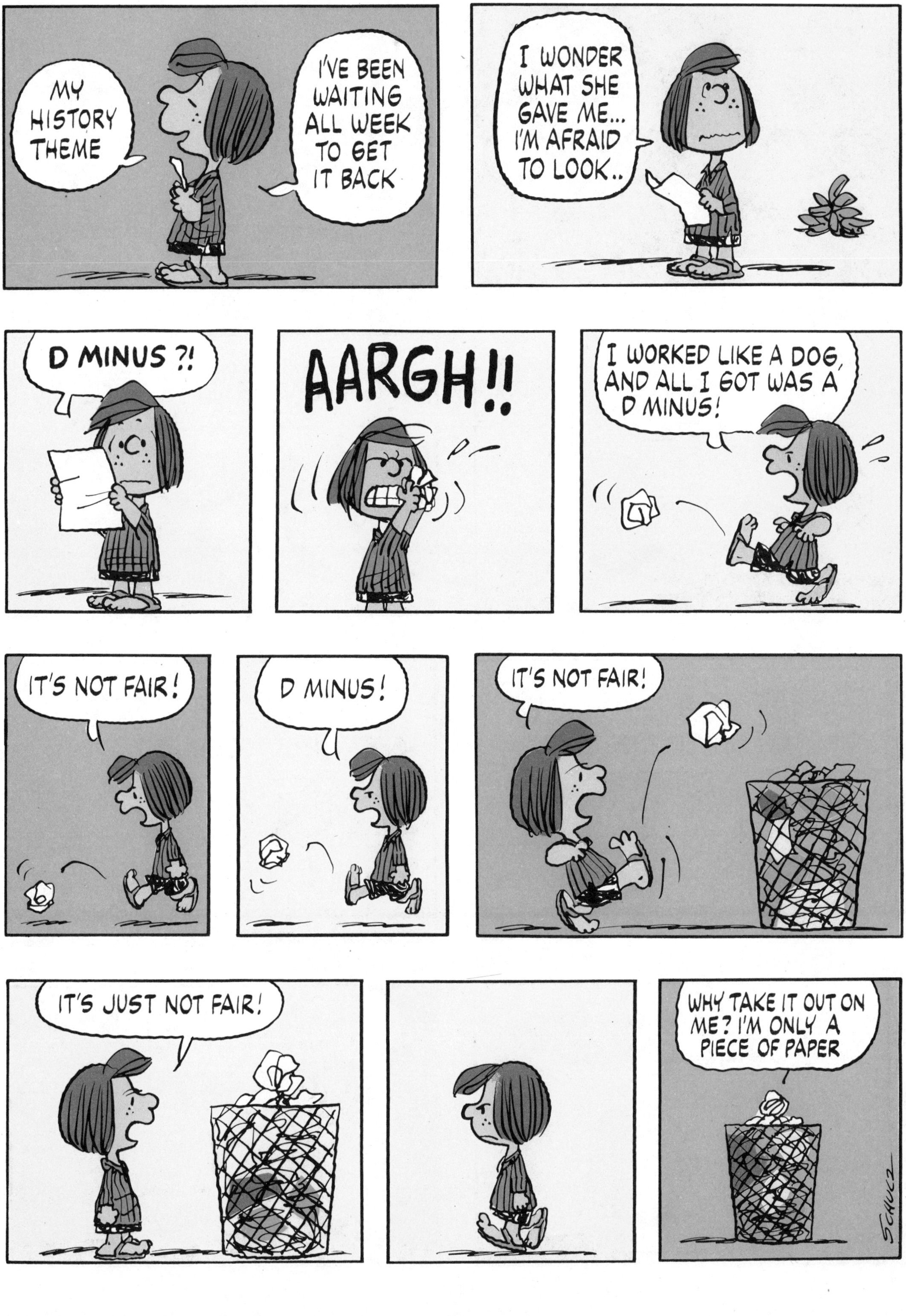

MY HISTORY THEME
I'VE BEEN WAITING ALL WEEK TO GET IT BACK
I WONDER WHAT SHE GAVE ME... I'M AFRAID TO LOOK..
D MINUS ?!
AARGH!!
I WORKED LIKE A DOG, AND ALL I GOT WAS A D MINUS!
IT'S NOT FAIR!
D MINUS!
IT'S NOT FAIR!
IT'S JUST NOT FAIR!
WHY TAKE IT OUT ON ME? I'M ONLY A PIECE OF PAPER
SCHULZ

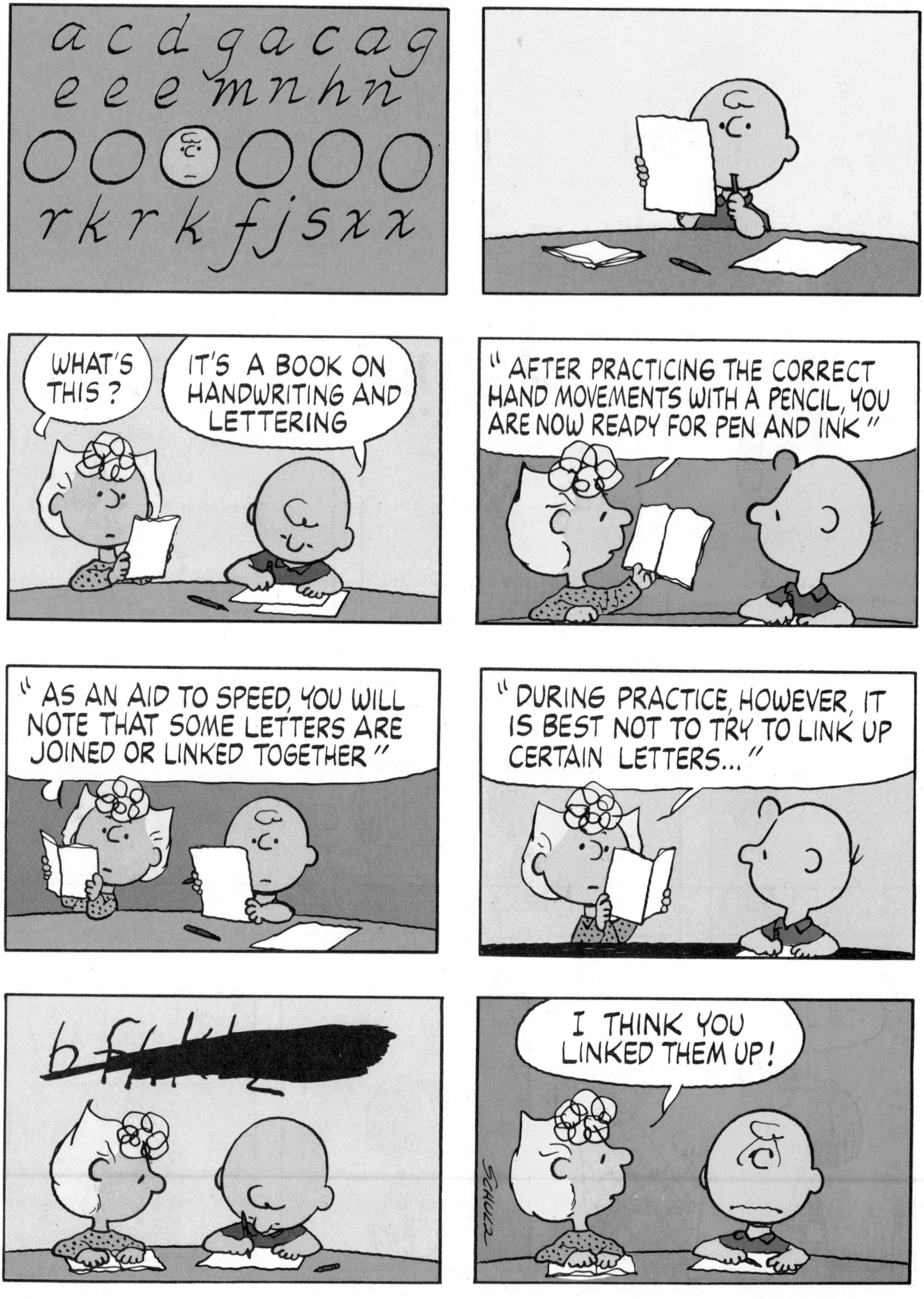
WHAT'S THIS ?
IT'S A BOOK ON HANDWRITING AND LETTERING
" AFTER PRACTICING THE CORRECT HAND MOVEMENTS WITH A PENCIL, YOU ARE NOW READY FOR PEN AND INK "
" AS AN AID TO SPEED, YOU WILL NOTE THAT SOME LETTERS ARE JOINED OR LINKED TOGETHER "
" DURING PRACTICE, HOWEVER, IT IS BEST NOT TO TRY TO LINK UP CERTAIN LETTERS... "
I THINK YOU LINKED THEM UP !

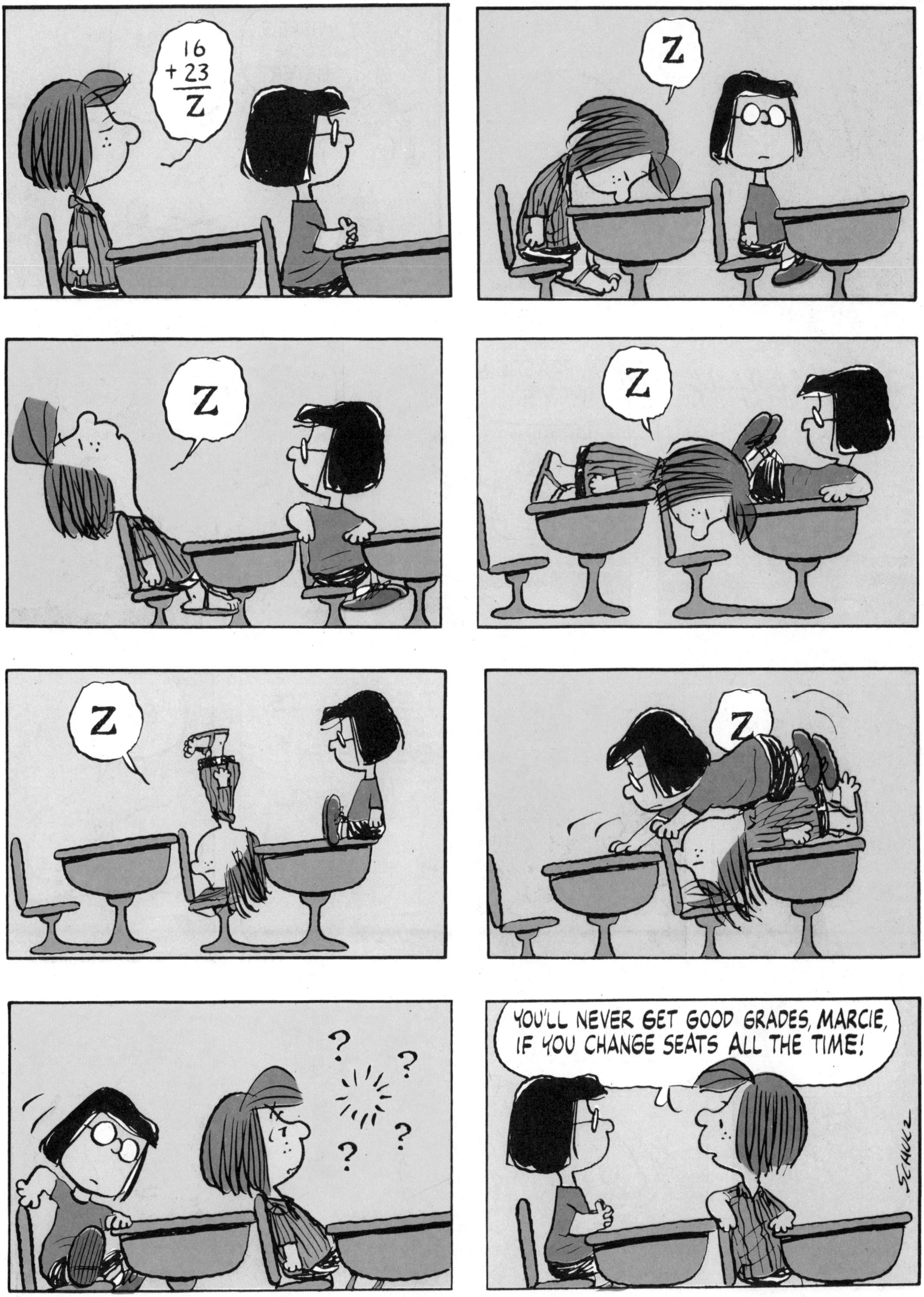
16
+ 23
Z
Z
Z
Z
Z
Z
? ? ? ?
YOU'LL NEVER GET GOOD GRADES, MARCIE, IF YOU CHANGE SEATS ALL THE TIME!
SCHULZ

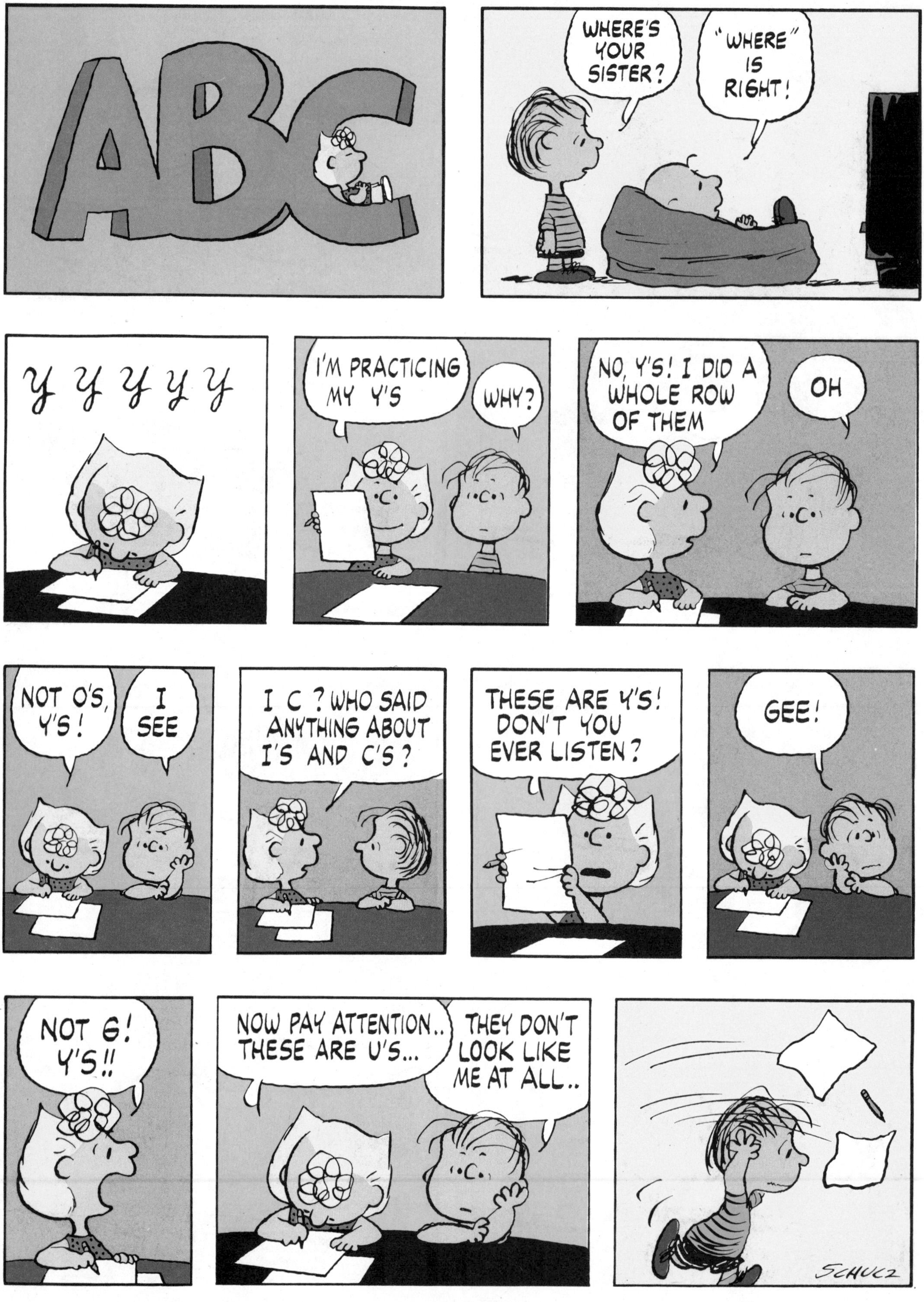
ABC
WHERE'S YOUR SISTER?
"WHERE" IS RIGHT!
I'M PRACTICING MY Y'S
WHY?
NO, Y'S! I DID A WHOLE ROW OF THEM
OH
NOT O'S, Y'S!
I SEE
I C ? WHO SAID ANYTHING ABOUT I'S AND C'S ?
THESE ARE Y'S! DON'T YOU EVER LISTEN?
GEE!
NOT G! Y'S!!
NOW PAY ATTENTION.. THESE ARE U'S...
THEY DON'T LOOK LIKE ME AT ALL..
SCHULZ

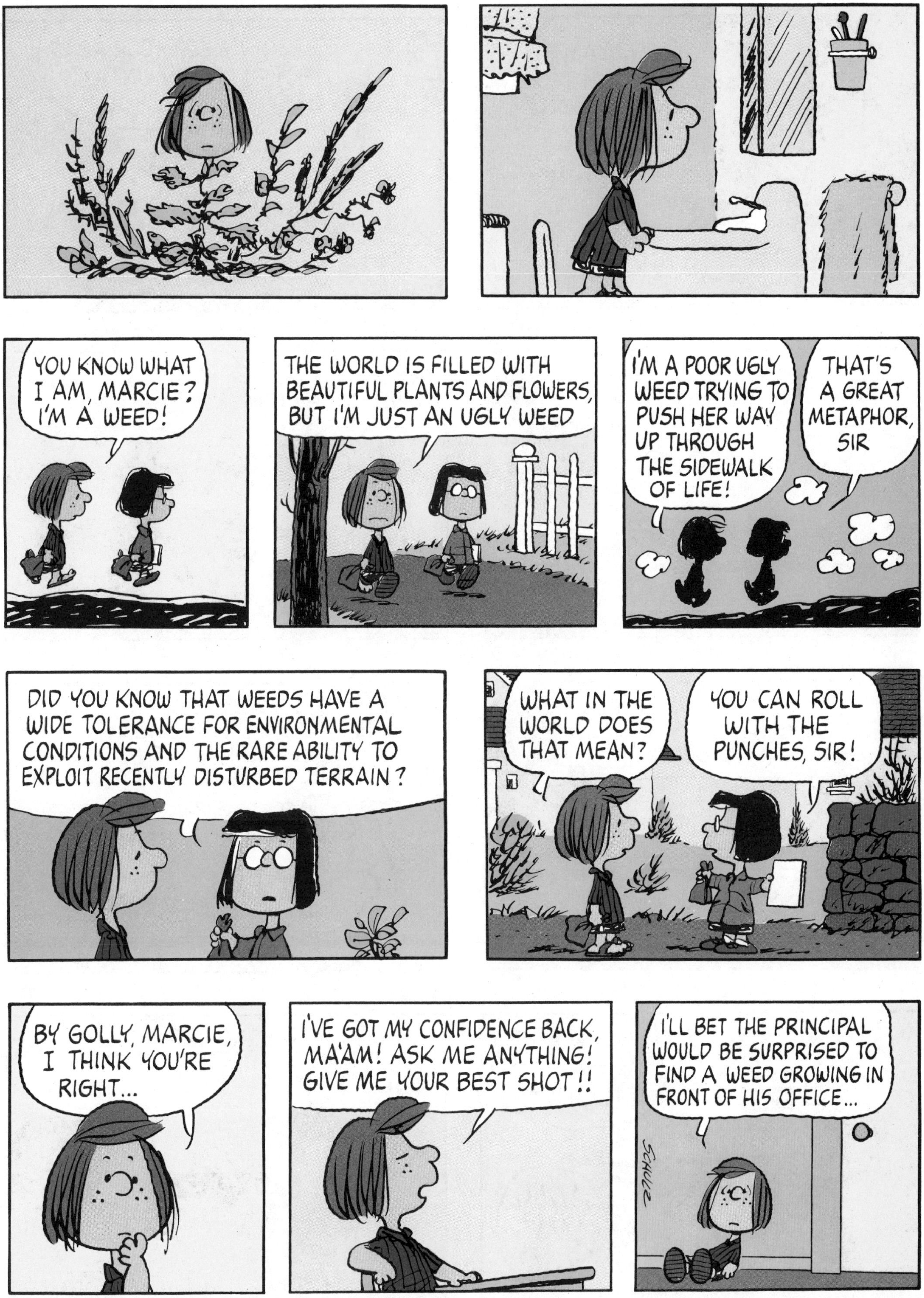
YOU KNOW WHAT I AM, MARCIE? I'M A WEED!
THE WORLD IS FILLED WITH BEAUTIFUL PLANTS AND FLOWERS, BUT I'M JUST AN UGLY WEED
I'M A POOR UGLY WEED TRYING TO PUSH HER WAY UP THROUGH THE SIDEWALK OF LIFE!
THAT'S A GREAT METAPHOR, SIR
DID YOU KNOW THAT WEEDS HAVE A WIDE TOLERANCE FOR ENVIRONMENTAL CONDITIONS AND THE RARE ABILITY TO EXPLOIT RECENTLY DISTURBED TERRAIN?
WHAT IN THE WORLD DOES THAT MEAN?
YOU CAN ROLL WITH THE PUNCHES, SIR!
BY GOLLY, MARCIE, I THINK YOU'RE RIGHT...
I'VE GOT MY CONFIDENCE BACK, MA'AM! ASK ME ANYTHING! GIVE ME YOUR BEST SHOT!!
I'LL BET THE PRINCIPAL WOULD BE SURPRISED TO FIND A WEED GROWING IN FRONT OF HIS OFFICE...
SCHULZ

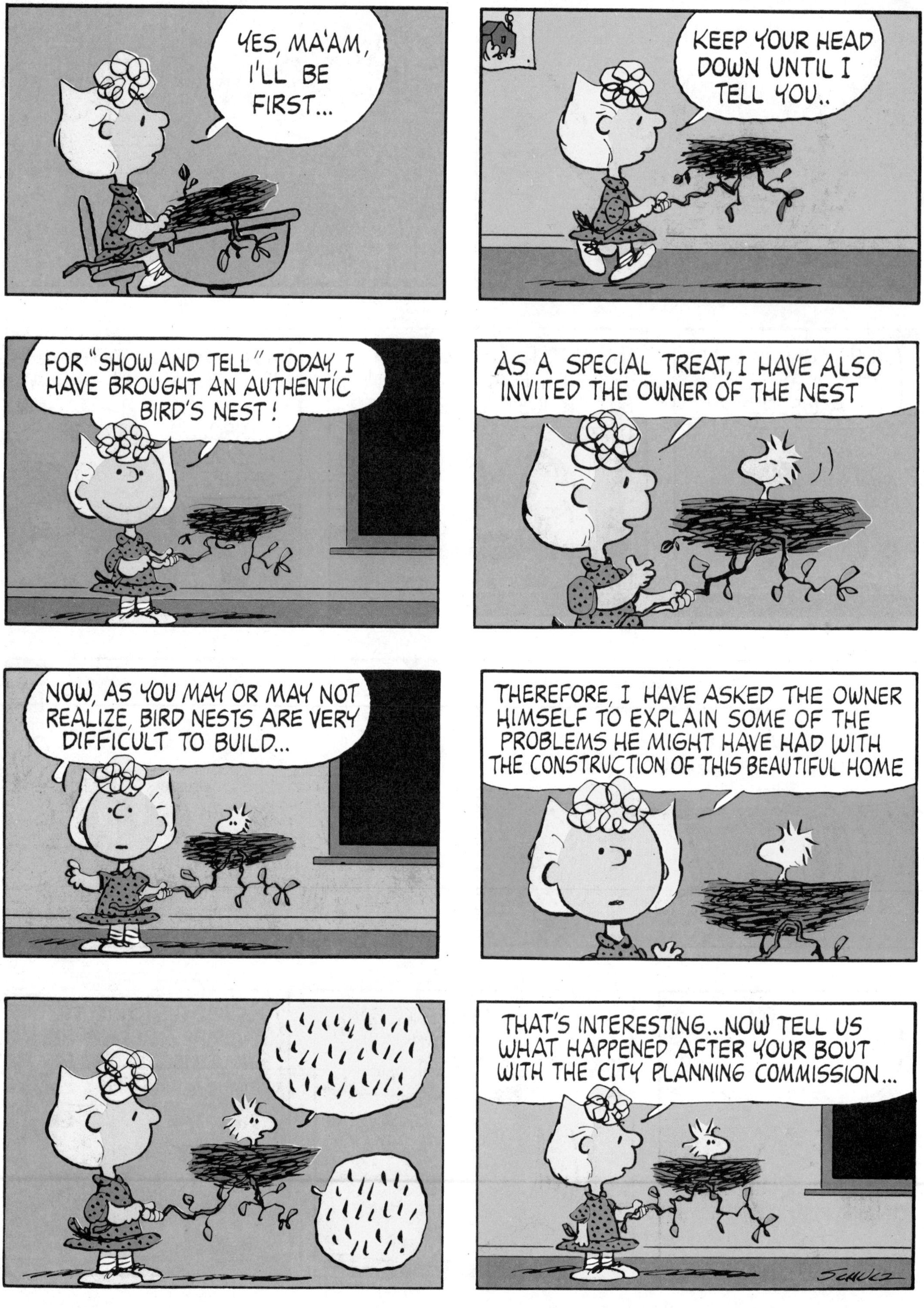
YES, MA'AM, I'LL BE FIRST...
KEEP YOUR HEAD DOWN UNTIL I TELL YOU..
FOR "SHOW AND TELL" TODAY, I HAVE BROUGHT AN AUTHENTIC BIRD'S NEST!
AS A SPECIAL TREAT, I HAVE ALSO INVITED THE OWNER OF THE NEST
NOW, AS YOU MAY OR MAY NOT REALIZE, BIRD NESTS ARE VERY DIFFICULT TO BUILD...
THEREFORE, I HAVE ASKED THE OWNER HIMSELF TO EXPLAIN SOME OF THE PROBLEMS HE MIGHT HAVE HAD WITH THE CONSTRUCTION OF THIS BEAUTIFUL HOME
THAT'S INTERESTING...NOW TELL US WHAT HAPPENED AFTER YOUR BOUT WITH THE CITY PLANNING COMMISSION...
SCHULZ

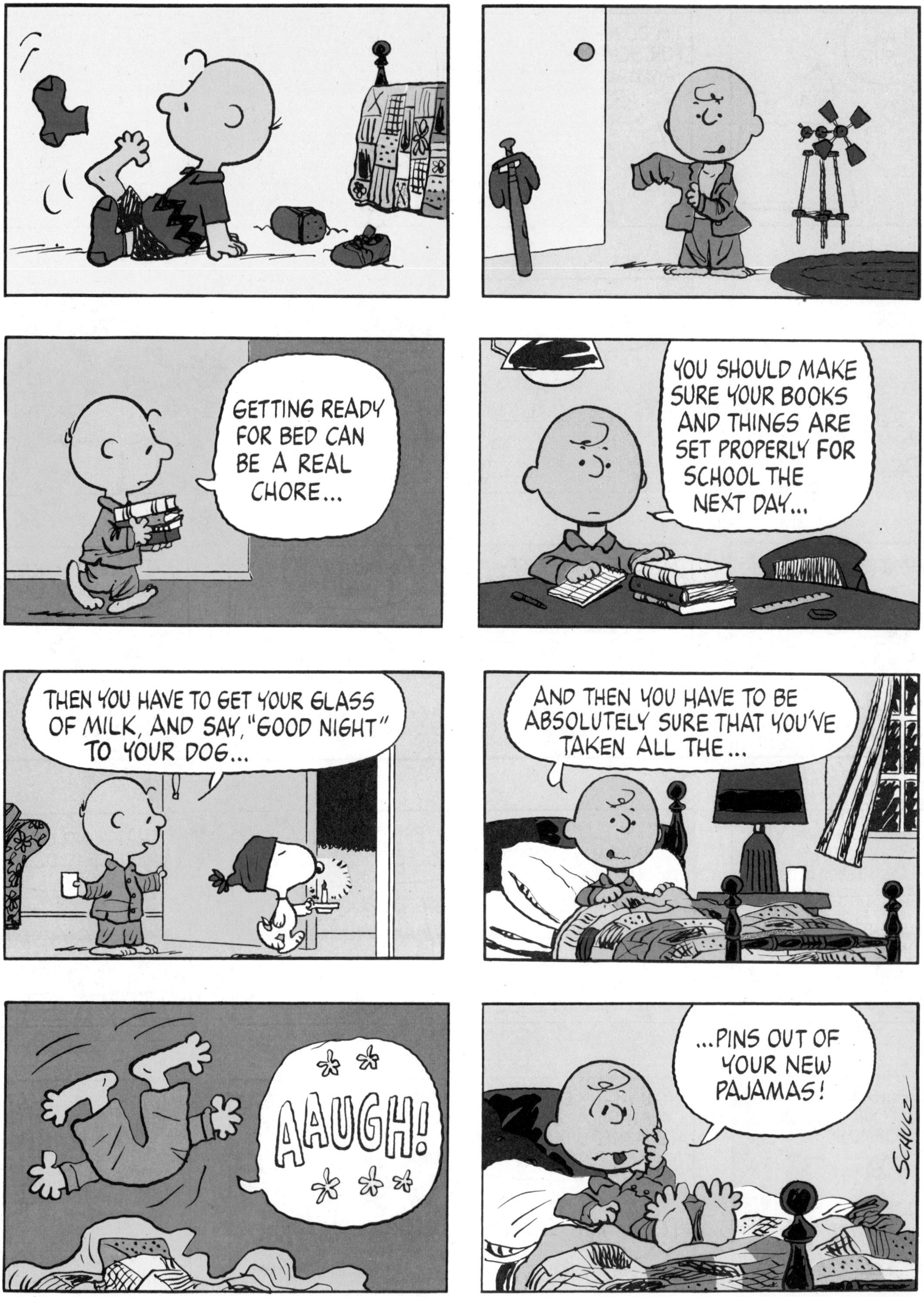
GETTING READY FOR BED CAN BE A REAL CHORE...
YOU SHOULD MAKE SURE YOUR BOOKS AND THINGS ARE SET PROPERLY FOR SCHOOL THE NEXT DAY...
THEN YOU HAVE TO GET YOUR GLASS OF MILK, AND SAY, "GOOD NIGHT" TO YOUR DOG...
AND THEN YOU HAVE TO BE ABSOLUTELY SURE THAT YOU'VE TAKEN ALL THE...
AAUGH!
...PINS OUT OF YOUR NEW PAJAMAS!
SCHULZ

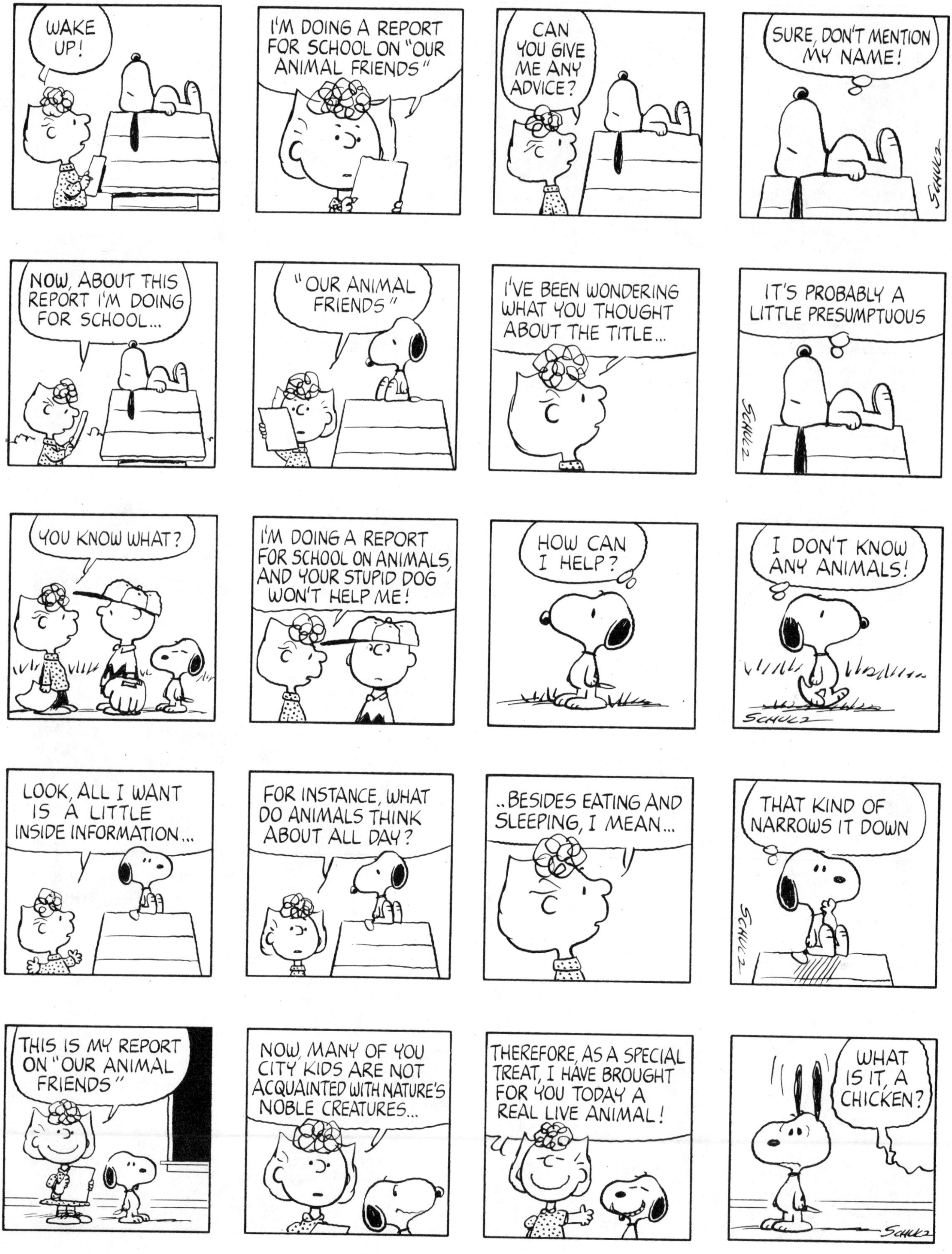

WAKE UP!
I'M DOING A REPORT FOR SCHOOL ON "OUR ANIMAL FRIENDS"
CAN YOU GIVE ME ANY ADVICE?
SURE, DON'T MENTION MY NAME!
SCHULZ
NOW, ABOUT THIS REPORT I'M DOING FOR SCHOOL...
"OUR ANIMAL FRIENDS"
I'VE BEEN WONDERING WHAT YOU THOUGHT ABOUT THE TITLE...
IT'S PROBABLY A LITTLE PRESUMPTUOUS
SCHULZ
YOU KNOW WHAT?
I'M DOING A REPORT FOR SCHOOL ON ANIMALS, AND YOUR STUPID DOG WON'T HELP ME!
HOW CAN I HELP?
I DON'T KNOW ANY ANIMALS!
SCHULZ
LOOK, ALL I WANT IS A LITTLE INSIDE INFORMATION...
FOR INSTANCE, WHAT DO ANIMALS THINK ABOUT ALL DAY?
..BESIDES EATING AND SLEEPING, I MEAN...
THAT KIND OF NARROWS IT DOWN
SCHULZ
THIS IS MY REPORT ON "OUR ANIMAL FRIENDS"
NOW, MANY OF YOU CITY KIDS ARE NOT ACQUAINTED WITH NATURE'S NOBLE CREATURES...
THEREFORE, AS A SPECIAL TREAT, I HAVE BROUGHT FOR YOU TODAY A REAL LIVE ANIMAL!
WHAT IS IT, A CHICKEN?
SCHULZ

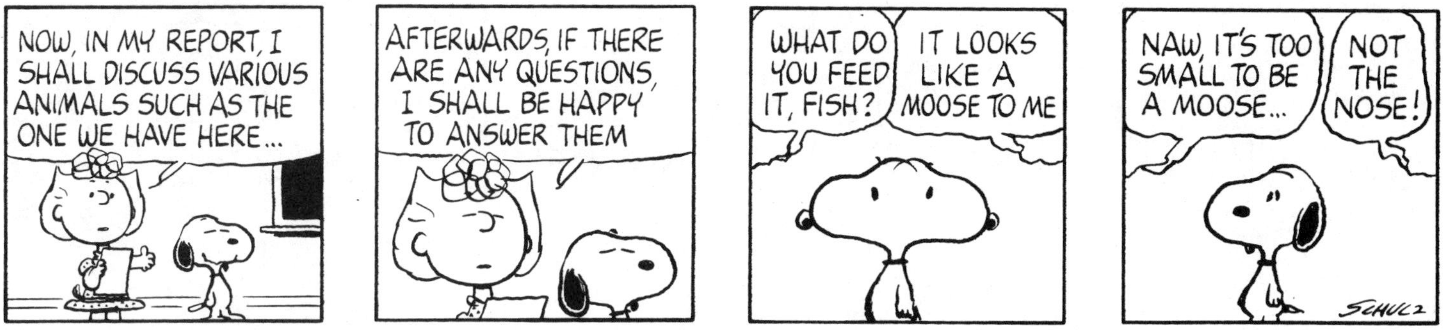
NOW, IN MY REPORT, I SHALL DISCUSS VARIOUS ANIMALS SUCH AS THE ONE WE HAVE HERE...
AFTERWARDS, IF THERE ARE ANY QUESTIONS, I SHALL BE HAPPY TO ANSWER THEM
WHAT DO YOU FEED IT, FISH?
IT LOOKS LIKE A MOOSE TO ME
NAW, IT'S TOO SMALL TO BE A MOOSE...
NOT THE NOSE!
SCHULZ

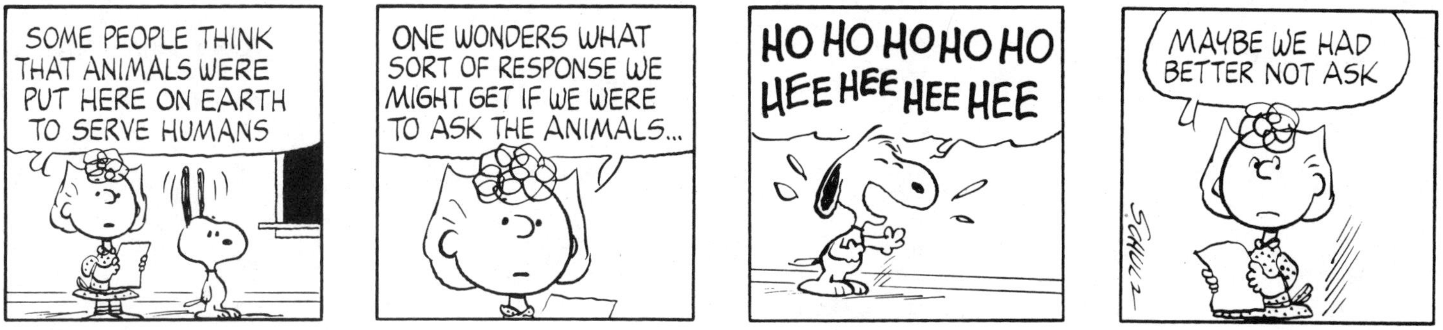
SOME PEOPLE THINK THAT ANIMALS WERE PUT HERE ON EARTH TO SERVE HUMANS
ONE WONDERS WHAT SORT OF RESPONSE WE MIGHT GET IF WE WERE TO ASK THE ANIMALS...
HO HO HO HO HO
HEE HEE HEE HEE
MAYBE WE HAD BETTER NOT ASK
SCHULZ

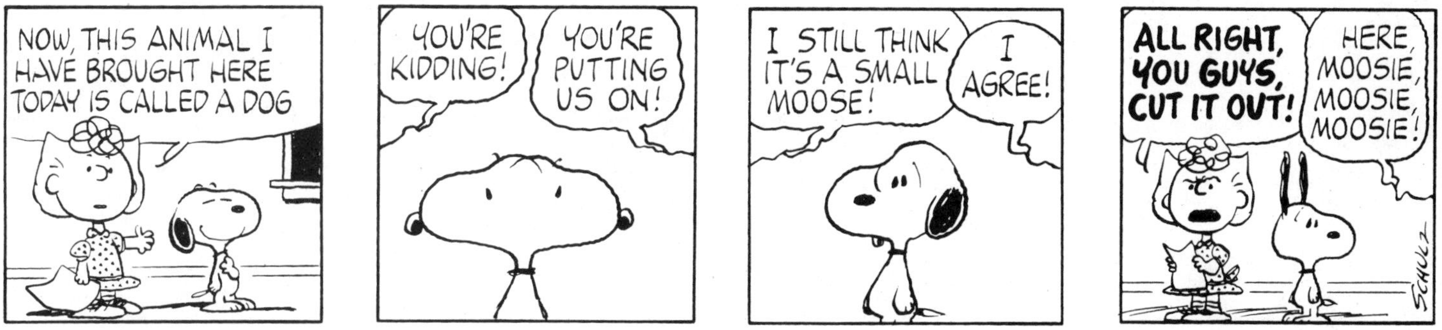
NOW, THIS ANIMAL I HAVE BROUGHT HERE TODAY IS CALLED A DOG
YOU'RE KIDDING!
YOU'RE PUTTING US ON!
I STILL THINK IT'S A SMALL MOOSE!
I AGREE!
ALL RIGHT, YOU GUYS, CUT IT OUT!
HERE, MOOSIE, MOOSIE, MOOSIE!
SCHULZ

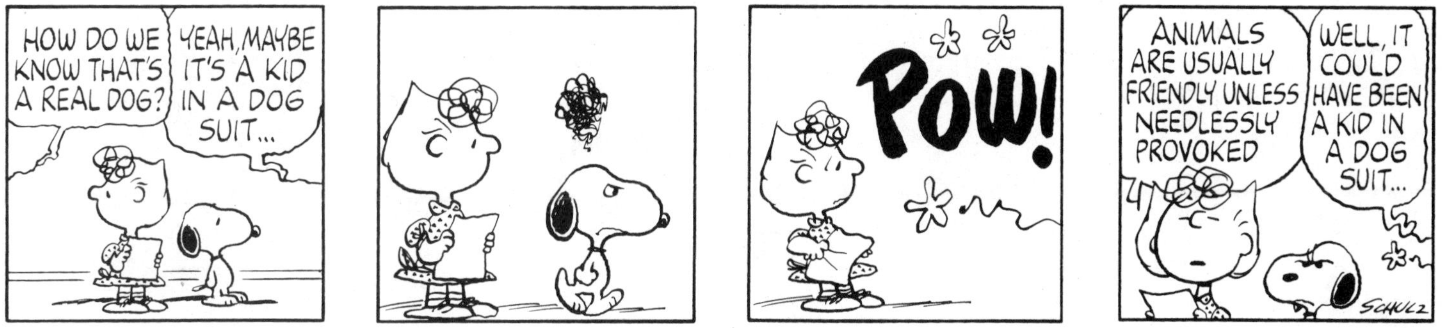
HOW DO WE KNOW THAT'S A REAL DOG?
YEAH, MAYBE IT'S A KID IN A DOG SUIT...
POW!
ANIMALS ARE USUALLY FRIENDLY UNLESS NEEDLESSLY PROVOKED
WELL, IT COULD HAVE BEEN A KID IN A DOG SUIT...
SCHULZ

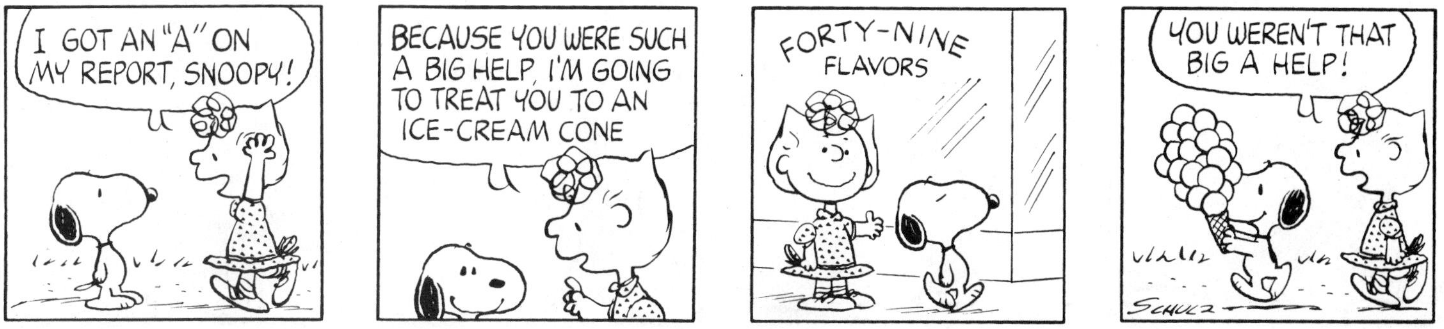
I GOT AN "A" ON MY REPORT, SNOOPY!
BECAUSE YOU WERE SUCH A BIG HELP, I'M GOING TO TREAT YOU TO AN ICE-CREAM CONE
FORTY-NINE FLAVORS
YOU WEREN'T THAT BIG A HELP!
SCHULZ

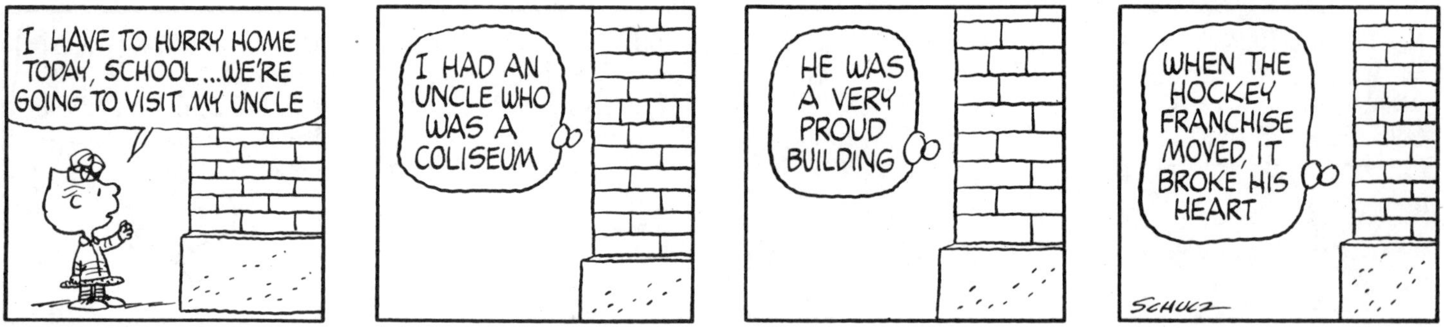
I HAVE TO HURRY HOME TODAY, SCHOOL...WE'RE GOING TO VISIT MY UNCLE
I HAD AN UNCLE WHO WAS A COLISEUM
HE WAS A VERY PROUD BUILDING
WHEN THE HOCKEY FRANCHISE MOVED, IT BROKE HIS HEART
SCHULZ

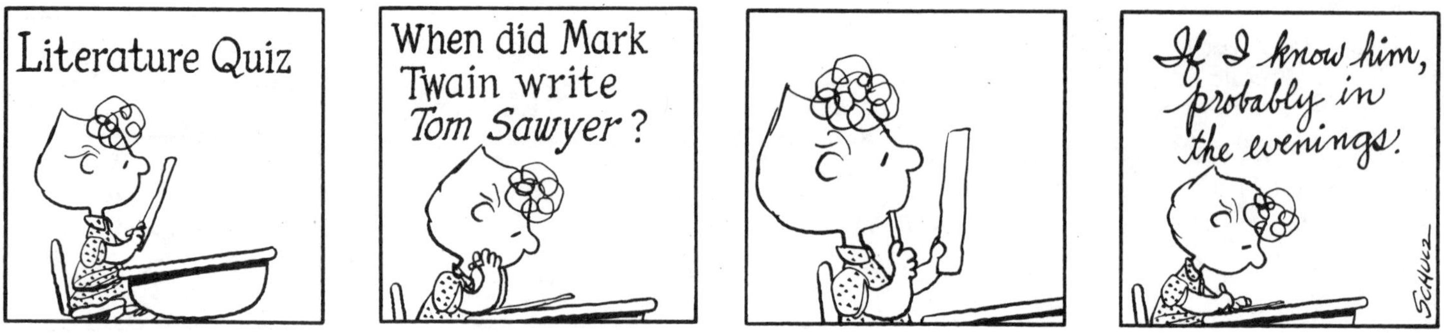
Literature Quiz
When did Mark Twain write *Tom Sawyer*?
If I know him, probably in the evenings.
SCHULZ

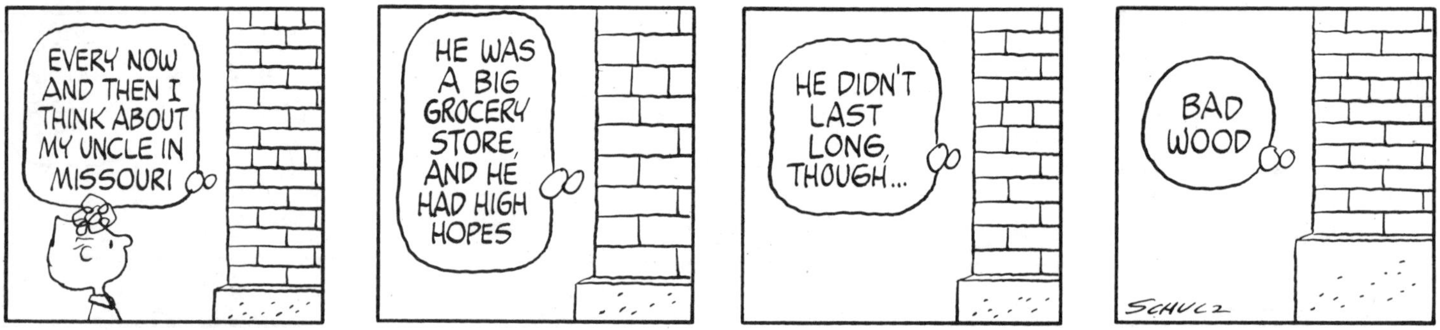
EVERY NOW AND THEN I THINK ABOUT MY UNCLE IN MISSOURI
HE WAS A BIG GROCERY STORE, AND HE HAD HIGH HOPES
HE DIDN'T LAST LONG, THOUGH...
BAD WOOD
SCHULZ

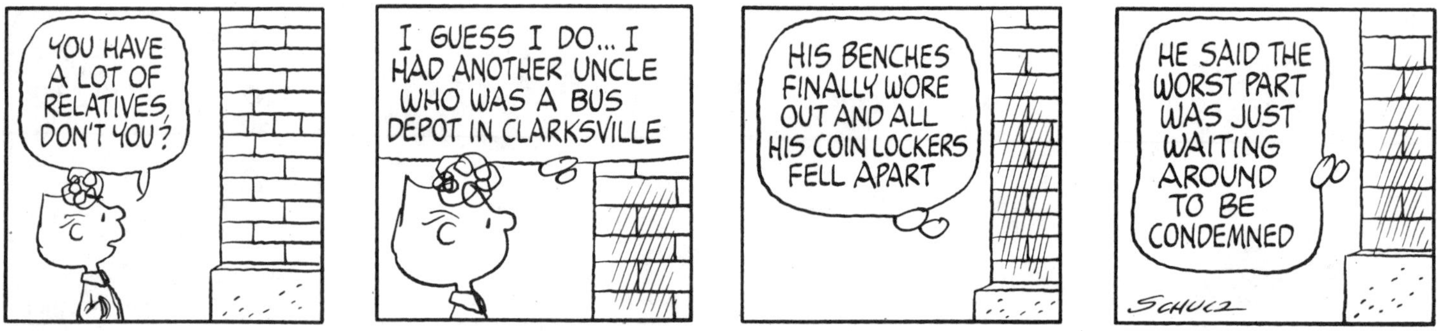
YOU HAVE A LOT OF RELATIVES, DON'T YOU?
I GUESS I DO... I HAD ANOTHER UNCLE WHO WAS A BUS DEPOT IN CLARKSVILLE
HIS BENCHES FINALLY WORE OUT AND ALL HIS COIN LOCKERS FELL APART
HE SAID THE WORST PART WAS JUST WAITING AROUND TO BE CONDEMNED
SCHULZ

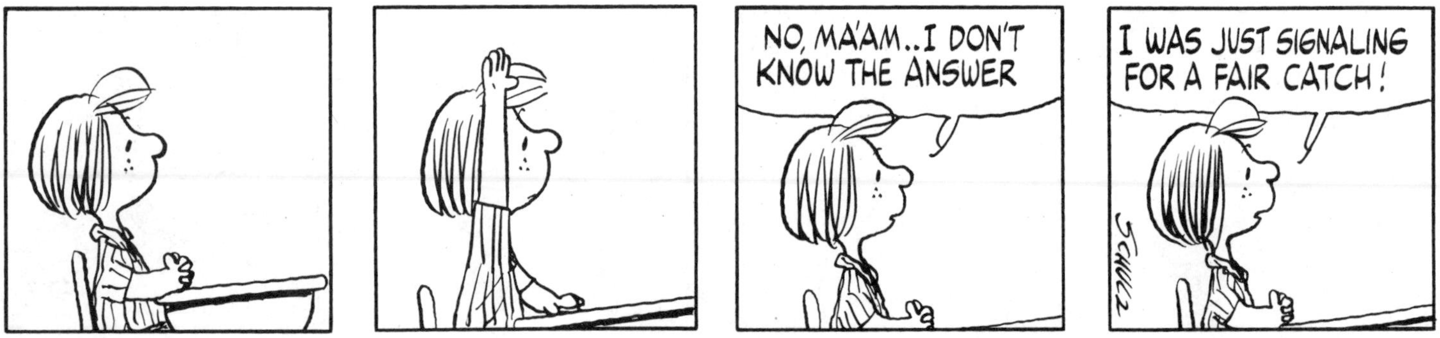
NO, MA'AM..I DON'T KNOW THE ANSWER
I WAS JUST SIGNALING FOR A FAIR CATCH!
SCHULZ

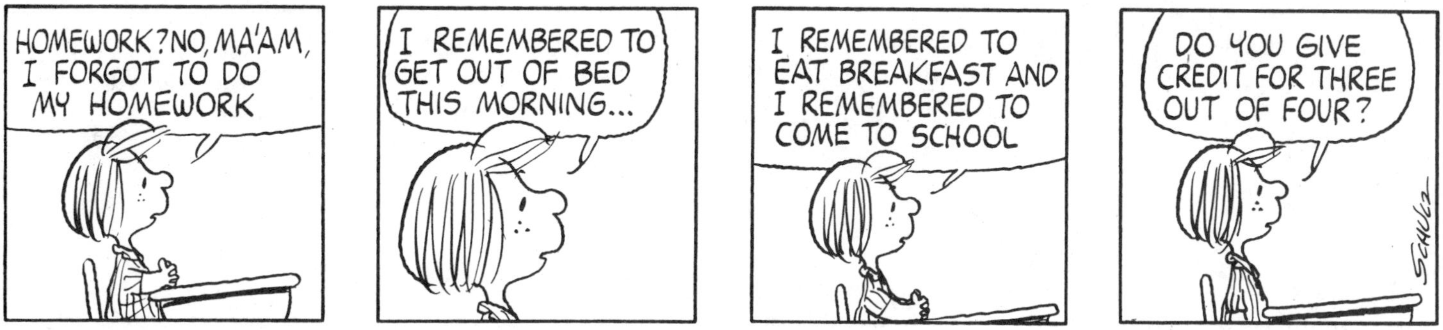
HOMEWORK? NO, MA'AM, I FORGOT TO DO MY HOMEWORK
I REMEMBERED TO GET OUT OF BED THIS MORNING...
I REMEMBERED TO EAT BREAKFAST AND I REMEMBERED TO COME TO SCHOOL
DO YOU GIVE CREDIT FOR THREE OUT OF FOUR?

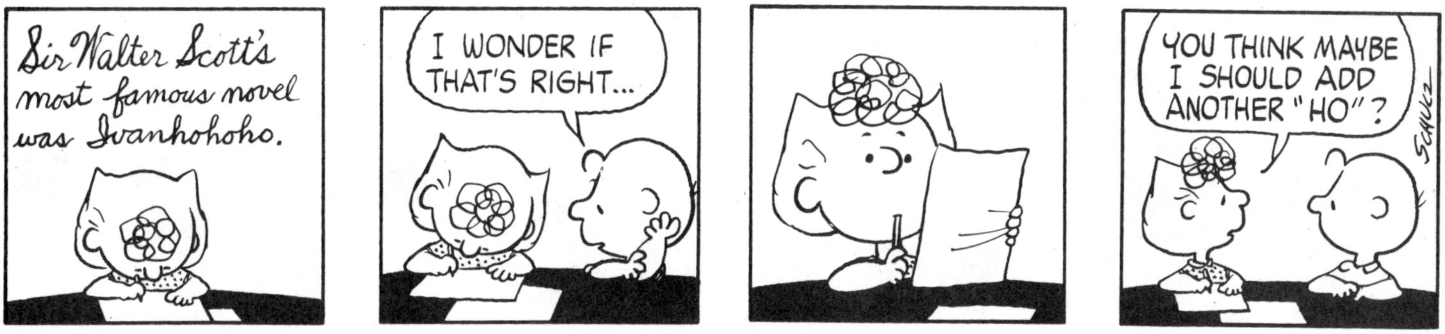
Sir Walter Scott's most famous novel was Ivanhohoho.
I WONDER IF THAT'S RIGHT...
YOU THINK MAYBE I SHOULD ADD ANOTHER "HO"?

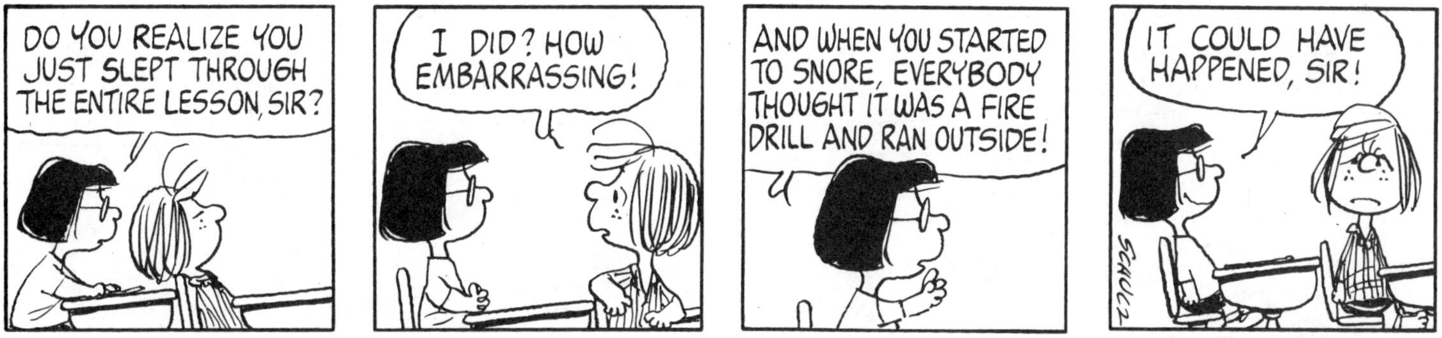
DO YOU REALIZE YOU JUST SLEPT THROUGH THE ENTIRE LESSON, SIR?
I DID? HOW EMBARRASSING!
AND WHEN YOU STARTED TO SNORE, EVERYBODY THOUGHT IT WAS A FIRE DRILL AND RAN OUTSIDE!
IT COULD HAVE HAPPENED, SIR!

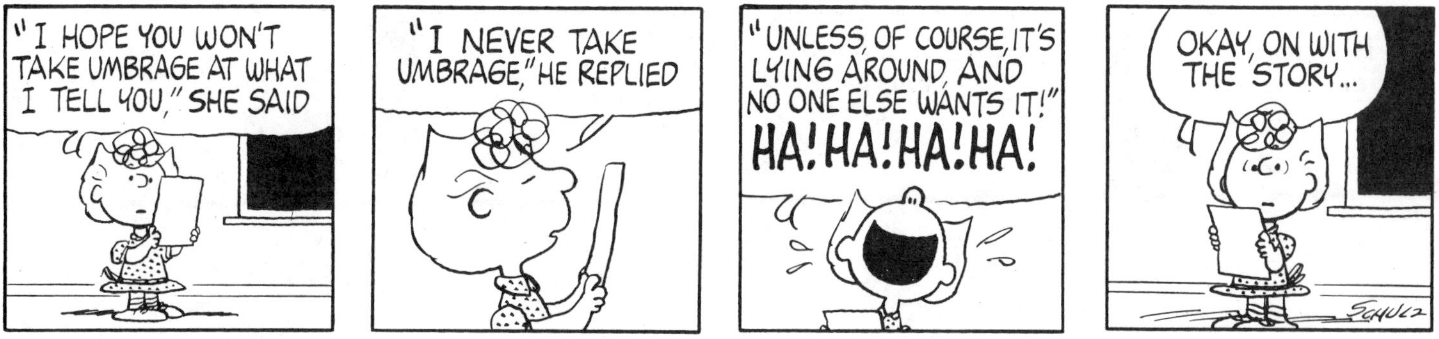
"I HOPE YOU WON'T TAKE UMBRAGE AT WHAT I TELL YOU," SHE SAID
"I NEVER TAKE UMBRAGE," HE REPLIED
"UNLESS, OF COURSE, IT'S LYING AROUND, AND NO ONE ELSE WANTS IT!"
HA! HA! HA! HA!
OKAY, ON WITH THE STORY...

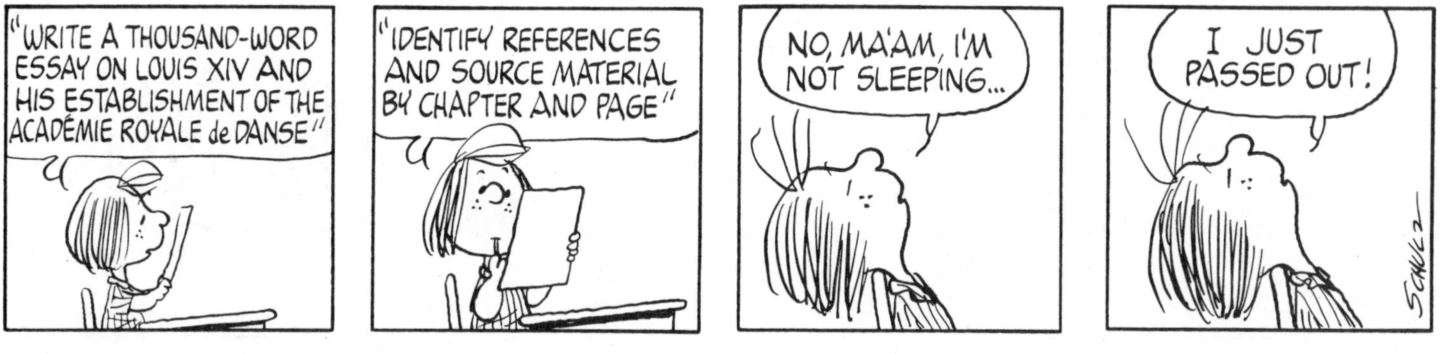
"WRITE A THOUSAND-WORD ESSAY ON LOUIS XIV AND HIS ESTABLISHMENT OF THE ACADÉMIE ROYALE de DANSE"
"IDENTIFY REFERENCES AND SOURCE MATERIAL BY CHAPTER AND PAGE"
NO, MA'AM, I'M NOT SLEEPING...
I JUST PASSED OUT!

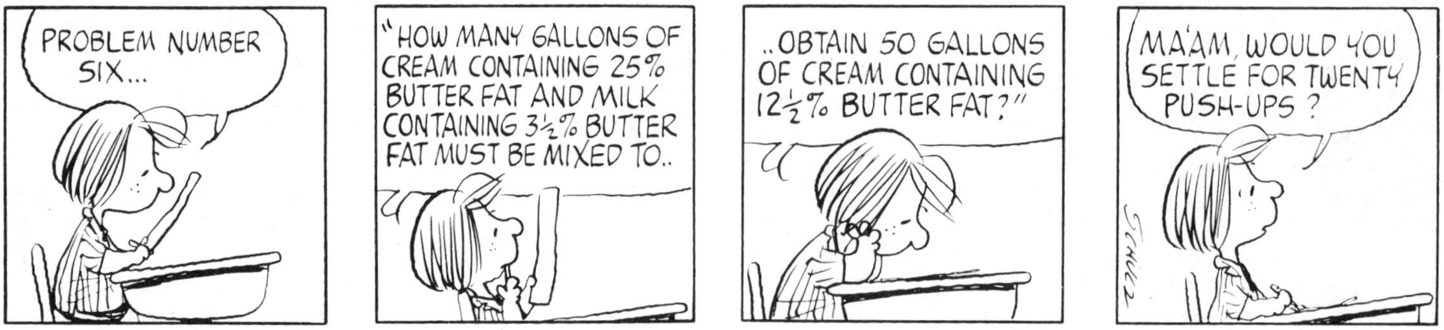
PROBLEM NUMBER SIX...
"HOW MANY GALLONS OF CREAM CONTAINING 25% BUTTER FAT AND MILK CONTAINING 3½% BUTTER FAT MUST BE MIXED TO..
..OBTAIN 50 GALLONS OF CREAM CONTAINING 12½% BUTTER FAT?"
MA'AM, WOULD YOU SETTLE FOR TWENTY PUSH-UPS ?
SCHULZ

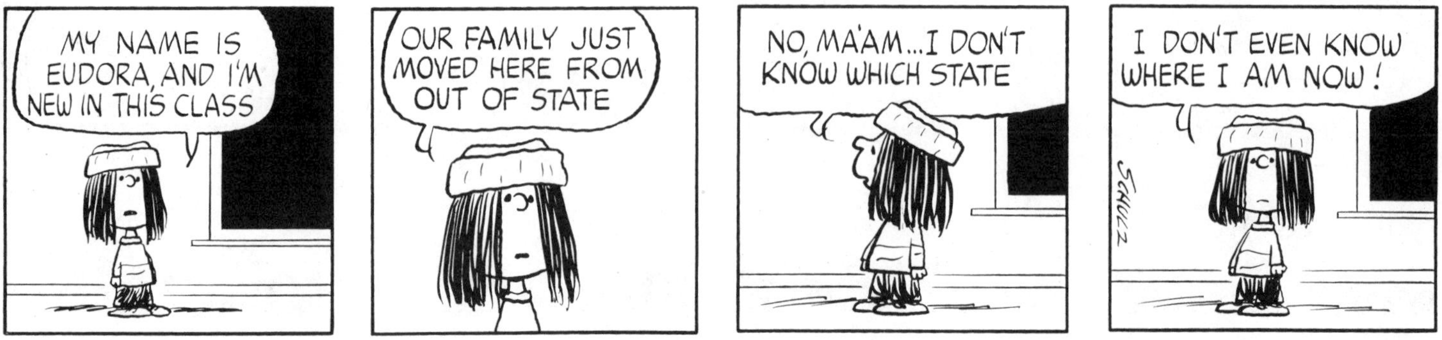
MY NAME IS EUDORA, AND I'M NEW IN THIS CLASS
OUR FAMILY JUST MOVED HERE FROM OUT OF STATE
NO, MA'AM...I DON'T KNOW WHICH STATE
I DON'T EVEN KNOW WHERE I AM NOW !
SCHULZ

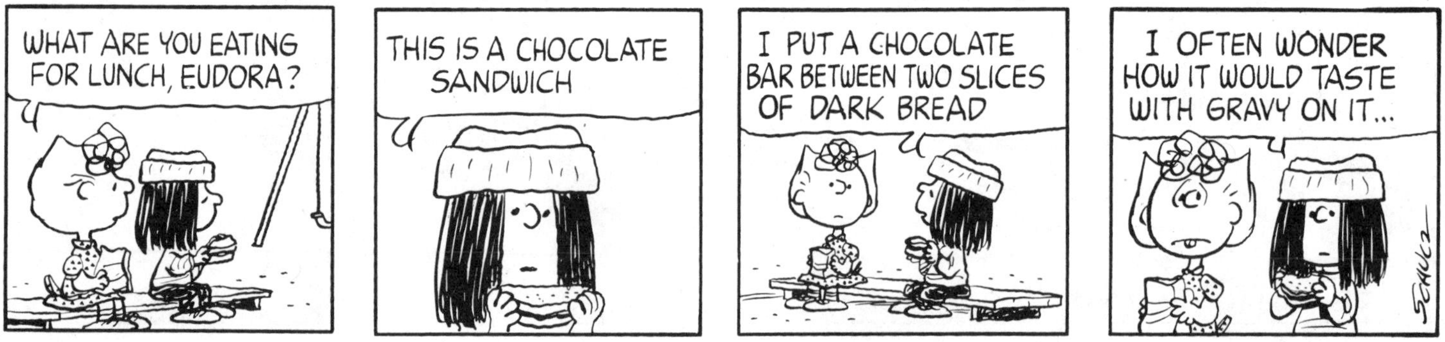
WHAT ARE YOU EATING FOR LUNCH, EUDORA ?
THIS IS A CHOCOLATE SANDWICH
I PUT A CHOCOLATE BAR BETWEEN TWO SLICES OF DARK BREAD
I OFTEN WONDER HOW IT WOULD TASTE WITH GRAVY ON IT...
SCHULZ

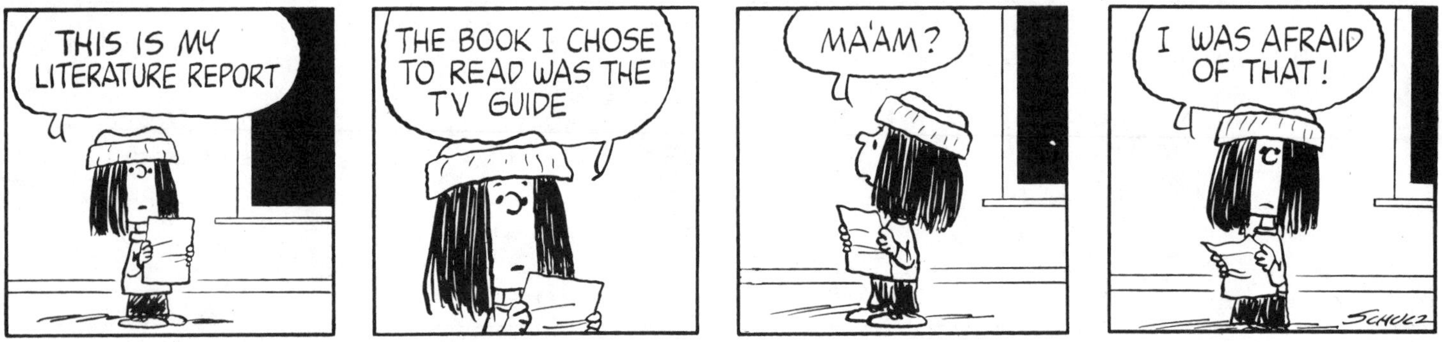
THIS IS MY LITERATURE REPORT
THE BOOK I CHOSE TO READ WAS THE TV GUIDE
MA'AM ?
I WAS AFRAID OF THAT !
SCHULZ

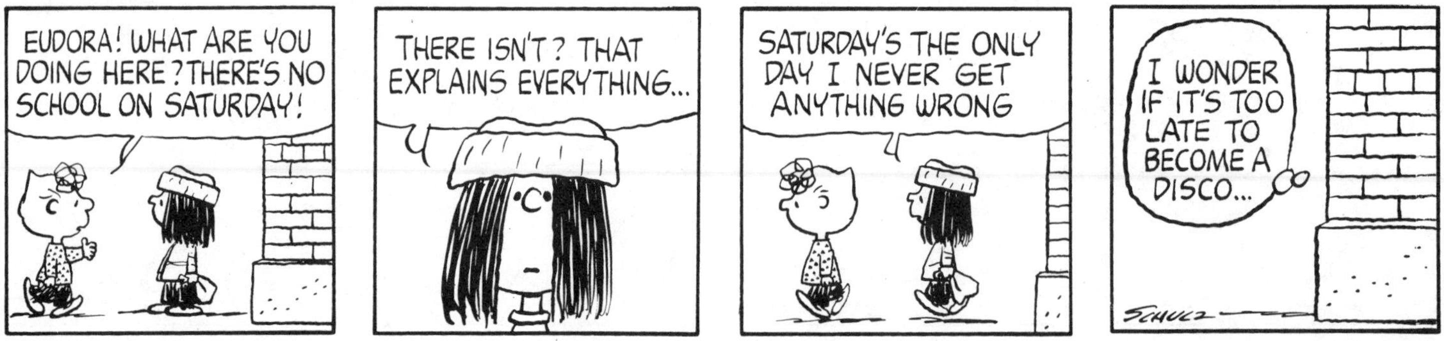
EUDORA! WHAT ARE YOU DOING HERE? THERE'S NO SCHOOL ON SATURDAY!
THERE ISN'T? THAT EXPLAINS EVERYTHING...
SATURDAY'S THE ONLY DAY I NEVER GET ANYTHING WRONG
I WONDER IF IT'S TOO LATE TO BECOME A DISCO...
SCHULZ

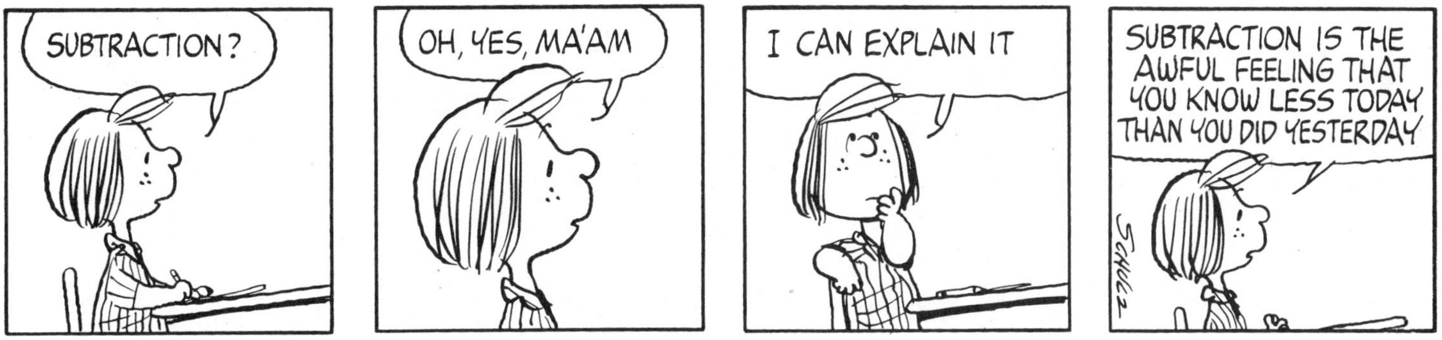
SUBTRACTION?
OH, YES, MA'AM
I CAN EXPLAIN IT
SUBTRACTION IS THE AWFUL FEELING THAT YOU KNOW LESS TODAY THAN YOU DID YESTERDAY
SCHULZ

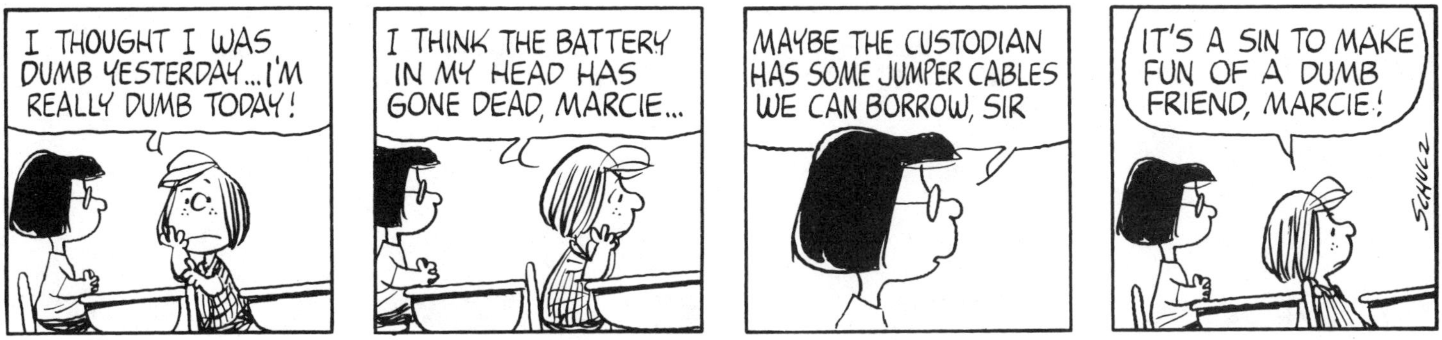
I THOUGHT I WAS DUMB YESTERDAY...I'M REALLY DUMB TODAY!
I THINK THE BATTERY IN MY HEAD HAS GONE DEAD, MARCIE...
MAYBE THE CUSTODIAN HAS SOME JUMPER CABLES WE CAN BORROW, SIR
IT'S A SIN TO MAKE FUN OF A DUMB FRIEND, MARCIE!
SCHULZ

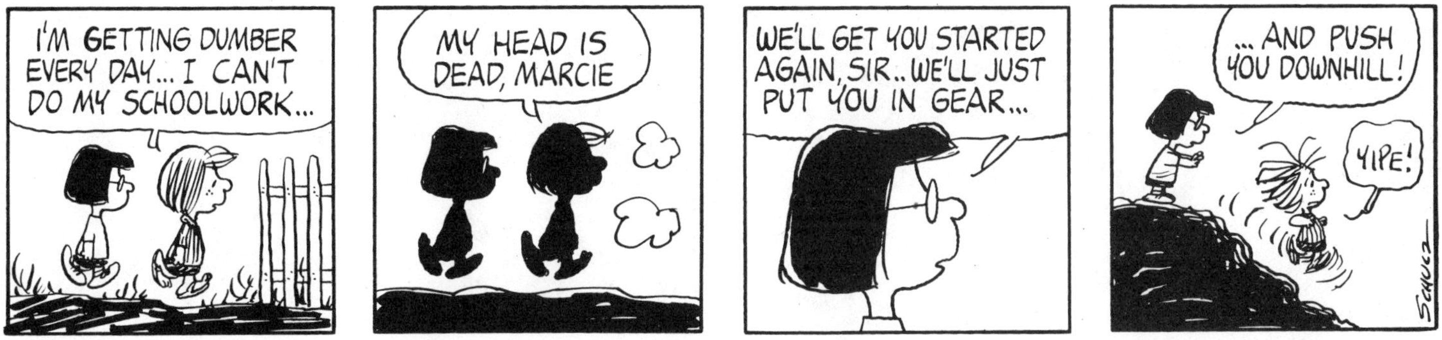
I'M GETTING DUMBER EVERY DAY... I CAN'T DO MY SCHOOLWORK...
MY HEAD IS DEAD, MARCIE
WE'LL GET YOU STARTED AGAIN, SIR.. WE'LL JUST PUT YOU IN GEAR...
... AND PUSH YOU DOWNHILL!
YIPE!
SCHULZ

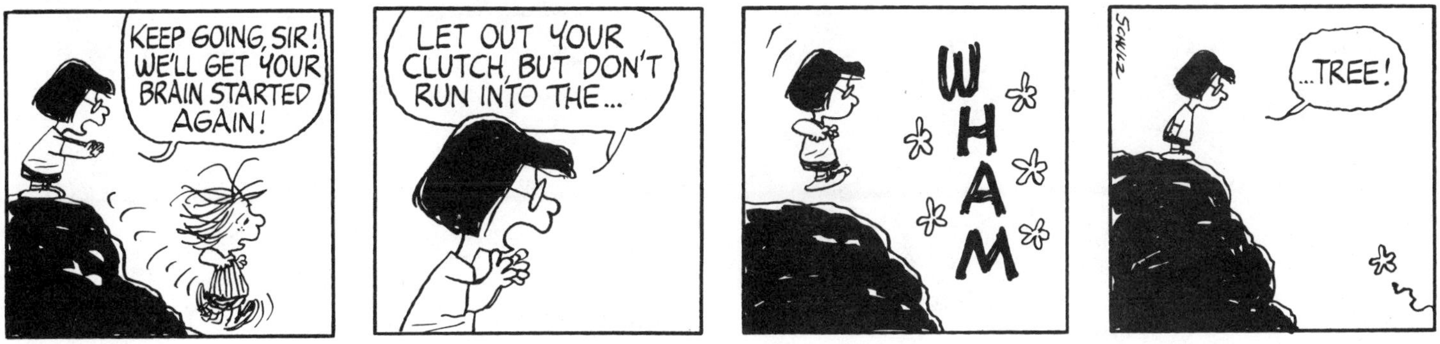
KEEP GOING, SIR! WE'LL GET YOUR BRAIN STARTED AGAIN!
LET OUT YOUR CLUTCH, BUT DON'T RUN INTO THE...
WHAM
SCHULZ
...TREE!

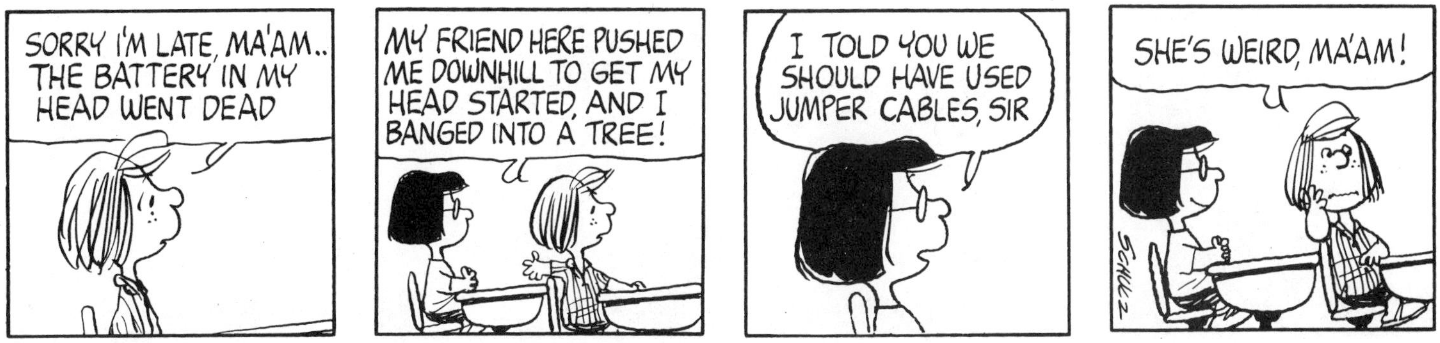
SORRY I'M LATE, MA'AM.. THE BATTERY IN MY HEAD WENT DEAD
MY FRIEND HERE PUSHED ME DOWNHILL TO GET MY HEAD STARTED, AND I BANGED INTO A TREE!
I TOLD YOU WE SHOULD HAVE USED JUMPER CABLES, SIR
SHE'S WEIRD, MA'AM!
SCHULZ

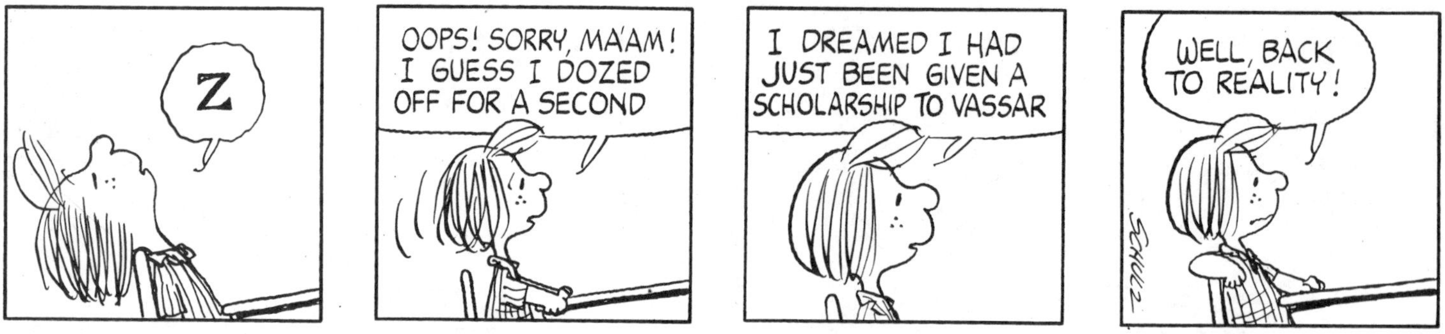
Z
OOPS! SORRY, MA'AM! I GUESS I DOZED OFF FOR A SECOND
I DREAMED I HAD JUST BEEN GIVEN A SCHOLARSHIP TO VASSAR
WELL, BACK TO REALITY!
SCHULZ

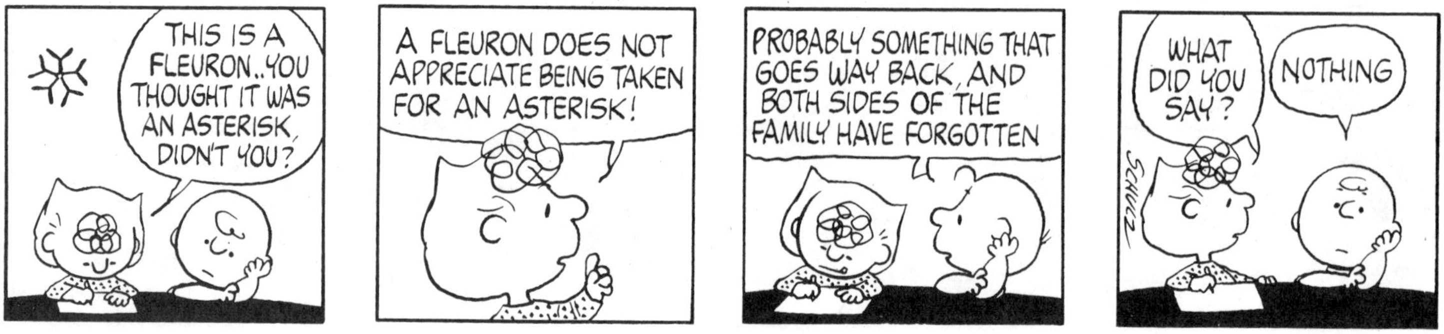
THIS IS A FLEURON..YOU THOUGHT IT WAS AN ASTERISK, DIDN'T YOU?
A FLEURON DOES NOT APPRECIATE BEING TAKEN FOR AN ASTERISK!
PROBABLY SOMETHING THAT GOES WAY BACK, AND BOTH SIDES OF THE FAMILY HAVE FORGOTTEN
WHAT DID YOU SAY?
NOTHING
SCHULZ

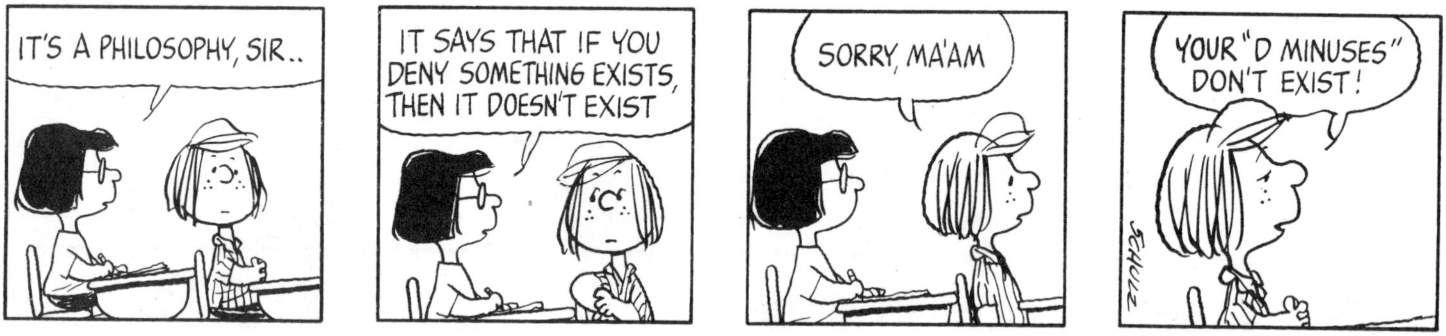
IT'S A PHILOSOPHY, SIR..
IT SAYS THAT IF YOU DENY SOMETHING EXISTS, THEN IT DOESN'T EXIST
SORRY, MA'AM
YOUR "D MINUSES" DON'T EXIST!
SCHULZ

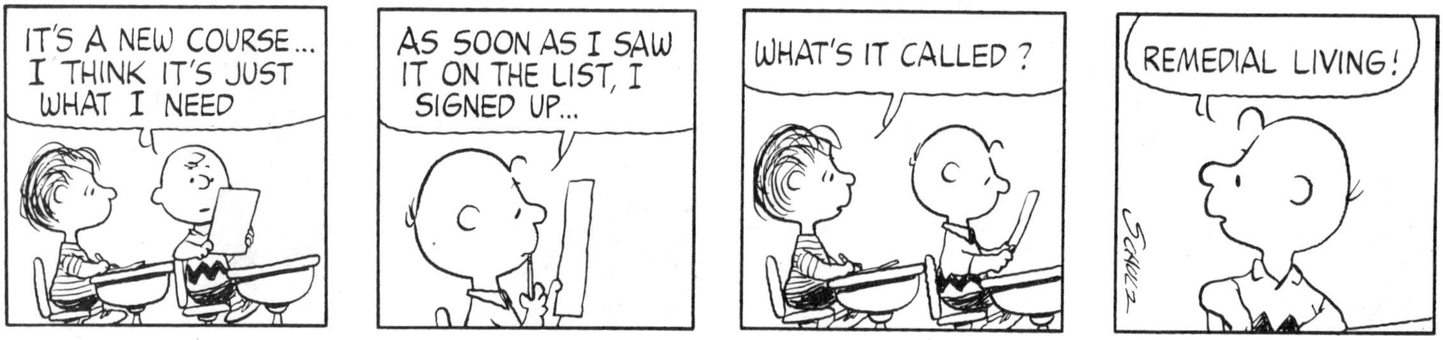
IT'S A NEW COURSE... I THINK IT'S JUST WHAT I NEED
AS SOON AS I SAW IT ON THE LIST, I SIGNED UP...
WHAT'S IT CALLED?
REMEDIAL LIVING!
SCHULZ

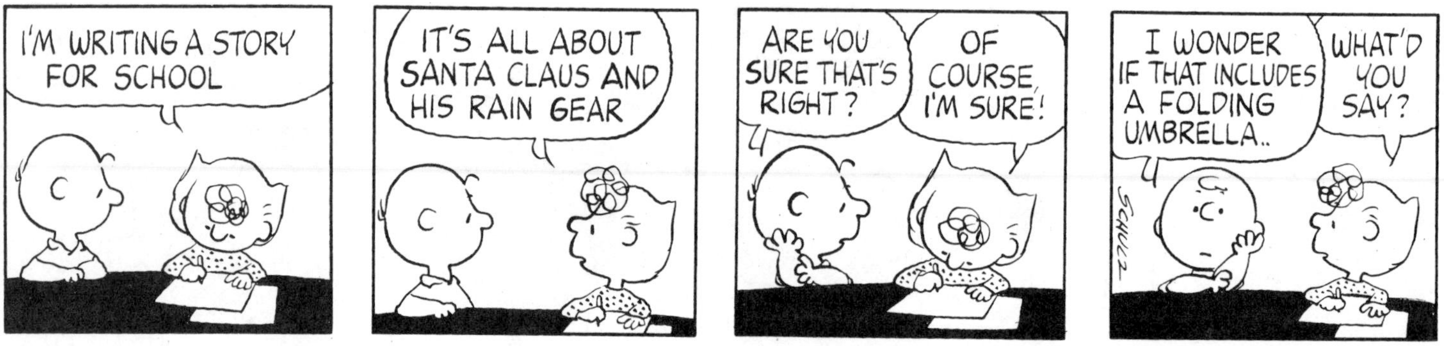
I'M WRITING A STORY FOR SCHOOL
IT'S ALL ABOUT SANTA CLAUS AND HIS RAIN GEAR
ARE YOU SURE THAT'S RIGHT?
OF COURSE, I'M SURE!
I WONDER IF THAT INCLUDES A FOLDING UMBRELLA..
WHAT'D YOU SAY?
SCHULZ

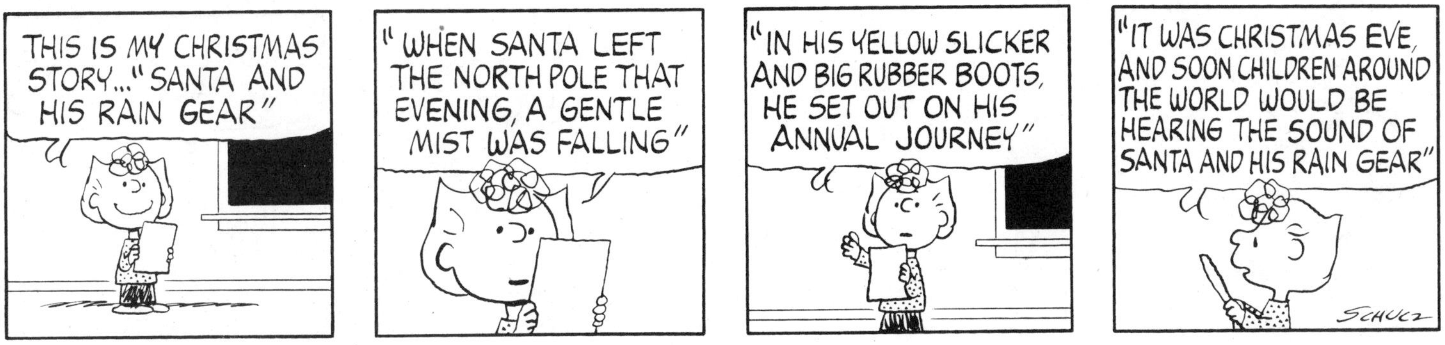
THIS IS MY CHRISTMAS STORY..." SANTA AND HIS RAIN GEAR"
" WHEN SANTA LEFT THE NORTH POLE THAT EVENING, A GENTLE MIST WAS FALLING"
"IN HIS YELLOW SLICKER AND BIG RUBBER BOOTS, HE SET OUT ON HIS ANNUAL JOURNEY"
"IT WAS CHRISTMAS EVE, AND SOON CHILDREN AROUND THE WORLD WOULD BE HEARING THE SOUND OF SANTA AND HIS RAIN GEAR"

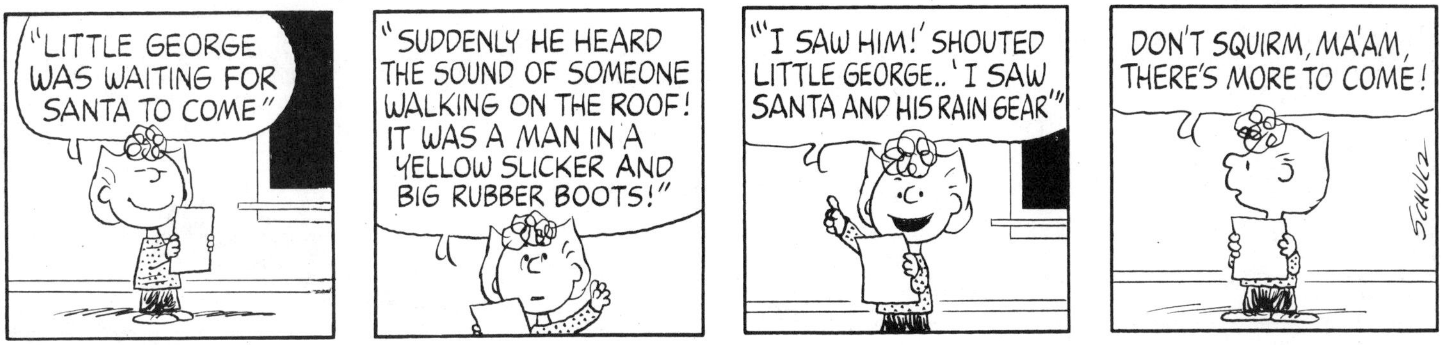
"LITTLE GEORGE WAS WAITING FOR SANTA TO COME"
"SUDDENLY HE HEARD THE SOUND OF SOMEONE WALKING ON THE ROOF! IT WAS A MAN IN A YELLOW SLICKER AND BIG RUBBER BOOTS!"
"'I SAW HIM!' SHOUTED LITTLE GEORGE..'I SAW SANTA AND HIS RAIN GEAR'"
DON'T SQUIRM, MA'AM, THERE'S MORE TO COME!

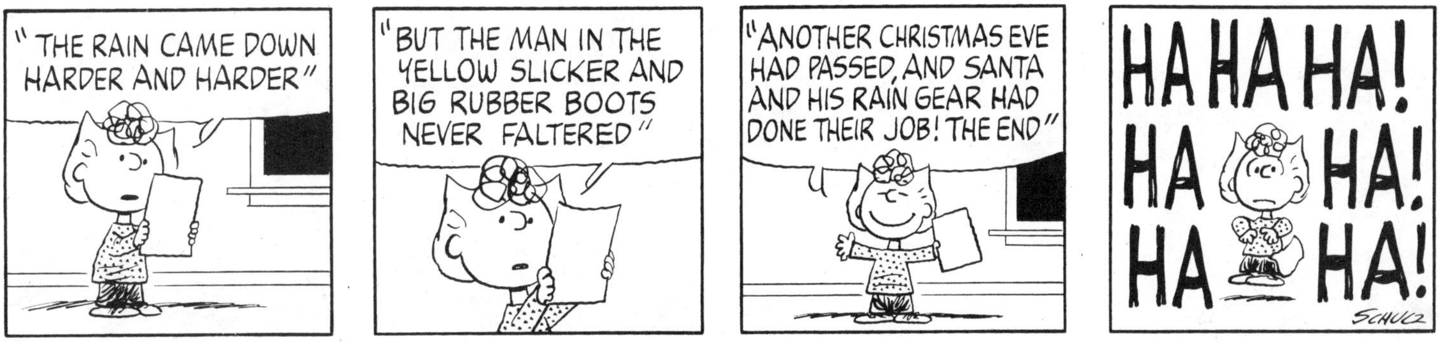
" THE RAIN CAME DOWN HARDER AND HARDER"
"BUT THE MAN IN THE YELLOW SLICKER AND BIG RUBBER BOOTS NEVER FALTERED"
"ANOTHER CHRISTMAS EVE HAD PASSED, AND SANTA AND HIS RAIN GEAR HAD DONE THEIR JOB! THE END"
HA HA HA! HA HA! HA HA!

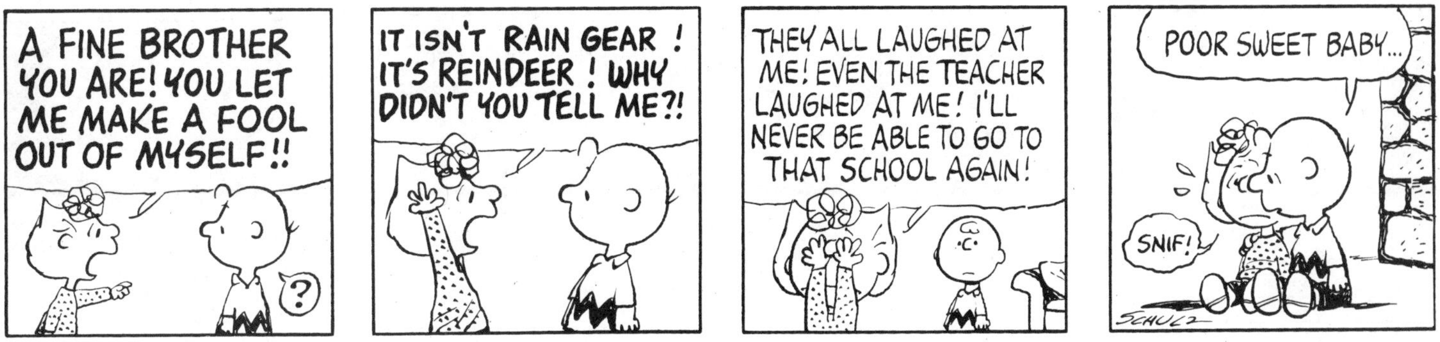
A FINE BROTHER YOU ARE! YOU LET ME MAKE A FOOL OUT OF MYSELF!!
?
IT ISN'T RAIN GEAR! IT'S REINDEER! WHY DIDN'T YOU TELL ME?!
THEY ALL LAUGHED AT ME! EVEN THE TEACHER LAUGHED AT ME! I'LL NEVER BE ABLE TO GO TO THAT SCHOOL AGAIN!
POOR SWEET BABY...
SNIF!

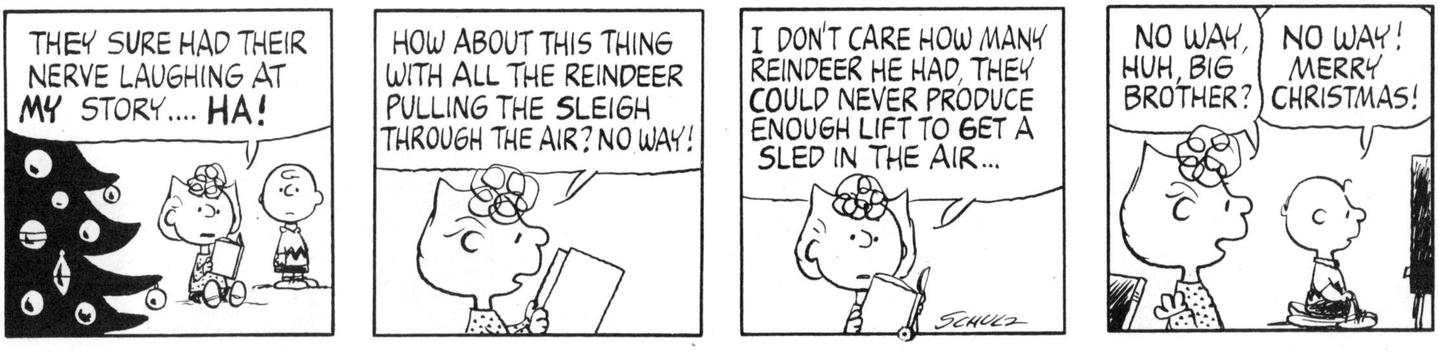
THEY SURE HAD THEIR NERVE LAUGHING AT MY STORY.... HA!
HOW ABOUT THIS THING WITH ALL THE REINDEER PULLING THE SLEIGH THROUGH THE AIR? NO WAY!
I DON'T CARE HOW MANY REINDEER HE HAD, THEY COULD NEVER PRODUCE ENOUGH LIFT TO GET A SLED IN THE AIR...
NO WAY, HUH, BIG BROTHER?
NO WAY! MERRY CHRISTMAS!

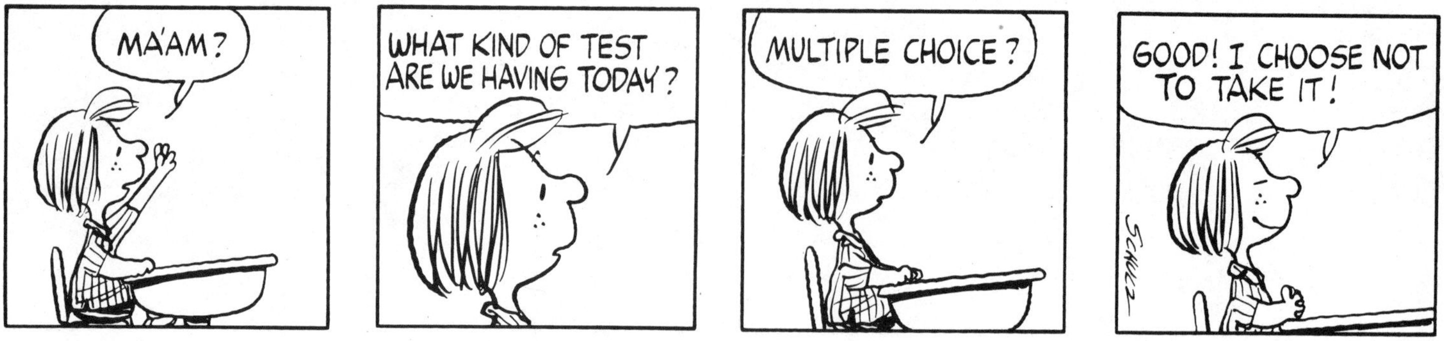
MA'AM?
WHAT KIND OF TEST ARE WE HAVING TODAY?
MULTIPLE CHOICE?
GOOD! I CHOOSE NOT TO TAKE IT!
SCHULZ

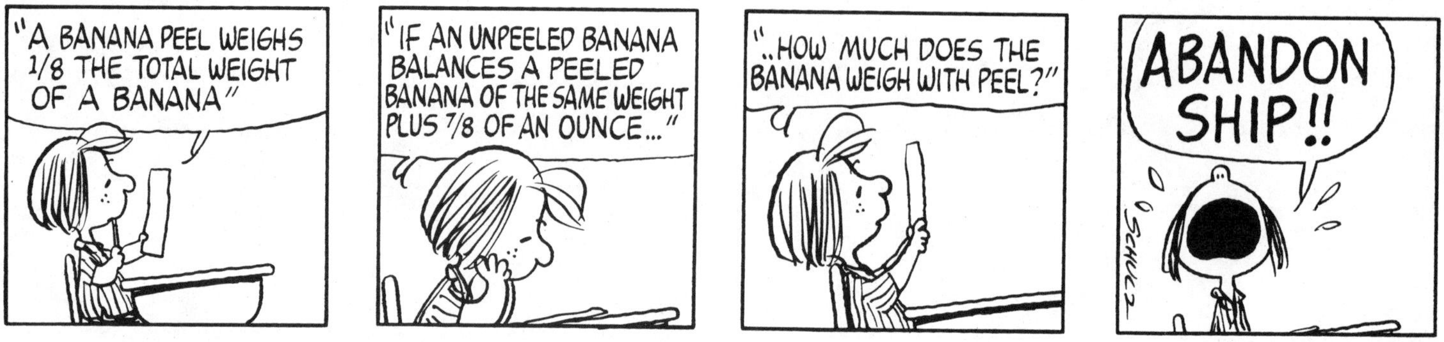
"A BANANA PEEL WEIGHS 1/8 THE TOTAL WEIGHT OF A BANANA"
"IF AN UNPEELED BANANA BALANCES A PEELED BANANA OF THE SAME WEIGHT PLUS 7/8 OF AN OUNCE..."
"..HOW MUCH DOES THE BANANA WEIGH WITH PEEL?"
ABANDON SHIP!!
SCHULZ

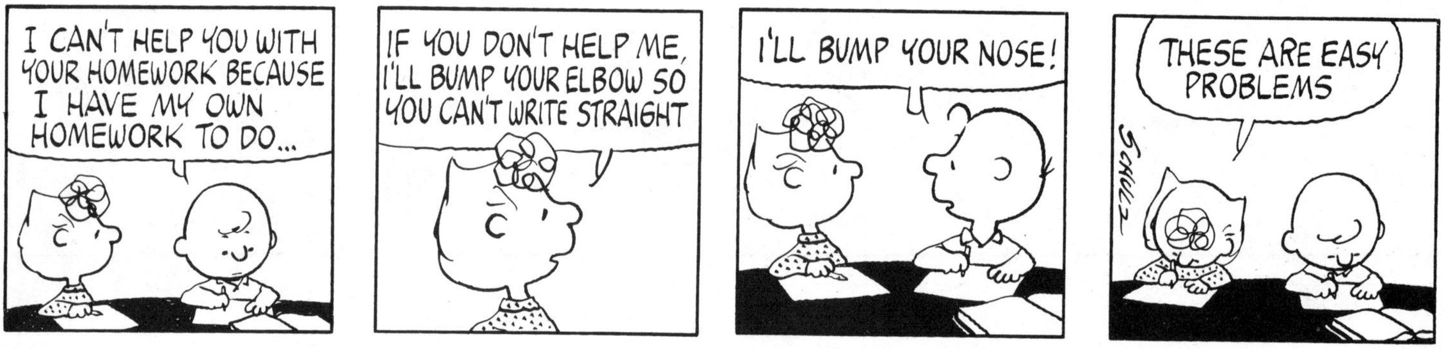
I CAN'T HELP YOU WITH YOUR HOMEWORK BECAUSE I HAVE MY OWN HOMEWORK TO DO...
IF YOU DON'T HELP ME, I'LL BUMP YOUR ELBOW SO YOU CAN'T WRITE STRAIGHT
I'LL BUMP YOUR NOSE!
THESE ARE EASY PROBLEMS
SCHULZ

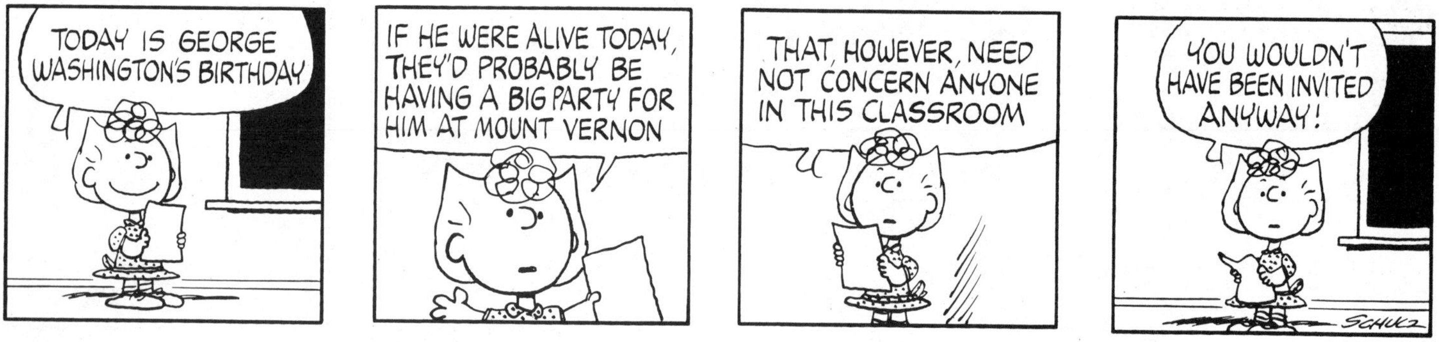
TODAY IS GEORGE WASHINGTON'S BIRTHDAY
IF HE WERE ALIVE TODAY, THEY'D PROBABLY BE HAVING A BIG PARTY FOR HIM AT MOUNT VERNON
THAT, HOWEVER, NEED NOT CONCERN ANYONE IN THIS CLASSROOM
YOU WOULDN'T HAVE BEEN INVITED ANYWAY!
SCHULZ

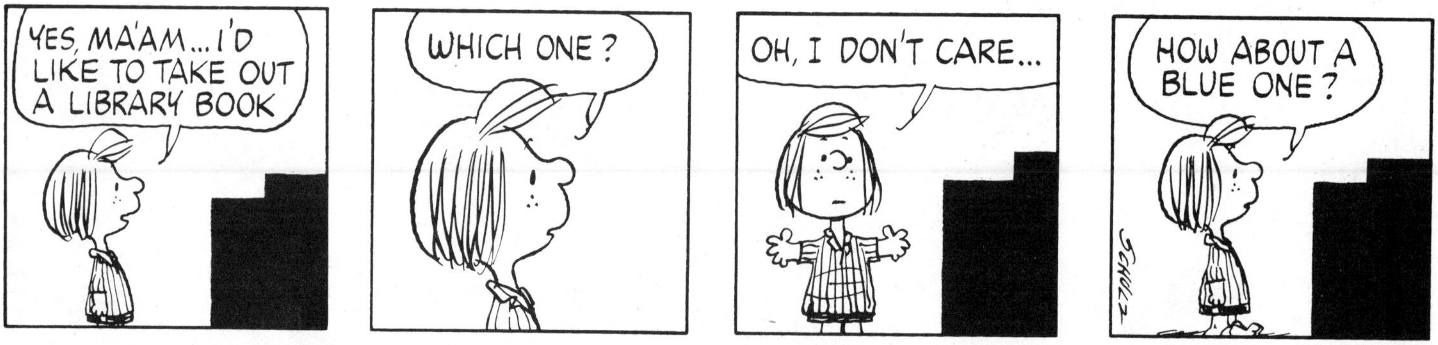
YES, MA'AM... I'D LIKE TO TAKE OUT A LIBRARY BOOK
WHICH ONE?
OH, I DON'T CARE...
HOW ABOUT A BLUE ONE?
SCHULZ

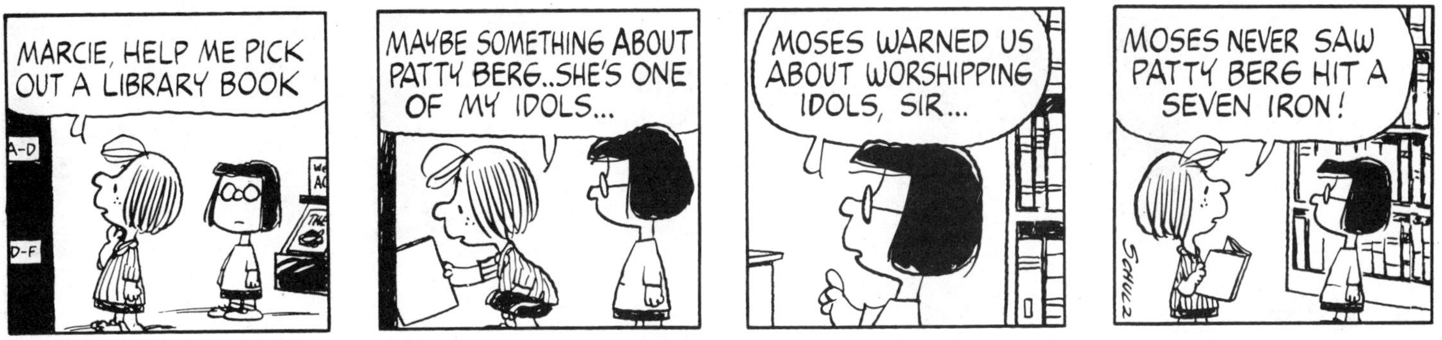
MARCIE, HELP ME PICK OUT A LIBRARY BOOK
A-D
D-F
MAYBE SOMETHING ABOUT PATTY BERG..SHE'S ONE OF MY IDOLS...
MOSES WARNED US ABOUT WORSHIPPING IDOLS, SIR...
MOSES NEVER SAW PATTY BERG HIT A SEVEN IRON!
SCHULZ

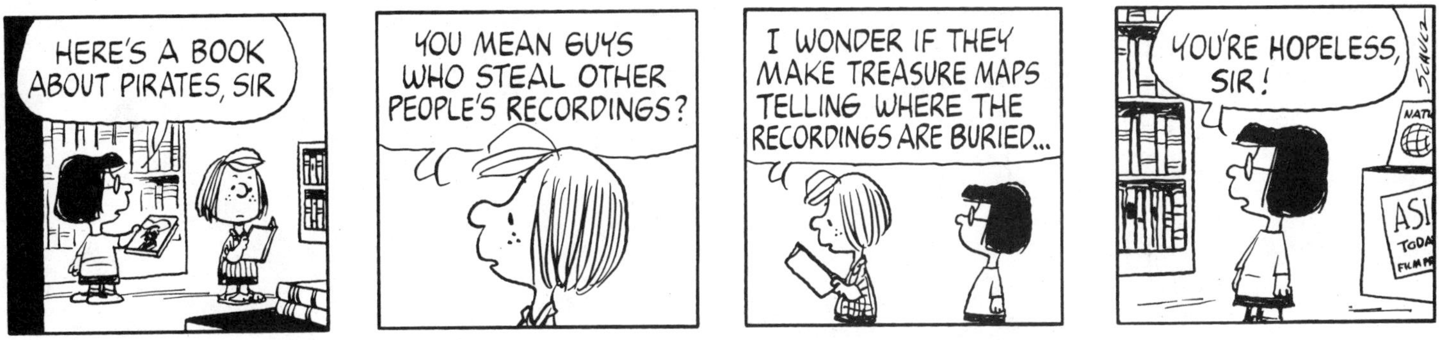
HERE'S A BOOK ABOUT PIRATES, SIR
YOU MEAN GUYS WHO STEAL OTHER PEOPLE'S RECORDINGS?
I WONDER IF THEY MAKE TREASURE MAPS TELLING WHERE THE RECORDINGS ARE BURIED...
YOU'RE HOPELESS, SIR!
SCHULZ

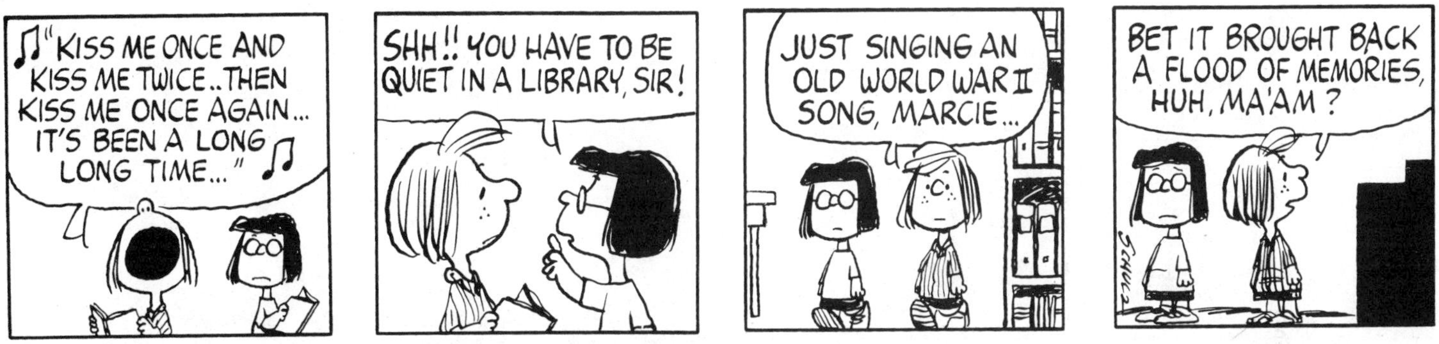
"KISS ME ONCE AND KISS ME TWICE..THEN KISS ME ONCE AGAIN... IT'S BEEN A LONG LONG TIME..."
SHH!! YOU HAVE TO BE QUIET IN A LIBRARY, SIR!
JUST SINGING AN OLD WORLD WAR II SONG, MARCIE...
BET IT BROUGHT BACK A FLOOD OF MEMORIES, HUH, MA'AM?
SCHULZ

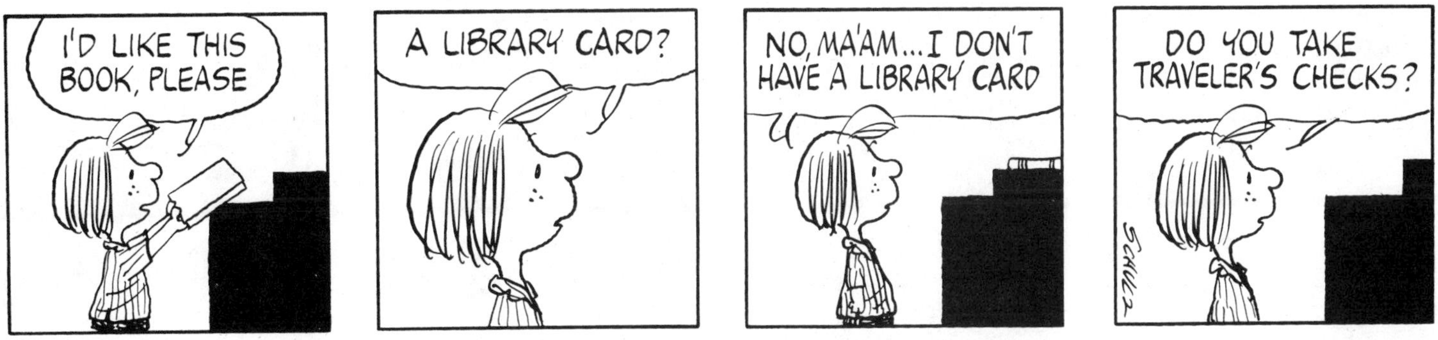
I'D LIKE THIS BOOK, PLEASE
A LIBRARY CARD?
NO, MA'AM...I DON'T HAVE A LIBRARY CARD
DO YOU TAKE TRAVELER'S CHECKS?
SCHULZ

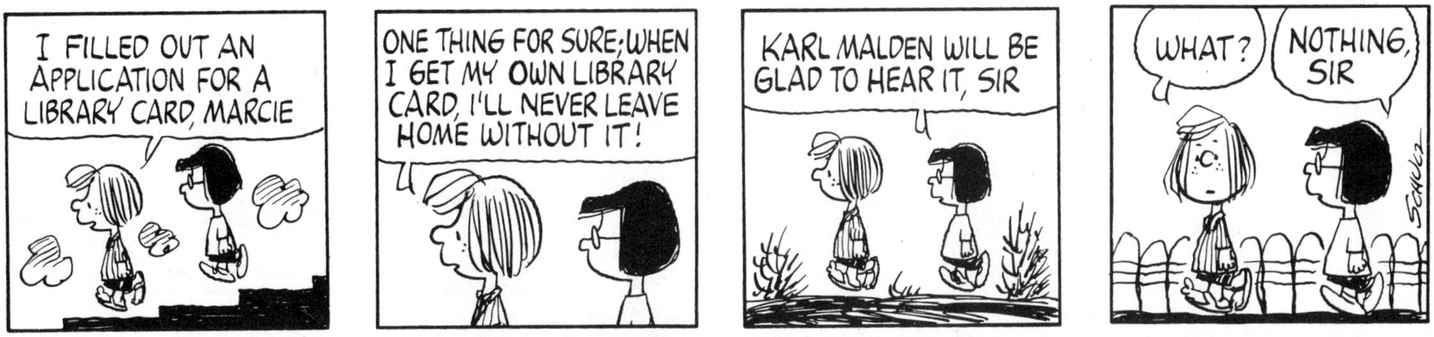
I FILLED OUT AN APPLICATION FOR A LIBRARY CARD, MARCIE
ONE THING FOR SURE; WHEN I GET MY OWN LIBRARY CARD, I'LL NEVER LEAVE HOME WITHOUT IT!
KARL MALDEN WILL BE GLAD TO HEAR IT, SIR
WHAT?
NOTHING, SIR
SCHULZ

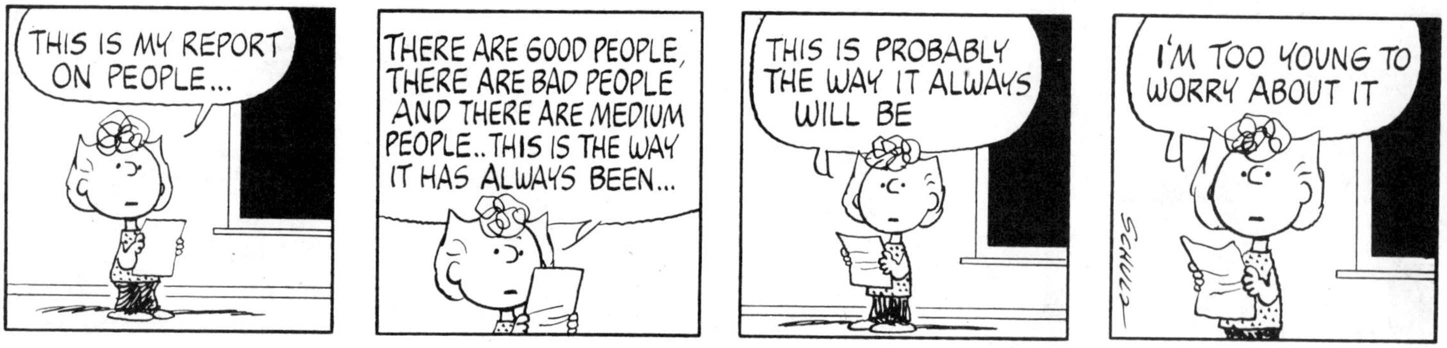
THIS IS MY REPORT ON PEOPLE...
THERE ARE GOOD PEOPLE, THERE ARE BAD PEOPLE AND THERE ARE MEDIUM PEOPLE.. THIS IS THE WAY IT HAS ALWAYS BEEN...
THIS IS PROBABLY THE WAY IT ALWAYS WILL BE
I'M TOO YOUNG TO WORRY ABOUT IT
SCHULZ

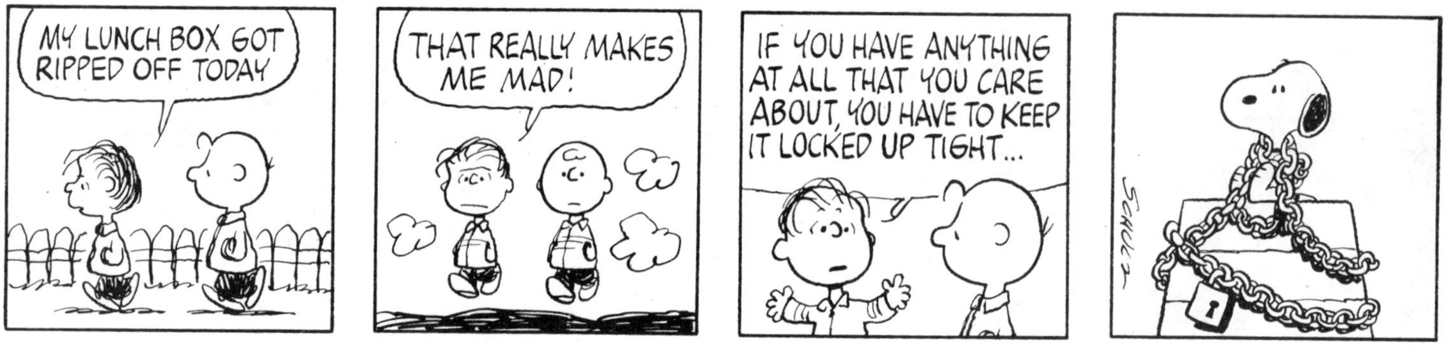
MY LUNCH BOX GOT RIPPED OFF TODAY
THAT REALLY MAKES ME MAD!
IF YOU HAVE ANYTHING AT ALL THAT YOU CARE ABOUT, YOU HAVE TO KEEP IT LOCKED UP TIGHT...
SCHULZ

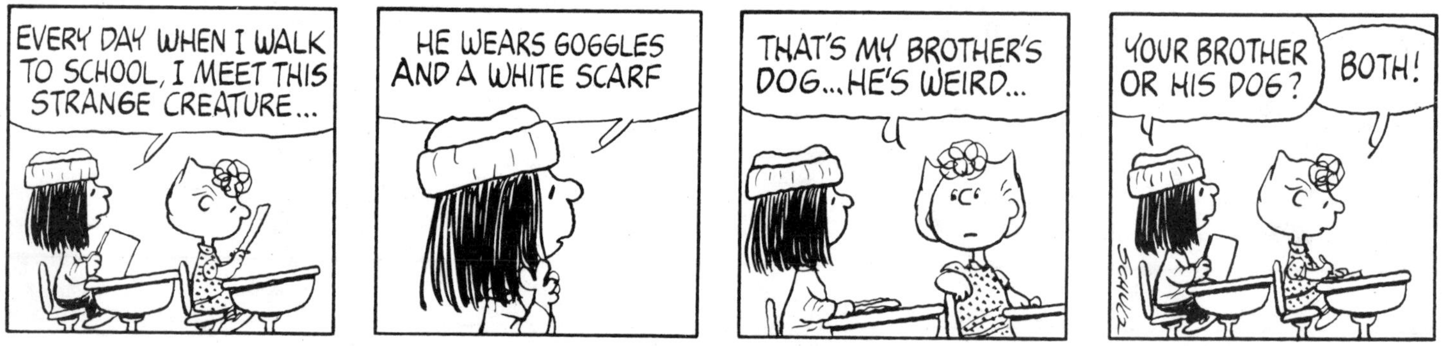
EVERY DAY WHEN I WALK TO SCHOOL, I MEET THIS STRANGE CREATURE...
HE WEARS GOGGLES AND A WHITE SCARF
THAT'S MY BROTHER'S DOG...HE'S WEIRD...
YOUR BROTHER OR HIS DOG?
BOTH!
SCHULZ

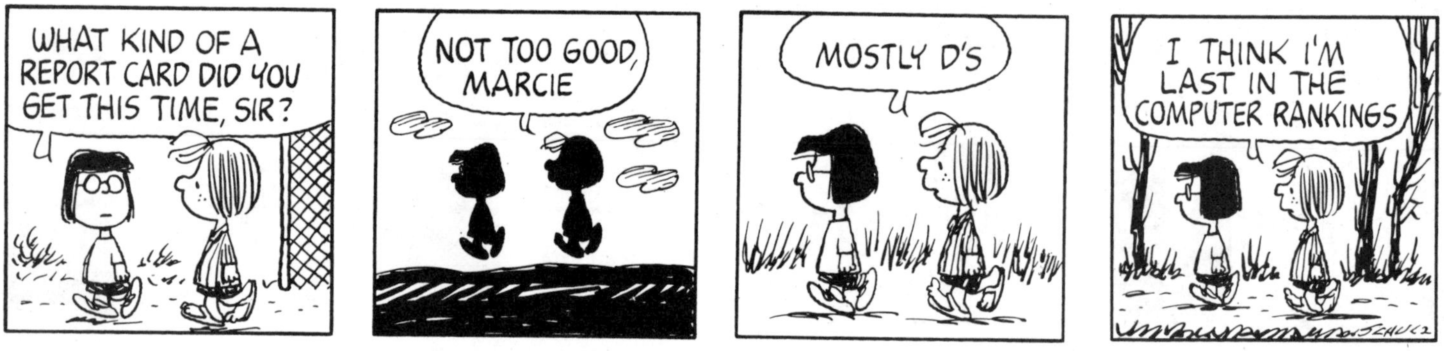
WHAT KIND OF A REPORT CARD DID YOU GET THIS TIME, SIR?
NOT TOO GOOD, MARCIE
MOSTLY D'S
I THINK I'M LAST IN THE COMPUTER RANKINGS
SCHULZ

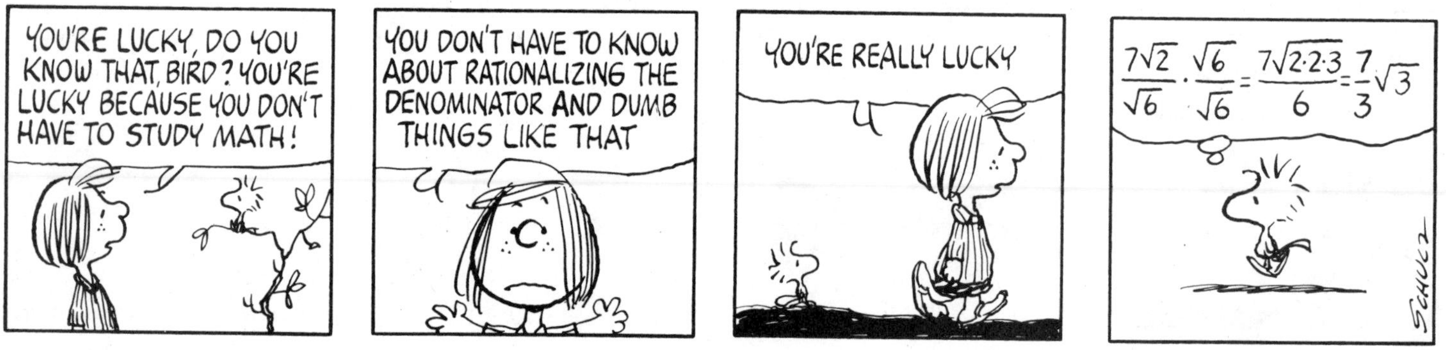
YOU'RE LUCKY, DO YOU KNOW THAT, BIRD? YOU'RE LUCKY BECAUSE YOU DON'T HAVE TO STUDY MATH!
YOU DON'T HAVE TO KNOW ABOUT RATIONALIZING THE DENOMINATOR AND DUMB THINGS LIKE THAT
YOU'RE REALLY LUCKY
$\frac{7\sqrt{2}}{\sqrt{6}} \cdot \frac{\sqrt{6}}{\sqrt{6}} = \frac{7\sqrt{2 \cdot 2 \cdot 3}}{6} = \frac{7}{3}\sqrt{3}$
SCHULZ

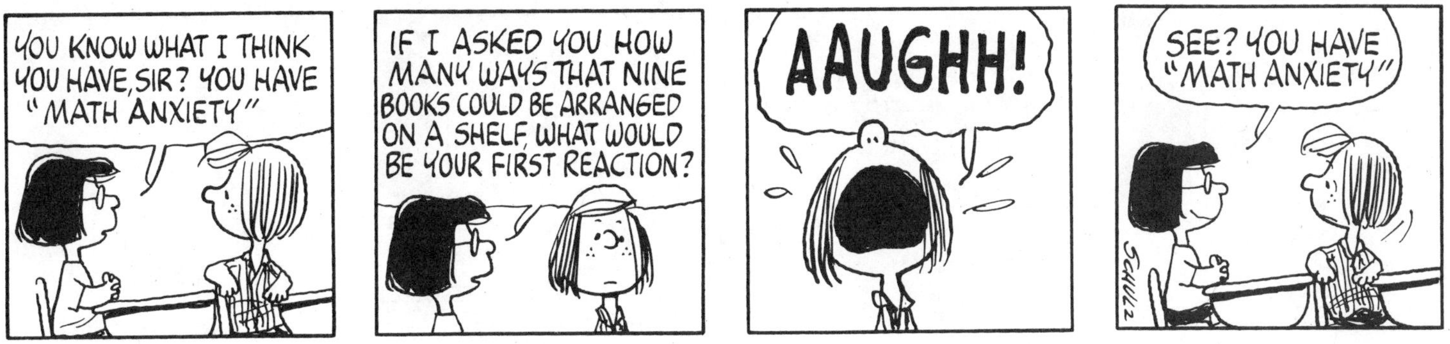
YOU KNOW WHAT I THINK YOU HAVE, SIR? YOU HAVE "MATH ANXIETY"
IF I ASKED YOU HOW MANY WAYS THAT NINE BOOKS COULD BE ARRANGED ON A SHELF, WHAT WOULD BE YOUR FIRST REACTION?
AAUGHH!
SEE? YOU HAVE "MATH ANXIETY"
SCHULZ

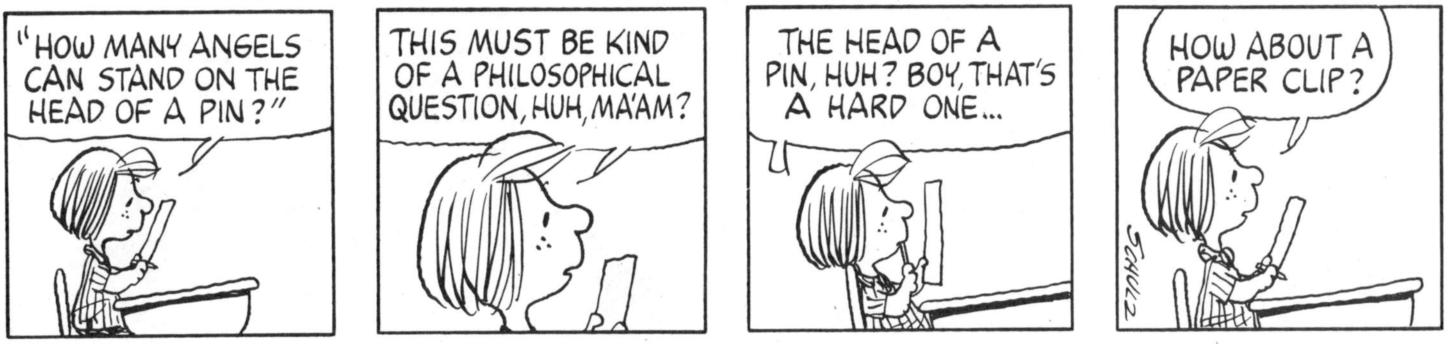
"HOW MANY ANGELS CAN STAND ON THE HEAD OF A PIN?"
THIS MUST BE KIND OF A PHILOSOPHICAL QUESTION, HUH, MA'AM?
THE HEAD OF A PIN, HUH? BOY, THAT'S A HARD ONE...
HOW ABOUT A PAPER CLIP?
SCHULZ

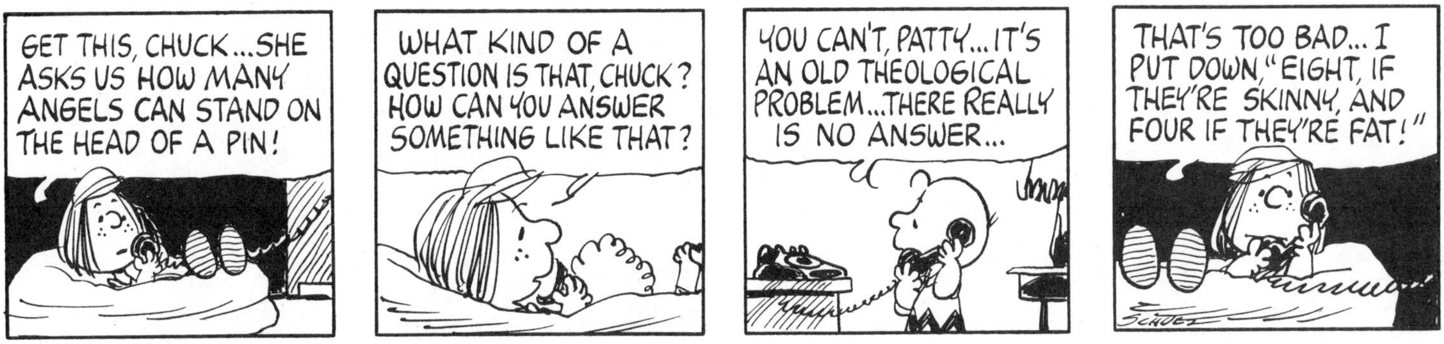
GET THIS, CHUCK...SHE ASKS US HOW MANY ANGELS CAN STAND ON THE HEAD OF A PIN!
WHAT KIND OF A QUESTION IS THAT, CHUCK? HOW CAN YOU ANSWER SOMETHING LIKE THAT?
YOU CAN'T, PATTY...IT'S AN OLD THEOLOGICAL PROBLEM...THERE REALLY IS NO ANSWER...
THAT'S TOO BAD... I PUT DOWN, "EIGHT, IF THEY'RE SKINNY, AND FOUR IF THEY'RE FAT!"
SCHULZ

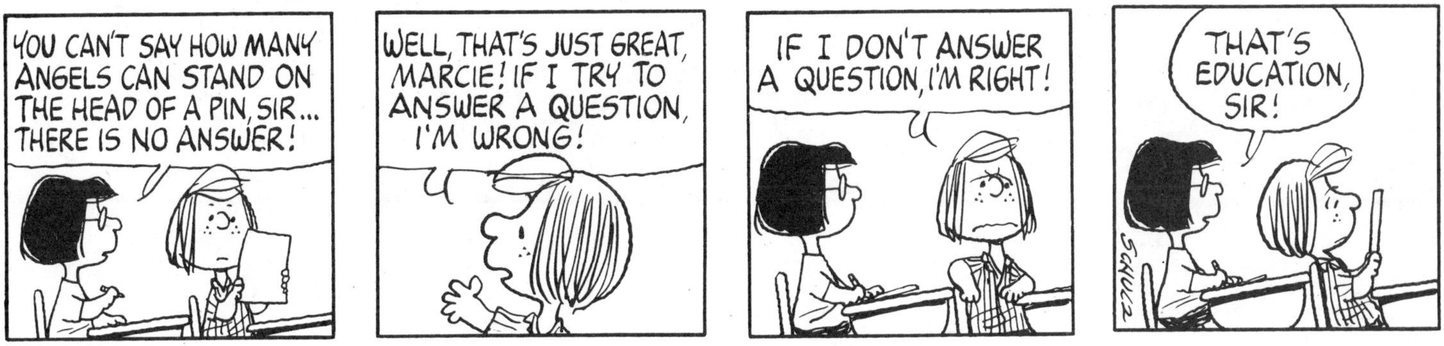
YOU CAN'T SAY HOW MANY ANGELS CAN STAND ON THE HEAD OF A PIN, SIR... THERE IS NO ANSWER!
WELL, THAT'S JUST GREAT, MARCIE! IF I TRY TO ANSWER A QUESTION, I'M WRONG!
IF I DON'T ANSWER A QUESTION, I'M RIGHT!
THAT'S EDUCATION, SIR!
SCHULZ

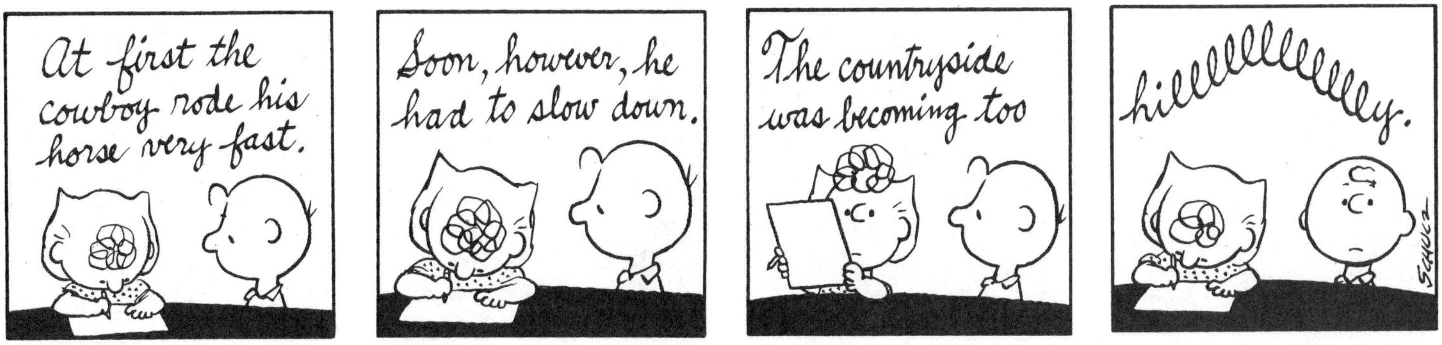
At first the cowboy rode his horse very fast.
Soon, however, he had to slow down.
The countryside was becoming too
hilllllllllllly.
SCHULZ

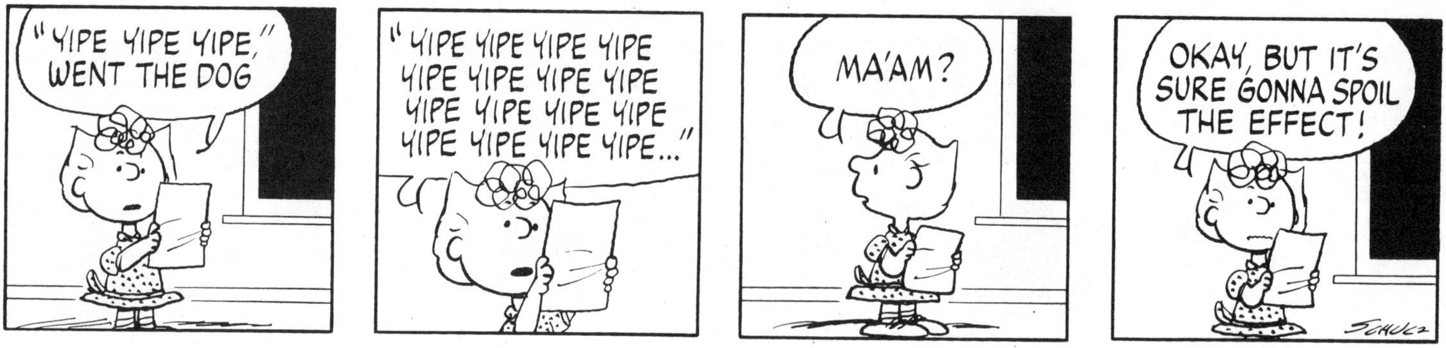
"YIPE YIPE YIPE," WENT THE DOG
"YIPE YIPE YIPE YIPE YIPE YIPE YIPE YIPE YIPE YIPE YIPE YIPE YIPE YIPE YIPE YIPE..."
MA'AM?
OKAY, BUT IT'S SURE GONNA SPOIL THE EFFECT!
SCHULZ

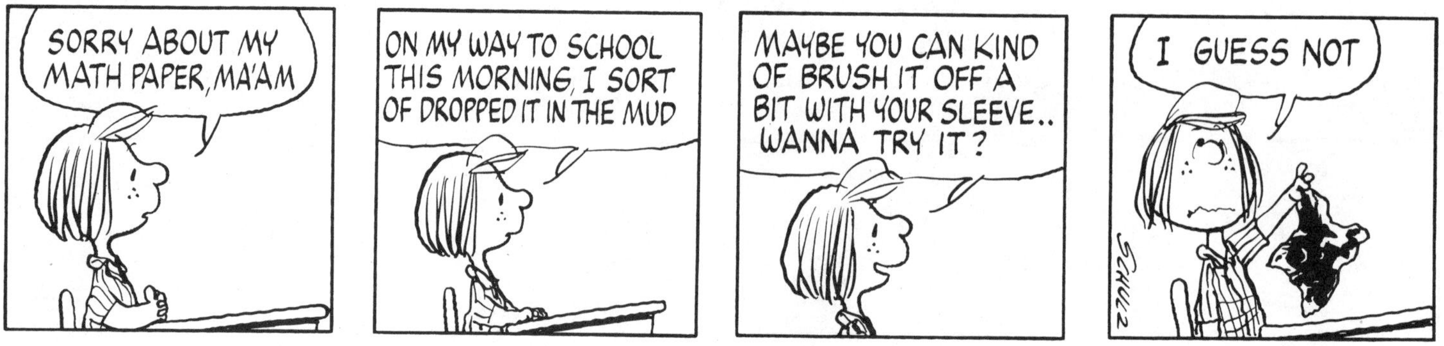
SORRY ABOUT MY MATH PAPER, MA'AM
ON MY WAY TO SCHOOL THIS MORNING, I SORT OF DROPPED IT IN THE MUD
MAYBE YOU CAN KIND OF BRUSH IT OFF A BIT WITH YOUR SLEEVE.. WANNA TRY IT?
I GUESS NOT
SCHULZ

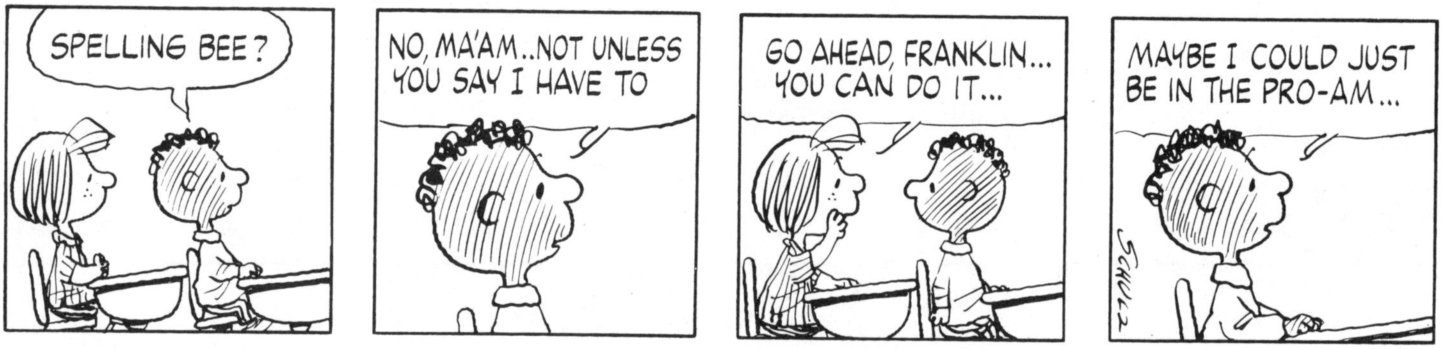
SPELLING BEE?
NO, MA'AM..NOT UNLESS YOU SAY I HAVE TO
GO AHEAD, FRANKLIN... YOU CAN DO IT...
MAYBE I COULD JUST BE IN THE PRO-AM...
SCHULZ

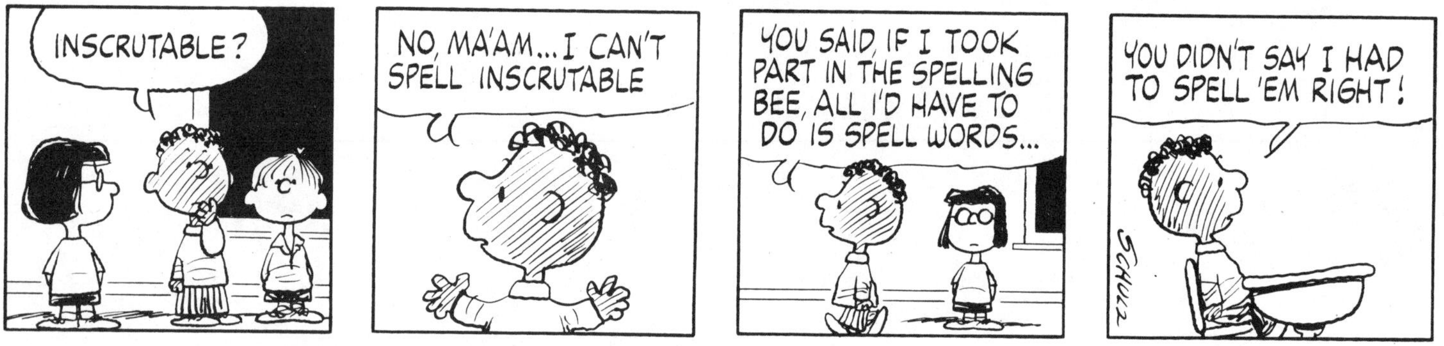
INSCRUTABLE?
NO, MA'AM...I CAN'T SPELL INSCRUTABLE
YOU SAID, IF I TOOK PART IN THE SPELLING BEE, ALL I'D HAVE TO DO IS SPELL WORDS...
YOU DIDN'T SAY I HAD TO SPELL 'EM RIGHT!
SCHULZ

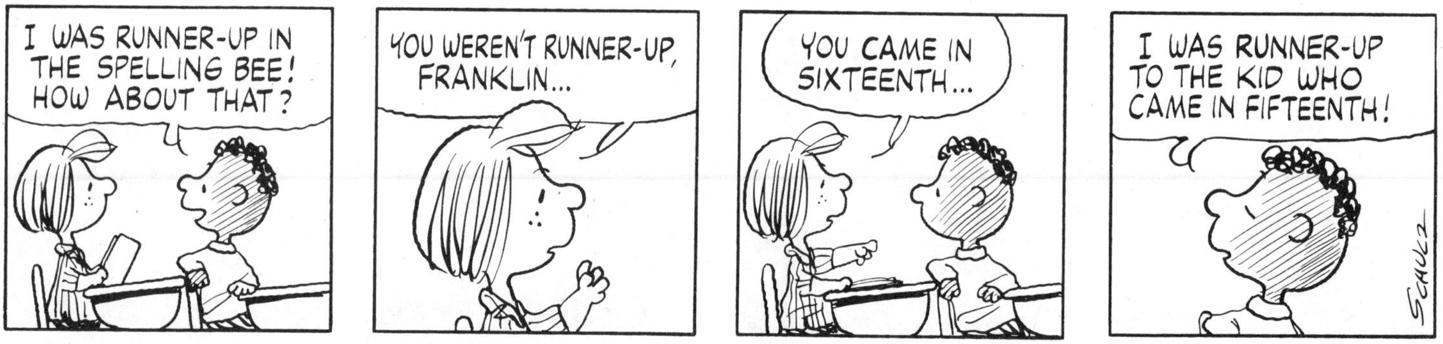
I WAS RUNNER-UP IN THE SPELLING BEE! HOW ABOUT THAT?
YOU WEREN'T RUNNER-UP, FRANKLIN...
YOU CAME IN SIXTEENTH...
I WAS RUNNER-UP TO THE KID WHO CAME IN FIFTEENTH!
SCHULZ

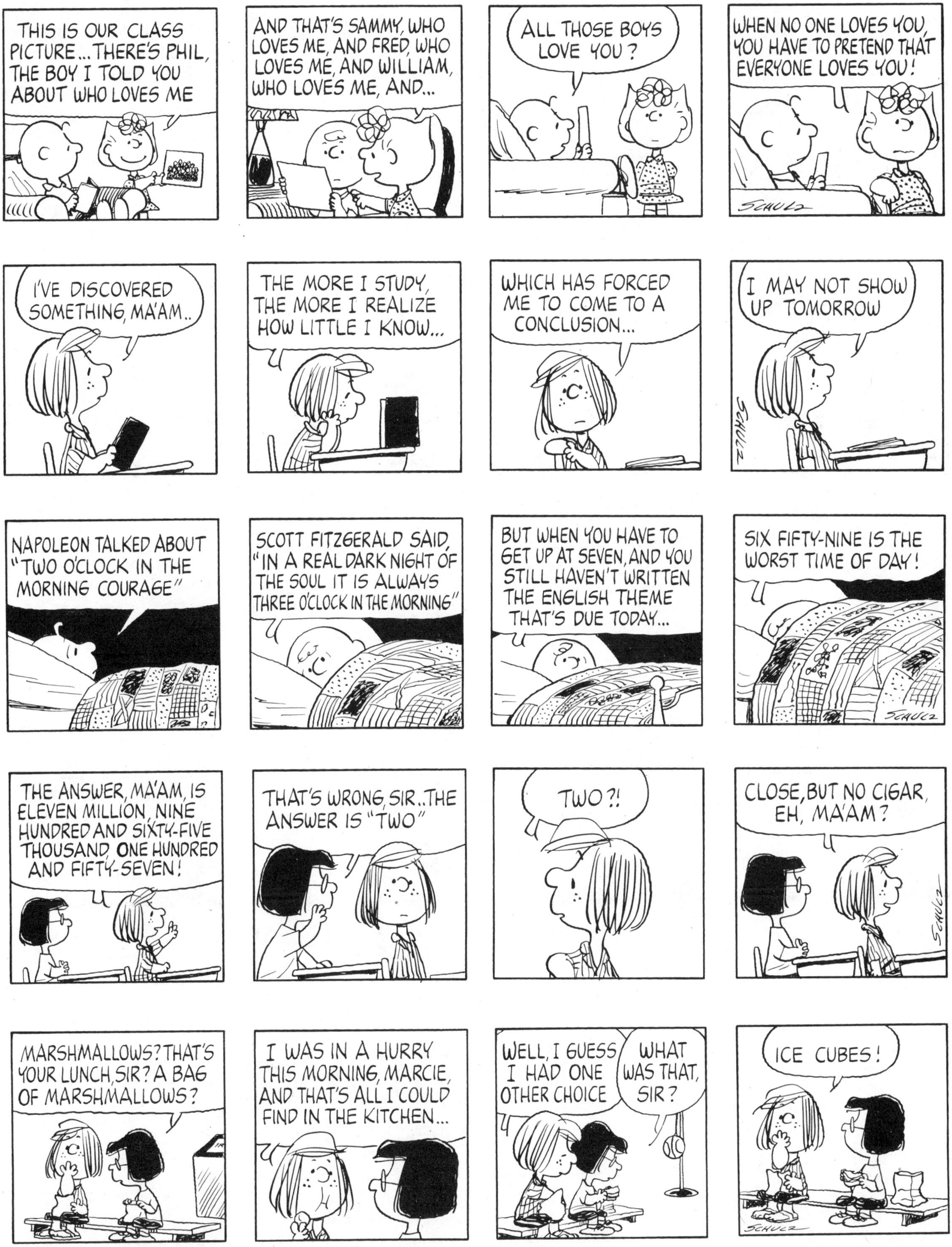
THIS IS OUR CLASS PICTURE...THERE'S PHIL, THE BOY I TOLD YOU ABOUT WHO LOVES ME
AND THAT'S SAMMY, WHO LOVES ME, AND FRED, WHO LOVES ME, AND WILLIAM, WHO LOVES ME, AND...
ALL THOSE BOYS LOVE YOU?
WHEN NO ONE LOVES YOU, YOU HAVE TO PRETEND THAT EVERYONE LOVES YOU!
SCHULZ
I'VE DISCOVERED SOMETHING, MA'AM..
THE MORE I STUDY, THE MORE I REALIZE HOW LITTLE I KNOW...
WHICH HAS FORCED ME TO COME TO A CONCLUSION...
I MAY NOT SHOW UP TOMORROW
SCHULZ
NAPOLEON TALKED ABOUT "TWO O'CLOCK IN THE MORNING COURAGE"
SCOTT FITZGERALD SAID, "IN A REAL DARK NIGHT OF THE SOUL IT IS ALWAYS THREE O'CLOCK IN THE MORNING"
BUT WHEN YOU HAVE TO GET UP AT SEVEN, AND YOU STILL HAVEN'T WRITTEN THE ENGLISH THEME THAT'S DUE TODAY...
SIX FIFTY-NINE IS THE WORST TIME OF DAY!
SCHULZ
THE ANSWER, MA'AM, IS ELEVEN MILLION, NINE HUNDRED AND SIXTY-FIVE THOUSAND, ONE HUNDRED AND FIFTY-SEVEN!
THAT'S WRONG, SIR..THE ANSWER IS "TWO"
TWO?!
CLOSE, BUT NO CIGAR, EH, MA'AM?
SCHULZ
MARSHMALLOWS? THAT'S YOUR LUNCH, SIR? A BAG OF MARSHMALLOWS?
I WAS IN A HURRY THIS MORNING, MARCIE, AND THAT'S ALL I COULD FIND IN THE KITCHEN...
WELL, I GUESS I HAD ONE OTHER CHOICE
WHAT WAS THAT, SIR?
ICE CUBES!
SCHULZ

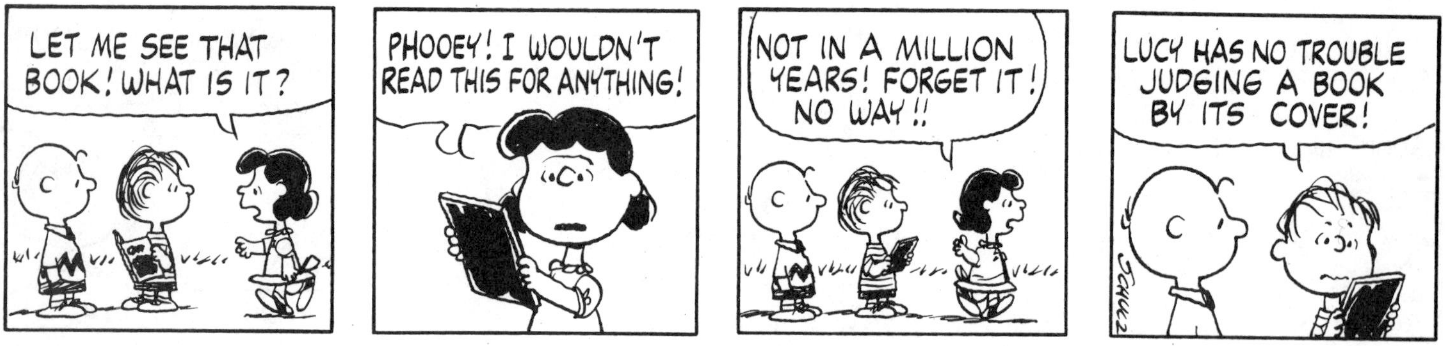
LET ME SEE THAT BOOK! WHAT IS IT?
PHOOEY! I WOULDN'T READ THIS FOR ANYTHING!
NOT IN A MILLION YEARS! FORGET IT! NO WAY!!
LUCY HAS NO TROUBLE JUDGING A BOOK BY ITS COVER!
SCHULZ

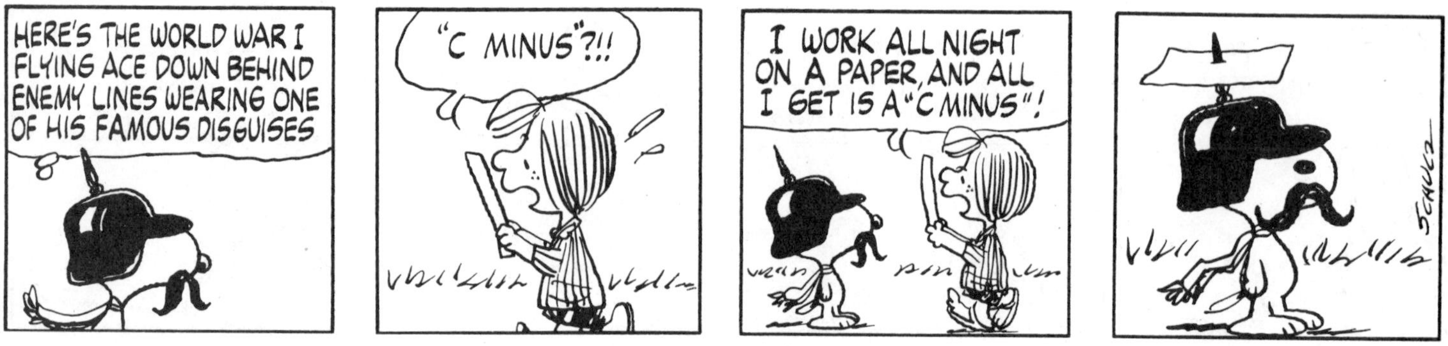
HERE'S THE WORLD WAR I FLYING ACE DOWN BEHIND ENEMY LINES WEARING ONE OF HIS FAMOUS DISGUISES
"C MINUS"?!!
I WORK ALL NIGHT ON A PAPER, AND ALL I GET IS A "C MINUS"!
SCHULZ

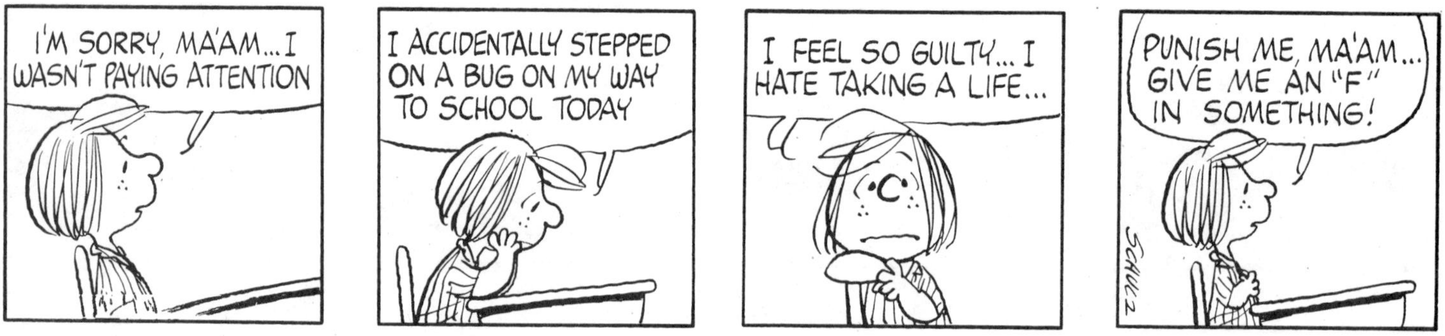
I'M SORRY, MA'AM... I WASN'T PAYING ATTENTION
I ACCIDENTALLY STEPPED ON A BUG ON MY WAY TO SCHOOL TODAY
I FEEL SO GUILTY... I HATE TAKING A LIFE...
PUNISH ME, MA'AM... GIVE ME AN "F" IN SOMETHING!
SCHULZ

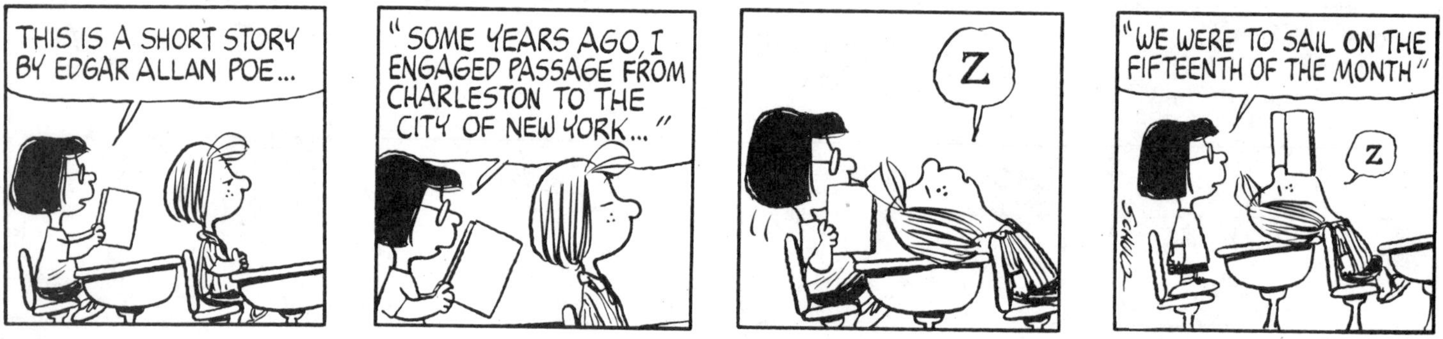
THIS IS A SHORT STORY BY EDGAR ALLAN POE...
"SOME YEARS AGO, I ENGAGED PASSAGE FROM CHARLESTON TO THE CITY OF NEW YORK..."
Z
"WE WERE TO SAIL ON THE FIFTEENTH OF THE MONTH"
Z
SCHULZ

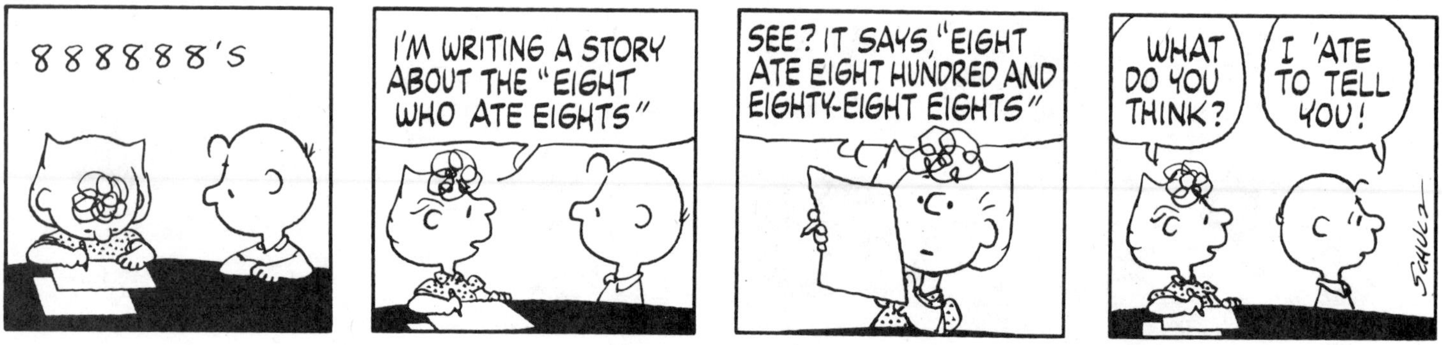
888888'S
I'M WRITING A STORY ABOUT THE "EIGHT WHO ATE EIGHTS"
SEE? IT SAYS, "EIGHT ATE EIGHT HUNDRED AND EIGHTY-EIGHT EIGHTS"
WHAT DO YOU THINK?
I 'ATE TO TELL YOU!
SCHULZ

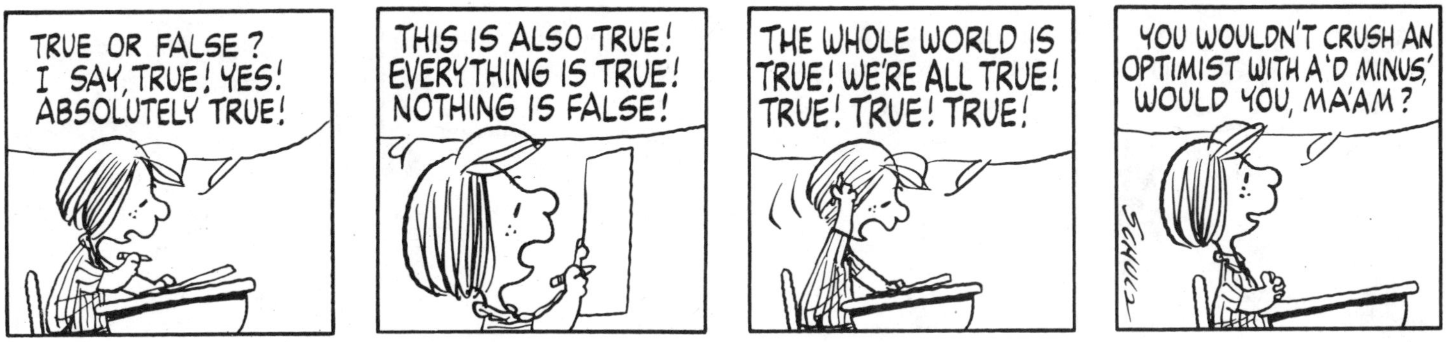
TRUE OR FALSE? I SAY, TRUE! YES! ABSOLUTELY TRUE!
THIS IS ALSO TRUE! EVERYTHING IS TRUE! NOTHING IS FALSE!
THE WHOLE WORLD IS TRUE! WE'RE ALL TRUE! TRUE! TRUE! TRUE!
YOU WOULDN'T CRUSH AN OPTIMIST WITH A 'D MINUS' WOULD YOU, MA'AM?
SCHULZ

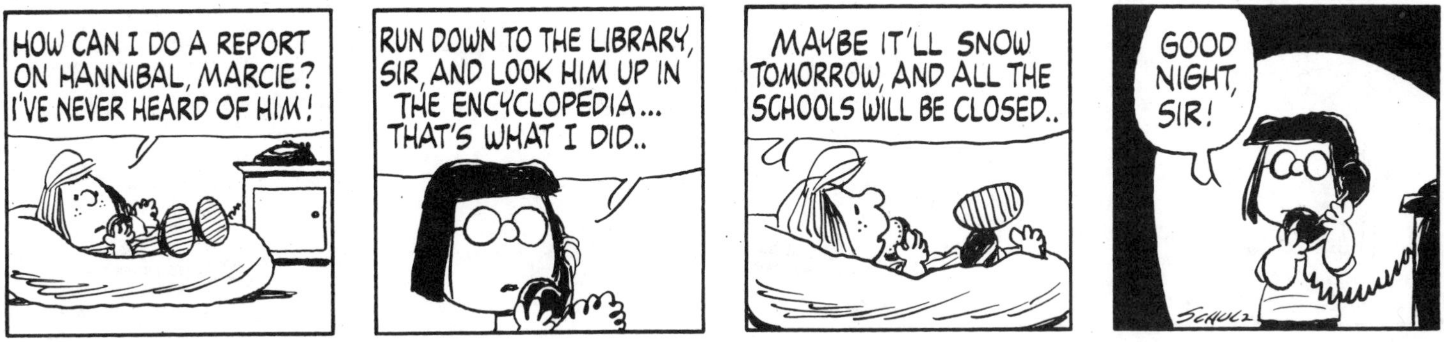
HOW CAN I DO A REPORT ON HANNIBAL, MARCIE? I'VE NEVER HEARD OF HIM!
RUN DOWN TO THE LIBRARY, SIR, AND LOOK HIM UP IN THE ENCYCLOPEDIA... THAT'S WHAT I DID..
MAYBE IT'LL SNOW TOMORROW, AND ALL THE SCHOOLS WILL BE CLOSED..
GOOD NIGHT, SIR!
SCHULZ

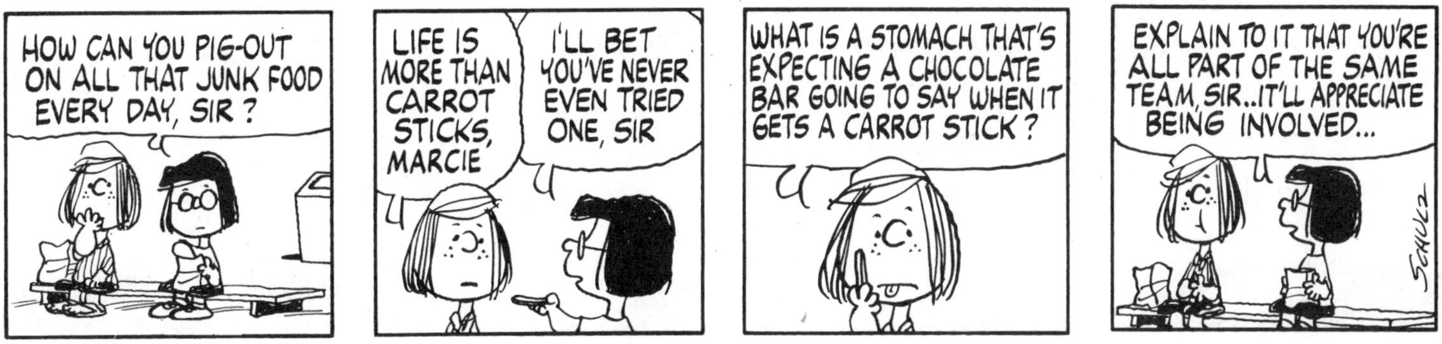
HOW CAN YOU PIG-OUT ON ALL THAT JUNK FOOD EVERY DAY, SIR?
LIFE IS MORE THAN CARROT STICKS, MARCIE
I'LL BET YOU'VE NEVER EVEN TRIED ONE, SIR
WHAT IS A STOMACH THAT'S EXPECTING A CHOCOLATE BAR GOING TO SAY WHEN IT GETS A CARROT STICK?
EXPLAIN TO IT THAT YOU'RE ALL PART OF THE SAME TEAM, SIR...IT'LL APPRECIATE BEING INVOLVED...
SCHULZ

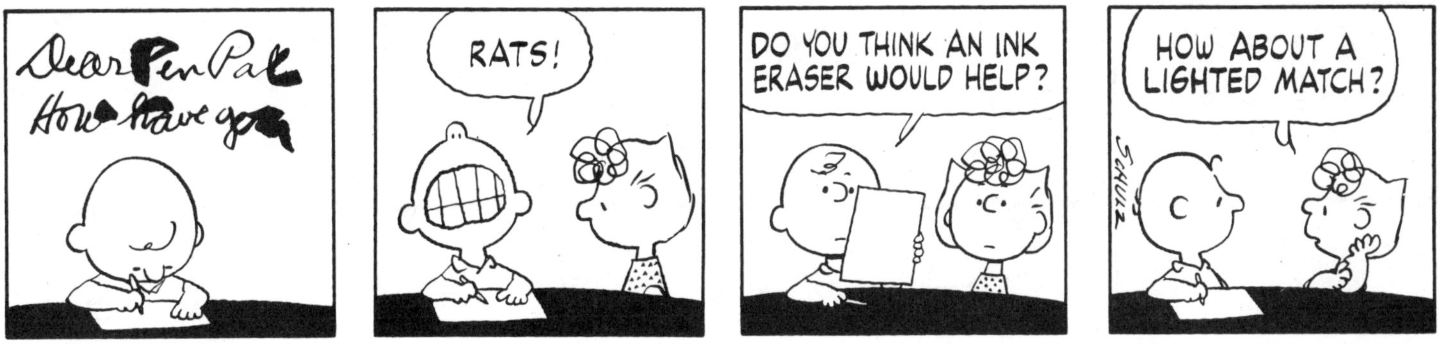
Dear Pen Pal
How have
RATS!
DO YOU THINK AN INK ERASER WOULD HELP?
HOW ABOUT A LIGHTED MATCH?
SCHULZ

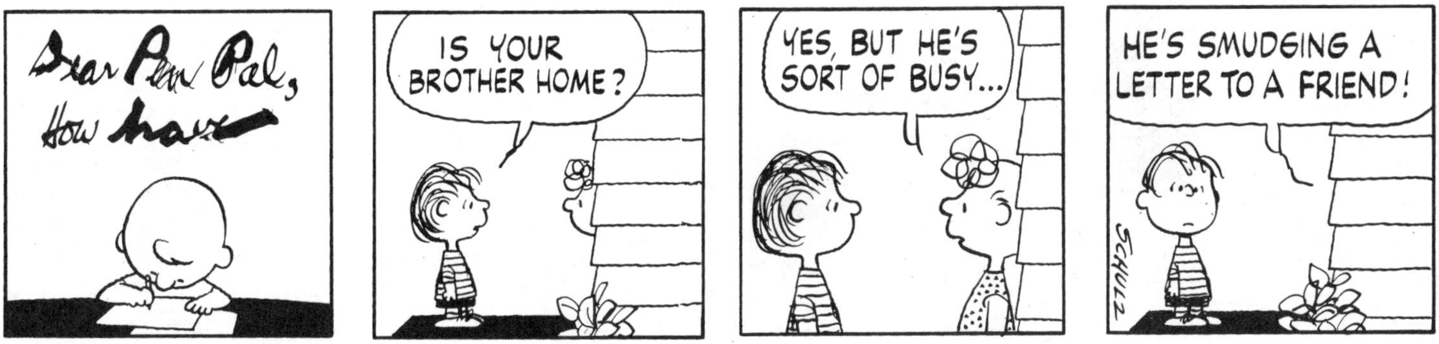
Dear Pen Pal,
How
IS YOUR BROTHER HOME?
YES, BUT HE'S SORT OF BUSY...
HE'S SMUDGING A LETTER TO A FRIEND!
SCHULZ

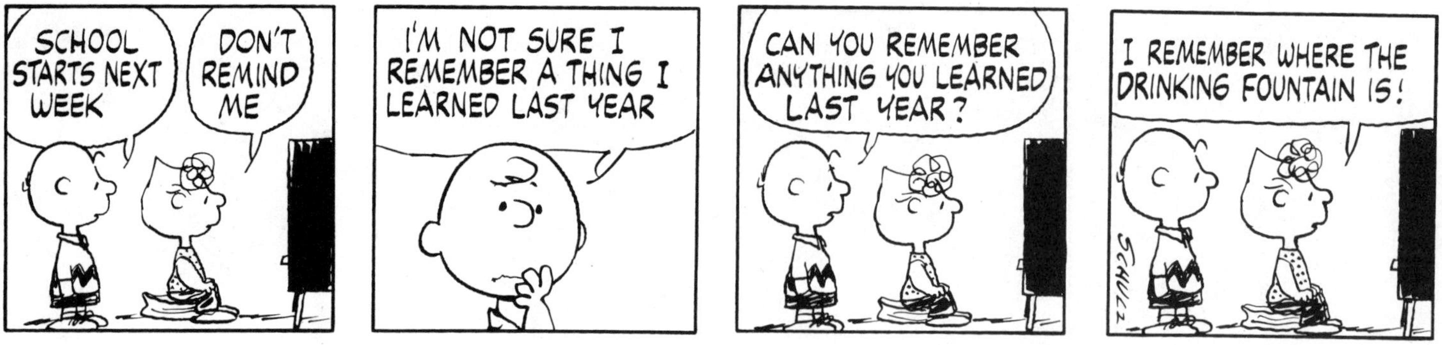
SCHOOL STARTS NEXT WEEK
DON'T REMIND ME
I'M NOT SURE I REMEMBER A THING I LEARNED LAST YEAR
CAN YOU REMEMBER ANYTHING YOU LEARNED LAST YEAR?
I REMEMBER WHERE THE DRINKING FOUNTAIN IS!
SCHULZ

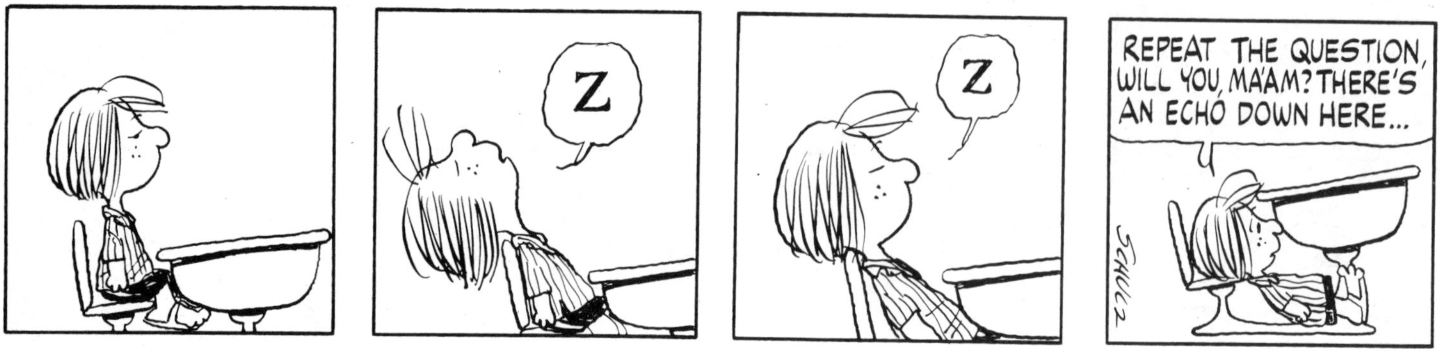
Z
Z
REPEAT THE QUESTION, WILL YOU, MA'AM? THERE'S AN ECHO DOWN HERE...
SCHULZ

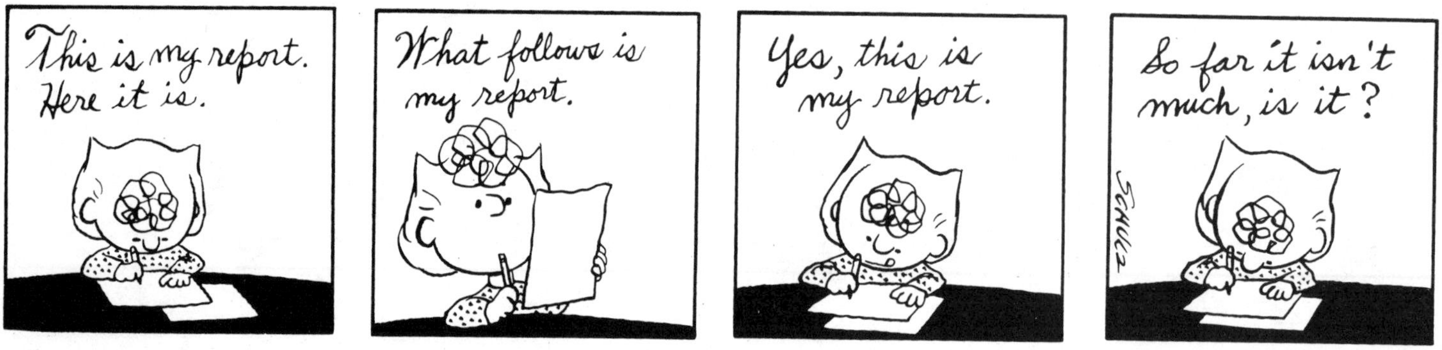
This is my report. Here it is.
What follows is my report.
Yes, this is my report.
So far it isn't much, is it?
SCHULZ

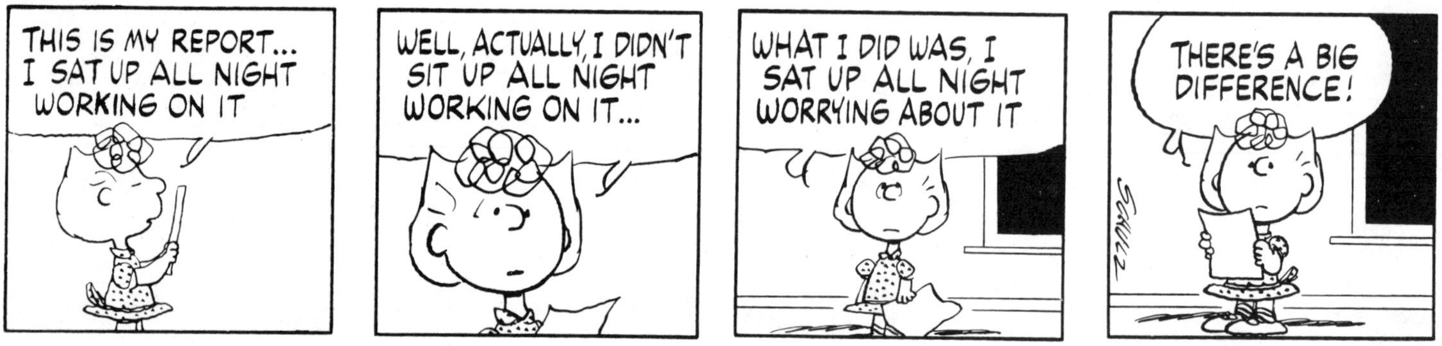
THIS IS MY REPORT... I SAT UP ALL NIGHT WORKING ON IT
WELL, ACTUALLY, I DIDN'T SIT UP ALL NIGHT WORKING ON IT...
WHAT I DID WAS, I SAT UP ALL NIGHT WORRYING ABOUT IT
THERE'S A BIG DIFFERENCE!
SCHULZ

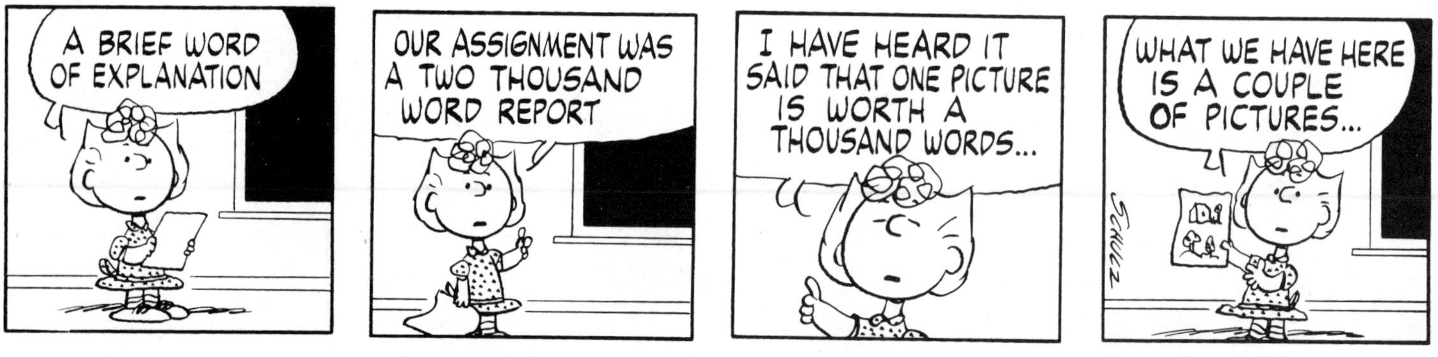
A BRIEF WORD OF EXPLANATION
OUR ASSIGNMENT WAS A TWO THOUSAND WORD REPORT
I HAVE HEARD IT SAID THAT ONE PICTURE IS WORTH A THOUSAND WORDS...
WHAT WE HAVE HERE IS A COUPLE OF PICTURES...
SCHULZ

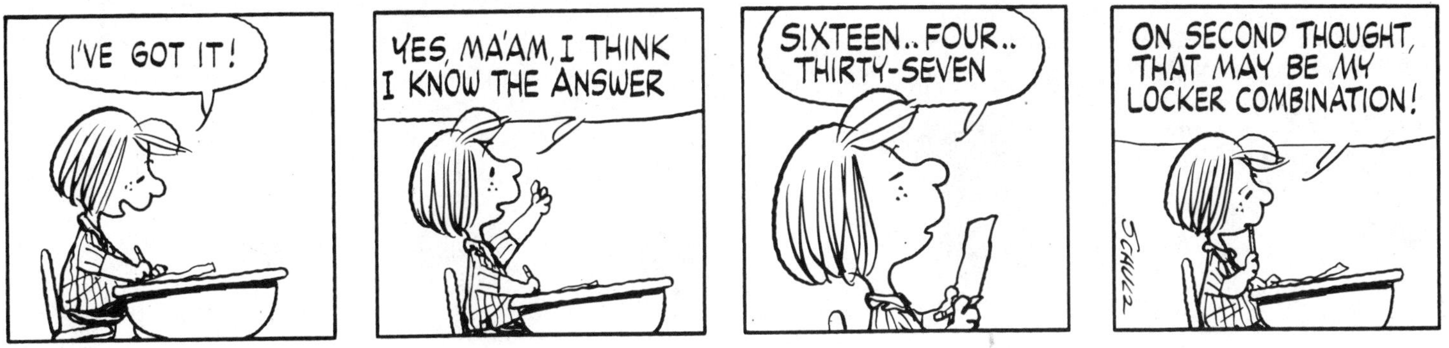
I'VE GOT IT!
YES, MA'AM, I THINK I KNOW THE ANSWER
SIXTEEN.. FOUR.. THIRTY-SEVEN
ON SECOND THOUGHT, THAT MAY BE MY LOCKER COMBINATION!

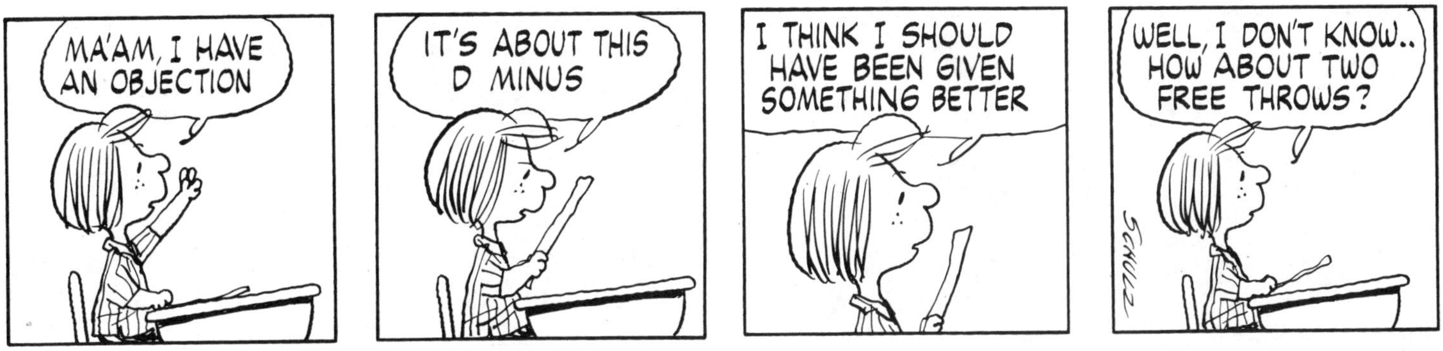
MA'AM, I HAVE AN OBJECTION
IT'S ABOUT THIS D MINUS
I THINK I SHOULD HAVE BEEN GIVEN SOMETHING BETTER
WELL, I DON'T KNOW.. HOW ABOUT TWO FREE THROWS?

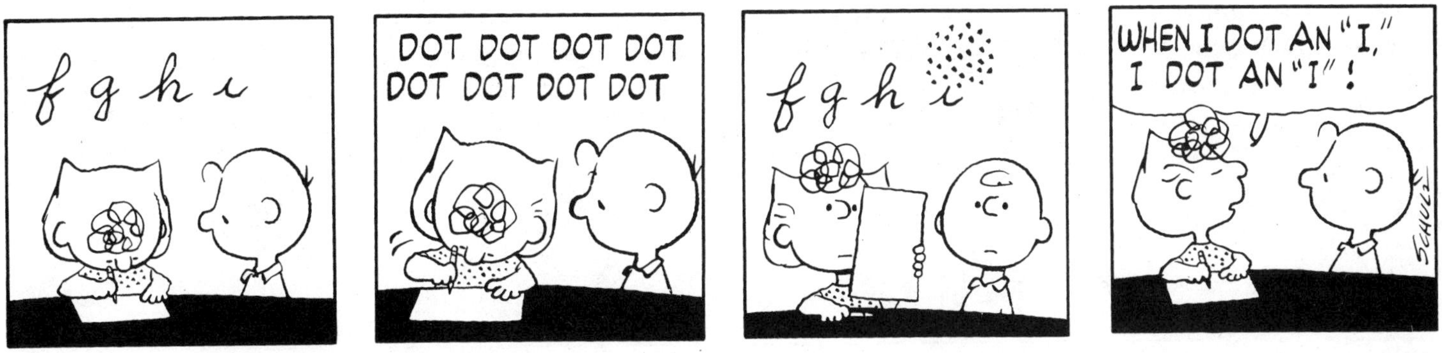
f g h i
DOT DOT DOT DOT DOT DOT DOT DOT
f g h i
WHEN I DOT AN "I," I DOT AN "I"!

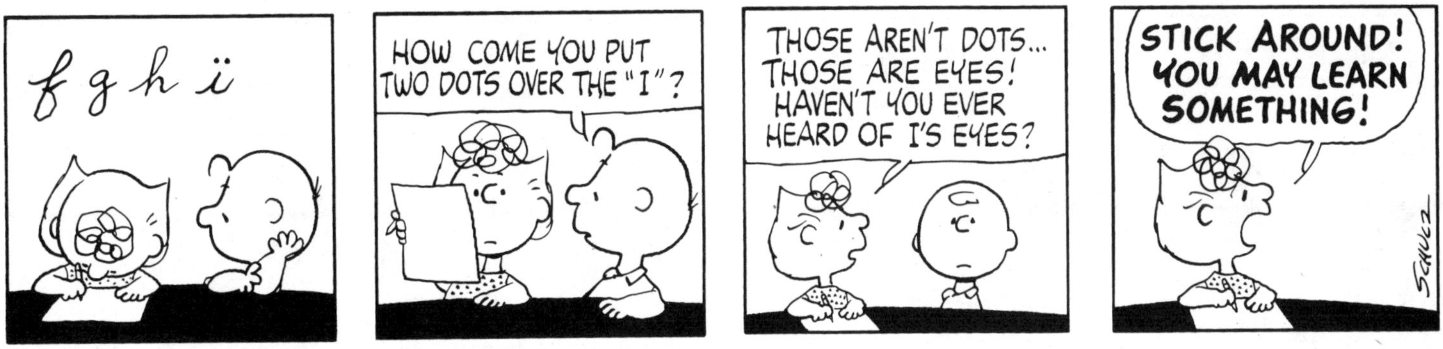
f g h ï
HOW COME YOU PUT TWO DOTS OVER THE "I"?
THOSE AREN'T DOTS... THOSE ARE EYES! HAVEN'T YOU EVER HEARD OF I'S EYES?
STICK AROUND! YOU MAY LEARN SOMETHING!

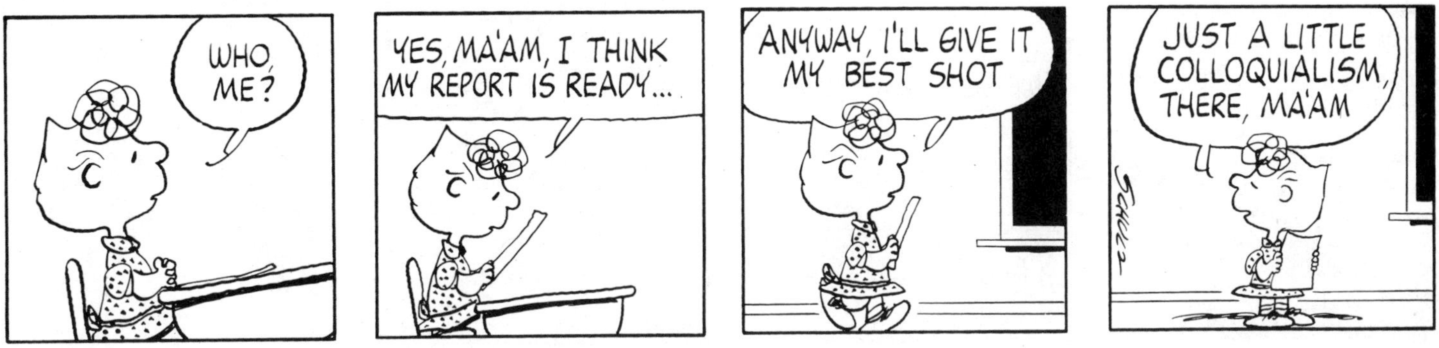
WHO, ME?
YES, MA'AM, I THINK MY REPORT IS READY...
ANYWAY, I'LL GIVE IT MY BEST SHOT
JUST A LITTLE COLLOQUIALISM, THERE, MA'AM

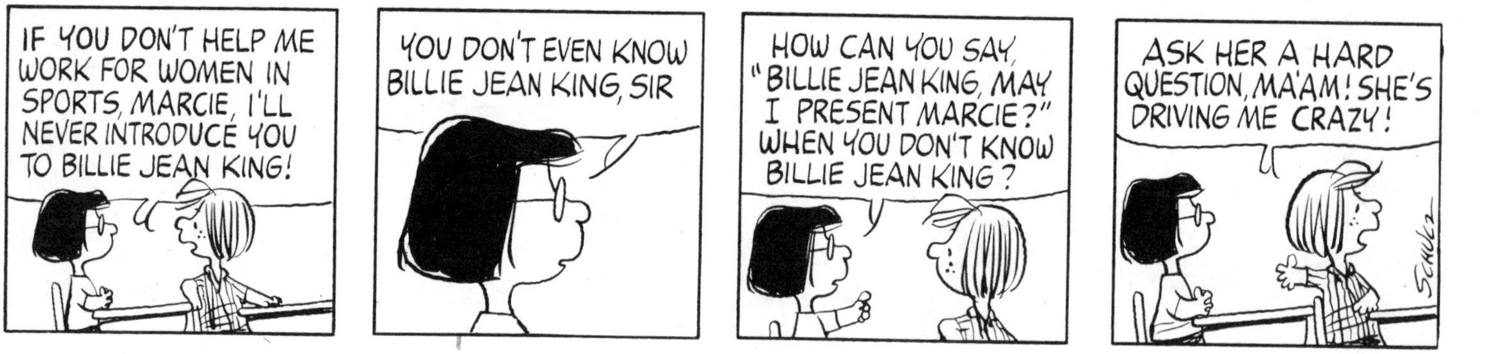
IF YOU DON'T HELP ME WORK FOR WOMEN IN SPORTS, MARCIE, I'LL NEVER INTRODUCE YOU TO BILLIE JEAN KING!
YOU DON'T EVEN KNOW BILLIE JEAN KING, SIR
HOW CAN YOU SAY, "BILLIE JEAN KING, MAY I PRESENT MARCIE?" WHEN YOU DON'T KNOW BILLIE JEAN KING?
ASK HER A HARD QUESTION, MA'AM! SHE'S DRIVING ME CRAZY!
SCHULZ

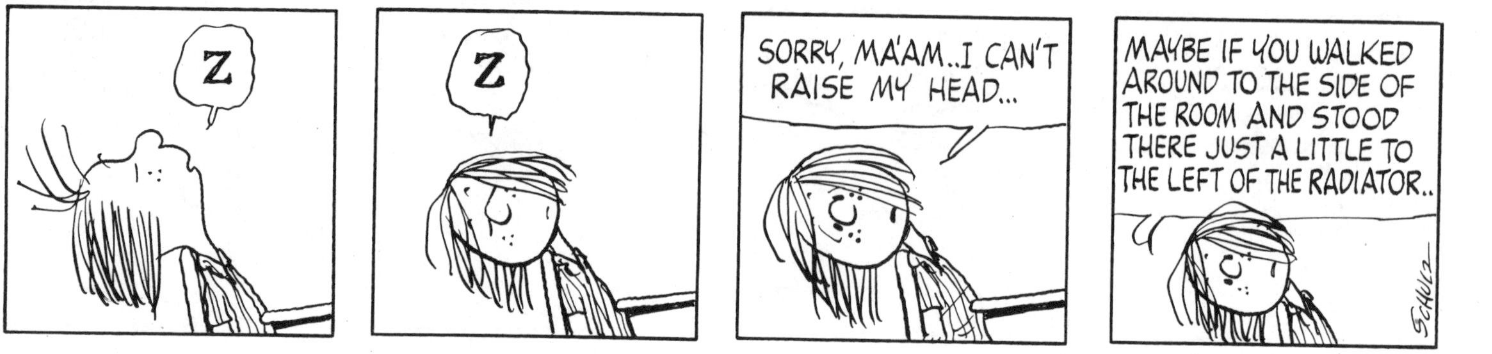
Z
Z
SORRY, MA'AM..I CAN'T RAISE MY HEAD...
MAYBE IF YOU WALKED AROUND TO THE SIDE OF THE ROOM AND STOOD THERE JUST A LITTLE TO THE LEFT OF THE RADIATOR..
SCHULZ

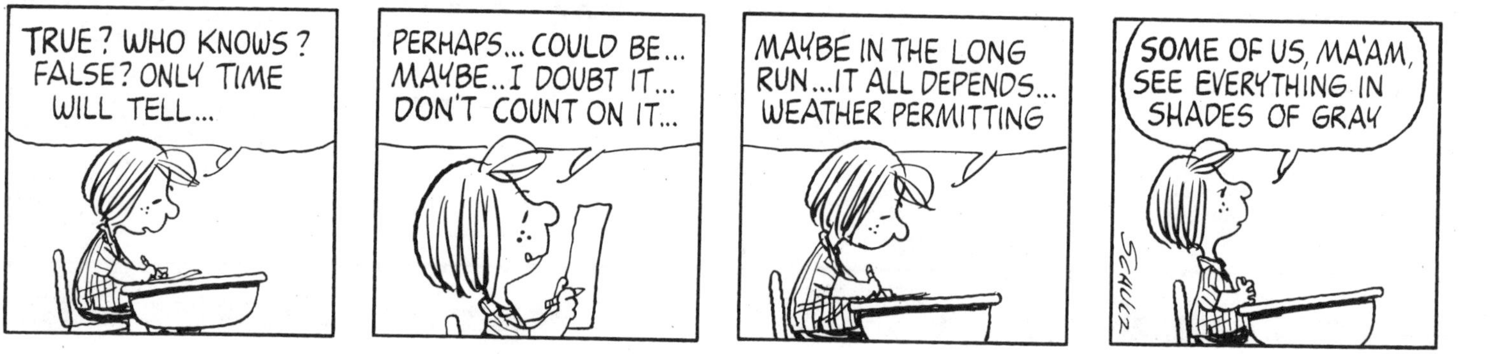
TRUE? WHO KNOWS? FALSE? ONLY TIME WILL TELL...
PERHAPS... COULD BE... MAYBE..I DOUBT IT... DON'T COUNT ON IT...
MAYBE IN THE LONG RUN...IT ALL DEPENDS... WEATHER PERMITTING
SOME OF US, MA'AM, SEE EVERYTHING IN SHADES OF GRAY
SCHULZ

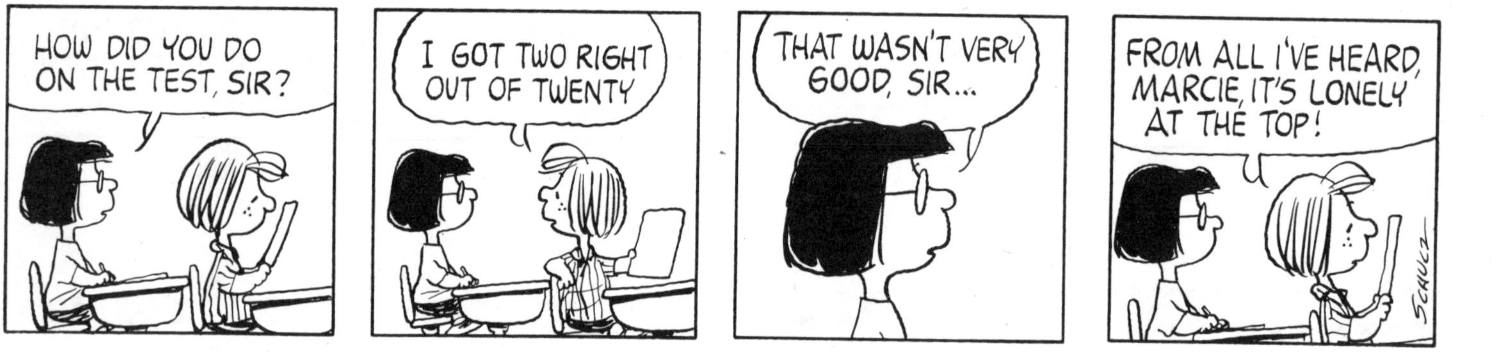
HOW DID YOU DO ON THE TEST, SIR?
I GOT TWO RIGHT OUT OF TWENTY
THAT WASN'T VERY GOOD, SIR...
FROM ALL I'VE HEARD, MARCIE, IT'S LONELY AT THE TOP!
SCHULZ

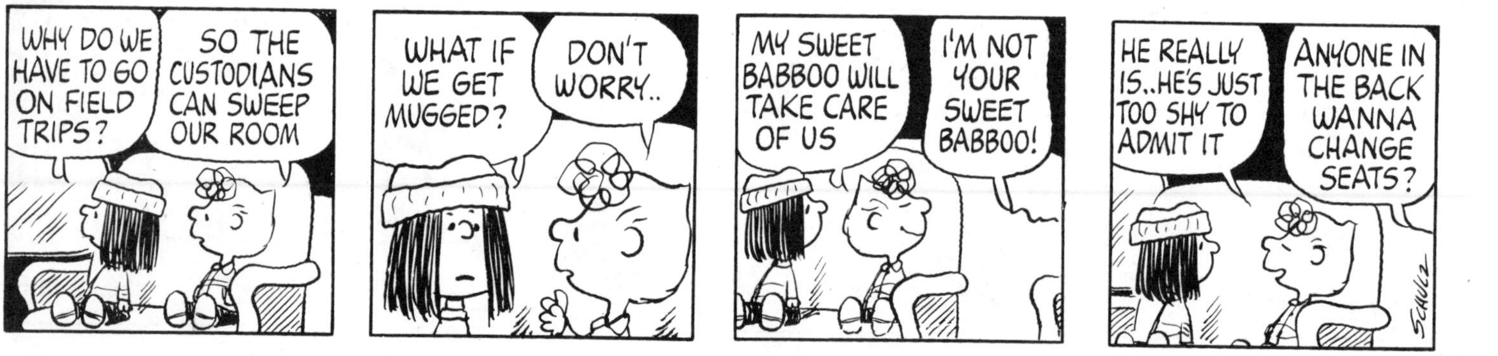
WHY DO WE HAVE TO GO ON FIELD TRIPS?
SO THE CUSTODIANS CAN SWEEP OUR ROOM
WHAT IF WE GET MUGGED?
DON'T WORRY..
MY SWEET BABBOO WILL TAKE CARE OF US
I'M NOT YOUR SWEET BABBOO!
HE REALLY IS..HE'S JUST TOO SHY TO ADMIT IT
ANYONE IN THE BACK WANNA CHANGE SEATS?
SCHULZ

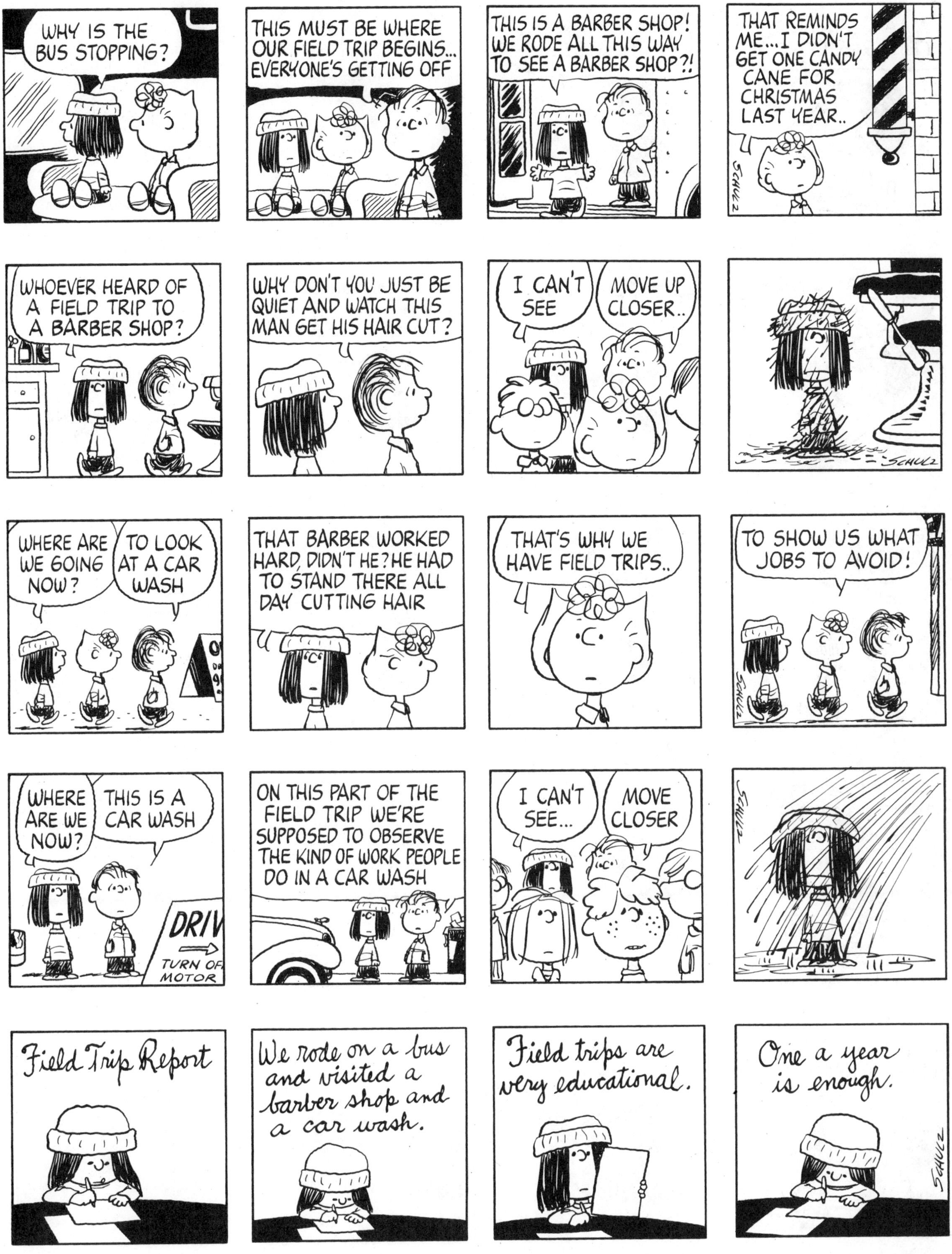
WHY IS THE BUS STOPPING?
THIS MUST BE WHERE OUR FIELD TRIP BEGINS... EVERYONE'S GETTING OFF
THIS IS A BARBER SHOP! WE RODE ALL THIS WAY TO SEE A BARBER SHOP?!
THAT REMINDS ME...I DIDN'T GET ONE CANDY CANE FOR CHRISTMAS LAST YEAR..
WHOEVER HEARD OF A FIELD TRIP TO A BARBER SHOP?
WHY DON'T YOU JUST BE QUIET AND WATCH THIS MAN GET HIS HAIR CUT?
I CAN'T SEE
MOVE UP CLOSER..
WHERE ARE WE GOING NOW?
TO LOOK AT A CAR WASH
THAT BARBER WORKED HARD, DIDN'T HE? HE HAD TO STAND THERE ALL DAY CUTTING HAIR
THAT'S WHY WE HAVE FIELD TRIPS..
TO SHOW US WHAT JOBS TO AVOID!
WHERE ARE WE NOW?
THIS IS A CAR WASH
DRIV
TURN OF
MOTOR
ON THIS PART OF THE FIELD TRIP WE'RE SUPPOSED TO OBSERVE THE KIND OF WORK PEOPLE DO IN A CAR WASH
I CAN'T SEE...
MOVE CLOSER
Field Trip Report
We rode on a bus and visited a barber shop and a car wash.
Field trips are very educational.
One a year is enough.

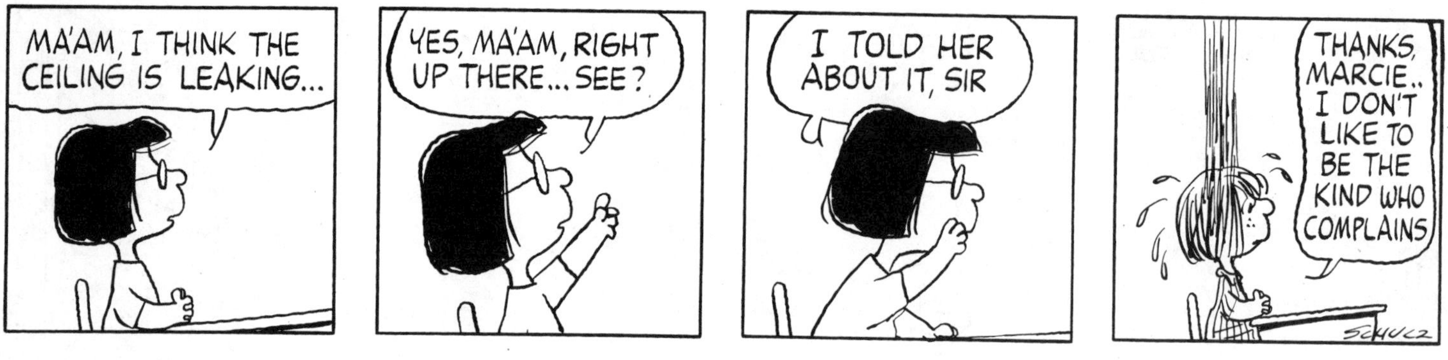
MA'AM, I THINK THE CEILING IS LEAKING...
YES, MA'AM, RIGHT UP THERE... SEE?
I TOLD HER ABOUT IT, SIR
THANKS, MARCIE.. I DON'T LIKE TO BE THE KIND WHO COMPLAINS
SCHULZ

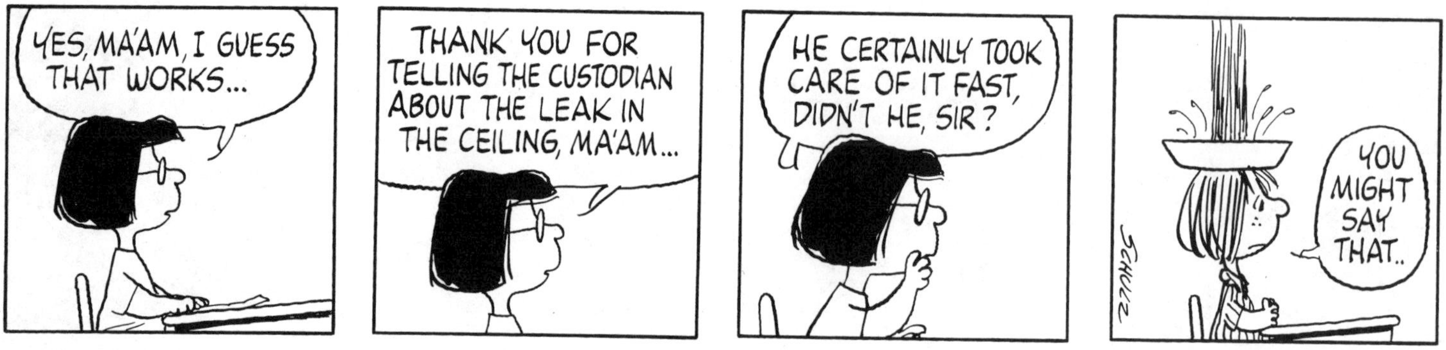
YES, MA'AM, I GUESS THAT WORKS...
THANK YOU FOR TELLING THE CUSTODIAN ABOUT THE LEAK IN THE CEILING, MA'AM...
HE CERTAINLY TOOK CARE OF IT FAST, DIDN'T HE, SIR?
SCHULZ
YOU MIGHT SAY THAT..

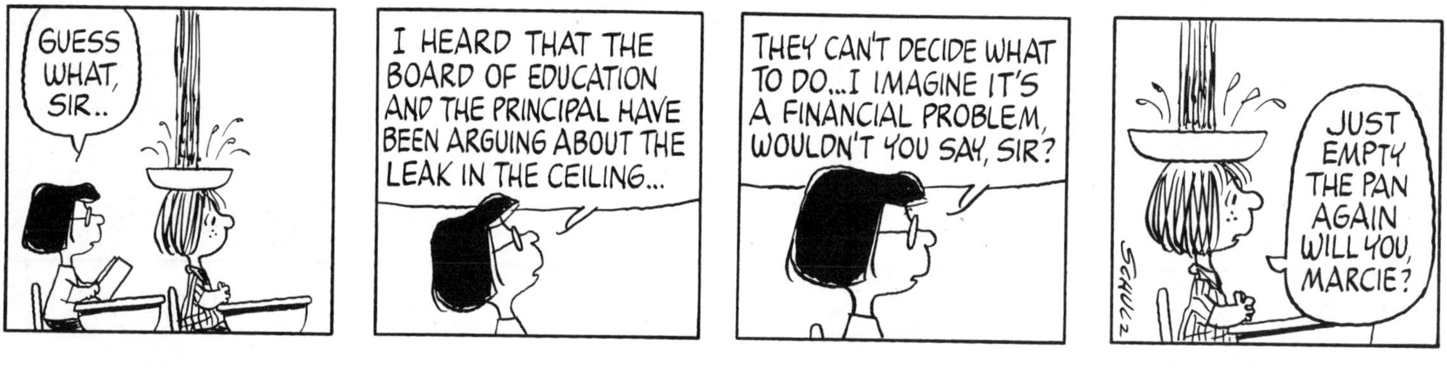
GUESS WHAT, SIR..
I HEARD THAT THE BOARD OF EDUCATION AND THE PRINCIPAL HAVE BEEN ARGUING ABOUT THE LEAK IN THE CEILING...
THEY CAN'T DECIDE WHAT TO DO...I IMAGINE IT'S A FINANCIAL PROBLEM, WOULDN'T YOU SAY, SIR?
SCHULZ
JUST EMPTY THE PAN AGAIN WILL YOU, MARCIE?

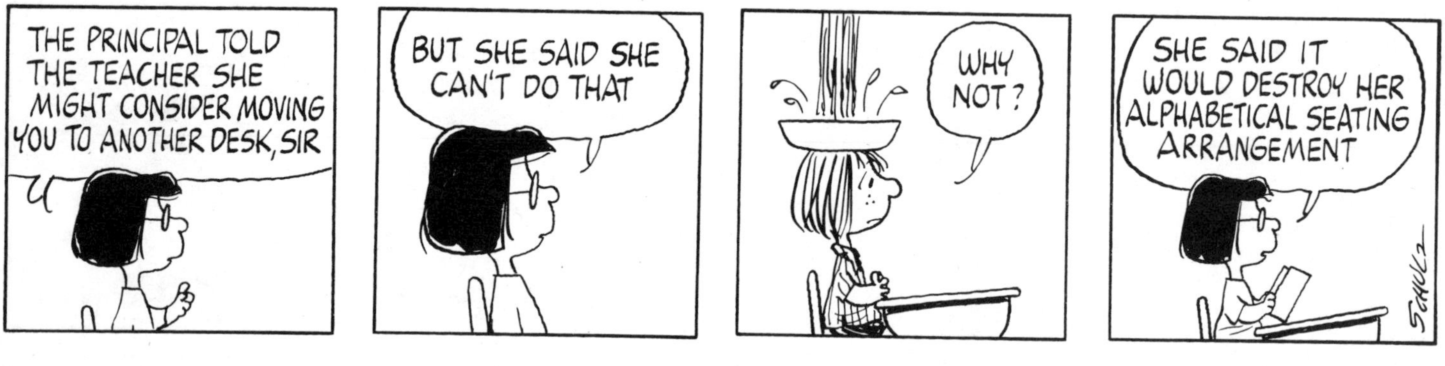
THE PRINCIPAL TOLD THE TEACHER SHE MIGHT CONSIDER MOVING YOU TO ANOTHER DESK, SIR
BUT SHE SAID SHE CAN'T DO THAT
WHY NOT?
SHE SAID IT WOULD DESTROY HER ALPHABETICAL SEATING ARRANGEMENT
SCHULZ

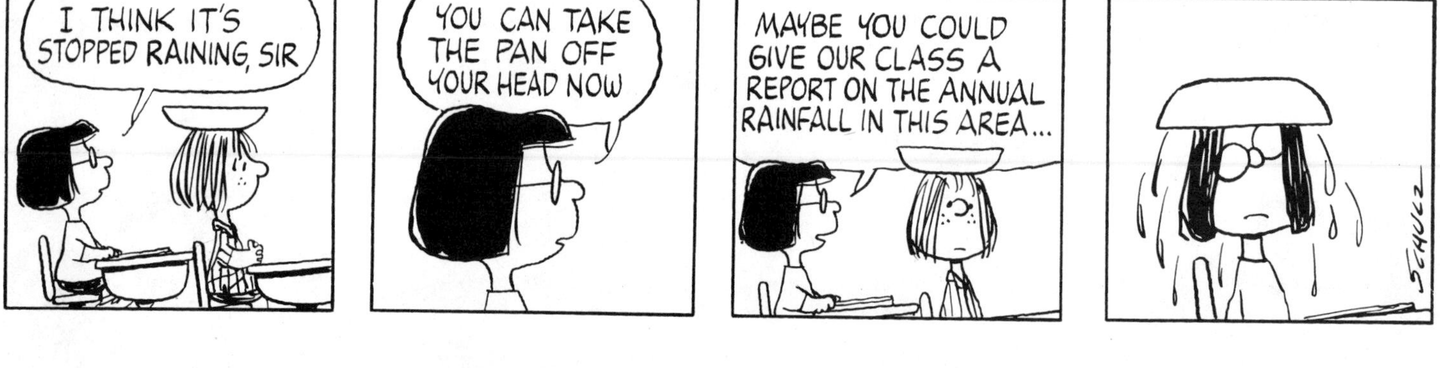
I THINK IT'S STOPPED RAINING, SIR
YOU CAN TAKE THE PAN OFF YOUR HEAD NOW
MAYBE YOU COULD GIVE OUR CLASS A REPORT ON THE ANNUAL RAINFALL IN THIS AREA...
SCHULZ

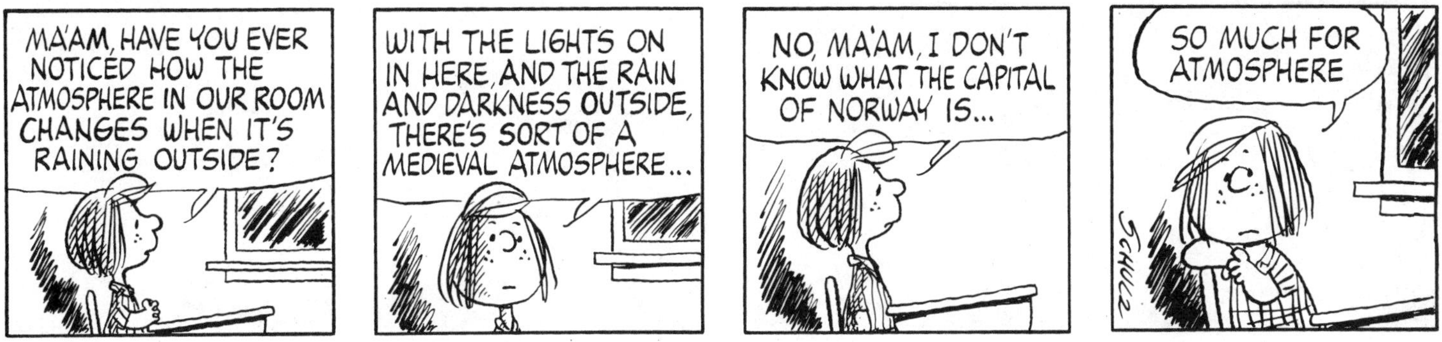
MA'AM, HAVE YOU EVER NOTICED HOW THE ATMOSPHERE IN OUR ROOM CHANGES WHEN IT'S RAINING OUTSIDE?
WITH THE LIGHTS ON IN HERE, AND THE RAIN AND DARKNESS OUTSIDE, THERE'S SORT OF A MEDIEVAL ATMOSPHERE...
NO, MA'AM, I DON'T KNOW WHAT THE CAPITAL OF NORWAY IS...
SO MUCH FOR ATMOSPHERE
SCHULZ

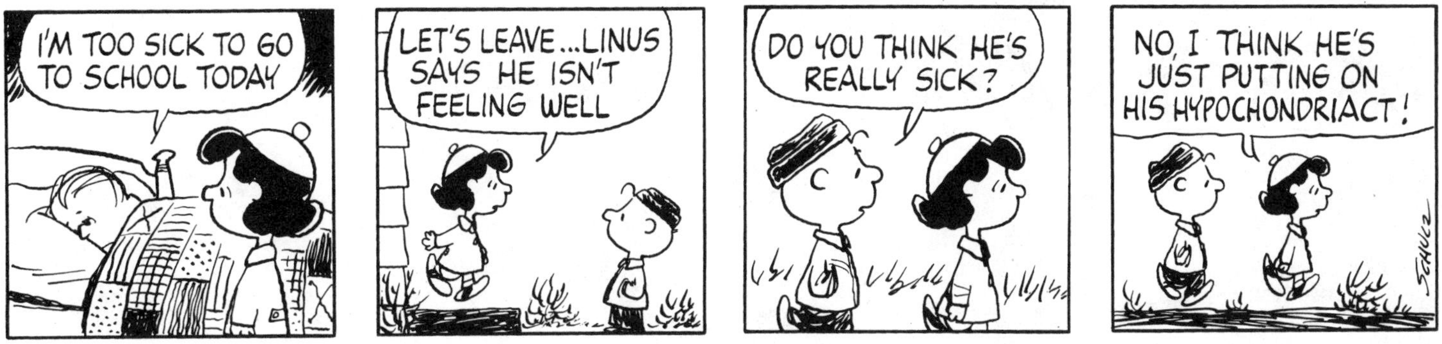
I'M TOO SICK TO GO TO SCHOOL TODAY
LET'S LEAVE...LINUS SAYS HE ISN'T FEELING WELL
DO YOU THINK HE'S REALLY SICK?
NO, I THINK HE'S JUST PUTTING ON HIS HYPOCHONDRIACT!
SCHULZ

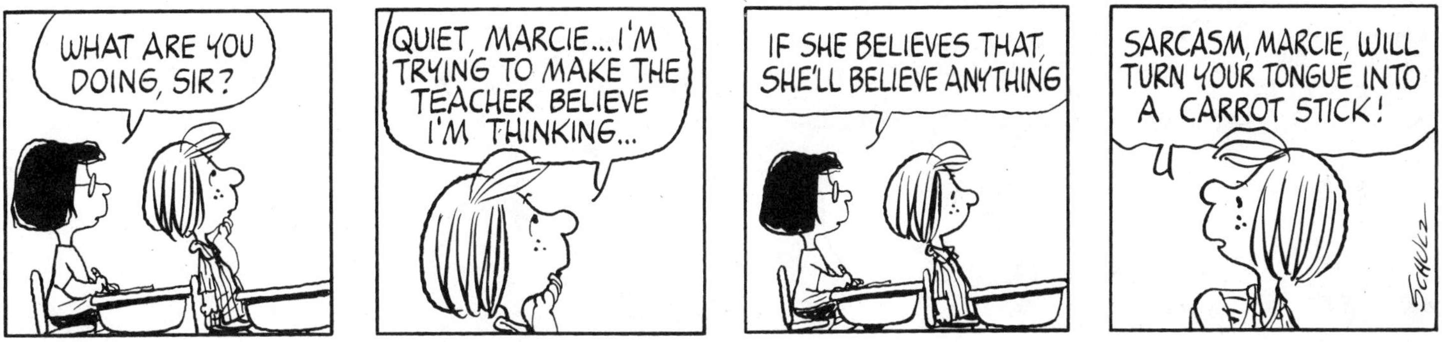
WHAT ARE YOU DOING, SIR?
QUIET, MARCIE...I'M TRYING TO MAKE THE TEACHER BELIEVE I'M THINKING...
IF SHE BELIEVES THAT, SHE'LL BELIEVE ANYTHING
SARCASM, MARCIE, WILL TURN YOUR TONGUE INTO A CARROT STICK!
SCHULZ

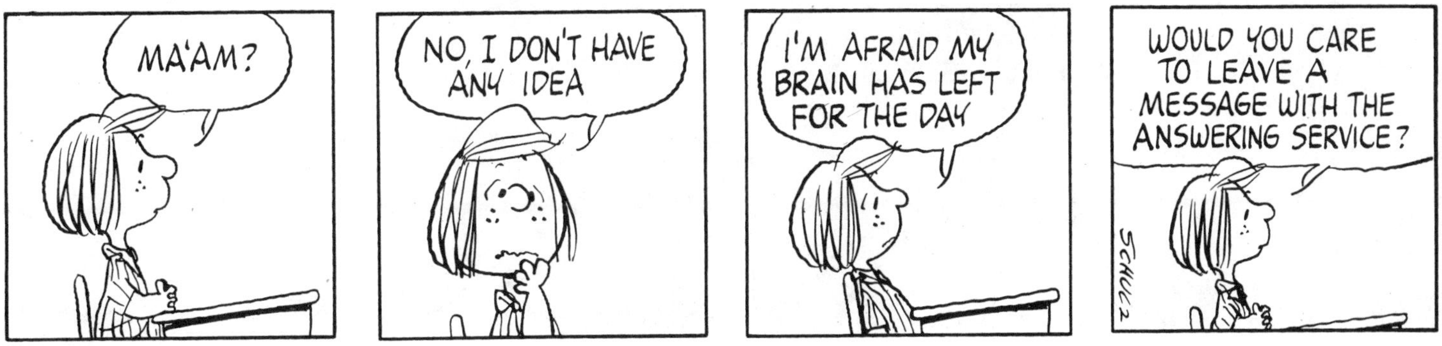
MA'AM?
NO, I DON'T HAVE ANY IDEA
I'M AFRAID MY BRAIN HAS LEFT FOR THE DAY
WOULD YOU CARE TO LEAVE A MESSAGE WITH THE ANSWERING SERVICE?
SCHULZ

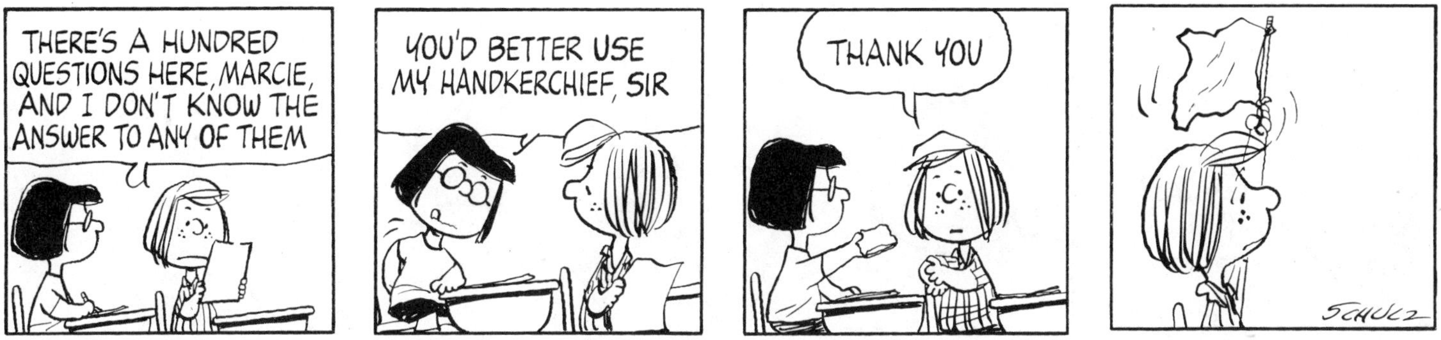
THERE'S A HUNDRED QUESTIONS HERE, MARCIE, AND I DON'T KNOW THE ANSWER TO ANY OF THEM
YOU'D BETTER USE MY HANDKERCHIEF, SIR
THANK YOU
SCHULZ

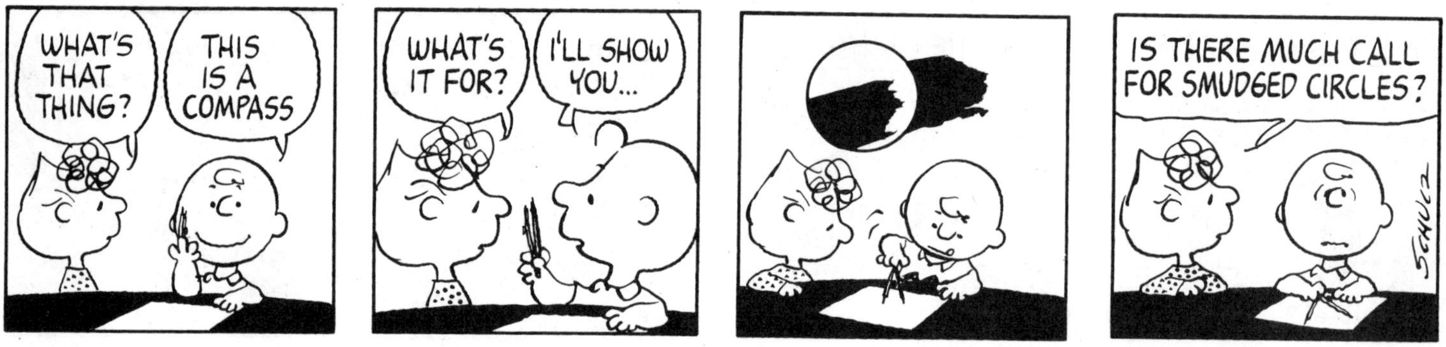
WHAT'S THAT THING?
THIS IS A COMPASS
WHAT'S IT FOR?
I'LL SHOW YOU...
IS THERE MUCH CALL FOR SMUDGED CIRCLES?
SCHULZ

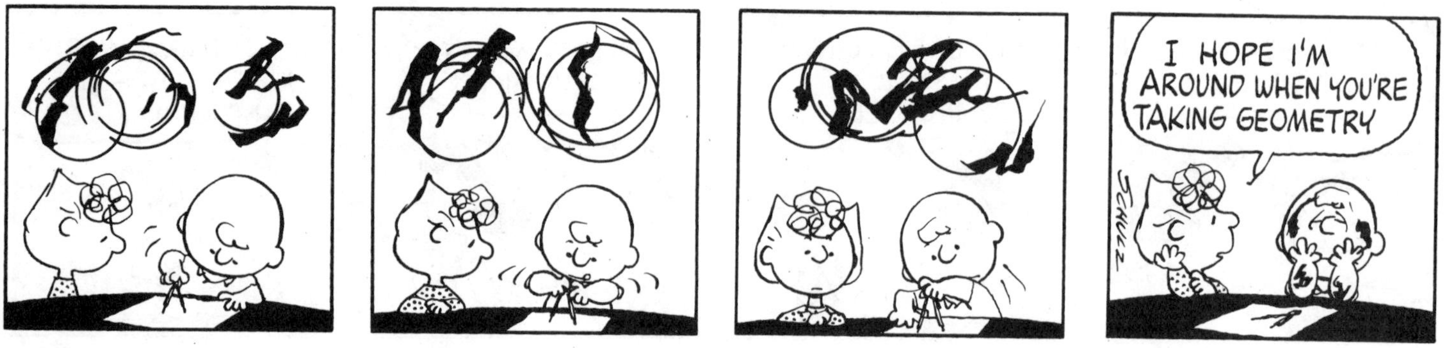
I HOPE I'M AROUND WHEN YOU'RE TAKING GEOMETRY
SCHULZ

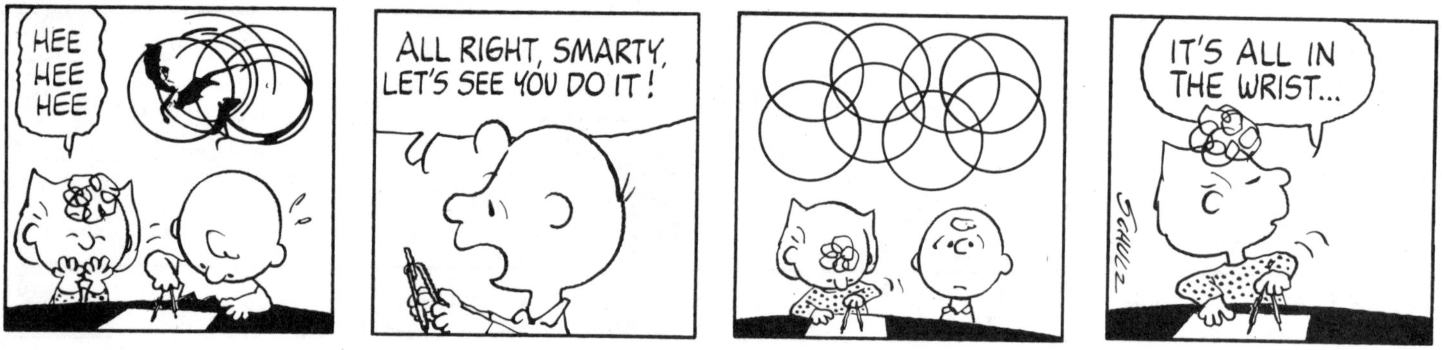
HEE HEE HEE
ALL RIGHT, SMARTY, LET'S SEE YOU DO IT!
IT'S ALL IN THE WRIST...
SCHULZ

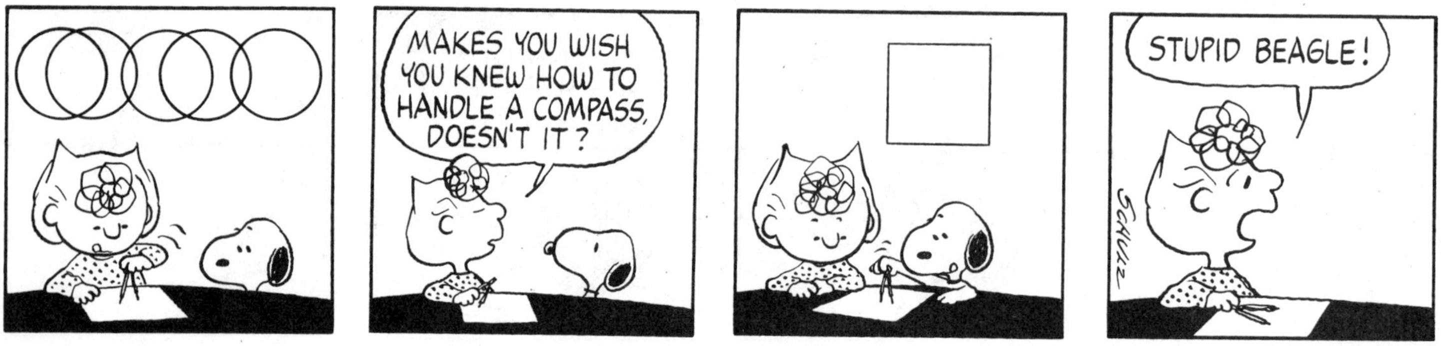
MAKES YOU WISH YOU KNEW HOW TO HANDLE A COMPASS, DOESN'T IT?
STUPID BEAGLE!
SCHULZ

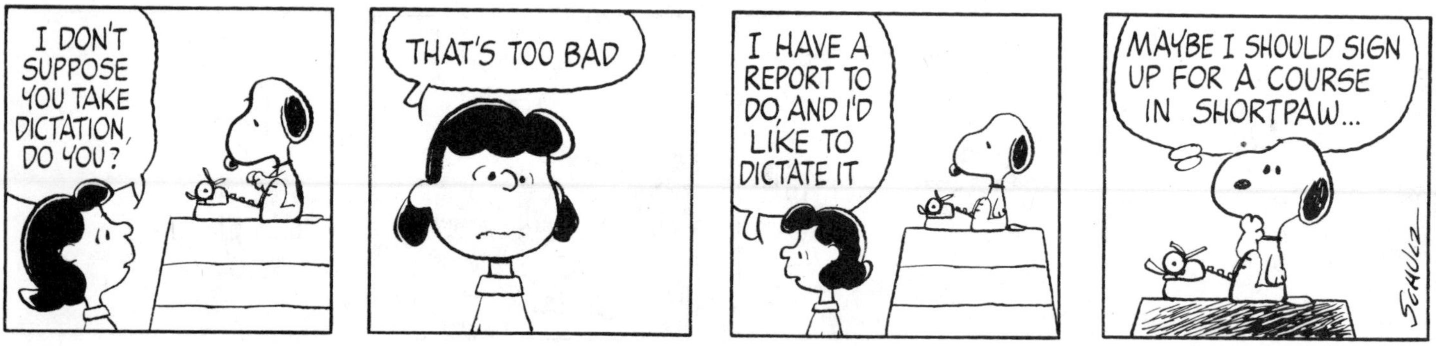
I DON'T SUPPOSE YOU TAKE DICTATION, DO YOU?
THAT'S TOO BAD
I HAVE A REPORT TO DO, AND I'D LIKE TO DICTATE IT
MAYBE I SHOULD SIGN UP FOR A COURSE IN SHORTPAW...
SCHULZ

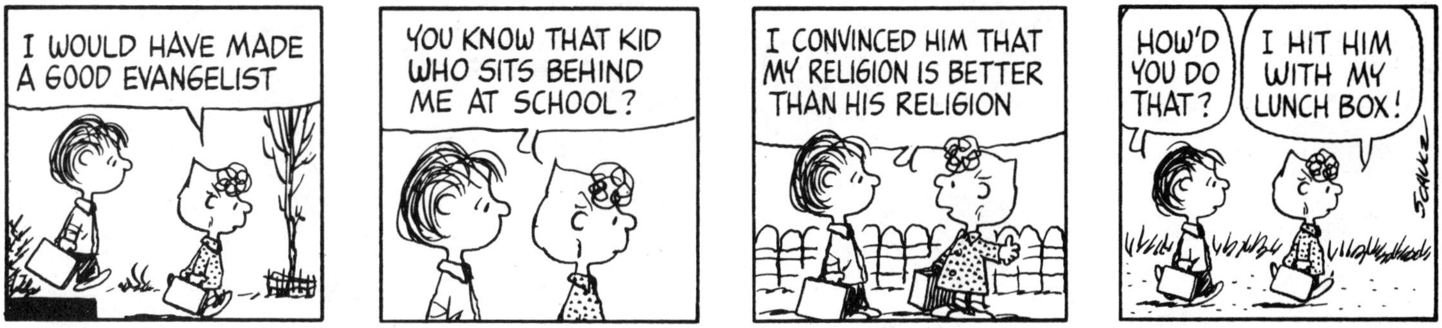
I WOULD HAVE MADE A GOOD EVANGELIST
YOU KNOW THAT KID WHO SITS BEHIND ME AT SCHOOL?
I CONVINCED HIM THAT MY RELIGION IS BETTER THAN HIS RELIGION
HOW'D YOU DO THAT?
I HIT HIM WITH MY LUNCH BOX!
SCHULZ

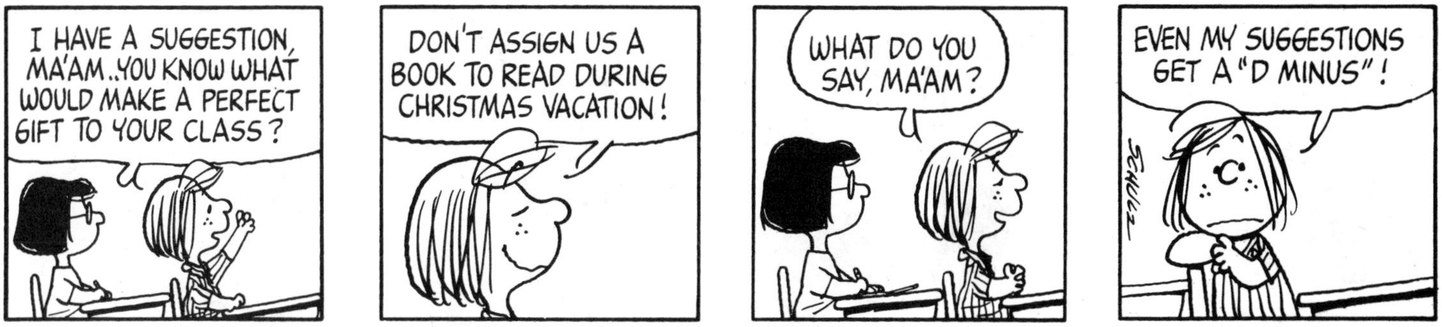
I HAVE A SUGGESTION, MA'AM..YOU KNOW WHAT WOULD MAKE A PERFECT GIFT TO YOUR CLASS?
DON'T ASSIGN US A BOOK TO READ DURING CHRISTMAS VACATION!
WHAT DO YOU SAY, MA'AM?
EVEN MY SUGGESTIONS GET A "D MINUS"!
SCHULZ

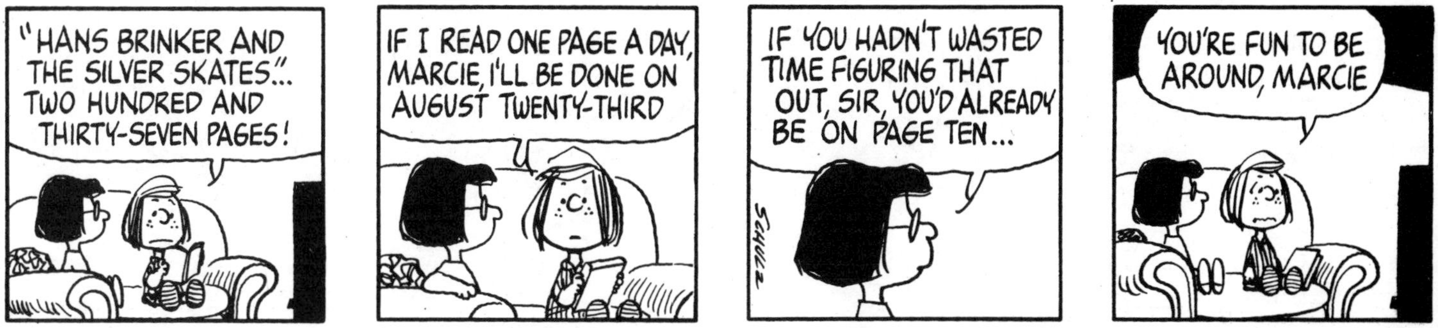
"HANS BRINKER AND THE SILVER SKATES"... TWO HUNDRED AND THIRTY-SEVEN PAGES!
IF I READ ONE PAGE A DAY, MARCIE, I'LL BE DONE ON AUGUST TWENTY-THIRD
IF YOU HADN'T WASTED TIME FIGURING THAT OUT, SIR, YOU'D ALREADY BE ON PAGE TEN...
SCHULZ
YOU'RE FUN TO BE AROUND, MARCIE

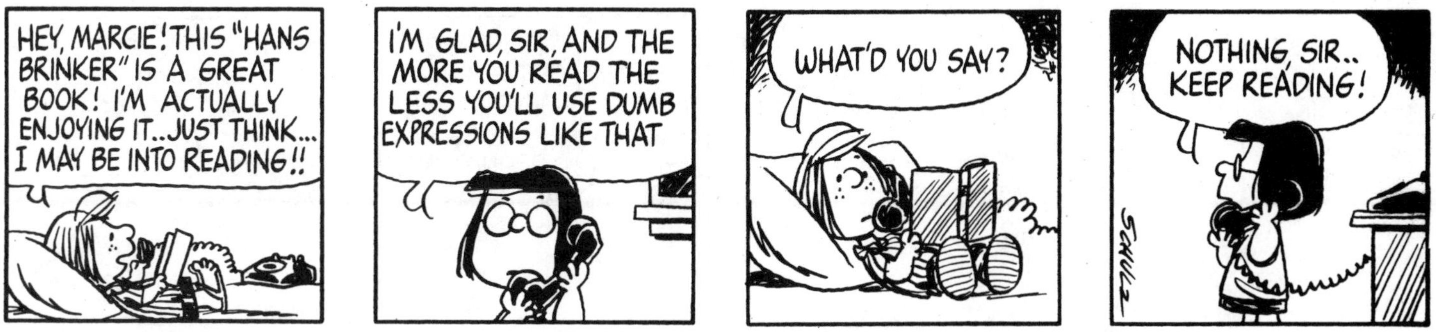
HEY, MARCIE! THIS "HANS BRINKER" IS A GREAT BOOK! I'M ACTUALLY ENJOYING IT..JUST THINK... I MAY BE INTO READING!!
I'M GLAD, SIR, AND THE MORE YOU READ THE LESS YOU'LL USE DUMB EXPRESSIONS LIKE THAT
WHAT'D YOU SAY?
NOTHING, SIR.. KEEP READING!
SCHULZ

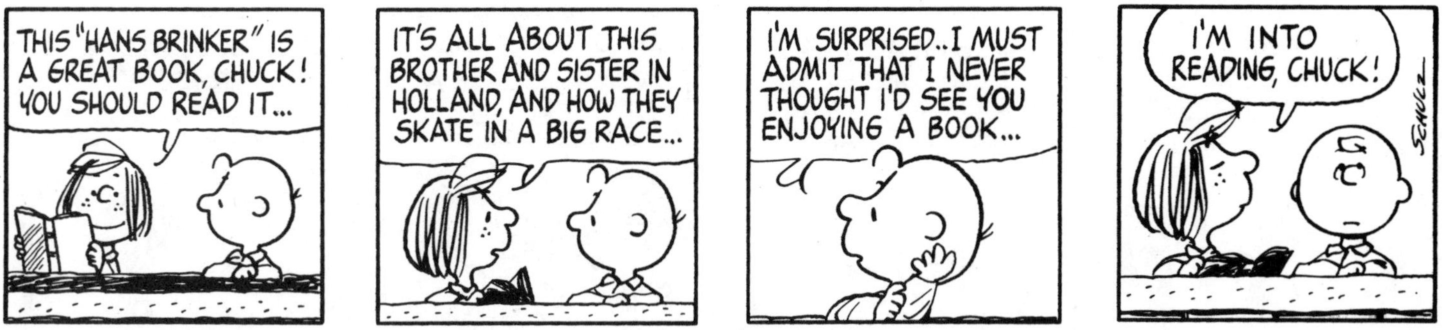
THIS "HANS BRINKER" IS A GREAT BOOK, CHUCK! YOU SHOULD READ IT...
IT'S ALL ABOUT THIS BROTHER AND SISTER IN HOLLAND, AND HOW THEY SKATE IN A BIG RACE...
I'M SURPRISED..I MUST ADMIT THAT I NEVER THOUGHT I'D SEE YOU ENJOYING A BOOK...
I'M INTO READING, CHUCK!
SCHULZ

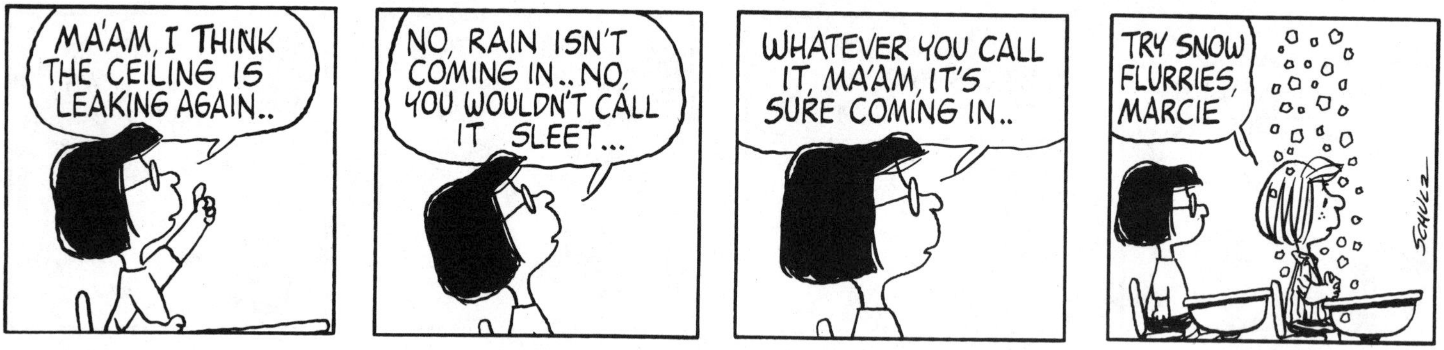
MA'AM, I THINK THE CEILING IS LEAKING AGAIN..
NO, RAIN ISN'T COMING IN..NO, YOU WOULDN'T CALL IT SLEET...
WHATEVER YOU CALL IT, MA'AM, IT'S SURE COMING IN..
TRY SNOW FLURRIES, MARCIE
SCHULZ

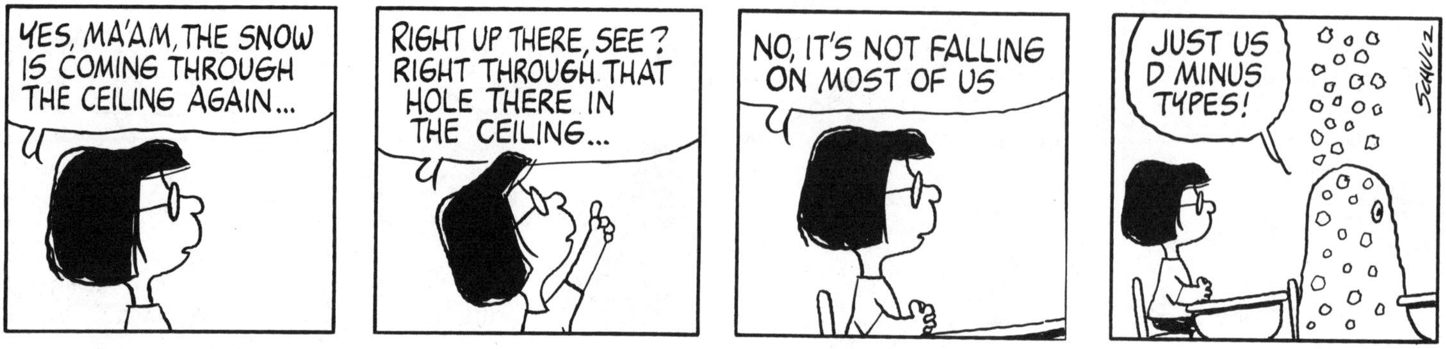
YES, MA'AM, THE SNOW IS COMING THROUGH THE CEILING AGAIN...
RIGHT UP THERE, SEE? RIGHT THROUGH THAT HOLE THERE IN THE CEILING...
NO, IT'S NOT FALLING ON MOST OF US
JUST US D MINUS TYPES!
SCHULZ

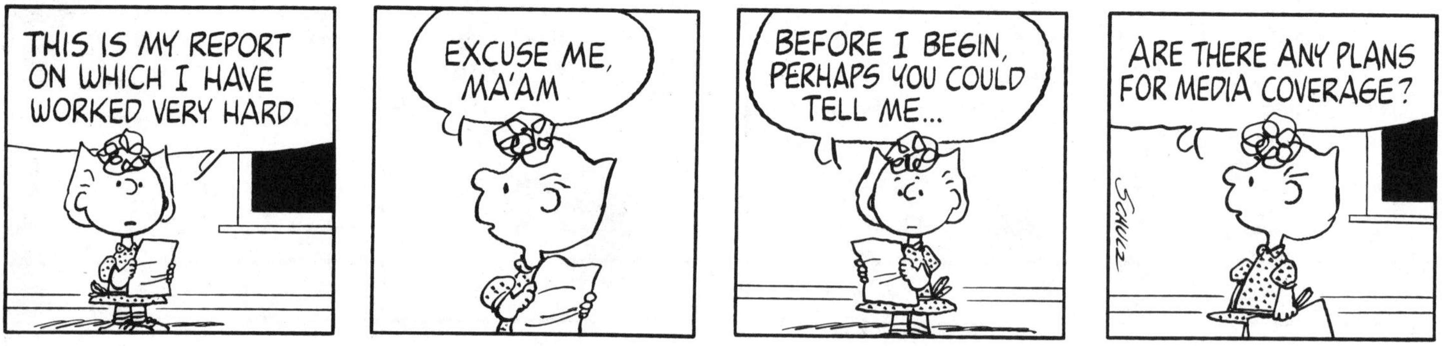
THIS IS MY REPORT ON WHICH I HAVE WORKED VERY HARD
EXCUSE ME, MA'AM
BEFORE I BEGIN, PERHAPS YOU COULD TELL ME...
ARE THERE ANY PLANS FOR MEDIA COVERAGE?
SCHULZ

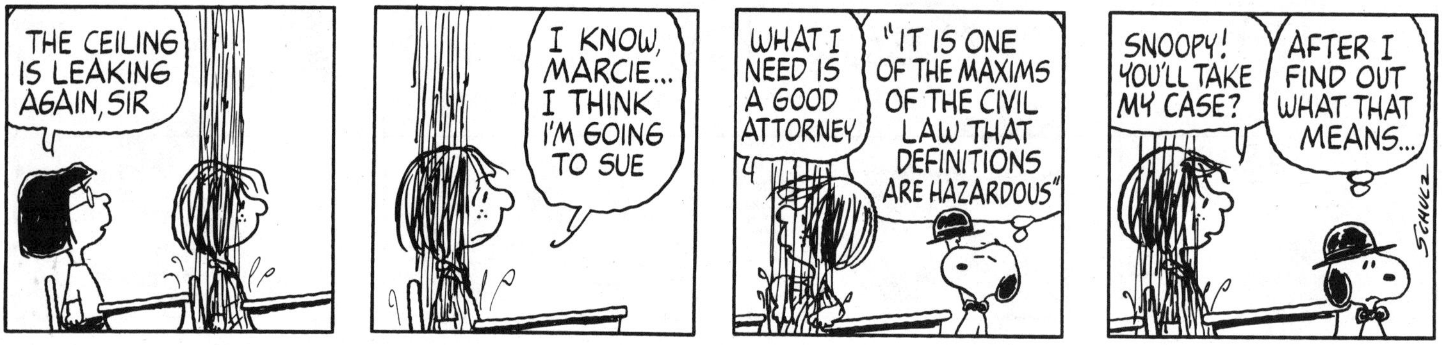
THE CEILING IS LEAKING AGAIN, SIR
I KNOW, MARCIE... I THINK I'M GOING TO SUE
WHAT I NEED IS A GOOD ATTORNEY
"IT IS ONE OF THE MAXIMS OF THE CIVIL LAW THAT DEFINITIONS ARE HAZARDOUS"
SNOOPY! YOU'LL TAKE MY CASE?
AFTER I FIND OUT WHAT THAT MEANS...
SCHULZ

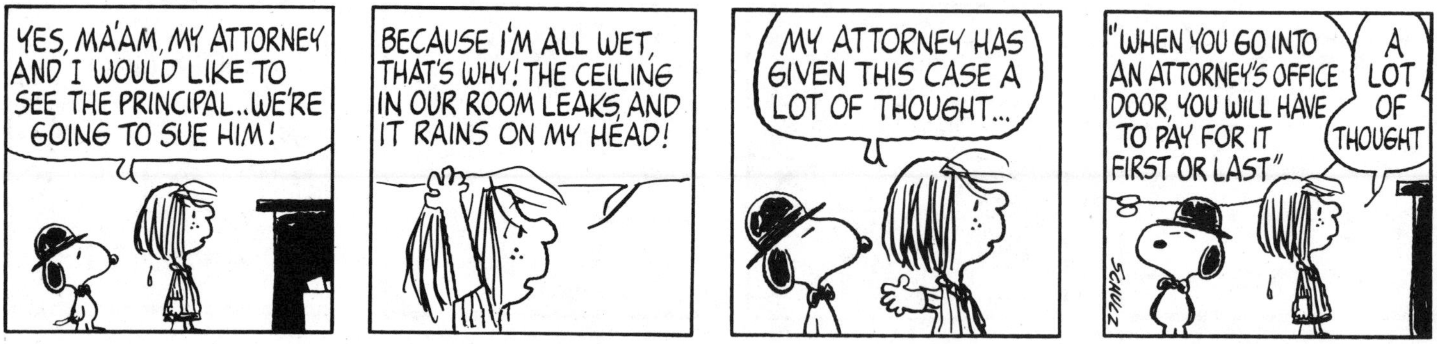
YES, MA'AM, MY ATTORNEY AND I WOULD LIKE TO SEE THE PRINCIPAL..WE'RE GOING TO SUE HIM!
BECAUSE I'M ALL WET, THAT'S WHY! THE CEILING IN OUR ROOM LEAKS, AND IT RAINS ON MY HEAD!
MY ATTORNEY HAS GIVEN THIS CASE A LOT OF THOUGHT...
"WHEN YOU GO INTO AN ATTORNEY'S OFFICE DOOR, YOU WILL HAVE TO PAY FOR IT FIRST OR LAST"
A LOT OF THOUGHT
SCHULZ

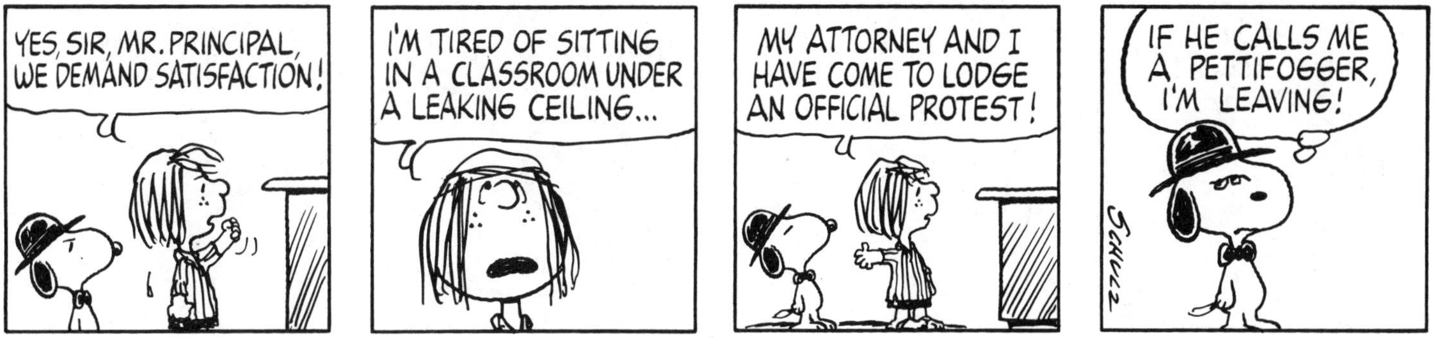
YES, SIR, MR. PRINCIPAL, WE DEMAND SATISFACTION!
I'M TIRED OF SITTING IN A CLASSROOM UNDER A LEAKING CEILING...
MY ATTORNEY AND I HAVE COME TO LODGE AN OFFICIAL PROTEST!
IF HE CALLS ME A PETTIFOGGER, I'M LEAVING!
SCHULZ

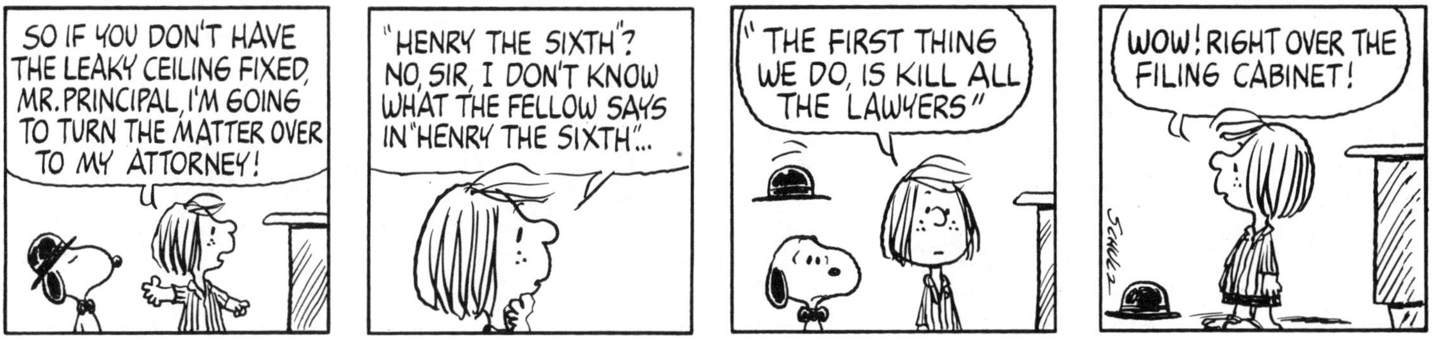
SO IF YOU DON'T HAVE THE LEAKY CEILING FIXED, MR. PRINCIPAL, I'M GOING TO TURN THE MATTER OVER TO MY ATTORNEY!
"HENRY THE SIXTH"? NO, SIR, I DON'T KNOW WHAT THE FELLOW SAYS IN "HENRY THE SIXTH"...
"THE FIRST THING WE DO, IS KILL ALL THE LAWYERS"
WOW! RIGHT OVER THE FILING CABINET!
SCHULZ

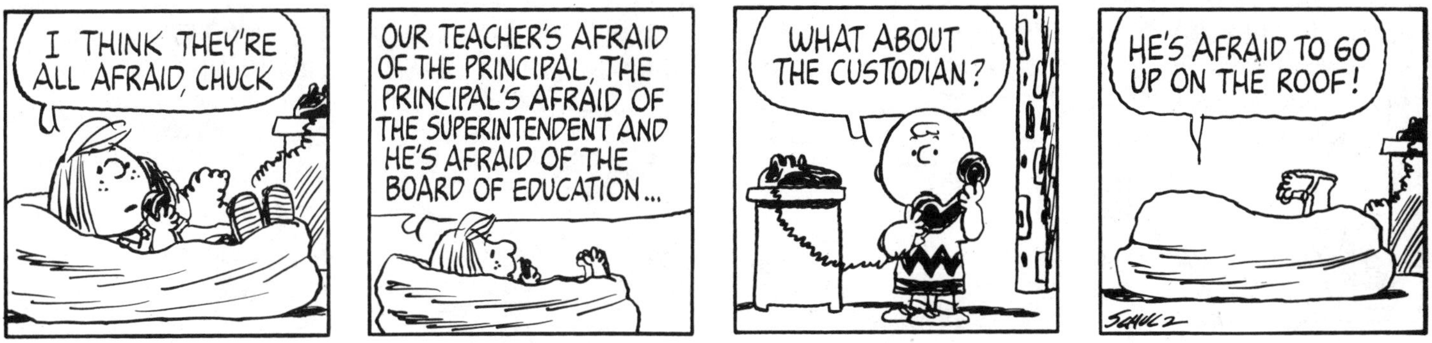
I THINK THEY'RE ALL AFRAID, CHUCK
OUR TEACHER'S AFRAID OF THE PRINCIPAL, THE PRINCIPAL'S AFRAID OF THE SUPERINTENDENT AND HE'S AFRAID OF THE BOARD OF EDUCATION...
WHAT ABOUT THE CUSTODIAN?
HE'S AFRAID TO GO UP ON THE ROOF!
SCHULZ

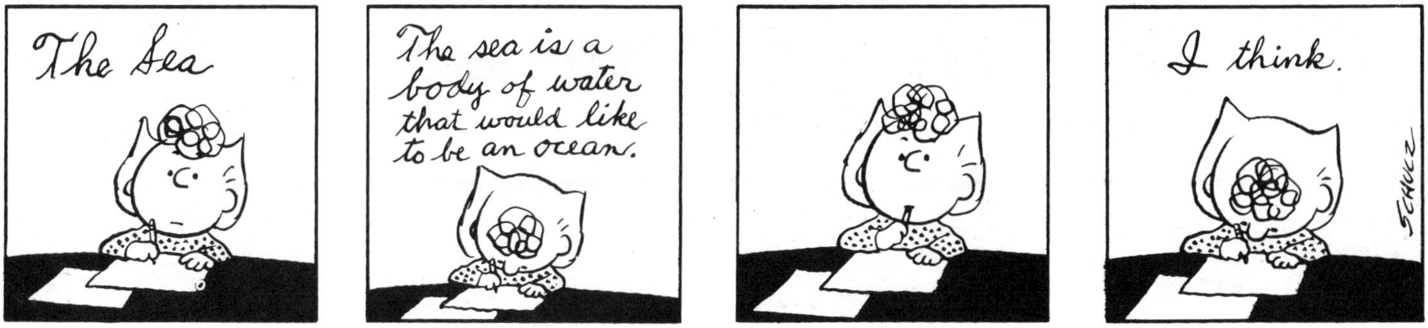
The Sea
The sea is a body of water that would like to be an ocean.
I think.
SCHULZ

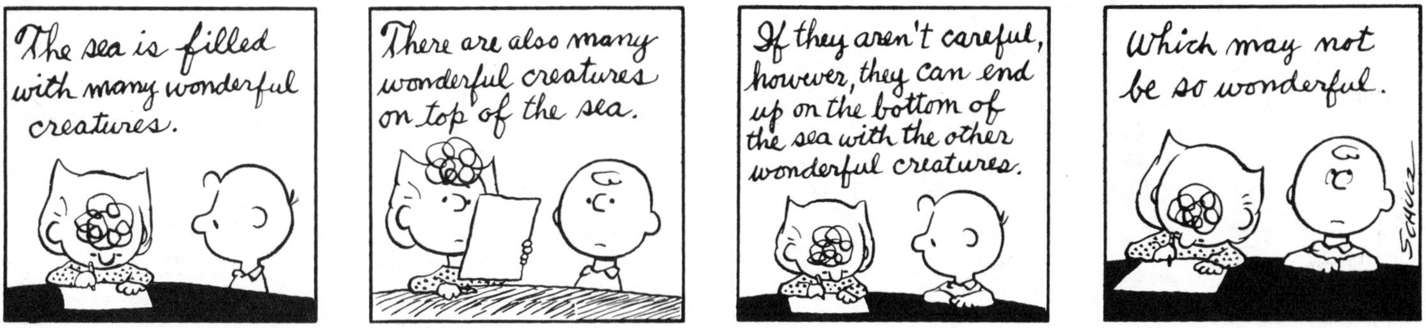
The sea is filled with many wonderful creatures.
There are also many wonderful creatures on top of the sea.
If they aren't careful, however, they can end up on the bottom of the sea with the other wonderful creatures.
Which may not be so wonderful.
SCHULZ

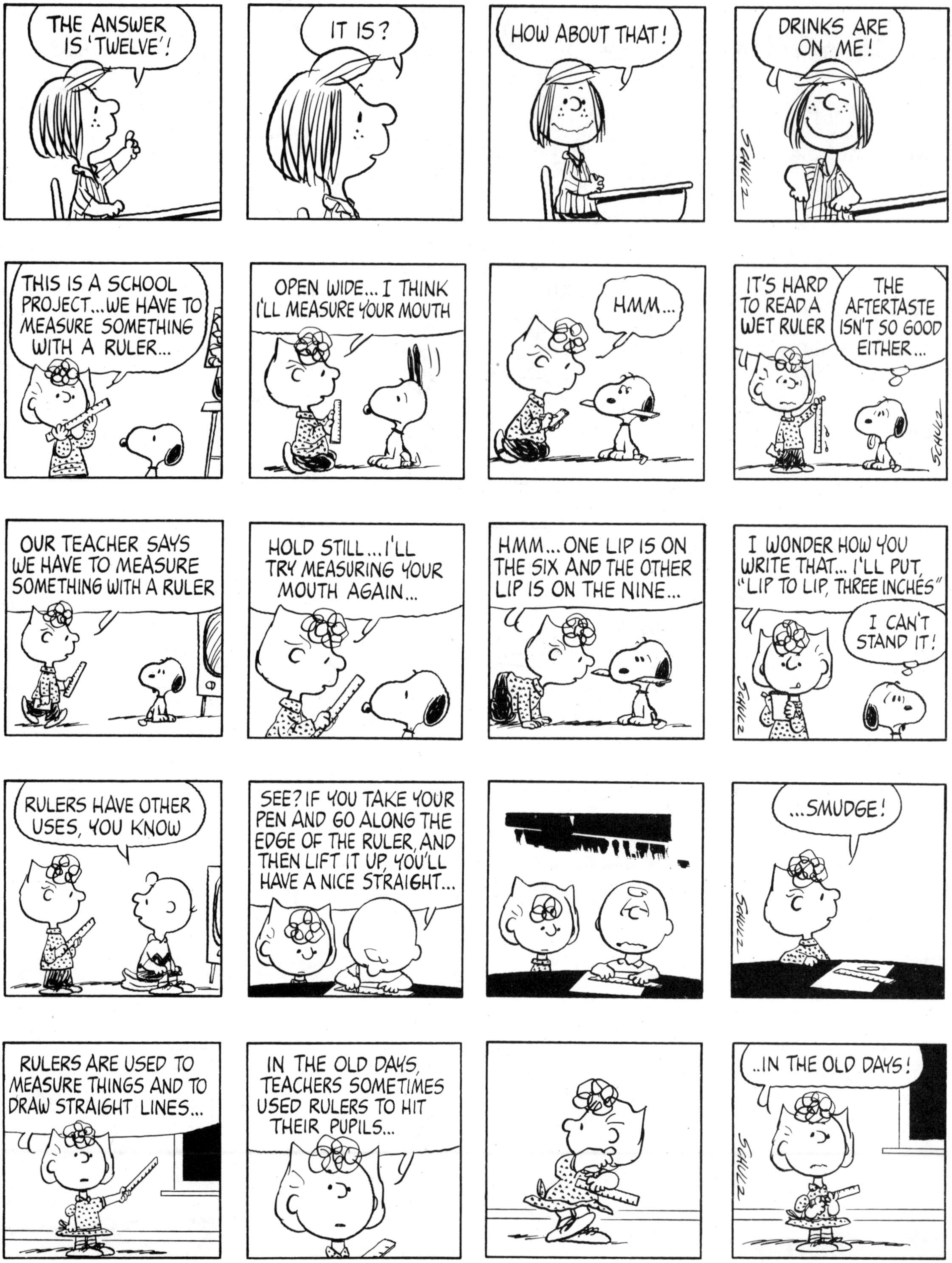
THE ANSWER IS 'TWELVE'!
IT IS?
HOW ABOUT THAT!
DRINKS ARE ON ME!
SCHULZ
THIS IS A SCHOOL PROJECT...WE HAVE TO MEASURE SOMETHING WITH A RULER...
OPEN WIDE... I THINK I'LL MEASURE YOUR MOUTH
HMM...
IT'S HARD TO READ A WET RULER
THE AFTERTASTE ISN'T SO GOOD EITHER...
SCHULZ
OUR TEACHER SAYS WE HAVE TO MEASURE SOMETHING WITH A RULER
HOLD STILL...I'LL TRY MEASURING YOUR MOUTH AGAIN...
HMM... ONE LIP IS ON THE SIX AND THE OTHER LIP IS ON THE NINE...
I WONDER HOW YOU WRITE THAT... I'LL PUT, "LIP TO LIP, THREE INCHES"
I CAN'T STAND IT!
SCHULZ
RULERS HAVE OTHER USES, YOU KNOW
SEE? IF YOU TAKE YOUR PEN AND GO ALONG THE EDGE OF THE RULER, AND THEN LIFT IT UP, YOU'LL HAVE A NICE STRAIGHT...
...SMUDGE!
SCHULZ
RULERS ARE USED TO MEASURE THINGS AND TO DRAW STRAIGHT LINES...
IN THE OLD DAYS, TEACHERS SOMETIMES USED RULERS TO HIT THEIR PUPILS...
..IN THE OLD DAYS!
SCHULZ

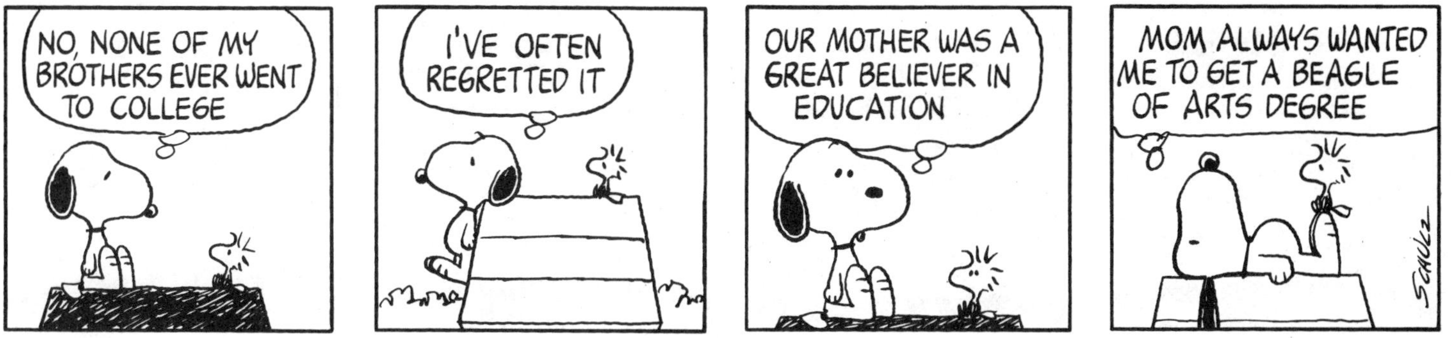
NO, NONE OF MY BROTHERS EVER WENT TO COLLEGE
I'VE OFTEN REGRETTED IT
OUR MOTHER WAS A GREAT BELIEVER IN EDUCATION
MOM ALWAYS WANTED ME TO GET A BEAGLE OF ARTS DEGREE
SCHULZ

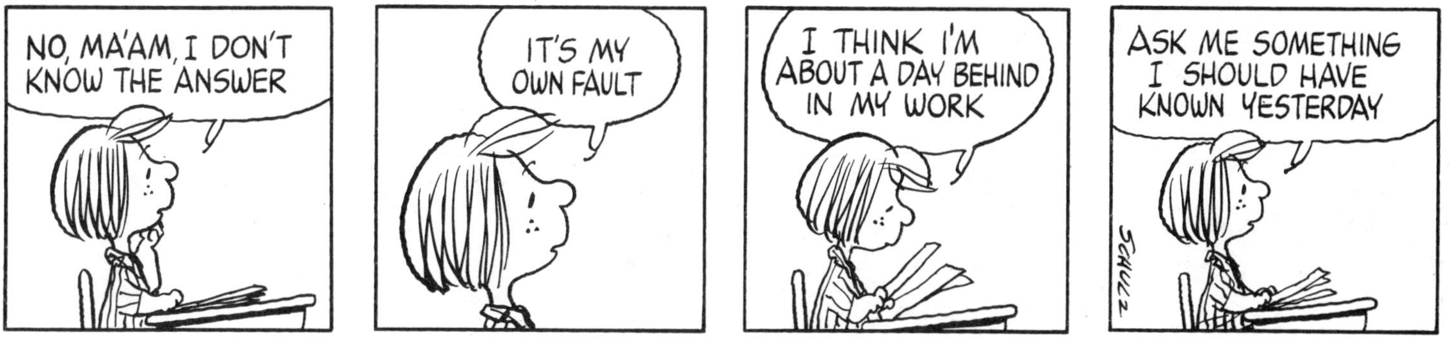
NO, MA'AM, I DON'T KNOW THE ANSWER
IT'S MY OWN FAULT
I THINK I'M ABOUT A DAY BEHIND IN MY WORK
ASK ME SOMETHING I SHOULD HAVE KNOWN YESTERDAY
SCHULZ

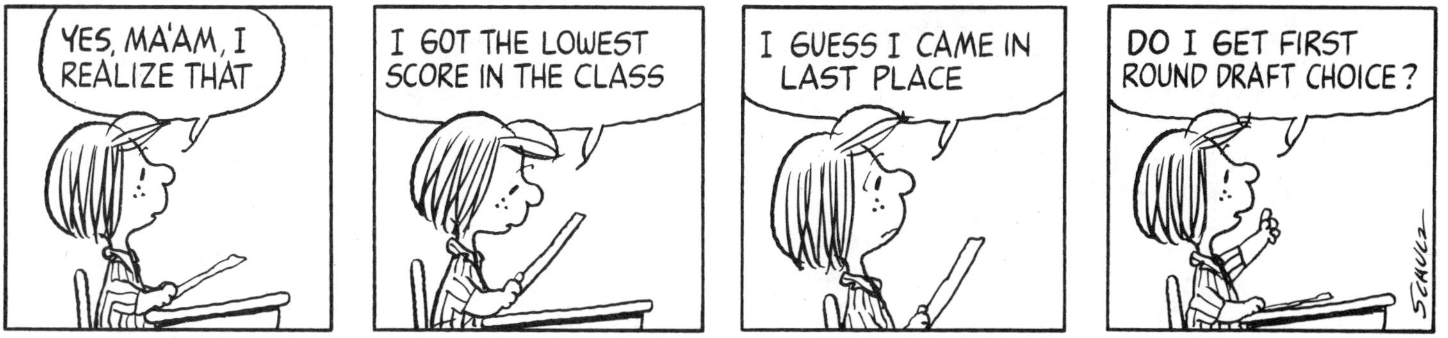
YES, MA'AM, I REALIZE THAT
I GOT THE LOWEST SCORE IN THE CLASS
I GUESS I CAME IN LAST PLACE
DO I GET FIRST ROUND DRAFT CHOICE?
SCHULZ

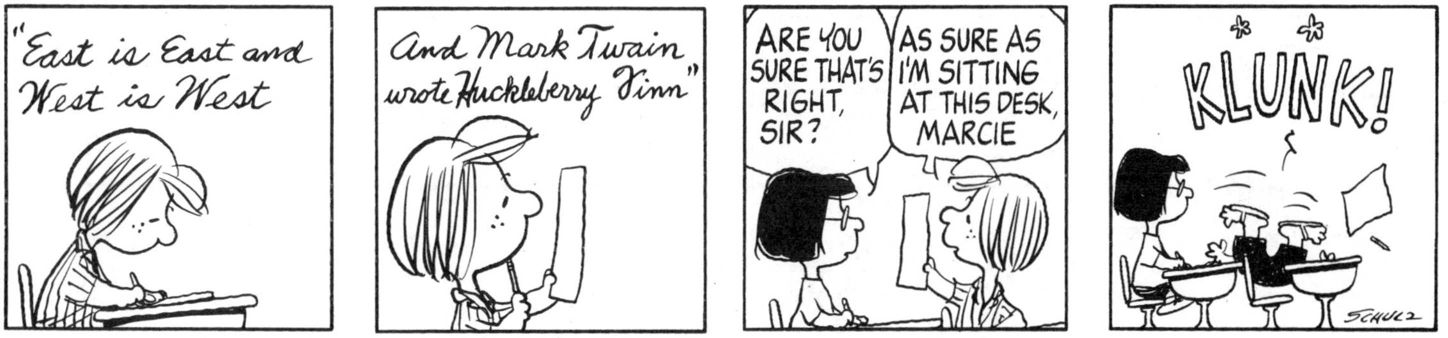
"East is East and West is West
And Mark Twain wrote Huckleberry Finn"
ARE YOU SURE THAT'S RIGHT, SIR?
AS SURE AS I'M SITTING AT THIS DESK, MARCIE
KLUNK!
SCHULZ

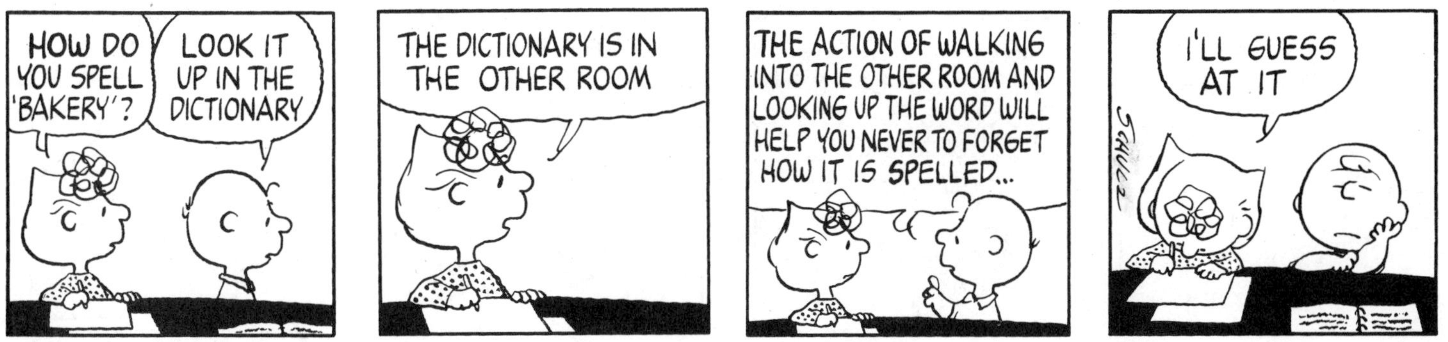
HOW DO YOU SPELL 'BAKERY'?
LOOK IT UP IN THE DICTIONARY
THE DICTIONARY IS IN THE OTHER ROOM
THE ACTION OF WALKING INTO THE OTHER ROOM AND LOOKING UP THE WORD WILL HELP YOU NEVER TO FORGET HOW IT IS SPELLED...
I'LL GUESS AT IT
SCHULZ

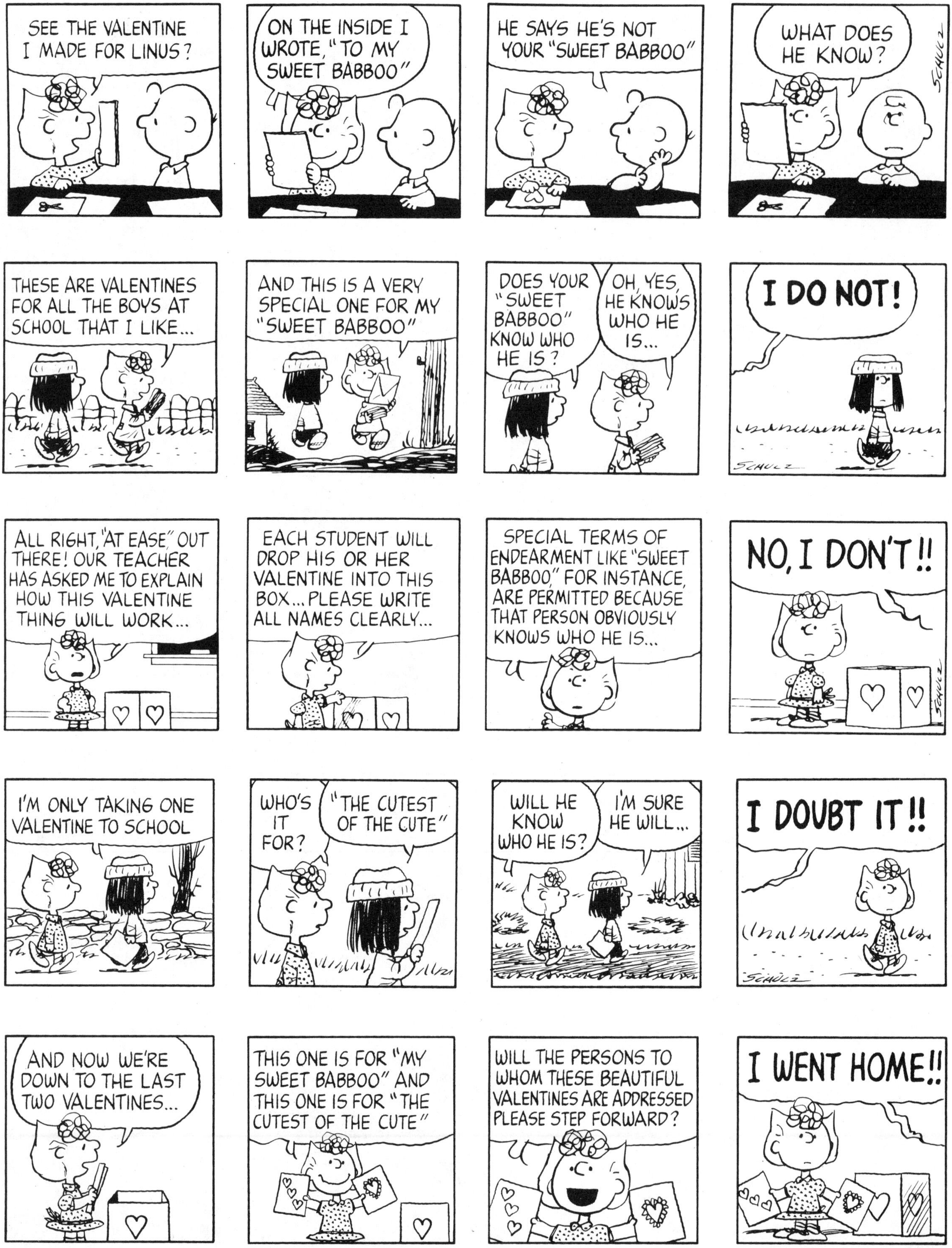
SEE THE VALENTINE I MADE FOR LINUS?
ON THE INSIDE I WROTE, "TO MY SWEET BABBOO"
HE SAYS HE'S NOT YOUR "SWEET BABBOO"
WHAT DOES HE KNOW?
SCHULZ
THESE ARE VALENTINES FOR ALL THE BOYS AT SCHOOL THAT I LIKE...
AND THIS IS A VERY SPECIAL ONE FOR MY "SWEET BABBOO"
DOES YOUR "SWEET BABBOO" KNOW WHO HE IS?
OH, YES, HE KNOWS WHO HE IS...
I DO NOT!
SCHULZ
ALL RIGHT, "AT EASE" OUT THERE! OUR TEACHER HAS ASKED ME TO EXPLAIN HOW THIS VALENTINE THING WILL WORK...
EACH STUDENT WILL DROP HIS OR HER VALENTINE INTO THIS BOX... PLEASE WRITE ALL NAMES CLEARLY...
SPECIAL TERMS OF ENDEARMENT LIKE "SWEET BABBOO," FOR INSTANCE, ARE PERMITTED BECAUSE THAT PERSON OBVIOUSLY KNOWS WHO HE IS...
NO, I DON'T!!
SCHULZ
I'M ONLY TAKING ONE VALENTINE TO SCHOOL
WHO'S IT FOR?
"THE CUTEST OF THE CUTE"
WILL HE KNOW WHO HE IS?
I'M SURE HE WILL...
I DOUBT IT!!
SCHULZ
AND NOW WE'RE DOWN TO THE LAST TWO VALENTINES...
THIS ONE IS FOR "MY SWEET BABBOO" AND THIS ONE IS FOR "THE CUTEST OF THE CUTE"
WILL THE PERSONS TO WHOM THESE BEAUTIFUL VALENTINES ARE ADDRESSED PLEASE STEP FORWARD?
I WENT HOME!!

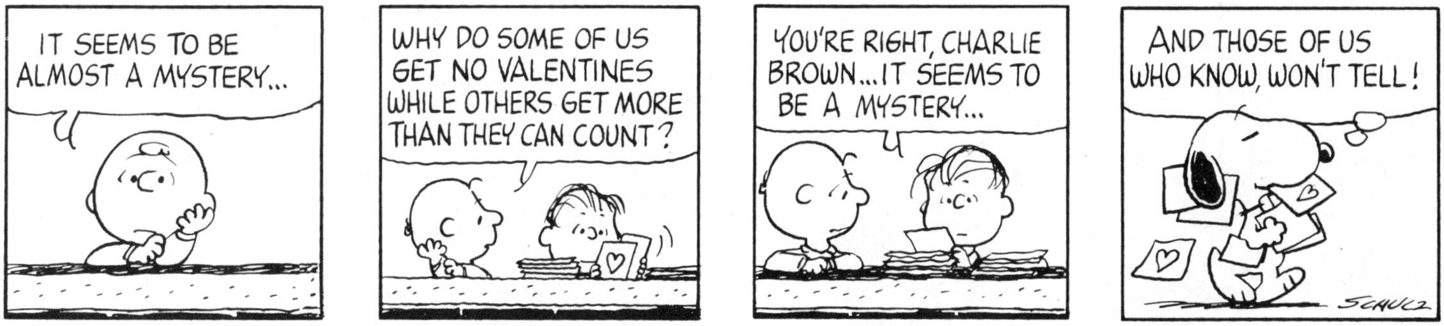
IT SEEMS TO BE ALMOST A MYSTERY...
WHY DO SOME OF US GET NO VALENTINES WHILE OTHERS GET MORE THAN THEY CAN COUNT?
YOU'RE RIGHT, CHARLIE BROWN... IT SEEMS TO BE A MYSTERY...
AND THOSE OF US WHO KNOW, WON'T TELL!
SCHULZ

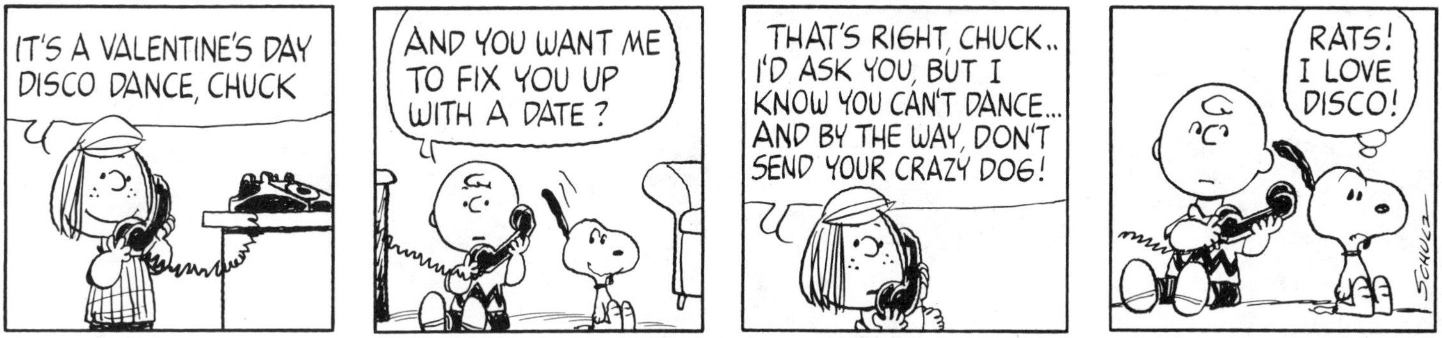
IT'S A VALENTINE'S DAY DISCO DANCE, CHUCK
AND YOU WANT ME TO FIX YOU UP WITH A DATE?
THAT'S RIGHT, CHUCK.. I'D ASK YOU, BUT I KNOW YOU CAN'T DANCE... AND BY THE WAY, DON'T SEND YOUR CRAZY DOG!
RATS! I LOVE DISCO!
SCHULZ

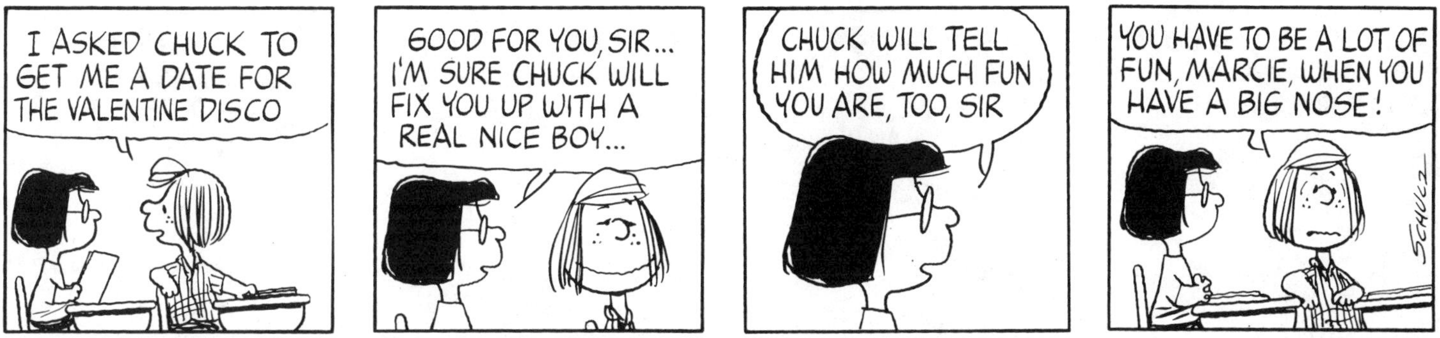
I ASKED CHUCK TO GET ME A DATE FOR THE VALENTINE DISCO
GOOD FOR YOU, SIR... I'M SURE CHUCK WILL FIX YOU UP WITH A REAL NICE BOY...
CHUCK WILL TELL HIM HOW MUCH FUN YOU ARE, TOO, SIR
YOU HAVE TO BE A LOT OF FUN, MARCIE, WHEN YOU HAVE A BIG NOSE!
SCHULZ

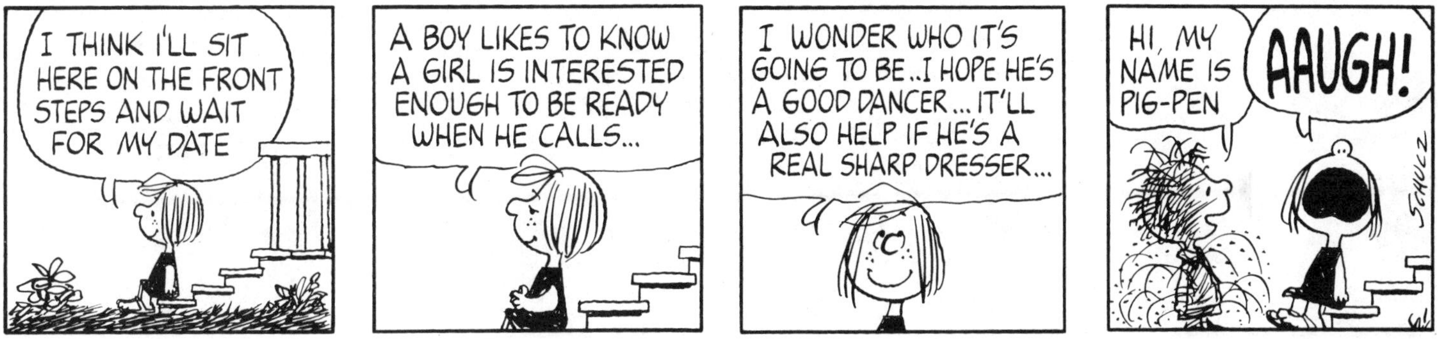
I THINK I'LL SIT HERE ON THE FRONT STEPS AND WAIT FOR MY DATE
A BOY LIKES TO KNOW A GIRL IS INTERESTED ENOUGH TO BE READY WHEN HE CALLS...
I WONDER WHO IT'S GOING TO BE.. I HOPE HE'S A GOOD DANCER... IT'LL ALSO HELP IF HE'S A REAL SHARP DRESSER...
HI, MY NAME IS PIG-PEN
AAUGH!
SCHULZ

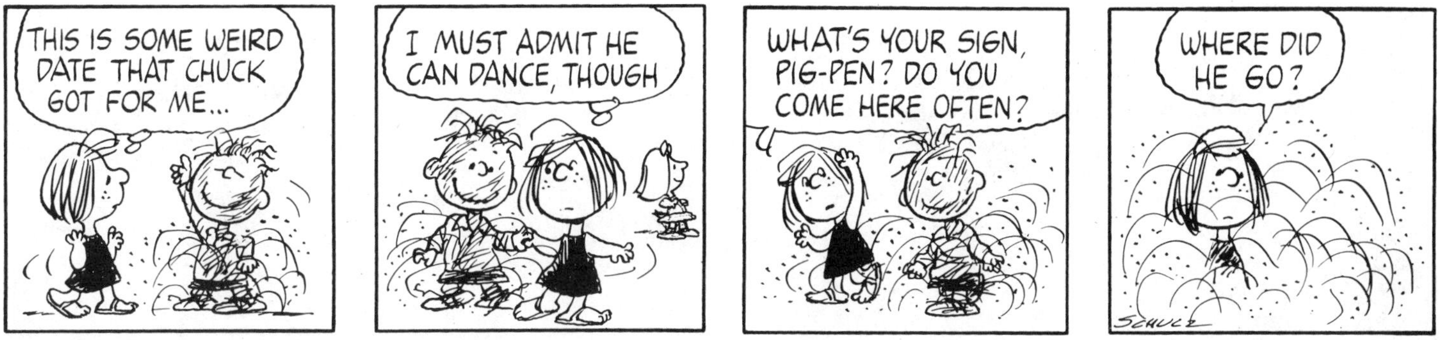
THIS IS SOME WEIRD DATE THAT CHUCK GOT FOR ME...
I MUST ADMIT HE CAN DANCE, THOUGH
WHAT'S YOUR SIGN, PIG-PEN? DO YOU COME HERE OFTEN?
WHERE DID HE GO?
SCHULZ

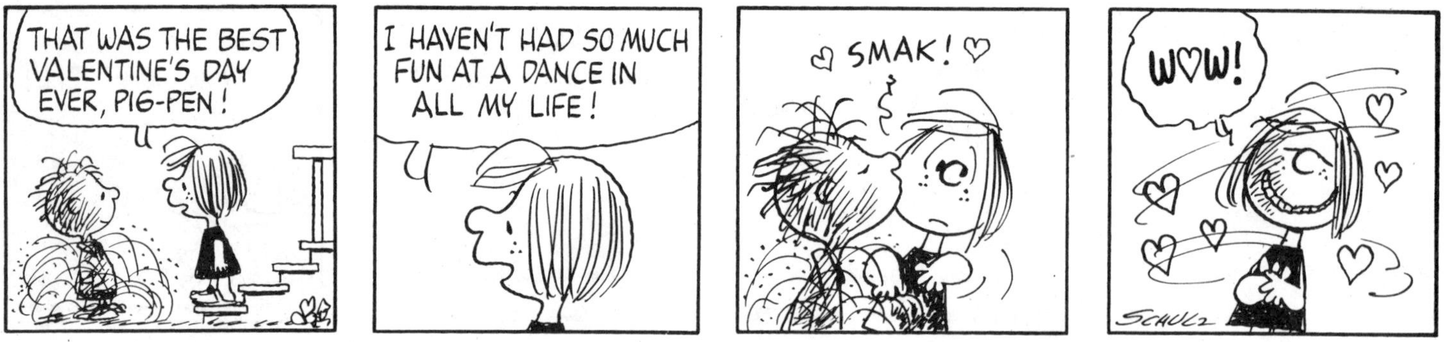
THAT WAS THE BEST VALENTINE'S DAY EVER, PIG-PEN!
I HAVEN'T HAD SO MUCH FUN AT A DANCE IN ALL MY LIFE!
SMAK!
WOW!
SCHULZ

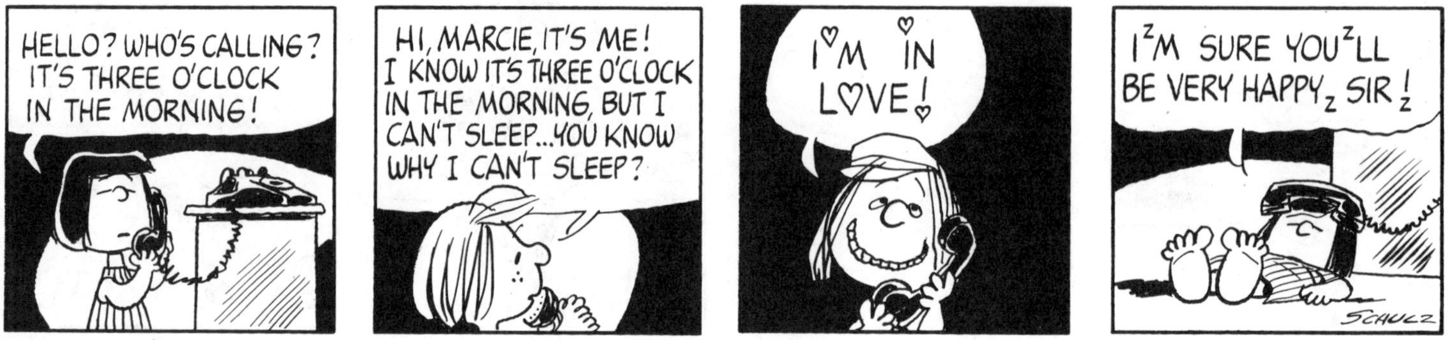
HELLO? WHO'S CALLING? IT'S THREE O'CLOCK IN THE MORNING!
HI, MARCIE, IT'S ME! I KNOW IT'S THREE O'CLOCK IN THE MORNING, BUT I CAN'T SLEEP...YOU KNOW WHY I CAN'T SLEEP?
I'M IN LOVE!
I'M SURE YOU'LL BE VERY HAPPY, SIR!
SCHULZ

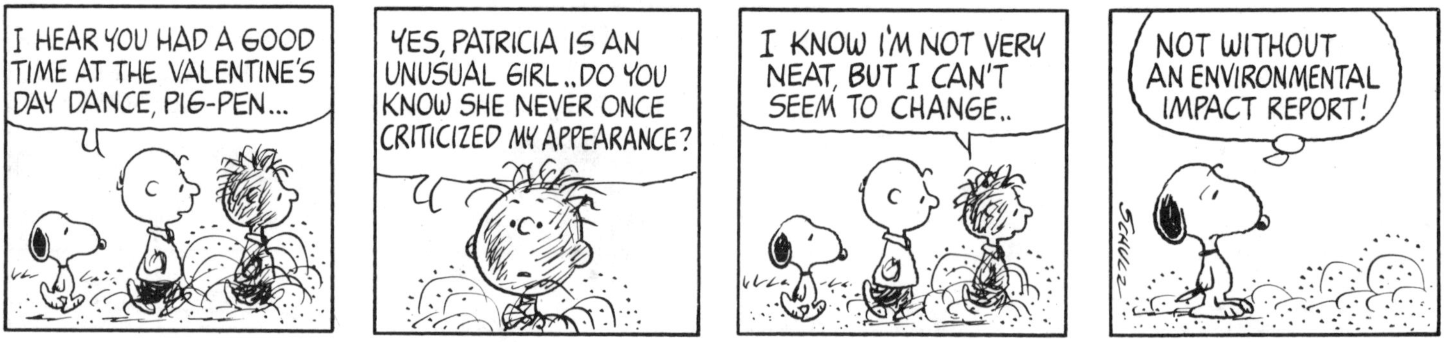
I HEAR YOU HAD A GOOD TIME AT THE VALENTINE'S DAY DANCE, PIG-PEN...
YES, PATRICIA IS AN UNUSUAL GIRL..DO YOU KNOW SHE NEVER ONCE CRITICIZED MY APPEARANCE?
I KNOW I'M NOT VERY NEAT, BUT I CAN'T SEEM TO CHANGE..
NOT WITHOUT AN ENVIRONMENTAL IMPACT REPORT!
SCHULZ

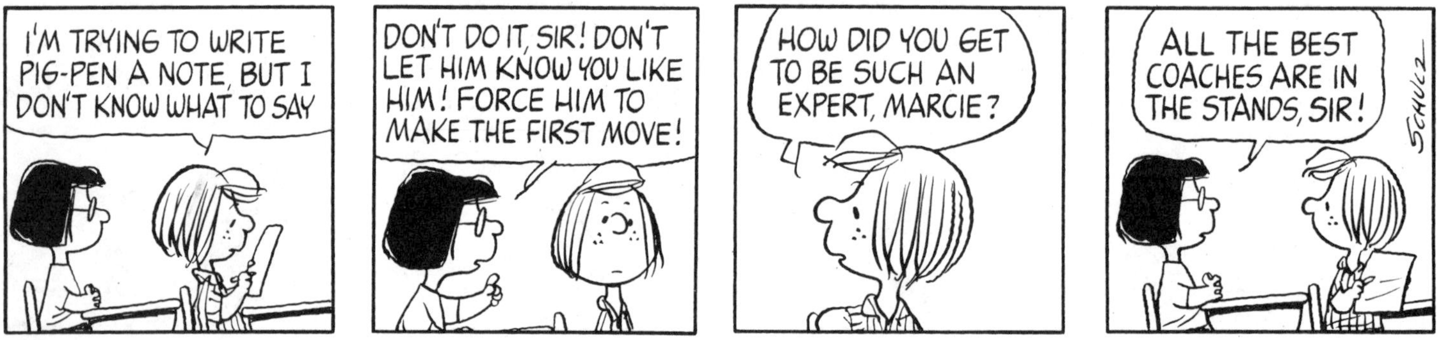
I'M TRYING TO WRITE PIG-PEN A NOTE, BUT I DON'T KNOW WHAT TO SAY
DON'T DO IT, SIR! DON'T LET HIM KNOW YOU LIKE HIM! FORCE HIM TO MAKE THE FIRST MOVE!
HOW DID YOU GET TO BE SUCH AN EXPERT, MARCIE?
ALL THE BEST COACHES ARE IN THE STANDS, SIR!
SCHULZ

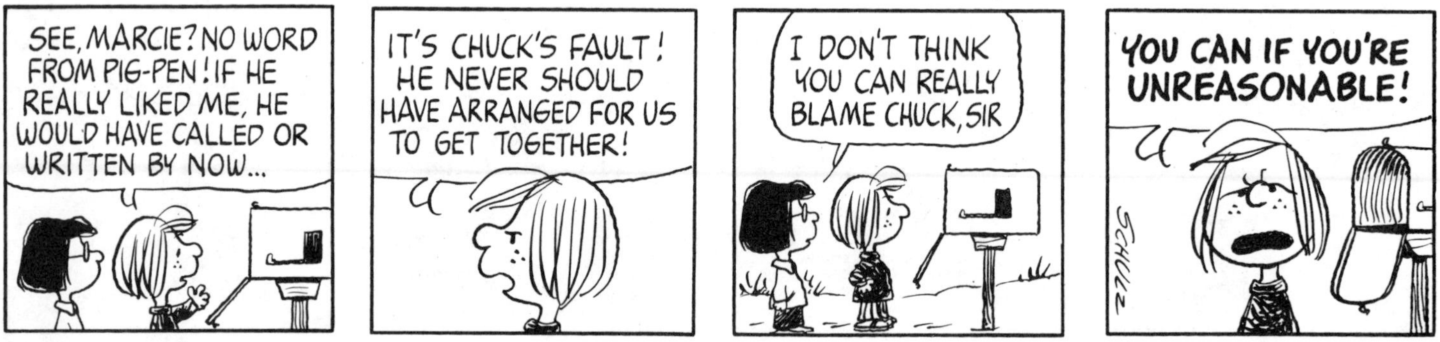
SEE, MARCIE? NO WORD FROM PIG-PEN! IF HE REALLY LIKED ME, HE WOULD HAVE CALLED OR WRITTEN BY NOW...
IT'S CHUCK'S FAULT! HE NEVER SHOULD HAVE ARRANGED FOR US TO GET TOGETHER!
I DON'T THINK YOU CAN REALLY BLAME CHUCK, SIR
YOU CAN IF YOU'RE UNREASONABLE!
SCHULZ

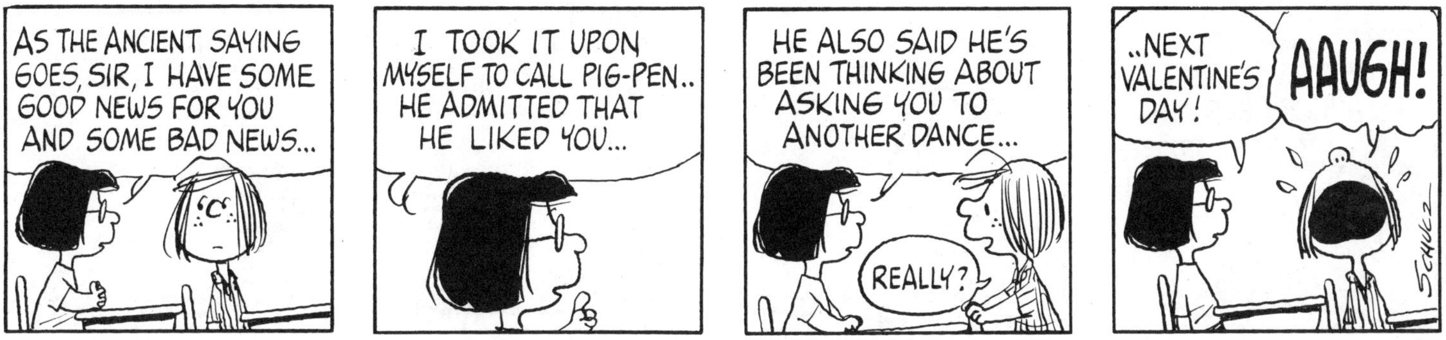
AS THE ANCIENT SAYING GOES, SIR, I HAVE SOME GOOD NEWS FOR YOU AND SOME BAD NEWS...
I TOOK IT UPON MYSELF TO CALL PIG-PEN.. HE ADMITTED THAT HE LIKED YOU...
HE ALSO SAID HE'S BEEN THINKING ABOUT ASKING YOU TO ANOTHER DANCE...
REALLY?
..NEXT VALENTINE'S DAY!
AAUGH!
SCHULZ

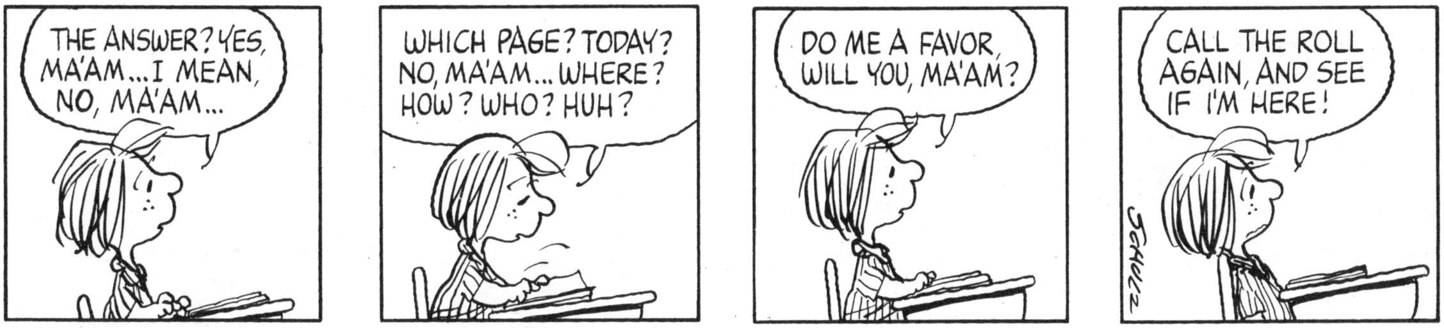
THE ANSWER? YES, MA'AM... I MEAN, NO, MA'AM...
WHICH PAGE? TODAY? NO, MA'AM... WHERE? HOW? WHO? HUH?
DO ME A FAVOR, WILL YOU, MA'AM?
SCHULZ
CALL THE ROLL AGAIN, AND SEE IF I'M HERE!

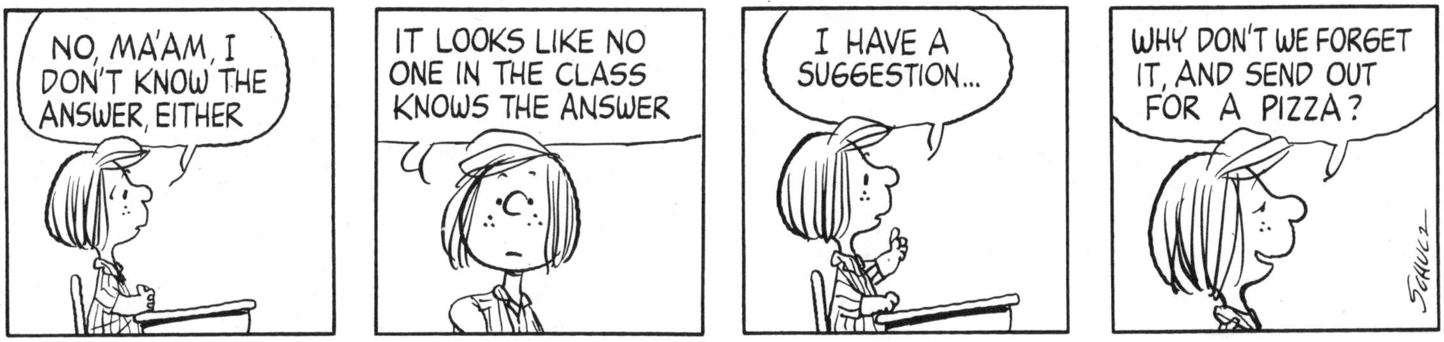
NO, MA'AM, I DON'T KNOW THE ANSWER, EITHER
IT LOOKS LIKE NO ONE IN THE CLASS KNOWS THE ANSWER
I HAVE A SUGGESTION...
WHY DON'T WE FORGET IT, AND SEND OUT FOR A PIZZA?
SCHULZ

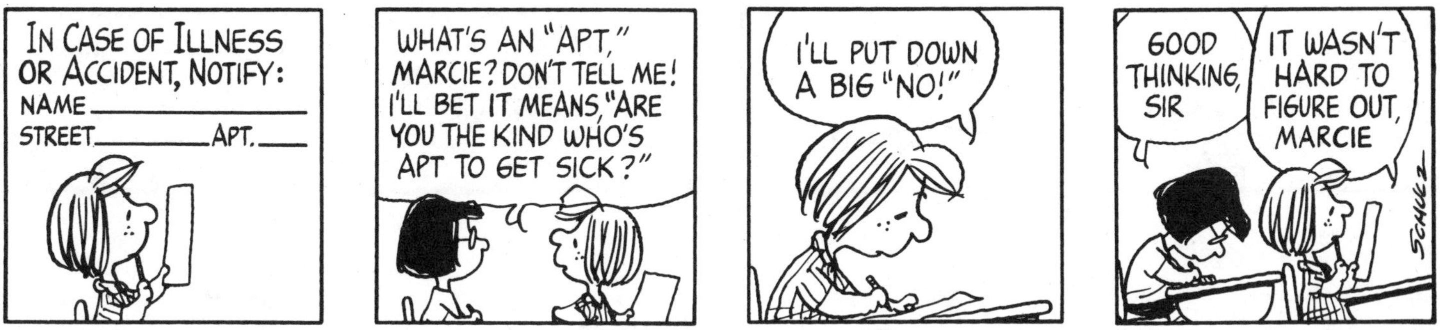
IN CASE OF ILLNESS OR ACCIDENT, NOTIFY:
NAME
STREET
APT.
WHAT'S AN "APT," MARCIE? DON'T TELL ME! I'LL BET IT MEANS, "ARE YOU THE KIND WHO'S APT TO GET SICK?"
I'LL PUT DOWN A BIG "NO!"
GOOD THINKING, SIR
IT WASN'T HARD TO FIGURE OUT, MARCIE
SCHULZ

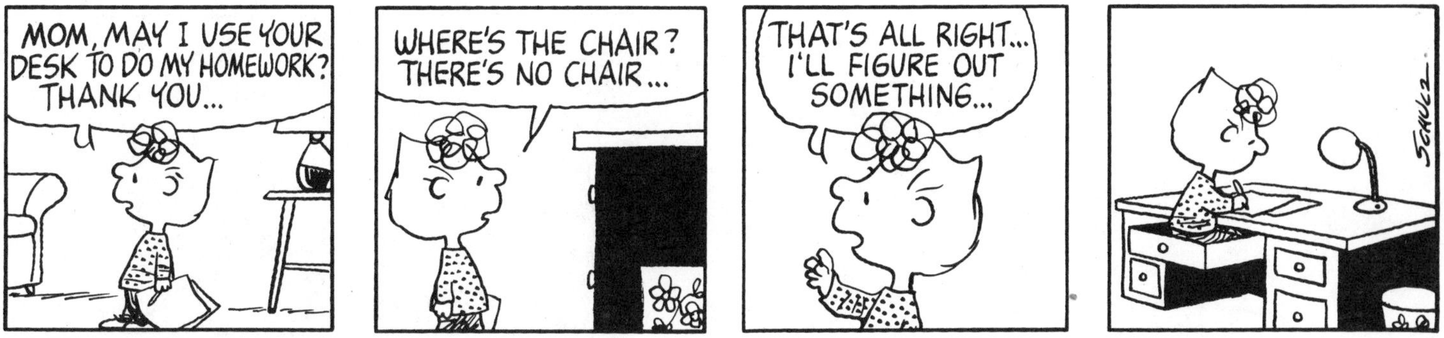
MOM, MAY I USE YOUR DESK TO DO MY HOMEWORK? THANK YOU...
WHERE'S THE CHAIR? THERE'S NO CHAIR...
THAT'S ALL RIGHT... I'LL FIGURE OUT SOMETHING...
SCHULZ

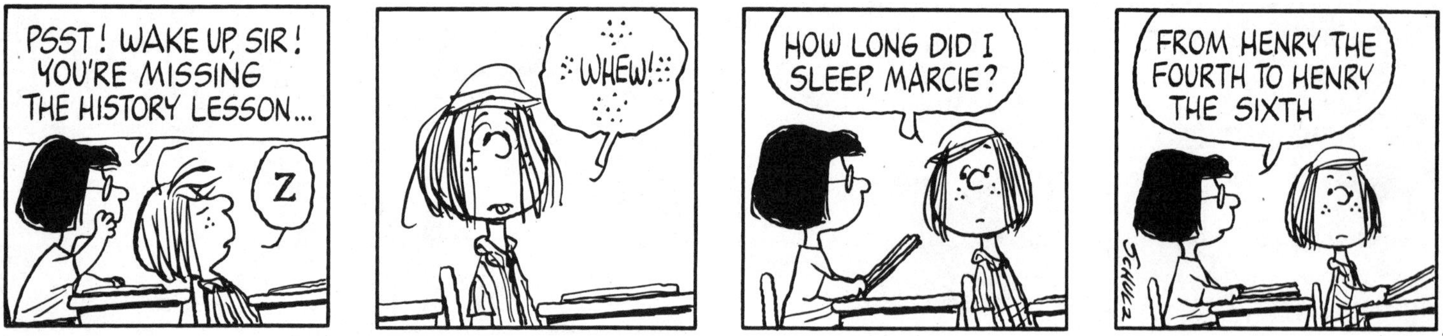
PSST! WAKE UP, SIR! YOU'RE MISSING THE HISTORY LESSON...
Z
WHEW!
HOW LONG DID I SLEEP, MARCIE?
FROM HENRY THE FOURTH TO HENRY THE SIXTH
SCHULZ

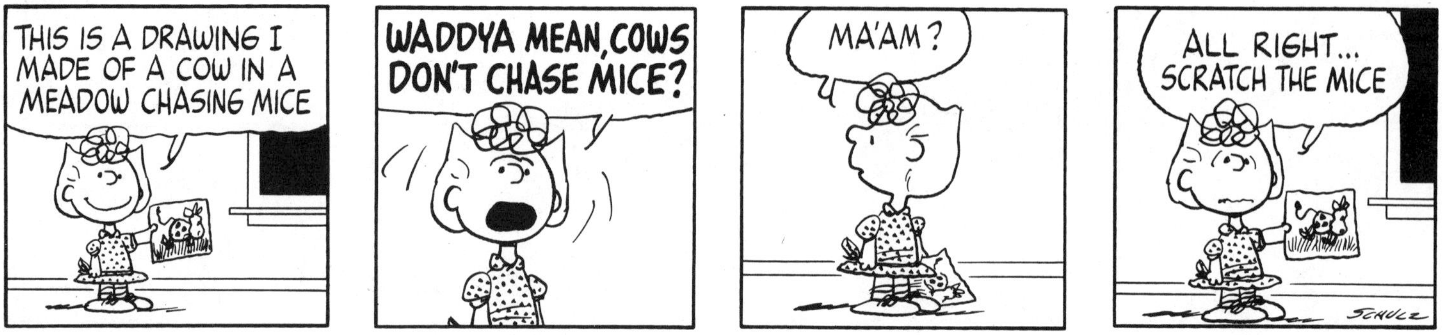
THIS IS A DRAWING I MADE OF A COW IN A MEADOW CHASING MICE
WADDYA MEAN, COWS DON'T CHASE MICE?
MA'AM?
ALL RIGHT... SCRATCH THE MICE
SCHULZ

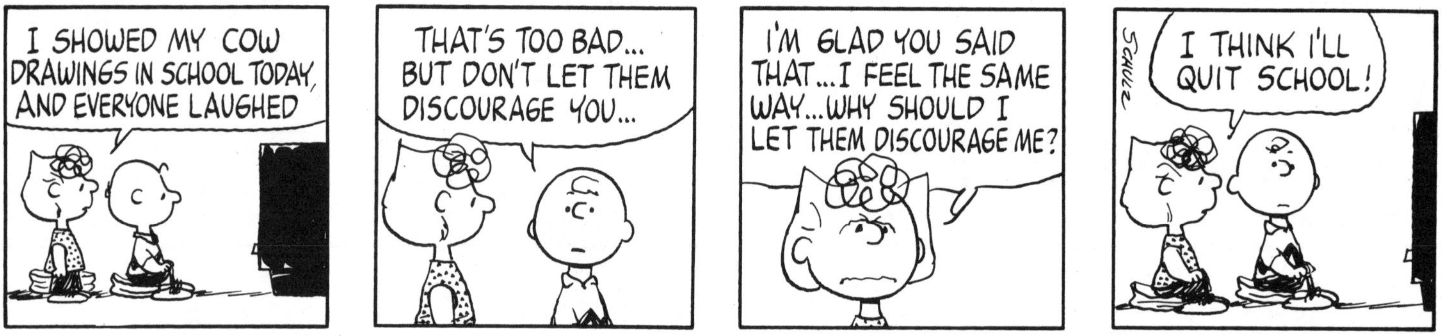
I SHOWED MY COW DRAWINGS IN SCHOOL TODAY, AND EVERYONE LAUGHED
THAT'S TOO BAD... BUT DON'T LET THEM DISCOURAGE YOU...
I'M GLAD YOU SAID THAT... I FEEL THE SAME WAY... WHY SHOULD I LET THEM DISCOURAGE ME?
SCHULZ
I THINK I'LL QUIT SCHOOL!

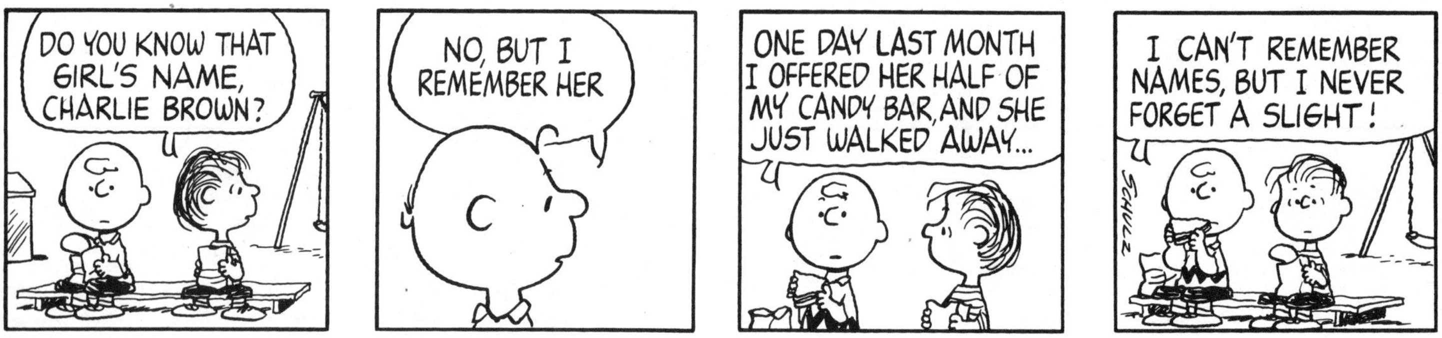
DO YOU KNOW THAT GIRL'S NAME, CHARLIE BROWN?
NO, BUT I REMEMBER HER
ONE DAY LAST MONTH I OFFERED HER HALF OF MY CANDY BAR, AND SHE JUST WALKED AWAY...
I CAN'T REMEMBER NAMES, BUT I NEVER FORGET A SLIGHT!
SCHULZ

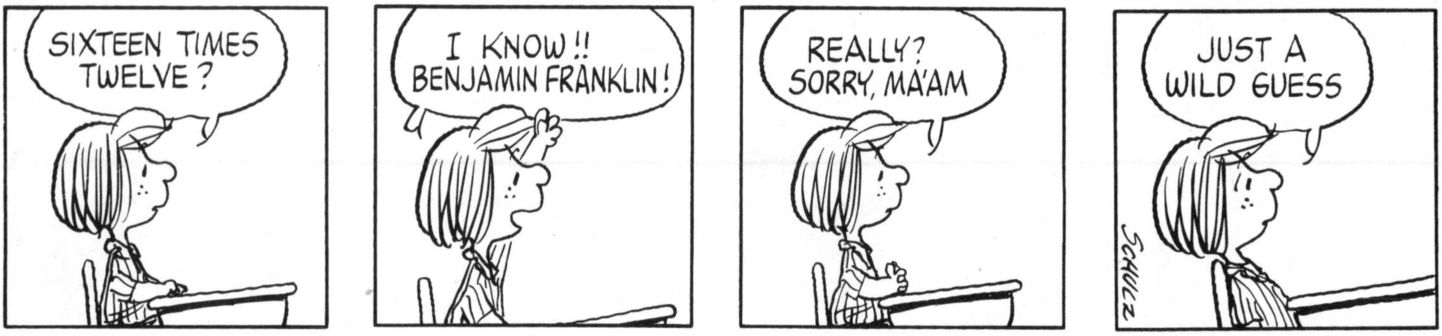
SIXTEEN TIMES TWELVE?
I KNOW!! BENJAMIN FRANKLIN!
REALLY? SORRY, MA'AM
SCHULZ
JUST A WILD GUESS

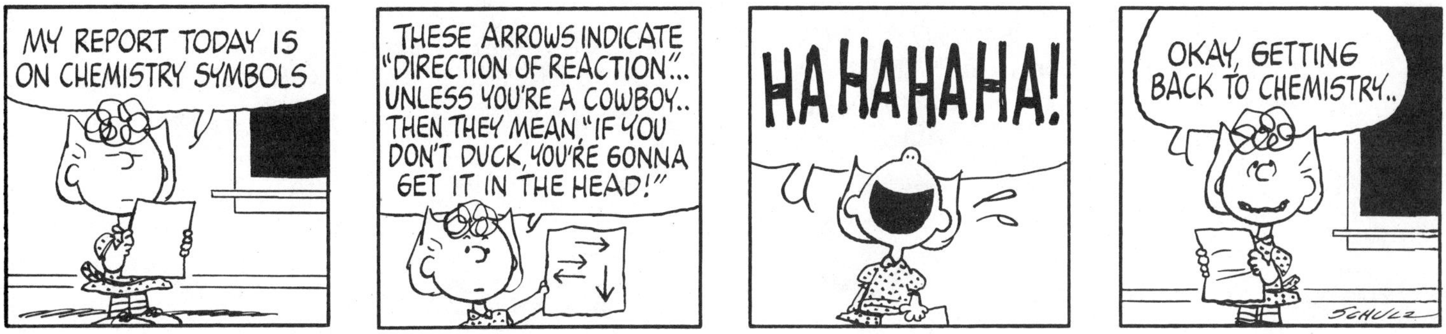
MY REPORT TODAY IS ON CHEMISTRY SYMBOLS
THESE ARROWS INDICATE "DIRECTION OF REACTION"... UNLESS YOU'RE A COWBOY.. THEN THEY MEAN, "IF YOU DON'T DUCK, YOU'RE GONNA GET IT IN THE HEAD!"
HAHAHAHA!
OKAY, GETTING BACK TO CHEMISTRY..
SCHULZ

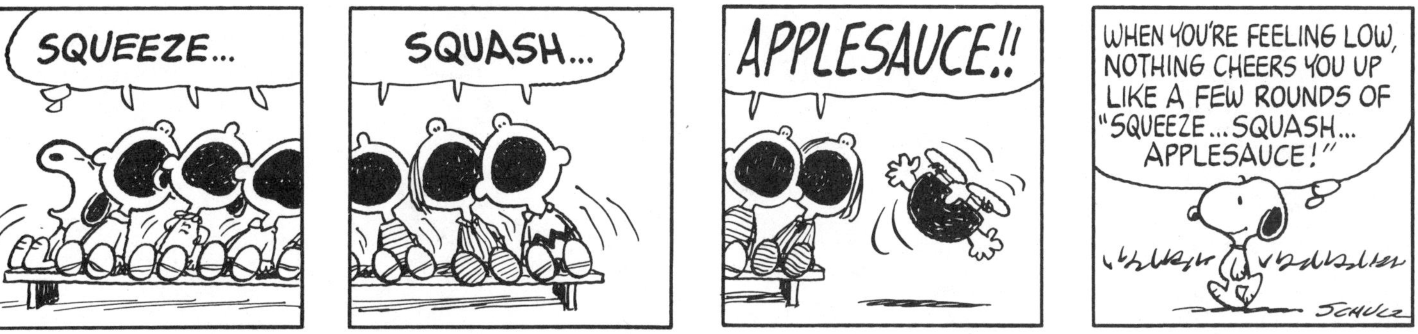
SQUEEZE...
SQUASH...
APPLESAUCE!!
WHEN YOU'RE FEELING LOW, NOTHING CHEERS YOU UP LIKE A FEW ROUNDS OF "SQUEEZE...SQUASH... APPLESAUCE!"
SCHULZ

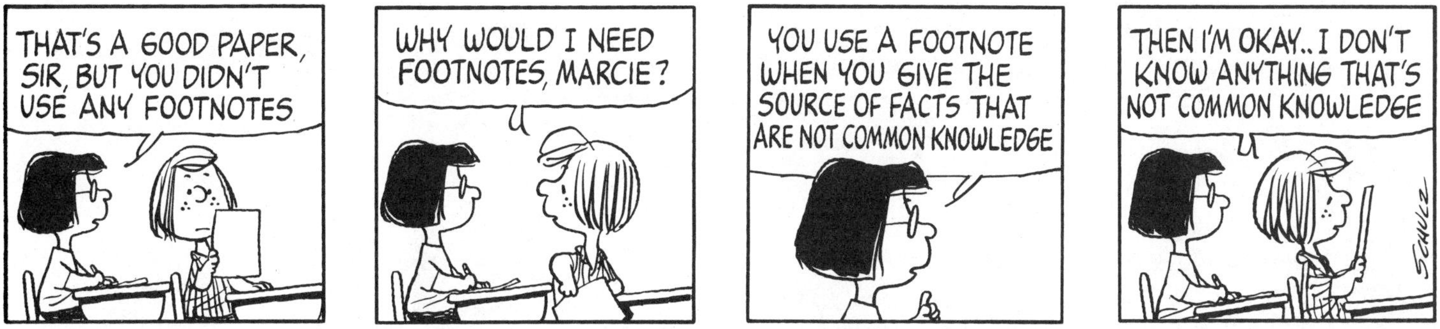
THAT'S A GOOD PAPER, SIR, BUT YOU DIDN'T USE ANY FOOTNOTES
WHY WOULD I NEED FOOTNOTES, MARCIE?
YOU USE A FOOTNOTE WHEN YOU GIVE THE SOURCE OF FACTS THAT ARE NOT COMMON KNOWLEDGE
THEN I'M OKAY.. I DON'T KNOW ANYTHING THAT'S NOT COMMON KNOWLEDGE
SCHULZ

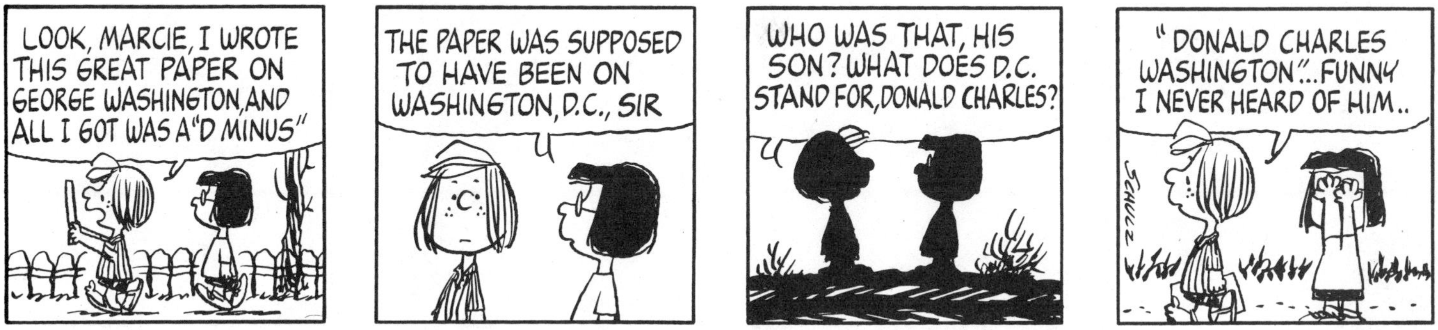
LOOK, MARCIE, I WROTE THIS GREAT PAPER ON GEORGE WASHINGTON, AND ALL I GOT WAS A "D MINUS"
THE PAPER WAS SUPPOSED TO HAVE BEEN ON WASHINGTON, D.C., SIR
WHO WAS THAT, HIS SON? WHAT DOES D.C. STAND FOR, DONALD CHARLES?
"DONALD CHARLES WASHINGTON"... FUNNY I NEVER HEARD OF HIM..
SCHULZ

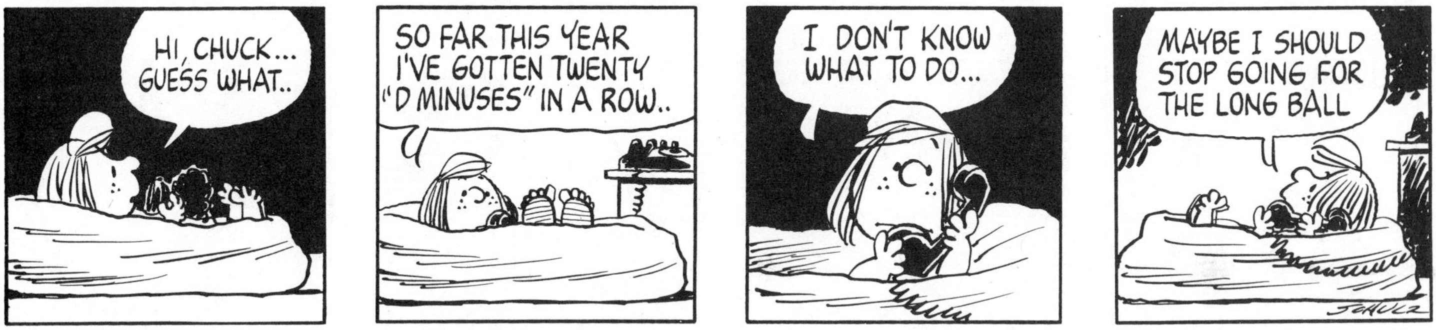
HI, CHUCK... GUESS WHAT..
SO FAR THIS YEAR I'VE GOTTEN TWENTY "D MINUSES" IN A ROW..
I DON'T KNOW WHAT TO DO...
MAYBE I SHOULD STOP GOING FOR THE LONG BALL
SCHULZ

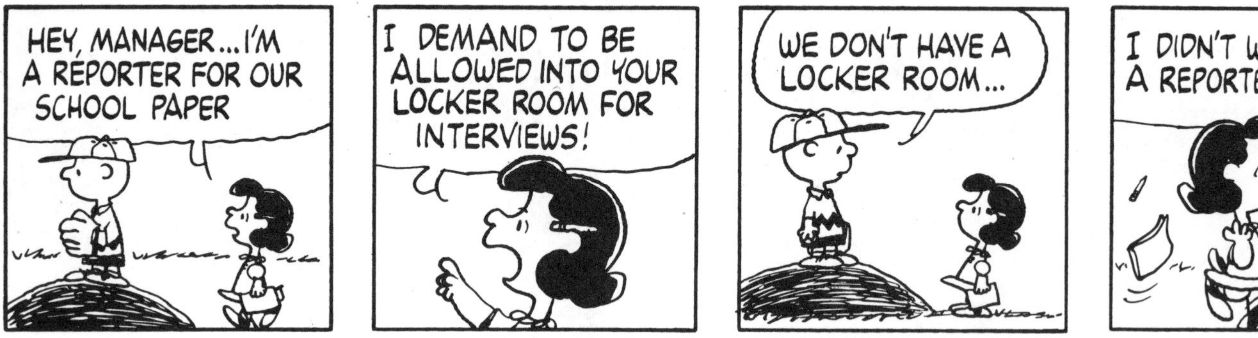
HEY, MANAGER...I'M A REPORTER FOR OUR SCHOOL PAPER
I DEMAND TO BE ALLOWED INTO YOUR LOCKER ROOM FOR INTERVIEWS!
WE DON'T HAVE A LOCKER ROOM...
I DIDN'T WANT TO BE A REPORTER ANYWAY
SCHULZ

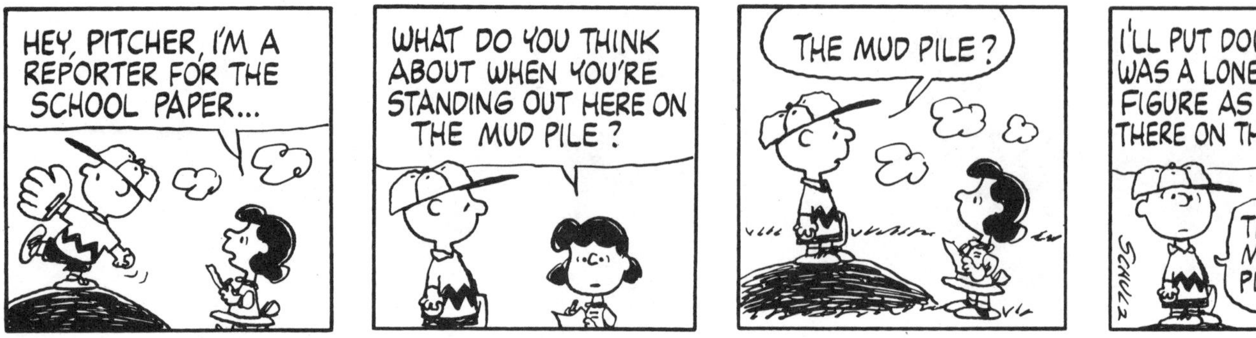
HEY, PITCHER, I'M A REPORTER FOR THE SCHOOL PAPER...
WHAT DO YOU THINK ABOUT WHEN YOU'RE STANDING OUT HERE ON THE MUD PILE?
THE MUD PILE?
I'LL PUT DOWN THAT HE WAS A LONELY LOOKING FIGURE AS HE STOOD THERE ON THE MUD PILE...
THE MUD PILE?
SCHULZ

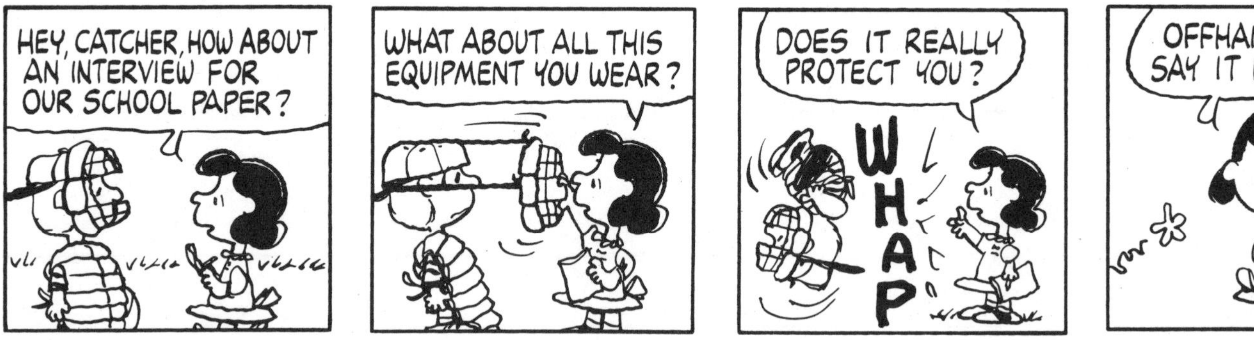
HEY, CATCHER, HOW ABOUT AN INTERVIEW FOR OUR SCHOOL PAPER?
WHAT ABOUT ALL THIS EQUIPMENT YOU WEAR?
DOES IT REALLY PROTECT YOU?
WHAP
OFFHAND, I'D SAY IT DOESN'T
SCHULZ

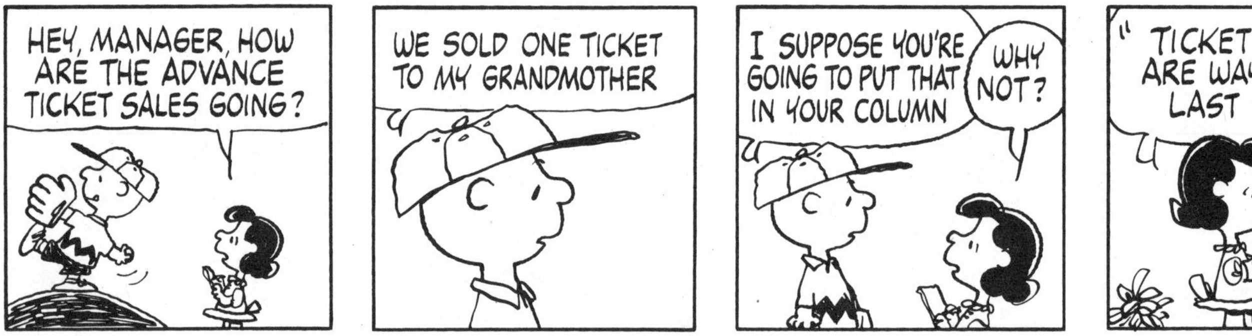
HEY, MANAGER, HOW ARE THE ADVANCE TICKET SALES GOING?
WE SOLD ONE TICKET TO MY GRANDMOTHER
I SUPPOSE YOU'RE GOING TO PUT THAT IN YOUR COLUMN
WHY NOT?
"TICKET SALES ARE WAY UP OVER LAST YEAR"
SCHULZ

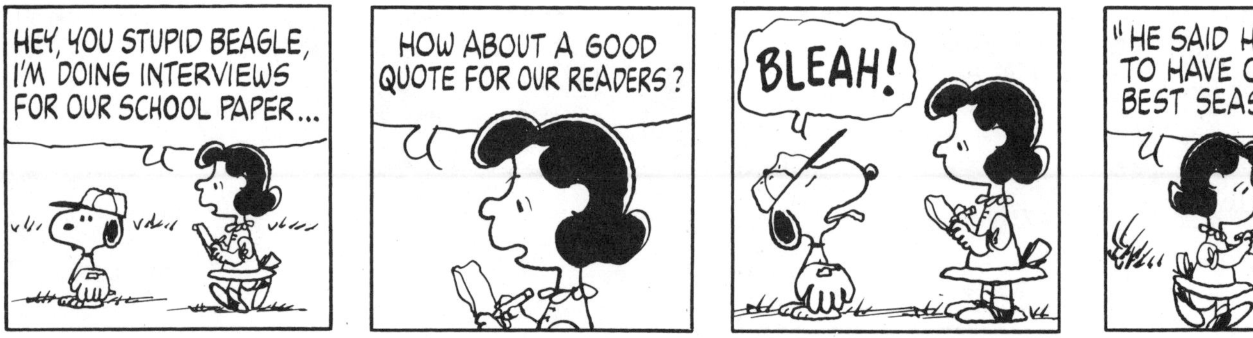
HEY, YOU STUPID BEAGLE, I'M DOING INTERVIEWS FOR OUR SCHOOL PAPER...
HOW ABOUT A GOOD QUOTE FOR OUR READERS?
BLEAH!
"HE SAID HE EXPECTS TO HAVE ONE OF HIS BEST SEASONS EVER"
SCHULZ

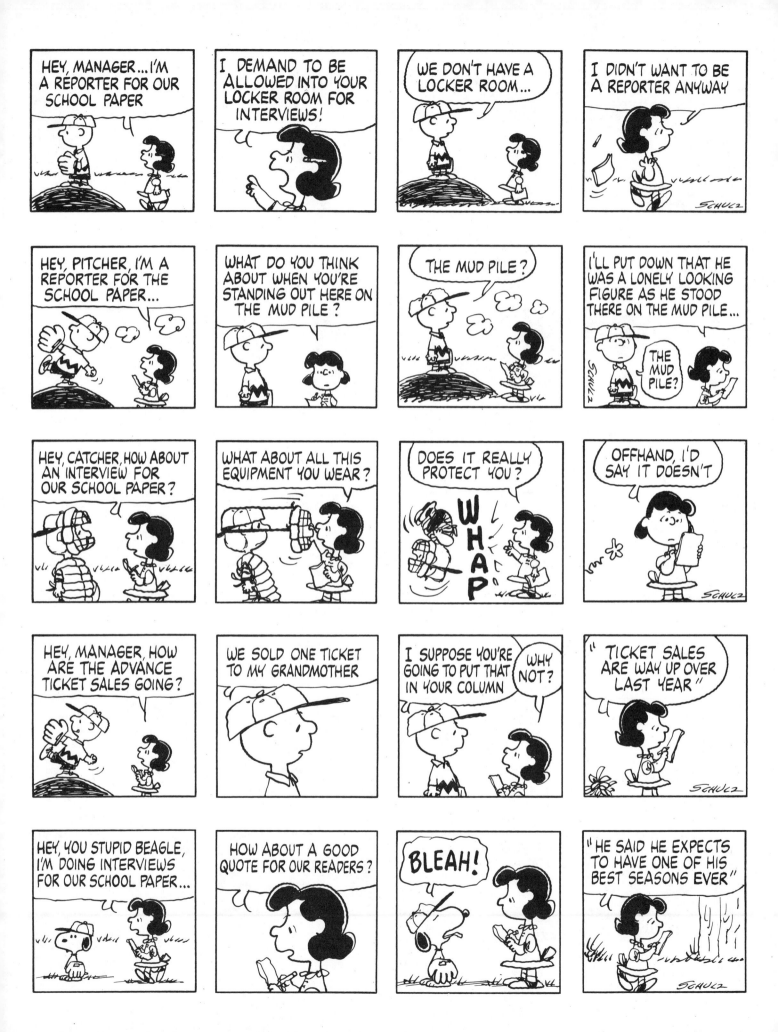

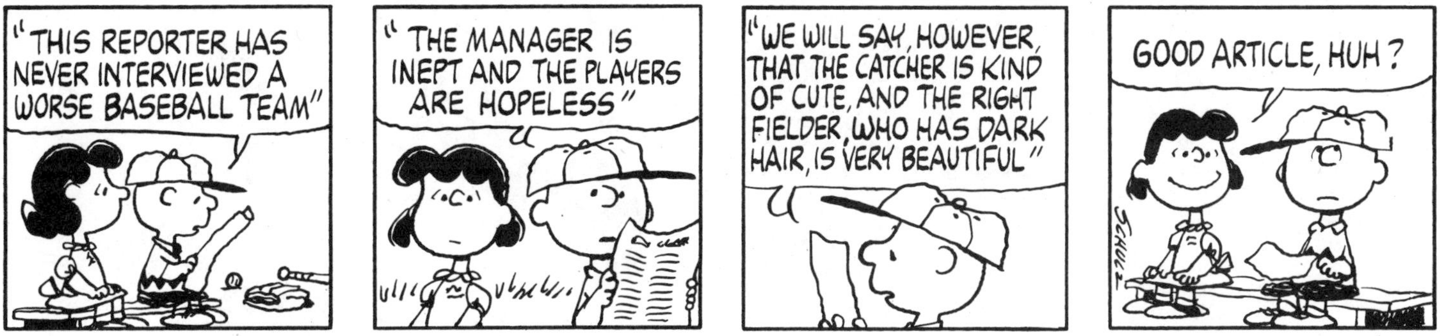
"THIS REPORTER HAS NEVER INTERVIEWED A WORSE BASEBALL TEAM"
"THE MANAGER IS INEPT AND THE PLAYERS ARE HOPELESS"
"WE WILL SAY, HOWEVER, THAT THE CATCHER IS KIND OF CUTE, AND THE RIGHT FIELDER, WHO HAS DARK HAIR, IS VERY BEAUTIFUL"
GOOD ARTICLE, HUH?
SCHULZ

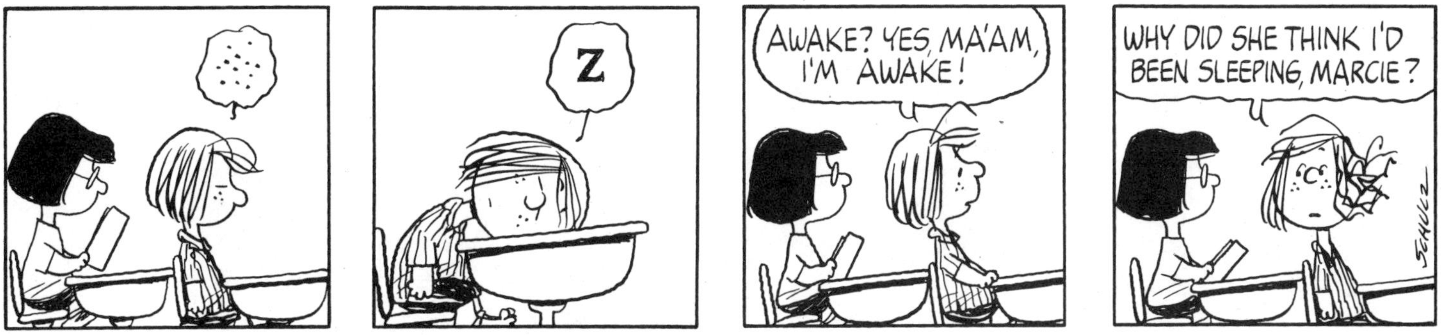
Z
AWAKE? YES, MA'AM, I'M AWAKE!
WHY DID SHE THINK I'D BEEN SLEEPING, MARCIE?
SCHULZ

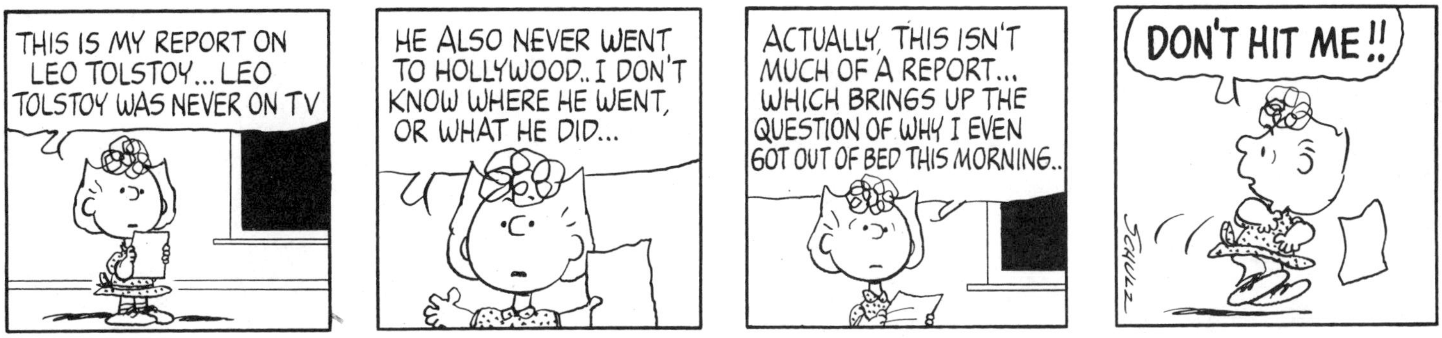
THIS IS MY REPORT ON LEO TOLSTOY... LEO TOLSTOY WAS NEVER ON TV
HE ALSO NEVER WENT TO HOLLYWOOD.. I DON'T KNOW WHERE HE WENT, OR WHAT HE DID...
ACTUALLY, THIS ISN'T MUCH OF A REPORT... WHICH BRINGS UP THE QUESTION OF WHY I EVEN GOT OUT OF BED THIS MORNING..
DON'T HIT ME!!
SCHULZ

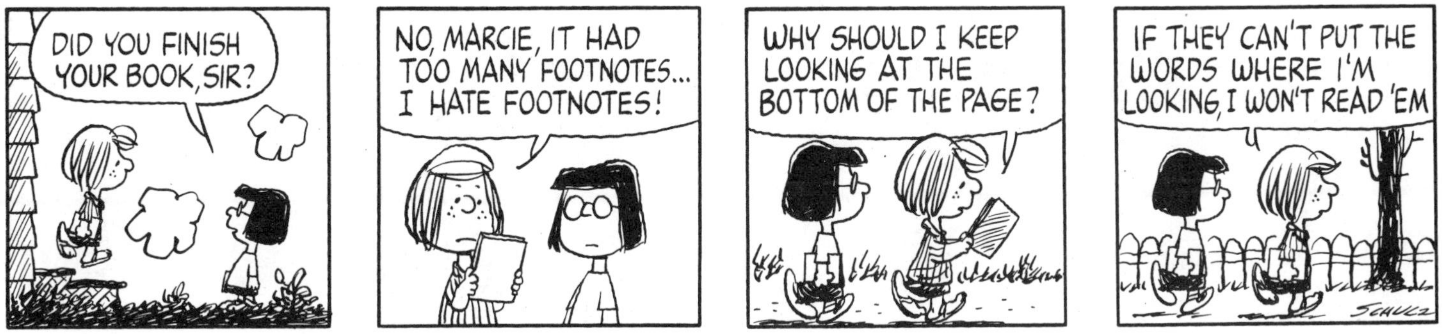
DID YOU FINISH YOUR BOOK, SIR?
NO, MARCIE, IT HAD TOO MANY FOOTNOTES... I HATE FOOTNOTES!
WHY SHOULD I KEEP LOOKING AT THE BOTTOM OF THE PAGE?
IF THEY CAN'T PUT THE WORDS WHERE I'M LOOKING, I WON'T READ 'EM
SCHULZ

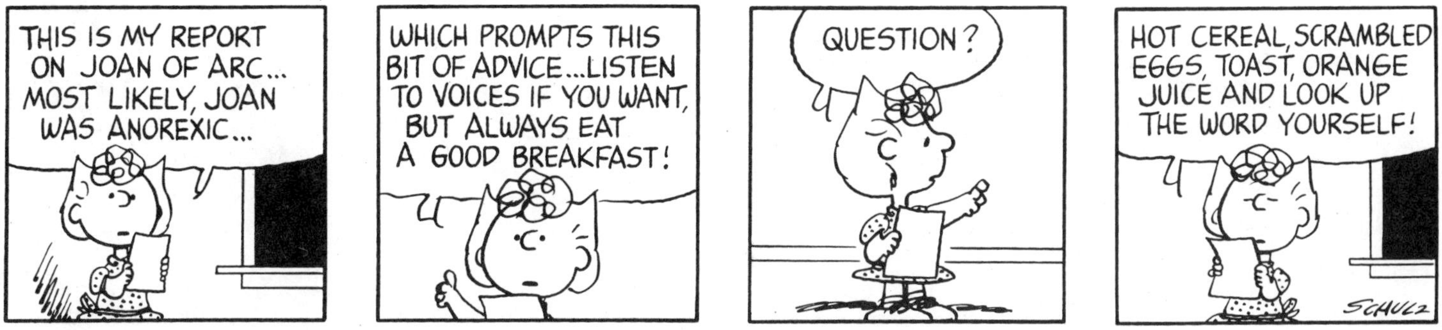
THIS IS MY REPORT ON JOAN OF ARC... MOST LIKELY, JOAN WAS ANOREXIC...
WHICH PROMPTS THIS BIT OF ADVICE...LISTEN TO VOICES IF YOU WANT, BUT ALWAYS EAT A GOOD BREAKFAST!
QUESTION?
HOT CEREAL, SCRAMBLED EGGS, TOAST, ORANGE JUICE AND LOOK UP THE WORD YOURSELF!
SCHULZ

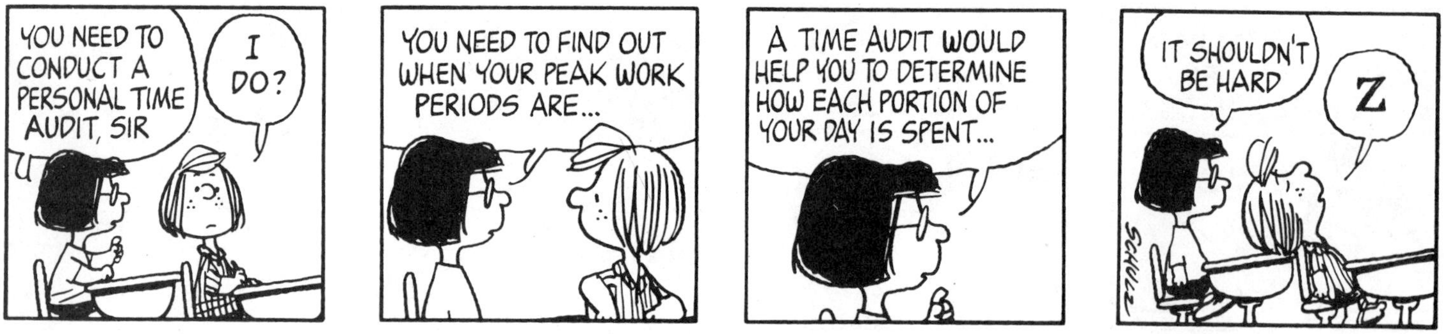
YOU NEED TO CONDUCT A PERSONAL TIME AUDIT, SIR
I DO?
YOU NEED TO FIND OUT WHEN YOUR PEAK WORK PERIODS ARE...
A TIME AUDIT WOULD HELP YOU TO DETERMINE HOW EACH PORTION OF YOUR DAY IS SPENT...
IT SHOULDN'T BE HARD
Z
SCHULZ

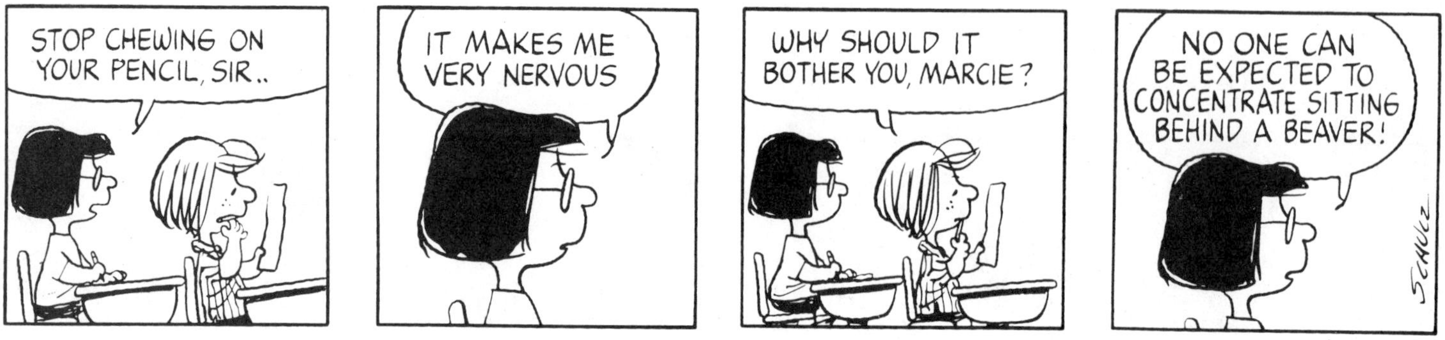
STOP CHEWING ON YOUR PENCIL, SIR..
IT MAKES ME VERY NERVOUS
WHY SHOULD IT BOTHER YOU, MARCIE?
NO ONE CAN BE EXPECTED TO CONCENTRATE SITTING BEHIND A BEAVER!
SCHULZ

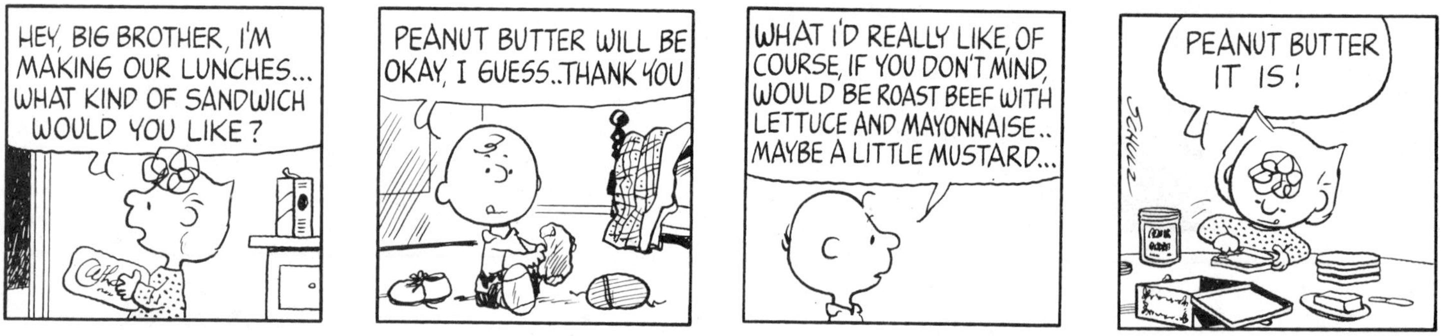
HEY, BIG BROTHER, I'M MAKING OUR LUNCHES... WHAT KIND OF SANDWICH WOULD YOU LIKE?
PEANUT BUTTER WILL BE OKAY, I GUESS..THANK YOU
WHAT I'D REALLY LIKE, OF COURSE, IF YOU DON'T MIND, WOULD BE ROAST BEEF WITH LETTUCE AND MAYONNAISE.. MAYBE A LITTLE MUSTARD...
PEANUT BUTTER IT IS!
SCHULZ

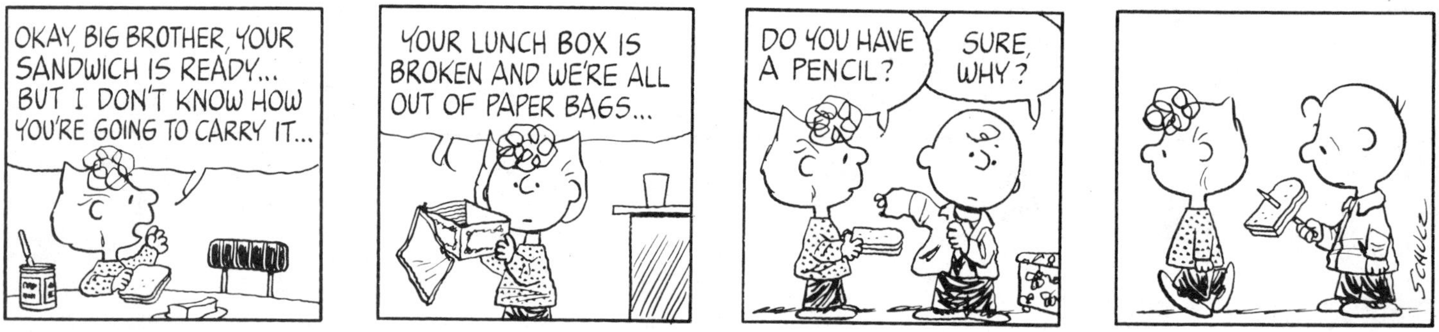
OKAY, BIG BROTHER, YOUR SANDWICH IS READY... BUT I DON'T KNOW HOW YOU'RE GOING TO CARRY IT...
YOUR LUNCH BOX IS BROKEN AND WE'RE ALL OUT OF PAPER BAGS...
DO YOU HAVE A PENCIL?
SURE, WHY?
SCHULZ

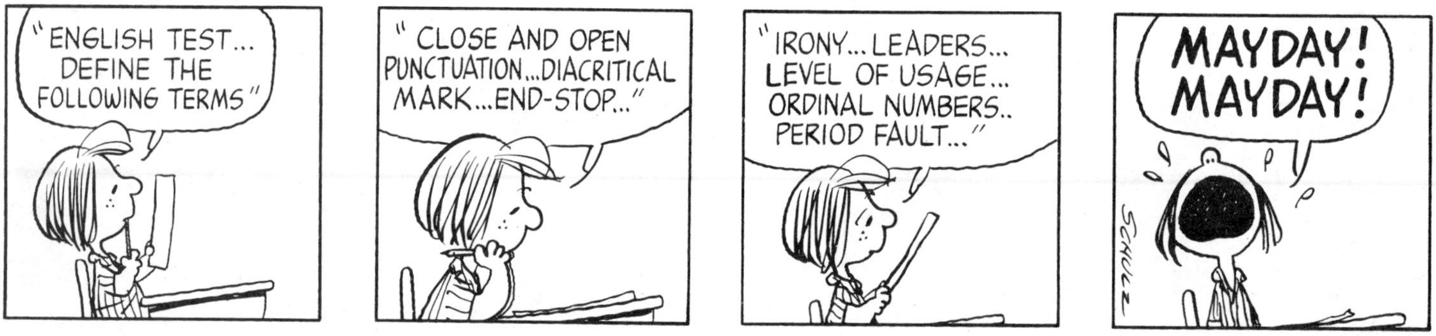
"ENGLISH TEST... DEFINE THE FOLLOWING TERMS"
"CLOSE AND OPEN PUNCTUATION...DIACRITICAL MARK...END-STOP..."
"IRONY... LEADERS... LEVEL OF USAGE... ORDINAL NUMBERS.. PERIOD FAULT..."
MAYDAY! MAYDAY!
SCHULZ

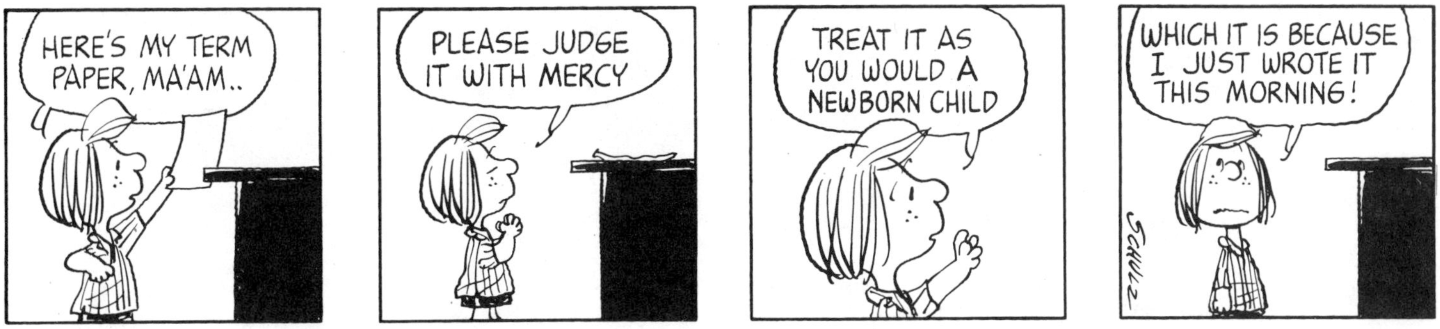
HERE'S MY TERM PAPER, MA'AM..
PLEASE JUDGE IT WITH MERCY
TREAT IT AS YOU WOULD A NEWBORN CHILD
WHICH IT IS BECAUSE I JUST WROTE IT THIS MORNING!
SCHULZ

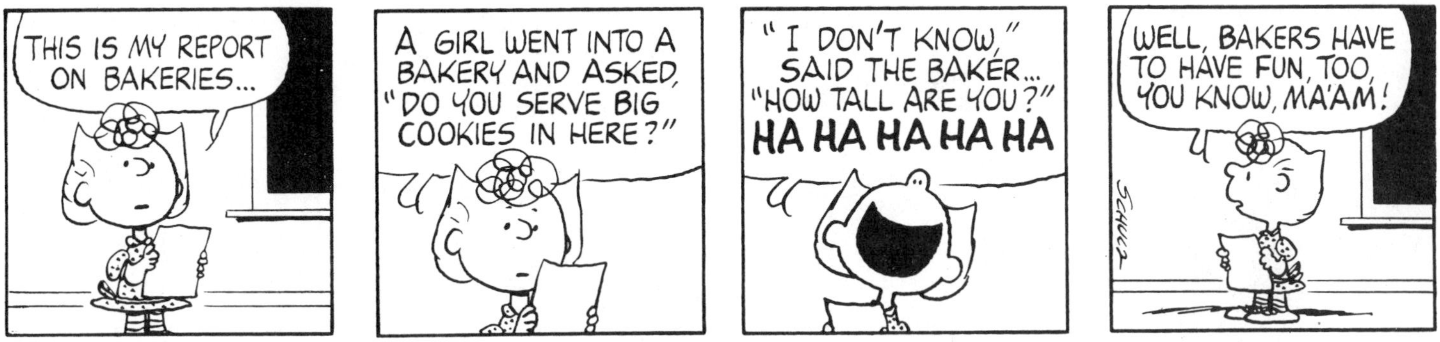
THIS IS MY REPORT ON BAKERIES...
A GIRL WENT INTO A BAKERY AND ASKED, "DO YOU SERVE BIG COOKIES IN HERE?"
"I DON'T KNOW," SAID THE BAKER... "HOW TALL ARE YOU?"
HA HA HA HA HA
WELL, BAKERS HAVE TO HAVE FUN, TOO, YOU KNOW, MA'AM!
SCHULZ

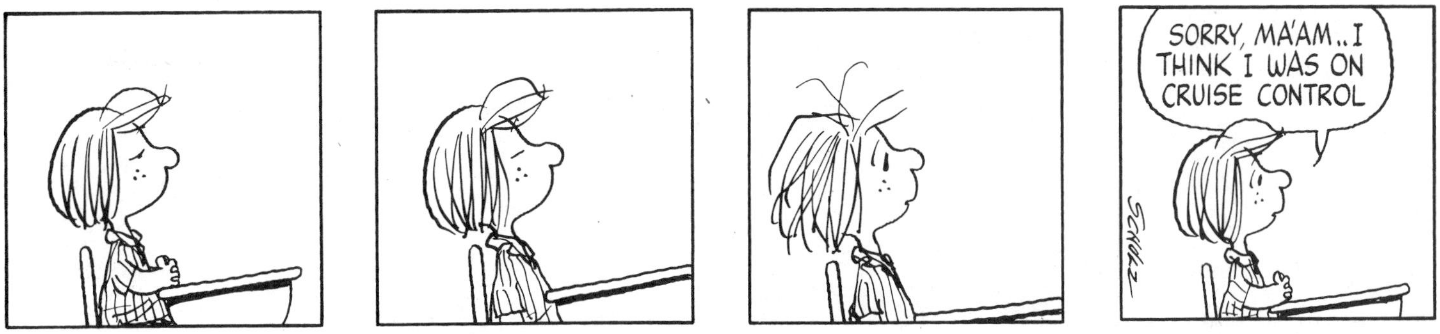
SORRY, MA'AM.. I THINK I WAS ON CRUISE CONTROL
SCHULZ

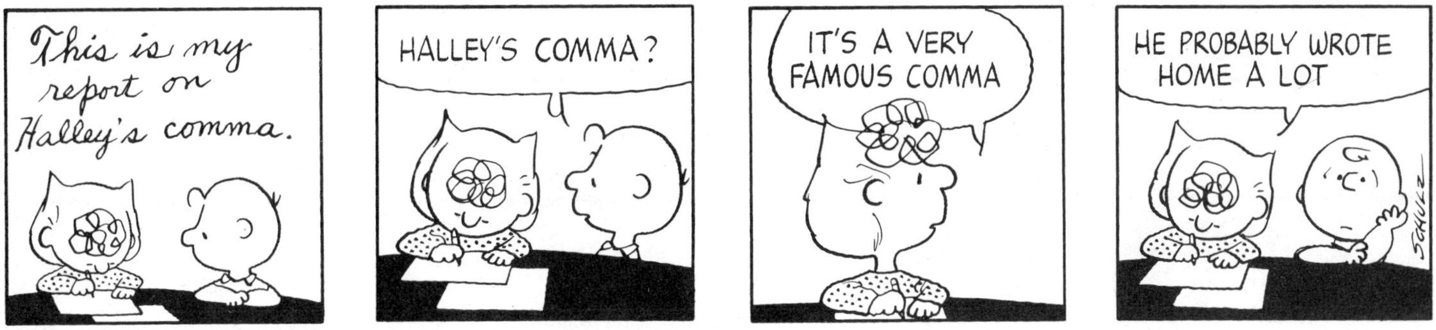
This is my report on Halley's comma.
HALLEY'S COMMA?
IT'S A VERY FAMOUS COMMA
HE PROBABLY WROTE HOME A LOT
SCHULZ

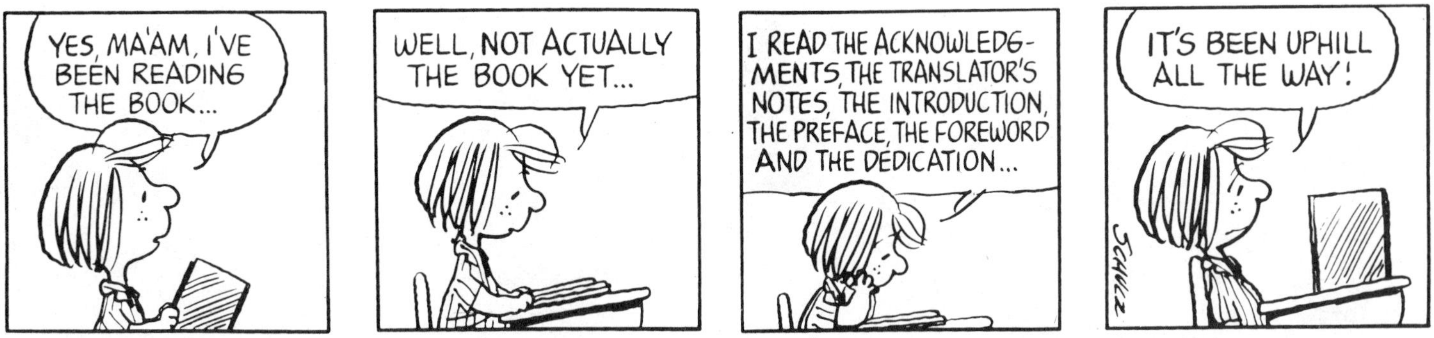
YES, MA'AM, I'VE BEEN READING THE BOOK...
WELL, NOT ACTUALLY THE BOOK YET...
I READ THE ACKNOWLEDGMENTS, THE TRANSLATOR'S NOTES, THE INTRODUCTION, THE PREFACE, THE FOREWORD AND THE DEDICATION...
IT'S BEEN UPHILL ALL THE WAY!
SCHULZ

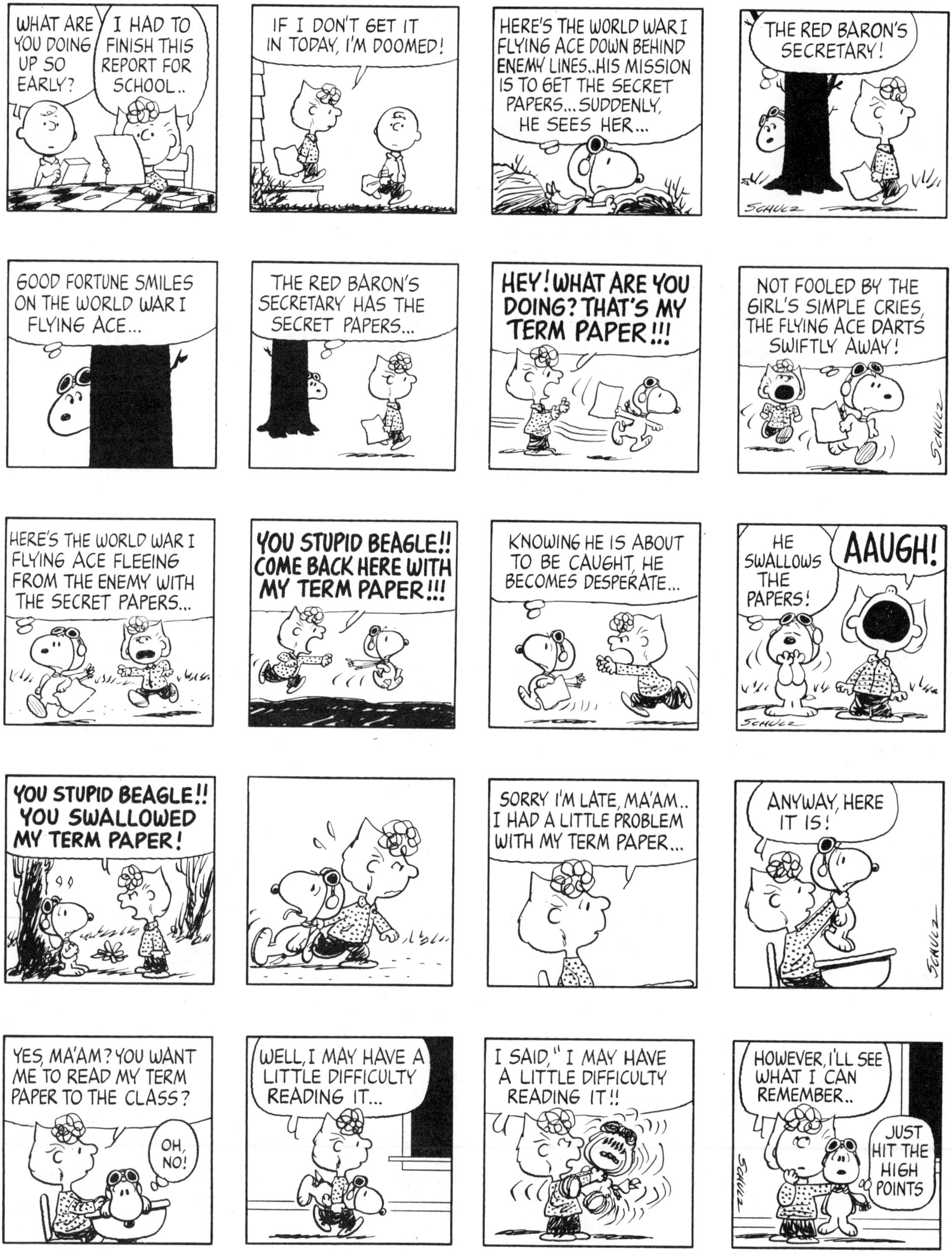
WHAT ARE YOU DOING UP SO EARLY?
I HAD TO FINISH THIS REPORT FOR SCHOOL..
IF I DON'T GET IT IN TODAY, I'M DOOMED!
HERE'S THE WORLD WAR I FLYING ACE DOWN BEHIND ENEMY LINES..HIS MISSION IS TO GET THE SECRET PAPERS... SUDDENLY, HE SEES HER...
THE RED BARON'S SECRETARY!
SCHULZ
GOOD FORTUNE SMILES ON THE WORLD WAR I FLYING ACE...
THE RED BARON'S SECRETARY HAS THE SECRET PAPERS...
HEY! WHAT ARE YOU DOING? THAT'S MY TERM PAPER!!!
NOT FOOLED BY THE GIRL'S SIMPLE CRIES, THE FLYING ACE DARTS SWIFTLY AWAY!
SCHULZ
HERE'S THE WORLD WAR I FLYING ACE FLEEING FROM THE ENEMY WITH THE SECRET PAPERS...
YOU STUPID BEAGLE!! COME BACK HERE WITH MY TERM PAPER!!!
KNOWING HE IS ABOUT TO BE CAUGHT, HE BECOMES DESPERATE...
HE SWALLOWS THE PAPERS!
AAUGH!
SCHULZ
YOU STUPID BEAGLE!! YOU SWALLOWED MY TERM PAPER!
SORRY I'M LATE, MA'AM.. I HAD A LITTLE PROBLEM WITH MY TERM PAPER...
ANYWAY, HERE IT IS!
SCHULZ
YES, MA'AM? YOU WANT ME TO READ MY TERM PAPER TO THE CLASS?
OH, NO!
WELL, I MAY HAVE A LITTLE DIFFICULTY READING IT...
I SAID, "I MAY HAVE A LITTLE DIFFICULTY READING IT!!
HOWEVER, I'LL SEE WHAT I CAN REMEMBER..
JUST HIT THE HIGH POINTS
SCHULZ

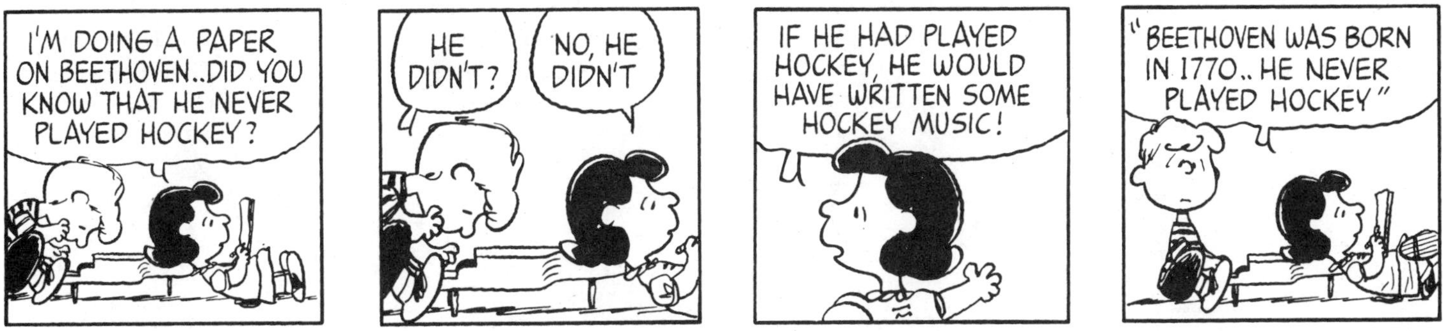
I'M DOING A PAPER ON BEETHOVEN..DID YOU KNOW THAT HE NEVER PLAYED HOCKEY?
HE DIDN'T?
NO, HE DIDN'T
IF HE HAD PLAYED HOCKEY, HE WOULD HAVE WRITTEN SOME HOCKEY MUSIC!
"BEETHOVEN WAS BORN IN 1770.. HE NEVER PLAYED HOCKEY"

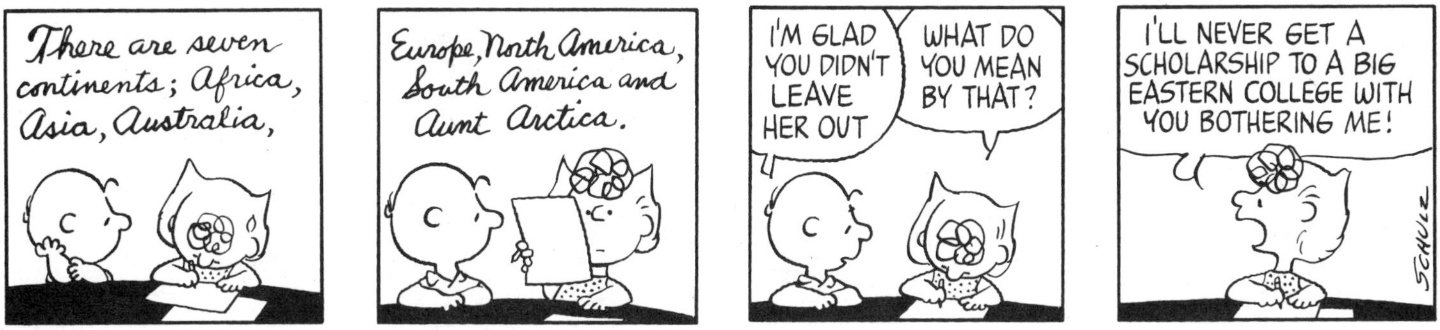
There are seven continents; Africa, Asia, Australia,
Europe, North America, South America and Aunt Arctica.
I'M GLAD YOU DIDN'T LEAVE HER OUT
WHAT DO YOU MEAN BY THAT?
I'LL NEVER GET A SCHOLARSHIP TO A BIG EASTERN COLLEGE WITH YOU BOTHERING ME!
SCHULZ

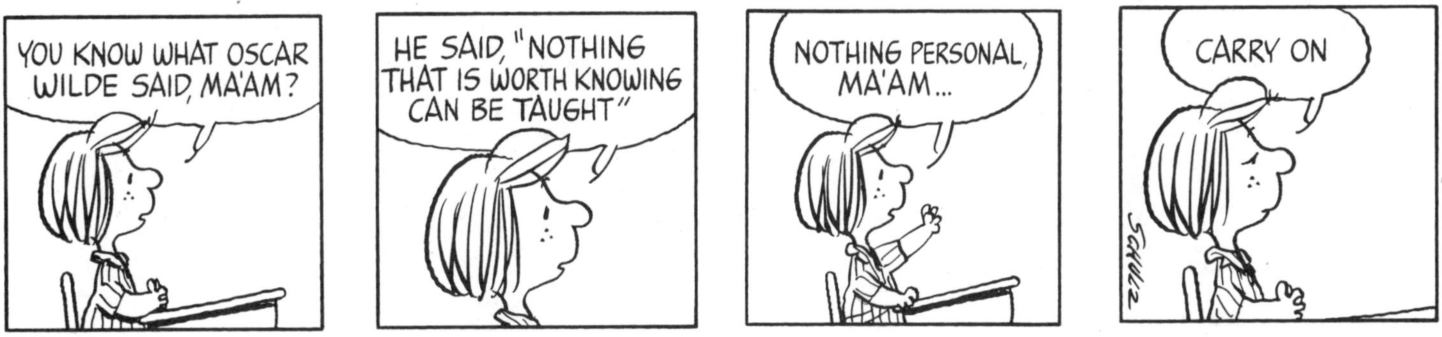
YOU KNOW WHAT OSCAR WILDE SAID, MA'AM?
HE SAID, "NOTHING THAT IS WORTH KNOWING CAN BE TAUGHT"
NOTHING PERSONAL, MA'AM...
SCHULZ
CARRY ON

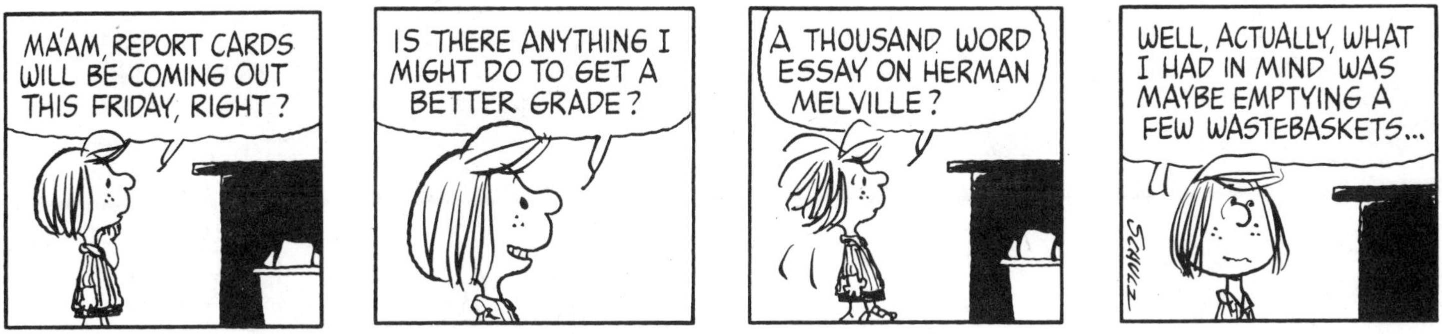
MA'AM, REPORT CARDS WILL BE COMING OUT THIS FRIDAY, RIGHT?
IS THERE ANYTHING I MIGHT DO TO GET A BETTER GRADE?
A THOUSAND WORD ESSAY ON HERMAN MELVILLE?
SCHULZ
WELL, ACTUALLY, WHAT I HAD IN MIND WAS MAYBE EMPTYING A FEW WASTEBASKETS...

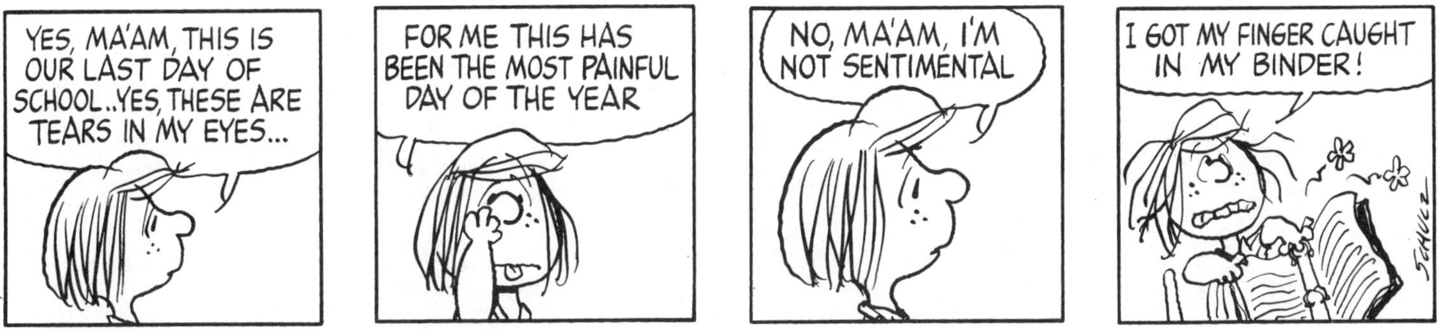
YES, MA'AM, THIS IS OUR LAST DAY OF SCHOOL..YES, THESE ARE TEARS IN MY EYES...
FOR ME THIS HAS BEEN THE MOST PAINFUL DAY OF THE YEAR
NO, MA'AM, I'M NOT SENTIMENTAL
I GOT MY FINGER CAUGHT IN MY BINDER!
SCHULZ

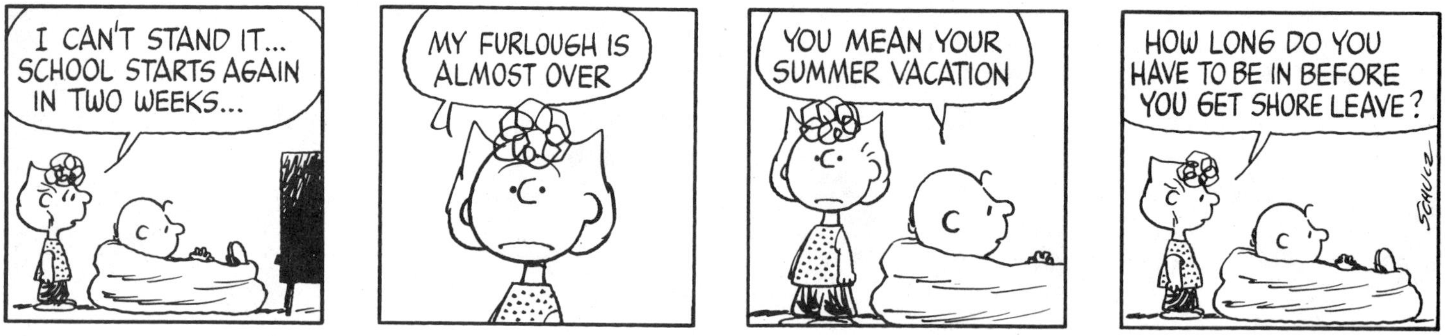
I CAN'T STAND IT... SCHOOL STARTS AGAIN IN TWO WEEKS...
MY FURLOUGH IS ALMOST OVER
YOU MEAN YOUR SUMMER VACATION
HOW LONG DO YOU HAVE TO BE IN BEFORE YOU GET SHORE LEAVE?
SCHULZ

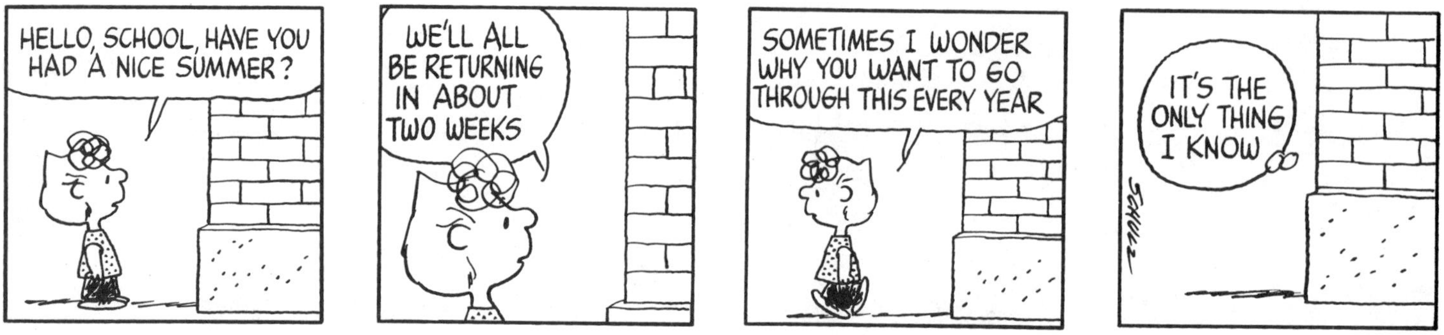
HELLO, SCHOOL, HAVE YOU HAD A NICE SUMMER?
WE'LL ALL BE RETURNING IN ABOUT TWO WEEKS
SOMETIMES I WONDER WHY YOU WANT TO GO THROUGH THIS EVERY YEAR
IT'S THE ONLY THING I KNOW
SCHULZ

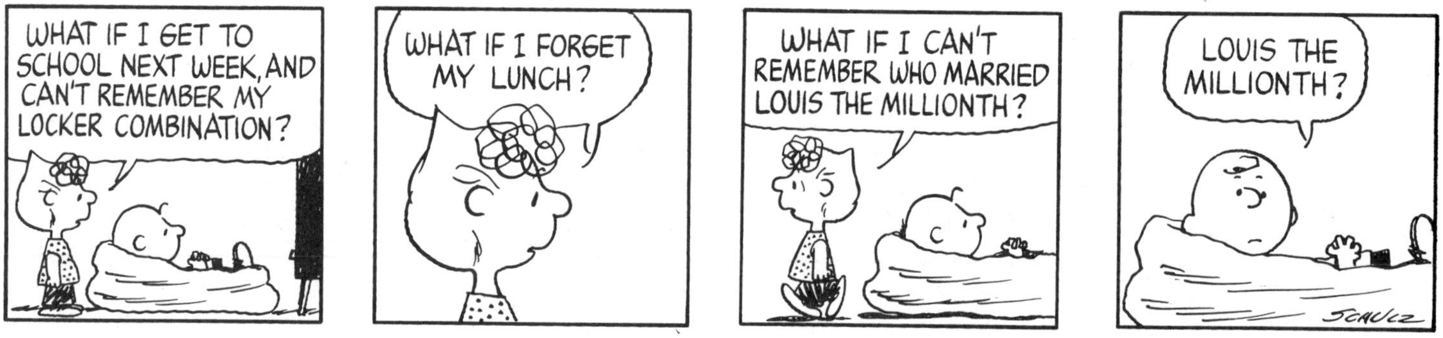
WHAT IF I GET TO SCHOOL NEXT WEEK, AND CAN'T REMEMBER MY LOCKER COMBINATION?
WHAT IF I FORGET MY LUNCH?
WHAT IF I CAN'T REMEMBER WHO MARRIED LOUIS THE MILLIONTH?
LOUIS THE MILLIONTH?
SCHULZ

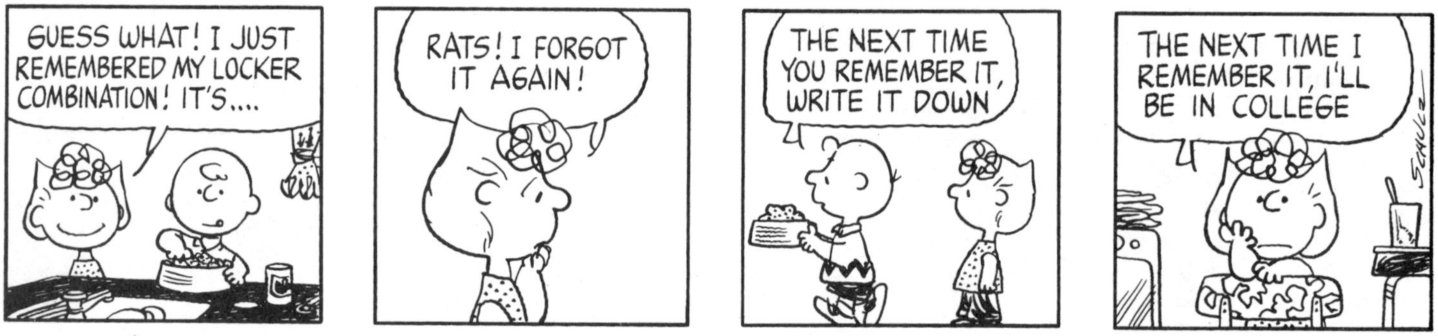
GUESS WHAT! I JUST REMEMBERED MY LOCKER COMBINATION! IT'S....
RATS! I FORGOT IT AGAIN!
THE NEXT TIME YOU REMEMBER IT, WRITE IT DOWN
THE NEXT TIME I REMEMBER IT, I'LL BE IN COLLEGE
SCHULZ

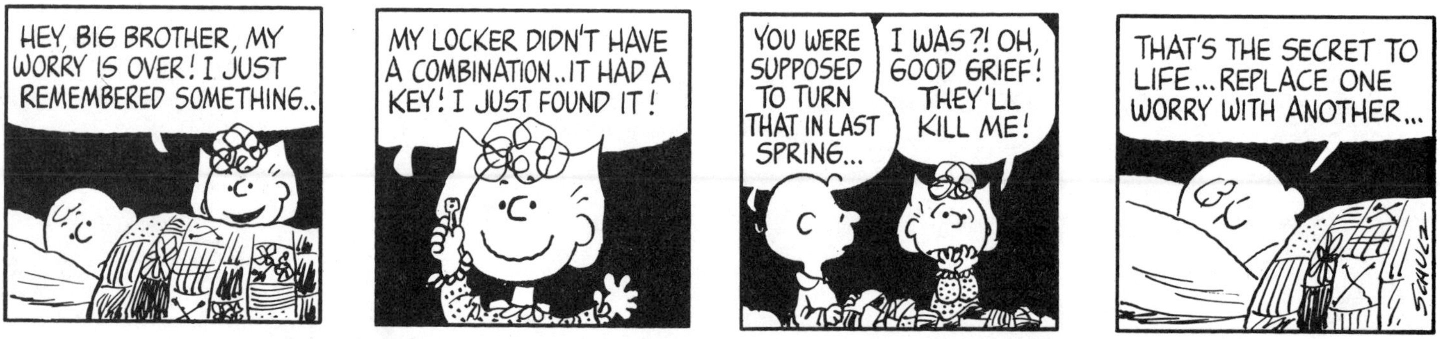
HEY, BIG BROTHER, MY WORRY IS OVER! I JUST REMEMBERED SOMETHING..
MY LOCKER DIDN'T HAVE A COMBINATION..IT HAD A KEY! I JUST FOUND IT!
YOU WERE SUPPOSED TO TURN THAT IN LAST SPRING...
I WAS?! OH, GOOD GRIEF! THEY'LL KILL ME!
THAT'S THE SECRET TO LIFE... REPLACE ONE WORRY WITH ANOTHER...
SCHULZ

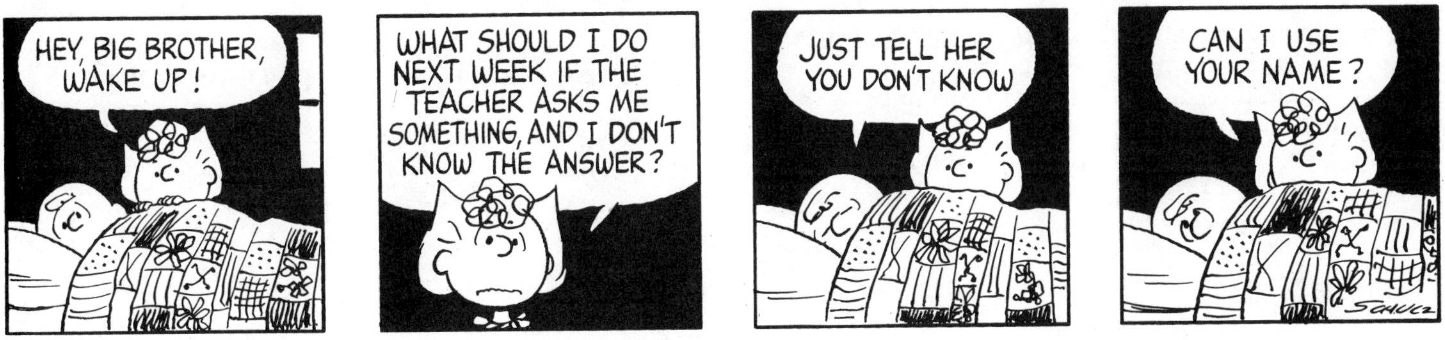
HEY, BIG BROTHER, WAKE UP!
WHAT SHOULD I DO NEXT WEEK IF THE TEACHER ASKS ME SOMETHING, AND I DON'T KNOW THE ANSWER?
JUST TELL HER YOU DON'T KNOW
CAN I USE YOUR NAME?
SCHULZ

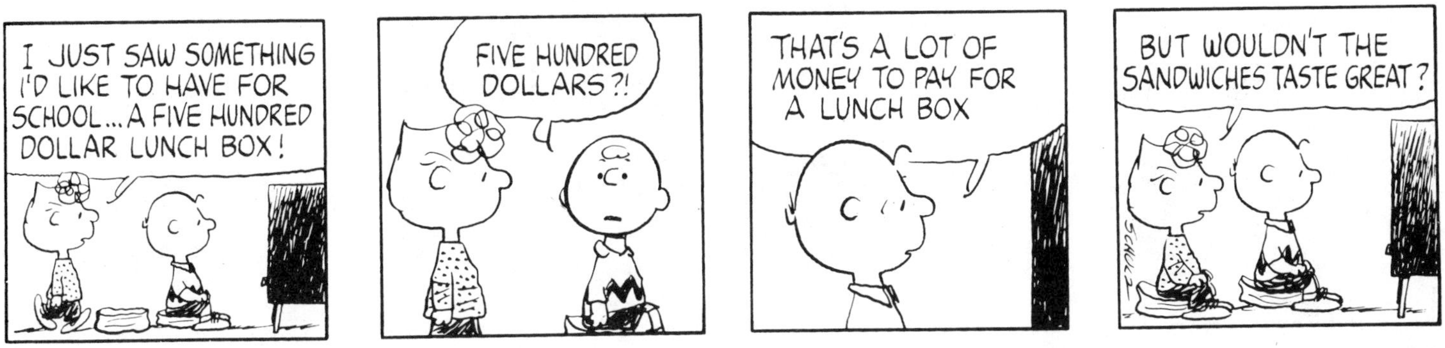
I JUST SAW SOMETHING I'D LIKE TO HAVE FOR SCHOOL... A FIVE HUNDRED DOLLAR LUNCH BOX!
FIVE HUNDRED DOLLARS?!
THAT'S A LOT OF MONEY TO PAY FOR A LUNCH BOX
BUT WOULDN'T THE SANDWICHES TASTE GREAT?
SCHULZ

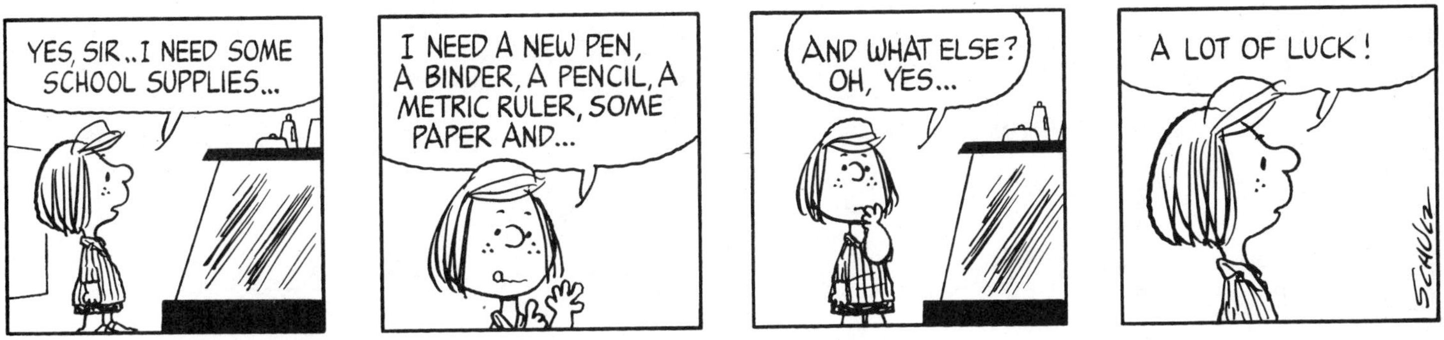
YES, SIR.. I NEED SOME SCHOOL SUPPLIES...
I NEED A NEW PEN, A BINDER, A PENCIL, A METRIC RULER, SOME PAPER AND...
AND WHAT ELSE? OH, YES...
A LOT OF LUCK!
SCHULZ

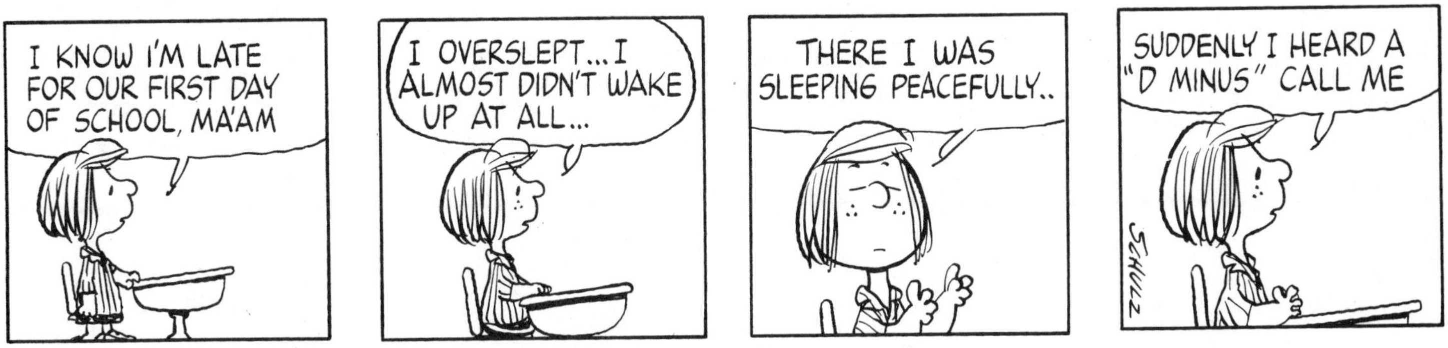
I KNOW I'M LATE FOR OUR FIRST DAY OF SCHOOL, MA'AM
I OVERSLEPT... I ALMOST DIDN'T WAKE UP AT ALL...
THERE I WAS SLEEPING PEACEFULLY..
SUDDENLY I HEARD A "D MINUS" CALL ME
SCHULZ

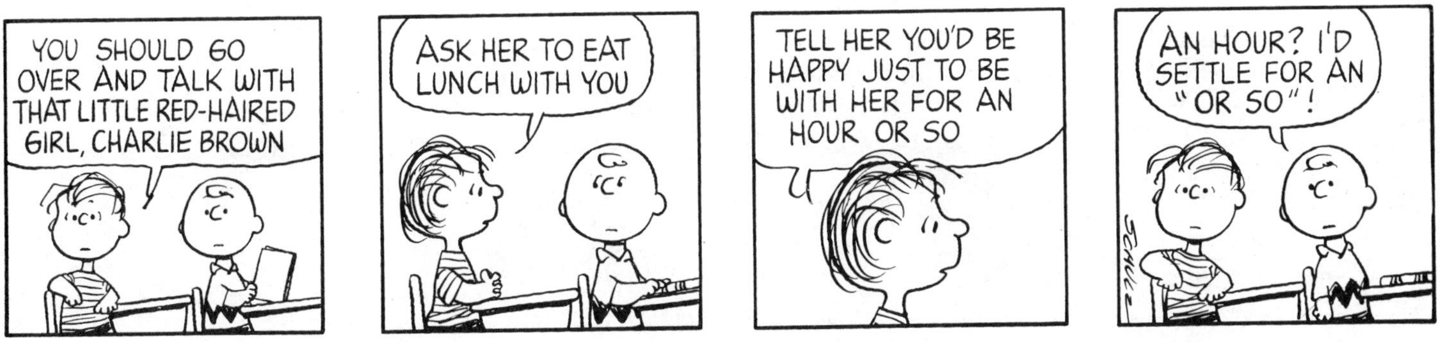
YOU SHOULD GO OVER AND TALK WITH THAT LITTLE RED-HAIRED GIRL, CHARLIE BROWN
ASK HER TO EAT LUNCH WITH YOU
TELL HER YOU'D BE HAPPY JUST TO BE WITH HER FOR AN HOUR OR SO
AN HOUR? I'D SETTLE FOR AN "OR SO"!
SCHULZ

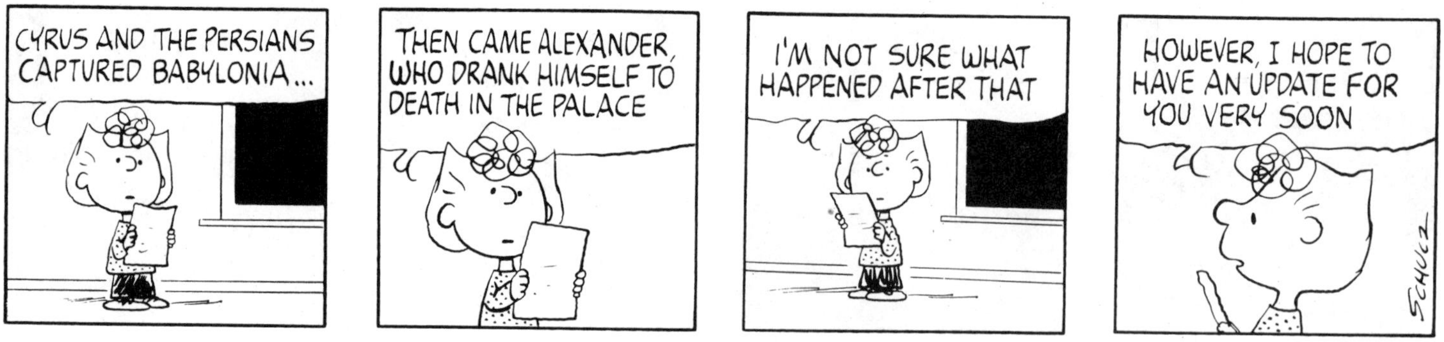
CYRUS AND THE PERSIANS CAPTURED BABYLONIA...
THEN CAME ALEXANDER, WHO DRANK HIMSELF TO DEATH IN THE PALACE
I'M NOT SURE WHAT HAPPENED AFTER THAT
HOWEVER, I HOPE TO HAVE AN UPDATE FOR YOU VERY SOON
SCHULZ

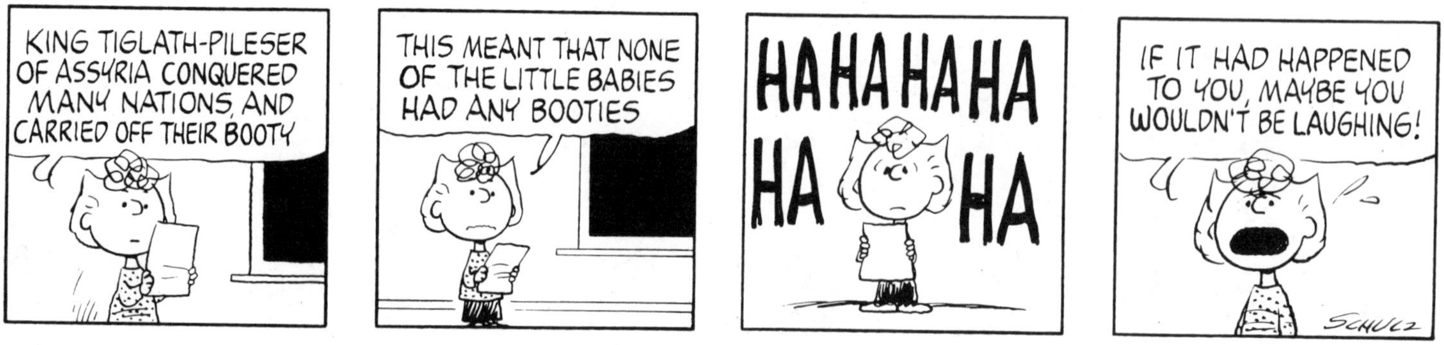
KING TIGLATH-PILESER OF ASSYRIA CONQUERED MANY NATIONS, AND CARRIED OFF THEIR BOOTY
THIS MEANT THAT NONE OF THE LITTLE BABIES HAD ANY BOOTIES
HAHAHAHA HA HA
IF IT HAD HAPPENED TO YOU, MAYBE YOU WOULDN'T BE LAUGHING!
SCHULZ

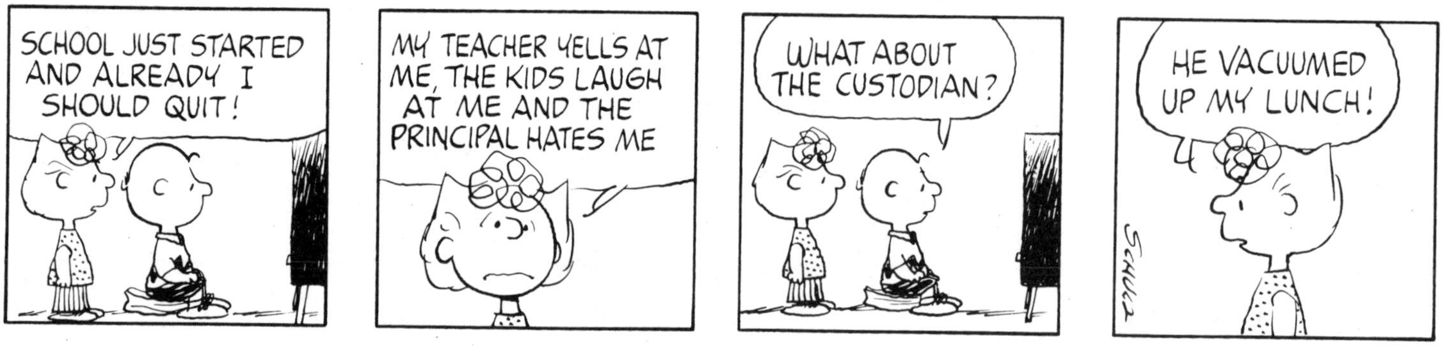
SCHOOL JUST STARTED AND ALREADY I SHOULD QUIT!
MY TEACHER YELLS AT ME, THE KIDS LAUGH AT ME AND THE PRINCIPAL HATES ME
WHAT ABOUT THE CUSTODIAN?
HE VACUUMED UP MY LUNCH!
SCHULZ

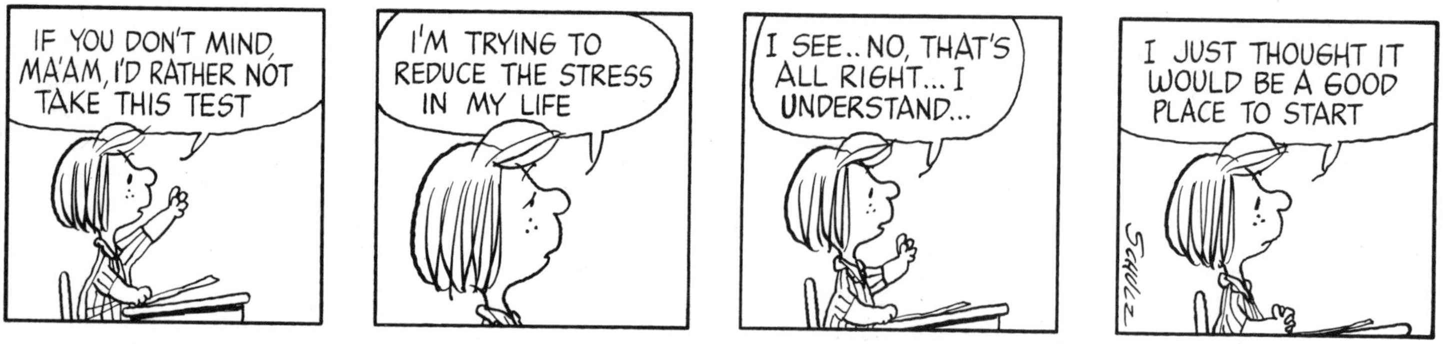
IF YOU DON'T MIND, MA'AM, I'D RATHER NOT TAKE THIS TEST
I'M TRYING TO REDUCE THE STRESS IN MY LIFE
I SEE.. NO, THAT'S ALL RIGHT... I UNDERSTAND...
I JUST THOUGHT IT WOULD BE A GOOD PLACE TO START
SCHULZ

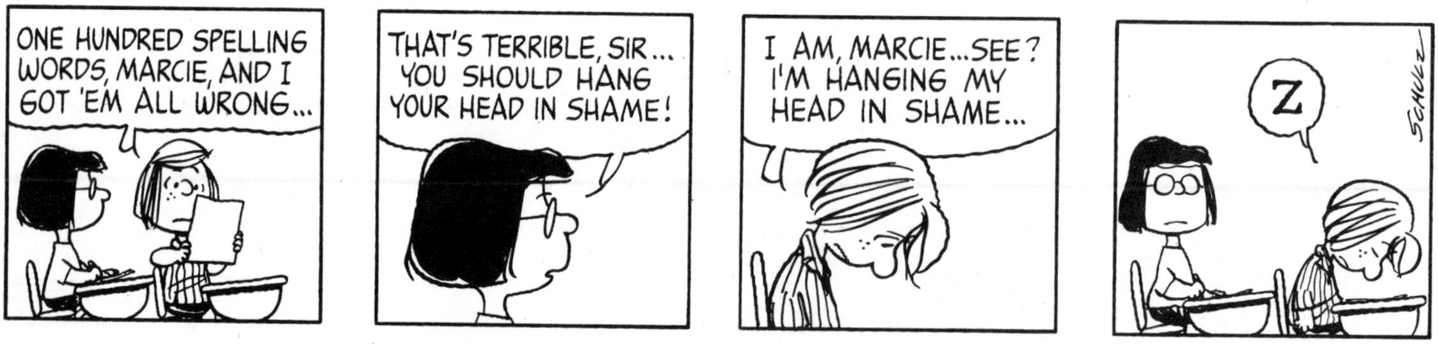
ONE HUNDRED SPELLING WORDS, MARCIE, AND I GOT 'EM ALL WRONG...
THAT'S TERRIBLE, SIR... YOU SHOULD HANG YOUR HEAD IN SHAME!
I AM, MARCIE...SEE? I'M HANGING MY HEAD IN SHAME...
Z
SCHULZ

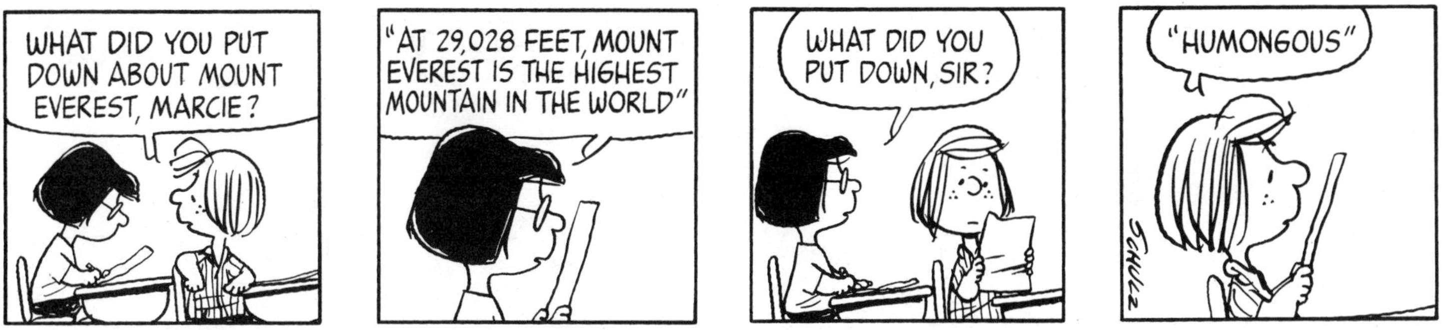
WHAT DID YOU PUT DOWN ABOUT MOUNT EVEREST, MARCIE?
"AT 29,028 FEET, MOUNT EVEREST IS THE HIGHEST MOUNTAIN IN THE WORLD"
WHAT DID YOU PUT DOWN, SIR?
"HUMONGOUS"
SCHULZ

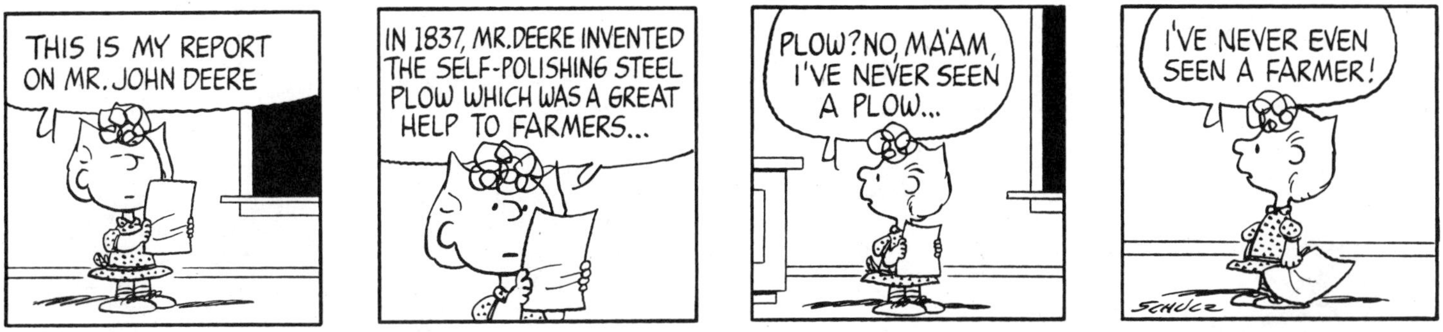
THIS IS MY REPORT ON MR. JOHN DEERE
IN 1837, MR. DEERE INVENTED THE SELF-POLISHING STEEL PLOW WHICH WAS A GREAT HELP TO FARMERS...
PLOW? NO, MA'AM, I'VE NEVER SEEN A PLOW...
I'VE NEVER EVEN SEEN A FARMER!
SCHULZ

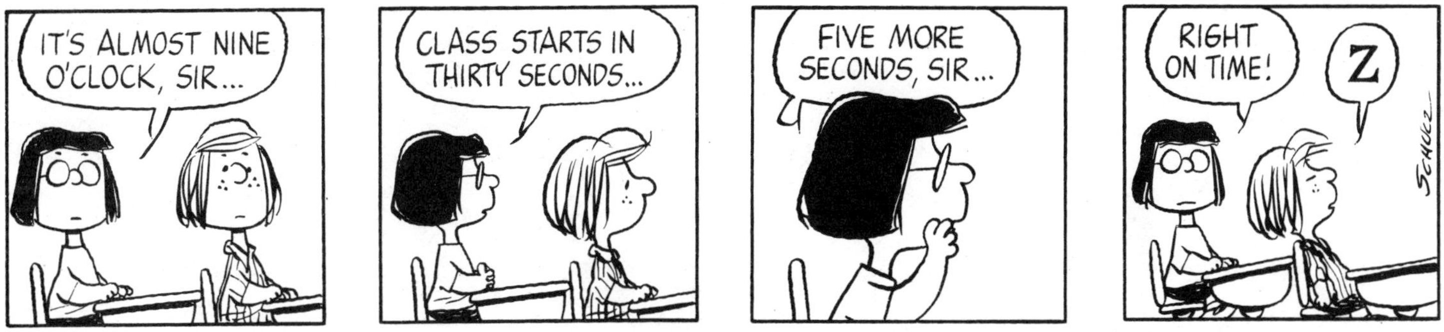
IT'S ALMOST NINE O'CLOCK, SIR...
CLASS STARTS IN THIRTY SECONDS...
FIVE MORE SECONDS, SIR...
RIGHT ON TIME!
Z
SCHULZ

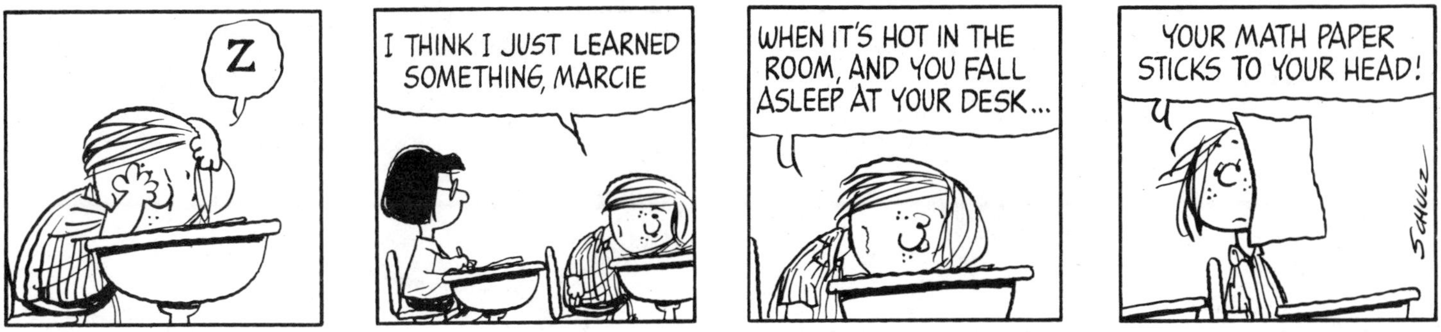
Z
I THINK I JUST LEARNED SOMETHING, MARCIE
WHEN IT'S HOT IN THE ROOM, AND YOU FALL ASLEEP AT YOUR DESK...
YOUR MATH PAPER STICKS TO YOUR HEAD!
SCHULZ

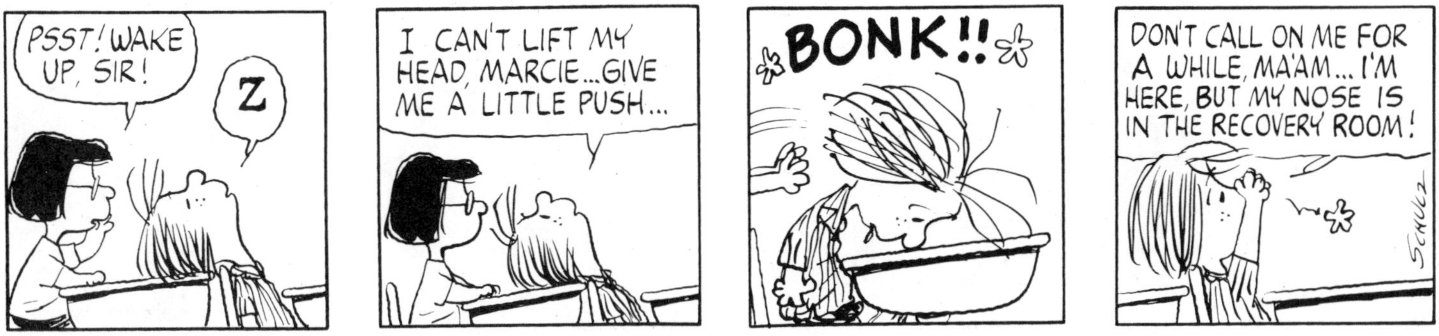
PSST! WAKE UP, SIR!
Z
I CAN'T LIFT MY HEAD, MARCIE...GIVE ME A LITTLE PUSH...
BONK!!
DON'T CALL ON ME FOR A WHILE, MA'AM... I'M HERE, BUT MY NOSE IS IN THE RECOVERY ROOM!
SCHULZ

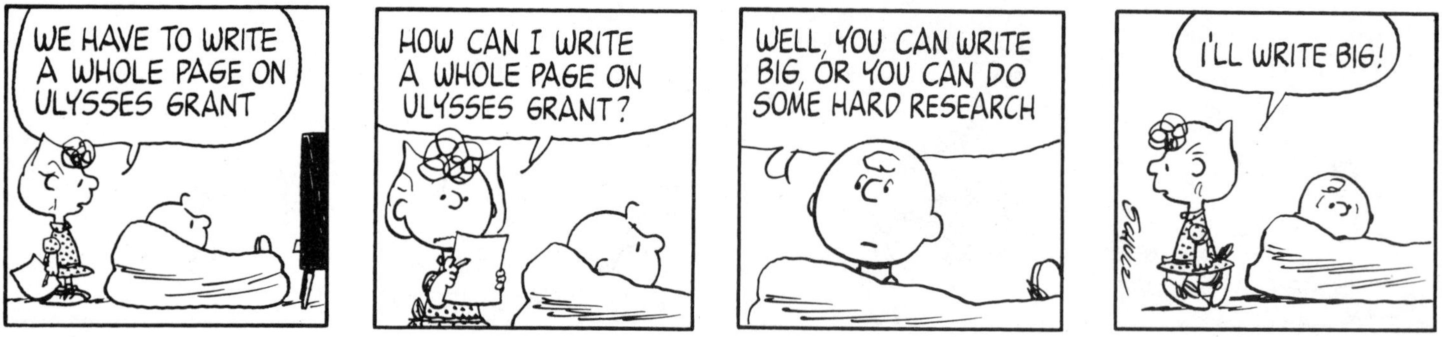
WE HAVE TO WRITE A WHOLE PAGE ON ULYSSES GRANT
HOW CAN I WRITE A WHOLE PAGE ON ULYSSES GRANT?
WELL, YOU CAN WRITE BIG, OR YOU CAN DO SOME HARD RESEARCH
I'LL WRITE BIG!

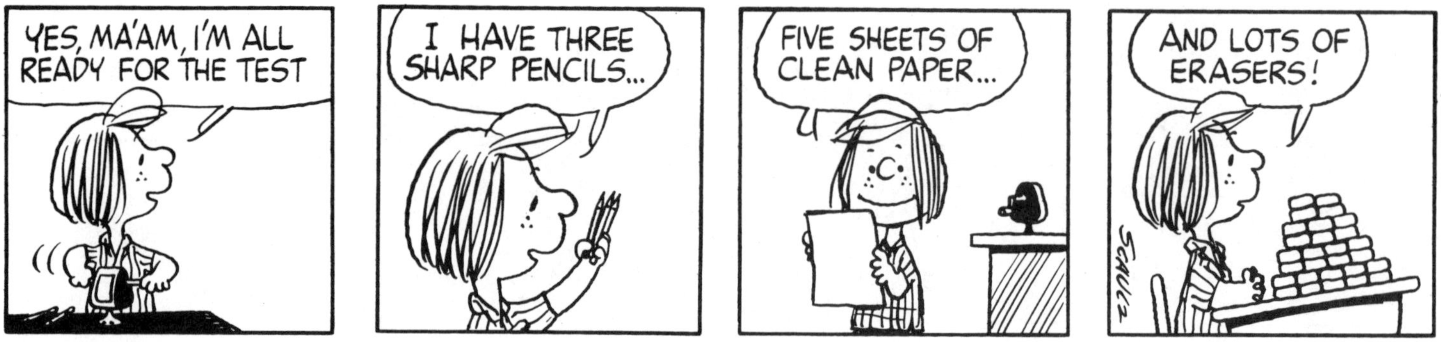
YES, MA'AM, I'M ALL READY FOR THE TEST
I HAVE THREE SHARP PENCILS...
FIVE SHEETS OF CLEAN PAPER...
AND LOTS OF ERASERS!

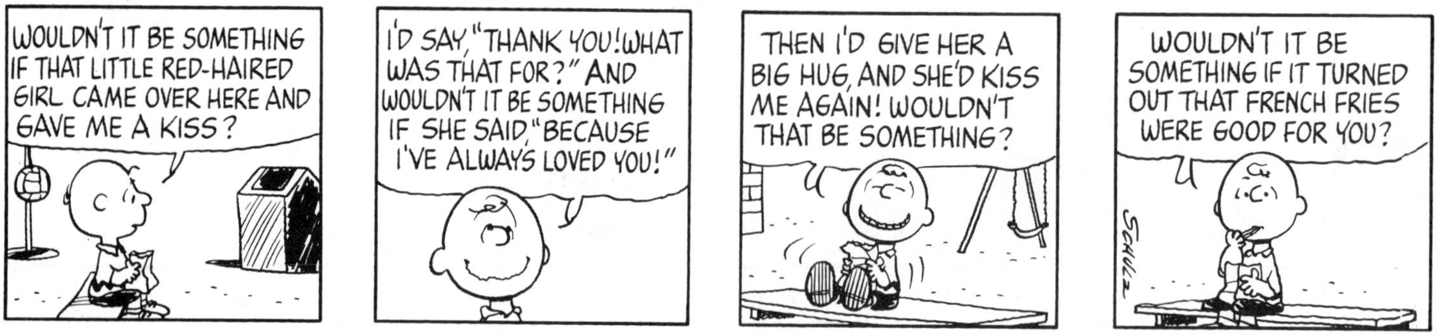
WOULDN'T IT BE SOMETHING IF THAT LITTLE RED-HAIRED GIRL CAME OVER HERE AND GAVE ME A KISS?
I'D SAY, "THANK YOU! WHAT WAS THAT FOR?" AND WOULDN'T IT BE SOMETHING IF SHE SAID, "BECAUSE I'VE ALWAYS LOVED YOU!"
THEN I'D GIVE HER A BIG HUG, AND SHE'D KISS ME AGAIN! WOULDN'T THAT BE SOMETHING?
WOULDN'T IT BE SOMETHING IF IT TURNED OUT THAT FRENCH FRIES WERE GOOD FOR YOU?

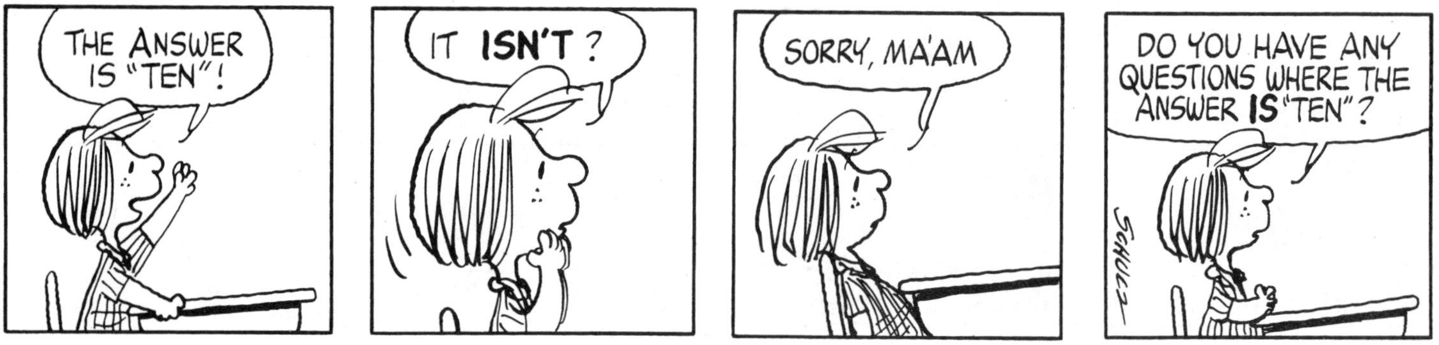
THE ANSWER IS "TEN"!
IT ISN'T?
SORRY, MA'AM
DO YOU HAVE ANY QUESTIONS WHERE THE ANSWER IS "TEN"?

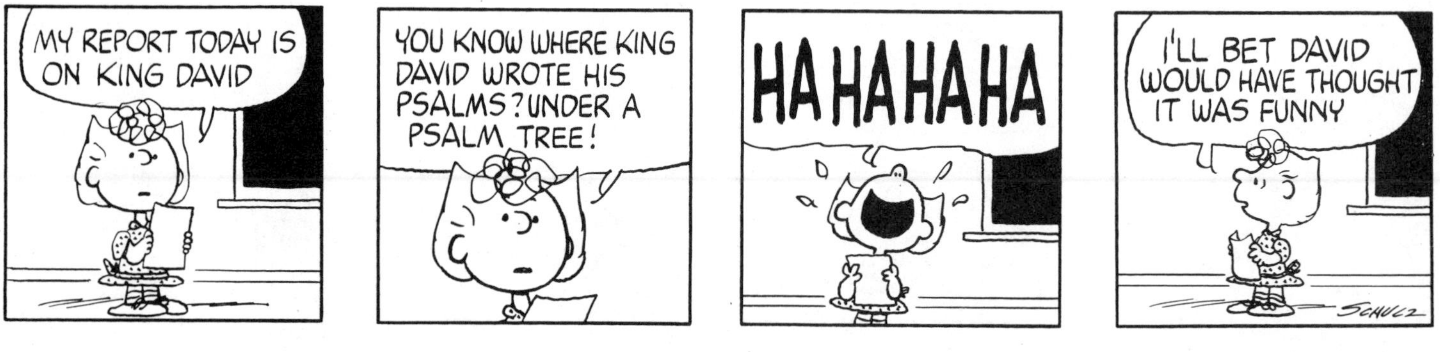
MY REPORT TODAY IS ON KING DAVID
YOU KNOW WHERE KING DAVID WROTE HIS PSALMS? UNDER A PSALM TREE!
HA HA HA HA
I'LL BET DAVID WOULD HAVE THOUGHT IT WAS FUNNY

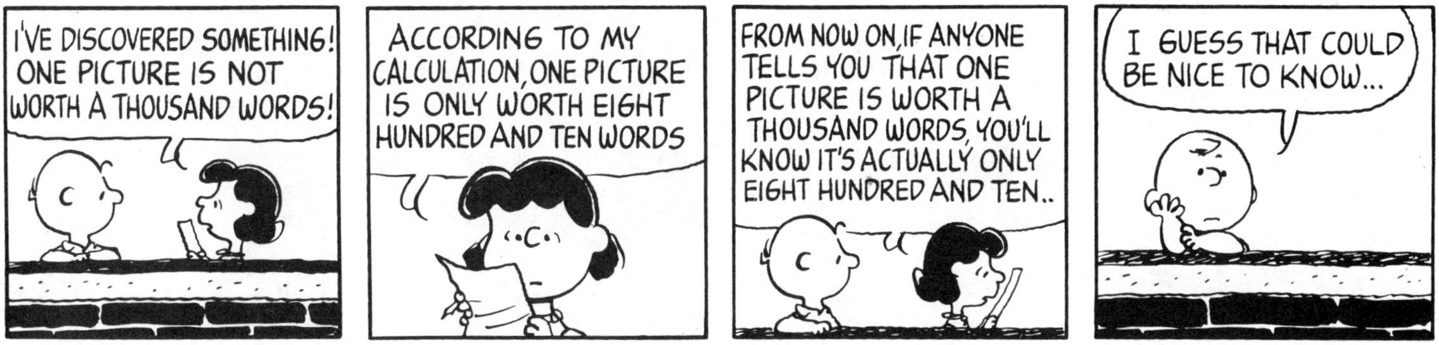
I'VE DISCOVERED SOMETHING! ONE PICTURE IS NOT WORTH A THOUSAND WORDS!
ACCORDING TO MY CALCULATION, ONE PICTURE IS ONLY WORTH EIGHT HUNDRED AND TEN WORDS
FROM NOW ON, IF ANYONE TELLS YOU THAT ONE PICTURE IS WORTH A THOUSAND WORDS, YOU'LL KNOW IT'S ACTUALLY ONLY EIGHT HUNDRED AND TEN..
I GUESS THAT COULD BE NICE TO KNOW...

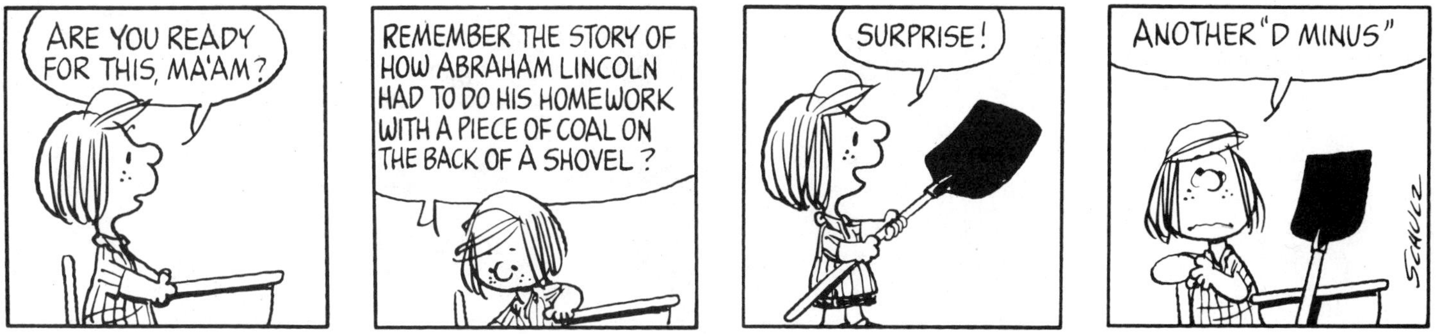
ARE YOU READY FOR THIS, MA'AM?
REMEMBER THE STORY OF HOW ABRAHAM LINCOLN HAD TO DO HIS HOMEWORK WITH A PIECE OF COAL ON THE BACK OF A SHOVEL?
SURPRISE!
ANOTHER "D MINUS"
SCHULZ

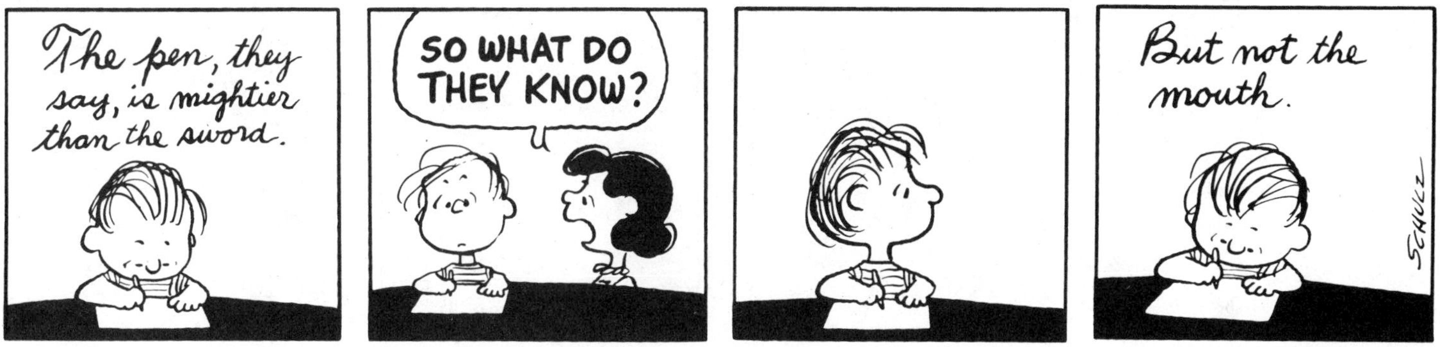
The pen, they say, is mightier than the sword.
SO WHAT DO THEY KNOW?
But not the mouth.
SCHULZ

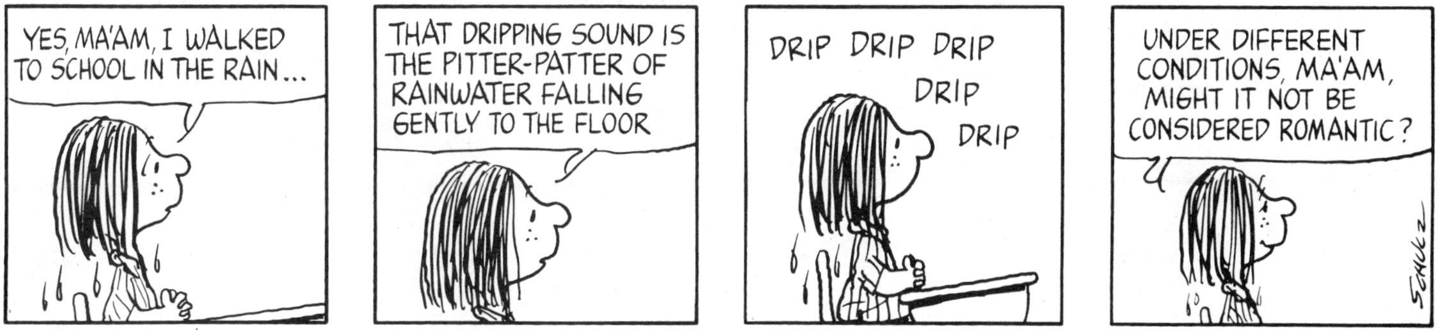
YES, MA'AM, I WALKED TO SCHOOL IN THE RAIN...
THAT DRIPPING SOUND IS THE PITTER-PATTER OF RAINWATER FALLING GENTLY TO THE FLOOR
DRIP DRIP DRIP DRIP DRIP
UNDER DIFFERENT CONDITIONS, MA'AM, MIGHT IT NOT BE CONSIDERED ROMANTIC?
SCHULZ

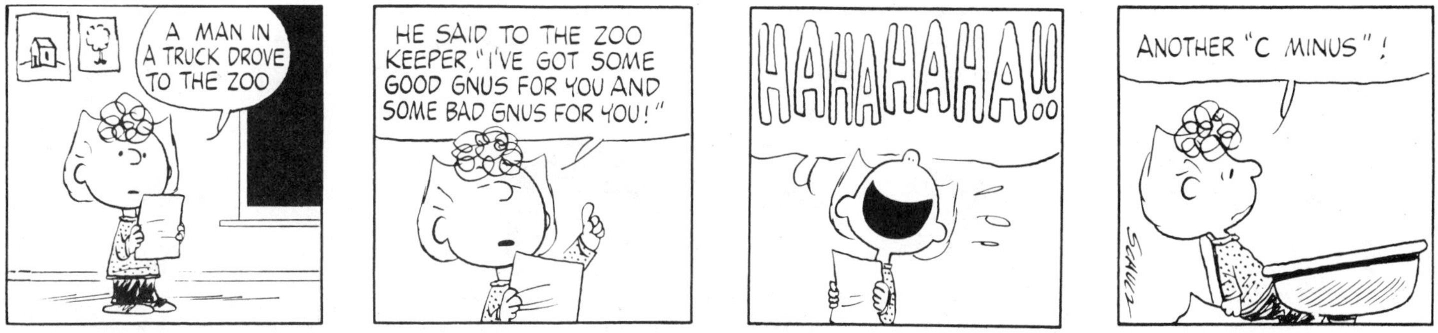
A MAN IN A TRUCK DROVE TO THE ZOO
HE SAID TO THE ZOO KEEPER, "I'VE GOT SOME GOOD GNUS FOR YOU AND SOME BAD GNUS FOR YOU!"
HAHAHAHA!!
ANOTHER "C MINUS"!
SCHULZ

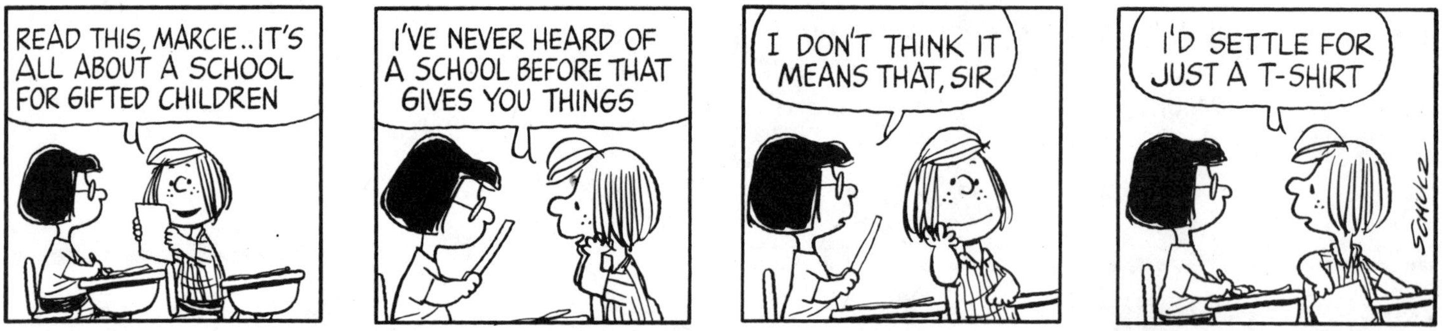
READ THIS, MARCIE..IT'S ALL ABOUT A SCHOOL FOR GIFTED CHILDREN
I'VE NEVER HEARD OF A SCHOOL BEFORE THAT GIVES YOU THINGS
I DON'T THINK IT MEANS THAT, SIR
I'D SETTLE FOR JUST A T-SHIRT
SCHULZ

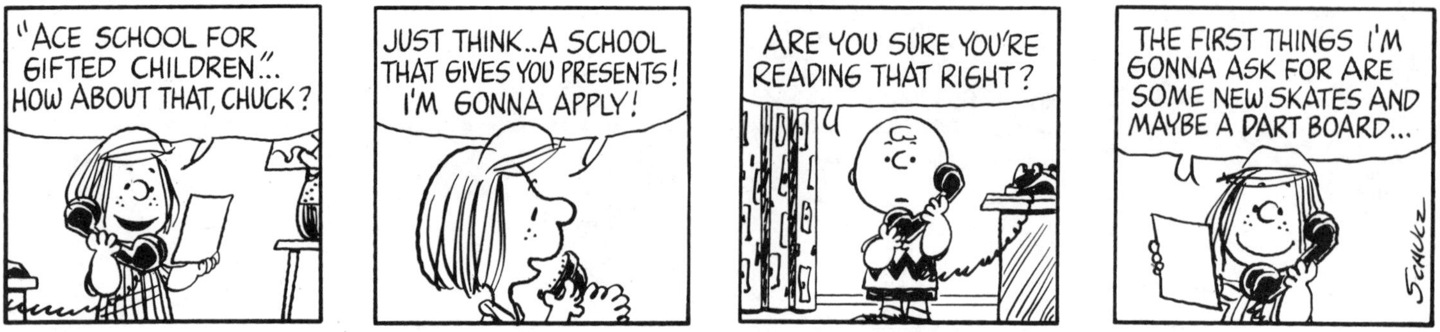
"ACE SCHOOL FOR GIFTED CHILDREN"..HOW ABOUT THAT, CHUCK?
JUST THINK..A SCHOOL THAT GIVES YOU PRESENTS! I'M GONNA APPLY!
ARE YOU SURE YOU'RE READING THAT RIGHT?
THE FIRST THINGS I'M GONNA ASK FOR ARE SOME NEW SKATES AND MAYBE A DART BOARD...
SCHULZ

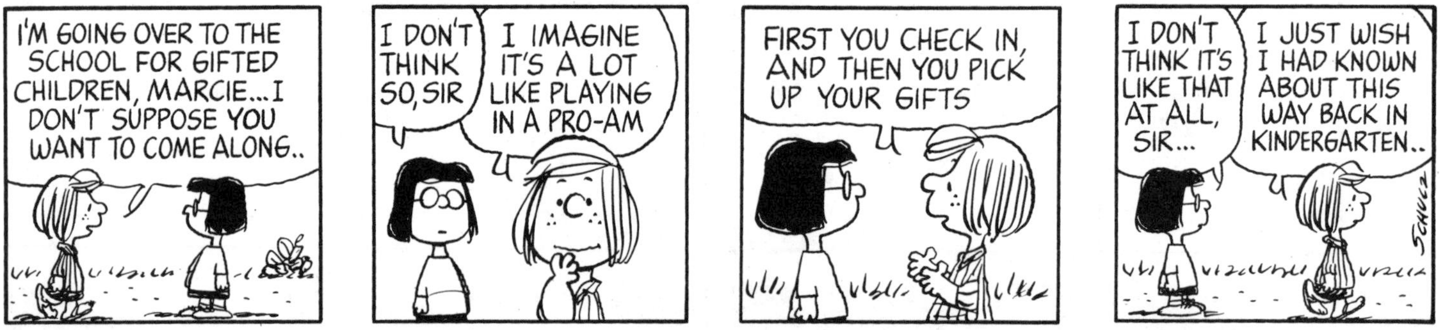
I'M GOING OVER TO THE SCHOOL FOR GIFTED CHILDREN, MARCIE...I DON'T SUPPOSE YOU WANT TO COME ALONG..
I DON'T THINK SO, SIR
I IMAGINE IT'S A LOT LIKE PLAYING IN A PRO-AM
FIRST YOU CHECK IN, AND THEN YOU PICK UP YOUR GIFTS
I DON'T THINK IT'S LIKE THAT AT ALL, SIR...
I JUST WISH I HAD KNOWN ABOUT THIS WAY BACK IN KINDERGARTEN..
SCHULZ

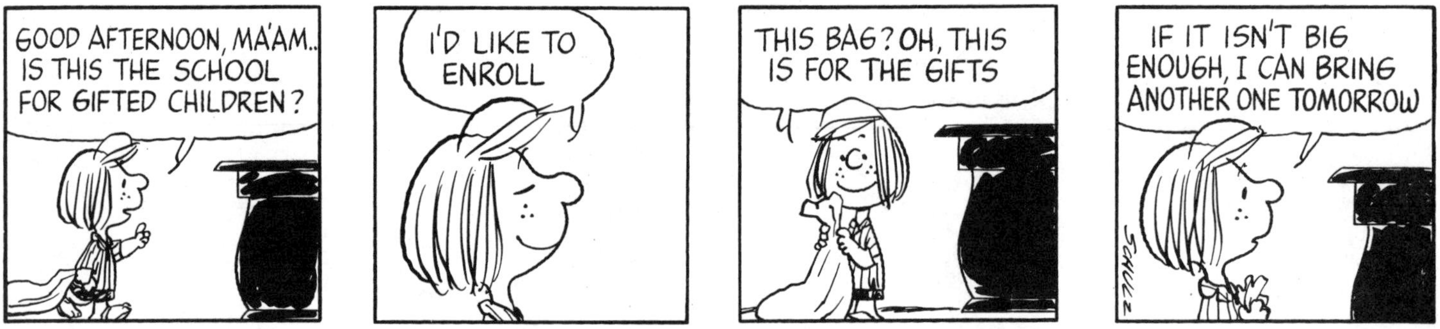
GOOD AFTERNOON, MA'AM.. IS THIS THE SCHOOL FOR GIFTED CHILDREN?
I'D LIKE TO ENROLL
THIS BAG? OH, THIS IS FOR THE GIFTS
IF IT ISN'T BIG ENOUGH, I CAN BRING ANOTHER ONE TOMORROW
SCHULZ

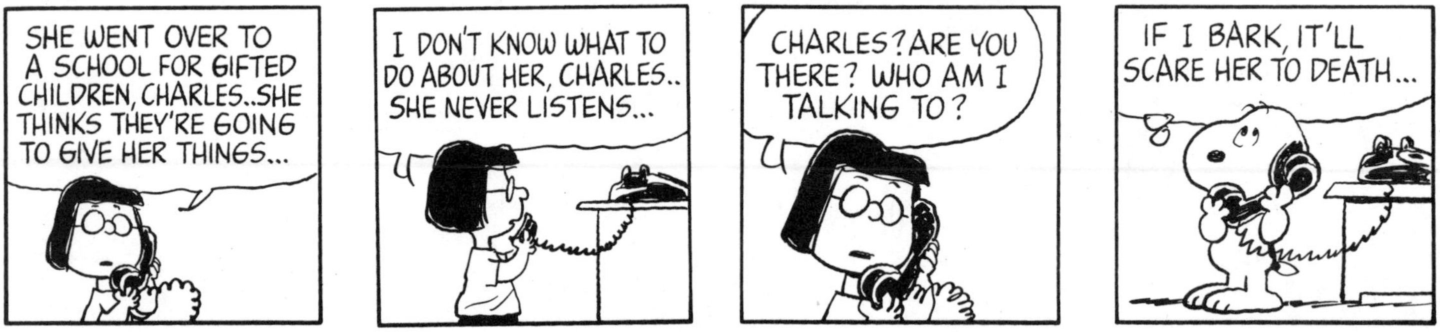
SHE WENT OVER TO A SCHOOL FOR GIFTED CHILDREN, CHARLES..SHE THINKS THEY'RE GOING TO GIVE HER THINGS...
I DON'T KNOW WHAT TO DO ABOUT HER, CHARLES.. SHE NEVER LISTENS...
CHARLES? ARE YOU THERE? WHO AM I TALKING TO?
IF I BARK, IT'LL SCARE HER TO DEATH...

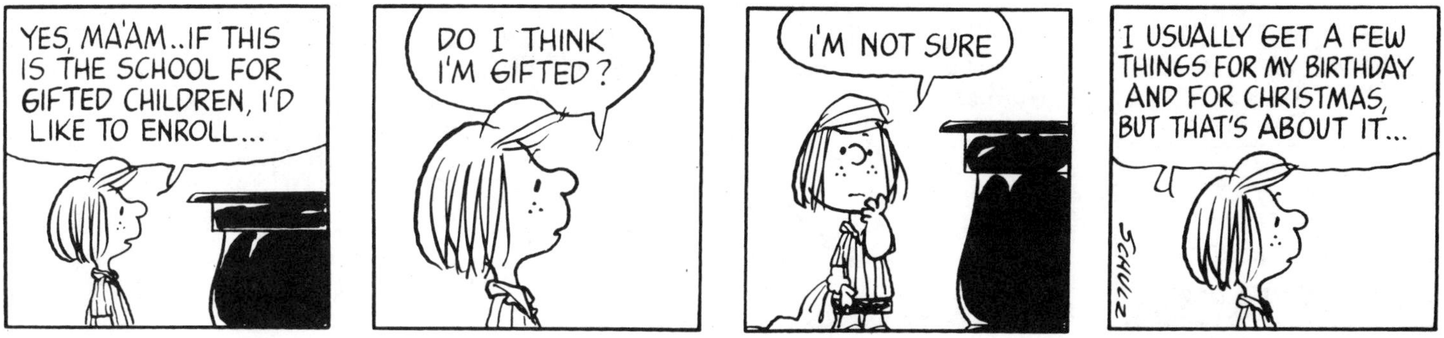
YES, MA'AM..IF THIS IS THE SCHOOL FOR GIFTED CHILDREN, I'D LIKE TO ENROLL...
DO I THINK I'M GIFTED?
I'M NOT SURE
I USUALLY GET A FEW THINGS FOR MY BIRTHDAY AND FOR CHRISTMAS, BUT THAT'S ABOUT IT...
SCHULZ

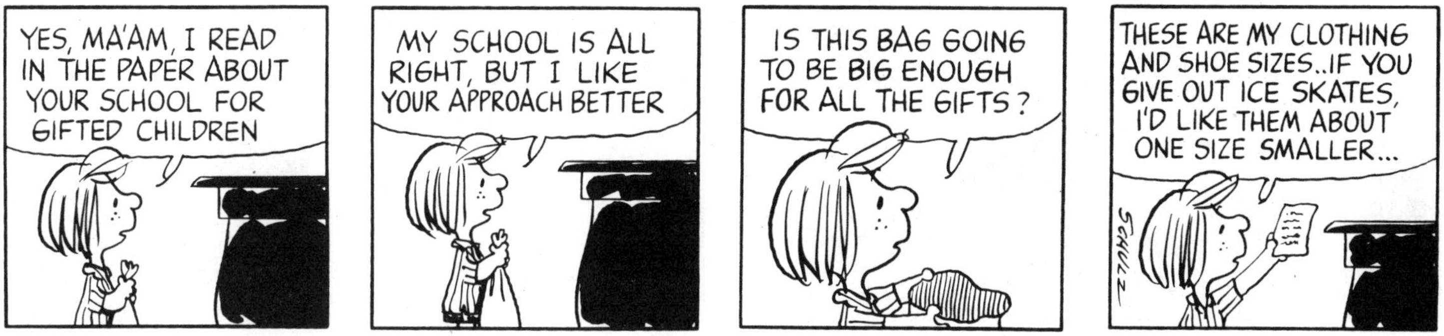
YES, MA'AM, I READ IN THE PAPER ABOUT YOUR SCHOOL FOR GIFTED CHILDREN
MY SCHOOL IS ALL RIGHT, BUT I LIKE YOUR APPROACH BETTER
IS THIS BAG GOING TO BE BIG ENOUGH FOR ALL THE GIFTS?
THESE ARE MY CLOTHING AND SHOE SIZES..IF YOU GIVE OUT ICE SKATES, I'D LIKE THEM ABOUT ONE SIZE SMALLER...
SCHULZ

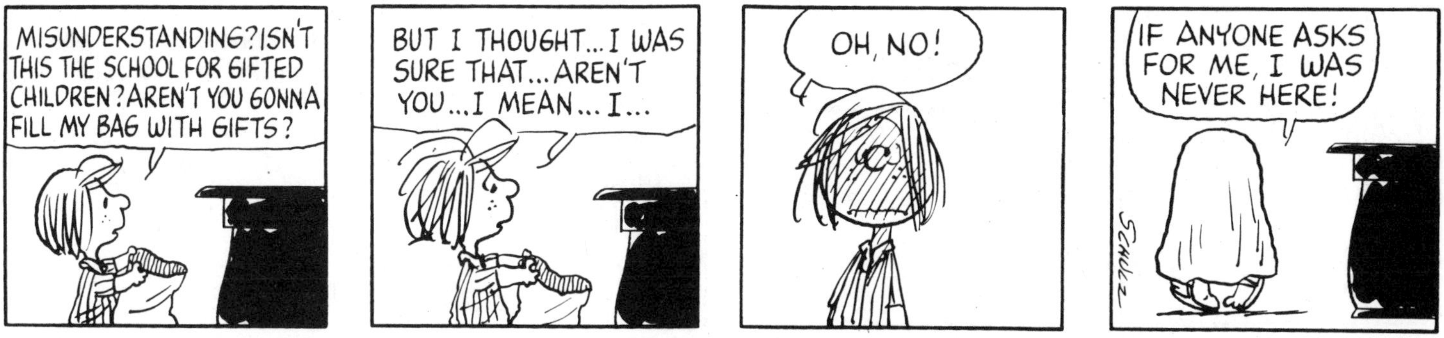
MISUNDERSTANDING? ISN'T THIS THE SCHOOL FOR GIFTED CHILDREN? AREN'T YOU GONNA FILL MY BAG WITH GIFTS?
BUT I THOUGHT... I WAS SURE THAT... AREN'T YOU... I MEAN... I...
OH, NO!
IF ANYONE ASKS FOR ME, I WAS NEVER HERE!
SCHULZ

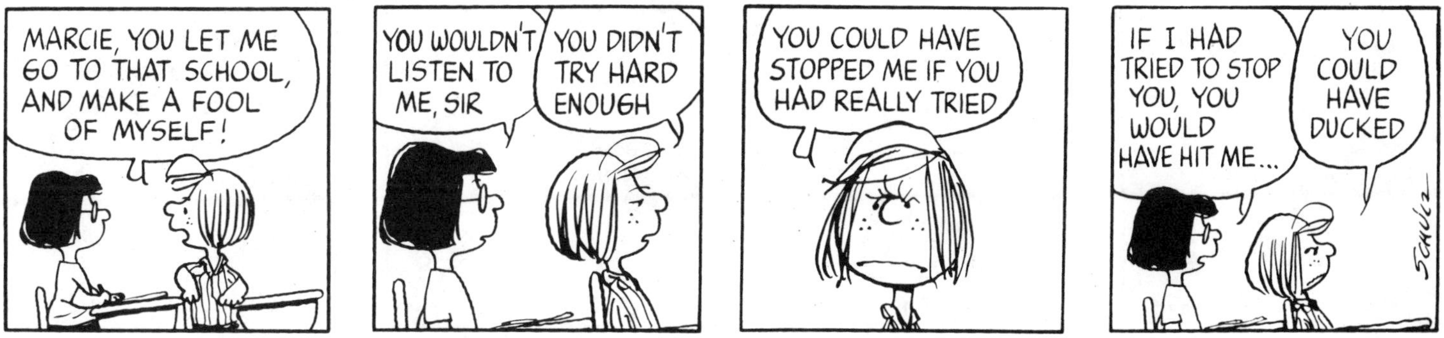
MARCIE, YOU LET ME GO TO THAT SCHOOL, AND MAKE A FOOL OF MYSELF!
YOU WOULDN'T LISTEN TO ME, SIR
YOU DIDN'T TRY HARD ENOUGH
YOU COULD HAVE STOPPED ME IF YOU HAD REALLY TRIED
IF I HAD TRIED TO STOP YOU, YOU WOULD HAVE HIT ME...
YOU COULD HAVE DUCKED
SCHULZ

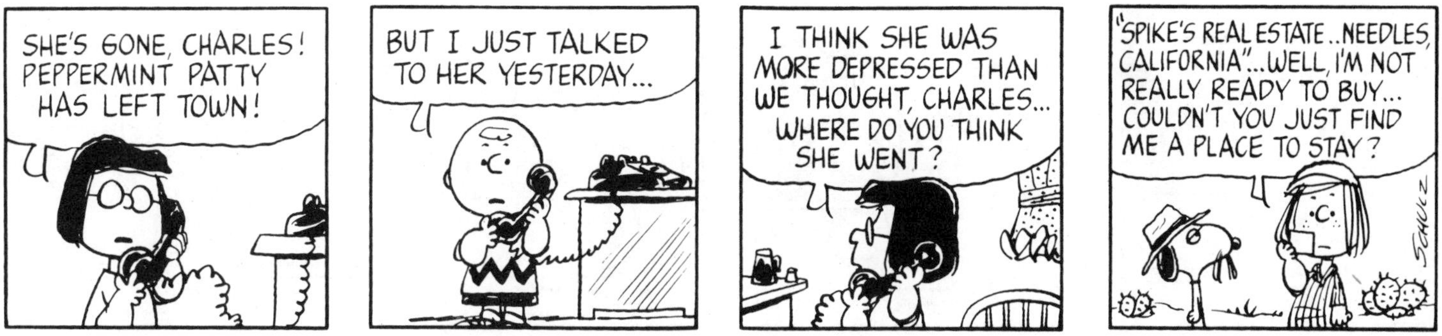
SHE'S GONE, CHARLES! PEPPERMINT PATTY HAS LEFT TOWN!
BUT I JUST TALKED TO HER YESTERDAY...
I THINK SHE WAS MORE DEPRESSED THAN WE THOUGHT, CHARLES... WHERE DO YOU THINK SHE WENT?
"SPIKE'S REAL ESTATE..NEEDLES, CALIFORNIA"...WELL, I'M NOT REALLY READY TO BUY... COULDN'T YOU JUST FIND ME A PLACE TO STAY?
SCHULZ

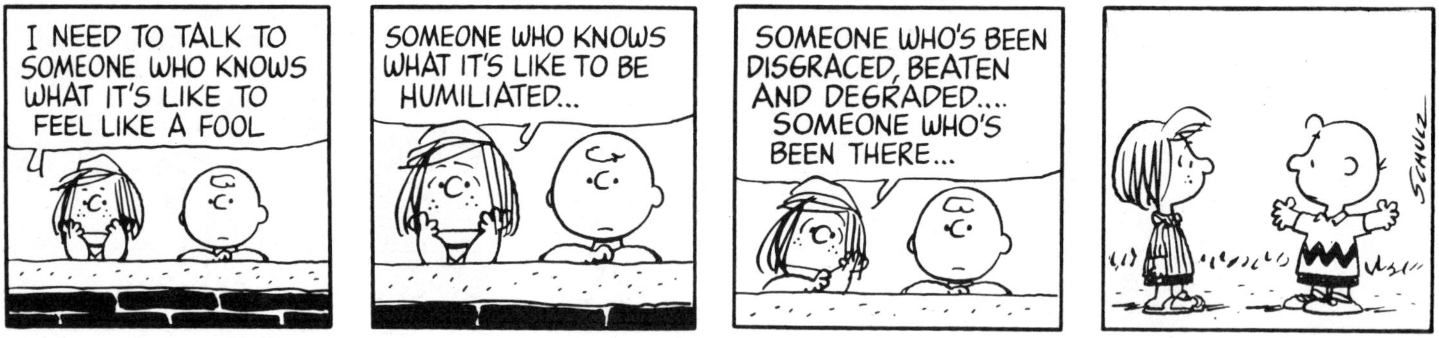
I NEED TO TALK TO SOMEONE WHO KNOWS WHAT IT'S LIKE TO FEEL LIKE A FOOL
SOMEONE WHO KNOWS WHAT IT'S LIKE TO BE HUMILIATED...
SOMEONE WHO'S BEEN DISGRACED, BEATEN AND DEGRADED.... SOMEONE WHO'S BEEN THERE...
SCHULZ

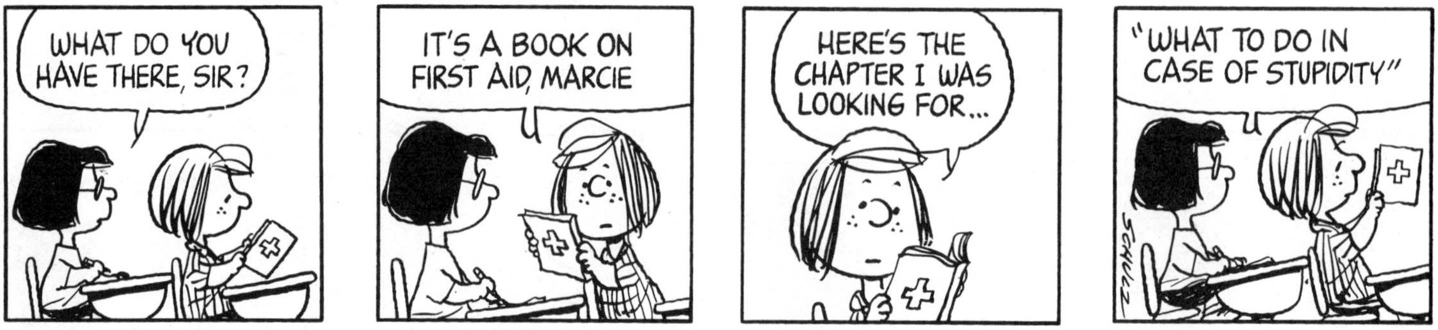
WHAT DO YOU HAVE THERE, SIR?
IT'S A BOOK ON FIRST AID, MARCIE
HERE'S THE CHAPTER I WAS LOOKING FOR...
"WHAT TO DO IN CASE OF STUPIDITY"
SCHULZ

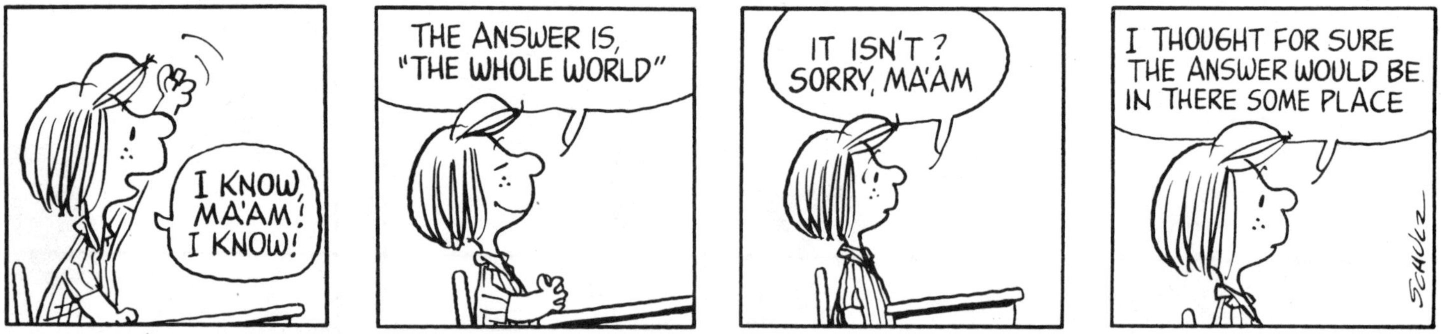
I KNOW, MA'AM! I KNOW!
THE ANSWER IS, "THE WHOLE WORLD"
IT ISN'T? SORRY, MA'AM
I THOUGHT FOR SURE THE ANSWER WOULD BE IN THERE SOME PLACE
SCHULZ

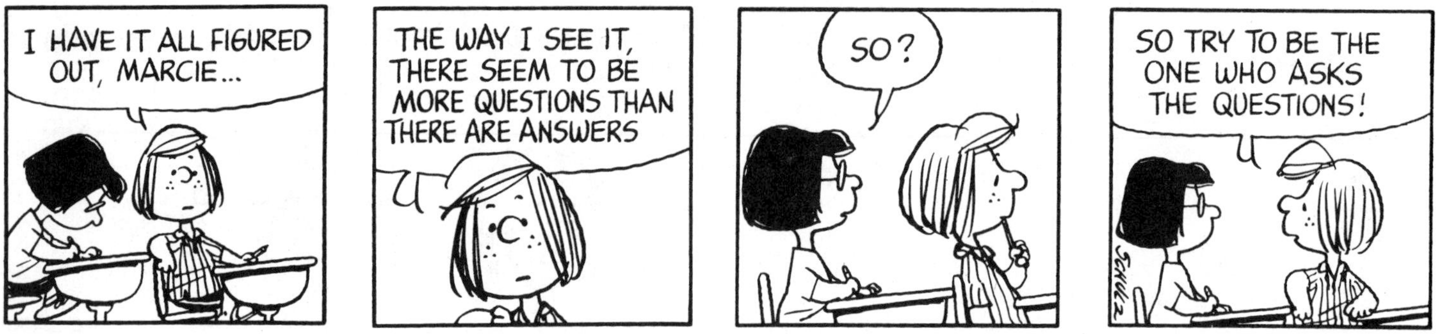
I HAVE IT ALL FIGURED OUT, MARCIE...
THE WAY I SEE IT, THERE SEEM TO BE MORE QUESTIONS THAN THERE ARE ANSWERS
SO?
SO TRY TO BE THE ONE WHO ASKS THE QUESTIONS!
SCHULZ

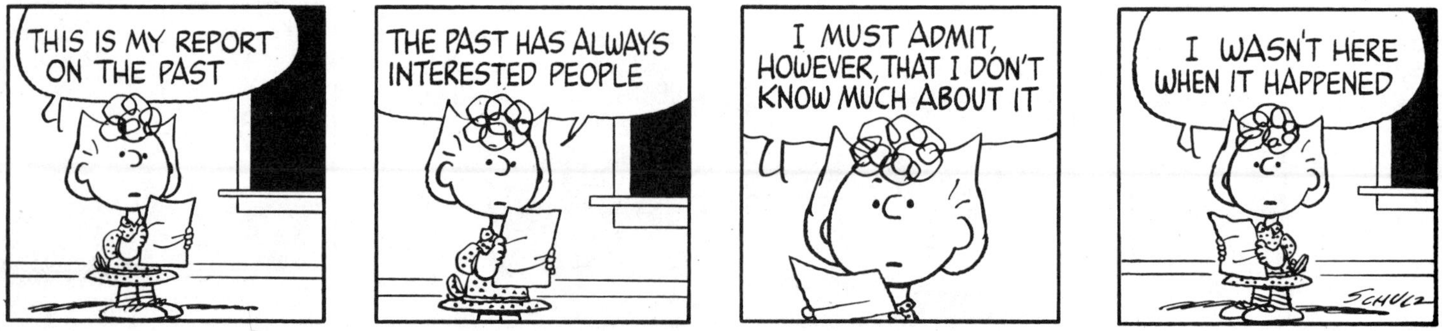
THIS IS MY REPORT ON THE PAST
THE PAST HAS ALWAYS INTERESTED PEOPLE
I MUST ADMIT, HOWEVER, THAT I DON'T KNOW MUCH ABOUT IT
I WASN'T HERE WHEN IT HAPPENED
SCHULZ

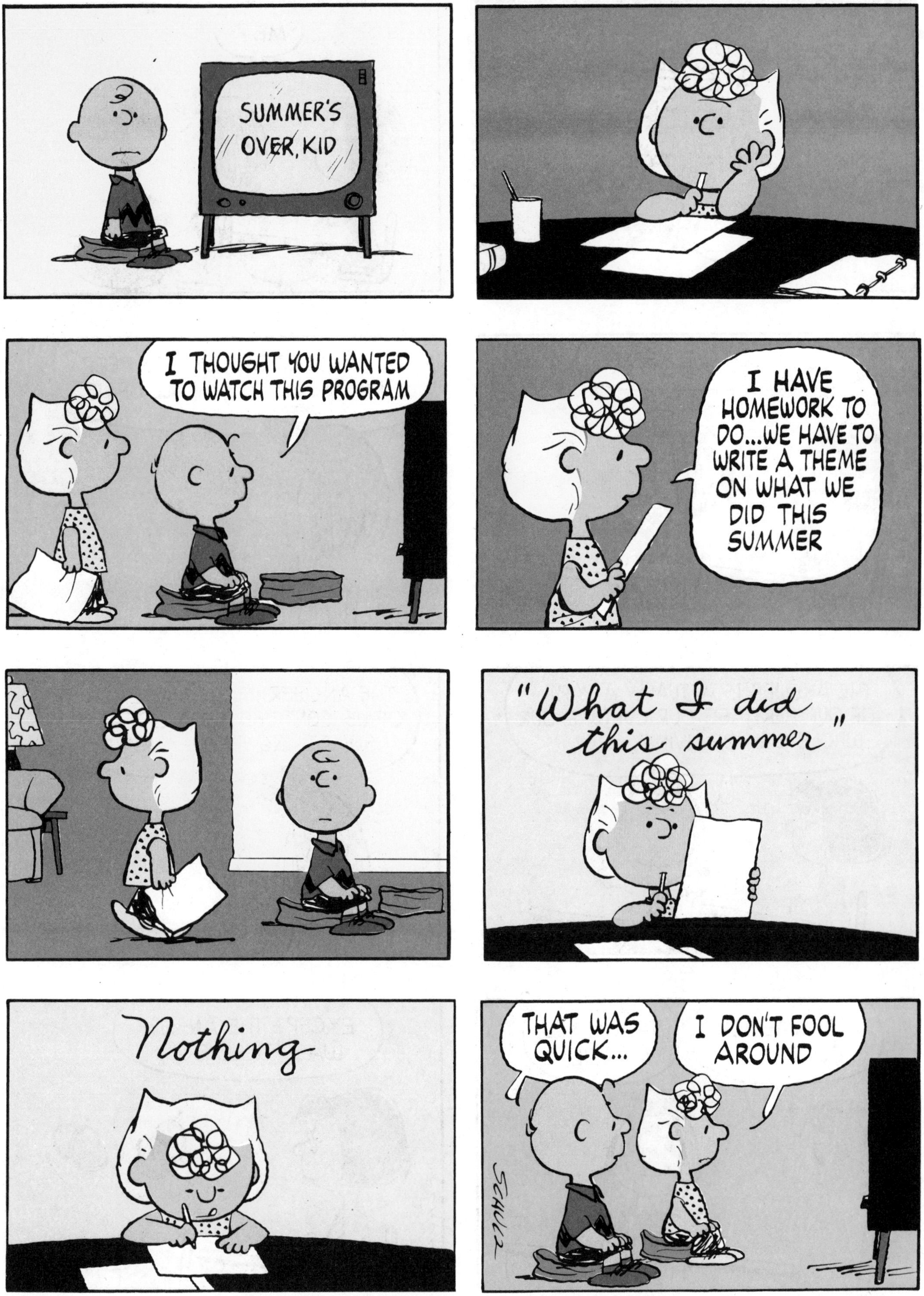
SUMMER'S OVER, KID
I THOUGHT YOU WANTED TO WATCH THIS PROGRAM
I HAVE HOMEWORK TO DO...WE HAVE TO WRITE A THEME ON WHAT WE DID THIS SUMMER
"What I did this summer"
Nothing
THAT WAS QUICK...
I DON'T FOOL AROUND
SCHULZ

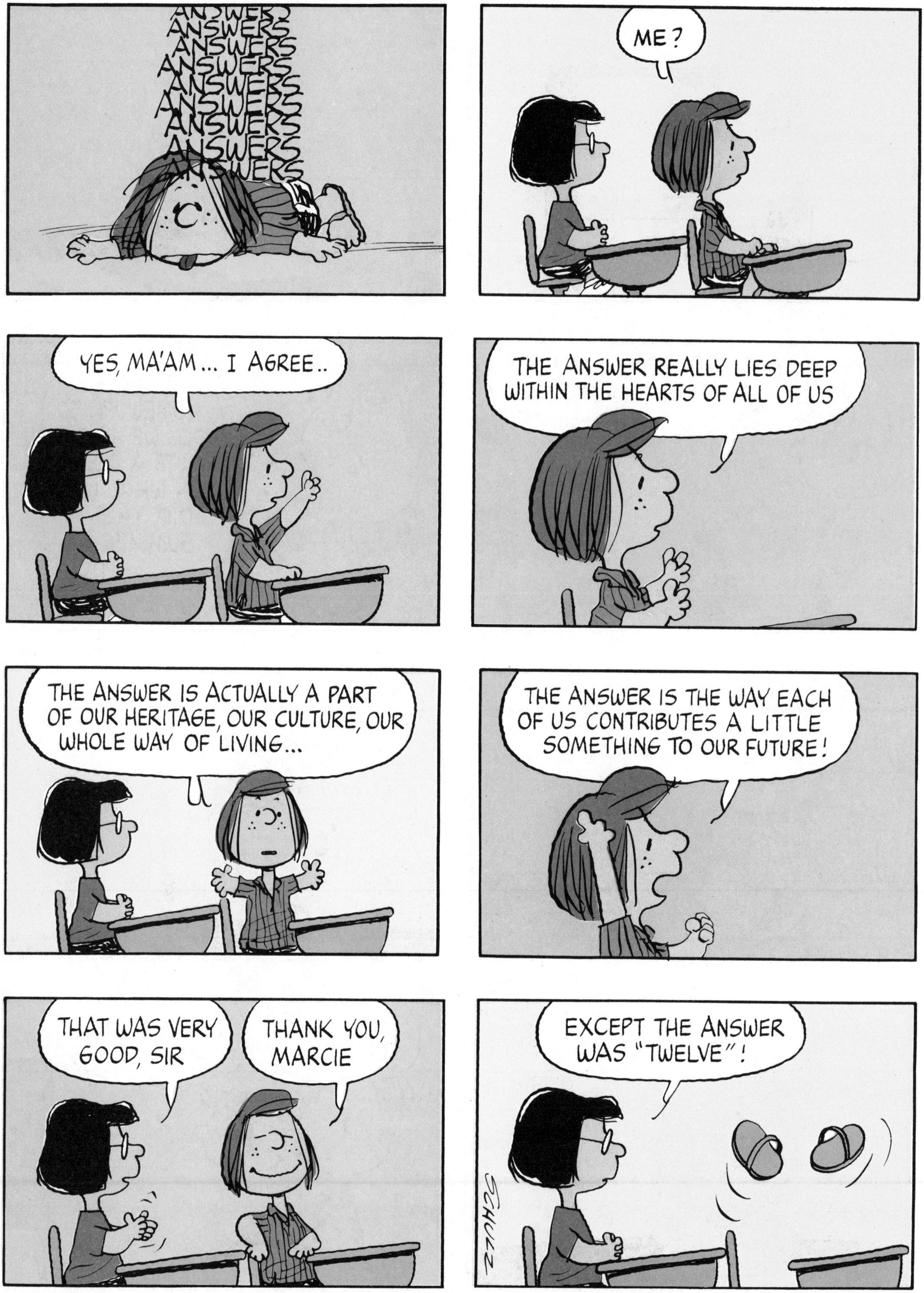
ANSWERS
ANSWERS
ANSWERS
ANSWERS
ANSWERS
ANSWERS
ANSWERS
ANSWERS
ME?
YES, MA'AM... I AGREE..
THE ANSWER REALLY LIES DEEP WITHIN THE HEARTS OF ALL OF US
THE ANSWER IS ACTUALLY A PART OF OUR HERITAGE, OUR CULTURE, OUR WHOLE WAY OF LIVING...
THE ANSWER IS THE WAY EACH OF US CONTRIBUTES A LITTLE SOMETHING TO OUR FUTURE!
THAT WAS VERY GOOD, SIR
THANK YOU, MARCIE
EXCEPT THE ANSWER WAS "TWELVE"!
SCHULZ

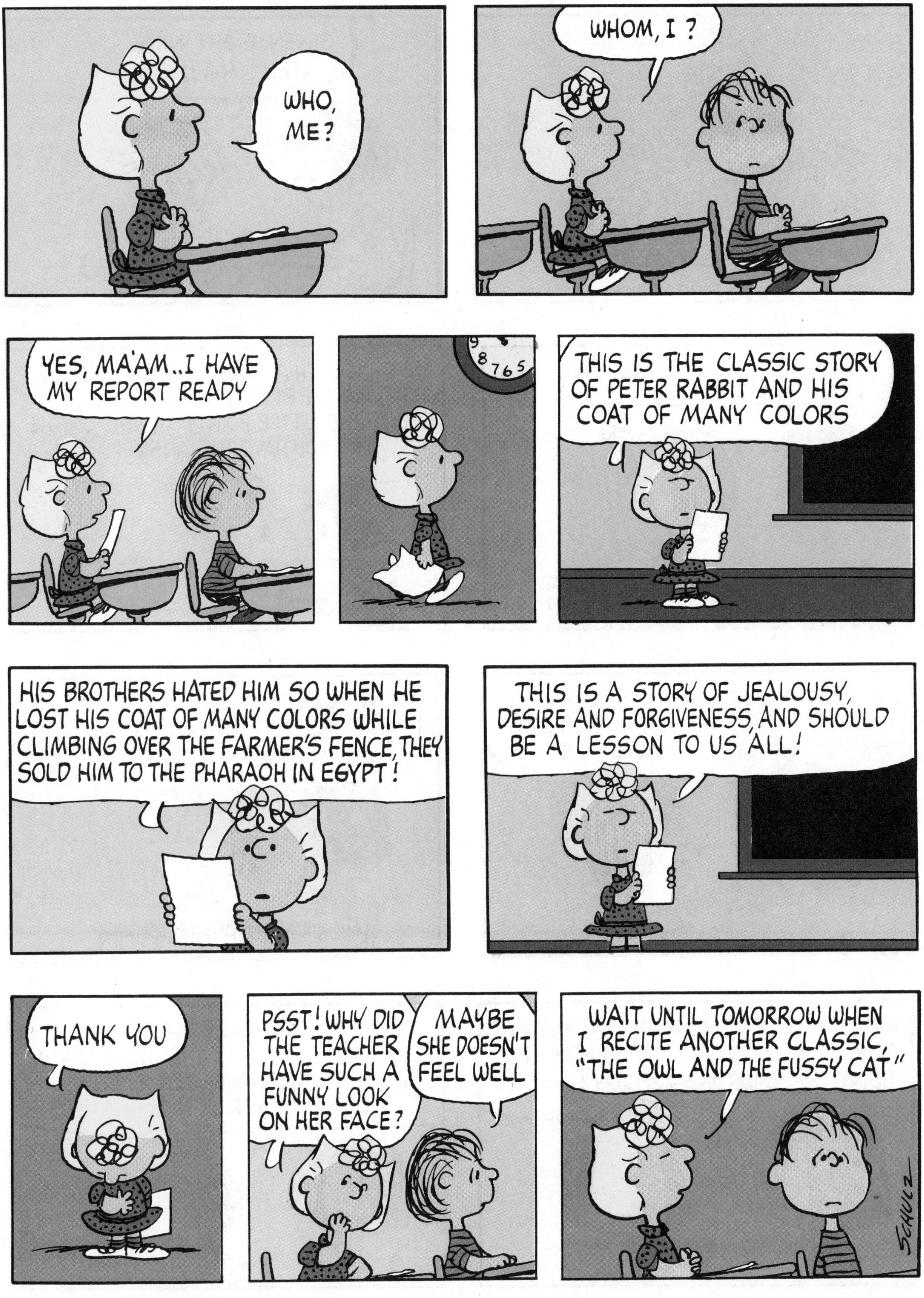
WHO, ME?
WHOM, I?
YES, MA'AM..I HAVE MY REPORT READY
THIS IS THE CLASSIC STORY OF PETER RABBIT AND HIS COAT OF MANY COLORS
HIS BROTHERS HATED HIM SO WHEN HE LOST HIS COAT OF MANY COLORS WHILE CLIMBING OVER THE FARMER'S FENCE, THEY SOLD HIM TO THE PHARAOH IN EGYPT!
THIS IS A STORY OF JEALOUSY, DESIRE AND FORGIVENESS, AND SHOULD BE A LESSON TO US ALL!
THANK YOU
PSST! WHY DID THE TEACHER HAVE SUCH A FUNNY LOOK ON HER FACE?
MAYBE SHE DOESN'T FEEL WELL
WAIT UNTIL TOMORROW WHEN I RECITE ANOTHER CLASSIC, "THE OWL AND THE FUSSY CAT"
SCHULZ

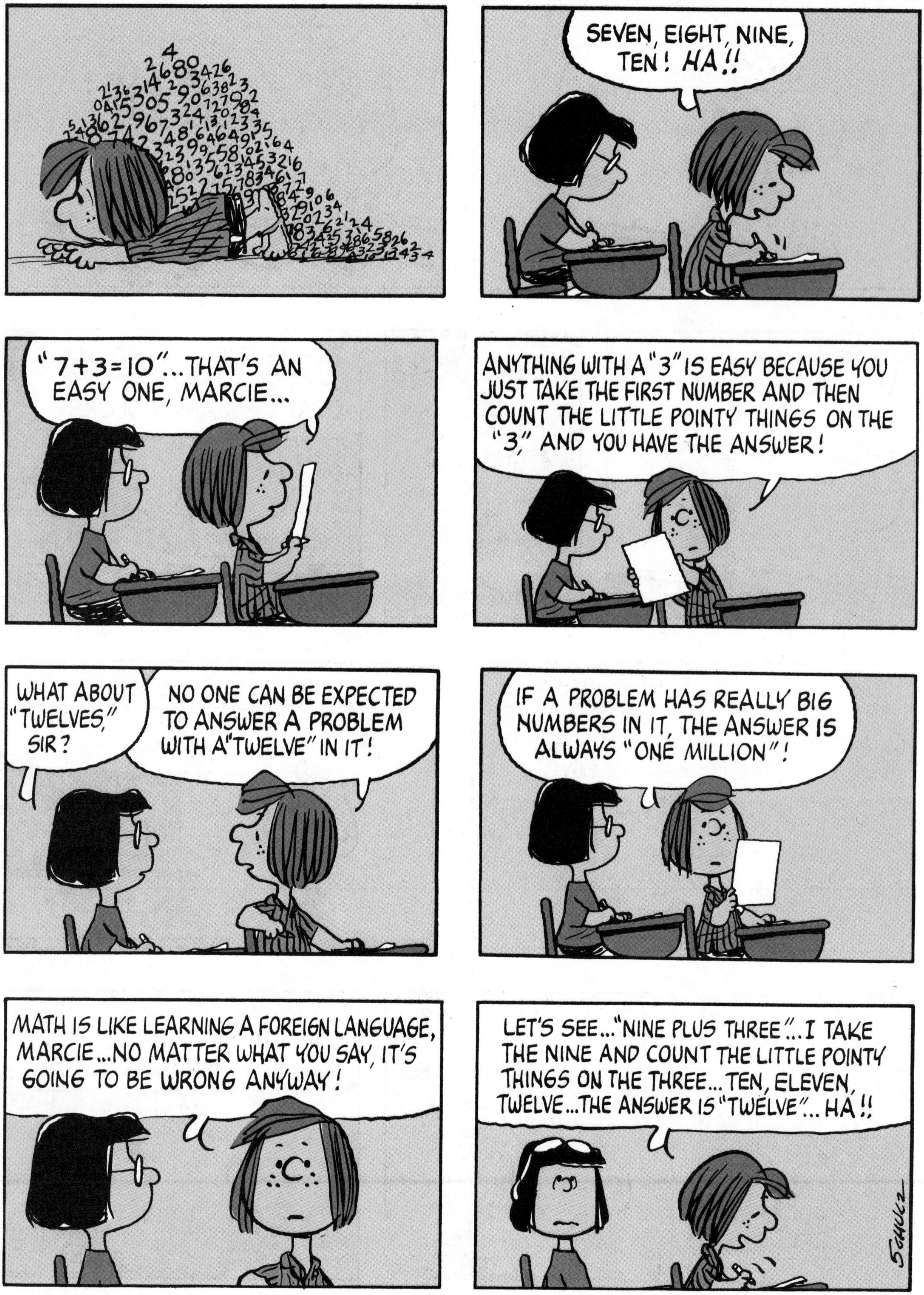

SEVEN, EIGHT, NINE, TEN! HA!!
"7+3=10"...THAT'S AN EASY ONE, MARCIE...
ANYTHING WITH A "3" IS EASY BECAUSE YOU JUST TAKE THE FIRST NUMBER AND THEN COUNT THE LITTLE POINTY THINGS ON THE "3," AND YOU HAVE THE ANSWER!
WHAT ABOUT "TWELVES," SIR?
NO ONE CAN BE EXPECTED TO ANSWER A PROBLEM WITH A "TWELVE" IN IT!
IF A PROBLEM HAS REALLY BIG NUMBERS IN IT, THE ANSWER IS ALWAYS "ONE MILLION"!
MATH IS LIKE LEARNING A FOREIGN LANGUAGE, MARCIE...NO MATTER WHAT YOU SAY, IT'S GOING TO BE WRONG ANYWAY!
LET'S SEE..."NINE PLUS THREE"...I TAKE THE NINE AND COUNT THE LITTLE POINTY THINGS ON THE THREE...TEN, ELEVEN, TWELVE...THE ANSWER IS "TWELVE"... HA!!

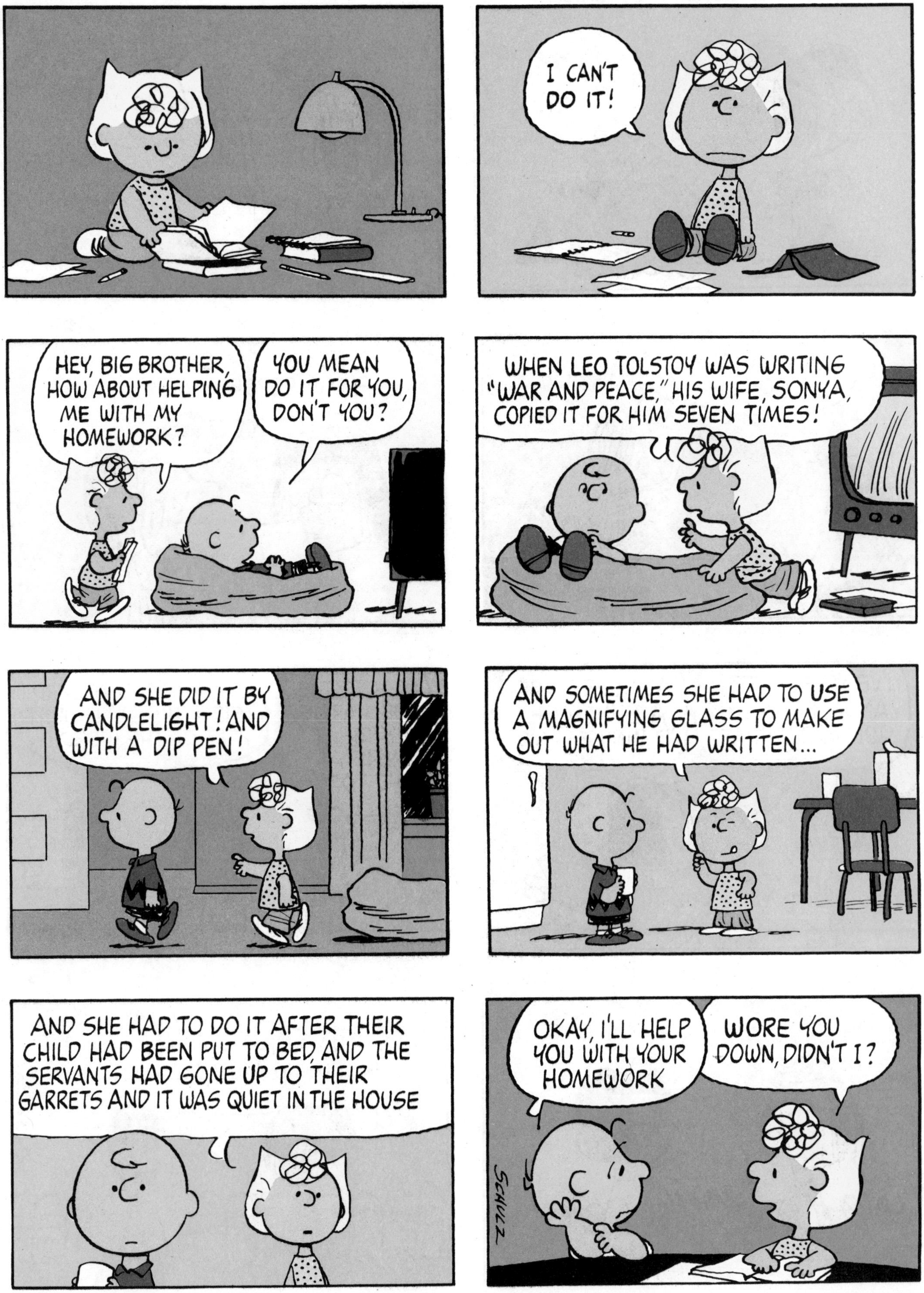
I CAN'T DO IT!
HEY, BIG BROTHER, HOW ABOUT HELPING ME WITH MY HOMEWORK?
YOU MEAN DO IT FOR YOU, DON'T YOU?
WHEN LEO TOLSTOY WAS WRITING "WAR AND PEACE," HIS WIFE, SONYA, COPIED IT FOR HIM SEVEN TIMES!
AND SHE DID IT BY CANDLELIGHT! AND WITH A DIP PEN!
AND SOMETIMES SHE HAD TO USE A MAGNIFYING GLASS TO MAKE OUT WHAT HE HAD WRITTEN...
AND SHE HAD TO DO IT AFTER THEIR CHILD HAD BEEN PUT TO BED, AND THE SERVANTS HAD GONE UP TO THEIR GARRETS AND IT WAS QUIET IN THE HOUSE
SCHULZ
OKAY, I'LL HELP YOU WITH YOUR HOMEWORK
WORE YOU DOWN, DIDN'T I?

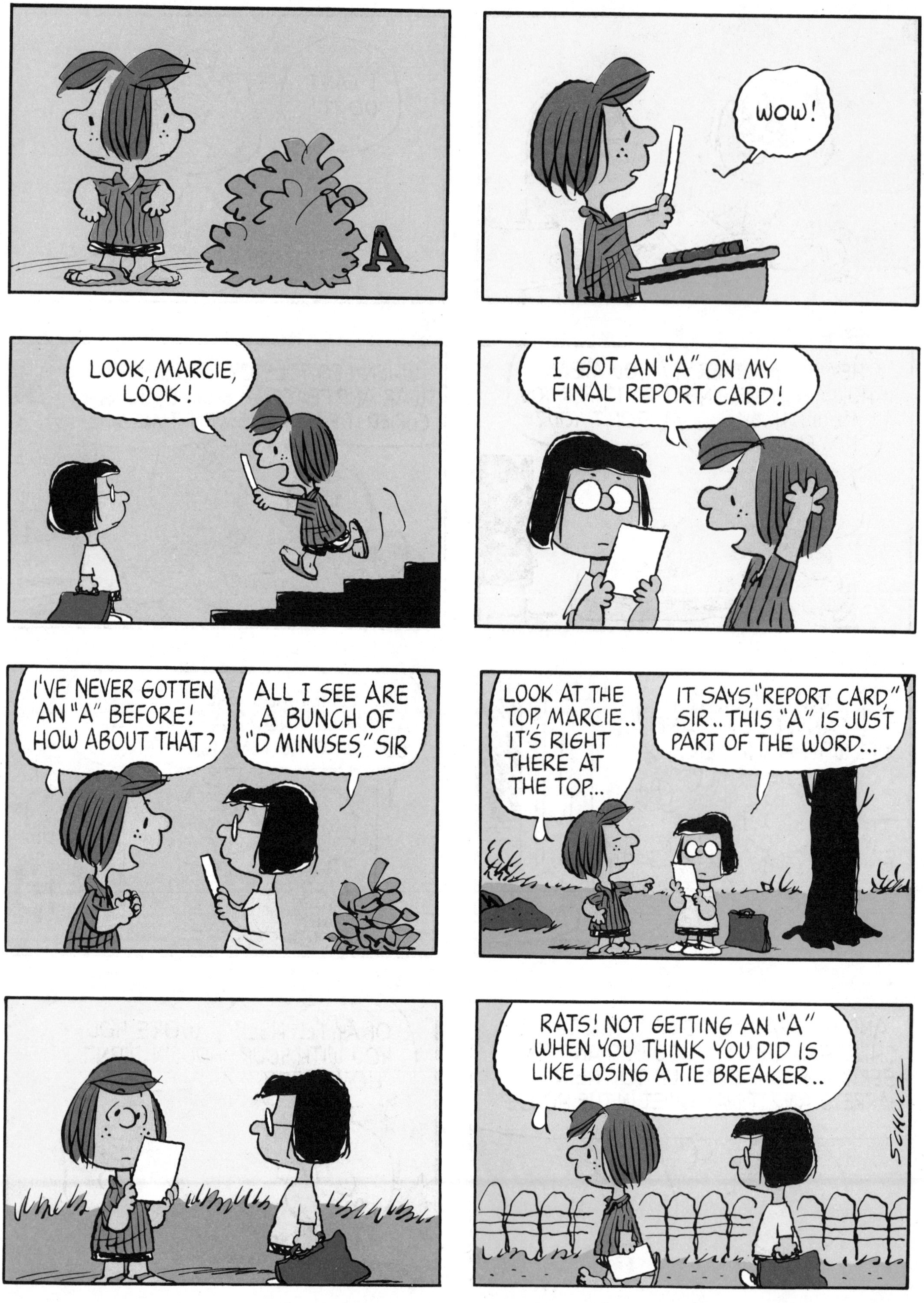
WOW!
LOOK, MARCIE, LOOK!
I GOT AN "A" ON MY FINAL REPORT CARD!
I'VE NEVER GOTTEN AN "A" BEFORE! HOW ABOUT THAT?
ALL I SEE ARE A BUNCH OF "D MINUSES," SIR
LOOK AT THE TOP, MARCIE.. IT'S RIGHT THERE AT THE TOP...
IT SAYS, "REPORT CARD," SIR.. THIS "A" IS JUST PART OF THE WORD...
RATS! NOT GETTING AN "A" WHEN YOU THINK YOU DID IS LIKE LOSING A TIE BREAKER..
SCHULZ

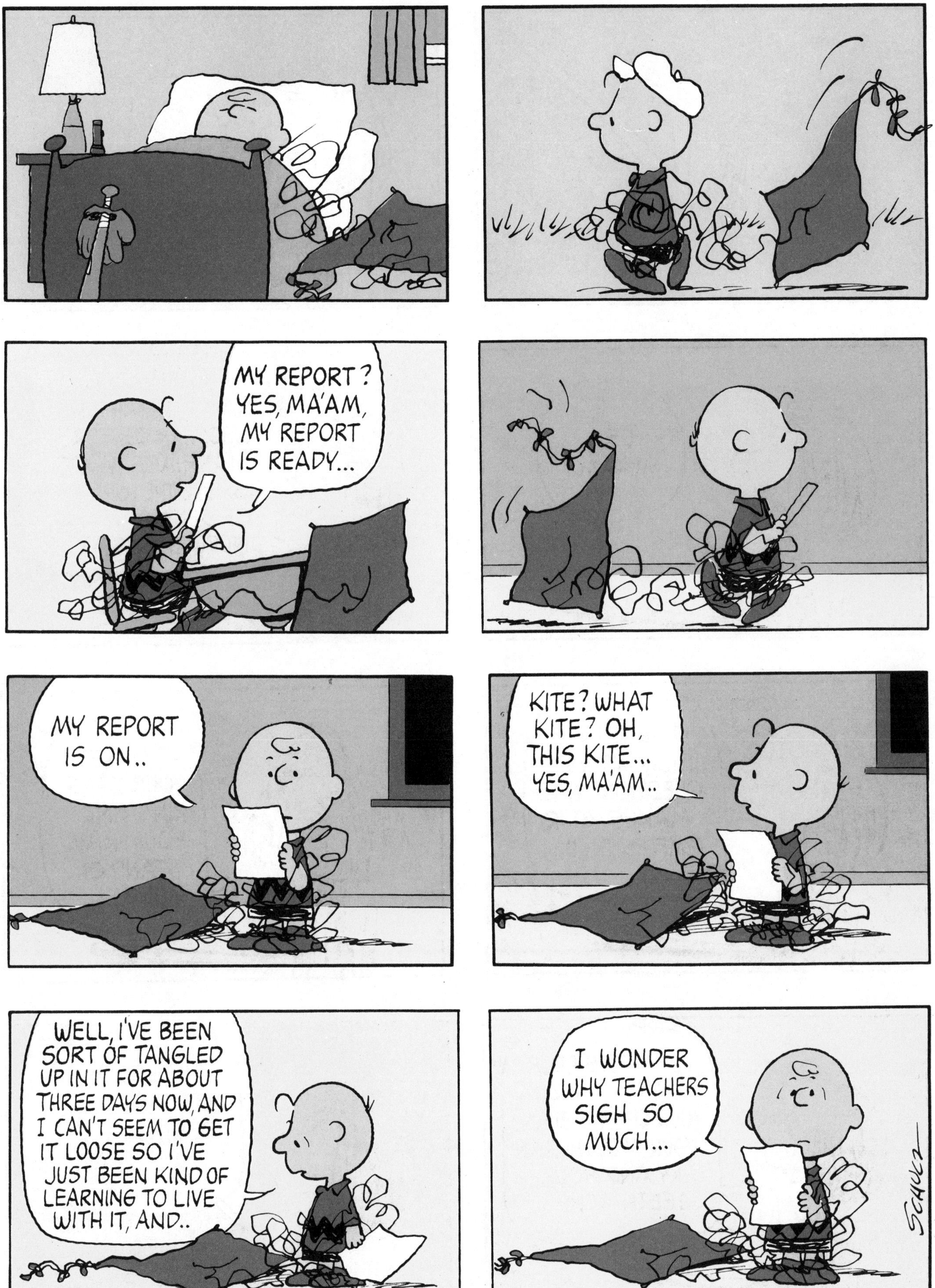
MY REPORT? YES, MA'AM, MY REPORT IS READY...
MY REPORT IS ON..
KITE? WHAT KITE? OH, THIS KITE... YES, MA'AM..
WELL, I'VE BEEN SORT OF TANGLED UP IN IT FOR ABOUT THREE DAYS NOW, AND I CAN'T SEEM TO GET IT LOOSE SO I'VE JUST BEEN KIND OF LEARNING TO LIVE WITH IT, AND..
I WONDER WHY TEACHERS SIGH SO MUCH...
SCHULZ

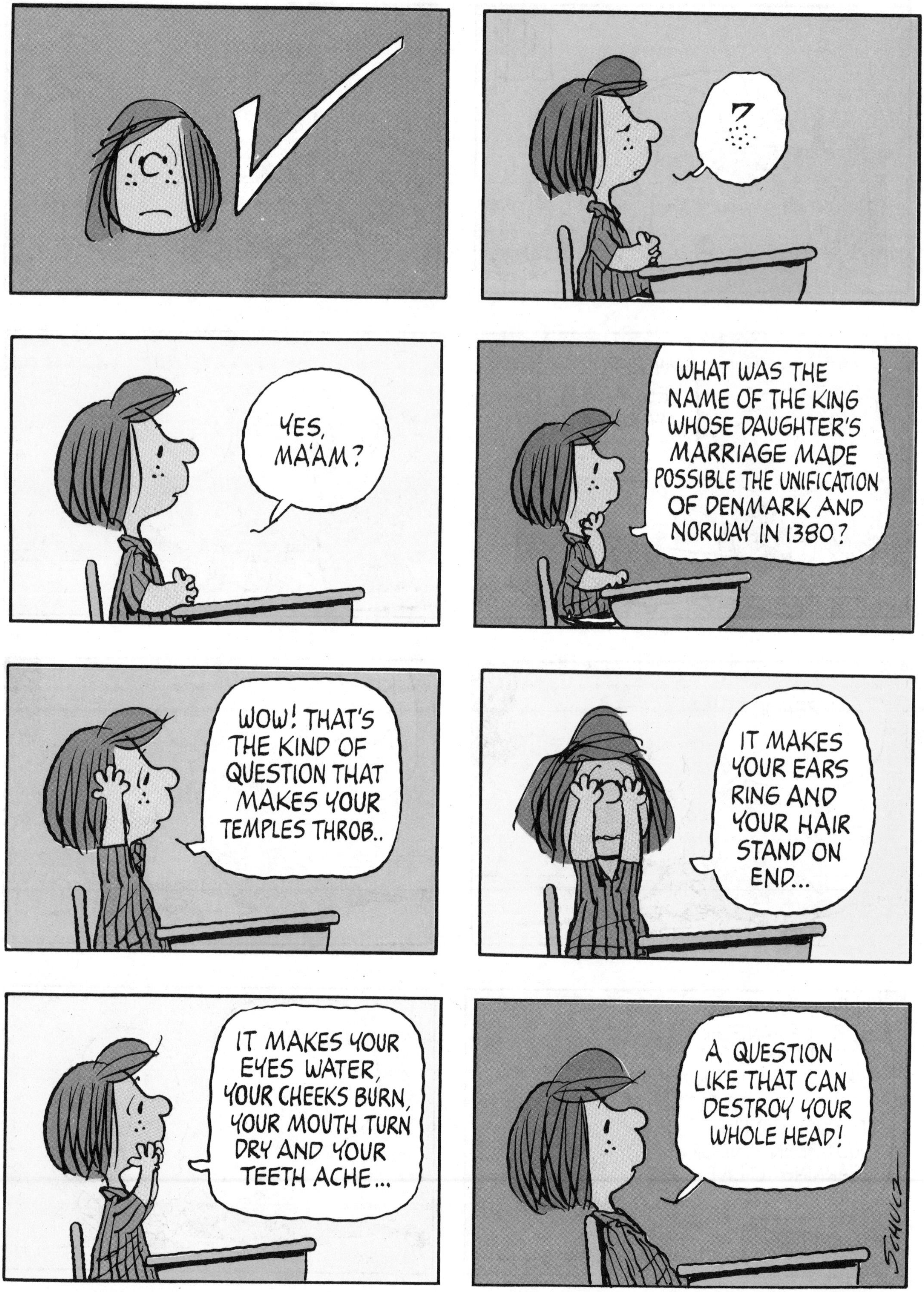
?
YES, MA'AM?
WHAT WAS THE NAME OF THE KING WHOSE DAUGHTER'S MARRIAGE MADE POSSIBLE THE UNIFICATION OF DENMARK AND NORWAY IN 1380?
WOW! THAT'S THE KIND OF QUESTION THAT MAKES YOUR TEMPLES THROB..
IT MAKES YOUR EARS RING AND YOUR HAIR STAND ON END...
IT MAKES YOUR EYES WATER, YOUR CHEEKS BURN, YOUR MOUTH TURN DRY AND YOUR TEETH ACHE...
A QUESTION LIKE THAT CAN DESTROY YOUR WHOLE HEAD!
SCHULZ

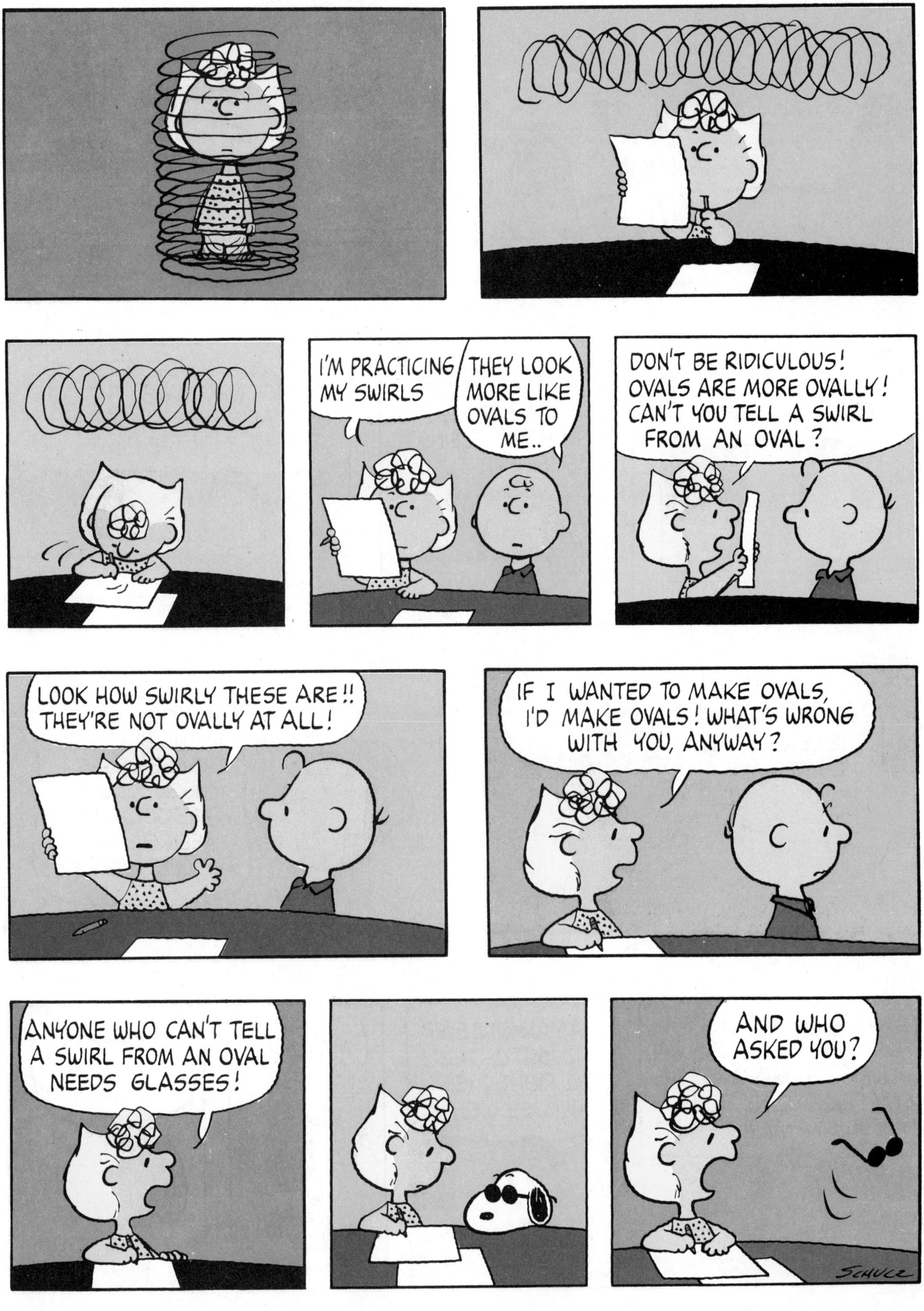
I'M PRACTICING MY SWIRLS
THEY LOOK MORE LIKE OVALS TO ME..
DON'T BE RIDICULOUS! OVALS ARE MORE OVALLY! CAN'T YOU TELL A SWIRL FROM AN OVAL?
LOOK HOW SWIRLY THESE ARE!! THEY'RE NOT OVALLY AT ALL!
IF I WANTED TO MAKE OVALS, I'D MAKE OVALS! WHAT'S WRONG WITH YOU, ANYWAY?
ANYONE WHO CAN'T TELL A SWIRL FROM AN OVAL NEEDS GLASSES!
AND WHO ASKED YOU?
SCHULZ

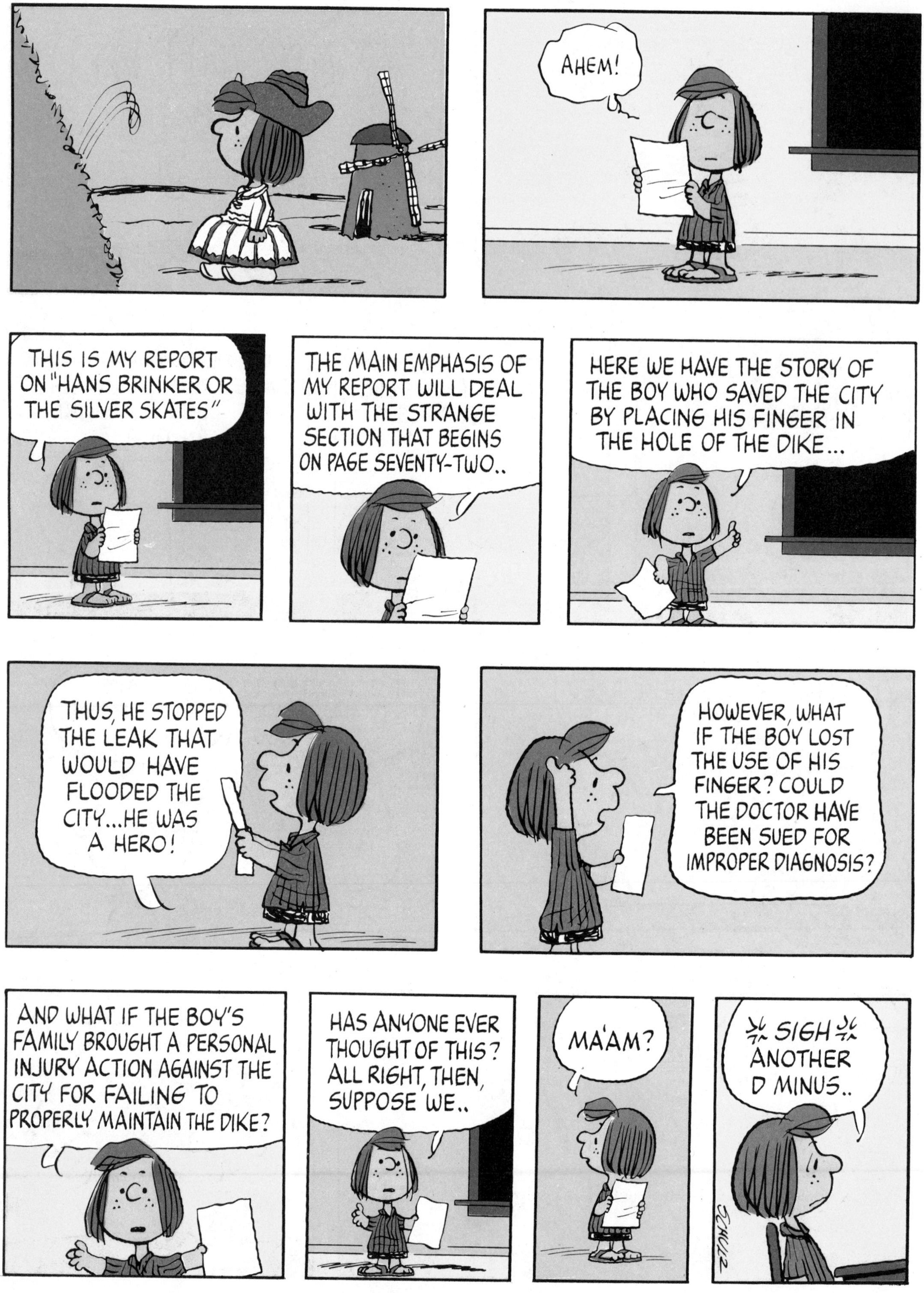
AHEM!
THIS IS MY REPORT ON "HANS BRINKER OR THE SILVER SKATES"
THE MAIN EMPHASIS OF MY REPORT WILL DEAL WITH THE STRANGE SECTION THAT BEGINS ON PAGE SEVENTY-TWO..
HERE WE HAVE THE STORY OF THE BOY WHO SAVED THE CITY BY PLACING HIS FINGER IN THE HOLE OF THE DIKE...
THUS, HE STOPPED THE LEAK THAT WOULD HAVE FLOODED THE CITY...HE WAS A HERO!
HOWEVER, WHAT IF THE BOY LOST THE USE OF HIS FINGER? COULD THE DOCTOR HAVE BEEN SUED FOR IMPROPER DIAGNOSIS?
AND WHAT IF THE BOY'S FAMILY BROUGHT A PERSONAL INJURY ACTION AGAINST THE CITY FOR FAILING TO PROPERLY MAINTAIN THE DIKE?
HAS ANYONE EVER THOUGHT OF THIS? ALL RIGHT, THEN, SUPPOSE WE..
MA'AM?
SIGH ANOTHER D MINUS..
SCHULZ

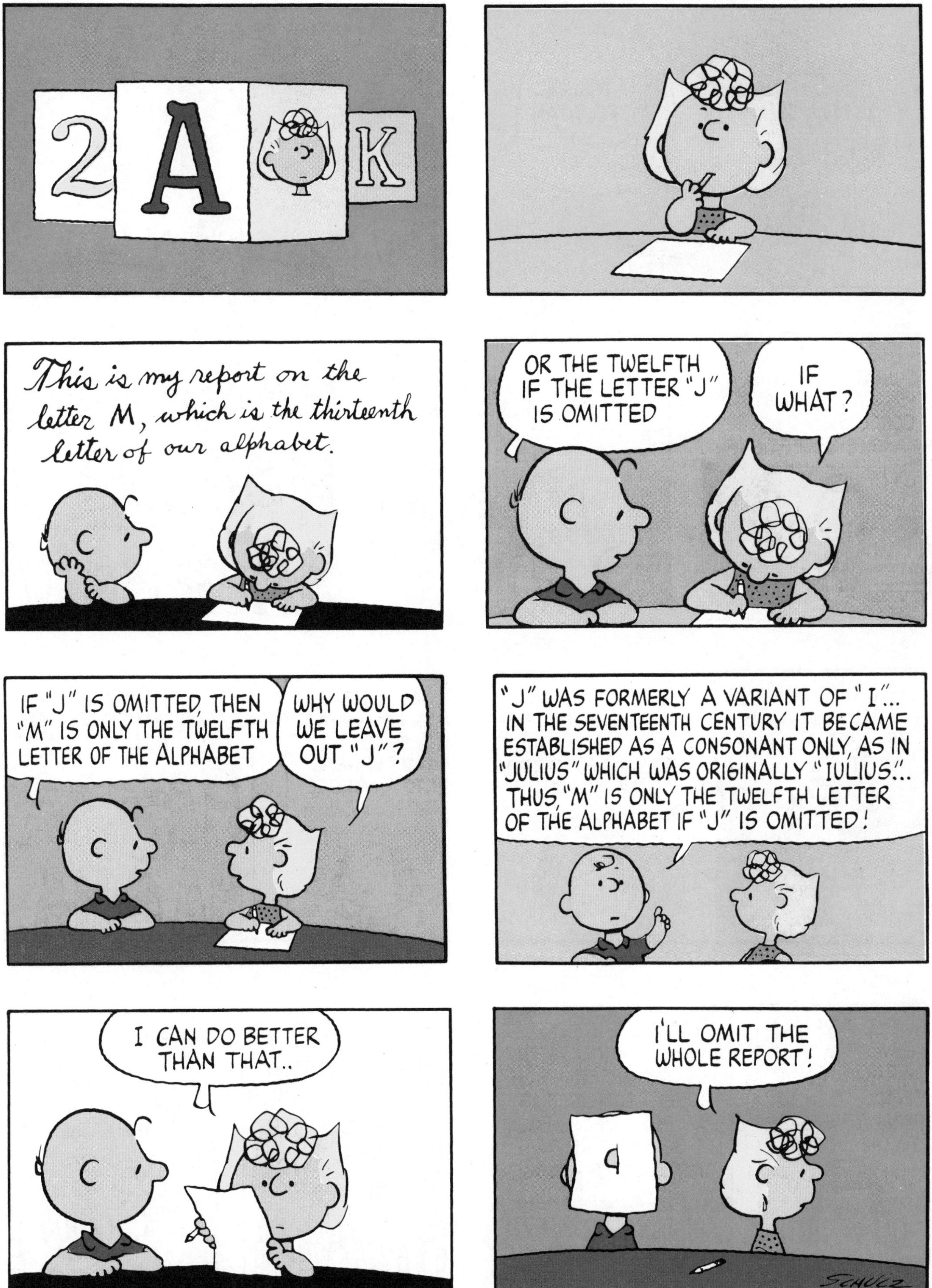
2
A
K
This is my report on the letter M, which is the thirteenth letter of our alphabet.
OR THE TWELFTH IF THE LETTER "J" IS OMITTED
IF WHAT?
IF "J" IS OMITTED, THEN "M" IS ONLY THE TWELFTH LETTER OF THE ALPHABET
WHY WOULD WE LEAVE OUT "J"?
"J" WAS FORMERLY A VARIANT OF "I"... IN THE SEVENTEENTH CENTURY IT BECAME ESTABLISHED AS A CONSONANT ONLY, AS IN "JULIUS" WHICH WAS ORIGINALLY "IULIUS"... THUS, "M" IS ONLY THE TWELFTH LETTER OF THE ALPHABET IF "J" IS OMITTED!
I CAN DO BETTER THAN THAT..
I'LL OMIT THE WHOLE REPORT!
SCHULZ

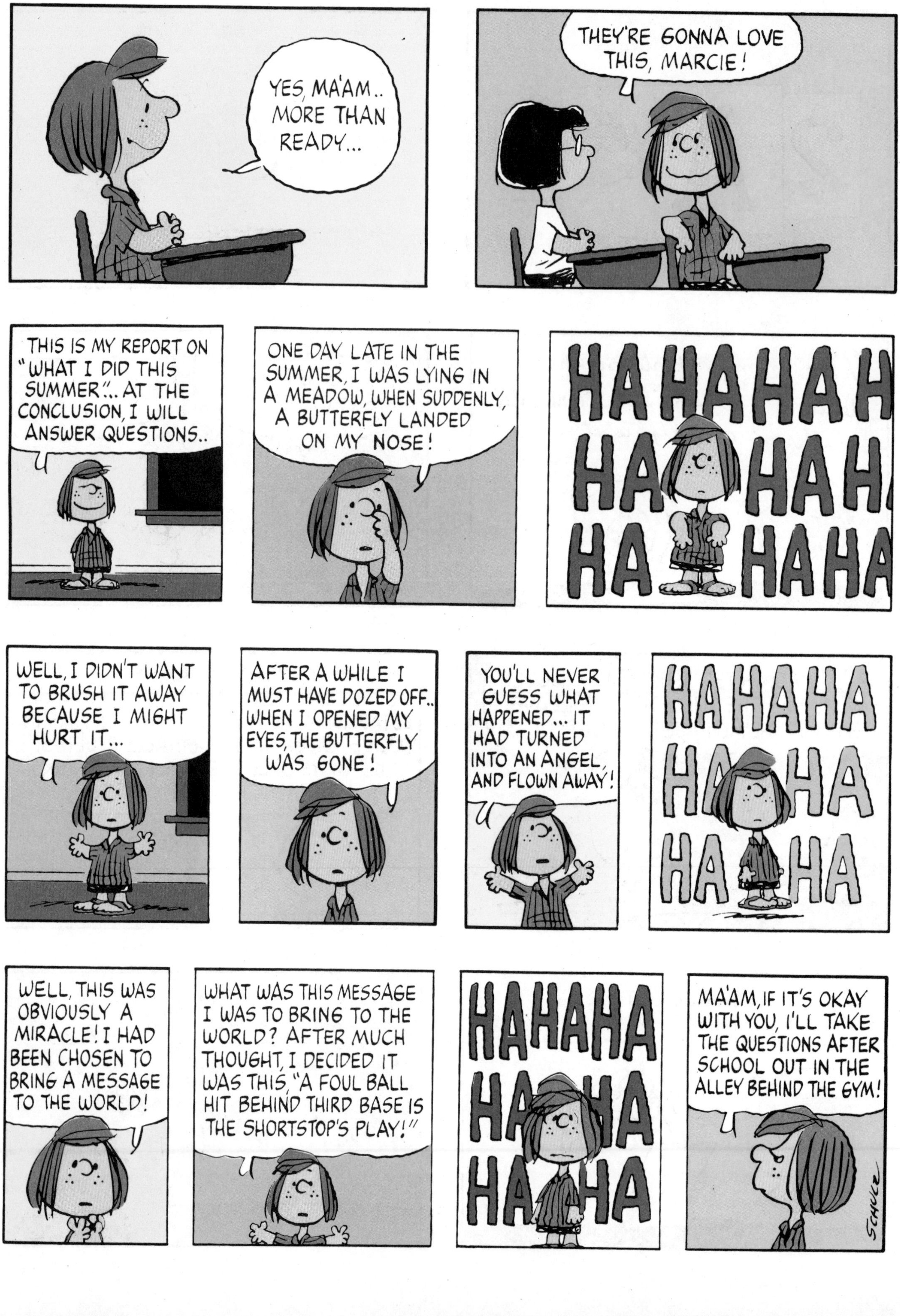
YES, MA'AM.. MORE THAN READY...
THEY'RE GONNA LOVE THIS, MARCIE!
THIS IS MY REPORT ON "WHAT I DID THIS SUMMER"... AT THE CONCLUSION, I WILL ANSWER QUESTIONS..
ONE DAY LATE IN THE SUMMER, I WAS LYING IN A MEADOW, WHEN SUDDENLY, A BUTTERFLY LANDED ON MY NOSE!
HA HA HA HA H HA HA HA HA HA HA
WELL, I DIDN'T WANT TO BRUSH IT AWAY BECAUSE I MIGHT HURT IT...
AFTER A WHILE I MUST HAVE DOZED OFF.. WHEN I OPENED MY EYES, THE BUTTERFLY WAS GONE!
YOU'LL NEVER GUESS WHAT HAPPENED... IT HAD TURNED INTO AN ANGEL, AND FLOWN AWAY!
HA HA HA HA HA HA HA
WELL, THIS WAS OBVIOUSLY A MIRACLE! I HAD BEEN CHOSEN TO BRING A MESSAGE TO THE WORLD!
WHAT WAS THIS MESSAGE I WAS TO BRING TO THE WORLD? AFTER MUCH THOUGHT, I DECIDED IT WAS THIS, "A FOUL BALL HIT BEHIND THIRD BASE IS THE SHORTSTOP'S PLAY!"
HA HA HA HA HA HA HA
MA'AM, IF IT'S OKAY WITH YOU, I'LL TAKE THE QUESTIONS AFTER SCHOOL OUT IN THE ALLEY BEHIND THE GYM!
SCHULZ

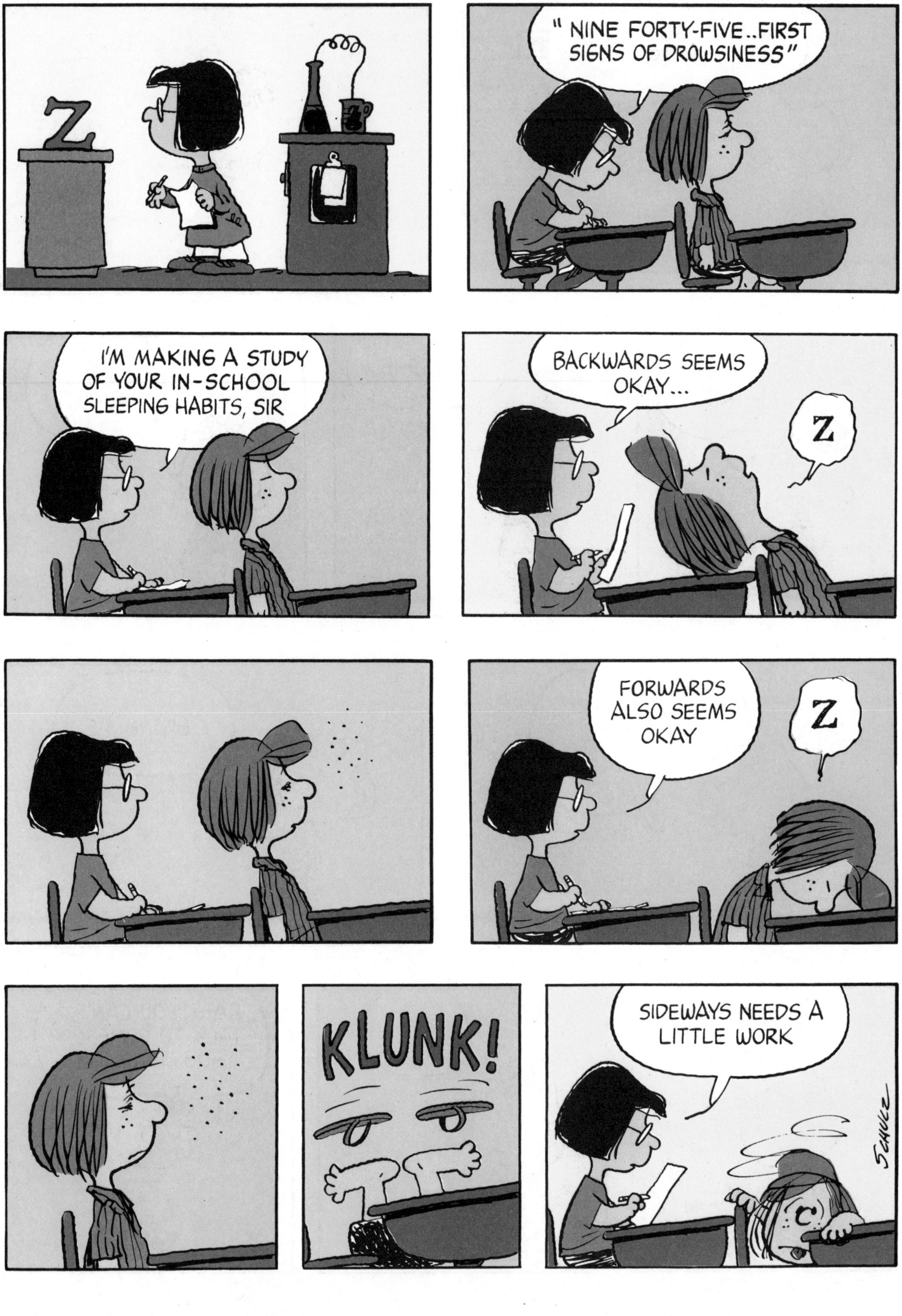
Z
" NINE FORTY-FIVE..FIRST SIGNS OF DROWSINESS"
I'M MAKING A STUDY OF YOUR IN-SCHOOL SLEEPING HABITS, SIR
BACKWARDS SEEMS OKAY...
Z
FORWARDS ALSO SEEMS OKAY
Z
KLUNK!
SIDEWAYS NEEDS A LITTLE WORK
SCHULZ

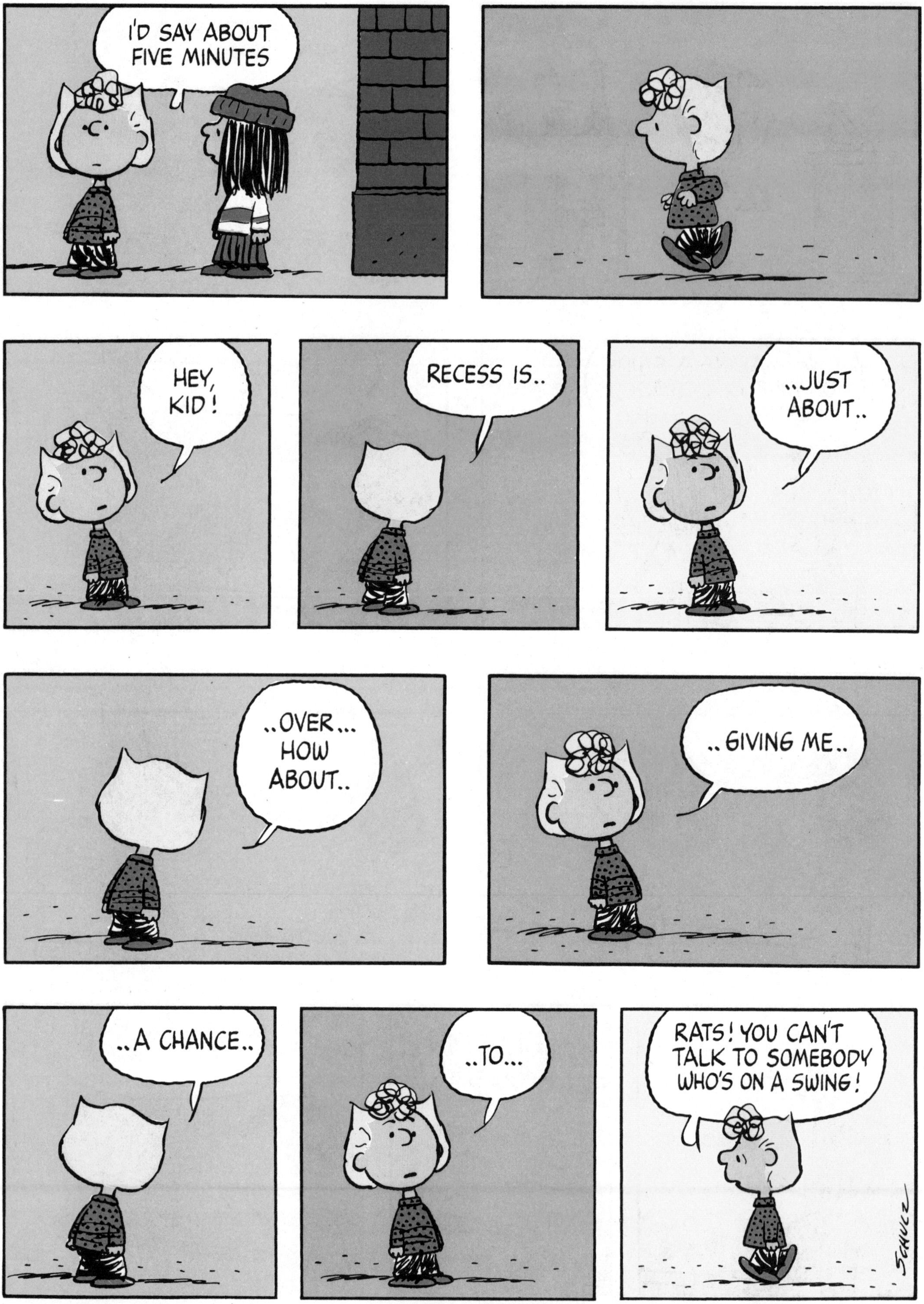
I'D SAY ABOUT FIVE MINUTES
HEY, KID!
RECESS IS..
..JUST ABOUT..
..OVER... HOW ABOUT..
..GIVING ME..
..A CHANCE..
..TO...
RATS! YOU CAN'T TALK TO SOMEBODY WHO'S ON A SWING!
SCHULZ

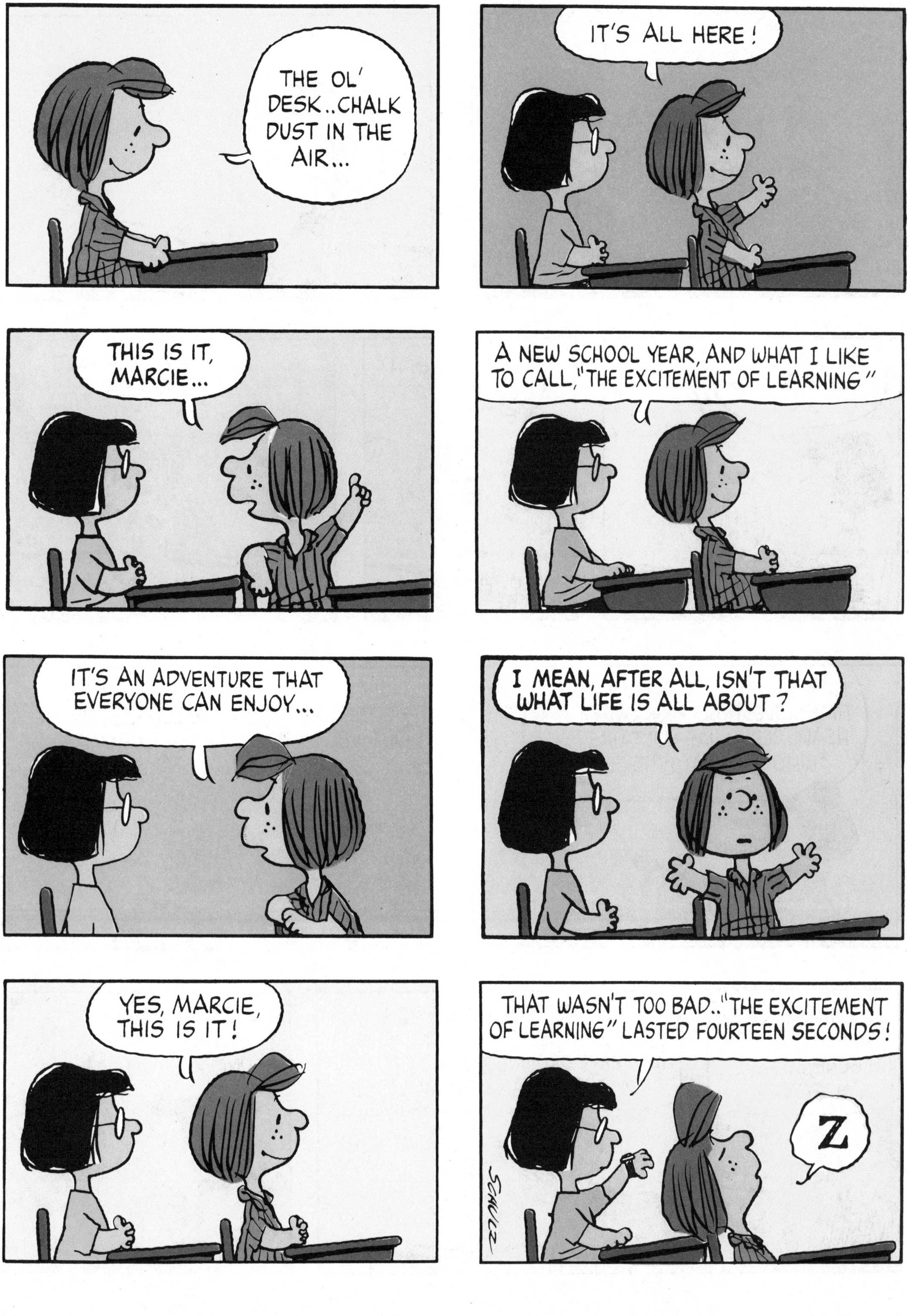
THE OL' DESK..CHALK DUST IN THE AIR...
IT'S ALL HERE!
THIS IS IT, MARCIE...
A NEW SCHOOL YEAR, AND WHAT I LIKE TO CALL, "THE EXCITEMENT OF LEARNING"
IT'S AN ADVENTURE THAT EVERYONE CAN ENJOY...
I MEAN, AFTER ALL, ISN'T THAT WHAT LIFE IS ALL ABOUT?
YES, MARCIE, THIS IS IT!
THAT WASN'T TOO BAD.."THE EXCITEMENT OF LEARNING" LASTED FOURTEEN SECONDS!
Z
SCHULZ

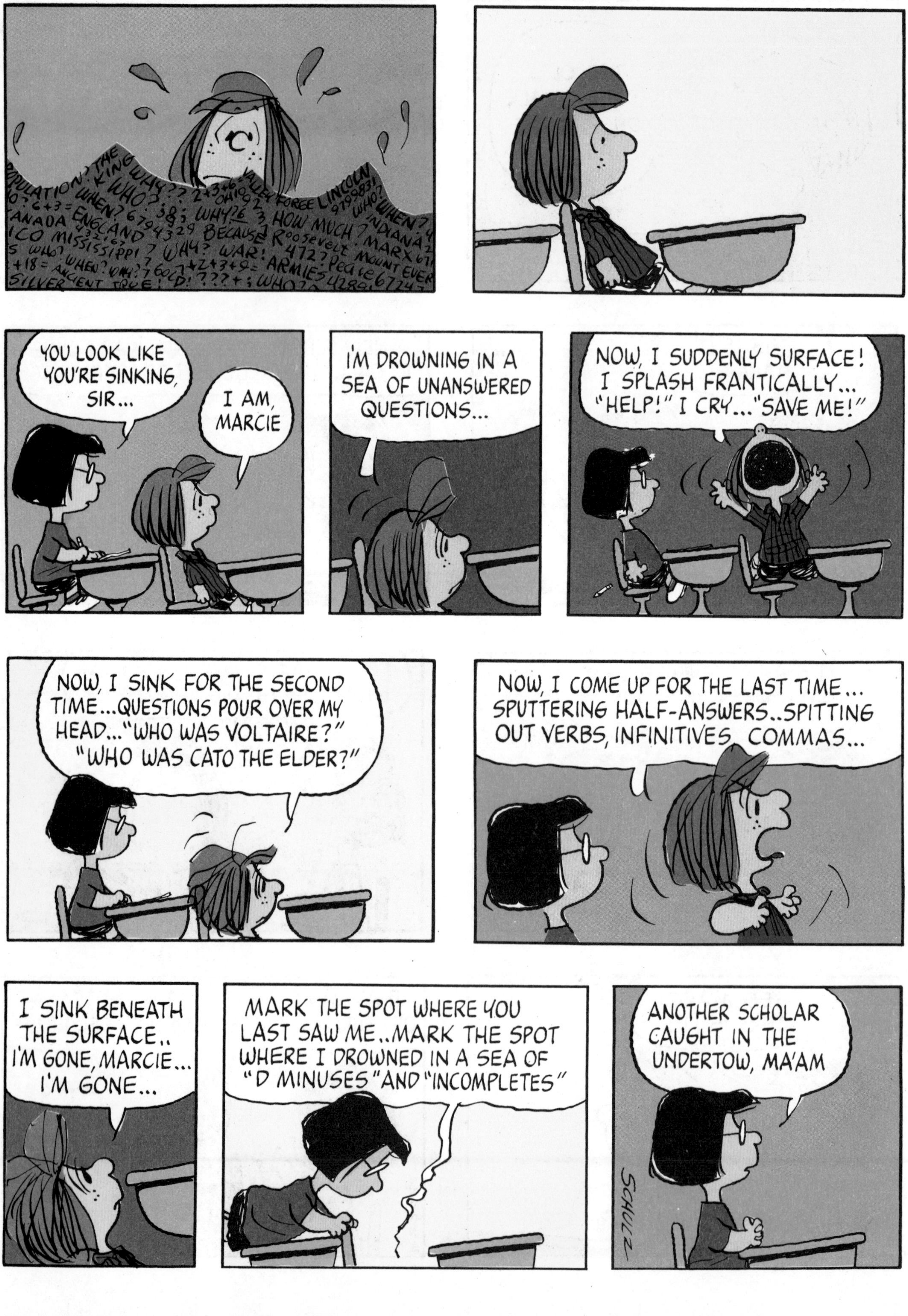
YOU LOOK LIKE YOU'RE SINKING, SIR...
I AM, MARCIE
I'M DROWNING IN A SEA OF UNANSWERED QUESTIONS...
NOW, I SUDDENLY SURFACE! I SPLASH FRANTICALLY... "HELP!" I CRY..."SAVE ME!"
NOW, I SINK FOR THE SECOND TIME...QUESTIONS POUR OVER MY HEAD..."WHO WAS VOLTAIRE?" "WHO WAS CATO THE ELDER?"
NOW, I COME UP FOR THE LAST TIME... SPUTTERING HALF-ANSWERS..SPITTING OUT VERBS, INFINITIVES COMMAS...
I SINK BENEATH THE SURFACE.. I'M GONE, MARCIE... I'M GONE...
MARK THE SPOT WHERE YOU LAST SAW ME..MARK THE SPOT WHERE I DROWNED IN A SEA OF "D MINUSES" AND "INCOMPLETES"
ANOTHER SCHOLAR CAUGHT IN THE UNDERTOW, MA'AM
SCHULZ